THE POSTWAR DEVELOPMENT OF JAPANESE STUDIES
IN THE UNITED STATES

BRILL'S JAPANESE STUDIES LIBRARY

EDITED BY

H. BOLITHO AND K.W. RADTKE

VOLUME 8

THE POSTWAR DEVELOPMENT OF JAPANESE STUDIES IN THE UNITED STATES

EDITED BY

HELEN HARDACRE

BRILL
LEIDEN · BOSTON · KÖLN
1998

This book is printed on acid-free paper.

Library of Congress Cataloging-in-Publication Data

The postwar development of Japanese studies in the United States /
  edited by Helen Hardacre.
    p.   cm. — (Brill's Japanese studies library,
  ISSN 0925-6512 ; v. 8)
  Includes index.
  ISBN 9004109811 (cloth : alk. papier)
  1. Japan—Study and teaching—United States.
  I. Hardacre, Helen, 1949. II. Series.
DS834.95.P67   1998
952'.007'073—dc21   98-15232
                                                                  CIP

Die Deutsche Bibliothek - CIP-Einheitsaufnahme

**The postwar development of Japanese studies in the
United States** / ed. by Helen Hardacre. - Leiden ; Boston ; Köln :
Brill 1998
  (Brill's Japanese studies library ; Vol 8)
  ISBN 90-04-10981-1
NE: GT

ISSN   0925-6512
ISBN   90 04 10981 1

© Copyright 1998 by Koninklijke Brill NV, Leiden, The Netherlands

All rights reserved. No part of this publication may be reproduced, translated, stored in
a retrieval system, or transmitted in any form or by any means, electronic,
mechanical, photocopying, recording or otherwise, without prior written
permission from the publisher.

Authorization to photocopy items for internal or personal
use is granted by Brill provided that
the appropriate fees are paid directly to The Copyright
Clearance Center, 222 Rosewood Drive, Suite 910
Danvers MA 01923, USA.
Fees are subject to change.

PRINTED IN THE NETHERLANDS

CONTENTS

Introduction	vii
HELEN HARDACRE	
Sizing Up (and Breaking Down) Japan	1
JOHN W. DOWER	
The Study of Japan's Early History	37
MARTIN COLLCUTT	
Tokugawa Japan: The Return of the Other?	85
HAROLD BOLITHO	
The Meiji Restoration: a Historiographical Overview	115
ALBERT M. CRAIG	
American Studies of Japanese Foreign Relations	143
AKIRA IRIYE	
Japanese Art Studies in America since 1945	161
JOHN M. ROSENFIELD	
The Postwar Development of Studies of Japanese Religions	195
HELEN HARDACRE	
"The Way of the World": Japanese Literary Studies in the Postwar United States	227
NORMA FIELD	
When and Where Japan Enters: American Anthropology since 1945	294
JENNIFER ROBERTSON	
The Turbulent Path to Social Science: Japanese Political Analysis in the 1990s	336
KENT E. CALDER	
The Development of Japanese Legal Studies in American Law Schools	354
FRANK K. UPHAM	
Taking Japanese Studies Seriously	387
ANDREW GORDON	
Index	407
List of Contributors	424

INTRODUCTION

Helen Hardacre

At the end of World War II, Japanese studies in the United States did not yet exist as a recognized area of study. Few universities offered instruction in the Japanese language, and fewer still offered more than a handful of courses on Japanese history, society, or culture. The available courses were frequently taught by non-specialists unable to read Japanese. Over the postwar decades, Japanese studies has developed markedly, so that now virtually all the country's major research universities, most of the state universities, and hundreds of private colleges and universities provide courses of study on Japan. The story of building the field's institutional infrastructure has been told in a number of important volumes.[1] While some of these also addressed the scholarly issues that defined research on Japan at the time of their compilation, or have assessed the "state of the field" in various disciplines from time to time, none to date has examined in detail the postwar development of scholarship across the spectrum of disciplines in which Japanese studies has become established.

This volume documents the postwar history of United States scholarship on Japan by presenting essays chronicling its historical development in each discipline or significant subfield, and reflecting upon the continuing task of strengthening the field's impact within the disciplines. Its separate essays put current debates in historical perspective and provide useful bibliographies. This volume should help to assess the field's achievements throughout the disciplines, to identify areas requiring more work, and to chart a direction for the future.

The essays in this volume suggest that Japanese studies in the United States has developed since 1945 in relation to several factors: social and political change in Japan and in the United States,

---

[1] See the following: Yasaka Takagi (1935); Social Science Research Council-American Council of Learned Societies Joint Committee on Japanese Studies (1970); Elizabeth T. Massey and Joseph A. Massey (1977); The Japan Foundation (1984, 1988); The Japan Foundation and the Association for Asian Studies (1996).

changes in the dominant scholarly concerns about Japan, and changing evaluations of area studies. This introduction provides a synthesis of this volume's findings, followed by an overview of the separate essays.

The period 1945 to 1960 saw the establishment of Japanese studies in the major research universities, staffed by a generation of scholars who had participated in World War II or the Allied Occupation of Japan after the war, often either raised in Japan or having their first instruction in Japanese language as part of their military experience. This generation of scholars cooperated closely with one another to promote the study of Japan, to build research library collections, and to create programs of undergraduate and graduate study. They set high standards of linguistic competence and encouraged their students to become widely read in all areas of Japanese history, culture, and society. At the time, the annual volume of publications on Japan was still small enough that one could realistically expect to read it all.

A subtext to the establishment of Japanese studies after World War II was the general ignorance about Japan in the United States and the continuing existence of racist attitudes toward Japan, an inevitable, ugly legacy of the war. There was a need to address these attitudes in order to establish the legitimacy of the study of Japan. The way found, probably not with conscious intention, was the creation of exotic, essentialized images of Japan and the Japanese people. Such wartime studies as Benedict's *The Chrysanthemum and the Sword* had identified a psychological profile supposedly valid for all Japanese in all times, a monolithic, stereotypical portrait which would sort out the essential differences between Japan and the West. The framework was implicitly comparative and straightforwardly essentialist. The circumstances of its undertaking were defined by the needs of military intelligence. Translations of literature emerging soon after the war dovetailed with Benedict's emphasis, stressing ahistorical, apolitical images of Japan rather than representing a cross-section of the actual literary world after World War II, which was riven with division, desperate to confront the question of war responsibility, and struggling to discern religious meaning in the tragedy of the atomic bombings. Zen emerged to epitomize popular American images of the entire culture of Japan. These various images combined to produce an exotic, aesthetically pleasing—even tantalizing, fascinating—counter to wartime attitudes, making it clear that Japan offered something eminently worthy of study, showing a cultural sophistication equal to the standards of Western history and culture.

Even in the social sciences, the study of Japan had a strong humanistic emphasis, and training in Japanese studies was assumed to necessitate broad knowledge of language, culture, history, and society. In the main, Japanese studies emphasized empirical scholarship, with correspondingly less stress upon conceptual or theoretical innovation. Perhaps because so many areas were and remain relatively unexplored, there was and is much excitement to be gained in empirical research, collecting and translating primary sources. This empirical emphasis has been affirmed by the general thrust of most scholarship in Japan as well.

It is well understood in Japanese studies that empirical scholarship is guided by a theoretical framework even if, in the worst case, it remains unexamined or unacknowledged. Similarly, it is understood that it is false to posit even the possibility of a complete disjuncture between empirical scholarship and the development and refinement of theory. Of the two, however, there is little question that most weight has been assigned to empirical work in the postwar history of Japanese studies. A similar pattern would probably be found in the history of area studies of any kind.

During the 1960s and 1970s, the belief arose that much of the value in studying Japan lay not in any additive contribution to Western theories, but, rather, precisely in pointing out either the impossibility of applying such theories to Japan, or putting Japan forward as "the exception that proves the rule." It was in this context that Japan's experience was principally interesting to modernization theorists other than Japan specialists.

For most of the postwar decades, modernization has provided the major framework for the study of Japan, establishing an enduring line of scholarship. The history of Japan since the Meiji Restoration of 1868 was conceptualized as the period of Japan's modernization, a century or so in which Japan was transformed from a premodern or "feudal" agricultural country to a modern, industrialized, urbanized society. In the process, political forms developed from an autocratic regime, with militaristic and imperialistic phases, to a democratic nation after 1945. The Japanese people were transformed by the experiences of compulsory education and political participation, and the previous regionalism was transcended in the development of a unified nation. Whereas these changes took centuries in the West, they were accomplished in about a century in Japan. Japan seemed to have achieved the social and political changes associated with modernization in a fraction of the time required in the West, with a minimum of social dislocation. How Japan accomplished such a monumental and thoroughgoing change in so short a time was a question that inspired many scholars of Japan since 1945 and pervasively influenced the entire field.

The question of Japan's modernization could be addressed in virtually any area of scholarship, from history to religion. Even in premodern fields, prior historical eras were examined to identify precursors or preparatory factors later facilitating modernization. Seeing Japan through the prism of modernization provided many opportunities for comparative scholarship and undoubtedly did much to bring Japan's relevance to the attention of the scholarly world as a whole. The pervasive influence of the modernization perspective also provided a unifying force within Japanese studies, even as each area of study became increasingly specialized.

In examinations of modernization around the globe, Japan specialists could enjoy the role of "spoiler" in theoretical discussions, usually able to show that, "Japan doesn't fit." From the standpoint of the disciplines, Japan was an interesting, odd "case," the source of endless puzzles, but rarely was it recognized as providing conceptual or theoretical innovation in its own right.

Through the 1960s and much of the 1970s, modernization was the major preoccupation of Japanese studies, and it remains highly influential. No alternative perspective of comparable power to connect Japan to other areas of academic inquiry has yet emerged, nor do subsequent paradigms show a comparable power to unite Japanese studies as a field.

In the 1980s, interest in pursuing studies of modernization was replaced by a variety of other theoretical frameworks. Not all of these derived from a critique of modernization, though as the influence of social and cultural history has grown in the American academy generally, many doubts have been raised about just how "painless" Japan's transition to modernity was. A natural sequel to such suspicions was the desire to study non-elite groups, for whom the transition to modernity was anything but painless. Structuralism, poststructuralism, deconstructionism, postmodernism, and rational choice theory have all found proponents in Japanese studies. The waxing and waning of these theoretical paradigms within Japanese studies' various fields follow diverse patterns, as this volume's essays demonstrate.

Concurrently, Japanese studies in each discipline became increasingly specialized, following a general pattern in the American academy. Graduate training was lengthened, making it possible for students to receive more advanced disciplinary training as well as requiring of them increasingly higher levels of competence in Japanese language and deeper knowledge of their particular subject within Japanese studies. Diverse attitudes towards the relative significance of theoretical and empirical work developed, sometimes a resignation in the face of short-lived theoretical movements, or even the suspicion that those who became caught up in them have done so in order to camouflage a weakness in their empirical knowledge of Japan or to mask a deficit in language skills.

Critiques of area studies based on the idea that they are inherently "Orientalist" began to make an impact on Asian studies as a whole, and on Japanese studies in particular during the 1980s. This is the view, originating with Edward Said, that the exotic images typical of Victorian scholarship on the Middle East produced an understanding of other societies as static, uncivilized backwaters requiring the adoption of Western reforms. "Oriental" in fact was equated with this benighted state. Not limited to studies of the Middle East, the critique of Orientalism found exponents in Japanese studies as well. As the authors of this volume's essays describe the situation, many early studies of Japan in fact incorporated the assumptions of the Orientalist perspective, misguidedly perpetuating an implicit binarism, a tacitly comparative perspective tending to caricature Japan. The charge laid by this critique was a call for a thorough re-examination of basic presuppositions. One such presupposition was that it would be "good" for Japan to become more like the West.

Postmodernism incorporates and extends critiques of area studies based on Orientalism. It goes without saying that postmodernism emphasizes different ideas in different disciplines. It is not a simple matter to summarize its main points as they have affected the study of Japan. Nevertheless, at the risk of being overly general, we can say that postmodernism prescribes attention to relations of power, examination of the periphery as well as the center, nonelite groups instead of a single focus on social elites. The essays of this volume suggest that postmodernism's appeal within Japanese studies shows a generational pattern, such that many younger scholars find it constructive and illuminating, whereas their elders typically find it undermining and inimical.

The 1980s advent of postmodernism revealed divisions in the field. The modernization perspective, which had functioned to unify Japanese studies up until the late 1970s, ceased to provide such a unifying focus. Furthermore, the field was growing in size and diversity. The level of specialization expected in the disciplines was rising to the point that it was not always easy for, say, a political scientist of Japan to understand and appreciate the efforts of literary scholars, and vice versa. Japanese studies in the disciplines of economics and linguistics became so technical that other Japan specialists could scarcely claim to comprehend their aims and methods.

The Occupation generation of Japan scholars had succeeded so well in creating support for Japanese studies that their students were emerging with different skills than their teachers. Those beginning their academic careers in the 1980s had been better funded as graduate students, and they had had the opportunity to study language (often with government grant support) for much longer than their predecessors, under more professional teachers, using better texts, and held to a higher standard. They were able to study in Japan for longer periods, and to develop extensive contacts with Japanese scholars. As a result, they took their first teaching positions not in their late twenties, but in their early or mid-thirties.

Although their undergraduate years coincided with the Vietnam War, almost none had military experience, though many had the experience of civil disobedience in opposition to that war or in the context of the civil rights or feminist movements. Almost no one was in sympathy with the proposition that area studies could or should contribute to intelligence work. Their experience channelled them toward iconoclasm and attracted them to the debunking potential of new theoretical writings. They did not shy from the parricidal potential of the Orientalism debate, postmodernism, and rational choice theory. In their scholarship they were less respectful of Japanese society's taboos on unwelcome topics (discrimination against women, the Burakumin, or studies of the imperial house, crime, minorities, etc.).

Those in the social sciences were trained in advanced theoretical and statistical methods. There were more outlets for publications, and, in part because they were also members of the "baby boom" generation, higher expectations of publication were imposed on their decisions for academic tenure. They faced little competition from European or British scholarship on Japan, and indeed, European and British scholars, foreseeing the decline of their own university systems, came to this country in significant numbers.

With the end of the Cold War, a variety of dissonant images of Japan has proliferated to replace exotic, essentialized portraits. Japan is no longer the "younger brother" to be instructed (an attitude lasting into the 1970s), nor does anyone expect it to become the next world hegemon (a much-feared scenario of the 1980s). Current theoretical debate in Japanese studies centers on postmodernism in the humanities and on rational choice theory in the social sciences, with no over-arching, unifying perspective yet having arisen to replace the modernization framework. There is much interest in comparative scholarship, and postmodernism offers some scope to comparative work. Similarly, the resurgence of a pan-Asian perspective in public discourse within Japan itself has led to renewed interest among Japanese scholars in comparative scholarship. Japanese studies' increasing specialization within the disciplines in United States universities is a mark of its increasing sophistication and acceptance, even as specialization and professionalization make it unlikely that a single perspective could emerge to capture the attention of the whole field again.

This volume's essays were written between 1994 and 1997, just as implications for area studies of all kinds of the end of the Cold War were being debated. One long-standing criticism of area studies held that they were originally sponsored in order to assist government and military intelligence operations and hence lack academic independence and integrity. On this view, levelled most pointedly at Southeast Asian studies and Soviet studies, the end of the Cold War should signal the end of a need for area studies. From a different perspective, however, it is argued that "globalization" and the increasing economic integration of nations produce a much-increased need for deep understanding of the history, society, language, and culture of other nations, underlining the continued, even increased need for sophisticated area studies.

With these debates about the meaning of the end of the Cold War for area studies forming the geopolitical background, academic scholarship both inside and outside area studies has been swept by currents of theoretical debate which would seem to undermine the value of area studies education, which stresses extensive language work and broad, detailed understanding of other nations' history, society, and culture. These debates are allied with postmodernism in the humanities and with rational choice theory in the social sciences.

It should be pointed out, however, that some areas of Japanese studies are still struggling to achieve a "critical mass" of scholars and distinct lines of cumulative research (law, pre-1600 history) and are thus not uniformly affected by these theoretical currents. Japanese studies of anthropology, nominally a social science, has developed much like a humanities discipline. While anthropological studies of Japan have been much affected by postmodernism, rational choice theory has not made a significant impact. It must also be noted that Japanese studies has never really become established in academic departments of psychology, and that it has declined conspicuously in sociology and economics, with the result that neither sociology, economics, nor psychology is addressed in this volume's essays. It is also worthy of note that in such areas of Japanese studies as Restoration history, foreign relations, and religion, the existence of parallel lines of scholarship in the United States and Japan has produced research trajectories incorporating a variety of theoretical debates, without producing any sense that studies of Japan are incongruent with disciplinary expectations in the United States.

Rational choice theory challenges all area studies through its claim that humanity everywhere obeys unitary rules of human behavior, implying that more specific considerations of particular histories, societies, and cultures are merely epiphenomena of no determinative value. In other words, it might be "nice" to know precisely how, say, Japanese politicians, bureaucrats, and corporations maintain their relationships through "gift-giving," socializing on the golf course, and carousing in nightclubs, but we can achieve a much more accurate understanding of how political corruption operates in Japan through the application to the situation of universal rules having nothing to do with Japan. These rules would emphasize the estimation of economic advantage and other factors at a trans-cultural level. In other words, theory-making can and should be "content-free." Local knowledge on this view becomes almost an obstacle to understanding rather than a precondition of it. The discipline most affected by the rational choice perspective is political science, and some areas within modern history. Rational choice has few outright proponents in Japanese studies, but this volume's essays suggest that, at least among younger scholars, there is a growing interest and a belief that it must be addressed straightforwardly.

Japanese studies in the United States today is a large and flourishing area of scholarship, contributing strongly to global research on Japan, fully established in the humanities and in most social sciences disciplines of American universities. By comparison with other branches of area studies, Japanese studies has developed steadily and expanded without major setbacks since 1945. The great outpouring of scholarship on Japan, far beyond the capacity of a single scholar even to monitor, let alone read and digest, testifies to the vitality of the field and to its record of cumulative scholarship throughout the disciplines.

Yet when seen from the perspective of the influence of Japanese studies within separate disciplines or subfields, many scholars would say that it has yet to achieve its full potential, that the broader significance of insights gained in the study of Japan is too seldom recognized by those outside Japanese studies, and that scholars of Japan have hardly ever succeeded in altering the Eurocentric perspectives which prevail in most disciplines. In other words, Japanese studies' quantitative and institutional growth has not been matched by a corresponding theoretical impact, in the view of some scholars.

Nevertheless, other factors have emerged to mitigate this situation, not all of them of a scholarly nature. With the advance of "globalization," convergences between Japanese and Western society have become apparent. Much like American young people, Japanese youth are currently fascinated by questions of personal identity and the potential for recreation, personal transformation, and social change to be found in religion, pop culture, and technology. Current literature displays similar themes. There is little idealization of tradition, no essential self, and no firm barrier between humanity and the technology it creates. In this situation, it is hardly to be expected that anyone could seriously entertain the idea of a monolithic national essence. National boundaries have become less relevant, and this means that it is more difficult to sustain thoroughgoing distinctions of cultural boundaries, and that it is more appealing to place the study of Japan within a global-comparative or at least pan-Asian context. Though the connections are indistinct and indirect, the concerns of contemporary culture thus seem to echo the postmodern or rational choice perspectives of the rising generations of scholars of Japan.

Overview of the Essays in This Volume

This volume is based on the Twenty-fifth Anniversary Symposium of the Edwin O. Reischauer Institute of Japanese Studies, Harvard University, a series of lectures during 1996 and 1997 in which the authors of this volume's essays presented their work before an audience of scholars and students of Japan at Harvard. The authors themselves were largely drawn from Harvard (Bolitho, Craig, Gordon, Hardacre, Iriye, Rosenfield), along with others representing significant centers of Japanese studies in the United States: Calder/ Princeton University; Collcutt/ Princeton University; Dower/ Massachusetts Institute of Technology; Field/ The University of Chicago; Robertson/ University of Michigan; Upham/ New York University. The lectures were later revised for inclusion in this volume.[2]

Scholarship by Japanese studies' specialists has contributed to virtually all the disciplines of the humanities and social sciences, and this volume attempts to reflect and to explore the full range

---

[2] Founded in 1973 as the Japan Institute and renamed in 1985 in honor of its founder, the Reischauer Institute exists to expand and strengthen Japanese studies at Harvard and throughout the international community of scholars of Japan. To that end, it sponsors academic research, the publication of monographs on Japan, fellowship programs, the establishment of professorships, and cultural events relating to Japan, while encouraging communication, cooperation, and understanding between the United States and Japan. It strives to provide the pre-eminent locus for Japanese studies in the United States and the Western world. Previous Institute publications documenting the history and present state of Japanese studies include those by Deptula and Hess (1996) and Hardacre and Kern, eds. (1997).

of that contribution. Historical studies of Japan today encompass a very wide expanse of humanistic scholarship, with important links to other disciplines, and historical study provides the conceptual framework for most areas of the study of Japan. In recognition of the central importance of history within Japanese studies, this volume devotes several studies to it, including a comprehensive survey of postwar historical scholarship on Japan (Dower), studies of diplomatic history (Iriye), art history (Rosenfield), and religious history (Hardacre), and separate essays on prehistory and ancient Japan (Collcutt), the Edo Period (Bolitho), and the Meiji Restoration (Craig). This volume also addresses Japanese studies within anthropology (Robertson), literary studies (Field), law (Upham), and political science (Calder). The volume's final essay discusses the situation of Japanese studies within contemporary debates on the post-Cold War future of area studies (Gordon).

John Dower addresses the larger political context of postwar historical studies of Japan, showing how the character of political relations between the United States and Japan has continually colored evaluations of Japanese history. Modernization theory applied to Japan resulted in a sweeping revision of earlier assessments of premodern history, especially, casting out earlier views of the Tokugawa period as "feudal," in favor of upbeat portrayals of it as progressing inexorably toward modernity and "free enterprise." This emphasis on the convergence of Japanese and Western historical trajectories was displaced in the 1980s, however, with the retreat of modernization theory and Japan's emergence as a challenge to Western economic hegemony. "Divergence" rather than convergence seemed to provide a more convincing explanatory framework. Dower holds that the new emphasis on divergence ironically harks back to outlooks prevailing before modernization theory's vogue, but with the significant difference that in important areas of study, "Japan's departures from the Western norm often are evaluated positively." In fact, scholars like Ronald Dore and Ezra Vogel proclaimed that the West had much to learn from Japan. Subsequent to that development, however, came a new approach to modern Japanese culture showing how much of Japanese "tradition" in fact is "socially constructed, ideologically charged, and part of a constant process of invention and reinvention." Attention to social construction focused on social division and conflict, virtually for the first time in Japanese studies, and since the mid-1970s this perspective has steadily gained strength and momentum. Thus, modernization theory seems now to have been decisively displaced by a "postmodern" perspective of multiple causalities and sources of power.

Martin Collcutt's treatment of the study of prehistory, ancient, and medieval Japan engages an area of scholarship in which interaction between Western and Japanese scholarship has been a sustained feature of the postwar decades. Prehistory and the ancient period are known in large part through the work of archaeologists, and while this field is "extremely active and well-funded" in Japan, Western archaeologists of Japan have always been a very small group, tending to fall between the stools of history and anthropology. As Collcutt shows, the development of archaeological scholarship on Japanese prehistory and the ancient period has been slow to develop. As a consequence, our understanding of early Japanese history is limited in many respects. Nevertheless, recent finds have significantly revised received knowledge on several important topics. For example, the earliest human habitation of the islands has been pushed back by finds at Kami Takamori (Miyagi Prefecture) to 600,000 B.C. Excavations at Sannai Maruyama (Aomori Prefecture) reveal a much more complex society during the Jōmon Period than was understood only a few years ago: village "long houses," separate burial sites for children and adults, and evidence that this site was part of a large trading network in obsidian, encompassing northern Honshū and Hokkaidō. Also, Yoshinogari (Saga Prefecture) has emerged as the leading contender for the Yamatai capital of Queen Himiko. Collcutt documents ongoing debate on the nature of ancient contact between Japan and the Korean peninsula, beginning with Egami Namio's "Horserider Thesis." However these debates are resolved, it is now indisputable that "Japan's early history cannot be understood in isolation from that of the rest of Asia and especially the Korean peninsula." It remains the case, nevertheless, that studies of ancient Japan have yet to muster a "critical mass" outside Japan itself. By contrast, studies of medieval history have flourished in recent years, stimulated by the field's ongoing revival in Japan, the so-called "*chūsei* boom." While many important topics remain unexplored, there are clear lines of interpretation for the period's overall historical development, with a vigorous group of scholars.

In his discussion of historical studies of the Tokugawa period, Harold Bolitho shows how assessments of the period have changed radically since 1945. At the end of World War II, both Japanese and Western scholarship agreed in the view that the period was a static and alien one, with little that could withstand comparison to Western history of the same era. As he describes the situation, the period was mostly viewed as "Other," remote from modern concerns and largely antithetical to them. However, as the modernization paradigm took shape, a new generation of scholars looked to the Tokugawa period for the antecedents of Japan's modernization, for the templates that made possible its transition to modernity. This emphasis produced more favorable assessments of the period. This optimistic trend has been continued, in part, by a cohort of scholars writing during the 1970s and 1980s, which wishes in addition to examine the dispersion of power from the center to the periphery, the variety of society and culture. This latter inquiry has tended to undercut earlier images of Tokugawa period society and culture as monolithic and static. In Bolitho's view, while these studies of sociocultural variety and resistance to authority may serve the intellectual agenda of postmodernism, the result is to re-enforce the view of the period as "Other," if a more likeable and approachable one. This contemporary impetus also fails, in Bolitho's opinion, to engage the fundamental questions about economic and institutional change which would allow us to link the period more convincingly to the modern era.

Albert Craig's essay on the Meiji Restoration identifies a central question running through the history of studies of this complex event: how the Restoration's multi-faceted reforms could have been carried out so rapidly. To locate promising areas of study for answering that question, he engages three main topics of investigation: commoners and Restoration history, the Restoration movement, and the period's cultural revolution. Craig discusses significant scholarship on late Tokugawa rural society, beginning with the work of Hugh Borton and Thomas Smith and continued by scholars in the 1980s and 1990s. These studies agree on certain central points bearing on the Restoration: that Tokugawa period uprisings were rare, not indicative of permanent divisions, and that they were basically irrelevant to the Restoration. While the rise of the market economy led to intensified social stratification, and while, for example, landlordism created severe tensions, society was highly stable, and this stability in rural society was the immediate backdrop to the Restoration. Unfortunately, Craig notes, as yet we have no study of urban society during the last days of the Tokugawa period, and it was in the cities that the major events of the Restoration occurred. As for the Restoration itself, there has been a consistent drive to refine our understanding of the many elements contributing to the whole: the role of foreign pressure, the roles of individual domains, the imperial house, the shogunate's demise, and biographical studies of the main actors. Nevertheless, a gap remains in our understanding of the economic history of the period 1850 to 1880. The general importance of cultural change is obvious, but no clear line of interpretation regarding the great diversity of thought during the period has yet emerged.

Akira Iriye's essay treats American studies of Japanese foreign relations. Iriye notes that American scholarship has dominated this field, probably because of the legacy of World War II. James William Morley made a great contribution through the translation of a major compilation of primary sources on the road to war, and he set his stamp on the field through the Hakone conference of 1960, inspiring a generation of younger historians. American students of Japan's foreign relations have worked so extensively in Japanese primary sources, and engage so closely with their Japanese colleagues that in this area we can see the emergence of a unified trajectory of scholarship. This integration is extremely stimulating for both sides. Americans are fortunate in avoiding the emotional politicization of discussion of Japanese imperialism to be seen, for example, in other East Asian contexts. Unfortunately, however, American studies of Japanese foreign relations have had little impact on the broader discipline of foreign relations, and studies of Japanese imperialism have not yet offered striking innovations. Nevertheless, recent discussions of the implications of culture for foreign relations may offer new opportunities to influence the discipline's future development.

John Rosenfield's study of Japanese art history shows that this area of scholarship has enjoyed rapid growth, but he also identifies significant areas of concern. Japanese arts played a crucial role in the evolution of Modern Art in Europe and America from 1850 until well into the postwar period. In this connection, Japanese arts were viewed as exciting alternatives to the formalism of European classicism. But when the perspective of modernism was superseded by postmodernism, a gap emerged in the nature of professional training and career expectations between specialists on Japan, on the one hand, and their disciplinary colleagues, on the other, for whom the theoretical perspective of postmodernism was becoming increasingly central. This gap occurred, paradoxically, because of the growing sophistication of training of American students in Japan, in which they were increasingly integrated into the academic lineages and traditions of art-historical training in Japan, which emphasizes minute, empirical description and technical specialization to a degree which would be understood in this country as hyper-developed, too concerned with tiny details ever to have a hope of producing theoretical insights. Furthermore, whereas the great corpus of Japanese Buddhist art offers endless opportunity for a researcher, the dominant attitude in the postmodernist perspective is anti-religious, according to Rosenfield, and thus hostile from the outset to the sort of insights likely to emerge from the study of this central sector of the arts of Japan. Concerned as postmodernism is with issues of colonialism, there is a suspicion among postmodernist scholars of art history that studies of Japan are Orientalist and distorted by colonialist attitudes. There is an impatience with the focus upon technique and with a well-established tradition of publishing exhibition catalogues instead of scholarly monographs, and pressure for art historians of Japan to make the leap more quickly from description to theoretical generalization. But these attitudes conflict with all that a young scholar is liable to be taught in Japan during the formative period of training. Seen in this light, there is a fundamental antagonism between the increasingly sophisticated training of the art historian of Japan and the paradigm currently enjoying hegemony in art history as a discipline. Rosenfield closes with the hope that the turbulent succession of theoretical fashions in America will not entirely destroy the expressive encounter and appreciation which must motivate commitment to the study of art history.

Hardacre's examination of the history of studies of Japanese religions shows a steady growth and diversification of this field. In terms of quantity, studies of Buddhism have far outnumbered studies of Shintō, Confucianism, Japanese Christianity, or other sectors of religious life in Japan. Before the mid-1950s, most studies of Japanese Buddhism concerned the Pure Land or True Pure Land sects, but with the appearance in English of the works of D. T. Suzuki, along with Suzuki's personal influence among American scholars, there began a great outpouring of scholarship on Zen. The result is an imbalance between the development of Zen studies, in itself a highly positive thing, and the historical reality of Zen's existence as one among many, equally important traditions of Buddhism in Japan. For example, studies of the equally significant Tendai and Shingon schools number only a handful, and studies of the Pure Land tradition have languished badly. Likewise, there was a short while in the 1960s and 1970s when Zen was idealized as representing the essence of all Japanese religions, if not all Japanese culture, paralleling anthropological studies essentializing the Japanese people as fundamentally homogenous. Thankfully, that episode seems to be finally laid to rest. Similarly, it is only in the late 1980s and after that one sees significant studies of Shintō and shrine life, Confucianism, or Japanese Christianity, though a few biographical studies had earlier shown the way. Studies of the new religions parallel their growing social and political importance, engaging increasing numbers of younger scholars, and creating fruitful connections with scholars in Japan. Japanese studies of religion have achieved recognition within religious studies, especially in the areas of studies of religion and gender (where connections to studies of Christianity in the medieval period have been the locus for exciting interchange with scholars of medieval European Christianity), and religion and politics, where the larger relevance of the study of Shintō is well understood. Studies of Japanese Buddhism have much potential to influence Buddhist studies as a whole, not least because the academic study of Buddhism is better developed in Japan than anywhere else. Perhaps because the study of religion itself is inherently interdisciplinary, the sort of Eurocentrism and disciplinary chauvinism which marginalize studies of Japan in other areas can be straightforwardly interrogated and the tables turned.

Norma Field discusses the ways that studies of Japanese literature have mediated between the scholarly concerns of American and Japanese academies. The postwar study of Japanese literature was launched from 1945 to 1960 through the publication of translations of a small group of Japanese prose authors, mainly Tanizaki,

Kawabata, and Mishima, and translations of haiku also were found to appeal to Western readers. This selection gave rise to exotic, ahistorical images of the Japanese people, while tending to marginalize and ignore more politically engaged literature or literary scholarship. The lacuna created thereby meant that studies of Japanese literature in the United States privileged an image of Japanese literature as ahistorical and apolitical, in spite of the urgent concern in Japan itself to deal with the war, its aftermath, and a sense of literature's complicity.

From the late 1960s in Japan, the student movement produced the Monoken school of literary criticism, which appropriated postmodern theory in order to establish a break with the past and to interrogate the roles of power and politics within academic literary scholarship. Meanwhile, literary scholarship on Japan in the United States flourished from the 1960s, influenced greatly by Konishi's "Association and Progression" and reflected in the works of Earl Miner; a high standard for both formal and contextual analysis was established. Translations of premodern prose and poetic works continued, though these have been marked by qualities of disconnected miscellany and pedantry, except for studies of *The Tale of Genji*, which show a stronger rationale and cumulative character. Nowadays postmodern theory provides the dominant paradigm for literary scholars both in the United States and Japan, and it has led to a fruitful questioning of stale, binary frameworks insisting on discussing Japanese literature within a "West vs. non-West" model.

Jennifer Robertson's study of anthropological studies of Japan identifies a persistent binarism, an implicit comparison between Japan and the United States which has an important point of origin in the work of Ruth Benedict. Benedict's study, published as *The Chrysanthemum and the Sword*, was based on interviews with Japanese and Japanese-Americans interned during World War II, and was quite self-consciously designed to assist the war effort against Japan. It compiled a unitary, static, and homogenous portrait of the Japanese people. For a time, Japan presented in this way occupied a central place in anthropological studies as a whole, but while that centrality has been displaced, the inherent binarism remains and even encourages essentializing, pseudo-academic studies of Japanese cultural identity in Japan itself, called *nihonjinron*. Anthropologists of Japan have made a concerted effort to introject the viewpoint from Japan to theoretical discussion, for example, at annual meetings of the American Anthropological Association. But while various papers on Japan may be presented in such settings, this effort has not yet produced an awareness of the potential of Japan as an area where theoretical innovation might be made. Instead, Japan anthropologists are not unlikely to be accused of whining that "Japan doesn't fit" the paradigms derived from the study of other areas. The received essentialized image of Japan as homogeneous and unitary seemingly must be unseated over and over again in a Sisyphean display, before attention can be directed to the questions of greater interest to specialists. Nevertheless, promising lines of research on gender and ethnic identity extend the possibility of destablizing the older images and connecting more forcefully with other Western anthropological concerns regarding self-reflection and expurgation of the discipline's colonialist past.

Kent Calder surveys the history of the study of Japanese politics and the Japanese political system, identifying five trends in the postwar development of this field: methodological innovation, a growing emphasis on comparative studies, an increasing tendency to contention and vigorous debate, the emergence of new forms of scholarly dialogue, especially via the Internet, and an increasing integration of foreign and Japanese analyses. These trends have been accompanied by the emergence of problems for the field as well, such as a paucity of cumulative research (except in the area of political economy) and a declining quality of information made available to scholars, as debate about Japanese politics becomes increasingly politicized and implicated in the making of national government policy in the United States. The current emphasis on comparison and theory in graduate school training undermines an earlier priority upon achieving a broad and deep understanding of Japanese culture and history.

Early postwar analysis of Japan's politics and political system began as a humanistic inquiry, exemplified in the works of Maruyama Masao. On this model, area specialists strove to situate their analyses in a culturally and historically informed framework. It was fully accepted among political scientists of Japan, according to Calder, that "...[u]nderstanding the distinctive historical-institutional circumstances in which Japan entered the modern global economy is a crucial precondition" for understanding modern

Japanese politics. This humanistic or culturalist framework was linked to an optimistic perspective on Japan:

> ...The prevailing interpretation [of Japanese politics and Japan's political system] until the late 1980s typically neglected the darker side of Japanese politics and presented an optimistic view of Japan's capacity and propensity to change in ways congruent with American interests.

By contrast, until recently the field showed little interest in building and testing of hypotheses or other hallmarks of social science methodology. Perhaps because of this disinterest, Japanese political scientists are regarded in their discipline as having made few conceptual or theoretical innovations, though Japan specialists contributed a great deal to modernization theory. Quantitative studies have been rare, except in studies of elections.

More recently, however, Japanese political science finds itself facing a growing pressure to become more like the harder social sciences, and to distance itself from its earlier humanistic moorings. Political science as a whole is moving in this direction, and younger scholars, in particular, gravitate more to a comparative perspective than to one solely based in Japan. Thus political science studies on Japan are seen to become more "scientific" the less obvious is their grounding in a deep knowledge of culture and history. Rational choice theory's appearance in Japanese political analysis is the most important phenomenon fueling this current trend to "content-free theorizing." While the applicability and value of rational choice theory are furiously debated among Japan specialists, the perspective has begun to acquire "a critical mass of adherents." The appeal of rational choice theory is linked to a critical, rather pessimistic perspective on Japanese society, its politics and political system, or, at least, to a determination not to shy away from Japanese politics's "dark side."

Frank Upham examines the most recently developed area of Japanese studies, Japanese legal studies. Japanese and American legal scholars began a sustained collaboration after World War II, intended to result in the incorporation of Western legal principles to Japan's postwar legal system. Important conferences and publications in the 1950s sustained these connections. The University of Washington emerged as the most comprehensive program of Japanese legal studies, offering both J.D. and L.L.M. degrees, but Harvard has produced most of the scholars currently teaching Japanese law in American universities today. The field of Japanese law has developed significantly since the 1970s, but even now there are only a dozen United States scholars of Japanese law able to utilize Japanese-language research materials.

Japanese legal studies has been closely connected with Japanese studies, exhibiting a commitment to area studies rare among scholars of comparative law. Japanese legal specialists highly value the area specialist's extensive training in history and culture and appreciate that the distinctiveness of Japanese law emerges from the country's history, society, and culture. But at the same time, "cultural" explanations of Japanese legal culture, mostly by non-specialists, have paradoxically created problems for the field. Japanese legal studies has had to struggle against Orientalizing, monolithic stereotypes about Japan and the Japanese people, to the effect that they are so dedicated to harmony and consensus, and so reluctant to enter litigation of any kind that law is essentially irrelevant to the study of Japan. Superficially informed "cultural explanations" are overly general, often inaccurate, and too frequently fail to establish any meaningful distinction between Japanese and American law. Not to put too fine a point on it, "the result sometimes verges on silliness," Upham writes, when cultural explanations are advanced as a substitute for an examination of institutional and social-structural similarities.

Japanese legal studies are unencumbered with debates on the relative merits of area studies and theory, a state of affairs arising from a combination of factors probably unique to legal education.

> Despite their close relationship with Japanese studies, professors of Japanese law have not suffered from the tension between area studies and theory building that has plagued their colleagues in the social sciences. In the first place, legal education retains a professional as well as an academic function, and at even the most elite schools there are faculty who argue for an emphasis on teaching and practical training.

This volume's final essay by Andrew Gordon addresses the place of Japanese studies within contemporary debates on area studies. He notes that the current controversy is not new, but renews older arguments. In the social sciences, area studies have long tended to be subordinated to, and have had to struggle against disciplinary theories claiming universal relevance. The presupposition of such debates is that, by comparison with a universal frame of reference, area studies can only produce partial, idiosyncratic data which at best serve as the basic material out of which theories are made. But this dichotomy is false, in Gordon's view. Theoretical knowledge is inseparable from area knowledge, and the data of some particular time and place are always, in practice, inevitably integrated with theory building.

If it could be shown that Japanese studies had never contributed concepts of broader theoretical relevance, then critiques of area studies might have some basis, but there are numerous examples of such contributions. For example, one might cite Thomas Smith's study of time and work discipline in Tokugawa Japan (which called into question E. P. Thompson's ideas about casual attitudes to time among all premodern peoples) or Takeshi Fujitani's study of the Japanese monarchy (which revises Foucault's concept of power) or Anne Allison's study of *manga* (which undermines Freudian interpretations of the male gaze). While these examples show how Japanese studies can identify useful revisions to established Western theoretical works, there are other examples of conceptual innovation which themselves give rise to universal-level theoretical debate, such as Chalmers Johnson's idea of the developmental state or Doi Takeo's concept of *amae*.

Taking Japanese studies seriously in this sense is a question of situating the enterprise of theorizing in the context of actual human behavior. The origins of the impasse between this perspective and rational choice theory can be seen to lie in that theory's assumption that theory can and should be "content-free." This most recent version of the bias against area studies is rooted in the political and cultural structure of academic life and is unlikely to change. Nevertheless, the expansion of the global economy is likely to produce more recognition of the depth of local particularism, though the specifics of any particular society should neither be marginalized nor romanticized.

Acknowledgments

A volume such as this could hardly be published without accumulating many debts. First, the volume is greatly indebted to the Reischauer Institute for its sponsorship of the Twenty-fifth Anniversary Symposium which produced the essays here, and also to E. J. Brill for accepting the volume as part of its Japanese Studies Library, and especially to Professor Harold Bolitho, the series' United States editor. At the Reischauer Institute the manuscript was compiled by Margot Chamberlain and Galen Amstutz, with assistance from Hiromi Maeda. Tonia Myers and Mary Amstutz gave valuable copyediting support. Finally, this book could have been published only with the intellectual contribution and sustained support of the essays' authors.

Unless otherwise specified, the place of publication of Japanese-language materials (including translations of same) is Tokyo. Romanization of Japanese terms follows the orthography used in Kenkyūsha's *New Japanese-English Dictionary*, 4th ed. References to the *Kodansha Encyclopedia of Japan* are from the 1983 edition published in Tokyo by Kodansha International. Japanese names follow either Japanese or English order, depending upon the language of publication, with the exception of the index, where English format is used exclusively. Bibliographies have not been indexed.

Bibliography

Deptula, Nancy Monteith, and Michael Hess. 1996. *The Edwin O. Reischauer Institute of Japanese Studies: A Twenty-Year Chronicle*. Cambridge: Reischauer Institute, Harvard University.

Hardacre, Helen, and Adam L. Kern, eds. 1997. *New Directions in the Study of Meiji Japan*. Leiden: E. J. Brill.

Japan Foundation. 1984. *Japanese Studies in the United States: The 1980s*. Tokyo: The Japan Foundation.

———. 1988. *Japanese Studies in the United States: Part I, History and Present Condition*. Japanese Studies Series XVII, edited by Marius B. Jansen. Ann Arbor: Association for Asian Studies.

Japan Foundation, and the Association for Asian Studies. 1996. *Japanese Studies in the United States: The 1990s*. Japanese Studies Series XXVI. Ann Arbor: Association for Asian Studies.

Massey, Elizabeth T., and Joseph A. Massey. 1977. *CULCON Report on Japanese Studies at Colleges and Universities in the United States in the Mid-70s*. New York: The Japan Society, Inc.

Social Science Research Council-American Council of Learned Societies Joint Committee on Japanese Studies. February, 1970. *Japanese Studies in the United States: A Report on the State of the Field, Current Resources and Future Needs*. New York: Social Science Research Council.

Takagi, Yasaka. 1935. *Japanese Studies in the Universities and Colleges of the United States*. LaJolla: Institute of Pacific Relations.

SIZING UP (AND BREAKING DOWN) JAPAN*

John W. Dower

One of the most ambitious undertakings in English-language historical scholarship is the Cambridge University Press series of national histories. The multi-volume *Cambridge History of This Country* and *Cambridge History of That Country* are presented to the public as authoritative. They occupy library shelves as if they were themselves historical monuments.

The first and only *Cambridge History of Japan* was published in six volumes beginning in the late 1980s. It was planned and supervised by four general editors: the American historians John W. Hall and Marius Jansen; Denis Twitchett of Great Britain, a specialist in medieval Chinese history; and Kanai Madoka of Japan. Professor Hall was the co-editor with James McClain of the fourth volume of the series (1991); Professor Jansen edited the fifth volume (1989); and Peter Duus, another American, the final volume (1988). All six volumes, covering from prehistoric times to the twentieth century (and averaging around eight hundred pages each), had the same elegant design on the dust jacket: a reproduction of a Tokugawa-period painting by Utagawa Toyoharu of Ryōgoku Bridge on the Sumida River in Edo.

The dust jacket tells a great deal about popular Western perceptions of Japan. It is aesthetically tasteful. It is exotic—a frozen image of late-feudal culture, replete with fans and paper umbrellas, kimono and lanterns, graceful wooden bridges and archaic man-powered boats. And it conveys the clear impression of a fundamentally unchanging society. The same visual image covers every

---

* This is the edited version of an essay, prepared in 1994, which appeared under the title "Nihon Shakaizō no Genzai-Rekishi Ishiki no Hensen" in *Rekishi Ishiki no Genzai*, bessatsu 1 of *Nihon Tsūshi: Iwanami Kōza* (Iwanami shoten, 1995). An expanded version appeared in the September and October 1995 issues of *Shisō* under the title "Nihon o Hakaru: Eigoken ni okeru Nihon Kenkyū no Rekishi Jojutsu." For a detailed bibliography of English-language scholarship on Japan, see John W. Dower with Timothy George, eds., *Japanese History and Culture from Ancient to Modern Times: Seven Basic Bibliographies*, 2nd ed. (Princeton: Markus Wiener Publishers, 1995).

period of Japanese history, from Jōmon and Yayoi right up to the present day.

Culture, Power, and Ideology

The message implicit in this all-too-typical wrapping is that a unique, unchanging cultural essence pervades the entire history of Japan. This is nonsense, of course, but it reveals a problematic concern in current scholarly as well as popular discourse. How do we deal with "culture?" Indeed, what do we even mean by this ambiguous term? As historians and social scientists, how heavily should we weigh culture (or "tradition") as opposed to other social, political, and economic considerations?

These are old issues, but they have taken on new meaning in recent decades as Japan has emerged as a powerful capitalist state. In the comparative study of Japan and other modern societies, such questions have become entangled with larger issues of difference on the one hand and apparent similarity on the other. These "divergence/convergence" debates in turn raise fundamental questions concerning the values and dynamics that drive individual and collective action in Japan and elsewhere.

It is in this context that the Cambridge dust jacket is noteworthy. In the terms of contemporary cultural criticism, the fact that such a distinguished publishing house chose to wrap twentieth-century Japan with an exotic scene from the Tokugawa period can be seen as emblematic of Euro-American "Orientalist" attitudes in general. The Orientalism concept, introduced by Edward Said in 1978, gave a fine gloss and memorable label to what previously had been identified in plainer terms as Western ethnocentrism vis-à-vis cultures and societies outside the Judaeo-Christian sphere. Beginning with the earliest contacts between Europeans and non-Europeans, Westerners at all levels of society, as Said demonstrated (mostly by examining European writings on the Middle East), have tended to exoticize and caricature non-Westerners and to emphasize how their values and experiences differ fundamentally from those of the West. From this perspective, the repetitive dust jacket for the *Cambridge History of Japan* is splendidly Orientalist, for it conveys the impression of a society that is (1) unchanging in essence, and (2) fundamentally divergent from the European or Euro-American experience. Needless to say, by wrapping Japan's modern century with Toyoharu's depiction of late-eighteenth-century Edo, the impression also is conveyed that modern and even contemporary Japan remains backward and even feudalistic.[1]

This is an astonishing stereotype when we consider the vigor of Japanese capitalism in the late 1980s, when the Cambridge volumes began appearing, and the advanced technological and technocratic competence on which these economic accomplishments rested. Yet if we turn from the scholarly British publisher to popular depictions in the U.S. media in this same period, much the same Orientalist imagery is to be found. It was a rare political cartoonist or magazine illustrator indeed who could resist depicting Japan's industrial and financial power with exotic, traditionalistic, culture-saturated images.

By far the most popular of such graphic images was a giant sumo wrestler looming over Wall Street or towering over Uncle Sam. This was a witty way of representing Japan's huge financial clout, as well as its enormous trade surplus, but it also carried a potent subliminal message. Like Toyoharu's "Ryōgoku Bridge," the sumo-capitalist suggested that contemporary Japanese practices, even in the realm of high finance and cutting-edge technology, remain fundamentally rooted in the Tokugawa period. More significant yet, such popular iconography implied that Japan plays the modern game of capitalism by old and culture-bound rules unfamiliar to Westerners—for Europeans and Americans, of course, do not play or comprehend sumo. The symbolic sumo wrestler became an almost irresistible metaphor for affirming that in capitalism, as in virtually everything else, the Japanese "play by different rules."

After this exotic behemoth, the most clichéd image American cartoonists and illustrators turned to was the samurai—again seizing Wall Street, or somehow incongruously meshed with modern

---

[1] Edward Said (1978). A comparably stereotyped "Orientalist" impression is conveyed by the dust jacket of *The Cambridge Encyclopedia of Japan*, edited by Richard Bowring and Peter Kornicki (1993). The front of the jacket displays a large photograph of Mt. Fuji, the spine features a geisha, and four photographs appear on the back: a masked *kendō* swordsman, mothers and children in festive New Year's kimono, a pagoda, and a McDonald's fast-food restaurant. It is doubtful that even a contest to produce the most banal clichés possible could have surpassed this.

Western clothing or high-tech appurtenances. The quintessential Japanese salaryman or capitalist almost invariably is depicted in a manner evocative of feudal culture. At the same time, of course—and this is particularly evident in mass-media graphics—it also is always clear that this representative figure is physically (that is, racially) "Oriental."[2]

Do these images really matter greatly if we wish to discuss more thoughtful perceptions of modern Japanese history and society? Yes and no. One of the striking features of even serious writings on Japan since before World War II has been the almost indivisible relationship between such writings and current political and ideological concerns. This is particularly true of the mainstream of American scholarship—even while the writers of such commentaries may be proclaiming a commitment to "value-free" or "non-ideological" analysis. In a detailed overview of studies in political science, published in 1992, for example, the American scholar Richard Samuels concluded that "[t]he intellectual history of Japanese political studies in this country reflects closely the changes in the foreign relations of the United States and Japan. The predominant images of Japan in U.S. scholarship have been positive when U.S.-Japan relations have been friendly and have turned critical when the relationship has been more adversarial. Indeed, American Japan scholarship has been more deeply embedded in the political culture of the bilateral relationship than in social science itself."[3]

This is not a surprising observation, although in American and other academic circles the politics of scholarship usually has been obscured by evocations of "objectivity." Many years ago, E. H. Carr advised readers to study the historian before engaging what he or she wrote, a caution that applies to academics generally. Scholars, no less than anyone else, are products of their times and circumstances.

---

[2] The popular imagery of U.S.-Japan relations since World War II is discussed and illustrated in John W. Dower (1994), 287-335.

[3] Richard J. Samuels (1992), 17-56. The British historian W. G. Beasley made a similar point in a (1988) review of Edwin O. Reischauer's (1986) autobiography, emphasizing that Reischauer's influential writings on Japanese history and society reflected "differing perceptions of *contemporary* Japanese society" and "not pure scholarship."

Modernization and "Convergence"

From the 1930s into the 1950s, English-language writings about Japan were predictably critical and dwelled (much as *Kōzaha* scholarship within Japan did) on the profound differences between Japan and "the West." Pernicious "feudal legacies" and inherently antidemocratic "cultural values," coupled with the haste of the country's relatively late development as a modern nation, it was argued, led to the creation of an authoritarian state and made the militarism of the 1930s all but inevitable. Ruth Benedict's wartime studies of the "national character" of the Japanese, conducted secretly for the U.S. Office of War Information and summarized in her classic 1946 book *The Chrysanthemum and the Sword*, established the basic paradigm of Japanese cultural divergence from the more "universalistic" Western norm. Japan, in this analysis, was a "shame" rather than "guilt" culture, and its moral or ethical codes tended to be situational and particularistic rather than transcendent and universally binding in all situations. In historical studies, the Canadian historian E. H. Norman, drawing eclectically on both *Rōnōha* and *Kōzaha* scholarship in Japanese, offered an eloquent critique of the authoritarian feudal background of the modern state. The early reform agenda of the Allied Occupation of Japan was firmly grounded on such critical perceptions of an "incomplete" transition to modernity.

Beginning in the mid-1950s, as Japan became America's essential Cold War ally in Asia, English-language scholarship changed dramatically. Under the rubric of "modernization theory," which remained fashionable until roughly the mid- or late 1970s, the feudal culture of pre-Meiji society was re-evaluated in a manner that accentuated its "positive" contributions to the country's modern development. Indeed, it was under the influence of American modernization theorists such as John Hall that the terminology used to periodize the Tokugawa era itself was changed from "late feudal" to "early modern"—a significant revision designed to signify the dynamic and fundamentally admirable nature of the pre-Meiji era.[4] The positive thrust of modernization theory also led Western scholars to treat the oppression and aggression of the

---

[4] In volume 4 of *The Cambridge History of Japan* (John W. Hall and James McClain, eds., 1991), the "early modern" designation is extended back to the late Sengoku period.

prewar state as having been, by and large, an aberration—or, at best, a "dilemma of growth" rather than a fundamental and almost inevitable outcome of the peculiar path of "modernization" that was followed in the wake of the Meiji Restoration.

The difference between the modernization-theory approach and earlier scholarship was thus striking. The old critique of "feudal legacies" was by and large repudiated. Pre-Meiji values and practices were praised as providing a solid baseline for subsequent modernization. The authoritarian legacies of the Meiji era were minimized, and the rigorous sense of inherent "contradictions" in the system leading to the repression and militarism of the 1930s was abandoned. "Taishō democracy" in the relatively narrow sense of parliamentary party politics was identified as a meaningful baseline for postwar democracy in Japan. The prewar economy was evaluated as having made fundamentally sound and impressive progress toward the attainment of "MEG" (Modern Economic Growth). "Free enterprise," as Edwin O. Reischauer put it in 1964, speaking of the prewar period, "accounted for the bulk of Japan's earlier economic modernization."[5]

This was a drastic revision of the analysis developed by E. H. Norman and the earlier generation of scholars—not merely because it offered such a positive evaluation of the "early modern" and "modern" experience, but also because it emphasized Japan's ever increasing *similarity* to the more developed capitalist nations of the West. In the Cold War milieu, modernization theory represented an anti-Marxist and highly ethnocentric theoretical model, in which it was presumed that all non-communist countries would and should become increasingly similar to the advanced nations of Europe and the United States as they "modernized" along capitalist lines. The modernization theorists, in short, stressed the manner in which Japan's trajectory of social, political, and economic development signaled convergence with the Western model.[6]

It is now apparent that this predominantly American formulation of convergence was riddled with a double hubris. Thus, it

---

[5] Edwin Reischauer (1964). This essay was written for *Life* magazine's special issue on Japan, published in conjunction with the Tokyo Olympics when Reischauer was serving as ambassador to Tokyo.

[6] For an annotated critical study of Norman's writings and the later modernization theorists, see the introductory essay on "E. H. Norman, Japan, and the Uses of History" in Dower, ed. (1975).

was not only assumed that Japan would develop in essentially the same manner and direction as the more advanced capitalist nations, but also taken for granted that it could not ever actually catch up with the United States. Japan was not merely a "late developer." It also was destined to play catch-up eternally; and as a consequence, it behooved Americans to treat their loyal and earnest ally with patience and generosity. This paternalistic condescension emerged with striking frankness in an unpublished report on the state of political studies of Japan prepared for the Social Science Research Council in 1968. William Steslicke, the author, criticized the "vulgar cultural determinism" of earlier Western writings and described the research agenda of the 1960s as a "realistic liberal, social scientific, progressive" perspective. He then went on to identify the following nine assumptions as constituting the premises of this new perspective:

1) The United States has a great stake in Japan because Japan is the key to Asia's future.
2) Japan is America's number one ally in the Pacific.
3) The alliance cannot be taken for granted.
4) U.S. specialists have an obligation to explain Japan's position and to encourage Americans to be patient with Japan.
5) Do not expect U.S.-style democracy to flourish in Japan.
6) Japanese democracy is not mature.
7) Japanese tend to be too idealistic and emotional; they need to be more pragmatic.
8) We should help Japan, since the Japanese have so much to learn from us.
9) Japan has little to teach us.

This nicely captures the intellectual milieu of the time. Politics and scholarship were inseparable. Privately, the proponents of convergence theory held grave reservations concerning the prospects for democracy in Japan. And as late as 1968, even political scientists specializing in Japan assumed that "Japan has little to teach us."[7]

The decline of modernization theory in the 1970s coincided with Japan's unanticipated emergence as an economic power. Obviously, nothing in the modernization paradigms had prepared Americans or Europeans (or Japanese, for that matter) for a Jap-

---

[7] William E. Steslicke (1968), as reproduced in Samuels (1992), 26-27.

anese *challenge* to Western hegemony over the global political economy. Nor were the modernization theorists prepared to contemplate such a seeming anomaly as a "Japanese model" for practicing capitalism. It is in this context of confrontation by an unexpectedly strong "non-Western" state that much English-language scholarly as well as popular writing began to assume a more critical tenor—and to emphasize not points of convergence between the Japanese and Western experiences, but, once again, points of significant difference and divergence.

The Japanese Challenge and "Divergence"

Recent Western scholarship is vastly more diverse and nuanced than it was a half century ago. Nonetheless, the "third stage" of postwar discourse that followed modernization theory calls to mind the writings of the wartime and early postwar years in two provocative ways: much of this scholarship is preoccupied with Japan's divergence from Euro-American models and, at the same time, closely attentive to "culture." This can be seen across the spectrum of recent historical and social scientific studies.

As Japan emerged as a formidable economic power, for example, "revisionist" political scientists began to emphasize its distinctive qualities as a "capitalist developmental state." Chalmers Johnson's 1982 study of the Ministry of International Trade and Industry, which included detailed historical analysis of MITI's prewar institutional roots, was a landmark publication in this regard and is sometimes described as the most influential political science study of Japan ever published in English. Johnson's emphasis on the role of the bureaucratic state in promoting industrial policy did not merely challenge earlier notions about "convergence," but also called into question the so-called universal principles of both Marxism and market-oriented neoclassical economics. Thus, in a typically provocative statement, Johnson observed in a 1987 essay that "[w]e are only beginning to recognize that Japan has invented and put together the institutions of capitalism in new ways, ways that neither Adam Smith nor Karl Marx would recognize or understand."[8]

---

[8] Chalmers Johnson (1982). The quotation appears in his (1987) article at

Similar revisionism has become influential in other disciplines as well. In legal studies, for example, American scholars such as Frank Upham and John Haley have offered closely documented analyses that reach conclusions comparable to those commonly heard in the decades prior to the vogue of modernization theory—namely, that although Japan has adopted Western legal norms, it does not put them into practice as Westerners do. In his important 1987 book, Upham advanced the thesis that conservative hostility to Western ideals of "rule-centered law" and "judge-centered law" has influenced the Japanese legal process "in such a way that it has evolved in directions largely different from either of our Western models." Through well-entrenched processes of "bureaucratic informalism," Upham contends, the dominant elites (the bureaucracy, big business, and Liberal Democratic Party) "use legal rules and institutions to manage and direct conflict and control change at a social level."[9]

This perception of fundamentally divergent attitudes toward law was expressed in even more sweeping terms in a favorable review by the German scholar Carl Steenstrup, published in the leading English-language journal of Japanese studies in 1993. In terms reminiscent of Ruth Benedict, Steenstrup offered this as the "bottom line" in John Haley's analysis of law and authority in Japan: "Japan has 'consensual' and power-diffusing government. 'Law' has decorative and warning functions. 'Morals' are situational. Power is held by groups, exercised by group leaders, and sanctioned by the threat of expulsion. There are no absolute standards of fairness, particularly not toward outsiders: group loyalty is the paramount value. Inter-group power balance decides most issues. 'Law,' being individualistic and egalitarian, since of Western parentage, is *not* a basis of the Japanese state. Pressure is normal, formal coercion rare."[10]

---

420. Johnson (1988) discusses the theoretical implications of his argument that Japan practices a different sort of capitalism than other countries. This last publication appears in a volume that also includes commentaries on U.S. scholarship on Japanese history (Marius Jansen), literature (Edwin McClellan), and anthropology and sociology (L. Keith Brown).

[9] Frank K. Upham (1987). See especially chapter 1 on "Models of Law and Social Change."

[10] Carl Steenstrup (1993): 485. For generally positive commentary on other studies contrasting the practice of law in Japan and the West, see *Journal of Japanese Studies* 19, no. 1 (Winter 1993): 212, and 18, no. 2 (Summer 1992): 552-56.

Scholars supportive of such postmodernization-theory revisionism often evoke the Japanese vocabulary of *tatemae* (appearance) and *honne* (reality). "Westernization" is *tatemae*, the argument goes, while conformity to elite pressure and group social controls is *honne*. Anthropologists and sociologists thus have renewed their emphasis on the continued primacy of the group over the individual, and the way Japanese distinguish respect for individuality (*kosei*) but not for individualism (*kojinshugi*).[11] From a political perspective, such low regard for individualism—coupled with the immense influence wielded by the "iron triangle" of bureaucracy, big business, and until recently the Liberal Democratic Party—represents another conspicuous divergence from Western norms and values. The paternalistic democracy of postwar Japan thus is seen as differing in significant ways from the tenets and practices of Western-style liberal democracy. As the 1968 report to the Social Science Research Council revealed, reservations about the prospects for "U.S.-style democracy" were widespread even at the height of the modernization-theory vogue. Now, however, when emphasis on divergence is more fashionable, such criticism has become a staple of academic as well as popular discourse.[12] In a very different field of inquiry, literary critics disdainful of the "universalistic" presumptions of modernization theory also have shown renewed interest in "the variance and peculiarity" of such distinctive Japanese genres as the *shishōsetsu* ("I-novel" or "I-fiction").[13]

The resemblance between this "third stage" preoccupation with divergence from Western models and the wartime and early postwar writings seems, at first glance, even more striking when "culture" is factored in—for whether dealing with capitalism or law, politics or literary aesthetics, the divergence theorists inevitably

---

[11] See, for example, Harumi Befu (1993).

[12] See Samuels (1992): 37-39, for a summary of Western political science writings beginning in the early 1960s which debated "whether or not the Japanese are *capable* of becoming democrats."

[13] Masao Miyoshi (1988). This special issue was republished as a book a year later (Miyoshi and Harootunian, 1989). The essay also is included in Miyoshi's *Off Center* (1991). Miyoshi rejects the notion that the Japanese even respect individuality (*shutaisei*). "There seems to be little question," he writes, "that individuality in personality, autonomy in action, and freedom in thought and expression are not characteristic of modern Japanese." In his view, there is nothing wrong with this, since *shutaisei* is a Western value that in practice has contributed to great exploitation of others; see *Off Center*, esp. 122-25.

must address basic questions about cultural values. Emphasis on such purportedly "Japanese" characteristics as the group model, acquiescence to authority, situational ethics, esteem for "individuality" rather than "individualism," and the like does indeed share common ground with Ruth Benedict's preoccupation with "national character" and distinctive "patterns of culture." At the same time, in emphasizing Japan's unique values and practices, divergence theorists also on occasion seem to be adopting a position similar to that of conservative *nihonjinron* theorists in Japan.

Such resemblances are misleading, however, for the recent Western literature is far more complex and nuanced than this. To appreciate how the new scholarship differs from the old—and differs from nationalistic writings about Japan's unique cultural essence as well—we must begin at an elemental level by recalling the difference between the country's obvious failure in the 1940s and early 1950s and its successful accomplishments in recent decades. The "first-stage" divergence theorists and cultural determinists were writing in the milieu of war, when it was apparent that the initial attempt to "modernize" had ended in disaster. Their writings naturally represented a thoroughgoing critique of both feudal legacies and the authoritarianism of the modern state.

The "third-stage" divergence theorists who began to make their voices heard beginning in the mid- and late 1970s write from a dramatically different perspective. They are, with few exceptions, impressed by many of Japan's postwar accomplishments. At the same time, they have rejected the Cold War hubris of the modernization theorists and generally write from a position of skepticism regarding Western hegemonism and cultural imperialism. As a consequence, the acknowledgment of important differences between Japan and "the West" does not necessarily reflect a negative judgment about Japan. It may be offered as a neutral observation. In areas such as industrial relations, social policy, and preuniversity education, Japan's departures from the Western norm often are evaluated positively.

The seminal book in the latter category was *Japan As Number One*, published in 1979 by the Harvard sociologist Ezra Vogel. Although criticized at the time by many Japan specialists, Vogel essentially overturned the tables of popular discourse by suggesting what previously had been heresy: that "the West" might learn from "the East"—and not merely about values, but about practical ways of organizing a modern society.[14]

Much the same thesis has been developed in detail by the eminent British sociologist Ronald Dore, who essentially merged "divergence theory" and "convergence theory" in ways shocking to neoclassical theorists by arguing that the Japanese had created institutions and social practices which Western industrial societies might well attempt to emulate. Dore's intimation of a "Japanese model" actually was conveyed in a comparative study of British and Japanese factory structure published as early as 1973. He later elaborated on this with specific reference to the moral and rational appeal of non-Western values (1987).[15] Robert Cole, an American sociologist well known since the early 1970s for his empirical and comparative studies of industrial relations, likewise has argued (1979, 1988) that in many areas Japanese firms make better use of their human resources than their American counterparts.

Many other third-stage divergence theorists similarly reversed the traditional notion of "learning from the West" to argue that it might be possible to learn from Japan—either directly, by emulation, or indirectly, by at least acknowledging that Japan had changed the rules of modern capitalism and nation building. Chalmers Johnson's study of MITI spawned a veritable cottage industry of both popular and scholarly debate about the necessity and desirability of having the state engage in some sort of "industrial policy." Legal scholars such as John Haley suggested that Japan's hierarchical social structure was not necessarily inferior to the grossly inequitable class structure of the United States.[16] Many Western commentators, particularly in the United States, praised

---

[14] For samples of the critical response to Vogel's bestseller by American Japan specialists, see reviews published in 1980 by Edward Seidensticker and Donald Hellman. At the popular level, two noteworthy English-language books actually preceded Vogel's in calling attention to Japan's positive postwar accomplishments, the first comprised of articles by correspondents of the British weekly magazine *The Economist* (1963), and the second by Herman Kahn (1970).

[15] Dore (1987) stresses Confucian ideals such as benevolence and virtue more than duty or discipline in creating "institutions designed to protect a general sense of the fairness of social arrangements." See also Dore's (1979) essay.

[16] John Haley (1991). See especially the chapter on "The Fallacy of America As Model."

the Japanese penchant for avoiding litigation—once derided as "premodern"—as an estimable practice. In 1984, the attorney general of Connecticut actually presented this argument in the *New York Times* in an essay titled "Give Confucius a Chance."[17] A prize-winning theoretical book in criminology and sociology published by John Braithwaite in 1989 took the Japanese practice of "shaming" (Ruth Benedict's core concept) as a model for effective community participation in controlling crime. Thomas Rohlen, an American who did field work in a Japanese bank, was among the earliest anthropologists to suggest that Confucian ideals of "harmony" might be more effective for modern organizations than the American ideal of individualism (1974).

In a 1991 study of the Japanese software industry, Michael Cusumano, a specialist in Japanese business history and practices, added his voice to those who argue that Americans could learn from factory practices followed in Japan. In the process, Cusumano also turned old East-West formulas inside out by depicting the craft mode of software development in the United States as an "art," as opposed to the more "scientific" factory approach followed in Japan.[18] In the familiar "Orientalist" approach, of course, it is always the other way round: Westerners are supposed to approach manufacture scientifically, non-Westerners more in the mode of arts and crafts. So voluminous is the contemporary literature of this sort that it is startling indeed to recall that in 1968 American social scientists were operating on the premise that "Japan has little to teach us."

Postmodernism and "Culture"

Where "culture" per se is concerned, the divergence theories of the postmodernization-theory period reflect the influence of a number of critical theories fashionable among European and American social scientists. For example, the "invention of tradition"—a phrase popularized by Eric Hobsbawm and Terence Ranger in an influential 1983 collection of essays on European history—became a dynamic concept for re-evaluating the ideological

---

[17] Joseph Lieberman (1984).
[18] See also the review of Cusumano by Marie Anchordoguy (1992).

construction of "tradition" and "culture" in modern and contemporary Japanese society.[19] Indeed, as anthropologists were quick to observe, the practice of inventing traditions already had been flamboyantly acknowledged in Japanese popular culture itself in the 1970s vogue of *furusato zukuri* ("recreating native places"). Heightened sensitivity to the pervasiveness of invented traditions in all societies provided Western Japan specialists with a firmer theoretical basis for criticizing *nihonjinron*-style arguments. Thus, they called attention to the careful and adroit manner by which elites and the molders of popular opinion, in Japan as elsewhere, routinely create modern myths under the rubric of "tradition" or cultural uniqueness—whether these be myths involving the emperor, or an idealized hierarchical "family system," or a code of "obedience and filial piety," or a harmonious "traditional employment system," or a simple and egalitarian rural community, or a pure "national essence" rooted deep in the past before the corruption of foreign influences from China and the West.[20]

From an early date, English-language scholarship on Japan has revealed competing views concerning the persistence of so-called traditional values on the one hand and, on the other hand, the ideological manipulation of an imagined and highly romanticized past for contemporary purposes of social control and regimentation. Sumiya Mikio's work on the Meiji-era creation of myths of enterprise "familyism," for example, was known to Western scholars.[21] Earlier writings on Japanese ideology and politics, particu-

---

[19] Also conceptually influential was the related concept of "imagined communities" introduced that same year in a study of nationalism by the American Southeast Asia specialist Benedict Anderson (1983). These were not, of course, new concepts in the social sciences; Karl Mannheim had discussed the phenomenon of intellectual movements of "return" to an idealized earlier time decades earlier (1936).

[20] For English-language critiques of the invention of "tradition" as seen in contemporary *nihonjinron* writings by Japanese, see Harumi Befu (1980); Ross Mouer and Yoshio Sugimoto (1986); Peter N. Dale (1986); the "Symposium on *Ie* Society" (1985), involving five responses to the "*ie* society" thesis advanced by Murakami Yasusuke, et al.; David Plath's review of Kawai Hayao's theories concerning fairy tales and the Japanese psyche (1992); and John Whittier Treat's (1992) review of Ikegami Yoshihiko's (1991) work.

[21] See Sumiya's essays in Kazuo Okochi, Bernard Karsh, and Solomon Levine, eds. (1974), 15-87. The historical emergence of the modern Japanese employment system is delineated in essays published in 1978 by Sydney Crawcour, Robert Cole, and W. Mark Fruin. See also Fruin's (1980) article, as well as his (1983) monograph. Scholars of Japanese industrial relations such as Robert Cole, Ronald

larly before the modernization-theory vogue, when E. H. Norman's influence was still strong, had dwelled at some length on the essentially authoritarian "reinvention" of the emperor and emperor system in the *bakumatsu* and Meiji periods. Studies of prewar and wartime indoctrination (also generally marginalized during the vogue of modernization theory) naturally were attentive to the militaristic and ultranationalistic uses of the past that reached a disastrous peak in the early decades of the Shōwa era. Nonetheless, the re-emergence of emphasis on manufactured or invented "traditions" became a conspicuous feature of Western scholarship beginning around the mid-1980s. Carol Gluck's important 1985 study of late-Meiji ideology, significantly titled *Japan's Modern Myths*, epitomized this new sensitivity.[22]

The intellectual thrust of such writings is that much of what is presented as "unique" and supposedly unchanging cultural values in the writings of Euro-American "Orientalists" as well as the "self-Orientalizing" Japanese proponents of *nihonjinron* is socially constructed, ideologically charged, and part of a constant process of invention and reinvention. And in this, there is nothing at all unique about Japan: all societies and cultures operate or function similarly. There is disagreement concerning how much weight to assign "culture" in trying to explain the social, political, and economic dynamics of modern Japan. Chalmers Johnson treats culture as being of negligible influence compared to bureaucratic rationality and control, for example, while Ronald Dore urges Westerners to take Confucian practices seriously. Virtually all contemporary scholarship, however, is sensitive to the manufacture of traditions and modernization of myths.

The playful paradoxes involved in speaking of the commonality of uniqueness or the invention of tradition reflect an analytical approach that has exerted immense influence in the humanities

---

Dore, and Andrew Gordon also emphasize how employment practices have evolved through persistent social, political, and cultural contestation.

[22] W. Dean Kinzley's (1991) study of the theories of industrial harmony promoted by the Taishō period Kyōchōkai appropriated the concept of "invented tradition" directly. Anthropological studies of Japan also have emphasized this theme. See works by William Kelly (1986); Theodore C. Bestor (1989); Helen Hardacre (1989); and Jennifer Robertson (1991). A major research conference organized by Stephen Vlastos and explicitly devoted to "Invention of Japanese Tradition," held in September 1994, similarly takes its title from the work of Hobsbawm and Ranger (1993).

and social sciences since the 1970s. This mode of analysis has been presented under various labels: "poststructuralism," "deconstruction," "postmodernism," "cultural criticism," even simply (and pretentiously) "critical theory." The language employed by devotees of the new critical approaches is often opaque and incomprehensible to non-initiates. Nonetheless, the grand preoccupations of poststructuralist or postmodernist thought probably reflect better than any other single mode of analysis the *Zeitgeist* of Western academics in the period since modernization theory declined and the economic rise of Japan and other East Asian nations helped call into question the hegemonic power of the West that had been taken for granted for centuries.

The iconoclastic American sociologist C. Wright Mills once drew a distinction between theoretical Marxism and *plain* Marxism—meaning by the latter basic Marxist insights as non-specialists in Marxist theory might comprehend them. In the same spirit, it seems possible to identify several insights of *plain* "poststructuralism" as these have influenced Japanese studies. Critical attentiveness to modern mythmaking and the invention of traditions, as already noted, reflects renewed sensitivity to the social and ideological construction of "culture." At the same time, the decline of Western hegemonism in the more conventional sense of Euro-American domination of the global economy has been accompanied, in the new critical approaches, by sweeping criticism of Western *intellectual* hegemonism. Edward Said's denunciation of "Orientalism" is but a small corner of this broader critique, which repudiates the traditional Western conceit that the Judaeo-Christian experience reflects "universal" norms and properly represents an inevitable and desirable path of "modern" development.

The very term "postmodernism" itself is heavy with ambiguity as well as innuendo. It refers, to begin with, to both a stage of socio-economic development and a mode of analysis. In the former sense, postmodernism is an advanced stage of capitalist society, first attained in the United States and Europe and now extended to Japan. In this narrow construction, "postmodern" Japan is essentially synonymous with contemporary Japan, and as such may be subjected to conspicuously varying evaluations. To many outsiders as well as Japanese, Japanese "postmodernism" represents a highly successful outcome of the "modernization" process that began in the Tokugawa period and began to accelerate rapidly in

Meiji. To harsher critics, postmodern Japan, like other late-capitalist or post-industrial societies, is more noteworthy as an example of the manner in which "culture" has been "commodified." The first sustained critique of Japan in these terms appeared in 1988 in the form of a collection of essays edited by Masao Miyoshi and H. D. Harootunian.[23] Miyoshi himself has offered the most doomsday vision of Japan as a postmodern cultural wasteland in which "the collective nonindividuals of Japan seem to be leading the whole pack of peoples and nations, in both the West and the Rest, to a fantastic dystopia of self-emptied, idea-vacated, and purpose-lost production, consumption, and daydreaming."[24]

Japan and the Critique of Western Hegemonism

In the introduction to their book, Miyoshi and Harootunian characterize postmodernism as entailing a critical perspective on "interiority, subject/object binarism, centrality, universalism, logocentricity, masculine neutrality—all such hegemonic traits that have ranged over the whole paradigm of the Enlightenment." As postmodernism replaces modernism, they explain, "playfulness, gaming, spectacle, tentativeness, alterity, reproduction, and pastiche are offered to guide the new age. Such terms are intent on dispersal, maintaining a sensitive aversion for any form of concentration." This is playful language in itself, but it points to the critical spirit that has permeated much recent scholarship on Japan, even where individual authors may not use (or even really understand) such specialized jargon.

The core of the new criticism in this regard is a profound skepticism toward "metanarratives"—that is, toward grand theories or all-embracing systems of any sort. This is what Miyoshi and Harootunian have in mind in attacking the "hegemonic traits" associated with the Enlightenment, and in referring to "a sensitive aversion for any form of concentration." The "universal" pretentions of Euro-American values and practices represent the grandest and most vulnerable of such metanarratives (thus extending the post-

---

[23] See the extended reviews of this collection by John Whittier Treat (1990) and David Pollack (1989).
[24] Masao Miyoshi (1991), 124.

modernist critique to all post-Enlightenment pretensions to "objectivity" and "rationality," and rejecting traditional constructions of linear "progress"). Modernization theory, as a transparent manifestation of such Eurocentric "universalism," naturally is repudiated. So too are the "metanarratives" associated with Hegel and Marx (although many poststructuralist intellectuals still associate themselves with a nebulous "Left"). Freudian analysis also becomes a discredited metanarrative. Needless to say, this critique of "totalizing" systems is severe in its dismissal of *nihonjinron*-type attempts to explain Japan's experience and accomplishments in terms of some "master code" of immutable cultural values. At the same time, however—and here the ideological ambiguity of such criticism reveals itself most graphically—the attack on Western "hegemonism" and "universalism" that is central to this critical mode often calls to mind the denunciations of the West expressed by prewar as well as postwar Japanese nationalists.

This resonance emerges vividly in the volume in *The Cambridge History of Japan* devoted to the twentieth century, which concludes with an incisive essay by Tetsuo Najita and H. D. Harootunian entitled "Japanese Revolt Against the West: Political and Cultural Criticism in the Twentieth Century." Najita and Harootunian are associated with a "Chicago school" of Japan specialists who are firmly grounded in contemporary critical theory, and their essay makes the case that from the very beginning of the Meiji Restoration, "distrust of the West accompanied the act of state building in Japan." Addressing a binary paradigm that is of great interest in contemporary criticism, namely constructions of "Self" and "Other," the authors begin by observing that modern Japan has persistently and obsessively defined itself vis-à-vis the dominant West (just as it defined itself vis-à-vis China in earlier centuries). To "cosmopolitan" Japanese this meant primarily catching up with the West—and, ideally, surpassing it to make a unique contribution to world civilization by combining the best of "East" and "West." Even among sincere prewar Japanese "Westernizers," that is, there resided the seeds of a preoccupation with uniqueness. To patriots more attuned to the Euro-American *threat*, both materially and culturally, the Western "Other" became more simply a dark mirror by which to clarify, by contrast, Japan's own unique cultural "Self."

By the late 1930s, most cosmopolitan Japanese Westernizers had caved in to the ultranationalists, of course, and ideological tracts issued by the state, such as *Kokutai no hongi* (Cardinal Principles of the National Polity) and *Shinmin no michi* (The Way of the Subject), laid down in unmistakable terms the absolutely fundamental difference between the corrupt and imperialistic "universal" values of the West on the one hand (individualism, democracy, liberalism, materialism, utilitarianism, etc.) and the unique, pure, communal, emperor-centered "traditional" values of the Japanese on the other hand. I myself have analyzed the violent hatreds of World War II in comparative terms of race, power, and ideology (1986). Najita and Harootunian, however, approach the Self/Other dichotomy differently. They are not interested here in comparison or the formal texts of state indoctrination such as *Kokutai no hongi* and *Shinmin no michi*, but concentrate instead on the abiding—and passionate—intellectual tradition of anti-Western thought. Their essay provides the best synthesis in English of the nationalistic and ultranationalistic critique of Western-style "modernization"—beginning with Restoration realists such as Kido Takayoshi and extending through Okakura Tenshin, Kita Ikki, Gondō Seikei, Tachibana Kosaburō, Nakano Seigō, Ōkawa Shūmei, the Kyoto School philosophers (Miki Kiyoshi on the one hand, and Nishida Kitarō, Kōyama Iwao, Kōsaka Masaaki, Suzuki Shigetaka, and Nishitani Keiji on the other), Watsuji Tetsurō, Yanagida Kunio, Tanizaki Jun'ichirō, the *Romanha* writers, and the numerous intellectuals engaged in the early 1940s debate on "overcoming the modern" (*kindai no chōkoku*). "Japan's proper cultural place," Najita and Harootunian conclude, also "remained as the central intellectual issue for the postwar period."[25]

The intellectuals discussed by Najita and Harootunian were by no means unknown to Westerners interested in Japan, but never before had they been presented in such a scholarly manner as being so *central* a thread in the fabric of modern Japanese thought. Their critique of the West was presented in detail, and taken seriously. Only the Kyoto School intellectuals were really treated harshly and described as "fascist" (a concept otherwise virtually absent from *The Cambridge History of Japan*). The impression left by this provocative final chapter in the Cambridge history was that the most potent strain of political and cultural criticism in mod-

---

[25] Tetsuo Najita and H. D. Harootunian (1988).

ern Japan was neither liberal nor leftist. To the contrary, it entailed an incisive and often uncompromising critique of "the threat of the West."[26]

There are more than a few ironies embedded in this discourse. One lies in the fact that contemporary Western critics of Euro-American "modernism" and cultural imperialism now take renewed interest not merely in figures such as Yanagida and Tanizaki, who devoted themselves to recording and preserving Japanese traditions, but also in intellectuals once dismissed more casually as right-wing extremists. Ironic too is the fact that much of what tends to impress present-day Western critics as being "unique" in contemporary Japanese society—activities such as the intrusive role of the bureaucracy, the practice of industrial policy, and the exceptional powers of the *zaibatsu* and *keiretsu* in the private sector—are in fact adaptations of Western practices which the prewar cultural and political critics denounced as being classic manifestations of the intrusive, corrupting capitalistic and materialistic civilization of the West. When all is said and done, after all, what the prewar traditionalists and ultranationalists were appalled by—whether they were *nōhonshugisha* (exponents of traditional agrarianism) or European-trained philosophy professors determined to "overthrow the modern"—was the depredation of Western-style capitalism. What impresses most contemporary commentators on Japan is just the opposite of this. They are impressed by how adroitly and "uniquely" Japan has *done* capitalism. Preoccupation with divergence from Western norms and practices thus leads, in itself, in numerous divergent directions.

"Decentering" Japanese History

What does all this mean where Western studies of Japan are concerned? It does not mean that poststructuralist or postmodernist thought has become a new orthodoxy. But the spirit of "deconstruction" or "decentering" has penetrated the field as a whole. There is no center. There are no grand integrating theories com-

---

[26] The penultimate chapter in *The Cambridge History of Japan*, by Peter Duus and Irwin Scheiner, dealt with "Socialism, Liberalism, and Marxism, 1901-1931." This treated prewar Japanese liberals and leftists seriously, but did not make the case that these Western traditions had taken deep root in Japan.

parable to Norman's eclectic Marxism in the first stage or modernization theory in the second stage. Thus, John Whittier Treat refers to "our centrifugally disintegrating profession." Mary Elizabeth Berry speaks of "the collapse of paradigmatic analysis."[27] In the place of overarching theories, we now operate in a middle ground of multiple themes and topics. And the Japan field is, as a result, both richer and poorer.

Several of these themes and preoccupations do interlock in suggestive ways. Before turning to these, however, two features of contemporary studies deserve attention. The field is, to begin with, cosmopolitan in a way undreamed of a half century ago, in that an extremely large portion of the serious scholarship available in English is by Japanese. To speak of "English-language writings on Japan" no longer connotes just writings by Anglo-Americans. Beyond this, moreover, since the 1960s the work of younger Western specialists has shown increasing familiarity with and indebtedness to the writings of Japanese scholars.

Also notable is the lingering influence of the old modernization paradigm. The clearest example of this is to be found in *The Cambridge History of Japan* itself, which generally was received with polite disappointment by reviewers. Cambridge University Press takes pride in presenting its histories as reflections of the current state of knowledge in each respective field, but the critical reception the Japan volumes received made clear that they were caught in a time warp. Although published in the late 1980s and 1990s, the volumes clearly reflected their genesis in the 1970s. The Cambridge histories were themselves historical artifacts, in a manner of speaking, and reviewers treated them accordingly—not so much by criticizing what was addressed as by lamenting what was missing.

Long review essays in the mainstream *Journal of Japanese Studies* conveyed the generational tension in the field. Thus, Mary Elizabeth Berry, reviewing the volume on medieval history (edited by Kozo Yamamura), observed that it reflected "the continuing concern with institutional history that has dominated the scholarship both of Americans and those Japanese most translated into En-

---

[27] Treat's comment appears in an interesting review of postmodernism and Japan (1990). For Berry, see her (1992) article, in which she applied the notion of a collapse of paradigmatic analysis to Japanese as well as Western historical scholarship.

glish," as well as "the primacy of high politics." Upheavals such as *ikki* received only passing attention, Berry noted, and the general impression left by the volume was "that of a development akin to 'progress' that accorded more gains than losses to most medieval people." William Hauser, reviewing the volume on "early modern Japan" co-edited by his mentor John Hall, characterized the overall approach as reflecting a traditional and conservative "1970s conception of the field." Among other things, he noted, this volume (which covered from the mid-sixteenth century to the end of the eighteenth century) failed to address seriously such topics as local history, family history, women's history, or the history of peasant protest and social conflict. Hauser also wondered why seventy-two pages were devoted to "Christianity and the Daimyō," while Buddhism and Shintō received a mere seventeen pages in passing. Here, for any good cultural critic, was surely an egregious example of Western bias.

Henry Smith II's review of the Cambridge coverage of the nineteenth century (edited by Marius Jansen) identified this too as reflective of "the 'modernization' approach," and found astonishing Jansen's introductory defense of modernization as "an effort to avoid politics." This was to be understood, Smith explained, as a reflection of "the virulence of the initial American reaction to Japanese Marxist scholarship." The essence of this modernization approach, as Smith nicely put it, was apparent in the tendency "to see the Meiji Restoration as a political blip in a steadily ascending curve of gradualist socioeconomic 'transition.'" Only one essay, by H. D. Harootunian, portrayed the Restoration as revolutionary potential that remained unfulfilled, rather than as a mere "transition." Only one essay, by Stephen Vlastos, really hinted at "people's history." Just as Berry and Hauser had criticized the scholarly preoccupation with developments at the more elite levels of society, so Smith also observed that "the English-language history of nineteenth-century Japan remains heavily concentrated at the center." There were no sharp societal cleavages in this sort of history. There were no passions. There was little sense of choice.

The final volume in the Cambridge series, dealing with the twentieth century, was reviewed by Andrew Gordon. Like the reviewers of other volumes, he praised individual essays, deplored the manner in which historiographic controversy was largely ignored, regretted the editors' adoption of "the 'modernization' approach to Japanese history," and devoted much of his review to what failed to be addressed. Among the controversies skirted were debates about "Taishō democracy," the emperor system, fascism, and the "reverse course" in the postsurrender Occupation period. "Both the style and substance of many articles," Gordon observed, "tend to downplay conflict and the operation of power in history as well as to downplay controversy in historiography." There also was a general tendency to neglect the historical experience of women and ordinary Japanese in general—and, indeed, to fail to address "the relationship between civil society, broadly conceived, and the state."[28]

These criticisms, by scholars a generation younger than Hall and Jansen, the American general editors, reflected not merely ennui at the "modernization" fixation on gradualist institutional history and elitist developments at the political and socioeconomic center, but also surprise that the old guard had failed to accomodate new avenues of inquiry that already were apparent in the 1970s, when the Cambridge histories were planned. I myself had published the first frontal critique of modernization theory and its "uses of history" in the Japan field in 1975, in a long introduction to a new edition of writings by E. H. Norman.[29] Almost simultaneously with this, new scholarship began to appear that departed conspicuously from the modernizationist fixation on gradual "transition" and convergence toward the Western capitalist model. The new scholarship focused on political, social, and cultural activity peripheral to the centers of power; on tensions, conflict, and oppression; on not merely the protests of "marginal" groups, but also the complicated reciprocal relationships between the state

---

[28] See the reviews published in 1992 by Berry, Hauser, and Smith (479-514, inclusive). For Gordon's review, see (1991b). See also reviews by Herbert Bix (1991), Takashi Fujitani (1991), and Laura Hein (1990). I also benefited in preparing this essay from an unpublished 1992 draft essay by Professor Hein. The manner in which English-language scholarly writings on Japan in the "modernization" vogue tend to avoid serious discussion of historiographical issues and controversies is quite striking. For a departure from this, explicitly emphasizing contending interpretations, see Harry Wray and Hilary Conroy, eds. (1983).

[29] "E. H. Norman, Japan, and the Uses of History," in Dower, ed. (1975), 3-101.

and civil society; on conservative as well as dynamic legacies from Tokugawa to Meiji and from prewar to postwar Japan; on tensions and problems within the U.S.-Japan relationship; and on issues of choice and roads not taken.

These emerging concerns generally attracted younger scholars who were developing their research agendas in the turbulent years when the Cold War erupted into the violence of the Vietnam conflict, and when contentious popular movements were arising in a variety of causes throughout the advanced capitalist world. Civil disorder in Japan as well as the United States and Europe—manifest in university upheavals and a variety of grassroots citizens' movements—obviously undercut the model of Japanese harmony and consensus while at the same time calling attention to political and social dynamics outside the conspicuous centers of power. The fact that many of Japan's most impressive *shimin undō*, or "citizens' movements," were directed against environmental destruction caused by rapid industrialization further discredited the developmental optimism associated with modernization theory. The dynamic grassroots upheavals of the 1960s and 1970s similarly undermined the "gradualist" and "institutional" fixations associated with prevailing models—although, on the other side of the coin, the ability of the government successfully to weather these and other upheavals also drew scholarly attention to Japan's emergence as a "strong state."

These new conceptual preoccupations resulted in a spate of historically-oriented studies dealing with tension and conflict. Tetsuo Najita set a high standard for such inquiries with the publication in 1974 of a short, eloquent interpretation of "the intellectual foundations of modern Japanese politics." Through close analysis of a range of political philosophers, Najita advanced a bold thesis of interlocking strains of bureaucratic and iconoclastic thought that helped explain the dynamic tension between system maintenance and radical transformation in the country's modern development. This was followed in 1978 (the year *The Cambridge History of Japan* was planned) by a collection of essays edited by Najita and Irwin Scheiner on "methods and metaphors" in Tokugawa thought in which tensions and alternatives rather than some stable code of "cultural values" were again emphasized. A symposium on the turn-of-the-century Ashio mine pollution struggle was published in the second issue of the then new *Journal of Japanese*

Studies in 1975, and was soon followed by other historical studies of citizen protest.[30]

Beginning in 1976, Najita and J. Victor Koschmann began work on organizing a conference on "the neglected tradition" of conflict. Eventually published in 1982, this conference volume was prefaced with a precise critique of the thrust of prior Japan scholarship. "We have been accustomed to viewing human time as a consensual flow or movement," Najita and Koschmann wrote, "regulated by certain stylized relationships such as loyalty to the group or superiors in Japan, and moving along in a mainstream or on a central track. Although the metaphors vary, the basic idea is the same. History proceeds in a causal or purposeful sequence. Those parts that do not conform easily to that central flow are put aside as insignificant, as peripheral, or as evidence of ineffectualness." Without denying the importance of consensuality, the numerous contributors to this volume chose to examine instead "the obverse of consensus, which is dissent, secession, and conflict." In Najita's introduction, he went further to make the theoretical point "that in their claim to objectivity vis-à-vis factual materials, historians have tended to resist a basic truth about the discontinuous and ultimately chaotic character of the historical reality they confront." His call for greater attention to discontinuity and "synchronic systems of events" was another challenge to the gradualist, institutional, centripetal focus of the modernization approach.

Since the mid-1970s, conflict and protest have remained central to the agenda of scholars working on early modern and modern Japan. This has resulted in an impressive number of detailed case studies of such topics as peasant protest, landlord-tenant conflict, popular social and political movements (including labor and women), urban riots, prewar leftwing politics and doctrinal disputes (including the great "*Rōnō-Kōza*" debates on the nature of Japanese capitalism), the imperial state's mechanisms of repression, and the social costs of modernization generally.[31] "People's

---

[30] See articles published in 1975 by Kenneth Pyle, Fred Notehelfer, and Alan Stone. See also Kenneth Strong (1978) and J. Victor Koschmann, ed. (1978).

[31] These developments are summarized and annotated in fuller detail in a longer version of this essay that appears in Japanese in the September and October 1995 issues of *Shisō*. In general, since the mid-1970s major historical studies have been published on peasant protest by William W. Kelly, Herbert P. Bix, Anne Walthall, and Stephen Vlastos; on the *jiyū minken* (liberty and people's rights)

history" made a conspicuous debut in 1982, when Mikiso Hane published an influential text on "the underside of modern Japan" that drew extensively on informal writings such as diaries, reminiscences, and prison notes to let such individuals as poor farmers, women factory workers, prostitutes, miners, and Burakumin outcastes tell their own stories in their own words.

"Many Japans": The State and Civil Society

In his 1982 text, Hane posited the notion of "two Japans," thus essentially cleaving the consensus model into two unequal parts: the state and privileged elites counterpoised against the great number of ordinary people who paid dearly for Japan's rush into industrialization, imperialism, and war. This was an effective emphasis at the time Hane was writing. By no means, however, does the "two Japans" paradigm reflect the overall thrust of contemporary scholarship. On the contrary, what is emerging out of the new and decentered approach is a complex sense of "*many* Japans"—a sense, that is, of a society (like most societies) in which conflicts and tensions exist at innumerable levels; in which interactions between the state and civil society are reciprocal even if inequitable; and in which the agents of change (and of resistance to change) are multiple.

The ramifications of such an outlook are enormous, for this more fragmented perception of "many Japans" has meant that neither "the state" nor "the people" can be seen as monolithic or essentially homogeneous entities. To speak simply of the state or ruling groups on the one hand and a more-or-less homogenized and victimized "people" on the other hand amounts, as it were, to a kind of two-headed *nihonjinron*—or, indeed, two-headed Orientalism—in which elite Japanese exemplify one monolithic mode of behavior and the non-elites another. In the more interesting recent writings by historians and social scientists, simple hegemonic

---

movement by Roger Bowen; on landlord-tenant relations by Ann Waswo and Richard Smethurst; on the 1918 rice riots by Michael Lewis; on industrial relations and the labor movement by Andrew Gordon, Joe B. Moore, Sheldon Garon, and others; on the *Rōnō-Kōza* debates by Germaine A. Hoston; on women in modern Japanese history by Sharon Sievers, E. Patricia Tsurumi, Gail Bernstein, and Mikiso Hane; and on the control mechanisms of the Home Ministry and Justice Ministry by Richard Mitchell.

concepts of the state have been challenged and "the people" have become, not only more humanized and personalized, but also more diversified and *responsible.*

In T. J. Pempel's phrase, when the Japanese state is "unbundled," it is revealed to be a congeries of fractious and contentious parts. Much recent scholarship thus has tended to focus on competition and conflict within the prewar and postwar bureaucracies, among civilian elites such as the big-business community, and between the public and private sectors. Where contending interests are reconciled, this represents, in the phrase of Richard Samuels, a carefully brokered "politics of reciprocal consent." The revisionism inherent in such scholarship lies in qualifying the role of the state, repudiating assumptions of inherent harmony and common interests in the body politic, and emphasizing complex patterns of compromise and conflict resolution.[32]

In perhaps surprising ways, certain specialized new fields of inquiry such as business history also have contributed to these "antihegemonic" scholarly trends. Since the early 1970s, for example, the East Asian Studies program at Harvard University has promoted what Albert Craig calls "a new kind of scholarship" devoted to the "History of Japanese Business and Industry." While such scholarship bears obvious ties to studies in the modernization-theory mode, in more subtle ways it also reflects the discrete "case-study" fragmentation associated with postmodernism. Thus, the Harvard-trained Canadian historian William Wray, a leading promoter of Japanese business history, emphasizes that these micro-level approaches tend to challenge not only Marxist analysis, but also the macroeconomic aggregate analysis emphasized in most neoclassical economics.[33]

Such revisionist scholarship on the bureaucracy and big busi-

---

[32] Pempel's "unbundling" thesis appeared in 1987, but the major article initiating this debate was published by Haruhiro Fukui in 1977. For a recent summary of these arguments, see Samuels (1992). Samuels's "reciprocal consent" model is presented in his (1987) volume. In the internal debates on these matters, scholars such as Chalmers Johnson continue to place greater emphasis on the bureaucracy and strong state. For a major contribution to this decentered model of postwar and contemporary Japan, see Kent Calder's (1988) study.

[33] See, for example, the (1989) volume edited by William D. Wray. This is a good example of the new approaches to business and industry history, and Wray's comments on methodology can be found in both the introduction and afterword. Another recent historical study by William Miles Fletcher III (1989) emphasizes both conflict and reciprocity between the imperial government and the *zaikai*.

ness is best seen as part of a broader emerging interest not only in the nature of conflict and conflict resolution in prewar and postwar Japan, but also in the nature of "reciprocity" between the state and civil society in general. From this perspective, "the people" also have been rendered more fragmented and complex. At the same time, ordinary Japanese have been assigned more responsibility for their fate and the fate of their country.

This is a double-edged revisionism. On the one hand, ordinary people increasingly emerge as knowledgeable individuals who often have expressed their feelings and influenced the course of events. In a prize-winning 1991 study, for example, Andrew Gordon argued (much as Matsuo Takayoshi and Shinobu Seizaburō had done decades earlier) that a meaningful impetus toward democracy emerged in Japan around 1905 and came not merely from bourgeois intellectuals and politicians, but also from "the energies of common people throughout the nation." Gordon's sympathetic analysis of crowds, riots, and early labor agitation also led him to postulate the existence of a significant "tradition of protest" or "dispute culture" in prewar Japan.

Explicit in this analysis is what Gordon calls "a dialectic of challenge from and response to popular forces" that continued through the demise of Imperial Japan into the postwar era. Put differently, the same civil society that could take credit for promoting democratic trends in the early twentieth century also bore at least some degree of responsibility for the later turn toward militarism and fascism. It is here that the double edge of the argument lies: if "the people" can be given credit for progressive developments, then by the same token they also must bear some responsibility for reactionary trends and repressive behavior. A people found to be increasingly active and informed into the 1920s cannot suddenly be dismissed as completely helpless, hapless, silenced, and deceived when things fall terribly apart. In this most sensitive of all issues pertaining to prewar Japan, this means that responsibility for oppression at home and aggression and atrocity abroad extends to all Japanese along a gradient that is (and always will be) exceedingly difficult to define. Hane's brutalized women and men had scant control over their status, for example, but many of them also brutalized others—both in their own families and communities and abroad in Korea, China, and eventually Southeast Asia.

In essence, this line of argument represents a challenge to the thesis, familiar among Japanese historians, that the modern state imposed a hegemonic "emperor-state ideology" upon the people. Carol Gluck's 1985 work on Meiji Japan's "modern myths" essentially laid the groundwork for reconsidering the relationship between state and society, coercion and "suasion." Even in late Meiji, she argued, there existed "a plural ideological universe." Moreover, where the emperor-centered ideology was concerned, "the strongest line—the hard line—often came from outside the government." Sheldon Garon, another influential historian, has pursued similar themes in the 1930s and 1940s, arguing (1986, 1987, 1993) that militaristic government policies toward labor, religion, and women all reflected input from non-elite representatives of civil society—indeed, from labor, religious groups, and women's organizations themselves.

These new constructions of reciprocity and responsibility do not minimize the importance of the state's intensified regimentation beginning in the mid-1920s. They do, however, call attention to a more complex infrastructure of repression and indoctrination that involved not only bureaucrats, militarists, big businessmen, and national-level politicians, but also the mass media, intellectuals, labor leaders, small entrepreneurs, local elites, and grassroots organizations. Of particular interest in this regard has been the role played by intellectuals and other public figures. Contrary to the influential argument advanced shortly after the war by Maruyama Masao and others, to the effect that the chief support for fascism and aggression came from the petty bourgeoisie and other non-elite elements, recent studies have tended to dwell on how scholars, journalists, politicians, and elite university-trained technocrats of the post-World War I era emerged as active participants in the unfolding tragedy of the 1930s.

Such writings commonly take very seriously the intellectual, ideological, and psychological crises that public figures faced in the 1920s and 1930s. Indeed, as already noted, the critique of Euro-American "hegemonism" that characterizes much contemporary scholarship casts prewar Japanese nationalism in a new light for many scholars. At the same time, the intellectual elites of the post-World War I era—lightly chided by Maruyama—increasingly are seen as *active* participants in the rise of militarism. Whereas earlier scholarship tended to emphasize the "failure" of such public figures to oppose repression and aggression, more recent studies have examined how—in responding to the multiple crises that confronted them—these individuals interacted positively with the state and, with but rare exceptions, abetted its overseas aggression.[34]

At the same time, in keeping with the critical tenor of our present day, these intellectuals of more than a half century ago also have attracted new attention because of the light they may shed on the crisis of "modernity" itself.

Prewar/Transwar/Postwar

Two overriding questions dominate historical scholarship on modern Japan: how do we explain the road to war? And how, at the same time, can we best explain Japan's postwar experiences and attainments? Obviously, these questions are not separable from one another. As we have seen, moreover, current academic approaches reject simple or "centered" explanations. Most historians and social scientists now look not for laws, models, grand theories, or "metanarratives," but for multicausality. Where Imperial Japan's road to war is concerned, this is reflected in several broad interpretive trends. The critique of Western hegemonism has done more than just stimulate renewed interest in prewar critiques of "the West," and in concrete or imagined departures from the Western model at all levels of state and society. It also has made academics more attentive to the global milieu of capitalism and imperialism in which accelerated Japanese militarism and aggression occurred.

Such approaches complicate the issue of war responsibility. Globally, Western colonialism and imperialism now receive more critical emphasis than was customary in earlier writings, and Japanese expansion and aggression are more routinely seen in a comparative and competitive context. In addition, sensitivity to the potent psychological and political consequences of binary postu-

---

[34] Some of the more influential intellectual studies include William Miles Fletcher III's study of the Shōwa Kenkyūkai (1982); Sharon Minichiello's study of Nagai Ryūtarō (1984); Joshua A. Fogel's volume (1984); Atsuko Hirai's monograph (1987); Andrew Barshay's study of Nanbara Shigeru and Hasegawa Nyozekan (1988); and J. Thomas Rimer's edited volume (1990). Germaine Hoston has addressed the problem of support of imperialism and national socialism by ex-Communists in a number of publications.

lations of "Self" and "Other" has drawn attention not only to the deep currents of Euro-American racism and white supremacism, but also to the differing ways "modernizing" Japanese have defined themselves vis-à-vis other Asians as well as Caucasians.[35] At the same time, while the authoritarian state still bears primary onus for the road to war, the burden of responsibility has been extended to virtually the entire society.

In recent scholarship, the prewar and postwar experiences are linked in various ways. Methodologically, the same decentered, case-study approach is directed to both periods, and the same attentiveness to complex interaction between the state and civil society prevails. Topically, there has emerged since the late 1970s a growing emphasis on the centrality of wartime or "transwar" legacies to postwar and contemporary society. This represents repudiation of the old notion of a "new Japan," risen like a phoenix from the rubble of World War II. At the same time, it also is more precisely focused than the vague notion of "prewar" legacies, calling attention in particular to the far-reaching transformations of state and society that occurred in the 1930s and early 1940s under mobilization for total war.

For understandable reasons, both Japanese and non-Japanese scholars until recently have associated the first two decades of Shōwa almost exclusively with repression and war. Now, looking back from the vantage point of over a half century later, it has become apparent that these terrible years witnessed extraordinary changes in almost every aspect of life—technologically, technocratically, economically, politically, and—not least—in the realm of popular consciousness. My own work, published in 1979, on the conservative position exemplified by the prewar diplomat and postwar prime minister Yoshida Shigeru was motivated by a desire to explore, at an essentially political and ideological level, the linkages between the presurrender and postsurrender periods. Chalmers Johnson's work on MITI, published in 1982, covered the period 1925 to 1975 and devoted almost half of its treatment to developments prior to Japan's surrender. Johnson's focus, of course,

---

[35] My 1986 book was the first extended comparative study of this. See also the essays "Race, Language, and War in Two Cultures" and "Fear and Prejudice in U.S.-Japan Relations," with accompanying illustrations, in Dower (1994), 257-338. The concept of "Orient" as developed by Shiratori Kurakichi and other early twentieth-century Japanese academics is addressed by Stefan Tanaka (1993).

was on the emergence of a bureaucracy-led industrial policy. Numerous case studies since then have called attention to wartime or transwar legacies in labor-management relations, industrial structure, economic and financial policy, and—at the popular level—democratic and antiwar sentiments. In this revisionist perspective, the horrors of the war remain unaltered, but it also is recognized that in the cold calculus of history this was, in many respects, a "useful war" for Japan. Indeed, in interesting ways, the relationship between the "fifteen-year war" of 1931-1945 and postwar Japan is emerging as comparable in historical significance to the relationship between the *bakumatsu* period (1853-1868) and the Restoration and post-Restoration era.[36] The "postwar" period per se (which generally is taken to cover from 1945 to the simultaneous end of Shōwa and end of the Cold War in 1989) still awaits its historians.[37]

What, in conclusion, can we say about the overall impression of Japan that emerges from recent English-language scholarly literature? We can say, perhaps, that we have gained immeasurably in detail but lost any real sense of organizing principle; that we no longer have a clear conception of the structures of power, but rather are confronted by a world of fragmentation and multiple causality; and that greater emphasis is now placed on the ways in which Japan diverges from so-called Western patterns of thought and behavior than on its convergence. To each of these assertions there are of course conspicuous exceptions. The "strong state" theorists challenge the pluralists and decenterers; neoclassical economists downplay divergence and remind us that the name of the game is still markets and capitalism; and old-fashioned humanists still hope that it may be possible to salvage some notion of shared values and ideals that transcend power and profits. No one, however, can any longer point to a dominant paradigm governing Western perceptions of Japan.

---

[36] Dower (1979); Johnson (1982). I have summarized much of the literature pertaining to war legacies in "The Useful War," originally published in the Summer 1990 issue of *Daedalus*, and reprinted in Dower (1994), 9-32.

[37] The major historically-oriented publication to date on postwar Japan is a collection edited by Andrew Gordon, ed. (1993). Contributors to this volume, who generally represent a "postmodernization theory" outlook, include Gary Allinson, Sandra Buckley, Bruce Cumings, John Dower, Sheldon Garon, Carol Gluck, Laura Hein, Charles Horioka, Marilyn Ivy, William Kelly, J. Victor Koschmann, Mike Mochizuki, Koji Taira, Kathleen Uno, Frank Upham, and James White.

Bibliography

Anchordoguy, Marie. Summer 1992. Review of Cusumano (1991). *Journal of Japanese Studies* 18, no. 2: 599-603.
Anderson, Benedict. 1983. *Imagined Communities: Reflections on the Origin and Spread of Nationalism*. London: Verso.
Barshay, Andrew. 1988. *State and Intellectual in Imperial Japan: The Public Man in Crisis*. Berkeley: University of California Press.
Beaseley, W. G. Winter 1988. Review of Reischauer (1986). *Journal of Japanese Studies* 14, no. 1: 189-93.
Befu, Harumi. December 1980. "A Critique of the Group Model of Japanese Society." *Social Analysis*, no. 5-6 (Special edition on *Japanese Society*): 29-43.
———. Winter 1993. Review of Kuniko Miyanaga, *The Creative Edge: Emerging Individualism in Japan*, 1991. *Journal of Japanese Studies* 19, no. 2: 451-52.
Berry, Mary Elizabeth. Summer 1992. Review of Yamamura, ed. (1990). *Journal of Japanese Studies* 18, no. 2.
Bestor, Theodore C. 1989. *Neighborhood Tokyo*. Stanford: Stanford University Press.
Bix, Herbert. April-June 1991. Review of Jansen, ed. (1989) and Duus, ed. (1988). *Bulletin of Concerned Asian Scholars* 23, no. 2: 84-89.
Bowring, Richard, and Peter Kornicki, eds. 1993. *The Cambridge Encyclopedia of Japan*. Cambridge: Cambridge University Press.
Braithwaite, John. 1989. *Crime, Shame and Reintegration*. Cambridge: Cambridge University Press.
Calder, Kent. 1988. *Crisis and Compensation: Public Policy and Political Stability in Japan, 1949-1986*. Princeton: Princeton University Press.
Cole, Robert. Summer 1978. "The Late-Developer Hypothesis: An Evaluation of Its Relevance for Japanese Employment Patterns." *Journal of Japanese Studies* 4, no. 2: 247-65.
———. 1979. *Work, Mobility, and Participation: A Comparative Study of American and Japanese Industry*. Berkeley: University of California Press.
———. 1988. *Strategies for Learning: Small-Group Activities in American, Japanese, and Swedish Industry*. Berkeley: University of California Press.
Crawcour, Sydney. Summer 1978. "The Japanese Employment System." *Journal of Japanese Studies* 4, no. 2: 225-45.
Cusumano, Michael A. 1991. *Japan's Software Factories: A Challenge to U.S. Management*. Oxford: Oxford University Press.
Dale, Peter N. 1986. *The Myth of Japanese Uniqueness*. Kent, U.K.: Croom Helm.
Dore, Ronald. 1973. *British Factory-Japanese Factory*. Berkeley: University of California Press.
———. Winter 1979. "More About Late Development." *Journal of Japanese Studies* 5, no. 1: 137-51.
———. 1987. *Taking Japan Seriously: A Confucian Perspective on Leading Economic Issues*. Stanford: Stanford University Press.
Dower, John W. 1979. *Empire and Aftermath: Yoshida Shigeru and the Japanese Experience, 1878-1954*. Cambridge: Council on East Asian Studies, Harvard University.
———. 1986. *War Without Mercy: Race and Power in the Pacific War*. New York: Pantheon.
———. 1994. *Japan in War and Peace: Selected Essays*. New York: New Press.
Dower, John W., ed. 1975. *Emergence of the Modern Japanese State: Selected Writings of E. H. Norman*. New York: Pantheon.

Duus, Peter, ed. 1988. *The Twentieth Century.* Vol. 6 of *The Cambridge History of Japan.* Cambridge: Cambridge University Press.
The Economist. 1963. *Consider Japan.* London: Duckworth.
Fogel, Joshua A. 1984. *Politics and Sinology: The Case of Naitō Kōnan, 1866-1934.* Cambridge: Harvard University Press.
Fletcher, William Miles III. 1982. *The Search for a New Order: Intellectuals and Fascism in Prewar Japan.* Chapel Hill: University of North Carolina Press.
———. 1989. *The Japanese Business Community and National Trade Policy, 1920-1942.* Chapel Hill: University of North Carolina Press.
Fruin, W. Mark. Summer 1978. "The Japanese Company Controversy: Ideology and Organization in a Historical Perspective." *Journal of Japanese Studies* 4, no. 2: 267-300.
———. 1980. "The Family as a Firm and the Firm as a Family: The Case of Kikkōman Shōyu Company Limited." *Journal of Family History* 5, no. 4: 432-49.
———. 1983. *Kikkōman: Company, Clan, and Community.* Cambridge: Harvard University Press.
Fujitani, Takashi. May 1991. Review of Jansen, ed. (1989). *Journal of Asian Studies* 50, no. 2: 412-14.
Fukui, Haruhiro. 1977. "Studies in Policymaking: A Review of the Literature." In *Policymaking in Contemporary Japan,* edited by T. J. Pempel. Ithaca: Cornell University Press.
Garon, Sheldon. Summer 1986. "State and Religion in Imperial Japan, 1912-1945." *Journal of Japanese Studies* 12, no. 2: 273-302.
———. 1987. *The State and Labor in Modern Japan.* Berkeley: University of California Press.
———. Winter 1993. "Women's Groups and the Japanese State: Contending Approaches to Political Integration, 1890-1945." *Journal of Japanese Studies* 19, no. 1: 5-41.
Gluck, Carol. 1985. *Japan's Modern Myths: Ideology in the Late Meiji Period.* Princeton: Princeton University Press.
Gordon, Andrew. 1991a. *Labor and Imperial Democracy in Prewar Japan.* Berkeley: University of California Press.
———. Winter 1991b. Review of Duus, ed. (1988). *Journal of Japanese Studies* 17, no. 1: 143-57.
Gordon, Andrew, ed. 1993. *Postwar Japan As History.* Berkeley: University of California Press.
Haley, John Owen. 1991. *Authority without Power: Law and the Japanese Paradox.* New York: Oxford University Press.
Hall, John W., and James McClain, eds. 1991. *Early Modern Japan.* Vol. 4 of *The Cambridge History of Japan.* Cambridge: Cambridge University Press.
Hane, Mikiso. 1982. *Peasants, Rebels, and Outcastes: The Underside of Modern Japan.* New York: Pantheon.
Hardacre, Helen. 1989. *Shintō and the State, 1868-1988.* Princeton: Princeton University Press.
Hauser, William. Summer 1992. Review of Hall and McClain, eds. (1991). *Journal of Japanese Studies* 18, no. 2: 492-503.
Hein, Laura. November 1990. Review of Duus, ed. (1988). *Journal of Asian Studies* 49, no. 4: 933-35.
———. Unpublished draft, 1992. "Modernization Theory, Difference, and Japan Revisited."
Hellman, Donald. Summer 1980. Review of Vogel (1979). *Journal of Japanese Studies* 6, no. 2: 424-31.

Hirai, Atsuko. 1987. *Individualism and Socialism: Kawai Eijirō's Life and Thought, 1891-1944*. Cambridge: Council on East Asian Studies, Harvard University.
Hobsbawm, Eric, and Terence Ranger, eds. 1983. *The Invention of Tradition*. Cambridge: Cambridge University Press.
Ikegami, Yoshihiko, ed. 1991. *The Empire of Signs: Semiotic Essays on Japanese Culture*. Amsterdam: J. Benjamin.
Jansen, Marius B., ed. 1989. *The Nineteenth Century*. Vol. 5 of *The Cambridge History of Japan*. Cambridge: Cambridge University Press.
Johnson, Chalmers. 1982. *MITI and the Japanese Miracle: The Growth of Industrial Policy, 1925-1975*. Stanford: Stanford University Press.
——. Summer 1987. "How to Think About Economic Competition from Japan." *Journal of Japanese Studies* 13, no. 2: 415-27.
——. 1988. "Study of Japanese Political Economy: A Crisis in Theory." In *Japanese Studies in the United States: Part I—History and Present Condition*, edited by The Japan Foundation, 95-113. Ann Arbor: Association for Asian Studies.
Kahn, Herman. 1970. *The Emerging Japanese Superstate: Challenges and Response*. Englewood Hills, N.J.: Prentice-Hall.
Kazuo, Okochi, Bernard Karsh, and Solomon Levine, eds. 1974. *Workers and Employers in Japan: The Japanese Employment Relations System*. Princeton: Princeton University Press.
Kelly, William. 1986. "Rationalization and Nostalgia: Cultural Dynamics of New Middle Class Japan." *American Ethnologist* 13, no. 4: 603-18.
Kinzley, W. Dean. 1991. *Industrial Harmony in Modern Japan: The Invention of a Tradition*. London: Routledge.
Koschmann, J. Victor, ed. 1978. *Authority and the Individual in Japan: Citizen Protest in Historical Perspective*. Tokyo: University of Tokyo Press.
Lieberman, Joseph. 9 July 1984. "Give Confucius a Chance." *New York Times*.
Mannheim, Karl. 1936. *Ideology and Utopia: an Introduction to the Sociology of Knowledge*. Translated by Louis Wirth and Edward Shils. New York: Harcourt, Brace and World.
Minichiello, Sharon. 1984. *Retreat from Reform: Patterns of Political Behavior in Interwar Japan*. Honolulu: University of Hawai'i Press.
Miyoshi, Masao. Summer 1988. "Against the Native Grain: The Japanese Novel and the 'Postmodern' West." In a collection of essays on "Postmodernism and Japan." *South Atlantic Quarterly* 87, no. 3.
——. 1991. *Off Center: Power and Culture Relations between Japan and the United States*. Cambridge: Harvard University Press.
Miyoshi, Masao, and H. D. Harootunian, eds. 1989. *Postmodernism and Japan*. Durham: Duke University Press.
Mouer, Ross, and Yoshio Sugimoto. 1986. *Images of Japanese Society: A Study in the Structure of Social Reality*. London: KPI.
Najita, Tetsuo. 1974. *Japan: The Intellectual Foundations of Modern Japanese Politics*. Chicago: University of Chicago Press.
Najita, Tetsuo, and H. D. Harootunian. 1988. "Japanese Revolt Against the West: Political and Cultural Criticism in the Twentieth Century." In Peter Duus, ed. (1988), 711-74.
Najita, Tetsuo, and Irwin Scheiner, eds. 1978. *Japanese Thought in the Tokugawa Period: Methods and Metaphors*. Chicago: University of Chicago Press.
Najita, Tetsuo, and J. Victor Koschmann, eds. 1982. *Conflict in Modern Japanese History: The Neglected Tradition*. Princeton: Princeton University Press.
Notehelfer, Fred. Spring 1975. "Japan's First Pollution Incident." *Journal of Japanese Studies* 1, no. 2: 351-83.

Pempel, T. J. Summer 1987. "Unbundling Japan." *Journal of Japanese Studies* 13, no. 2: 271-306.
Plath, David. Winter 1992. Review of Kawai Hayao. *Journal of Japanese Studies* 18, no. 1: 240-42.
Pollack, David. Spring 1989. Review of Miyoshi and Harootunian, eds. (1989). *Monumenta Nipponica* 44, no. 1: 75-97.
Pyle, Kenneth. Spring 1975. "Introduction: Japan Faces Her Future." *Journal of Japanese Studies* 1, no. 2: 347-50.
Reischauer, Edwin O. 11 September 1964. "Inevitable Partners." *Life*, 27-28.
———. 1986. *My Life Between Japan and America*. New York: Harper and Row.
Rimer, J. Thomas, ed. 1990. *Culture and Identity: Japanese Intellectuals During the Interwar Years*. Princeton: Princeton University Press.
Robertson, Jennifer. 1991. *Native and Newcomer: Making and Remaking a Japanese City*. Berkeley: University of California Press.
Rohlen, Thomas. 1974. *For Harmony and Strength*. Berkeley: University of California Press.
Said, Edward. 1978. *Orientalism*. New York: Pantheon.
Samuels, Richard J. 1987. *The Business of the Japanese State: Energy Markets in Comparative and Historical Perspective*. Ithaca: Cornell University Press.
———. 1992. "Japanese Political Studies and the Myth of the Independent Intellectual." In *The Political Culture of Foreign Area and International Studies: Essays in Honor of Lucian W. Pye*, edited by Richard J. Samuels and Myron Weiner, 17-56. Washington: Brassey's.
Seidensticker, Edward. Summer 1980. Review of Vogel (1979). *Journal of Japanese Studies* 6, no. 2: 15-47.
Smith, Henry II. Summer 1992. Review of Jansen, ed. (1989). *Journal of Japanese Studies* 18, no. 2: 503-14.
Steenstrup, Carl. Summer 1993. Review of Haley (1991). *Journal of Japanese Studies* 19, no. 2: 481-85.
Stone, Alan. Spring 1975. "The Japanese Muckrakers." *Journal of Japanese Studies* 1, no. 2: 385-407.
Strong, Kenneth. 1978. *Ox Against the Storm: A Biography of Tanaka Shōzō—Japan's Conservationist Pioneer*. Victoria: University of British Columbia Press.
"Symposium on *Ie* Society." Winter 1985. *Journal of Japanese Studies* 11, no. 1: 1-69.
Tanaka, Stefan. 1993. *Japan's Orient: Rendering Pasts into History*. Berkeley: University of California Press.
Treat, John Whittier. Summer 1990. Review of Miyoshi and Harootunian, eds. (1989). *Journal of Japanese Studies* 16, no. 2: 481-89.
———. Summer 1992. Review of Ikegami, ed. (1991). *Journal of Japanese Studies* 18, no. 2: 536-44.
Upham, Frank K. 1987. *Law and Social Change in Postwar Japan*. Cambridge: Harvard University Press.
Vogel, Ezra. 1979. *Japan As Number One*. Cambridge: Harvard University Press.
Wray, Harry, and Hilary Conroy, eds. 1983. *Japan Examined: Perspectives on Modern Japanese History*. Honolulu: University of Hawai'i Press.
Wray, William D., ed. 1989. *Managing Industrial Enterprise: Cases from Japan's Prewar Experience*. Cambridge: Council on East Asian Studies, Harvard University.
Yamamura, Kozo, ed. 1990. *Medieval Japan*. Vol. 3 of *The Cambridge History of Japan*. Cambridge: Cambridge University Press.

THE STUDY OF JAPAN'S EARLY HISTORY

Martin Collcutt

This bibliographic essay surveys the research on Japan to 1600 produced in the past three or four decades. It focuses on work written in English. This includes many translations in English of research papers by Japanese scholars in the English language journals in the field. It should, of course, be remembered that there is a mountain of research in this field in Japanese and a substantial amount in European languages. The essay begins by introducing some of the quite startling recent developments in prehistoric archaeology and then goes on to consider the Proto-historic phase, the Nara and Heian periods, the medieval centuries, and the very vital sixteenth century.

Recent Study of Japan's Prehistory: Paleolithic, Jōmon, and Yayoi

Prehistoric archaeology, a very active field in Japan, has contributed enormously to the understanding of origins of human activity in Japan, early subsistence economy, and the formation of the earliest Japanese political units. Within only the past decade or so, the accepted origins of human settlement in the islands has been pushed back in time by several hundred thousand years on the basis of finds at the Kami-Takamori lower Paleolithic site in Miyagi Prefecture. Much more is now known about the earliest relations with China, Korea, and North Asia.

The practice and methods of Japanese Archaeology have been discussed in a number of recent essays. In them some Western participant-observers have questioned the relationship between scientific archaeology and Japanese notions of their cultural identity.[1]

Scholars such as J. E. Kidder, Jr., Richard Pearson, and Gina Barnes, and half a dozen others listed in the readings below, have combined professional archaeological expertise and knowledge

---

[1] See, for instance, works by Richard Pearson (1992b) and Clare Fawcett (1995, 1996).

of many of the sites with a historical interest in the place of pre- and Proto-historic Japanese culture in Asia and in the overall development of Japanese history. Their writings, and the exhibits they have organized in the West, have helped bring archaeological findings within the orbit of early Japanese history. The recently developed Yoshinogari site (Saga Prefecture), for instance, has revised and enhanced our understanding of the Yayoi period and early continental contacts, and added fuel to the long running debate over the possible location of Yamatai and early state formation in Japan.

However, having recognized the real contributions made by the few active Western archaeologists of Japan, and by the very few historians interested in archaeological findings and approaches, it must be stated that Western understanding of, and involvement with, Japanese archaeology is quite limited. This, in turn, has a negative impact on our understanding of early Japanese history.

Although the scientific study of Japanese archaeology was initiated by an American, S. E. Morse, who excavated the Ōmori shell middens in the 1870s, the field has long since come to be dominated by Japanese researchers. For many decades now the Western contribution to the illumination of Japan's prehistory has been slight, and with few archaeologists of Japan being trained in the West today, and few Western students getting rigorous on-site experience in Japan, its prospects for the future seem quite dim. This is in marked contrast to the situation in Japan. It is also a source of weakness in the Western study of Japanese early history in general, where so much depends on being in touch with material as well as documentary sources.

The Japanese people are fascinated by their origins. When did humans first come to the islands? What kind of lives did they lead? What was their social organization, religion, art? When did Japanese culture take shape? Etc. Interest is expressed in all the major early phases: the pre-ceramic Paleolithic or old stone age phase (prior to ca. 10,000 B.C.E.), the Jōmon ceramic culture phase (ca. 10,000 B.C.E. to 300 B.C.E.), the brief but important rice agriculture diffusion phase known as Yayoi (ca. 300 B.C.E. to 300 C.E.). With the appearance of huge mounded tombs from around 300 C.E. Japan moved into what many historians think of as the Proto-historic age of the great tombs (ca. 300-700 C.E.). This phase will be considered briefly in the following section.

Archaeology in Japan is extremely active and well-funded. Japanese specialists are digging up and analyzing the buried Japanese past at a prodigious rate. Hardly a day goes by without some new "find" being introduced in newspapers and television programs. Much of this funding comes from the Ministry of Education, including its Agency for Cultural Affairs, prefectural education committees, university departments, and especially the large corporations and the Ministry of Construction (Kensetsuchō), one of the richest ministries in Japan. Archaeological excavations are being carried on constantly all over Japan, from Hokkaido in the north to Okinawa and the islands to the south. These digs are supervised by professional archaeologists attached to universities, museums, prefectural education authorities, and the Ministry of Education. In any one year thousands of people are excavating sites all over Japan, analyzing data, writing research reports, books, and newspaper articles, or preparing TV documentaries and museum exhibitions. Archaeology, in this sense, is a tremendously broad, complex, and active enterprise in Japan.

In the past decade there have been many important, and some spectacular finds, for each of the major prehistoric phases. Here there is room to mention only a few that have drastically changed our understanding of the prehistoric origins of Japan. These include:

Kami-Takamori site, Miyagi Prefecture (Pacific Coast, N.E. Japan)

Excavations during 1995-96 exposed physical evidence for human presence in the Japanese archipelago from a much earlier period than hitherto believed. What are believed to be stone tools found at the lowest stratum of the Kami-Takamori site have been dated to as early as 600,000 B.P. This pushes the origins of the earliest inhabitants of the Japanese islands back by some 400,000 years from the conventional dating of from 30,000-200,000 years ago accepted just a few years ago.

Sannai Maruyama site, Aomori Prefecture (N.E. Japan)

Now the largest restored Jōmon site in Japan. Provides evidence of extensive settlement over a long period of time with buildings that used great timber posts, a village "long house," storehouses, grave sites, and a separate children's burial area close to the residential sites. Center of a complex trading economy in obsidian and other materials embracing northeastern Japan and southern Hokkaido.

Yoshinogari site, Saga Prefecture (Kyushu)

Developed over the past decade and now one of the most visited archaeological sites in Japan. A restored Yayoi period village complete with wooden enclosure and two-story watch towers. Some assert that this was the Yamatai capital of Queen Himiko mentioned in the Chinese dynastic chronicles. This had added fuel to the long running debate over the location of Yamatai, tipping the scales temporarily in favor of Kyushu as the location of that elusive Kingdom of Queen Himiko.

At these and other sites professional archaeologists are assisted by devoted and painstaking bands of paid "diggers," some of whom are students and many of whom are retirees. The pay (4,000-6,000 yen a day) is not great by current Japanese standards, but it gets people into the fresh air, gives them a social experience, the excitement of a hunt, and a sense of participation in the clarification of Japan's early past. They can be seen on all the major sites in Japan, squatting and painstakingly scraping the earth away from any find as the dig goes down. The materials are washed, sorted, examined, and graphed on site. Some are then sent to appropriate research laboratories and museums where they are subjected to the most advanced scientific testing including infra-red, x-rays, pollen trace, floral opal, Carbon 14, and DNA tests. Not surprisingly, the Japanese are leaders in the field of technical archaeological analysis. In some cases new "discoveries" are made when previously tested objects are brought under the analysis of newly developed technologies.

Before construction work can begin on any major housing project, factory development, road, industrial park, or subway line a site evaluation must be conducted by archaeologists. Often money is poured in to get the evaluation completed and the materials classified and moved into museums so that construction work can proceed. Sometimes a major archaeological find can seriously delay, or even halt, construction of a planned development, as at Sannai Maruyama and Yoshinogari. The governor and prefectural government of Aomori, for example, recently canceled work that had already been started on a baseball and soccer stadium complex when an extensive Jōmon site was unearthed nearby at Sannai Maruyama. It was decided that an archaeological Jōmon theme park would be more beneficial to the prefectural economy and culture than a stadium. The site has captured the attention of Aomori residents and created something of a Jōmon boom in 1996. In Saga, plans for an industrial park were shelved when excavations revealed the extent and the importance of the Yoshinogari Yayoi period site.

Over the past decade or so archaeological interest has moved to embrace not only the pre-historic and ancient periods but also medieval and early modern Japan, and there is a growing undersea band of marine archaeologists working on wrecks. Some of the major finds in the medieval and early modern phase include such urban sites as Kusado Sengen and Tosa Minato, wrecked trading vessels, castles, and urban architecture.

In this way, understanding of the Japanese past is constantly being revised, extended, and deepened, sometimes overturned, by the relentless application of scientific archaeology to history. However, the results of this enormous archaeological research effort filter only slowly into the Western understanding of Japan's past. Probably ninety-nine percent, or more, of this archaeological research is conducted by Japanese archaeologists. There are no more than a handful of Western archaeologists who are active on the ground in Japan on a regular, systematic basis. The archaeology of Japan is hardly offered in American or European Ph.D. programs, and what is presented to undergraduates and the general public is often a few years out of date. We tend to read about the "latest" findings some years after they have been introduced to the Japanese public. The Jōmon period Sannai Maruyama site, for instance, was in the news in Japan for four or five years before its scale and importance became known in the West. Even at the time of writing, it is still not widely known, even among Japan specialists. This is a sad, but hardly surprising, state of affairs. It is extremely difficult to teach full-time in the United States or Europe and be fully engaged in the Japanese archeological effort. There are few scholars to report on the latest developments in Japanese archaeology, and most Western journalists in Japan are more interested in the current economy than the ancient past.

For introductions to the state of research in the late 1980s and early 1990s the reader can consult Richard Pearson (1992a). Gina L. Barnes (1993) provides a continental perspective on Japan's prehistory. Pearson, Barnes, and Hutterer's work (1986) is now a little dated but contains informative essays. Hudson and Barnes (1991) provide a helpful introduction to the important Yayoi period Yoshinogari site in Kyushu. We still await good studies in English of the more recent finds at Sannai Maruyama, Kami-Takamori, and many other sites, the evidence from which is rapidly reshaping the understanding of Japanese prehistory in Japan. The excavations at Yoshinogari and the extensive scale of that site raised once again the long-running debate over the location of Yamatai and early continental connections. Finds at Sannai Maruyama and other Jōmon sites have raised the question of the extent to which something that might be called "agriculture," or at least systematic plant husbandry, existed in the late Jōmon period. For an introduction to this debate see the article by Crawford and Takamiya (1990). Some of the work on dentition and physical differences between Jōmon and Yayoi peoples is now finding its way into the Western literature (Hanihara, 1993).

Other, more specialized research is listed in the bibliography. Perhaps the best access to the most recent findings is via the Internet, aiming a web browser at the English language newspapers published in Japan and searching from there. There is, of course, an enormous body of material available in Japanese, much more than one person could ever hope to command. Even on single sites, or controversial new developments or theories, there is often a mass of reports, articles, books, reviews, newspaper articles, and television programs. Perhaps the best access to these Japanese data is via the summaries of each year's major findings presented by the Asahi Publishing Co., *Hakkutsu sareta Nihon rettō* (published annually in June).

The Proto-historic, Tumulus, and Asuka Periods

The period from the close of the Yayoi era (300 B.C.E. to 300 C.E.) to the foundation of Nara in 710 marks the transition from prehistory, where existing evidence is principally archaeological, to historical time, where the material evidence is increasingly supported by written records in Chinese, Japanese, and Korean. By the close of this period many of the elite were attaining literacy, Buddhist texts were being studied, poetry was being written, and government documents and records were being produced. This phase is referred to variously as the Tumulus, or *kofun*, period, in reference to the vast tombs that were built in many parts of Japan, especially in the Yamato district centering on the Asuka-Nara region. Part of it is also referred to as the Asuka period, especially the years 552-710, emphasizing the development of political and cultural institutions in and around Asuka under Empress Suiko, the young regent Prince Shōtoku, and his successors. It is also sometimes referred to as the age of the Yamato State, *Yamato kokka*, focusing on the political regime centered in the Yamato region at the eastern end of the Inland Sea that seemed to dominate much of central and western Japan in these centuries.

Because of the paucity of documentary materials, the period remains somewhat hazy, but within the haze many important developments were clearly taking place. Rice agriculture, metal technology, weaving, use of Chinese characters and elite literacy, social stratification, small state formation, the acceptance of Buddhism, Buddhist institutions, culture, and art, Confucian and Taoist teachings and practices, all seem to have been spreading. Although its precise boundaries of power are unclear, a centralized ruling regime seems to have been taking shape in the Yamato region. Compared with the preceding prehistoric phase, in which many petty village states or local families vied for power, something that we may think of as an early Japanese hegemonic "state" or regime was taking shape in Yamato, out of which emerged the Japanese imperial line.

The number of Western scholars working in this area of the field has never been great, but important work has been done. Serious attention to this period probably dates from Robert Reischauer's work published in 1937, reflecting prewar Japanese scholarship. Since 1945 there have been efforts by Western historians to illuminate this haze, drawing on the insights of the many Japanese historians and archaeologists who devote their energies to clarifying this crucial phase of Japan's early history. Those areas which seem to have received most attention have been the great tombs and tomb culture, social structure and rankings in clan society, the notion of an invasion by horseriding warriors, the contribution of Prince Shōtoku, Chinese-style reform efforts, the Taika Reform of 645, the introduction and diffusion of Buddhism and Confucianism, early Shintō, mythology, continental relations, especially with Korea, and the lessons of Korean history for the clarification of early Japanese history.

Historiography and Primary Sources

During this period Japan, or land of the *Wa* people as it was known, figures prominently in Chinese dynastic records. Continental visitors brought knowledge of the Chinese writing system to Japan. Some Japanese began to master it and overlay it on their spoken language. Written historical records began to be produced. These took the form of inscriptions of statues and tombs, records on wooden slips (*mokkan*), commentaries on Buddhist texts, genealogies, gazetteers (*fudoki*), and from the early eighth century the earliest chronicles, the *Kojiki* and *Nihon shoki*, both of which purported to present the history of Japan from the Age of the Gods. A number of these early written texts have been made available in translation. There are now two translations of the *Kojiki*. Unfortunately, there has been little Western study of the *Nihon shoki*, and we are still left with a single, Victorian, translation of that important work. Apart from the translation by John Brownlee of earlier Japanese research (Sakamoto, 1991), little has been done on the historiography, or historical sources, for this period since Beasley and Pulleyblank (1961).

The Great Tombs

The Proto-historic period was characterized by the construction of massive stone and earthen tombs, many of them keyhole shaped, built with enforced labor in Yamato and other regions of Japan. Tombs continued to be built on a lavish scale well into the eighth century, although their funereal function was by then being taken over by Buddhist temples. J. Edward Kidder (1964, 1972a, 1990) has provided some of the best introductions to the world of the tombs and the excavations of several very famous tombs: Fujinoki *kofun* and Takamatsuzuka *kofun*.

Horserider Invasion Thesis

Quite a lot of heat has been generated around the fourth century "horserider invasion" thesis proposed by Egami Namio from the 1940s. Although few Japanese archaeologists or ancient historians support the idea of a single decisive invasion by horseriding warriors from the Korean peninsula, the thesis, in revised form, had some support in the Western literature on early Japan. Gari Ledyard (1975) and Walter Edwards (1983) have made the most telling presentations. Edwards has stressed the idea of process rather than a single event and adjusted the timing of the "invasion" to coincide more closely with the dated archaeological evidence from the tombs themselves.

Political and Social History

One of the first American scholars to take this Proto-historic period seriously was Robert Karl Reischauer. In 1937 he published his two-volume study of *Early Japanese History* (ca. 40 B.C.-A.D. 1169). This drew heavily on the work of the Japanese historian Kuroita Katsumi, especially his *Kotei kokushi no kenkyū* (1931). George Sansom (1958) provides a standard introductory account. This was deepened by John W. Hall, who in 1966 provided a view of social organization focused on *uji, be,* and *yatsuko,* in early Bizen and in Yamato prior to the surge of reforms in the seventh and eighth centuries. J. E. Kidder (1983a) provides a useful brief survey of the period from the mid-6th century to 710.

Prince Shōtoku remains an intriguing but little-researched figure. In spite of several newish biographical studies in Japanese, there has been little new work in English. The basic documentary source remains the *Nihon shoki* (Aston translation, 1972 [1896]). The best introduction to Shōtoku from a religious perspective is probably Hanayama (1987). The Hōryūji and its treasures have been presented in several books or exhibition catalogues, including Kurata Bunsaku (trans. 1981).

Useful work on pre-Taika reform-era social organization and political hierarchy was done by Richard J. Miller in his descriptions of the *uji* and *kabane* ranking systems (1953, 1974). If there is a weakness in the earlier work, it is a tendency to take documents pointing to "centralization" at face value, to overstate the political reach of the Yamato regime, and to underestimate regional and local resistance to centralization. Some of the most insightful study has been done by Cornelius Kiley on the early Yamato state (1973) and the *uji-kabane* system (1977); Kiley significantly deepened the discussion. Two recent important studies of the Yamato regime are Gina Barnes's monograph (1988) and Joan Piggot's recent study (1997) of early Japanese "kingship," some of which deals with Yamato chieftains. John W. Hall's (1966) work still provides one of the best brief introductions to social organization in the age of the great tombs. On the whole, the second half of the seventh century, the decades after the Taika Reform, the prelude to the establishment of the Fujiwara and Heijō capitals remain understudied in the Western literature on ancient Japan.

Introduction of Buddhism

During this period Buddhism was introduced to Japan and began to take root as part of the larger-scale adoption of continental institutions. J. Edward Kidder's study (1972a), though dated, is still a useful introduction. J. H. Kamstra (1967) offered an early, and controversial, attempt to deal with the complex process of the adoption of Buddhism. Among the Buddhist temples built in the first surge of Buddhism, the Hōryūji has received most attention. Kurata (trans. 1981) provides a nice visual introduction. The whole topic of the early acceptance and acculturations of Buddhism in Asuka cries out for serious attention from researchers steeped in Japanese Buddhist history and gifted with command of Chinese and Korean sources. In this respect, Stanley Weinstein's work (1987) on Chinese Buddhism has insights to offer for students of early Japan.

Continental Relations/Korea

Part of the attractiveness of the "Horserider Invasion Thesis" mentioned above is that it gives a dynamic role to the Korean peninsula in the shaping of early Japan. In general Japanese historians have stressed domestic development and a presence for Japan in the colony of Mimana (Kaya) in the southern part of the peninsula (for instance Suematsu Yasukazu, 1958). Korean historians, and a few Japanese historians, have tended to reject the evidence of a Mimana colony and any claims to extended

Japanese presence in the peninsula, stressing instead Korean contributions to political, religious, and cultural development during the Proto-historic phase (James Ash, 1971). This is an ongoing debate but the mounting evidence strengthens claims for an extensive cultural influx from the peninsula. Hatada (1979) provides a thoughtful analysis of the controversial King Kwangaeto stele inscription, source of many claims and counter-claims. Hirano (1977) provides a basic introduction to Yamato's connections with the Korean peninsula in the earlier Proto-historic centuries. In this area, the best hope for future research lies in the developing collaborative efforts at excavation and analysis by joint Korean-Japanese research efforts, and the participation of Western scholars in this dialogue. Whatever one may believe about the Horseriders, Japan's early history cannot be understood in isolation from that of the rest of Asia and especially the Korean peninsula.

The Nara Period and the Early Ritsuryō *System*

The eighth century saw the establishment of a more permanent capital city, Heijō-kyō, or Nara as it was later known, serving as the home of a centralized bureaucratic imperial regime based on Chinese administrative codes, *ritsu* and *ryō*. From the late seventh century the older clan system of Yamato was overlaid with a heavy lattice of regularized, centralized taxation, census, land, and military systems. This is often referred to as the "*Ritsuryō* System" or the "*Ritsuryō* State."

Western historians looking at the history of the Nara period, 710-784, have analyzed the *ritsuryō* codes that provided the basis of the bureaucratic system, studied the establishment of the new capital and the working of the bureaucracy, charted responses in provincial society to these changes in central organization, and tried to assess how deep these changes really went. Some researchers have explored Japan's close relationship with China embodied in the missions to T'ang China (*kentōshi*) making Japan an eastern terminus of the silk road, while others have been impressed by the promotion of Buddhism in the great temples of Nara and the flowering of culture reflected in the images and objects surviving in Tōdaiji, Kōfukuji, and the Shōsō'in, in the writing of poetry, in the performance of music and dance, in the study of Confucianism, or in the compilation of histories and chronicles.

Much of the earlier work on the Nara period sought to explain the adoption of the Chinese legal codes and the workings of the central bureaucracy and administrative institutions. Here the work of George Sansom (1924, 1932), J. I. Crump (1952), and Richard J. Miller (1978) did much to clarify the administrative framework. A recent, clear, statement of the findings of this administrative and political approach is provided by Naoki Kōjirō (1993).

It has become increasingly clear that the great changes evident in the early Nara period did not come about suddenly with the establishment of Heijō-kyō in 710 but were the product of reform efforts of the mid- and late seventh century. In this area we are still heavily dependent on the contributions of Japanese scholars. For a good introduction to the surge of reforms of the seventh century, placing them in the context of East Asian history, see Inoue Mitsusada with Delmer M. Brown (1993).

Some historians have looked at the Nara court, the rise of the Fujiwara family and the intensifying struggles among nobles and clerics, culminating in the Dōkyō incident. Although there is as yet no good, detailed, study of the early Fujiwara family, or of other Nara bureaucrats, in English, there has been some research on the imperial family. This has tended to cluster around the more active male members of the lineage: Prince Shōtoku, and emperors Temmu, Tenchi, Shōmu and Kammu. This tendency has been critiqued by Patricia Tsurumi who has asked (1983) why so much attention has been focused on male rulers and so little on female emperors who were influential until the end of the Nara period. Ross Bender (1979) exposes the factional infighting between nobles and clerics in Nara around the time of the Dōkyō Incident (770). He links the cult of Hachiman to the rise and fall of the monk Dōkyō, who gained such influence over Empress Shōtoku that she sought to make him her consort.

Perhaps the most interesting work on the Nara period by Western historians in the past few decades has been in the areas of social and economic history. John W. Hall's volume (1966) still provides one of the most coherent accounts of the actual, on the ground, working of the *ritsuryō* system and of the relationship between changes in the provinces and pressures from the center. In Chapter 2, "The Imperial State System," Hall examines the transformation of Japan in the seventh and eighth centuries. He concludes: "There is no question that Japan had been transformed from a loose federation of *uji* in the fifth century to an empire on the order of imperial China in the eighth. A new theory of state and a new structure of government supported the Japanese sovereign in the style and with the powers of an absolute monarch."[2]

In practice what this meant, according to Hall, was that:

> The traditional political and economic relationships which had comprised the *uji* system were now channeled through a rationally conceived state apparatus with legally defined official functions and precedents. The landed surface of the Japanese islands had been surveyed, classed according to type, and registered according to use. The various claims upon the land, short of sovereignty, whether of ownership, proprietorship, right of cultivation, or right to income were defined by administrative practice, and any changes made subject to official process. All of this was most advantageous to the official class and was instrumental in creating a new aristocracy which was both synonymous with the state and strategically placed to benefit most from the activities of the state, now systematically supported by tax income from the entire country. The great public works, the palaces, government offices, temples, roads, and irrigation works which marked the heyday of the Nara period were the visible signs of a new concentration of power. Japan had entered upon an age of cultural achievement under the leadership of a new aristocracy, an age which was to last for over four centuries.[3]

In "Bizen: The Institutions of Taihō" (Chapter 3), Hall shows how the administrative reforms emanating from Yamato after 646 were slowly adopted in Bizen Province and a new provincial administration, tax, and land system was imposed on the old local *uji* aristocracy. While there may have been local resistance to these changes there does not seem to have been open revolt. Dana Morris (1980) looks at the peasantry as they were affected by these sweeping changes in social and economic organization.

Where Hall and many of the Japanese historians have given a generally positive, dynamic, assessment of the *ritsuryō* changes—the impression of a society growing in population, scale, density, and complexity as it became more of an imperial state—Wayne Farris (1985) has warned that Nara/early Heian society was also beset by problems. Analyzing census data, tax, and land records,

---

[2] John W. Hall (1966), 63.
[3] Ibid., 64.

Farris shows that epidemic disease had negative effects on population growth and that in many places land, which had been painfully brought into cultivation, was often allowed to return to the wild as the labor supply dwindled or absconded under the burden of taxes. Hall, Farris, and Dana Morris all comment on the early phases of the privatization of land within the officially public *ritsuryō* system. This was to lead to the proliferation of *shōen* holdings, and the ultimate erosion of the public land allocation system.

Buddhism, Confucianism, and Shintō all saw significant developments during the Nara period. As the study of Japanese religion is discussed elsewhere in this volume by Professor Helen Hardacre, this section confines itself to works that have a historical thrust to them. Considering some of the art-historical, institutional, and historical aspects of Buddhism, useful introductions will be found in volumes by Kidder (1972a) and John Rosenfield (1986). Joan Piggot's dissertation (1987) provides a more detailed study of the role of the important temple Tōdaiji within the Nara state. Y. Chiyonobu (1992) introduces the results of continuing research into the history of Tōdaiji. Tōdaiji's extensive landholdings in the Nara and Heian periods receive some attention from Elizabeth Satō (1974). Less research has been devoted to early Shintō shrines than to Buddhist temples, especially Tōdaiji. Two valuable works with sections devoted to important shrines during the Nara period are by William Coaldrake, ed. (1996) and Alan Grapard (1992). It will be evident from the above references that there has been a tendency to concentrate on a few of the most prestigious temples and shrines. There is a great need for studies of less well known religious institutions, and for temples in the provinces as well as in the capital. The whole *kokubunji* system deserves at least a monograph in English. Confucian and Taoist ideas and practices, which were also finding acceptance in Japan during the seventh and eighth centuries, have not yet been well researched by Western scholars. A brief introduction to Confucianism can be found in an article by Kaizuka (1959).

The Nara period, under direct Chinese influence, witnessed a surge in literacy, literature (including the *Manyōshū* anthology of poetry), and the writing of historical chronicles and gazetteers. The most useful recent introductions to Nara period literacy, literature, and historical consciousness have been provided by Edwin

Cranston (1993) and Delmer M. Brown (1993a). On Nara-period historical writing the reader may also consult G. W. Robinson (1961) and Sakamoto Tarō (1991). Joan Piggot (1990) has introduced some of the tens of thousands of wooden tally slips (*mokkan*), found in ever increasing numbers, and especially important for understanding economic history.

The great political, social, religious, intellectual, and cultural changes taking place in all areas of Japanese life in the early *ritsuryō* period were stimulated and sustained by the strong continental connection. There are plenty of general accounts of the large embassies to T'ang China initiated in the seventh century and repeated through the eighth and ninth centuries. Perhaps the most searching recent study has been by Wang Zhen-ping (1989), who has closely examined the rhetoric of Sino-Japanese diplomacy, which he sees to have been based, from the Japanese point of view at least, on a claim for "reciprocity."

The Nara period was brought to a close between 784 and 794 by the determination of Emperor Kammu to abandon the Heijō capital and build a new capital further north, first at Nagaoka-kyō, then at Heian-kyō. The reasons behind this sudden decision have been examined by Ronald Toby (1985).

The Heian Period

The long Heian period (794-1185) opened in the late eighth century with the shift of the capital city from Heijō-kyō to Heian-kyō ("capital of peace and tranquility") and efforts at administrative reform aimed at pulling the *ritsuryō* system together again. The ensuing centuries, however, saw further erosion of the centralized bureaucratic government. Imperial power was restricted and eclipsed by struggles for power at court attending the rise of the Fujiwara family. The Fujiwara nobles entrenched themselves by the establishment of extra-legal offices not envisioned in the original *ritsuryō* codes. Notions of public land and public authority gave way to private claims on land and people. These centuries witnessed the beginnings of the proliferation of privatized land holdings known as *shōen*, and the re-emergence of privatized personal authority in the form of warrior bands (*bushidan*). The *ritsuryō* administrative structure survived, but over these centuries it became increasingly a hollow shell. Changes in politics were accompanied by developments in Buddhism, Shintō, and fine and literary arts. Contact with the continent began strong with large official embassies continuing to import ideas and institutions in the early ninth century, but waned to a trickle between the tenth and twelfth centuries.

While the movement of the capital and the building of a new capital at Heian-kyō were enormous undertakings for Emperor Kammu and the court[4] and seemed to mark a major break with the preceding Nara period, when we look closely at the movement of history, early Heian was still very much a continuation of the imperial and aristocratic centralized bureaucratic *ritsuryō*-centered authority of the Nara period. The big shift from "public" to "private" authority may actually have come later, from around the year 1000, when the central imperial court, weakened by Fujiwara influence and the rivalry between cloistered emperors (*in*), and Fujiwara, began to lose control of the provinces, and the deterioration of the *ritsuryō* system was confirmed by the proliferation of *shōen* and the increasing provincial ascendancy of warriors.

Although there is much in these centuries still to clarify, study of Heian period history in the West has lagged behind the study of its literature and art. It is to be expected that the superb literature of Heian would draw many talented translators and critics. While we have been blessed with fine translations of Heian tales, *monogatari*, literary diaries, and poetry, by Donald Keene, Ivan Morris, Edward Seidensticker, Helen and William McCullough, Robert Brower, Earl Miner, Edward Kamens, and Richard Bowring, and with searching critical studies of *monogatari* by Haruo Shirane, Richard Okada, and Norma Field, to name only a few, there have not been comparable translations of historical texts and political diaries; nor have there been many recent strong studies of society, politics, or the changing economy. The most creative work has probably been in the area of military history, especially the emergence of the samurai.

Among the few recent translations of Heian period historical chronicles, the best have been provided by Helen and William McCullough (notably 1979 [a translation of the *Eiga monogatari*], 1980). Both of these quasi-historical texts focus on the exploits

---

[4] On this see Ronald Toby (1985).

and munificent life of Fujiwara Michinaga. Both translations contain useful introductions and notes on Heian institutions and court life. Felicia Bock's translations of the several books of the *Engishiki* (1970) have made that basic compendium of court and religious ritual accessible to a wider readership. Judith Rabinovitch's translation of the *Shōmonki* (1986) gives valuable insight into the abortive but unsettling uprising by Taira no Masakado in the eastern provinces around 940, an event which shook the already teetering Heian imperial court authority.

Not surprisingly, the imperial court during the Heian period has received the most attention from Western historians, although even that has been sporadic rather than systematic. Emperor Kammu's decision to move his court from Heijō to Heian has been discussed in a brief article by Ronald Toby (1985). Ivan Morris (1964) looks at the court around the year 1000, the age of Lady Murasaki. Based mainly on the *Tale of Genji* and other literary materials, this book does not pretend to go very deeply into historical issues, and presents many stereotypes of Heian history, but it is readable, and still probably the most widely-known introduction to Heian court society. Much more useful as institutional history have been the now aging essays edited by Hall and Mass (1974). This volume contains durable essays on the city of Heian (Kyoto) by Hall, and on the Heian court by Kiley and Hurst. Robert Borgen's study (1986) of Sugawara Michizane gives the political as well as the literary aspect of that ill-treated statesman. We await a full-scale study in English of Fujiwara Michinaga, or indeed any other Fujiwara nobleman, although there is a brief study of Michinaga's "maladies" by Cameron Hurst (1979). The best work on the structure and functioning of the Heian court in its later phase, when cloistered emperors struggled with Fujiwara regents to assume leadership, has been done by Hurst in his several studies of *insei* (1974a, 1974b). Especially noteworthy is his essay on "The Structure of the Heian Court," in which he applies Hall's notion of "familial authority" as a means of laying bare the structural dynamics of the court.

Shifting the focus from the court to the provinces during the Heian period, the main issues debated by historians have been the erosion of the *ritsuryō* system, the privatization of land holdings and the proliferation of *shōen*, the emergence of warrior bands (*bushidan*), and the growth of local and regional disorder. The terms of debate for *shōen* and *bushi* were set by John W. Hall,[5] who looked at the situation in Bizen during the Heian period. Here he makes it clear that the proliferation of *shōen* and the emergence of warriors (*bushi*), were interrelated events, that the emergence of warriors depended on the creation of *shōen*, and that the privatization of land ultimately may have had the most far-reaching impact on social change:

> Historians have speculated upon a number of causes which help to explain the decline of the central authority particularly over the provinces. Two appear critical. First, the gradual abandonment of provisions for state control of rice lands led ultimately to the growth of vast private proprietorships (*shōen*) through which the aristocratic houses and religious establishments of the capital were able to absorb many of the powers and functions of the central government. Second, abandonment of the principle of public conscription led to the emergence of a provincial military class (*bushi*) which increasingly took over the military and police functions of the state on a hereditary basis and by the thirteenth century began to encroach upon the civil authority of provincial administration as well. Of the two, the spread of the *shōen* system was the first to manifest itself and in the long run was to have the most far-reaching effects upon the political structure of Japan. While it is conceivable that the *bushi* might have attained their political dominance in Japan without the prior existence of the *shōen* system, in actual fact it greatly accelerated the appearance of independent military groups within the provinces.[6]

On the Heian period *shōen*, useful essays have also been contributed by Elizabeth Satō (1974), Neil Kiley (1974), and Kozo Yamamura (1974). Kiley's essay presents an analytical attempt to distinguish in legal terms between Heian notions of "estate" and "property." Yamamura argues that the rapid decline of the *ritsuryō* system in late Heian was brought about by "market forces" expressed in the competition from nobles, temples, and shrines as they privatized land and attracted labor from the public domain by setting relatively lighter tax burdens. In the 1980s and early 1990s the focus of attention shifted from the debate over *shōen* to a series of skirmishes between Wayne Farris and Karl Friday over the origins and emergence of the samurai. Books and articles by both these authors have challenged much of the received wisdom on Japan's early

---

[5] In his chapter "The *Shōen* System and the Return to Familial Authority" (in 1966).

[6] Ibid., 101.

military tradition and opened up the field of military history. These works, and others on the history of the samurai were recently reviewed by Martin Collcutt (1996).

Heian culture is perhaps the crowning achievement of early Japan. Buddhism took deeper root and was enriched by the devotion to the *Lotus Sutra* and the depth and power of esoteric teachings and mandalas. Priests like Saichō, Kūkai, and Ennin, all of whom studied in China, built influential monasteries and promoted powerful new religious currents within Japan. Tendai, Shingon, and Pure Land Buddhism ran strongly through the Heian period. Buddhism is discussed elsewhere by Professor Hardacre. Here it is sufficient to remind readers of the fine studies of Saichō, Kūkai, and Ennin by Groner (1984), Hakeda (1972), and Reischauer (1955). De Visser's *Early Buddhism in Japan* still wears well. Nakamura's (1973) translation of the *Nihon ryōiki* by Kyōkai gives some insight into the powerful appeal of karmic belief in the Nara and Heian periods.

Japan's relations with China during the Heian centuries—state-sponsored and very active in the early period, much diminished after the ninth century—have not yet been fully explored. The best studies are probably Borgen's essay (1982) and Wang Zhenping's dissertation (1989), which explores the language of Sino-Japanese relations during this period using the notion of "reciprocity" to challenge that of a "Sino-centric world order."

As of writing, we await Volume 2 of the *Cambridge History of Japan*. When this volume appears it should provide systematic coverage of the period and allow us to take better stock of the achievements of the past twenty years in Heian historical studies.

The Medieval Age: Kamakura and Muromachi Periods to ca. 1500

The long span of Japanese history between the tenth and sixteenth centuries, embracing the late Heian, Kamakura, and Muromachi periods, is generally referred to as Japan's medieval age (*chūsei*). Looking beneath historical details we can distinguish broad, long-term currents of change in politics, society, religion, and the arts. A few might be described as distinctively "medieval"; most, however, had antecedents well before the tenth century, or continued to be felt long after the sixteenth. Because the intermingling of these various currents shaped the larger features of traditional Japanese society, and since, in many cases, their impact can still be detected today, it is no exaggeration to say that the *chūsei* heritage is as important for Japan as the medieval heritage has been for the history of any European society.

As a field of historical research, the medieval centuries have fared better than the preceding Heian period. Research in the United States has been stimulated by several important conferences, involving leading Japanese as well as Western scholars, on the Kamakura, Nanbokuchō, Muromachi, and Sengoku periods. There have been important art exhibits, including the "Age of Daimyo Culture" at the National Gallery in Washington, D.C. (Shimizu, 1988) and "Momoyama, Japan's Golden Age" in Dallas in 1997. The development of the field can be gauged from several useful "state of the field essays." These include those by Conrad Totman (1979), Kozo Yamamura (1990b), and John W. Hall (1991).

Politically, historians have distinguished three long-term currents in the medieval age: the transfer of political leadership to a new elite; the erosion of stable central authority into decentralization and civil war; and, when political fragmentation had reached an extreme, a fierce drive back through warfare to reunification. The first of these phases involved a shift in political power from the imperial court to warrior chieftains in the thirteenth and fourteenth centuries, with the establishment of warrior governments (*bakufu*) on the one hand and the erosion of imperial authority and the power of the court nobility on the other. Whereas the early phases of warrior government, the Kamakura and early Muromachi *bakufu*, were relatively strong and stable, the late fifteenth and early sixteenth centuries saw a loss of central control by the Muromachi *bakufu* accompanied by provincial unrest, endemic warfare, and local control. This process has been referred to as the "lower toppling the upper" (*gekokujō*) in an age of provincial wars. Eventually, from the ruck of warring barons there emerged men such as Oda Nobunaga and Toyotomi Hideyoshi, who were impelled by a larger vision of national unification.

For the late twelfth and thirteenth centuries, historians have sought to explain the growing ascendancy of warriors in Japanese society. This has involved close studies of the Kamakura *bakufu*, its organs of government, especially *shugo* and *jitō*, and its relationship with the imperial court and with other major landed proprietors including temples and shrines. Here the work of Jeffrey P. Mass has set the pace and energized the field. Emphasizing the novelty of "Warrior Government" in his early work (1974b), he has since come to view "*bakufu*" and "court," with religious institutions, in a more interactive and intricate balance of power, tilting in favor of warriors throughout the thirteenth century.[7] In addition to the work of Mass, important contributions to the understanding of the dynamics of Kamakura *bakufu* rule have been provided by Hall (1966), Varley (1982), Steenstrup (1979), Hurst (1982) and Kiley (1982).

The decline of the Kamakura *bakufu*, its overthrow by Emperor Go-Daigo, the short-lived Kenmu Restoration, and the early Muromachi *bakufu* under the Ashikaga line of shoguns have drawn the attention of a number of scholars including Hori Kyotsu (1974), Prescott B. Wintersteen, Jr. (1974a), H. Paul Varley (1971), Kenneth Grossberg (1981), and most recently Andrew Goble (1996). Where Varley presented Go-Daigo's Kenmu Restoration as an anachronistic failure, for instance, Goble's recent book gives Go-Daigo greater credit for attempting new initiatives in government and land policy, even if they could not be brought to fruition. The best studies of the Ashikaga shoguns focus on Ashikaga Yoshimitsu[8] and emphasize his cultural role. We await good studies of the political and economic aspects of Ashikaga rule. The most sustained attempt so far in English has been by Kenneth Grossberg (1981). His book is thought-provoking but claims more for shogunal authority— "kingship" as Grossberg thinks of it—in the form of military power, personal bureaucracy, and mercantilist reach than the documents will support. Moving into the fifteenth century, as the Ashikaga shogunal grip on power is seen to be loosening, historians have looked closely at *bakufu*-daimyo relations, the competition between *shugo* daimyo and the *kokujin*-level warriors beneath, and the emergence of those powerful local warriors known as the "daimyo of the age of war" (*sengoku daimyō*). Here, Hall (1966, 1968), Arnesen (1979), and Birt (1985) have all made important contributions.

For an introduction to recent trends in the political history of the Kamakura and Muromachi periods the reader can consult four or five readily accessible collections of essays: Yamamura, ed. (1990),

---

[7] See for instance the essays by Jeffrey Mass and others in Mass, ed. (1982).
[8] See Paul Varley (1977), and Varley and Isao Kumakura, eds. (1989).

Hall and Mass, eds. (1974), Mass, ed. (1982), Hall and Toyoda, eds. (1977), and a new volume, forthcoming from Stanford University Press, on Japan in the fourteenth century, edited by Jeffrey Mass. Not all the attention of political historians has been focused on central institutions of court and *bakufu*. They have also looked at changing relationships in the provinces. In some cases this has taken the forms of studies of the erosion of the *shōen* system.[9] In others, it has involved study of local lordship or proprietorship.[10] More recently attention is being directed at struggles on the land.[11] There is still room for considerable work on medieval *ikki*, including *ikkō-ikki*. Now the attention of historians is moving in the direction of status as well as conflict. Nagahara's essay (1979) is a harbinger for further research in this area.

There has also been significant work on the institutional aspects of religious history in the Kamakura and Muromachi periods—medieval temples, shrines, centers of pilgrimages, and fundraising—by Piggot, Goodwin, Grapard, Tyler, Collcutt, and others. Younger scholars are now looking at Enryakuji and Kōfukuji, with their extensive land holdings, moneylending activities, commercial interests, and military forces. Stanley Weinstein's studies of Jōdo Shinshū religious development, combined with those of Michael Solomon, James Dobbins, and Galen Amstutz, have insights for historians, as does the work of Donald McCallum on Zenkōji, and William Bodiford's study of medieval Sōtō Zen. Multiple studies of Zen by Bernard Faure and Carl Bielefeldt have provided invaluable theoretical stimulus for students of history as well as those of Japanese religion. This is a fertile area, with room for many more interesting studies.

In the areas of social and economic life, the medieval age saw the emergence of new classes, new patterns of landholding, growing agricultural production, increased market activity, more extensive commerce, greater use of coinage, and substantial urban development, all of which contributed to, and benefited from, the release of new economic and commercial energies. The best brief overviews of the changing medieval economy are probably by Kozo Yamamura (1990a) and Takeshi Toyoda and Hiroshi Sugiyama (1977). Haruko Wakita's essay (1975) is also well worth consulting. Hitomi Tono-

---

[9] Hall, Mass, and Yamamura, eds. (1981), and Kyōhei Oyama (1990).
[10] Arnesen's studies of Suō (1982) and of the Ōuchi as medieval daimyo (1979).
[11] Lorraine Harrington (1982).

mura (1992) has written a fine book which looks at the changes in the villages around Kyoto and takes the story into the sixteenth century.

Urban growth in the Kamakura and Muromachi periods has been studied mainly in terms of Kyoto, Sakai, and the temple towns. Good studies include those by Hall (1974), T. Hayashiya (1977), Dixon Morris (1970, 1977, 1981), and Haruko Wakita (1981). Such smaller medieval towns as Kusado Sengen and Tosa Minato, excavated in the past two decades by Japanese archaeologists and extensively written about in Japan, have yet to be enfolded into the English language literature on medieval urban life.

Until recently medieval cultural history tended to be directed at the elite, emperors, shoguns, nobles, and influential prelates. Paul Varley's study of Yoshimitsu (1977) and his essay on "Cultural Life in Medieval Japan" (1990) are strong examples of this. Martin Collcutt (1988) extends the notion of elite cultural patronage to the educated elite of warrior society. Popular culture has attracted attention only recently, especially in the fine work of Barbara Ruch (1977, 1990). Hopefully, this will be a precursor to many more studies of the cultural lives of ordinary people.

With the exception of the decades around the Mongol Invasion attempts, Japan was in fairly close contact with Korea and China during these centuries. Some of this contact was official—trade missions by *bakufu* or daimyo, or journeys in search of the *dharma* by monks, and so forth. Some of it would fall under the heading of "freebooting" or marauding by pirates and petty merchants, *wakō* as they were called elsewhere in Asia. Relatively little work has been done by American scholars in this area since Wang Yi-Tung's (1953) article and a 1967 essay by Benjamin Hazard. The best recent introductions are probably the translated essays by Takeo Tanaka (1977) and Shōji Kawazoe's "Japan and East Asia" (1990).

The Sixteenth Century: From the Age of Wars, Sengoku, to the Golden Age of Momoyama. Warfare, Political Consolidation, and Economic Growth

There is now a considerable and rapidly growing body of historical research on Japan in the sixteenth century. While much of the earlier research tended to stress the first contacts with the West, as in Sir George Sansom's classic volume (1950) or C. R. Boxer's work (1951), more recent research has looked for internal dynamics and inter-Asian connections. While the motive of explaining the subsequent "Tokugawa period" through clarification of the sixteenth century is still strong, there are some scholars who view the sixteenth century for its own sake. There has also been a shift from a view of the period as one of unbridled warfare and violence to one that sees the warfare, pursued by Sengoku daimyo, as a kind of tempering process, a forge, in which old institutions were finally broken down, ready for re-formation, or reunification, by strong hegemons like Oda Nobunaga and Toyotomi Hideyoshi. While interest in the ruling elite remains strong, recent scholarship is looking more closely at popular culture, religion, cultural patronage, and material culture, especially that relating to excavated ceramics and the world of tea.

The sixteenth century was a time of upheaval and disorder, but at century's end Japan was substantially unified and pacified. This was the result of three trends. The first was a gradual growth in the size of domains that local figures with retainer armies were carving out. Warfare, alliance, and marriage politics helped pacify the principal geographic divisions. Larger riparian works made it possible for local rulers to extend their control to more efficiently sized economic units; in the process their political potential grew accordingly. Second, the entrance of new foreign technology changed the face of warfare and brought the victory to leaders who had access to firearms. Larger forces of professional soldiery ruled out the extremes of political participation that had been possible in a world of arrows, spears, and mounted samurai. Third, a generation of formidable war lords brought a new ruthlessness and thoroughness to their campaigns. The greatest of these were Oda Nobunaga, Toyotomi Hideyoshi, and Tokugawa Ieyasu.[12]

For much of the sixteenth century the Ashikaga shoguns were still nominally in control of the country, though neither they nor the imperial court had better than a tattered legitimacy; and any remnant of power they retained did not extend beyond Kyoto. There are still some scholars who view the century prior to

---

[12] Helpful bibliographic overviews and introductions to the period will be found in Bardwell Smith (1981). This can be updated from Hall's "Introduction" (1991). The process of political and military reunification is discussed in a number of studies. One of the most accessible is by Asao Naohiro (1991).

Hideyoshi as "late medieval" and see him as the architect of social changes that shifted Japan in the direction of what many Western historians call an "early modern" (*kinsei*) experience. Most scholars, however, now seem inclined to consider the "sixteenth century" as a unit of about a century and a half from around 1500 to 1650, the early Tokugawa period, in which the political map of Japan was reshaped in war, and the country was being reunified in surges under increasingly far-reaching regimes and growing economically in ways it had not experienced before. John W. Hall (1981b) has called this whole phenomenon "the sixteenth century revolution."

Some scholars have stressed the importance of the contribution made by the warrior lords of the age of wars (*sengoku daimyō*) to the notion of the "state" in their assertion of their domains as "realms" under their public authority (*kōgi*). This notion of *kōgi* has received considerable attention, for instance from Nagahara (1985) and Katsumata (1981). There have been many fine studies of Sengoku daimyo rule. Among them readers will find especially helpful Marius Jansen's work on Tosa (1968), John Hall's on Bizen under the Akamatsu, Matsuda, Urakami and Ukita houses,[13] Peter Arnesen's studies of the Ōuchi and Mōri (1979, 1982); Michael Birt's dissertation on the Odawara Hōjō (1985), and James Kanda's study of the Date family law code, the *Jinkaishū* (1974).

The impact of warfare itself has only recently begun to receive serious attention. Delmer Brown made an early start with his essay (1948). More recently, and more ambitiously, Geoffrey Parker, a historian of Europe, has introduced his notion of a "military revolution" to the sixteenth-century Japanese arena (1988).

Although we do not yet have recent detailed biographies of Oda Nobunaga and Tokugawa Ieyasu, Elizabeth Berry has provided a fine biography of Toyotomi Hideyoshi, stressing the "federalist" character of his political settlement (1982). Fujiki Hisashi (1981), George Elison (Jurgis Elisonas) (1981a, 1981b), and Osamu Wakita (1981a) have given us, among them, more than half a dozen telling studies of differing aspects of the policies of Nobunaga and Hideyoshi.

The entrenched military power of the older Buddhist temples and the cohesive determination of sectarian followers of the True Pure Land groups, and Lotus devotees in Kyoto, presented to

---

[13] Hall (1966), 238-320.

anybody intent on conquering the country resistance as fierce as that of any daimyo. The struggle between the unifiers and Buddhist opponents in the sixteenth century is being told in increasing detail by McMullin (1984) as well as students of True Pure Land Buddhism, including Stanley Weinstein, Michael Solomon, David Davis, James Dobbins, and more recently Elizabeth Berry, Galen Amstutz, and Carol Richmond. Through their studies we are beginning to come to a clearer picture of resistance to authority and the nature of sixteenth-century *ikki*. We are still, however, far from understanding what precise "religious" beliefs, if any, lay behind the fierce resistance to Nobunaga made by the *ikkō-ikki*.

The general assumption in many of the studies of Hideyoshi that his social policies (sword hunts, separation of samurai and farmers, cadastral surveys, and land registration policies) were rapidly enforced has been challenged by Philip Brown (1993). Herman Ooms's recent work (1996) on "village practice" looks at the effects of these changes from the village level.

The burgeoning, war-driven economy of the sixteenth and early seventeenth century has attracted considerable attention. Wealth was being created at a rate hitherto unknown in Japan. Ostentation among warlords and merchants was the order of the day and the Momoyama era has rightly earned a reputation as a "golden age." European visitors of the day commented on the wealth in bullion and the gilded character of late sixteenth-century Japanese life. Exhibitions of Japanese art and culture in our own day are mounted around the theme of Golden Momoyama. The best work on the Japanese coinages, bullion, mines, and mining has probably been done by Japanese scholars led by Kobata (1965). Delmer Brown published an early study in English on the "money economy in medieval Japan" (1951). Kozo Yamamura (1981a) has presented the most daringly argued synoptic view of a thriving economy driven increasingly by accumulating political unification and "market forces." William Atwell has placed Japan in the larger context of Asian and world economic history with his fine studies of ups and downs of bullion flows from Mexico to Japan and China and the "Seventeenth Century Crisis" (1986), and Iwao Seiichi has written on Japan's foreign trade in the sixteenth and seventeenth centuries (1976).

In such a gilded age, elite patronage was on a grandiose scale. Much interesting recent work can be grouped under the heading of "cultural patronage." This was seen in grandiose castle design, grandiloquent performances and receptions, lavish temple decoration, and ostentatious tea ceremonies, to name only a few examples. Oda Nobunaga's patronage of Kanō Eitoku and their grand design at Azuchi was visualized by Carolyn Wheelwright (1981). Hideyoshi's munificent patronage is discussed in many sources including Berry (1975) and Elison (1981b). The patronage and politics surrounding the tea ceremony are the focus of essays by Bodart-Bailey (1977), Louise Cort (1982), and Andrew Watsky (1995). Literary patronage in this period is discussed by Stephen D. Carter (1993) and Janet Yuba (1993). In many respects the recent Momoyama exhibition in Dallas and the catalogue to it comprised an extended discussion of the manifestations of patronage in late sixteenth-century Japan.

Interest in patronage at the elite level has been counterbalanced by a growing interest in the lives of ordinary citizens living in a turbulent age. Mary Berry's is the most extended recent discussion of this topic (1994). Michael Cooper's edited accounts by visiting foreigners have added vignettes to the obscure picture of everyday life (1965). Popular culture is also being explored through the studies of early Kabuki, music, and dance, and through work on religious currents in the age. But it still remains a poorly-studied area of sixteenth-century Japanese life.

Japan's relations with the West have not been forgotten. Over the past several decades, the work of Sansom and Boxer has been deepened by that of Michael Cooper, George Elison, and Derek Massarella, to name only three among many who work in this field. Cooper's translations (1965, 1973) have provided wonderfully observant glimpses of all aspects of Japanese society. Elison's remains one of the most thoughtful and enduring studies of the encounter between Christianity and Japan (1973), and Massarella's work (1990) on the East India Company reveals how that enterprise actually worked and shows the English as well as the Portuguese, Spanish, and Dutch, to have been active protagonists in sixteenth-century Japan. There have been many fine studies of the Catholic Mission effort, the church, its various denominations, and its leaders during the sixteenth and early seventeenth centuries. On a different front, that of the sword rather than the cross, Geoffrey Parker's work (1988) has stressed military interactions between

Europe and Japan. Donald Lach (1968) has been reminding us that Japan, as well as China and other Asian countries, loomed large in the eyes not only of Europeans who visited Japan but of many of those who never left Europe.

More work recently has been done on Asian connections. Ronald Toby's questioning of *sakoku* and the whole notion of a "closed country" from the seventeenth century has opened up the door for study of Japan's contacts with Asia, as well as the West, from the sixteenth century on. The ongoing work of Toby, William Atwell, and younger scholars is placing sixteenth-century Japan in the context of contemporary Asian and world history. Inter-Asian trade and bullion flows have been analyzed by Iwao and Atwell. The precise nature and results of Hideyoshi's invasions are being exposed by scholars like Elison (1988), and in Andrew Maske's studies (1994, 1996) of the forced introduction of Korean potters and ceramic technology during the invasions. Growing interest in inter-Asian connections may perhaps be indicated by the lively panel on this topic at the 1997 Association for Asian Studies meeting in Chicago and by the interest shown in the touring exhibition, sponsored by the Government of the Philippines, of the galleon *San Diego*, sunk off Manila in 1600 and brought up from the seabed only recently. The objects recovered from the *San Diego* show clearly the inter-connections within Asia and of Asia with Europe in the late sixteenth century.

BIBLIOGRAPHY

Acta Asiatica/Bushi. 1985. "Japanese Warriors." *Acta Asiatica* 49.
Acta Asiatica/Medieval. 1983. "Medieval Social History." *Acta Asiatica* 44.
Akamatsu, Toshihide. 1977. "Muromachi Zen and the Gozan System." In Hall and Toyoda, eds. (1977), 313-29.
Akazawa, Takeru, and C. Melvin Aikens. 1986. *Prehistoric Hunter-gatherers in Japan.* Tokyo: University of Tokyo Press and New York: Columbia University Press.
Amakasu, Ken. 1977. "The Significance of the Formation and Distribution of Kofun." *Acta Asiatica* 31: 24-50.
Amino, Yoshihiko. 1983. "Some Problems Concerning the History of Popular Life in Medieval Japan." *Acta Asiatica* 44: 77-97.
———. 1992. "Deconstructing Japan." *East Asian History* 3: 121-42.
Amstutz, Galen. 1991. "The Honganji Institution 1500-1570: The Politics of Pure Land Buddhism in Medieval Japan." Ph.D. diss., Princeton University.
Anderson, Jennifer L. 1991. *An Introduction to Japanese Tea Ritual.* Albany: State University of New York Press.

Anesaki, Masaharu. 1931. "Writings on Martyrdom in Kirishitan Literature." *Transactions of the Asiatic Society of Japan*, 2nd series 8: 20-65.
——. 1963. *History of Japanese Religion*. Rutland, Vt.: Charles E. Tuttle.
——. 1964. "Japanese Mythology." In *Mythology of All Races*, edited by L. H. Gray, 205-400. New York: Cooper Square.
Aoki, Michiko Yamaguchi, trans. *Izumo Fudoki*. Edited by Monumenta Nipponica Monographs. Sophia University, 1971.
Arnesen, Peter Judd. 1979. *The Medieval Japanese Daimyo: The Ōuchi Family's rule of Suō and Nagato*. New Haven: Yale University Press.
——. 1982. "Suō Province in the Age of Kamakura." In Mass, ed. (1982), 92-120.
——. 1985. "The Provincial Vassals of the Muromachi Shoguns." In Mass and Hauser, eds. (1985), 99-129.
Asakawa, Kanichi. 1918. "Some Aspects of Japanese Feudal Institutions." *Transactions of the Asiatic Society of Japan*, 1st series 46: 76-102.
——. 1919. "The Life of a Monastic *shō* in Medieval Japan." *Annual Report of the American Historical Association for 1916 I*: 311-46.
——. 1955 [1929]. *The Documents of Iriki, Illustrative of the Development of the Feudal Institution in Japan*. Tokyo: Japan Society for the Promotion of Science.
——. 1965a [1911]. "Notes on Village Government in Japan after 1600." In Asakawa (1965c).
——. 1965b [1918]. "Some Aspects of Japanese Feudal Institutions." In Asakawa (1965c).
——. 1965c. *Land and Society in Medieval Japan*, compiled and edited by the Committee for the Publication of Dr. K. I. Asakawa's Works. Tokyo: Japan Society for the Promotion of Science.
Asao, Naohiro. 1981. "Shogun and Tennō." In Hall, ed. (1981).
——. 1991. "The Sixteenth-Century Unification." In Hall and McClain, eds. (1991), 40-95.
Ash, James K. 1971. "Korea in the Making of the Early Japanese State." *Journal of Social Sciences and Humanities*.
Aston, William G., trans. 1972 [1896]. *Nihongi: Chronicles of Japan from Earliest Times to A.D. 697*. Rutland, Vt.: Charles E. Tuttle.
Atwell, William. 1986. "Some Observations on the 'Seventeenth Century Crisis' in China and Japan." *Journal of Asian Studies* 45, no. 2: 223-44.
Barnes, Gina L. 1983. "Kofun (Tomb Mounds)." *Kodansha Encyclopedia of Japan*: 244-46.
——. 1988. *Proto-historic Yamato: Archeology of the First Japanese State*. Michigan Papers in Japanese Studies, 17. Museum of Anthropology, Anthropological Papers, 78. Ann Arbor: University of Michigan.
——. 1990a. *Bibliographic Reviews of Far Eastern Archaeology*. Oxford: Oxbow.
——. 1990b. *Hoabinihian, Jomon, Yayoi, Early Korean States*. Oxford: Oxbow.
——. 1990c. "The Idea of Prehistory in Japan." *Antiquity* 64, no. 245: 929-39.
——. 1993. *China, Korea and Japan: The Rise of Civilization in East Asia*. London: Thames and Hudson.
Barnes, Gina L., and Timothy Reynold. 1984. "The Japanese Palaeolithic: a Review." *Proceedings of the Prehistoric Society* 50.
Beardsley, Richard K. 1955. "Japan Before History: A Survey of the Archeological Record." *Far Eastern Quarterly* 14: 317-46.
Beasley, W. G., and E. G. Pulleyblank. 1961. *Historians of China and Japan*. London: Oxford University Press.
Befu, Harumi, and Chester S. Chard. 1960. "Pre-Ceramic Cultures in Japan." *American Anthropologist* 62, no.4: 815-49.

Bender, Ross. 1979. "The Hachiman Cult and the Dōkyō Incident." *Monumenta Nipponica* 34, no. 2: 125-54.
Berry, Mary Elizabeth. 1975. *Hideyoshi in Kyoto: The Arts of Peace*. Cambridge: Harvard University Press.
——. 1982. *Hideyoshi*. Cambridge: Council on East Asian Studies, Harvard University.
——. 1983. "Restoring the Past: The Documents of Hideyoshi's Magistrate in Kyoto." *Harvard Journal of Asiatic Studies* 43, no. 1: 57-95.
——. 1986. "Public Peace and Private Attachment: The Goals and Conduct of Power in Early Modern Japan." *Journal of Japanese Studies* 12: 237-71.
——. 1994. *The Culture of Civil War in Kyoto*. Berkeley: University of California Press.
Birt, Michael P. 1985. "Samurai in Passage: Transformation of the Sixteenth Century Kanto." *Journal of Japanese Studies* 11: 369-89.
Bleed, Peter. 1972. "Yayoi Cultures of Japan." *Arctic Anthropology* 9, no. 2: 1-20.
——. 1983a. "Prehistoric Archaeology." *Kodansha Encyclopedia of Japan*.
——. 1983b. "Prehistory." *Kodansha Encyclopedia of Japan*.
——. 1986. "Almost Archaeology: Early Archaeological Interest in Japan." In Pearson, Barnes, and Hutterer, eds. (1986).
Bock, Felicia Gressit, trans. 1970. *"Engi-shiki": Procedures of the Engi Era, Books I-V*. Tokyo: Sophia University Press.
Bodart-Bailey, Beatrice M. 1977. "Tea and Counsel: The Political Role of Sen no Rikyū." *Monumenta Nipponica* 32, no. 1: 49-74.
Bodiford, William M. 1993. *Sōtō Zen in Medieval Japan*. Honolulu: University of Hawai'i Press.
Borgen, Robert. 1982. "The Japanese Mission to China 801-806." *Monumenta Nipponica* 37, no. 1: 1-28.
——. 1986. *Sugawara no Michizane and the Early Heian Court*. Cambridge: Council on East Asian Studies, Harvard University.
Boscaro, Adriana. 1973. *Sixteenth Century European Printed Works on the First Japanese Mission to Europe: a Descriptive Bibliography*. Leiden: E. J. Brill.
——. 1975. *101 letters of Hideyoshi: The Private Correspondence of Toyotomi Hideyoshi*. Tokyo: Sophia University Press.
Bottomley, Ian, and Anthony Hopson. 1988. *Arms and Armour of the Samurai: The History of Weaponry in Ancient Japan*. Greenwich: Bison.
Bowles, Gordon T. 1983. "Origins of the Japanese People." *Kodansha Encyclopedia of Japan*: 33-35.
Boxer, Charles R. 1931. "Notes on Early European Military Influence in Japan, 1543-1853." *Transactions of the Asiatic Society of Japan*, 2nd series 8: 67-75 especially.
——. 1935. "Hosokawa Tadaoki and the Jesuits, 1587-1645." *Transactions and Proceedings of the Japan Society* [London] 32: 79-119.
——. 1951. *The Christian Century in Japan, 1549-1650*. Berkeley: University of California Press.
——. 1963. *The Great Ship from Amacon: Annals of Macao and the Old Japan Trade, 1555-1640*. Lisbon: Centro de Estudos Históricos Ultramarinos.
——. 1968 [1948]. *Fidalgos in the Far East, 1550-1770*. Reprint. Oxford: Oxford University Press.
Brown, Delmer M. 1947. "The Importation of Gold into Japan by the Portuguese During the Sixteenth Century." *Pacific Historical Review* 16, no. 2: 125-33.
——. 1948. "The Impact of Firearms on Japanese Warfare, 1543-98." *Far Eastern Quarterly* 7, no. 3: 236-53.

———. 1951. *Money Economy in Medieval Japan: A Study in the Use of Coins.* New Haven: Institute of Far Eastern Languages, Yale University.
———. 1993a. "The Early Evolution of Historical Consciousness." In Brown, ed. (1993), 504-48.
———. 1993b. "Introduction: Ancient Japan." In Brown, ed. (1993).
———. 1993c. "The Yamato Kingdom." In Brown, ed. (1993), 108-162.
Brown, Delmer, ed. 1993. *Ancient Japan.* Vol. 1 of *The Cambridge History of Japan.* Cambridge: Cambridge University Press.
Brown, Delmer, and Ichirō Ishida. 1979. *The Future and the Past.* Berkeley: University of California Press.
Brown, Philip. 1993. *Central Authority and Local Autonomy in the Formation of Early Modern Japan.* Stanford: Stanford University Press.
Brownlee, John. 1975. "Crisis as Reinforcement of the Imperial Institution: The Case of the Jōkyū Incident, 1221." *Monumenta Nipponica* 30, no. 2: 193-202.
———. 1991. *Political Thought in Japanese Historical Writing: from "Kojiki" (712) to "Tokushi Yoron" (1712).* Toronto: Wilfrid Laurier University Press.
Bunshi, Nanpō. 1964. "Teppō-ki [Record of firearms]." In Tsunoda, de Bary, and Keene, eds. (1964).
Butler, Kenneth Dean. 1969. "The *Heike monogatari* and the Japanese Warrior Ethic." *Harvard Journal of Asiatic Studies* 29: 93-108.
Carter, Stephen D. 1993. *Literary Patronage in Late Medieval Japan.* Ann Arbor: Center for Japanese Studies, University of Michigan.
Castile, Rand. 1971. *The Way of Tea.* New York: Weatherhill.
Chamberlain, Basil Hall, trans. 1973 [1883]. *"Kojiki": or Records of Ancient Matters.* Reprint. Rutland, Vt.: Charles E. Tuttle.
Chiyonobu, Yoshimasa. 1992. "Recent Archeological Excavations at Tōdaiji." *The Japanese Journal of Religious Studies* 19, nos. 2-3: 245-54.
Cieslik, Hubert, S.J. 1954. "Early Jesuit Missionaries in Japan." *The Missionary Bulletin* 8-10.
Coaldrake, William H. 1996a. "The Grand Shrines of Ise and Izumo: The Appropriation of Vernacular Architecture by Early Ruling Authority." In Coaldrake, ed. (1996), 16-51.
———. 1996b. "Great Halls of Religion and State: Architecture and the Creation of the Nara Imperial Order." In Coaldrake, ed. (1996), 52-80.
Coaldrake, William H., ed. 1996. *Architecture and Authority in Japan.* London: Routledge.
Coates, Harper Havelock, and Ryugaku Ishizuka. 1925. *Honen, the Buddhist Saint: his Life and Teachings.* Kyoto: Chionin.
Collcutt, Martin. 1981. *Five Mountains, the Rinzai Zen Monastic Institution in Medieval Japan.* Cambridge: Harvard University Press.
———. 1982a. "Kings of Japan? The Political Authority of the Ashikaga Shoguns." *Monumenta Nipponica* 37, no. 4: 523-30.
———. 1982b. "The Zen Monastery in Kamakura Society." In Mass, ed. (1982).
———. 1983. "Muromachi History." *Kodansha Encyclopedia of Japan*: 172-77.
———. 1987. "Medieval Society." In *Thousand Cranes: Treasures of Japanese Art,* edited by Seattle Art Museum. Seattle: Seattle Art Museum.
———. 1988. "Daimyo and Daimyo Culture." In Shimizu, ed. (1988).
———. 1990. "Zen and the Gozan." In Yamamura, ed. (1990). Examines the development of Rinzai Zen in medieval Japan, the distinction between the *gozan* and the *rinka* monasteries, economy and adminstration, and changes in Zen practice, culture, and monastic life. Traces the history of Rinzai Zen from its earliest transmission to Japan in the Heian period, to the institutional

rooting of the five mountains system in the Kamakura period, and the flowering of Rinzai Zen and Zen culture in the Muromachi period. Looks at the Zen monastic economy and administration, changes in Zen practice, culture, and the monastic life.

———. 1995. "Premodern Japan (A Bibliographic Guide)." In *Guide to Historical Literature*. Vol. 1, edited by M. B. Norton, 355-82. New York: Oxford University Press.

———. 1996. "The Emergence of the Samurai and the Military History of Early Japan." *Harvard Journal of Asiatic Studies*.

Collcutt, Martin, Marius B. Jansen, and Isao Kumakura. 1988. *A Cultural Atlas of Japan*. Oxford: Equinox and New York: Facts on File.

Cooper, Michael, S.J. 1972. "The Mechanics of the Macao-Nagasaki Silk Trade." *Monumenta Nipponica* 27, no. 4: 423-33.

———. 1974. *Rodrigues the Interpreter: An Early Jesuit in China and Japan*. New York: Weatherhill.

———. 1989. "The Early Europeans and Tea." In Varley and Kumakura, eds. (1989), 101-34.

Cooper, Michael, S.J., ed. 1965. *They Came to Japan: An Anthology of European Reports on Japan, 1543-1640*. London: Thames and Hudson.

———, 1971. *The Southern Barbarians: The First Europeans in Japan*. Tokyo: Kodansha International.

Cooper, Michael, S.J., ed. and trans. 1973. *This Island of Japon: Joao Rodriques' Account of 16th Century Japan*. Tokyo: Kodansha International.

Cort, Louise Allison. 1982. "The Grand Kitano Tea Gathering." *Chanoyu Quarterly* 31: 15-44.

Covell, Jon Carter. 1980. *Unraveling Zen's Red Thread: Ikkyū's Controversial Way*. Seoul, Korea, Elizabeth, N.J.: Hollym Corp.

Covell, Jon Carter, and Sōbin Yamada. 1974. *Zen at Daitokuji*. Tokyo: Kodansha International.

Cranston, Edwin. 1993. "Asuka and Nara Culture: Literacy, Literature, and Music." In Brown, ed. (1993), 453-503.

Crawford, Gary W. 1983. *Paleoethnobotany of the Kameda Peninsula Jomon*. Ann Arbor: Museum of Anthropology, University of Michigan.

———. 1992. "Plant Domestication in East Asia." *The Origins of Agriculture in International Perspective*, edited by C. W. Cowan and P. J. Watson. Washington, D.C.: Smithsonian Institution Press.

Crawford, Gary W., and Hiroto Takamiya. 1990. "The Origins and Implications of Late Prehistoric Plant Husbandry in Northern Japan." *Antiquity* 64: 889-911.

Crump, J. I. 1952. "Borrowed T'ang Titles and Offices in the Yoro Code." *Occasional Papers of the Center for Japanese Studies*. Ann Arbor: Center for Japanese Studies, University of Michigan 2: 35-58.

Cunningham, Michael, and Norio Suzuki. 1991. *The Triumph of Japanese Style: 16th Century Art in Japan*. Cleveland: Cleveland Museum of Art and Bloomington: Indiana University Press.

Davis, David L. 1974. "Ikki in Late Medieval Japan." In Hall and Mass, eds. (1974), 221-47.

de Visser, Marinus Willem. 1935. *Ancient Buddhism in Japan: Sutras and Ceremonies in Use in the Seventh and Eighth Centuries A.D. and their History in Later Times*. 2 vols. Leiden: E. J. Brill.

Dobbins, James C. 1989. *Jōdo Shinshū: Shin Buddhism in Medieval Japan*. Bloomington: Indiana University Press.

Douglas, John H. 1978. "The Horsemen of Yamato." *Science News* 113, no. 32: 364-66.
Duus, Peter. 1993 [1969]. *Feudalism in Japan.* 3rd ed. New York: McGraw Hill.
Earhart, H. Byron. 1982. *Japanese Religion: Unity and Diversity.* Belmont, Calif.: Wadsworth.
Ebisawa, Arimichi. 1959. "The Jesuits and their Cultural Activities in the Far East." *Cahiers d'histoire mondiale (Journal of World History)* 5, no. 2: 344-74.
Edwards, Walter. 1983. "Event and Process in the Founding of Japan: The Horserider Theory in Archeological Perspective." *Journal of Japanese Studies* 9, no. 2: 265-95.
Egami, Namio. 1962. "Light on Japanese Cultural Origins from Historical Archaeology and Legend." In *Japanese Culture: Its Development and Characteristics,* edited by R. J. Smith and R. K. Beardsley. Chicago: Aldine.
——. 1964. "The Formation of the People and the Origins of the State in Japan." *Memoirs of the Toyo Bunko* 23: 35-70.
Elison, George. 1973. *Deus Destroyed: The Image of Christianity in Early Modern Japan.* Cambridge: Harvard University Press.
——. 1981a. "The Cross and the Sword: Patterns of Momoyama History." In Elison and Smith, eds. (1981), 56-85.
——. 1981b. "Hideyoshi, The Bountiful Minister." In Elison and Smith, eds. (1981), 223-44.
——. 1981c. "Introduction: Japan in the Sixteenth Century." In Elison and Smith, eds. (1981), 1-6.
——. 1988. "The Priest Keinen and his Account of the Campaign in Korea, 1597-1598: An Introduction." In *Nihon Kyōikushi Ronsō,* edited by M. Y. K. t. k. r. h. iinkai. Kyoto: Shibunkaku shuppan.
Elison, George, and Bardwell L. Smith, eds. 1981. *Warlords, Artists, and Commoners: Japan in the Sixteenth Century.* Honolulu: University of Hawai'i Press.
Elisonas, Jurgis (Elison, George). 1991. "Christianity and the Daimyo." In Hall and McClain, eds. (1991), 301-72.
Farris, William Wayne. 1985. *Population, Disease, and Land in Early Japan, 645-900.* Cambridge: Harvard University Press.
——. 1992a. *Heavenly Warriors: The Evolution of Japan's Military, 500-1300.* Cambridge: Council on East Asian Studies, Harvard University.
——. 1992b. "The History of Disease in Japan." In *The Cambridge World History of Human Disease,* edited by K. Kipple. Cambridge: Cambridge University Press.
——. Forthcoming. *Sacred Texts and Buried Treasures: Essays in the Historical Archaeology of Ancient Japan.* Honolulu: University of Hawai'i Press.
Fawcett, Clare. 1995. "Nationalism and Postwar Japanese Archaeology." In *Nationalism and Postwar Japanese Archaeology,* edited by P. L. Kohl and C. Fawcett, 232-46. Cambridge: Cambridge University Press.
——. 1996. "Archaeology and Japanese Identity." In *Multicultural Japan: Paleolithic to Postmodern,* edited by D. e. a. Denoon, 60-77. Cambridge: Cambridge University Press.
Foard, James Harlan. 1977. *Ippen Shōnin and Popular Buddhism in Kamakura Japan.* Ann Arbor: University Microfilms.
Formanek, Susanne. 1988. "Old Age in the Pre-Nara and Nara Periods." *Nachrichten der Ostasientischen Gesellschaft* 144: 11-27.
Foulk, T. Griffith, and Robert H. Sharf. 1993/94. "On the Ritual Use of Ch'an Portraiture in China." *Cahiers d'extreme orient* 7.
Frédéric, Louis. 1973 [1968]. *Daily Life in Japan at the Time of the Samurai, 1185-1603.* Edited by E. Lowe. Rutland, Vt.: Charles E. Tuttle.

Friday, Karl F. 1992. *Hired Swords: The Rise of Private Warrior Power in Early Japan.* Stanford: Stanford University Press.
Fujiki, Hisashi. 1981. "The Political Posture of Oda Nobunaga." In Hall, Nagahara, and Yamamura, eds. (1981), 149-93.
Gay, Suzanne. 1985. "Muromachi Rule in Kyoto: Administrative and Judicial Aspects." In Mass and Hauser, eds. (1985).
Goble, Andrew. 1982. "The Hōjō and Consultative Government." In Mass, ed. (1982).
———. 1987. "Go-Daigo and the Kenmu Restoration." Ph.D. diss., Stanford University.
———. 1989. "Truth, Contradiction, and Harmony in Medieval Japan." *Journal of the International Association of Buddhist Studies* 12, no. 1: 21-65.
———. 1996. *Kenmu: Go-Daigo's Revolution.* Cambridge: Council on East Asian Studies, Harvard University.
Goodrich, Carrington L., and R. Tsunoda. 1951. "Japan in the Chinese Dynastic Histories: Later Han through Ming Dynasties." Pasadena, Calif.: Perkins.
Goodwin, Janet R. 1993. *Alms and Vagabonds: Buddhist Temples And Popular Patronage in Medieval Japan.* Honolulu: University of Hawai'i Press.
Grapard, Allan G. 1992. *The Protocol of the Gods: a Study of the Kasuga Cult in Japanese History.* Berkeley: University of California Press.
Groner, Paul. 1984. *Saichō: The Establishment of the Japanese Tendai School.* Berkeley: Center for South and Southeast Asian Studies, University of California/ Institute for Buddhist Studies.
Grossberg, Kenneth A. 1976a. "Bakufu Bugyōnin: the Size of the Lower Bureaucracy in Muromachi Japan." *Journal of Asian Studies* 35: 651-54.
———. 1976b. "From Feudal Chieftain to Secular Monarch." *Monumenta Nipponica* 31, no 1: 29-49.
———. 1977. "Central Government in Medieval Japan." Ph.D. diss., Harvard University.
———. 1981. *Japan's Renaissance: the Politics of the Muromachi Bakufu.* Cambridge: Council on East Asian Studies, Harvard University.
Grossberg, Kenneth A., and Nobuhisa Kanamoto. 1981. *The Laws of the Muromachi Bakufu: "Kenmu shikimoku" (1336) and Muromachi Bakufu Tsuika-hō.* Tokyo: Sophia University Press.
Gubbins, J. H. 1880. "Hideyoshi and the Satsuma Clan in the Sixteenth Century." *Transactions of the Asiatic Society of Japan* 8: 92-143.
Hakeda, Yoshito, trans., with commentary. 1972. *Kukai: Major Works.* New York: Columbia University Press.
Hall, John Carey. 1906. "Japanese Feudal Laws: the Institute of Judicature: Being a Translation of *Go seibai shikimoku.*" *Transactions of the Asiatic Society of Japan,* 1st series 34: 1-44.
Hall, John W. 1966. *Government and Local Power in Japan, 500-1700: A Study Based on Bizen Province.* Princeton: Princeton University Press.
———. 1968a. "Foundations of the Modern Japanese Daimyō." In Hall and Jansen, eds. (1968).
———. 1968b. "The Ikeda House and its Retainers in Bizen." In Hall and Jansen, eds. (1968).
———. 1971 [1970]. *Japan: From Prehistory to Modern Times.* Reprint. Rutland, Vt.: Charles E. Tuttle.
———. 1974a. "Kyoto as Historical Background." In Hall and Mass, eds. (1974), 3-38.

———. 1974b. "Rule by Status in Tokugawa Japan." *Journal of Japanese Studies* 1, no. 1: 39-49.
———. 1977a. "The Muromachi Age in Japanese History." In Hall and Toyoda, eds. (1977), 1-8.
———. 1977b. "The Muromachi Power Structure." In Hall and Toyoda, eds. (1977), 39-43.
———. 1981a. "Hideyoshi's Domestic Policies." In Hall, Nagahara, and Yamamura, eds. (1981), 194-223.
———. 1981b. "Japan's Sixteenth Century Revolution." In Elison and Smith, eds. (1981), 7-21.
———. 1982. "Epilogue." In Mass, ed. (1982).
———. 1983. "Terms and Concepts in Medieval Japanese History: An Inquiry into the Problems of Translation." *Journal of Japanese Studies* 9: 1-32.
———. 1990. "The Muromachi Bakufu." In Yamamura, ed. (1990), 175-230.
———. 1991. "Introduction: Early Modern Japan." In Hall and McClain, eds. (1991), 1-39.
Hall, John W., and Marius B. Jansen, eds. 1968. *Studies in the Institutional History of Early Modern Japan*. Princeton: Princeton University Press.
Hall, John W., and Jeffrey P. Mass, eds. 1974. *Medieval Japan: Essays in Institutional History*. New Haven: Yale University Press.
Hall, John W., and Takeshi Toyoda, eds. 1977. *Japan in the Muromachi Age*. Berkeley: University of California Press.
Hall, John W., Keiji Nagahara, and Kozo Yamamura, eds. 1981. *Japan before Tokugawa: Political Consolidation and Economic Growth, 1500-1650*. Princeton: Princeton University Press.
Hall, John W., Marius B. Jansen, Madoka Kanai, and Denis Twitchett, eds. 1990. *The Cambridge History of Japan*. 6 vols. Cambridge: Cambridge University Press.
Hall, John W., and James McClain, eds. 1991. *Early Modern Japan*. Vol. 4 of *The Cambridge History of Japan*. Cambridge: Cambridge University Press.
Hane, Mikiso. 1972. *Japan: A Historical Survey*. New York: Scribners.
Hanihara, Kazuro. 1993. "Biological Relationship between the Jōmon-Ainu and Pacific Population Groups." *Japan Review (Bulletin of International Research Center for Japanese Studies)* 4.
Harich-Schneider, Eta. 1973. *A History of Japanese Music*. Oxford: Oxford University Press.
Harrington, Lorraine. 1982. "Social Control and the Significance of the Akutō." In Mass, ed. (1982), 221-50.
———. 1985. "Regional Outposts of Muromachi Bakufu Rule: The Kanto and Kyushu." In Mass and Hauser, eds. (1985), 66-99.
Hashimoto Fumio. 1981. *Architecture in the Shoin Style: Japanese Feudal Residences*. Translated by H. Mack Horton. Kodansha and Shibundo.
Hatada, Takashi. 1979. "An Interpretation of the King Kwangaet'o Inscription." *Korean Studies* 3: 1-17.
Hayashiya, Seizo. 1979. *Chanoyu: Japanese Tea Ceremony*. New York: Japan Society.
Hayashiya, Tatsusaburo. 1977. "Kyoto in the Muromachi Age." In Hall and Toyoda, eds. (1977), 15-37.
Hayashiya, Tatsusaburo, Masao Nakamura, and Seizo Hayashiya. 1974. *Japanese Arts and the Tea Ceremony*. New York: Weatherhill.
Hazard, Benjamin H. 1967. "The Formative Years of the Wakō." *Monumenta Nipponica* 22, nos. 3-4: 260-77.
———. 1983. "Korea and Japan, Premodern Relations (to 1875)." *Kodansha Encyclopedia of Japan*: 276-79.

Hickman, Money L. 1996. *Japan's Golden Age: Momoyama*. Dallas: Museum of Art.
Hirai, Kiyoshi. 1973. *Feudal Architecture in Japan*. Edited by S. Hiroaki and J. Ciliota. New York: Weatherhill and Tokyo: Heibonsha.
Hirai, Naofusa. 1987. "Shintō." *Encylopedia of Religion*, edited by M. Eliade: 280-94.
Hirano, Kunio. 1977. "The Yamato State and Korea in the Fourth and Fifth Centuries." *Acta Asiatica* 31: 51-82.
Hisamatsu Shin'ichi. 1971. *Zen and the Fine Arts*. Translated and edited by Gishin Tokiwa. Kodansha International.
Hori, Kyotsu. 1967. "The Mongol Invasions and the Kamakura Bakufu." Ph.D. diss., Columbia University.
———. 1974. "The Economic and Political Effects of the Mongol Wars." In Hall and Mass, eds. (1974), 184-98.
Hudson, Mark. 1990. "Recent Review of Yayoi Archaeology." In *Bibliographic Reviews of Far Eastern Archaeology*, edited by G. L. Barnes. Oxford: Oxbow.
Hudson, Mark, and Gina L. Barnes. 1991. "Yoshinogari: A Yayoi Settlement in Northern Kyushu." *Monumenta Nipponica* 46, no. 2: 211-35.
Hurst, G. Cameron III. 1974a. "The Development of Insei: A Problem in Japanese History and Historiography." In Hall and Mass, eds. (1974).
———. 1974b. "The Structure of the Heian Court: Some Thoughts on the Nature of 'Familial Authority' in Heian Japan." In Hall and Mass, eds. (1974), 39-59.
———. 1979. "Michinaga's Maladies: a Medical Report on Fujiwara Michinaga." *Monumenta Nipponica* 34: 101-12.
———. 1982. "The Kōbu Polity: Court-Bakufu Relations in Kamakura Japan." In Mass, ed. (1982), 3-28.
Ikawa-Smith, Fumiko. 1974. *Early Palaeolithic of South and East Asia*. The Hague: Mouton.
———. 1980. "Current Issues in Japanese Archaeology." *American Scientist* 68, no. 2: 134-45.
Ikegami, Eiko. 1995. *The Taming of the Samurai: Honorific Individualism and the Making of Modern Japan*. Cambridge: Harvard University Press.
Imatani, Akira. 1990. "Muromachi Local Government: Shugo and Kokujin." In Yamamura, ed. (1990), 231-59.
Inoue, Mitsusada. 1977. "The Ritsuryō System in Japan." *Acta Asiatica* 31: 83-112.
Inoue, Mitsusada, with Delmer M. Brown. 1993. "The Century of Reform." In Brown, ed. (1993), 163-220.
Ishii, Ryōsuke. 1952. "On Japanese Possession of Real Property — a Study of Chigyō in the Middle Ages." *Japan Annual of Law and Politics* 1: 149-62.
———. 1978. "Japanese Feudalism." *Acta Asiatica* 35: 1-29.
Ishii, Susumu. 1990. "The Decline of the Kamakura Bakufu." In Yamamura, ed. (1990), 128-74.
Ishino, Hironobu. 1992. "Rites and Rituals of the Kofun Period." *Japanese Journal of Religious Studies* 19, nos. 2-3.
Itō, Teiji. 1977. "The Development of *Shoin* Style Architecture." In Hall and Toyoda, eds. (1977), 227-39.
Iwao, Seichi. 1976. "Japanese Foreign Trade in the 16th and 17th Centuries." *Acta Asiatica* 30: 1-18.
Jansen, Marius B. 1968. "Tosa in the Sixteenth Century: The 100 Article Code of Chosokabe Motochika." In Hall and Jansen, eds. (1968), 89-114.
Japan Society. 1985. *Spectacular Helmets of Japan, 16th -19th Century*. New York: Japan Society.

Jennes, Josef. 1973. *A History of the Catholic Church in Japan: From its Beginnings to the Early Meiji Era*. Tokyo: Oriens Institute for Religious Research.
Kaizuka, Shigeki. 1959. "Confucianism in Ancient Japan." *Cahiers d'histoire mondiale (Journal of World History)*: 41-58.
Kamikawa, Michio. 1990. "Accession Rituals and Buddhism in Medieval Japan." *Japanese Journal of Religious Studies* 17, no. 2-3.
Kamiki, T. 1966. "The Circulation of Commodities and the Use of Money in Early Medieval Japan." *Kobe University Economic Review* 12: 117-28.
Kamstra, J. H. 1967. *Encounter or Syncretism*. Leiden: E. J. Brill.
Kancho, Erika. 1966. "Japan: A Review of Yayoi Burial Practices." *Asian Perspectives* 9: 1-26.
Kanda, James. 1974. "Japanese Feudal Society in the Sixteenth Century as Seen Through the Jinkaishū and other Legal Codes." Ph.D. diss., Harvard University.
———. 1978. "Methods of Land Transfer in Medieval Japan." *Monumenta Nipponica* 33, no. 4: 375-405.
Kashiwahara Yūsen, and Kōyū Sonoda. 1994. *Shapers of Japanese Buddhism*. Translated by Gaynor Sekimori. Kōsei.
Kataoka, Yakichi. 1938. "Takayama Ukon." *Monumenta Nipponica* 1, no. 2: 159-72.
Katsumata, Shizuo. 1981. "The Development of Sengoku Law." In Hall, Nagahara, and Yamamura, eds. (1981), 101-24.
Kawaii, Masaharu. 1977. "Shogun and Shugo: the Provincial Aspects of Muromachi Politics." In Hall and Toyoda, eds. (1977), 65-88.
Kawazoe, Shōji. 1990. "Japan and East Asia." In Yamamura, ed. (1990), 396-446.
Kazar, Lajos. 1976. "Uralic-Japanese Language Comparison." *Ural-Altaishe Jahrbücher* 48-49: 127-50.
Keally, Charles, and Shizuo Oda. 1989. "A Critical Look at the Paleolithic and 'Lower Paleolithic' Research in Miyagi Prefecture, Japan." *Jinruigaku Zasshi* 94, no. 3: 325-61.
Keene, Donald. 1989. *Travelers of a Hundred Ages: the Japanese as Revealed Through 1,000 Years of Diaries*. New York: Holt.
Keirstead, Thomas. 1992. *The Geography of Power in Medieval Japan*. Princeton: Princeton University Press.
Kidder, Jonathan Edward, Jr. 1957. *The Jōmon Pottery of Japan*. Ascona: Artibus Asiae.
———. 1964. *Early Japanese Art: The Great Tombs and Treasures*. London: Thames and Hudson.
———. 1965. *The Birth of Japanese Art*. New York: Praeger.
———. 1966. *Japan before Buddhism (Ancient Peoples and Places, 10)*. London: Thames and Hudson and New York: Praeger.
———. 1968. *Prehistoric Japanese Arts: Jōmon Pottery*. Tokyo: Kodansha International.
———. 1972a. *Early Buddhist Japan*. London: Thames and Hudson.
———. 1972b. "The Newly Discovered Takamatsuzuka Tomb." *Monumenta Nipponica* 27, no. 3: 245-51.
———. 1977. *Ancient Japan: The Making of the Past*. Oxford: Elsevier-Phaidon.
———. 1983a. "Asuka History (Mid-Sixth Century-710)." *Kodansha Encyclopedia of Japan*: 161-63.
———. 1983b. "Jōmon Culture." *Kodansha Encyclopedia of Japan*.
———. 1990. "Saddle Bows and Rump Plumes: More on the Fujinoki Tomb." *Monumenta Nipponica* 45, no. 1: 80-85.
———. 1993. "The Earliest Societies in Japan." In Brown, ed. (1993), 48-108.

Kiley, Cornelius J. 1969. "A Note on the Surnames of Immigrant Officials in Nara Japan." *Harvard Journal of Asiatic Studies* 29: 177-89.
———. 1973. "State and Dynasty in Archaic Yamato." *Journal of Asian Studies* 33, no. 1: 25-49.
———. 1974. "Estate and Property in the Late Heian Period." In Hall and Mass, eds. (1974), 109-24.
———. 1977. "Uji and Kabane in Ancient Japan." *Monumenta Nipponica* 32, no. 3: 365-76.
———. 1982. "The Imperial Court as a Legal Authority in the Kamakura Age." In Mass, ed. (1982), 29-44.
———. 1983a. "Ritsuryō System." *Kodansha Encyclopedia of Japan*.
———. 1983b. "Uji-Kabane system." *Kodansha Encyclopedia of Japan*: 131-37.
Kiley, Neil. 1974. "Estate and Property in the Late Heian Period." In Hall and Mass, eds. (1974), 109-24.
Kirby, John B. 1962. *From Castle to Tea House: Japanese Architecture of the Momoyama Period*. Rutland, Vt.: Charles E. Tuttle.
Kitagawa, Joseph M. 1963. "Prehistoric Background of Japanese Religion." *History of Religions* 2: 292-328.
———. 1966. *Religion in Japanese History*. New York: Columbia University Press.
———. 1969. "Ainu Myths." In *Myths and Symbols: Studies in Honor of Mircea Eliade*, edited by J. M. Kitagawa and C. H. Long. Chicago: University of Chicago Press.
———. 1973. "The Japanese Kokutai [National Community] in Myth and History." *History of Religions* 13: 209-26.
———. 1980. "A Past of Things Present: Notes on Major Motifs in Early Japanese Religions." *History of Religions* 20: 27-42.
Klein, Bettina. 1984. *Japanese Kinbyōbu: The Gold-leafed Folding Screens of the Muromachi Period (1333-1573)*. Ascona: Artibus Asiae.
Knauth, Lotha. 1970. "Pacific Confrontation: Japan Encounters the Spanish Overseas Empire, 1542-1639." Ph.D. diss., Harvard University.
Kobata, Atsushi. 1965. "The Production and Uses of Gold and Silver in Sixteenth and Seventeenth-century Japan." *Economic History Review*. 2nd series 18, no. 1-3: 245-66.
Kobayashi, Tatsuo. 1974. "Behavioral Patterns Reflected in Pottery Remains: The Jōmon Period." *Arctic Anthropology*: 163-70.
Koike, Hiroko. 1980. *Seasonal Dating by Growth-Line Counting of the Clam Meretrix Lusoria: toward a Reconstruction of the Prehistoric Shell-collecting Activities in Japan*. Tokyo: Tokyo University Press.
Komatsu, Isao. 1962. *The Japanese People: Origins of the People and their Language*. Tokyo: Kokusai bunka shinkokai.
Kondō, Yoshirō. 1986. "The Keyhole Tumulus and its Relationship to Earlier Forms of Burial." In Pearson, Barnes, and Hutterer, eds. (1986).
Koyama, Shuzo, and David Thomas. 1981. *Affluent Foragers: Pacific Coasts East and West*. Senri, Osaka: National Museum of Ethnology.
Koyama, Yasunori. 1983. "Recent Trends in the Study of the Social and Economic History of Medieval Japan." *Acta Asiatica* 44: 98-126.
Kumakura, Isao. 1989. "Sen no Rikyū: Inquiries into his Life and Tea." In Varley and Kumakura, eds. (1989), 33-70.
Kurata Bunsaku. 1981. *Hōryūji: Temple of the Exalted Law: Early Buddhist Art from Japan*. Translated by W. Chie Ishibashi. New York: Japan Society.
Kuwayama, Kōnen. 1977. "The Bugyōnin System: A Closer Look." In Hall and Toyoda, eds. (1977), 53-63.

Kwan-u, Ch'ön. 1974. "A New Interpretation of the Problems of Minana." *Korea Journal* 14, nos. 2, 4: 9-23, 31-44.
Lach, Donald F. 1968. *Japan in the Eyes of Europe, the Sixteenth Century*. Chicago: University of Chicago Press.
Laures, Johannes, S.J. 1942. "Takayama Ukon: A Critical Essay." *Monumenta Nipponica* 5: 86-112.
———. 1943. "Were the Takayamas and the Naitōs involved in a Hideyori Plot?" *Monumenta Nipponica* 6, no. 1/2: 233-44.
———. 1959. *Two Japanese Christian Heroes: Justo Takayama Ukon and Gracia Hosokawa Tamako*. Rutland, Vt.: Charles E. Tuttle.
———. 1962. *The Catholic Church in Japan: a Short History*. Notre Dame, Ind.: University of Notre Dame Press.
Ledyard, Gari. 1975. "Galloping Along with the Horseriders: Looking for the Founders of Japan." *Journal of Japanese Studies* 1, no. 2: 217-54.
———. 1983. "Yamatai." *Kodansha Encyclopedia of Japan*: 305-7.
Lewin, Bruno. 1976. "Japanese and Korean: The Problems and History of a Linguistic Comparison." *Journal of Japanese Studies* 2, no. 2: 389-412.
Lu, David J. 1974. *Sources of Japanese History*. 2 vols. New York: McGraw Hill.
Ludwig, Theodore. 1974. "The Way of Tea: A Religio-aesthetic Mode of Life." *History of Religions* 14, no. 1: 28-50.
———. 1981. "Before Rikyū: Religious and Aesthetic Influences in the Early History of the Tea Ceremony." *Monumenta Nipponica* 36: 367-90.
———. 1989. "Chanoyu and Momoyama: Conflict and Transformation in Rikyū's Art." In Varley and Kumakura, eds. (1989), 71-100.
Machida, Hiroshi. 1992. "An Impact of Large-scale Explosive Volcanism on the Prehistoric World in Japan." *Newsletter of Environment and Civilization* 6: 20.
Malm, William P. 1981. "Music Cultures of Momoyama Japan." In Elison and Smith, eds. (1981), 163-85.
Maringer, Johannes. 1974. "Clay Figurines of the Jōmon Period: A Contribution to the History of Ancient Religion in Japan." *History of Religions* 14: 129-39.
Marra, Michele. 1991. *The Aesthetics of Discontent: Politics and Reclusion in Medieval Japanese Literature*. Honolulu: University of Hawai'i Press.
Maske, Andrew. 1994. "The Continental Origins of Takatori Ware: the Introduction of Korean Potters and Technology to Japan through the Invasions of 1592-1598." *Transactions of the Asiatic Society of Japan*, 4th series 9: 43-61.
———. 1996. "Advances in Tea Ceramic History: Recent Excavations of Tea Ware from Consumer Sites." *Chanoyu Quarterly* 70: 8-21.
Mass, Jeffrey P. 1974a. "The Emergence of the Kamakura Bakufu." In Hall and Mass, eds. (1974), 127-56.
———. 1974b. "Jitō Land Possession in the Thirteenth Century: The Case of Shitaji Chūbun." In Hall and Mass, eds. (1974).
———. 1974c. *Warrior Government in Early Medieval Japan: A Study of the Kamakura Bakufu, Shugo, and Jitō*. Stanford: Stanford University Press.
———. 1976. *The Kamakura Bakufu, A Study in Documents*. Stanford: Stanford University Press.
———. 1977. "The Origins of Kamakura Justice." *Journal of Japanese Studies* 3, no. 2: 299-332.
———. 1979. *The Development of Kamakura Rule, 1180-1250: A History with Documents*. Stanford: Stanford University Press.
———. 1982. "The Early Bakufu and Feudalism." In Mass, ed. (1982).
———. 1989. *Lordship and Inheritance in Early Medieval Japan: a Study of the Kamakura Soryō System*. Stanford: Stanford University Press.

———. 1990. "The Kamakura Bakufu." In Yamamura, ed. (1990), 46-88.
Mass, Jeffrey P., ed. 1982. *Court and Bakufu in Japan: Essays in Kamakura History*. New Haven: Yale University Press.
Mass, Jeffrey P., and William B. Hauser. 1985. *The Bakufu in Japanese History*. Stanford: Stanford University Press.
Massarella, Derek. 1990. *A World Elsewhere: Europe's Encounter with Japan in the Sixteenth and Seventeenth Centuries*. New Haven: Yale University Press.
Matsuda Kiichi. 1977. *Nichi-ō kōshō shi bunken mokuroku* (Catalogue of Studies on the History of the Relationship between Japan and Europe). Yūshōdō shoten.
Matsui Akira, and Yamamoto Tadanao. 1988. *Japanese-English Dictionary of Japanese Archaeology*. Nara: Nara kokuritsu bukazai kenkyūjo.
Matsunaga, Daigan, and Alicia Matsunaga. 1974. *Foundations of Japanese Buddhism*. Vol. 1: *The Aristocratic Age*. Los Angeles: Buddhist Books International.
———. 1976. *Foundations of Japanese Buddhism*. Vol 2: *The Mass Movement (Kamakura and Muromachi Periods)*. Los Angeles: Buddhist Books International.
Matsuoka, Hisato. 1981. "The Sengoku Daimyo of Western Japan: The Case of the Ōuchi." In Hall, Nagahara, and Yamamura, eds. (1981), 64-100.
McCallum, Donald F. 1994. *Zenkōji and its Icon: A Study in Medieval Japanese Relgious Art*. Princeton: Princeton University Press.
McClain, James L. 1980. "Castle Towns and Daimyo Authority: Kanazawa in the Years 1583-1630." *Journal of Japanese Studies* 6, no. 2: 267-99.
McCullough, Helen C., trans. 1966. *"Yoshitsune": A Fifteenth Century Chronicle*. Stanford: Stanford University Press.
———. 1979. *The "Taiheiki": A Chronicle of Medieval Japan*. Reprint. Princeton: Princeton University Press.
———. 1980. *Okagami, The Great Mirror: Fujiwara Michinaga (966-1027) and His Times: A Study and Translation*. Princeton: Princeton University Press.
———. 1988. *The "Tale of the Heike"*. Stanford: Stanford University Press.
McCullough, William. 1968. "The Azuma kagami account of the Shōkyū War." *Monumenta Nipponica* 32: 102-55.
McCullough, William, and Helen C. McCullough, trans. 1980. *A Tale of Flowering Fortunes*. Stanford: Stanford University Press.
McMullin, Neil. 1984. *Buddhism and the State in Sixteenth Century Japan*. Princeton: Princeton University Press.
Meech-Pekarik, Julia, and Andrew Pekarik. 1975. *Momoyama: Japanese Art in an Age of Grandeur*. New York: Metropolitan Museum of Art.
Miller, Alan, L. 1971. "Ritsuryō Japan: The State as Liturgical Community." *History of Religions* 11: 98-121.
Miller, Richard J. 1953. "A Study of the Development of a Centralized Japanese Government Prior to the Taika Reform (A.D. 645)." Ph.D. diss., University of California.
———. 1974. *Ancient Japanese Nobility: The Kabane Ranking System*. University of California Press.
———. 1978. *Japan's First Bureaucracy: A Study of Eighth Century Government*. Ithaca: Cornell University East Asia Program.
Miller, Roy A. 1974. "The Origins of Japanese." *Monumenta Nipponica* 29, no. 1: 93-102.
———. 1976. "The Relevance of Historical Linguistics for Japanese Studies." *Journal of Japanese Studies* 2, no. 2: 335-88.
———. 1980. *Origins of the Japanese Language*. Seattle: University of Washington Press.
Miura, Keiichi. 1983. "Villages and Trade in Medieval Japan." *Acta Asiatica* 44: 53-76.

Miyagawa, Mitsuru. 1977. "From Shōen to Chigyō, Proprietory Lordship and the Structure of Local Power." In Hall and Toyoda, eds. (1977), 89-105.
Miyazaki, Fumiko. 1992. "Religious Life of the Kamakura Bushi: Kumagai Naozane and his Descendants." *Monumenta Nipponica* 47, no. 4: 435-67.
Mizuno, Yu. 1974. "The Origins of the Japanese Race." *The East* 10, no. 4: 37-44.
Mizuo, Hiroshi. 1969. "Patterns of Kofun Culture." *Japan Quarterly* 16, no. 1: 71-77.
Mori, Katsumi. 1961. "International Relations between the 10th and 16th Century and the Development of Japanese International Consciousness." *Acta Asiatica* 2: 69-93.
———. 1972. "The Beginnings of Overseas Advance of Japanese Merchant Ships." *Acta Asiatica* 23: 1-24.
Morlar, Richard E. 1967. "Chronometric Dating in Japan." *Arctic Anthropology* 14, no. 2: 180-212.
Morrell, Robert E. 1987. *Early Kamakura Buddhism: A Minority Report*. Berkeley: Asian Humanities Press.
———. 1985. *Sand and Pebbles ("Shasekishū"): The Tales of Mujū Ichien, a Voice for Pluralism in Kamakura Buddhism*. Albany: State University of New York Press.
Morris, Dana R. 1980. *Peasant Economy in Early Japan, 650-950*. Berkeley: University of California Press.
Morris, Ivan. 1985 [1964]. *The World of the Shining Prince*. Reprint. Harmondsworth, U.K.: Penguin.
Morris, V. Dixon. 1970. "Sakai: the History of a City in Medieval Japan." Ph.D. diss., University of Washington.
———. 1977. "Sakai: From Shōen to Port City." In Hall and Toyoda, eds. (1977), 145-58.
———. 1981. "The City of Sakai and Urban Autonomy." In Ellison and Smith, eds. (1981), 23-54.
Murai, Yasuhiko. 1989. "The Development of Chanoyu: Before Rikyū." In Varley and Kumakura, eds. (1989), 3-32.
Murakami, Naojiro. 1943. "The Jesuit Seminary of Azuchi." *Monumenta Nipponica* 6: 375-90.
Murayama, Shichiro. 1976. "The Malayo-Polynesian Component in the Japanese Language." *Journal of Japanese Studies* 2, no. 2: 413-36.
Murayama, Shichiro, and Roy Andrew Miller. 1979. "The Inariyama Tumulus Sword Inscription." *Journal of Japanese Studies* 5, no. 2: 405-38.
Murdoch, James. 1925. *A History of Japan*. Vol. 2: *During the Century of Early Foreign Intercourse (1542-1651)*. London: Kegan Paul, Trench, Trubner.
Nagahara, Keiji. 1960. "The Social Structure of Early Medieval Japan." *Hitotsubashi Journal of Economics* 1: 90-97.
———. 1975. "Landownership Under the Shōen Kokugaryō System." *Journal of Japanese Studies* 1, no. 2: 269-96.
———. 1979. "The Medieval Origins of the Eta-hinin." *Journal of Japanese Studies* 5, no. 2: 385-403.
———. 1981. "The Sengoku Daimyo and the Kandaka System." In Hall, Nagahara, and Yamamura, eds. (1981), 27-63.
———. 1985. "The Lord-Vassal System and Public Authority (*Kōgi*): The Case of the Sengoku Daimyo." *Acta Asiatica* 49: 34-45.
———. 1990a. "The Decline of the Shōen System." Translated by Michael P. Birt. In Yamamura, ed. (1990).
———. 1990b. "The Medieval Peasant." In Yamamura, ed. (1990), 301-43.

Nagahara, Keiji, and Kozo Yamamura. 1977. "Village Communities and Daimyo Power." In Hall and Toyoda, eds. (1977).
Nakamura, Kyoko Motomichi, ed. and trans. 1973. *Miraculous Stories from the Japanese Buddhist Tradition: The "Nihon ryōiki" of the Monk Kyōkai.* Harvard Yenching Institute Monograph Series, vol. 20. Cambridge: Harvard University Press.
Naoki, Kōjiro. 1993. "The Nara State." In Brown, ed. (1993), 221-67.
Obayashi, Taryo. 1977. "The Structure of the Pantheon and the Concept of Sin in Ancient Japan." *Diogenes* 98: 117-32.
Okamoto, Yoshitomo. 1972. *The Namban Art of Japan.* Translated by Ronald K. Jones. Vol. 19 of *The Arts of Japan.* New York: Weatherhill and Tokyo: Heibonsha.
Okazaki, Takashi. 1993. "Japan and the Continent." In Brown, ed. (1993). 268-316.
Ono, Susumu. 1971. *The Origins of the Japanese Language.* Tokyo: Kokusai bunka shinkōkai.
Ooms, Herman. 1996. *Tokugawa Village Practice: Class, Status, Power, Law.* Berkeley: University of California Press.
Ortolani, Benito, S.J. 1962. "Okuni-Kabuki and Onna-Kabuki." *Monumenta Nipponica* 17: 161-213.
Osumi, Kazuo. 1990. "Buddhism in the Kamakura Period." In Yamamura, ed. (1990), 544-82.
Oyama, Kyōhei. 1990. "Medieval Shōen." In Yamamura, ed. (1990), 89-123.
Palmer, Edwina. 1991. "Land of the Rising Sun: The Predominant East-West Axis Among the Early Japanese." *Monumenta Nipponica* 46, no. 1: 69-90.
Park, Yune-hee. 1973. *Admiral Yi Sun-shin and his Turtle Boat Armada: A Comprehensive Account of the Resistance of Korea to the Sixteenth Century Japanese Invasion.* Seoul: Shinsaeng.
Parker, Geoffrey. 1988. *The Military Revolution: Military Innovation and the Rise of the West, 1500-1800.* Cambridge: Cambridge University Press.
Paske-Smith. 1914. "The Japanese Trade and Residence in the Philippines Before and During the Spanish Occupation." *Transactions of the Asiatic Society of Japan* 42: 685-710.
Pearson, Richard J. 1976. "The Contribution of Archaeology to Japanese Studies." *Journal of Japanese Studies* 2, no. 2: 305-27.
———. 1977. "Paleoenvironment and Human Settlement in Japan and Korea." *Science* 197: 1239-46.
———. 1992a. *Ancient Japan.* New York: Braziller.
———. 1992b. "The Nature of Japanese Archaeology." *Asian Perspectives* 31, no. 2: 115-27.
Pearson, Richard J., Gina L. Barnes, and Karl L. Hutterer. 1986. *Windows on the Japanese Past: Studies in Archaeology and Prehistory.* Ann Arbor: Center for Japanese Studies, University of Michigan.
Pelzel, John C. 1970. "Human Nature in the Japanese Myths." In *Personality in Japanese History*, edited by A. C. Craig and D. H. Shively, 29-59. Berkeley: University of California Press.
Perrin, Noel. 1979. *Giving Up the Gun: Japan's Reversion to the Sword, 1543-1879.* Boston: D. R. Godine.
Philippi, Donald L., trans. 1968. *Kojiki.* University of Tokyo Press.
———. 1979. *Songs of Gods, Songs of Humans: The Epic Tradition of the Ainu.* Princeton: Princeton University Press.
———. 1990. *Norito: A Translation of Ancient Japanese Ritual Prayers.* Princeton: Princeton University Press.

Piggot, Joan. 1982. "Hierarchy and Economics in Early Medieval Tōdaiji." In Mass, ed. (1982), 45-91.
———. 1987. "Tōdaiji and the Nara Imperium." Ph.D. diss., Stanford University.
———. 1989. "Sacral Kingship and Confederacy in Early Izumo." *Monumenta Nipponica* 44, no. 1: 45-74.
———. 1990. "Mokkan: Wooden Documents from the Nara Period." *Monumenta Nipponica* 45, no. 4: 449-.
———. 1997. *The Emergence of Japanese Kingship*. Stanford: Stanford University Press.
Ponsonby-Fane, Richard. 1931. *Kyoto: Its History and Vicissitudes since its Foundation*. Hong Kong.
———. 1979a. *The Fortunes of the Emperors: Studies in Revolution, Exile, Abdication, Usurpation, and Deposition in Ancient Japan*. Reprint. Washington, D.C.: University Publications of America, Greenwood.
———. 1979b [1930]. *Imperial Cities: the Capitals of Japan from the Oldest Times until 1229*. Reprint. Washington, D.C.: University Publications of America.
Rabinovitch, Judith, ed. and trans. 1986. *Shōmonki: the Story of Masakado's Rebellion*. Tokyo: Monumenta Nipponica, Sophia University.
Reischauer, Edwin O. 1955. *Ennin's Travels in Tang China*. New York: Ronald.
———. 1956. "Japanese Feudalism." In *Feudalism in History*, edited by R. Coulbourn, 26-48. Princeton: Princeton University Press.
Reischauer, Robert Karl. 1937. *Early Japanese History (ca. 40 B.C.-A.D. 1169)*. Princeton: Princeton University Press.
Robinson, G. W. 1961. "Early Japanese Chronicles: The Six National Histories." In Beasley and Pulleyblank, eds. (1961).
Rogers, Minor Lee, and Ann Rogers. 1992. *Rennyo, the Second Founder of Shin Buddhism*. Berkeley: Asian Humanity Press.
Rogers, Philip G. 1956. *The First Englishman in Japan: The Story of Will Adams*. London: Harvill Press.
Rosenfield, John M. 1986. *The Great Eastern Temple: Treasures of Japanese Art from Tōdaiji-ji*. Chicago: Art Institute of Chicago and Bloomington: Indiana University Press.
Ruch, Barbara. 1977. "Jongleurs and the Making of a National Literature." In Hall and Toyoda, eds. (1977).
———. 1990. "The Other Side of Culture in Medieval Japan." In Yamamura, ed. (1990), 500-43.
Sadler, A. L. 1978 [1937]. *The Life of Shogun Tokugawa Ieyasu: Maker of Modern Japan*. Reprint. Rutland, Vt.: Charles E. Tuttle.
Sahara, M., and H. Kanaseki. 1979. "The Yayoi Period." *Asian Perspectives* 19: 15-26.
Sakai, Atsuharu. 1940. "The Hitachi fudoki or Records of Customs and Land of Hitachi." *Cultural Nippon* 8, nos. 2, 3, 4: 145-85, 109-56, 137-86.
Sakakibara Kōzan. 1963 [1800]. *The Manufacture of Armour and Helmets in Sixteenth Century Japan*. Translated by H. Russell Robinson. London: Holland.
Sakamoto Tarō. 1991. *The Six National Histories*. Translated by John S. Brownlee. Vancouver: University of British Columbia Press.
Sansom, George B. 1924. "The Imperial Edicts in the Shoku-Nihongi (700-799 A.D.)." *Transactions of the Asiatic Society of Japan, 2nd series*: 5-39.
———. 1929. "An Outline of Recent Japanese Archaeological Research in Korea and its Bearing upon Early Japanese History." *Transactions of the Asiatic Society of Japan, 2nd series* 6: 5-19.
———. 1932. "Early Japanese Law and Administration." *Transactions of the Asiatic Society of Japan, 2nd series* 9, 11: 67-110, 117-50.

——. 1950. *The Western World and Japan: A Study in the Interaction of European and Asiatic Cultures.* New York: Alfred A. Knopf and Rutland, Vt.: Charles E. Tuttle (pbk).
——. 1958. *A History of Japan to 1334.* Stanford: Stanford University Press.
——. 1961. *A History of Japan, 1334-1615.* Stanford: Stanford University Press.
Sasaki, Ginya. 1981. "Sengoku Daimyo Rule and Commerce." In Hall, Nagahara, and Yamamura, eds. (1981), 125-48.
Sato, Elizabeth S. 1974. "The Early Development of Shōen." In Hall and Mass, eds. (1974), 91-108.
Satō, Shin'ichi. 1977. "The Ashikaga Shogun and the Muromachi Bakufu Administration." In Hall and Toyoda, eds. (1977), 45-52.
Satow, Ernest. 1874. "The Shinto Temples of Ise." *Transactions of the Asiatic Society of Japan, 1st series*: 113-19.
——. 1879. "Vicissitudes of the Church at Yamaguchi from 1550-1586." *Transactions of the Asiatic Society of Japan* 7: 131-56.
——. 1888. *The Jesuit Mission Press in Japan 1591-1610.* London: Privately printed.
——. 1890. "The Origins of Spanish and Portuguese Rivalry in Japan." *Transactions of the Asiatic Society of Japan* 18.
Saunders, E. Dale. 1961. "Japanese Mythology." In *Mythologies of the Ancient World*, edited by S. N. Kramer, 409-42. New York: Doubleday.
Shimizu, Yoshiaki, ed. 1988. *Japan: the Shaping of Daimyo Culture, 1185-1868.* New York: Braziller and Washington, D.C.: National Gallery of Art.
Shinoda, Minoru. 1960. *The Founding of the Kamakura Shogunate 1180-1185 — With Selected Translations from the "Azuma kagami".* New York: Columbia University Press.
——. 1983. "Kamakura History (1185-1333)." *Kodansha Encyclopedia of Japan*: 169-72.
Shiryō-Hensanjo, Tokyo Daigaku. 1961. *The Young Men's Embassy: Dai Nippon shiryō [Historical Documents of Japan].* Part 11, Supplementary Volumes (*bekkan*). 2 vols. Tokyo: Tokyo University Press.
Shulman, Frank, J. 1982. *Doctoral Dissertations on Japan and Korea, 1969-79, An Annotated Guide to Studies in Western Languages.* Seattle: University of Washington Press.
——. 1989. *World Bibliographical Series, Japan.* Oxford: Clio.
——. 1991. *Doctoral Dissertations on Asia.* Ann Arbor: Association for Asian Studies.
Smith, Bardwell L. 1981. "Japanese Society and Culture in the Momoyama Era: A Bibliographic Essay." In Elison and Smith, eds. (1981), 245-79.
Snellen, J. B. 1934. "Shoku Nihongi: Chronicles of Japan, Continued, from A.D. 697-791." *Transactions of the Asiatic Society of Japan, 2nd series* 11, 14: 151-239, 209-78.
So, Kwan-Wai. 1975. *Japanese Piracy in Ming China during the 16th Century.* East Lansing: Michigan State University Press.
Solomon, Ira Michael. 1972. "Rennyo and the Rise of Honganji in Muromachi Japan." Ph.D. diss., Columbia University.
——. 1974. "Kinship and the Transmission of Religious Charisma: The Case of Honganji." *Journal of Asian Studies* 33, no. 3.
——. 1978. "The Dilemma of Religious Power: Honganji and Hosokawa Masamoto." *Monumenta Nipponica* 33, no. 1.
Steenstrup, Carl. 1973. "The Imagawa Letter: A Muromachi Warrior's Code of Conduct which Became a Tokugawa Schoolbook." *Monumenta Nipponica* 28: 295-316.

———. 1974. "Hōjō Sōun's Twenty-One articles: The Code of Conduct of the Odawara Hōjō." *Monumenta Nipponica* 29: 283-303.
———. 1976. "Marsilius of Padua and the Post-Kemmu Reformers of Japan: Why Did Political Rationalism Emerge Simultaneously in Japan and in Western Europe in the Early Fourteenth Century?" Proceedings of the 30th International Congress of Human Sciences in Asia and North Africa, held in Mexico City.
———. 1979. *Hōjō Shigetoki (1198-1261) and his Role in the History of Political and Ethical Ideas in Japan*. London: Curzon.
———. 1980. "Pushing the Papers in Kamakura: the Nitty-Gritticists versus the Grand Sweeper." *Monumenta Nipponica* 35, no. 3: 337-46.
———. 1991a. *A History of Law in Japan until 1868*. Leiden: E. J. Brill.
———. 1991b. "The Middle Ages Surveyed." *Monumenta Nipponica* 46, no. 2: 237-52.
Steichen, M. 190?. *The Christian Daimyos: A Century of Religious and Political History in Japan, 1549-1650*. Tokyo: Rikkyo Gakuen Press.
Storry, Richard. 1978. *The Way of the Samurai*. New York: Putnam.
Stramigioli, Giuliana. 1954. "Hideyoshi's Expansionist Policy on the Asiatic Mainland." *Transactions of the Asiatic Society of Japan*, 2nd series 3, no. 1: 74-116.
Suematsu, Yasukazu. 1958. "Japan's Relations with the Asian Continent and the Korean Peninsula (Before 900 A.D.)." *Cahiers d'historie mondiale (Journal of World History)* 4, no. 3: 671-87.
Sugihara, Sosuke, and Tozawa Mitsumori. 1960. "Pre-Ceramic Age in Japan." *Acta Asiatica* 1: 1-28.
Sugimoto, Masayoshi, and David L. Swain. 1978. *Science and Culture in Traditional Japan, A.D. 600-1854*. Cambridge: MIT Press.
Susser, Bernard. 1985. "The Toyotomi Regime and the Daimyō." In Mass and Hauser, eds. (1985), 129-52.
Suzuki, Daisetz T. 1959. *Zen and Japanese Culture*. Princeton: Princeton University Press.
Suzuki, Hisashi, and Hanihara Kazuo, eds. 1982. *The Minatogawa Man: The Upper Pleistocene Man from the Island of Okinawa*. Tokyo: Tokyo University Press.
Sweet, C. F. 1916. "The Crucifixion of the Twenty-six in 1597." *Transactions of the Asiatic Society of Japan* 44: 20-45.
Takagi, Shōsaku. 1985. "'Hideyoshi's Peace' and the Transformation of the Bushi Class: The Dissolution of the Autonomy of the Medieval Bushi." *Acta Asiatica* 49: 46-77.
Takakura, Shinichirō. 1960. "The Ainu of Northern Japan." *Transactions of the American Philosophical Society* 50, no. 4.
Takase, Kōichirō. 1976. "Unauthorized Commercial Activities by Jesuit Missionaries in Japan." *Acta Asiatica* 30: 19-33.
Takayanagi, Shun'ichi. 1977. "The Glory That Was Azuchi." *Monumenta Nipponica* 32, no. 4: 515-24.
Takekoshi Yosaburo. 1930. *Economic Aspects of the History of the Civilization of Japan*. 3 vols. London: Allen and Unwin.
———. 1940. *The Story of the Wakō, Japanese Pioneers in Southern Regions*. Translated by Hideo Watanabe. Kenkyusha.
Takeshi, Matsumae. 1993. "Early Kami Worship." In Brown, ed. (1993), 317-58.
Takeuchi, Rizō. 1982. "Old and New Approaches to Kamakura History." In Mass, ed. (1982).
———. 1983. "Nara History (710-794)." *Kodansha Encyclopedia of Japan*.

Takizawa, Takeo. 1980. "Early Currency Policies of the Tokugawas, 1563-1608." *Acta Asiatica* 39: 21-41.
Tanabe, George Joji, Jr. 1983. "Myōe Shōnin (1173-1232): Tradition and Reform in Early Kamakura Buddhism." Ph.D. diss., Columbia University.
Tanaka, Takeo. 1977. "Japan's Relations with Overseas Countries." In Hall and Toyoda, eds. (1977), 159-78.
Toby, Ronald. 1985. "Why Leave Nara? Kammu and the Transfer of the Capital." *Monumenta Nipponica* 40, no. 3: 331-47.
Tonomura, Hitomi. 1992. *Community and Commerce in Late Medieval Japan: The Corporate Villages of Tokuchin-ho.* Stanford: Stanford University Press.
Torao, Toshiya. 1993. "Social and Economic Institutions of the Nara Period." In Brown, ed. (1993), 415-52.
Totman, Conrad. 1979. "English Language Studies of Medieval Japan: An Assessment." *Journal of Asian Studies* 38, no. 3: 541-51.
———. 1981. *Japan Before Perry: A Short History.* Berkeley: University of California Press.
———. 1983. *Tokugawa Ieyasu: Shogun.* Union City, Calif.: Heian International.
———. 1989. *The Green Archipelago: Forestry in Preindustrial Japan.* Berkeley: University of California Press.
Toyoda, Takeshi. 1969. *A History of Pre-Meiji Commerce in Japan.* Tokyo: Kokusai bunka shinkokai.
Toyoda, Takeshi, and Hiroshi Sugiyama. 1977. "The Growth of Commerce and the Trades." In Hall and Toyoda, eds. (1977), 129-44.
Tsubaki, Andrew T. 1977. "The Performing Arts of Sixteenth-Century Japan: A Prelude to Kabuki." *Educational Theatre Journal* 29, no 3: 299-309.
Tsuboi, Kiyotari. 1992. "Issues in Japanese Archaeology." *Acta Asiatica* 63: 1-20.
Tsuboi Kiyotari, and Migaku Tanaka. 1991. *The Historic City of Nara, an Archaeological Approach.* Translated by David W. Hughes and Gina L. Barnes. Tokyo: Center for East Asian Cultural Studies.
Tsuda, Sōkichi. 1963. "On the Stages of Formation of Japan as a Nation and the Origin of Belief in the Perpetuity of the Imperial Family." *Philosophical Studies of Japan* 4: 49-78.
Tsunoda, Ryusaku, William T. de Bary, and Donald Keene. 1964 [1958]. *Sources of Japanese Tradition.* New York: Columbia University Press.
Tsurumi, E. Patricia. 1983. "The Male Present versus the Female Past: Historians and Japan's Ancient Female Emperors." *Bulletin of Concerned Asian Scholars* 14, no. 4: 71-75.
Tubielewicz, Jolanta. 1980. *Superstition, Magic, and Mantic Practices in the Heian Period.* Warsaw: Warsaw University Press.
Turner, C. G. II. 1976. "Dental Evidence of the Origins of the Ainu and the Japanese." *Science* 193: 911-13.
———. 1989. "Teeth and Prehistory in Asia." *Scientific American* 263: 70-77.
Tyler, Royall. 1990. *The Miracles of the Kasuga Deity.* New York: Columbia University Press.
Tyler, Susan C. 1992. *The Cult of Kasuga as Seen through its Art.* Ann Arbor: Center for Japanese Studies, University of Michigan.
Varley, H. Paul. 1966. *The Onin War: A History of its Origins and Background with a Selective Translation of the Chronicle of Onin.* New York: Columbia University Press.
———. 1970. *The Samurai.* New York: Delacorte.
———. 1971. *Imperial Restoration in Medieval Japan.* New York: Columbia University Press.

------. 1974. "The Age of the Military Houses." In *An Introduction to Japanese Civilization*, edited by A. Tiedemann, 61-95. New York: Columbia University Press.

------. 1977. "Ashikaga Yoshimitsu and the World of Kitayama: Social Change and Shogunal Patronage in Early Muromachi Japan." In Hall and Toyoda, eds. (1977), 183-204.

------. 1980. *A Chronicle of Gods and Sovereigns, "Jinnō shōtōki" of Kitabatake Chikafusa*. New York: Columbia University Press.

------. 1982. "The Hōjō Family and Succession to Power." In Mass, ed. (1982), 143-67.

------. 1990. "Cultural Life in Medieval Japan." In Yamamura, ed. (1990), 447-99.

------. 1993. *Warriors of Japan, as Portrayed in the War Tales*. Honolulu: University Hawai'i Press.

Varley, H. Paul, and George Elison. 1981. "The Culture of Tea from its Origins to Sen no Rikyū." In Elison and Smith, eds. (1981), 187-222.

Varley, H. Paul, and Isao Kumakura. 1989. *Tea in Japan: Essays on the History of Chanoyu*. Honolulu: University of Hawai'i Press.

Waida, Manabu. 1976. "Sacred Kingship in Early Japan: A Historical Introduction." *History of Religions* 15: 319-42.

Wakita, Haruko. 1975. "Towards a Wider Perspective on Medieval Commerce." *Journal of Japanese Studies* 1, no. 2: 321-45.

------. 1981. "Dimensions of Development: Cities in Fifteenth and Sixteenth Century Japan." In Hall, Nagahara, and Yamamura, eds. (1981), 295-326.

------. 1983. "Cities in Medieval Japan." *Acta Asiatica* 44: 28-52.

------. 1984. "Marriage and Property in Premodern Japan from the Perspective of Women's History." *Journal of Japanese Studies* 10, no. 1: 73-99.

Wakita, Osamu. 1975. "The Kokudaka System: A Device for Unification." *Journal of Japanese Studies* 1, no. 2: 297-320.

------. 1981a. "The Commercial and Urban Policies of Oda Nobunaga and Toyotomi Hideyoshi." In Hall, Nagahara, and Yamamura, eds. (1981), 224-47.

------. 1981b. "The Social and Economic Consequences of Unification." In Hall and McClain, eds. (1981), 96-127.

------. Summer 1982. "The Emergence of the State in Sixteenth Century Japan: From Oda to Tokugawa." *Journal of Japanese Studies* 8: 343-67.

Wang, Yi-Tung. 1953. "Official Relations between China and Japan, 1368-1549." *Harvard Yenching Institute Studies*. Vol. 9. Cambridge: Harvard University Press.

Wang, Zhen-ping. 1989. "Sino-Japanese Relations before the 11th Century: Modes of Diplomatic Communication Re-examined in Terms of the Concept of Reciprocity." Ph.D. diss., Princeton University.

Watsky, Andrew M. 1995. "Commerce, Politics, and Tea: The Career of Imai Sōkyū." *Monumenta Nipponica* 50, no. 1.

Webb, Herschel. 1965. *Research in Japanese Sources*. New York: Columbia University Press.

Weeder, Erica H. 1990. *The Rise of a Great Tradition: Archaeological Ceramics from the Jomon through Heian Periods*. New York: Japan Society.

Weinstein, Stanley. 1977. "Rennyo and the Shinshū Revival." In Hall and Toyoda, eds. (1977), 331-59.

------. 1987. *Buddhism under the T'ang*. Cambridge: Cambridge University Press.

Wheatley, Paul, and Thomas See. 1978. *From Court to Capital: A Tentative Interpretation of the Origins of the Japanese Urban Tradition*. Chicago: University of Chicago Press.

Wheeler, Post, trans. and ed. 1952. *The Sacred Scriptures of the Japanese*. London: Allen and Unwin.
Wheelwright, Carolyn. 1981. "A Visualization of Eitoku's Lost Paintings at Azuchi Castle." In Elison and Smith, eds. (1981), 87-111.
Wilson, William S. 1982. *Ideals of the Samurai: Writings of the Japanese Warriors*. Burbank, Calif.: Ohara.
Wintersteen, Prescott, B. 1974a. "The Early Muromachi Bakufu in Kyoto." In Hall and Mass, eds. (1974).
——. 1974b. "The Muromachi Shugo and Hanzei." In Hall and Mass, eds. (1974), 210-20.
Yamamura, Kozo. 1972. "The Development of Za in Medieval Japan." *Business History Review* 47, no. 4: 438-65.
——. 1974. "The Decline of the Ritsuryō System: Hypotheses on Economic and Institutional Change." *Journal of Japanese Studies* 1, no. 1: 3-37.
——. 1975. "Workshop Papers on the Economic and Institutional History of Medieval Japan." *Journal of Japanese Studies* 1, no. 2: 255-345.
——. 1981a. "Returns on Unification: Economic Growth in Japan, 1550-1650." In Hall, Nagahara, and Yamamura, eds. (1981), 327-72.
——. 1981b. "Tara in Transition: a Study of a Kamakura Shōen." *Journal of Japanese Studies* 7: 349-91.
——. 1988. "From Coins to Rice: Hypotheses on the Kandaka and Kokudaka Systems." *Journal of Japanese Studies* 14: 348-67.
——. 1990a. "The Growth of Commerce in Medieval Japan." In Yamamura, ed. (1990), 344-95.
——. 1990b. "Introduction: Medieval Japan." In Yamamura, ed. (1990), 1-45.
Yamamura, Kozo, ed. 1990. *Medieval Japan*. Vol. 3 of *The Cambridge History of Japan*. Cambridge: Cambridge University Press.
Yasuda, Motohisa. 1965. "History of the Studies of the Formation of the Japanese Hōken System (Feudalism)." *Acta Asiatica* 8: 74-100.
Yasuda, Yoshinori. 1992. "Holocene Climatic Changes and the Transformations of Jōmon Culture in Japan." *Newsletter of Environment and Civilization* 6: 15-19.
Yazaki, Takeo. 1968. *Social Change and the City in Japan: From Earliest Times Through the Industrial Revolution*. Tokyo: Japan Publications.
Yoshida, Atsuhiko. 1977. "Japanese Mythology and the Indo-European Trifunctional System." *Diogenes* 98: 93-116.
Young, John. 1957. *The Location of Yamatai: A Case Study in Japanese Historiography*. Baltimore: Johns Hopkins University Press.
Yuba, Janet Ikeda. 1993. "Triumphant Survivor of Japan's Cultural Battlefield of the Sixteenth Century: Hosokawa Yūsai, 1534-1610, Warrior, Nijō Poet, and Guardian of the *kokin denju*." Ph.D. diss., Princeton University.

TOKUGAWA JAPAN: THE RETURN OF THE OTHER?

Harold Bolitho

In 1946 anybody searching for information on the subject of Tokugawa Japan in English would have been in for a disappointment. For a start, there were few primary sources available, the major collection being the series of translations edited by Wigmore (1891-1941) on the subject of Tokugawa legal practice. Otherwise the reader would have been left to make what he could of some stray translations of Tokugawa thinkers, as with N. Skene Smith's "An Introduction to Some Japanese Economic Writings of the 18th century" (1934), with its brief selections from Arai Hakuseki, Ogyū Sorai, and Miura Baien, or Galen M. Fisher's translation of Kumazawa Banzan's *Daigaku wakumon* (1938), or William Knox's work on Arai Hakuseki's *Oritaku shiba no ki* (1903). Perhaps the closest to an accessible primary source touching on life in Tokugawa Japan would have been the partial and, as it now turns out, often inaccurate translation of the observations of the German physician Engelbert Kaempfer, published in 1906.[1]

Scholarly monographs, if more plentiful, were only slightly so, represented by a scattering of articles in the *Transactions of the Asiatic Society of Japan* dating back to the 1870s. For the most part these were produced by people who, while knowledgeable and educated, and beneficiaries of lengthy periods of residence in Japan, were for the most part amateur scholars and, in the eyes of the hypothetical reader in 1946, untrained, unsophisticated, and uncritical. But there were some notable exceptions, and one of them was a very important one—Hugh Borton's 1938 paper on peasant rebellions, which was to remain the only substantial work on the subject for the better part of the next fifty years.

Tokugawa thought, recently hailed as "one of the liveliest and most interesting fields in Japanese studies in America,"[2] was in 1946, as it was to be for several decades to come, largely ignored, represented by a handful of papers on such thinkers as Nakae Tōju, Dazai Jun, and Kumazawa Banzan who, although not currently

---

[1] See also Beatrice Bodart-Bailey (1988).
[2] Samuel Hideo Yamashita (1996): 1.

disparaged, seem nevertheless to have yielded their places in the pantheon to more beguiling thinkers, Itō Jinsai, Ogyū Sorai, and Nakai Chikuzan among them.

If anything, Tokugawa Japan was even less adequately served in the area of biography, and this would certainly have appeared curious to an educated reader, who would have been conditioned to see this particular genre as the apex of the historian's craft. Such a reader coming from the study of the Western world would have been familiar with the major biographies—Morley's Gladstone, Abbott's Napoleon, and the like—and would therefore have been disappointed to find virtually nothing except Sadler's biography of Tokugawa Ieyasu (1937). The same reader, incidentally, fifty years later, would still be puzzled. Apart from studies of Tanuma Okitsugu and Matsudaira Sadanobu,[3] the Tokugawa political biography is still ignored, and biographical studies of other figures far from plentiful.

Monographs apart, Tokugawa Japan in 1946 was represented by a few chapters in general surveys of Japanese history, some of them dating back to the end of the nineteenth century. The best known would have been James Murdoch's three-volume survey (1926), but there were several others by historians like Walter Dickson (1898), David Murray (1894), and Ernest Clement (1915). By far the best of these, and certainly the best written, was George Sansom's *Japan: A Short Cultural History*, first published in 1931, later revised in 1943, and still, in 1997, worth reading.

While we must recognize the difficulties under which these early scholars worked, and applaud their achievements, it should be said that anyone in the year 1946 trying to build up a picture of Tokugawa Japan from these meager resources would have come away with a certain impression which we would now perceive as inaccurate. To be fair, it should also be acknowledged that the same reader, had he known Japanese, would have been little wiser, and gained much the same impression, albeit more detailed. The outlines of Tokugawa history had, after all, been generally accepted among Japanese scholars, and in the prewar period, when little was to be gained by challenging them, few seemed so inclined.

Tokugawa Japan, as it was depicted prior to 1946, was an extremely forbidding place in almost every respect. In government it was

---

[3] John Whitney Hall (1955); Herman Ooms (1975).

believed to be subject to a system of national dictatorship set in place by Tokugawa Ieyasu himself, a government based upon Confucian morality, and ruled—initially, at least—by able shogun, men who were both stern and just. Ultimately, as years of peace took their toll on national morale, Japan and its rulers succumbed to the temptations of idleness and extravagance, insulating themselves from the concerns of their subjects by a wall of cronies and toadies, and growing all the while more greedy and more repressive, but also less concerned with their obligations to the emperor and the rest of the nation. Controlling to the end, there was no part of life which the government did not attempt to regulate, announcing its intentions in a torrent of prohibitions, finely calibrated so that they might be applied differentially to separate sections of society.

That society itself was divided rigidly into four estates, of which the topmost, the samurai, were uniquely equipped by birth and training with virtues of restraint, frugality, and spiritual nobility. Insofar as they fell short of these ideals, which more and more they did, it was through forces over which they had no control—centuries of peace and soft urban living—and to the insidious activities of those cunning and unscrupulous members of the fourth, and least regarded estate, the merchants. Sandwiched uncomfortably between these two estates were the peasants, oppressed by tax-hungry rulers on the one hand and cheated by the profit-hungry merchants on the other.

Thus far Japanese and Western scholars were in agreement. The one issue on which they tended to divide was the influence of the one upon the other: not the influence of Japan on the West, but the influence of the West on Japan. Western historians, gravitating towards the familiar, usually preferred to see Tokugawa Japan refracted through the eyes of Western observers: Portuguese, Spanish, and Italian missionaries of the sixteenth century; English traders of the early seventeenth century; Dutch, German, and Swedish residents of Dejima; and finally those Americans who delivered Japan from her long isolation. If the tenth chapter of Ernest Clement's history of Japan, dealing with the years 1600-1853, or in other words virtually the entire Tokugawa period, is entitled "The Sleep of Japan," the eleventh, which covers the period 1853 to 1868, automatically becomes "The Awakening of Japan," as if nothing of significance had happened between the expulsion of most Westerners early in the seventeenth century and Commodore Perry's arrival two centuries or so later.

Behind all this early scholarship it is not difficult to discern an inchoate, unstated wish to portray Tokugawa Japan in a way that Western readers could readily grasp. Frequently this was achieved by reference to parallels familar to them. It is easy to understand the impulse, and to sympathize with it. Even as Japan was adapting itself to the world around it, those Western scholars who saw it in the late nineteenth and early twentieth centuries were nevertheless very conscious that it was an alien society. It lay on the margins of the modern world, its international significance still very much in the future. If it was strange in so many ways, its past, even its recent past, was still more so. To come to terms with it, therefore, and to explain it to a readership still less familiar with it, demanded that this small group of pioneer scholars reach for familiar comparisons, no matter how strained, in an effort to provide access to the inaccessible. Seeing Japan as essentially alien, the overwhelming temptation was to tame it by linking it with the safe and the familiar, much as wild horses may be broken in when paired with their domesticated cousins.

This strategy is apparent, for example, in the overtly Western perspective shared by most of the early scholarship. The emphasis, already noted, on Western visitors to Tokugawa Japan is an example of using the familiar to define the unfamiliar, seen at its most obvious, and least defensible, in the attention given to the otherwise insignificant figure of Will Adams, the English seaman who arrived in Japan in 1600 and lived out the remainder of his life there. Works which failed to mention such major Japanese figures as Tokugawa Yoshimune by name—or if they did refer to him did so only in passing—gave pages to a merchant seaman, and for no other reason than that he happened to be born in Kent, a county to which readers could relate more easily than to Edo, the city in which Adams ended his life.

It is also to be seen in the sometimes ludicrous tendency to offer legitimacy to Japanese figures by identifying them with Western referents—Chikamatsu Monzaemon as "the Shakespeare of Japan" is the best known of these, but one doesn't have to look far before one encounters Kanō Tanyū "the Whistler of Japan" and Takizawa Bakin "the Scott of Japan."[4] In each case the glib, patronizing comparison conceals much more than it reveals, and in each case, by

---

[4] See Ernest Clement (1915), chap. 10.

refusing to admit the enormous differences which exist between Chikamatsu and Shakespeare on almost every level except the most superficial, does justice to neither, and little to help understand Chikamatsu's enormous role in Tokugawa Japan's cultural life. Kenneth Kirkwood in his 1938 study of Genroku culture, in which he dealt with key figures of the period, Chikamatsu among them, also implicitly subscribed to this attitude, as the title of his work, *Renaissance in Japan,* indicates. Here too the comparison with a European cultural phenomenon obscured instead of explaining, by deflecting attention away from what was really noteworthy about Genroku, and raising expectations of its cultural life which could not be met without some distortion.

The Tokugawa Japan produced by these means, while it may have seemed comprehensible, was not necessarily an attractive place. There was also another set of Western preoccupations at work, and these showed a premodern Japan which was authoritarian, rigid, and punitive. Western scholars accustomed to parliamentary democracy and the rule of law saw in Tokugawa Japan the negation of all they held dear. Entering the enormous body of government documents, they saw a totalitarian state in which prohibition was piled upon prohibition, each more arbitrary and unreasonable than the one before. Themselves respectful of laws, they believed the proclamations of *bakufu* and daimyo, on the assumption that prohibitions so comprehensive and so copious would never have been written without the means and the intention of implementing them. If, too, the division of society into four estates were simply a fiction, why then would the government persist in that fiction to the end, never ceasing to differentiate between the rights and duties of the various classes? Inevitably, therefore, the threatening aspects of Tokugawa Japan came to the fore; unofficial documents—letters, diaries, and the like—which might have lightened the picture were largely ignored.

Beyond that, though, there were even more pressing reasons. For Japanese scholars of the Meiji period and later, the Tokugawa legacy was one which they had rightly sloughed off in favor of all that was up-to-date and good; Tokugawa Japan represented the bad old days. Western scholars, confident of the benefits of their own civilization, were already persuaded of this, and saw it readily confirmed by the primary documents most accessible to them. These were the eyewitness accounts of British and American observers who had come to Japan in the dying years of Tokugawa rule and whose experience was of a highly specific kind. The Japan they saw—effectively the narrow strip of coast running from Edo to Osaka—had, thanks to their intrusion, already become what later generations would call "contested terrain." The impressions of such men—Lawrence Oliphant, Townsend Harris, Henry Heusken, Ernest Satow, Algernon Mitford, and the like—were universally of the intransigence, incompetence, and inadequacy of a government which, although eager to keep them under observation at all times, was nevertheless unable to protect them. They also found it to be unresponsive to their demands, both diplomatic and commercial. Naturally, therefore, it had to go, and few Western observers shed tears on its passing.

It was all too easy for this unflattering appraisal of Tokugawa Japan to persist well into the twentieth century, and to preserve its dominance as late as 1946. The academic preoccupations of the first decades of this century were very much of a kind which reinforced the stereotype. In the late nineteenth and early twentieth centuries nobody would have needed much persuasion to see Tokugawa Ieyasu as did Sadler, as the one great man who by his vigor, courage, and wisdom could lay the foundations of Japan's longest-lasting and most powerful dynasty. A popular imagination dominated by figures like Washington, Napoleon, and Bismarck was enough to condition anybody to look for the great man and, once having identified him, then to accept almost anything consonant with that image. In the case of Ieyasu, it led to a universal and uncritical acceptance of apocrypha—the well-known story, for example, of the three unifiers and the bird, and most notably the document called "The Legacy of Ieyasu," now known to be an anachronistic counterfeit.

At the same time, however, it was also accepted that the achievements of single individuals, no matter how wise and forceful, were necessarily short-lived. Napoleons met their Waterloos, wise pilots like Bismarck were dropped by arrogant young Kaisers. So the scenario of decline and fall was a familiar one, and such shogun as Tsunayoshi, with his Nero-esque solicitude for the animal kingdom and his ambiguous sexuality, appeared to fit comfortably into it. So too did Ienari, with his numerous consorts and still more numerous progeny, especially if Walter Dickson's suggestion that "as he was subject to epileptic fits, and weakly in mind and body, he is not generally believed to have been the father of many of them"[5] is to be believed. Clearly with leaders of this kind the Tokugawa house was following the same trajectory as the later Caesars, the Stuarts (both earlier and later), the House of Bourbon, and the Romanovs. The cultural artifacts of late Tokugawa, with their presentation of the lubricious, the sensational, and the pornographic seemed also an integral part of dynastic decline, conveying unmistakable echoes of English culture on the eve of the Glorious Revolution.

This brings us to the issue of "the Other." I should say something about my use of this term; having employed it in my title, I can do no less. As generally interpreted, the Other is a construct, something we create as a way of defining ourselves. Whatever we are, the Other is not. It is normally the product of any combination of several reprehensible conditions—ignorance, fear, suspicion, chauvinism, and xenophobia among them. The most common guise in which the Other appears is a negative one, given our deplorable willingness to saddle specific groups with those attributes we most mistrust in ourselves. Jews, witches, *harijans*, Catholics, Nonconformists, Freemasons, Rosicrucians, African-Americans, Jehovah's Witnesses, Scientologists—the list is endless; everybody is somebody's Other. It is one way, and not a particularly pleasant one, of coping with difference.

But it is not the only way. There is another Other, which, while not encountered nearly so often, is no less a way of approaching the unfamiliar. In this case, however, rather than being kept at a distance, the Other is willy-nilly dragged closer, and so made more approachable. This Other, in its extreme form, is created when some different and distant group is credited with attributes we would like to have, but do not. Sir Thomas More took this to the limit, but Voltaire, in creating a China of his own imagination, was not too far behind. In its more moderate and most common form it is achieved when a different group is assigned those qualities with which we ourselves feel comfortable. It is a gentle and sympathetic way of dealing with difference, but nevertheless it is an implicit affirmation of precisely what it tries to deny—the Otherness of the Other.

To historians before 1946, Tokugawa Japan was the Other in

---

[5] Walter Dickson (1898), 235.

both the negative and positive senses. On the one hand it was demonized by those who perceived its political, social, and economic systems to be totally without redeeming features—a country in which the legitimate aspirations of its people were blocked by a cruel, authoritarian, and conservative government, one strong enough to impede progress of any kind, and devoted above all else to the preservation of an unjust system which guaranteed them privileges of a kind no longer warranted by their contribution to society. At the same time, and related to the same impulse, was the other Other, announcing itself by its generous feeling of solidarity with a people who in all essential ways were just like us, and whose legitimate aspirations to life, liberty, and the pursuit of happiness were crushed by such a system. References to the familiar—to the sailor from Kent as well as Shakespeare, Whistler, and Sir Walter Scott—played their part in creating this kinder, gentler Other.

This is the trap into which, with the best possible intentions, prewar historians of Tokugawa Japan often fell. But as one might have expected, the situation began to change rapidly in the wake of World War II, when those involved in this field of scholarship began to struggle out of it. The publications of scholars who had been led, or in some cases pushed, into Japanese studies largely through the exigencies of war displayed a new sensitivity to Tokugawa realities. This was the generation which gave us the first really detailed and sophisticated analyses of Tokugawa Japan, unclouded for the most part by notions of the Other. Toshio George Tsukahira's study of the *sankin kōtai* system (1966) offered the first comprehensive look at one of the Tokugawa polity's most distinctive and most durable features. John Whitney Hall, in his study of the eighteenth-century statesman Tanuma Okitsugu (1955) brought a refreshing critical rigor to the political biography. In intellectual history, Joseph Spae's study of Itō Jinsai (1948) was followed immediately by E. Herbert Norman's work on Andō Shōeki (1949). Then came Donald Keene's study of Honda Toshiaki (1952), Robert Bellah's treatment of a major variety of Tokugawa religion (1957), and J. R. McEwan on Ogyū Sorai (1962). Between them E. Herbert Norman (1940), Charles Sheldon (1958), and Thomas Smith (1959) drew attention in their several ways to developments in commerce and agriculture, and the social and political consequences they produced. Tokugawa culture received positive appraisals from Howard Hibbett (1959) and Donald Shively (1953) as, in the capable hands of Ronald Dore (1965), did the educational background.

The difference between these postwar works and their prewar forerunners is immediately apparent. They were far more nuanced, infinitely more detailed. Most of them, indeed, were of such quality and such eminence that even after thirty years they are still very much in use. Among them they erected a scaffolding in which the major constituent elements of Tokugawa Japan were identified and locked into place—government, society, thought, education, cultural life. Yet their scholarship was inevitably part of the intellectual mood of their times, and that, in the immediate postwar decades, was decidedly optimistic. All these works can be seen in their various ways searching for traces in traditional Japan which could be interpreted as positive, progressive, and rational, and therefore offering hope for the future. John Hall's study of Tanuma Okitsugu was accompanied by the revealing subtitle, "Forerunner of Modern Japan," and the Tanuma period itself was described as one in which Japan "first turned from subservience to her feudal past towards a realization that her future lay ahead of her."[6] To Donald Keene, Honda Toshiaki's writings, in particular, showed that "with him one has entered a new age, that of modern Japan. One finds in his books," Keene continued, "a new spirit, restless, curious and receptive."[7] Thomas Smith traced Japan's nineteenth-century modernization back to agrarian developments of the previous one hundred fifty years,[8] Robert Bellah looked to Shingaku for the light it could throw on "the rise of a modern industrial society,"[9] while the kind of education available to the people of Tokugawa Japan was, to Ronald Dore, "an essential precondition" of the same process.[10]

Given the general atmosphere of postwar optimism, especially in the United States, it is not surprising that there should have been this emphasis on the positive. After all, every one of these scholars had seen their lives and careers disrupted and refashioned by a Japan in which negative, reactionary, and irrational elements had appeared to predominate. It was therefore essential to salvage

---

[6] Hall (1955), vii.
[7] Donald Keene (1952), 1.
[8] Thomas C. Smith (1959), 201.
[9] Robert N. Bellah (1957), 3.
[10] Ronald Dore (1965), 3.

something of value from it. Just as the United States in particular was engaging in the postwar reconstruction of the physical Japan, so its scholars were engaged in reconstructing Japanese history, making the Tokugawa period, previously seen as feudal, stagnant, authoritarian, and xenophobic, appear rather more hopeful. Hall, Sheldon, Bellah, and Smith all pointed to Tokugawa Japan's accommodation with commerce, Hall to the diversity of political authority, Norman, Hibbett, and Shively to examples of cultural and intellectual freedom, Keene to an openness and curiosity about the outside world.

At the same time I should also add that insofar as the famous "Modernization Series" was concerned—since Tokugawa Japan featured in this as a precursor of the Meiji Restoration and all that followed—we should also factor in the preoccupations of the Cold War. To claim Japan for our side rather than theirs, it was also appropriate, in emphasizing the positive aspects of Japan's nineteenth-century development, to interpret the Tokugawa background in a more sympathetic fashion, to give a new and increasingly important ally a recognizably human face—one we could relate to.

There was consequently an undertone of Otherness in the work of this generation, but it was tempered by the extensive personal contact afforded by war and occupation. The experiences of these years inevitably produced familiarity with, and sympathy for, Japan and the Japanese. All of these scholars shared it. They had learnt the language, they had spent a large amount of time in the country, they had all managed to make contact with and befriend Japanese scholars. They were all able to take advantage—as previous generations had not been—of the work of a freshly-liberated Japanese historiography, the creation of those who even then were looking at their own history with new eyes. So the sense of Tokugawa Japan as "the Other" was naturally diminished. Which is not to say that it was gone entirely. Western models and Western parallels could still be found interposing themselves into the argument, to the detriment of the Japanese reality behind them. E. Herbert Norman was not above describing Arai Hakuseki as "the Francis Bacon of Japan."[11] Andō Shōeki, in Norman's treatment of him, was frequently hidden behind references to Montesquieu, John Ball

---

[11] E. H. Norman (1949), 4.

(14th-century England), Joss Fritz (16th-century Germany), Emanuel Kant, Denis Diderot, Critias (Athens, 5th century B.C.), Plato, Polybius, Epicurus, Gerrard Winstanley (17th-century Leveller), Plutarch, Cicero, Gassendi (17th-century Italian), Lucretius, Victor Cousin, Samuel Johnson, Richard Savage, Proudhon, Brissot, St. Paul, Erasmus, Thomas More, John Milton, Hobbes, Spinoza, Hippias, Alcidames, John Donne, and many more, to such an extent that Shōeki himself failed to emerge with any particular clarity. Bellah, too, while ostensibly dealing with Shingaku, was so preoccupied with Weber and the Protestant Ethic that he neglected to provide much information about the growth, organization, and influence of this variety of religion. Not until Jennifer Robertson's papers (1979, 1991) and Janine Sawada's book (1993), over twenty years later, did it become clear that there was very much more to the movement than Ishida Baigan.

In some cases, too, this tacit admission of Otherness was not so much due to a perception—and fear—of Tokugawa Japan as "the Other" as to rather more mundane considerations. That is, in struggling to win recognition for their scholarship in the eyes of obdurately Eurocentric colleagues, it was often necessary for academics to suppress or ignore the particularity of Japan and instead to emphasize such elements as might mesh with some kind of universal developmental scheme. Time which could more usefully have been devoted to seeing how Tokugawa Japan actually worked was spent trying to squeeze square Japanese pegs into round European holes labelled "feudalism," "early modern," and "modernity."

I have noted the tremendous significance for the field in the monographs produced during the 1950s and 1960s. It was indeed a major turning point. But there were not so very many of them—certainly they were few enough, to speak from my own experience, that even a graduate student could afford to buy them all. In that sense it was a happy time. In the 1970s and 1980s, however, the floodgates began to inch open as the students of those scholars who had come to prominence in the fifties and sixties came to establish themselves in their turn, and began filling in some of the interstices left in the scaffolding erected during the fifties and sixties. This is the cohort in which I would include myself, albeit at the senior end. Conrad Totman, whose *Politics in the Tokugawa Bakufu* was published in 1967, was the first of the next generation of Tokugawa specialists to make his mark. George Elison (1973),

William Hauser (1974), and myself (1974) came next, to be followed a little later by Herman Ooms (1975) and Ronald Toby (1983).

The 1980s produced still more work. Herbert Bix (1986) and Tetsuo Najita (1987), both of whom had previously published on later periods of Japanese history, turned their attention to the Tokugawa period, to the issue of peasant rebellions in one case, and to intellectual history in the other. At the same time a rather younger group of scholars emerged—Richard Rubinger (1982), James McClain (1982), Kate Nakai (1988), Ann Jannetta (1987), Anne Walthall (1986), William Kelly (1985), Stephen Vlastos (1986), and Bob Wakabayashi (1986). The list indeed stretches on to the present, since the work of such historians as Constantine Vaporis (1994), Philip Brown (1993), Gary Leupp (1992), Luke Roberts (forthcoming), David Howell (1995), and Janine Sawada (1993)—to name just a few—although published in the 1990s is identifiably in the same trajectory, although no doubt more sophisticated and informed by both the methodology and the lexicon of the social sciences.

All of us, whether old, middle-aged, or young, have been the beneficiaries—quite obviously so—of the achievements, efforts, contacts, and patronage of our teachers and predecessors. We have been beneficiaries, too (actually with the exception of myself, as a non-citizen, although I benefited in other ways) of government-funded fellowships which encouraged longer stays in Japan, better language training, and more leisurely preparation. Equally we profited from the enormous strides being made in Japanese scholarship, and in the ambitious publishing programs facilitated by Japan's economic miracle.

It would be idle to pretend that this group of scholars has not also brought its own preoccupations to the study of Tokugawa Japan. Most of us, in one way or another, are products of the 1960s, and we all know what that means. Journalists keep on telling us. Sex, drugs, and rock n' roll, yes. The Kennedy assassinations, yes. The death of Martin Luther King, yes. The Vietnam War, yes. The siege of Chicago, yes. The student movement, yes. Then, into the seventies, Watergate. All the clichés. Suspicion of authority, sympathy with the oppressed, cynicism about the system, tolerance for diversity, the search for new spiritual directions. Clichés they certainly are, and are very far from defining a particular generation and its heirs. Nevertheless, these themes can be discerned in what has been written on Tokugawa Japan since the 1960s. You can see their traces in the scholarship which came to fruition in the succeeding decades—the signs are more overt in some cases than in others, but they are there.

They are there in what is now the standard view of the Tokugawa political system. Where government in Tokugawa Japan had once been defined by what happened in the shogun's administration in Edo, together with the laws emerging from it, the emphasis has changed sharply. The *bakuhan taisei*, not the *bakufu*, is now the focus, with attention directed to the complex interaction between one government in Edo, and a large number of more or less independent regional governments, sometimes working towards the same ends, but often not. A comparable relationship is to be seen now between daimyo governments in their castle towns and villages, which were self-governing and not always amenable to external direction. The Tokugawa absolutism which was taken for granted in prewar scholarship has disappeared, and been replaced by a vision of government as something limited, contingent, and negotiable in nature. I attempted to indicate how the Tokugawa *bakufu*, as a central government, was eaten away from within by officials with regional interests of their own; Hauser, McClain, Brown, and Vaporis have pointed to government's failure to control different forms of activity—commerce, urban development, tax assessment, and travel. In each case these historians looked past statute to see just how government worked, or rather did not work, and to the way in which individuals, groups, and regions could, and did manage to serve their own interests.

A related development has been a new emphasis on the heterogeneity of Tokugawa Japan. The torrent of publications issuing from Japan's newly-affluent hamlets, towns, cities, counties, and prefectures from the 1960s onward made available, in legible form, materials of a kind which opened up new perspectives on the Tokugawa experience. John Hall, whose fascination with the history of Okayama[12] dated back to the 1950s, showed what could be done with local source materials, and he has been followed by a number of scholars whose attention is no longer on Edo and Osaka, but rather on the periphery. This has produced an explicit recognition of the difficulties inherent in generalizing about a country so diverse

---

[12] This was to bear fruit in his *Government and Local Power in Japan* (1966).

in topography and climate, so fragmented politically, and socially so multiform. In 1977 Susan Hanley and Kozo Yamamura demonstrated that different regions of Tokugawa Japan had their own patterns of economic development, and recent studies, like Kären Wigen's work on the growth and decline of the Ina region (1995), have confirmed this.

Interest in the common man has also emerged as a major theme in recent scholarship. Where once academic attention seldom strayed beyond the samurai class and its concerns, Tokugawa Japan's peasants and workers have now come to the forefront. Not that the samurai have completely disappeared, but it is significant that, with the exception of the absorbing samurai biography by Katsu Kokichi, *Musui's Story*, translated by Teruko Craig, Eiko Ikegami's *The Taming of the Samurai* (1995) is the first academic study of this class to appear since Kozo Yamamura published his work on samurai income over twenty years ago (1974). It is the Tokugawa underclass, farmers and laborers, who are the most studied. They provide the main focus for the demographic analyses of Thomas Smith (1977) and Susan Hanley,[13] but perhaps more significantly, in terms of productivity, it is their relationship with authority which has emerged as the predominant theme. The general framework of village life and power relations, based on the interaction of rich peasants with their poorer fellows, is still much as Thomas Smith described it in 1959, but there can be no doubt that peasant resistance has become the focus of attention. Irwin Scheiner and Patricia Sippel led the way in the 1970s, Scheiner with papers on peasant consciousness,[14] and Sippel with a (1977) study of the Bushū rising of 1866. They were followed by a spate of studies in the 1980s from William Kelly (1985), Stephen Vlastos (1986), Anne Walthall (1986), and Herbert Bix (1986). Most recently James White has also written on the subject (1995), while Herman Ooms (1996b) has contributed a work on resistance of a different kind, one carried on through lawsuits rather than riots. Gary Leupp, for the first time, has focused attention on urban poor (1992). All of this activity has offered fresh insights into the Tokugawa underclass. Where peasants were once seen as passive victims of a progression of rapacious authorities, stretching from overlords through magistrates and tax assessors

---

[13] Most recently her *Everyday Things in Premodern Japan* (1997).
[14] Irwin Scheiner (1973, 1978).

to village officials, they now appear in a more believable guise—still exploited to some extent, but not without resources, knowing that the system offered opportunities for a degree of intelligent manipulation through which certain advantages could be won and maintained.

The cultural life of Tokugawa Japan is also now seen as considerably more diverse than was once the case. This is true of Tokugawa education, although not to the extent of supplanting Ronald Dore's classic study, which still, after thirty years, offers unrivaled thematic breadth and unmatched command of Japanese sources. Nevertheless, where Dore concentrated on samurai education on the one hand, and basic education for commoners on the other, more recent writers have directed attention to other kinds of education. Richard Rubinger (1982) has described the different kinds of advanced education available to commoners in private academies, and one of these, Hirose Tansō's Kangien, has been analyzed in a recent study by Marleen Kassel (1996). Janine Sawada, too, has broadened our perception of Tokugawa education by showing that there was very much more to Shingaku than any role it might have played as premodern Japan's answer to Calvinism.

In the intellectual life of Tokugawa Japan there is a similar emphasis on diversity. It can now no longer be said quite so categorically that Confucianism was the predominant discourse. Herman Ooms (1984) demonstrated just how catholic the ruling ideology was, since it drew just as much from Buddhist and Shintō sources as it did from the Confucianism peddled by Hayashi Razan and his descendants. Confucianism itself is no longer the monolith that it was once assumed to be, as studies by Kate Nakai (1988), Tetsuo Najita (1987), and Bob Wakabayashi (1995) make clear. *Kokugaku*, too, the intellectual tradition which asserted the value of things Japanese over Chinese models, has re-emerged as an important strand in Tokugawa thought in the somewhat divergent approaches of Peter Nosco (1990) and Harry Harootunian (1988).

Two more areas of scholarly growth, albeit at opposite ends of the spectrum, are industry and sexuality. We have recently seen a cluster of works on the former—Conrad Totman's survey of the lumber industry (1995); studies of fishing in Kyushu and Hokkaido by Arne Kalland (1995) and David Howell (1995), respectively; and Kären Wigen's study of the rise and fall of the Ina Valley, to which I have already referred. All of these throw important light on areas of activity overlooked by earlier scholarship. Sexuality, a topic over which prewar scholars usually chose to pass in stony silence, has just begun to rear its head, with Cecilia Seigle's foray into the Edo brothel quarter (1993), and Gary Leupp's examination of Tokugawa homosexuality (1995). More along these lines is to be expected. The group of scholars gathered by Sumie Jones has already produced a small conference volume (1996), and promises to do more in its investigations of the erotic and its place in the life of Tokugawa Japan.

It could be complained that in all this activity the really big questions—how was Japan able to modernize, for example—have disappeared. I don't suppose that, for example, an analysis of bisexuality among Japanese men of the Tokugawa period can tell us an awful lot about Japan's transition to modernity, or at least not the sort of modernity focused on commerce and industry. Yet it would be difficult to deny that this diversity has been a useful development. On the major themes the waters may well have been muddied by the discovery of evidence resistant to tidy analysis, but at the same time our attention has been directed toward topics which might otherwise have been left lie fallow. These would include environmental matters of the kind Conrad Totman has introduced, for example, or the women's issues canvassed so successfully by Anne Walthall and Laurel Cornell.[15] What has resulted is a far richer and more varied picture of Tokugawa Japan than earlier scholars could have imagined.

For the most part—and I would like to emphasize that qualification—what has been written on Tokugawa Japan in English over the past quarter century has been cut recognizably from the same cloth. The sense of Tokugawa Japan as the Other, as alien, as needing to be viewed through Western filters before any sense can be made of it, has been muted. Research has become infinitely more detailed, connected more and more closely with the scholarship of Japanese colleagues, highly specific, and more than anything aimed at showing how Tokugawa Japan actually worked—how people at many different levels of society played politics, how they paid (or failed to pay) their taxes, how they complied (or failed to comply) with official directives, how they learnt, what they learnt, how they made their livings, what they thought of the

---

[15] See their contributions to Gail Lee Bernstein, ed. (1991).

world around them, how they ran their families, how they conducted their sex lives.

For the most part, too—and once again I would like to emphasize the qualification—while it is no doubt possible to divide scholars into conservatives and progressives, or, to use another formulation, into pragmatists and radicals, or realists and idealists, there is no doubt that whatever may divide us, we are linked by common presuppositions—what history is, what constitutes evidence, how documents can be used. If we disagree, we tend to do so in mutually intelligible ways. We may not say the same thing, but we speak the same language. In the work of the majority of these scholars there is no sense of anybody twisting the armature of Tokugawa history to conform to any explicit Western theoretical agenda. Of course, some fields are inevitably more technical than others—population studies, for example—but are no more dependent on Western models than Japanese work in the same fields. Bourgeois empiricism triumphant, you might say. That is still the dominant strain in the field of Tokugawa history, and as our acquaintance with Japan has grown, so has our acceptance of differences as well as similarities. If we all have our own set of presuppositions about our work, they seem to correspond very well with those of the Japanese scholars whose research is of such importance to us. We are at home with the Otherness of "the Other."

This is less true of those areas most influenced by the cultural studies movement, where scholars are programmed to sniff out the subversive, the transgressive, the eccentric, the disengaged, the alienated, and the liminal, to the exclusion of all else. These are preoccupations of the late twentieth century, so those who hunt for them in a Tokugawa context have a difficult task. Still it seems possible for some, after wading through the morass of evidence to the contrary, to find what they want, if only in attenuated form. *Gesaku* fiction, for example, the literary genre—facetious, punning, parodic, and fundamentally harmless—produced by a self-satisfied Edo coterie, has been hailed by one authority as "an expression of resistance and criticism."[16] Similarly the *aragoto* plays so popular in Tokugawa theater, with their uncritical admiration of the samurai class and its values, have been interpreted as "an open defiance towards samurai."[17] Yosa Buson the poet-painter

---

[16] Masao Miyoshi (1991), 19.
[17] C. Andrew Gerstle (1989), 35.

and Itō Jakuchū the profoundly religious artist, both professionals absorbed in their work, have nevertheless been thrust into the category of the alienated, eccentrics who "had lost faith in the present."[18] The list goes on. Love suicides become "a form of protest by a marginalized faction against the mainstream samurai values,"[19] while Edo's Rakanji, despite its financial support from *bakufu* and daimyo, is noted for the contrast it provides to a system "based on rank, privilege and degree."[20]

Can all of these really be lumped together as a gigantic indictment and subversion of the system? Some scholars would say yes. I am not convinced. Mikhail Bakhtin may very well see protest everywhere in popular culture, and LeRoy Ladurie believe that the world is turned upside down every time there is a carnival. But the fact is that conformity and acceptance were far more evident in Tokugawa culture than subversion, and in Japan, as elsewhere, the carnival is based upon a profoundly conservative understanding; once it is over, the world is quickly turned right side up again, just as at the end of every Celebrity Roast there is never any doubt who is, and who is not, the celebrity. In any case, it all tends to ignore the reality that the most trenchant criticism of Tokugawa Japan came from Confucian scholars and their fellow-travelers who, far from complaining that Tokugawa Japan was too repressive, declared that it was not nearly repressive enough. Buyō Inshi, often cited approvingly for his comprehensive dissatisfaction, is a case in point.

So there is something of a reverse course going on, and it is at its most conspicuous in the field of Tokugawa intellectual history, which ever since the mid-1980s has been in the process of splitting into two separate and contending—not to say contentious—streams. One of these is clearly the orthodox stream—that is, one which produces intellectual history written on the basis of certain assumptions which have in the past made up the dominant scholarly approach—the hegemonic discourse, if you like. Among those assumptions, I think it would be fair to say, you could include the following: that while it may never be possible to know with total certainty what writers from another age and cultural milieu thought, any attempt to understand them should be based on an informed and sensitive reading of what they wrote, and the background—

---

[18] Tetsuo Najita (1987), 189.
[19] Steven Heine (1994): 367.
[20] Timon Screech (1993): 407.

personal and institutional—from which they emerged. Any such conclusions may be partial, should be tentative, but must be based on such evidence as is available. It is an approach which is necessarily based upon documents—philosophical treatises of one kind or another—and therefore attaches great importance to accurate translation (which indeed assumes that such a thing is desirable, although difficult) and textual criticism, involving such issues as the comparison of variant texts and a consideration of the circumstances under which each document was compiled. It also, despite the sometimes arcane nature of its subject matter, has been concerned to make itself understood within the wider scholarly community.

There is no shortage of such works, focusing on the writings of the major figures of Tokugawa philosophy, and often incorporating substantial pieces of translation. Kaibara Ekken has been the subject of work by Mary Evelyn Tucker, in her translation and analysis of his *Yamato zokkun* (1989); Arai Hakuseki's life and thought received a masterly treatment from Kate Nakai (1988); Ogyū Sorai in particular has been given considerable attention, his *Seidan* analyzed by J. R. McEwan in 1962, his *Bendō* by Olof Lidin in 1973, his *Gakusoku* by Richard Minear in 1976, and his *Tōmonsho* by Samuel Yamashita in 1994. Michael Pye has translated and annotated Tominaga Nakamoto's *Okina no fumi* and *Shutsujōkōgō* (1990); Rosemary Mercer has done the same for Miura Baien's *Genkiron* and *Gengo* (1991); and Bob Wakabayashi has written major studies of both Yamagata Daini and Aizawa Seishisai, based on the former's *Ryūshi shinron* (1995) and the latter's *Shinron* (1986). The most recent of these orthodox approaches to intellectual history is Marleen Kassel's book on Hirose Tansō, which deals with both his *Ugen* and *Yakugen* (1996). Peter Nosco's (1990) study of *kokugaku* in the eighteenth century, while much larger in scope than any of these other works, since it deals with four thinkers rather than restricting itself to any single figure, is nevertheless also part of the orthodox tradition.

This kind of intellectual history has a distinguished lineage, but it clearly does not satisfy everybody, and the first indications of dissatisfaction emerged in 1978, with the publication of a collection of essays edited by Najita and Scheiner. Most of the papers in that collection were of a fairly conventional kind, involving the paraphrase and analysis of one or more texts—Robert Bellah on Ishida

Baigan's *Seirimondō*; Bito Masahide on some writings of Ogyū Sorai; Sakai Yukichi and Matsumoto Sannosuke on intellectual links between Tokugawa and Meiji. None of these papers would have raised a single orthodox eyebrow. Two, however, did—one written by Tetsuo Najita, and the other by Harry Harootunian. In the former, Najita sketched out what he saw to be new possibilities in the study of Tokugawa intellectual history, demonstrating his approach through a discussion of Kaiho Seiryō. Harootunian, in his paper, took the same theme into *kokugaku*. Together, the two papers heralded the advent of what has recently come to be called "the new intellectual history,"[21] and there was no mistaking that in almost every way they signaled a clear departure from the conventional approach.

They immediately provoked criticism, some from myself,[22] some from others, but I would have to say that while this new approach has not yet become the hegemonic discourse (at least in the eyes of many) in the field of Tokugawa intellectual history, it has nevertheless achieved a standing and a legitimacy which many of its original critics, myself included, would never have predicted. Beyond its two initial sponsors it has won several converts, albeit of varying degrees of commitment. Herman Ooms, for example, especially given his recent work, would have to be considered a moderate. Naoki Sakai (1991), on the other hand, could be said to have outstripped even his mentors, recently goading the more cautious Ooms into calling him to task for indulging in a "postmodernist romp" characterized by a "self-indulgent and impenetrable style...look-alike misprints and neologisms, jumbled footnotes, strained translations and interpretations stretched to the hermeneutic breaking point."[23] On the other hand, the movement has also won at least one apostate from conventional intellectual history; a comparison of Samuel Yamashita's orthodox study of Ogyū Sorai in 1994 with his breathless endorsement of the new intellectual history in general, and of Sakai in particular, only two years later[24] demonstrates how seductive the new approach can be.

---

[21] Yamashita (1996), 25.
[22] Harold Bolitho (1980).
[23] Herbert Ooms (1996a): 385.
[24] Yamashita (1996).

Just what the distinguishing characteristics of the new intellectual history are in the context of Tokugawa studies, however, is not so readily comprehended. Samuel Yamashita, in his flattering appraisal, offers little help: it is concerned, he says (with a succinctness uncharacteristic of the genre), with economic and social contexts, with power, and with human agency, especially as revealed in the subversive.[25] To those who might wish a little more explanation, he refers us to the work of those Western theorists on whom the new Tokugawa intellectual historians rely. If you wish to know why Najita writes as he does, then consult Quentin Skinner and J. G. A. Pocock, both of whom are "advocates of a contextualist approach to the study of ideas largely inspired by speech-act theory."[26] To see what Harootunian is about, turn to Louis Althusser's analysis of ideology.[27] The pea, it seems, is always under some other thimble.

On the whole the new intellectual history is more identifiable by what it denies than by what it affirms. The denials themselves are explicit. Tetsuo Najita, in 1978, was concerned to accentuate the negative: "We should not ask when something was first said and by whom. Nor should we attempt to distinguish who influenced whom or who begot whom in the manner displayed in traditional narratives of the genealogical trees of Tokugawa academies. Nor, for that matter, should we list how many persons were actually influenced by a system of thought.... Finally, we should not seek pure philosophical statements, exemplifications of syllogistic reasoning."[28]

To this austere inventory, with its unmistakable challenge to traditional intellectual history, Harry Harootunian was to add a few more caveats. The new theoretical strategies, Harootunian was to claim in 1988, should bear no relation to "historical common sense"—by which he meant the sort of expectations and preconceptions that the average person might bring to any historical problem. Not only that, historical documents do not "reflect an invariant reality," and it is impossible for us to "participate in the experience of texts rooted in historical imaginaries no longer available to us." For that matter, truth is not "invariant" but

[25] Ibid., 26.
[26] Ibid., 29.
[27] Ibid., 31.
[28] Tetsuo Najita (1978), 5.

"operational," language is never "neutral," but is always "ideologically charged." Attempting to uncover the past is itself pointless, since "the past can never be known."[29] Writing about it would seem to be more pointless still; stylistic impenetrability, of which Ooms is only the most recent to complain, is justified because "lucidity is illusory," for "words are...opaque, layered, filled with differing and contrary valences."[30]

One need not agree with these prohibitions to understand them and respect them. After all, they do possess a certain defiant Ozymandian grandeur. What is more difficult to understand, however, is why any scholars holding such beliefs should go to the trouble of writing about the unknowable past, or indeed—words themselves being snares—writing anything at all. There is also the baffling matter of internal contradictions, for it is obvious that, notwithstanding all the posturing, when the principles are translated into practice the postmodernist bite proves considerably less painful than its bark. Najita's subsequent work on the Kaitokudō (1987), in which he traced the genealogical tree of this particular academy from Miyake Sekian through Goi Ranjū to Nakai Chikuzan, et al., owed far more to the old intellectual history than the new, and the author apparently had little difficulty in paraphrasing texts from historical imaginaries no longer available to us. Similarly, Harootunian, for all his stridently-phrased reservations, was comfortable enough with language as a conveyor of meaning to fill over four hundred pages with it in his examination of *kokugaku*. He also seems confident that his own reading of texts has afforded him reliable insight into the minds of *kokugaku* thinkers like Hirata Atsutane. If so, then that is really an achievement. Many of Atsutane's contemporaries, despite their advantage of a much closer proximity to the same historical imaginary, did not know what he was talking about. One of them, Fujita Tōkō, was moved to declare Atsutane's writings to be "absurd, incoherent, frivolous, and arbitrary."[31]

My view of this development—the new intellectual history as it has come to be applied to Tokugawa Japan—is that it signifies in a subtle, but unmistakable way, a return to Tokugawa Japan as the Other. By this I mean not the pejorative Other, although

---

[29] Harry Harootunian (1988), 10.
[30] Ibid.
[31] Quoted by Kitajima Ken (1974).

elements of it are still very much alive. Behind the heroic subversives, after all, is still a ruthless and tyrannical system, little changed from 1946. It is the other Other, though, that is coming to the fore, with the heroic subversives depicted as subscribing to our beliefs and sharing our aspirations. This Other is produced first by a process of pasteurization, in which praiseworthy features are emphasized to the exclusion of others less flattering. So, for example, Najita's depiction of the Kaitokudō as "a sanctuary," an island of peace and safety in a hostile world, where scholars were able to reaffirm the worth of the merchant class, and freely exchange ideas in an atmosphere of intellectual equality, may well owe more to the ideal Kaitokudō than the real one. The notion of "sanctuary," for example, sits uncomfortably with an institution which was founded with official approval in 1724, and as much as seventy years later was still given government money to help with repairs. The Kaitokudō's commitment to commerce, a raison d'être, in a merchant academy, one would have thought, was oddly muted. Yamagata Bantō, one of the Kaitokudō's luminaries, had declared that "Agriculture should be encouraged while commerce should be discouraged,"[32] while Nakai Chikuzan, another, although prepared to allow commercial activity in Osaka, seems otherwise to have had serious reservations about both cities and commerce: Edo, which had outstripped his own city in commercial importance, he thought should be cut down to size, and cities in general he condemned as places where "simple and honest people lack food and clothing, while those who are vicious and corrupt make huge profits."[33] As for a community of equals, the Kaitokudō was no more devoted to this concept, desirable though it may be in twentieth-century eyes, than to any other Tokugawa-period institution. Heredity, not equality, governed succession to its leadership, as the progression from Nakai Shūan to his son Nakai Chikuzan and then to his grandson Nakai Shoen indicates. Similarly, the Kaitokudō's commitment to the ideal of a full and frank exchange of views, consonant with the standards of its own time rather than ours, may be judged by its expulsion of the fifteen-year-old Tominaga Nakamoto, who had written an essay disagreeing with his teachers.

---

[32] Quoted in Charles D. Sheldon (1958), 141 n. 32.
[33] Kobori Kazumasa (1984), 69-70.

The second way in which Tokugawa Japan is eased back towards the status of the Other is the amusing and familiar invocation ritual, in which postmodern scholars compete with each other to see who can claim the largest number of intellectual patrons. By it the historian summons up the spirits of Western theorists, many of them dead French men, to assist in the elucidation of Tokugawa reality—insofar, of course, as reality can be said to exist, or, if it exists, can ever be comprehended by those from a later historical imaginary. Traces of this practice were certainly not unknown in the past; we have seen E. Herbert Norman stalking Andō Shōeki from the concealment offered by a thicket of European worthies. In the main, however, it usually consisted of a brisk nod in the direction of Weber, or, to a lesser extent, Marx, before moving on to empirical work, and much of the best scholarship resisted the temptation altogether. Ronald Dore's *Education in Tokugawa Japan*, still very much in use, is an example. Over the entire 316 pages of this work Dore felt compelled to refer to just five books or papers not specifically related to the history of Japan, and named just two individuals from a non-Japanese context: one of them was Lord Baden-Powell, and the other Sir James Stephen.

Harry Harootunian, by contrast, pulls out all the postmodernist stops. Within the brief space of the twenty-two-page Prologue to his study of *kokugaku*, he manages, by hook or by crook, to declare his solidarity with the following: Louis Althusser, Michel Foucault, John Frow, Hayden White, Paul de Man, Emile Benveniste, Frederic Jameson, Catherine Belsey, Paul Ricoeur, Pierre Macherey, Pierre Bourdieu, Tony Bennett, Theodor Adorno, Julia Kristeva, Jacques Derrida, and Ernst Bloch—that's sixteen, and some of them are mentioned more than once. Well, you might say, it could be worse. He has omitted Saussure, Bakhtin, Roland Barthes, Jurgen Habermas, and Jacques Lacan. But actually the first two are mentioned, although only at second-hand, while Barthes, Habermas, and Lacan, not to be denied, emerge in later chapters, along with Perry Anderson, Kenneth Burke, Claude Lévi-Strauss, Terry Eagleton, and many more. Once more Tokugawa Japan receives a Western imprint, as if it cannot be decoded without the assistance of really respectable Western theorists.

All of this, it seems to me, is taking us not closer to Tokugawa Japan, but further away. What were the Japanese people of the time really like? There are two possible ways of looking at them.

One sees them as just like us; the other as not just like us. All of us who work in this field operate in the space offered between these two extremes. In some obvious respects, certainly, the people of Tokugawa Japan were much like ourselves. But that is far from the whole story. In other ways they were rather different, alien and, perhaps, when viewed from a Western standpoint, whether of the late nineteenth or the late twentieth century, not wholly admirable; they accepted some things which we would not wish to, did things of which we would not necessarily approve, believed things we cannot. To support one extreme, that of similarity, it is essential not to look too closely, for the closer you look the more the differences become apparent, and the nearer you edge towards the alien extreme. To acknowledge differences, on the other hand, to recognize what makes them (in our eyes, but not in theirs) strange, is to be accused of treating them as the Other. This could be interpreted as a form of discrimination—racist, perhaps, culture-bound, perhaps, lacking in sympathy, perhaps, and guilty of dismissively stuffing Tokugawa Japan into a box reserved for the exotic, the curious, and the comic.

Equally, however, I wonder if it might not also be treating Tokugawa Japan as the Other to concentrate too exclusively on what makes them like us. By straining to see the Japanese of the Tokugawa period as people just like ourselves, albeit with funny haircuts and somewhat undernourished, to see them as aspiring to the things to which we aspire, as sharing our sense of what is rational, of what is right and proper—this is also to see them as the Other, no less than the earlier habit of attributing to them deficiencies they did not deserve. The more we try to squeeze their world into a shape resembling ours, even with the best motives, the more we refuse them their individuality, their humanity, their right to be unlike us, the more we distance ourselves from them. It can lead to distortions of the Tokugawa past, but more than that, I think it denies the Japanese of the Tokugawa period their own place in the history of mankind.

The same can be said of engaging Tokugawa Japan from a distance, crouched behind a phalanx of European theorists, none of whom would wish to claim any particular knowledge of the subject. What is more, most of them would appear to have been consulted in translation, which raises another problem; if lucidity is illusory, and words are opaque and layered and all, how can you be sure, first, that the translator has understood the original, and second, that you have understood the translator? Even leaving aside the next step—how can you be sure your reader will understand you?—the mind, as they say, boggles at the complexities.

Fortunately, we still have Japanese scholars to show us how to approach the history of the Tokugawa period, and they seem to have no need of exotic stimulants. The eighteen-volume *Nihon no kinsei*,[34] published between 1991 and 1994, mentions just five non-Japanese theorists—Peter Laslett, Marc Bloch, Louis Mumford, Bruno Taut, and R. Whiting—in its thousands of pages. The five-volume *Atarashii kinsei shi*[35] increases the number to nine, Weber, Norman, Braudel, and Wallerstein among them, but not one would qualify for inclusion in the postmodern pantheon. In Japan, at least, the wave of the future does not seem to have overtaken the past.

Bibliography

Asao Naohiro, and Tsuji Tatsuya, eds. 1991-94. *Nihon no kinsei*. Chūō kōronsha.
Bellah, Robert N. 1957. *Tokugawa Religion: The Cultural Roots of Modern Japan*. Glencoe, Ill.: Free Press.
Bernstein, Gail Lee, ed. 1991. *Recreating Japanese Women, 1600-1945*. Berkeley: University of California Press.
Bix, Herbert P. 1986. *Peasant Protest in Japan, 1590-1884*. New Haven: Yale University Press.
Bodart-Bailey, Beatrice. 1998. "Kaempfer Restor'd." *Monumenta Nipponica* 43, no. 1.
Bolitho, Harold. 1974. *Treasures among Men: The Fudai Daimyo in Tokugawa Japan*. New Haven: Yale University Press.
———. 1980. "Concrete Discourse, Manifest Metaphor and the Tokugawa Intellectual Paradigm." *Monumenta Nipponica* 35, no. 1: 89-98.
Brown, Philip C. 1993. *Central Authority and Local Autonomy in the Formation of Early Modern Japan: The Case of Kaga Domain*. Stanford: Stanford University Press.
Clement, Ernest. 1915. *A Short History of Japan*. Chicago: University of Chicago Press.
Dickson, Walter. 1898. *Japan*. New York: P. F. Collier.
Dore, Ronald P. 1965. *Education in Tokugawa Japan*. Berkeley: University of California Press.
Elison, George. 1973. *Deus Destroyed: The Image of Christianity in Early Modern Japan*. Cambridge: Harvard University Press.

---

[34] Asao Naohiro and Tsuji Tatsuya, eds. (1991-94).
[35] Yamamoto Hirofumi, et al., eds. (1996).

Gerstle, C. Andrew, ed. 1989. *18th Century Japan: Culture and Society*. London: Allen and Unwin.
Hall, John Whitney. 1955. *Tanuma Okitsugu, 1719-1788, Forerunner of Modern Japan*. Cambridge: Harvard University Press.
———. 1966. *Government and Local Power in Japan, 500 to 1700: A Study Based on Bizan Province*. Princeton: Princeton University Press.
Hanley, Susan B. 1997. *Everday Things in Premodern Japan: The Hidden Legacy of Material Culture*. Berkeley: University of California Press.
Hanley, Susan, B., and Kozo Yamamura. 1977. *Economic and Demographic Change in Preindustrial Japan, 1600-1868*. Princeton: Princeton University Press.
Harootunian, H. D. 1988. *Things Seen and Unseen: Discourse and Ideology in Tokugawa Nativism*. Chicago: University of Chicago Press.
Hauser, William B. 1974. *Economic Institutional Change in Tokugawa Japan: Osaka and the Kinai Cotton Trade*. Cambridge: Cambridge University Press.
Heine, Steven. 1994. "Tragedy and Salvation in the Floating World: Chikamatsu's Double Suicide Drama as Millenarian Discourse." *Journal of Asian Studies* 53, no. 2: 367-93.
Hibbett, Howard. 1959. *The Floating World in Japanese Fiction*. New York: Oxford University Press.
Howell, David L. 1995. *Capitalism from Within: Economy, Society and the State in a Japanese Fishery*. Berkeley: University of California Press.
Ikegami, Eiko. 1995. *The Taming of the Samurai: Honorific Individualism and the Making of Modern Japan*. Cambridge: Harvard University Press.
Janetta, Ann Bowman. 1987. *Epidemics and Mortality in Early Modern Japan*. Princeton: Princeton University Press.
Jones, Sumie, ed. 1996. *Imaging Reading Eros: Proceedings for the Conference, Sexuality and Edo Culture, 1750-1850*. Bloomington: Indiana University Press.
Kaempfer, Engelbert. 1906. *History of Japan*. 3 vols. Glasgow: J. MacLehose.
Kalland, Arne. 1995. *Fishing Villages in Tokugawa Japan*. Honolulu: University of Hawai'i Press.
Kassel, Marleen. 1996. *Tokugawa Confucian Education: The Kangien Academy of Hirose Tanso (1782-1856)*. Albany: State University of New York Press.
Katsu, Kokichi. 1988. *Musui's Story: The Autobiography of a Tokugawa Samurai*. Translated by Teruko Craig. Tucson: University of Arizona Press.
Keene, Donald. 1952. *The Japanese Discovery of Europe: Honda Toshiaki and Other Discoverers, 1720-1978*. London: Routledge and Kegan Paul.
Kelly, William W. 1985. *Deference and Defiance in Nineteenth-Century Japan*. Princeton: Princeton University Press.
Kirkwood, Kenneth. 1938. *Renaissance in Japan: A Cultural Survey of the Seventeenth Century*. Tokyo: Meiji Press.
Kitajima Ken. 1974. *Hirata Atsutane to nyūgaku mondō. Hanpon Bunko*. Kokusho kankōkai.
Knox, G. William. 1903. "Autobiography of Arai Hakuseki." *Transactions of the Asiatic Society of Japan* 30.
Kobori Kazumasa. 1984. "Nakai Chikuzan no rekishikan — sono haibutsuron o chūshin toshite." In *Nihon kindai no seiritsu to tenkai*, edited by Umetani Akira kyōju taikan kinen rombunshū kankōkai, 57-76. Kyoto: Shibunkai.
Kumazawa Banzan. 1938. *Daigaku wakumon*. Translated by Galen M. Fisher as "Dai Gaku Wakumon. By Kumazawa Banzan." *Transactions of the Asiatic Society of Japan*, 2nd series 16.
Leupp, Gary P. 1992. *Servants, Shophands, and Laborers in the Cities of Tokugawa Japan*. Princeton: Princeton University Press.

———. 1995. *The Construction of Homosexuality in Tokugawa Japan*. Berkeley: University of California Press.
Lidin, Olof. 1973. *The Life of Ogyu Sorai, a Tokugawa Confucian Philosopher*. Lund: Scandinavian Institute of Asian Studies.
McClain, James L. 1982. *Kanazawa: A Seventeenth-Century Japanese Castle Town*. New Haven: Yale University Press.
McEwan, J. R. 1962. *The Political Writings of Ogyu Sorai*. Cambridge: Cambridge University Press.
Mercer, Rosemary. 1991. *Deep Words: Miura Baien's System of Natural Philosophy*. Leiden: E. J. Brill.
Minear, Richard H. 1976. "Ogyu Sorai's Instructions for Students: A Translation and Commentary." *Harvard Journal of Asiatic Studies* 36.
Miyoshi, Masao. 1991. *Off Center: Power and Cultural Relations Between Japan and the United States*. Cambridge: Harvard University Press.
Murdoch, James. 1926. *A History of Japan, Nation of the World*. London: P. F. Collier.
Murray, David. 1894. *Japan*. New York: G. P. Putnam and London: T. F. Unwin.
Najita, Tetsuo. 1978. "Method and Analysis in the Conceptual Portrayal of Tokugawa Intellectual History." In Najita and Scheiner, eds. (1978).
———. 1987. *Visions of Virtue in Tokugawa Japan: The Kaitokudo Merchant Academy of Osaka*. Chicago: University of Chicago Press.
Najita, Tetsuo, and Irwin Scheiner, eds. 1978. *Japanese Thought in the Tokugawa Period*. Chicago: University of Chicago Press.
Nakai, Kate Wildman. 1988. *Shogunal Politics: Arai Hakuseki and the Premises of Tokugawa Rule*. Cambridge: Harvard University Press.
Norman, E. Herbert. 1940. *Japan's Emergence as a Modern State: Political and Economic Problems of the Meiji Period*. New York: International Secretariat, Institute of Pacific Relations.
———. 1949. "Andō Shōeki and the Anatomy of Japanese Feudalism." *Transactions of the Asiatic Society of Japan, 3rd series* 2.
Nosco, Peter. 1990. *Remembering Paradise: Nativism and Nostalgia in Eighteenth-Century Japan*. Cambridge: Harvard University Press.
Ooms, Herman. 1975. *Charismatic Bureaucrat: A Political Biography of Matsudaira Sadanobu, 1758-1829*. Chicago: University of Chicago Press.
———. 1984. *Tokugawa Ideology: Early Constructs, 1570-1680*. Princeton: Princeton University Press.
———. 1996a. "Tokugawa Texts as a Playground for a Postmodern Romp." *Journal of Japanese Studies* 22, no. 2: 385-400.
———. 1996b. *Tokugawa Village Practice: Class, Status, Power, Law*. Berkeley: University of California Press.
Pye, Michael. 1990. *Emerging from Meditation*. Honolulu: University of Hawai'i Press.
Roberts, Luke. Forthcoming. *Imagined Economies: Economic Nationalism in Eighteenth-Century Tosa*. Cambridge: Harvard University Press.
Robertson, Jennifer. 1979. "Rooting the Pine: Shingaku Methods of Organization." *Monumenta Nipponica* 33, no. 4: 311-32.
———. 1991. "The Shingaku Woman: Straight from the Heart." In Bernstein, ed. (1991).
Rubinger, Richard. 1982. *Private Academies of Tokugawa Japan*. Princeton: Princeton University Press.
Sadler, Arthur Lindsay. 1937. *The Maker of Modern Japan: The Life of Tokugawa Ieyasu*. London: Allen and Unwin.
Sakai, Naoki. 1991. *Voices of the Past: The Status of Language in Eighteenth-Century Japan*. Ithaca: Cornell University Press.

Sansom, George. 1943 [1931]. *Japan: A Short Cultural History*. Rev. ed. New York: Appleton-Century-Crofts.
Sawada, Janine Anderson. 1993. *Confucian Values and Popular Zen: Sekimon Shingaku in Eighteenth-Century Japan*. Honolulu: University of Hawai'i Press.
Scheiner, Irwin. 1973. "The Mindful Peasant: Sketches for a Study of Rebellion." *Journal of Asian Studies* 32, no. 4.
———. 1978. "Benevolent Lords and Honorable Peasants: Rebellion and Peasant Consciousness in Tokugawa Japan." In Najita and Scheiner, eds. (1978), 39-62.
Screech, Timon. 1993. "The Strangest Place in Edo: The Temple of the Five Hundred Arhats." *Monumenta Nipponica* 48, no. 4: 407-28.
Seigle, Cecilia Segawa. 1993. *Yoshiwara: The Glittering World of the Japanese Courtesan*. Honolulu: University of Hawai'i Press.
Sheldon, Charles D. 1958. *The Rise of the Merchant Class in Tokugawa Japan, 1600-1868: An Introductory Survey*. Monographs of the Association for Asian Studies, no. 5. Locust Valley, N.Y.: J. J. Augustin; published for the Association for Asian Studies.
Shively, Donald H. 1953. *The Love Suicide at Amijima ["Shinjū tenno Amijima"]: A Study of a Japanese Domestic Tragedy*. Cambridge: Harvard University Press.
Sippel, Patricia. 1977. "Popular Protest in Early Modern Japan: The Bushū Outburst." *Harvard Journal of Asiatic Studies* 37.
Smith, Neil Skene. 1934. "An Introduction to Some Japanese Economic Writings of the 18th Century." *Transactions of the Asiatic Society of Japan*, 2nd series 11.
Smith, Thomas C. 1959. *The Agrarian Origins of Modern Japan*. Stanford: Stanford University Press.
———. 1977. *Nakahara: Family Farming and Population in a Japanese Village, 1717-1830*. Stanford: Stanford University Press.
Spae, Joseph J. 1948. *Ito Jinsai: A Philosopher, Educator and Sinologist of the Tokugawa Period*. Peiping: Catholic University of Peking.
Toby, Ronald P. 1983. *State and Diplomacy in Early Modern Japan: Asia in the Development of the Tokugawa Bakufu*. Princeton: Princeton University Press.
Totman, Conrad. 1967. *Politics in the Tokugawa Bakufu, 1600-1843*. Cambridge: Harvard University Press.
———. 1995. *The Lumber Industry in Early Modern Japan*. Honolulu: University of Hawai'i Press.
Tsukahira, Toshio George. 1966. *Feudal Control in Tokugawa Japan: The Sankin Kotai System*. Cambridge: Harvard University Press.
Tucker, Mary Evelyn. 1989. *Moral and Spiritual Cultivation in Japanese Neo-Confucianism: The Life and Thought of Kaibara Ekken (1630-1714)*. Albany: State University of New York Press.
Vaporis, Constantine Nomikos. 1994. *Breaking Barriers: Travel and the State in Early Modern Japan*. Cambridge: Harvard University Press.
Vlastos, Stephen. 1986. *Peasant Protests and Uprisings in Tokugawa Japan*. Berkeley: University of California Press.
Wakabayashi, Bob Tadashi. 1986. *Anti-Foreignism and Western Learning in Early-Modern Japan: The New Theses of 1825*. Cambridge: Harvard University Press.
———. 1995. *Japanese Loyalism Reconstructed: Yamagata Daini's "Ryūshi shinron" of 1759*. Honolulu: University of Hawai'i Press.
Walthall, Anne. 1986. *Social Protest and Popular Culture in Eighteenth-Century Japan*. Tucson: University of Arizona Press.
White, James W. 1995. *Ikki: Social Conflict and Political Protest in Early Modern Japan*. Ithaca: Cornell University Press.

Wigen, Kären. 1995. *The Making of a Japanese Periphery, 1750-1920*. Berkeley: University of California Press.

Wigmore, John Henry. 1996. *Law and Justice in Tokugawa Japan: Materials for the History of Japanese Law and Justice under the Tokugawa Shogunate*. Kokusai bunka shinkōkai, 1891-1941.

Yamamoto Hirofumi, et al., eds. *Atarashii kinsei shi*. Shinjinbutsu ōraisha.

Yamamura, Kozo. 1974. *A Study of Samurai Income and Entrepreneurship: Quantitative Analyses of Economic and Social Aspects of the Samurai in Tokugawa and Meiji Japan*. Cambridge: Harvard University Press.

Yamashita, Samuel Hideo. 1994. *Master Sorai's Responsals: An Annotated Translation of "Sorai sensei tōmonsho"*. Honolulu: University of Hawai'i Press.

———. 1996. "Reading the New Tokugawa Intellectual Histories." *Journal of Japanese Studies* 22, no. 1: 1-48.

THE MEIJI RESTORATION: A HISTORIOGRAPHICAL OVERVIEW

Albert M. Craig

The Meiji Restoration is the defining event in modern Japanese history. Crane Brinton once said that if he knew what a person thought of the French Revolution, he could predict their views on contemporary politics. Perhaps one can say this of the Meiji Restoration as well. Certainly, any comparison of the two events would have to admit that the Restoration led to changes of a far greater magnitude in Japan than those produced by the Revolution in France. For though it began as a modest rearrangement of political power—from daimyo under a shogun to daimyo under the emperor—it set in play forces that unleashed a cultural and social revolution in Japan.

In this chapter, I treat English language works on the Meiji Restoration, primarily those of American and British scholars, with an emphasis on post-World War II studies. This means I will omit any discussion of the writings of Perry, Harris, Heusken, Satow, Alcock, Baelz, Boisonnade, Francis Hall, or Clara Whitney. While important as primary sources, such works have little direct bearing on recent interpretations. I will also skip over the bulk of prewar Japanological studies of the kind represented by the *Transactions of the Asiatic Society of Japan*. These were mostly done by teachers, missionaries, businessmen, and diplomats who were resident in Japan. The best of their work, by McLaren, Skene Smith, and others, was admirable and is still useful. Even in treating postwar research, I will focus principally on the works that have influenced my own thinking, for writings on the Restoration era are so numerous that any attempt to be comprehensive would end up as an annotated bibliography.[1] From time to time, in the course of describing what has been accomplished, I also will try to point out areas where more research is needed.

Furthermore, I will not attempt to delineate even the contours of Japanese scholarship on the Restoration—except where they

---

[1] For a more complete listing of works, see the excellent bibliography by John Dower with Timothy George (1995).

bear directly on interpretations given in Western works. It would be too great a task. In every developed country the study of that country's history is a minor industry. This is as true of Japan as it is of the United States. Japanese studies of the transition from the late Tokugawa era to the early Meiji are like a river, broad, deep, and fed by a continuous flow of new studies. There is even a separate scholarly association (Meiji Ishin Shigakkai) solely for studies of the history of the Restoration. By way of contrast, Western studies of the period may be likened to pitchers of water dipped from the river.

This does not mean that Western studies of the Restoration are necessarily derivative: many are based solidly on primary sources. Some take issue with the findings of Japanese scholars. And, since they are interpreting Japan to the West, they inevitably have a somewhat different perspective. But even taking these points into account, it is also true that Western studies of Japan frequently take the form of an "interrupted discourse." That is to say, new research may largely ignore previous English language studies in favor of drawing fresh water directly from the river. Even today huge areas of Japanese monographic research still remain unexplored by Western scholarship.

Yet another factor affecting Western studies of the Restoration period is language. We read with ease the *Declaration of Independence*, which is over two hundred years old, and Locke's *Second Treatise of Government*, which is over three hundred years old. Whether we adequately grasp the ideas they contain or not, the language is about the same as present-day English. In contrast, the Japanese language has changed markedly during the past century or so since the Restoration. Present-day Japanese high school students usually cannot read historical documents written prior to the Restoration; they learn to read them while studying Japanese history at a university but not without a considerable effort. For the American or European scholar, the learning curve is steeper, the effort greater, and the result often meager. A Western scholar who reads modern newspapers with no difficulty whatever will spend long and painful hours plowing through the *Ōkubo kankei monjo*. Research on diplomatic history, as described by Akira Iriye, may have a level playing field, since Japanese scholars have almost as many difficulties with Western archives as we have with theirs. But for mid-nineteenth century Japanese history, the playing field is not level and will not become so in the foreseeable future.

For purposes of description, the historiography of the Restoration period might be broken down into three areas: the study of those who were not samurai, the study of those who were, and the study of changing currents of ideas and culture.

Commoners and Restoration History

In late Tokugawa Japan, about 85 percent of the population lived in villages, another 9 percent were non-samurai living in towns and cities, and the remaining 6 percent were samurai. Each of these demographic segments was diverse. Villagers included not only farmers and fishermen but priests, artisans, local merchants, schoolmasters, and others as well. City dwellers included such a great variety of mercantile, artisanal, and service establishments that any listing would be tedious. Moreover, each segment was highly stratified and regional differences were immense. Keeping in mind, then, the difficulties of generalization, the first question that might be posed is the role commoners played in the events leading up to the Restoration.

In English there is no book that deals specifically with urban society or urban commoner self-government during the *bakumatsu* (1853-1868) period.[2] This affects the way history is written. For example, when Chōshū troops tried to recapture Kyoto in 1864, they were driven back by the troops of Aizu, Kuwana, and other pro-*bakufu* domains. Descriptions of the event quite properly focus on the samurai combatants. But the Kyoto they fought in is presented as almost featureless. We are given no information about the actions of commoners and commoner officials. Presumably they were trying to stay out of the way of the fighting and attempting to put out the fires that destroyed two-thirds of the city. But we do not know. No scholar has addressed the issue. Much of the politicking of the *bakumatsu* era took place in cities, but we know little of the wards and local administration in Edo during the declining years of Tokugawa rule—to say nothing of Osaka, Nagasaki, and the many castletowns. As Tokugawa authority waned, did the authority of local commoner officials also wane, or did

---

[2] There are some articles, for example by William Steele (1990).

their self-government become stronger to compensate for the indecision at higher levels? Research is needed.

Future studies of *bakumatsu* urban society will no doubt turn directly to Japanese research. But they may begin by drawing on general studies of the Tokugawa city such as those by Noel Nouet (1961); Takeo Yazaki (1968); Gilbert Rozman (1973); Edward Seidensticker (1983); and James McClain, John Merriman, and Kaoru Ugawa, eds. (1994). Also important is the research, which has appeared in articles and chapters of books, by John Hall, Akira Hayami, Gilbert Rozman, Robert Smith, Henry Smith, William Steele, and others.[3]

One question of particular interest concerning late Tokugawa urban society is the measure of its social stability. Did the "crowd" play a role in *bakumatsu* history? Foreign visitors were uniformly amazed by the orderliness of the society, or, perhaps, by its compliance to the authority of officials. Alcock, together with several compatriots, at one point visited Odawara, a seacoast town to the southwest of Edo. All of the townspeople turned out to view the strange-looking foreigners. Alcock wrote, "a waving sea of heads seemed to bar our passage."

> I felt some curiosity as to the mode they would take to open a way through the dense mass of swaying bodies and excited heads, which looked all the more formidable the nearer we approached. My guides, however, seemed perfectly unembarrassed, and well they might be, for when within a few steps of the foremost ranks, there was a wave of a fan and a single word of command issued "Shitanirio" (kneel down), when, as if by magic, a wide path was opened, and every head dropped, the body disappearing in some marvelous way behind the legs and knees of its owner. Certainly Harlequin's wand or Aladdin's *sesame* never produced a more sudden or scenic effect. I could not help thinking how much more easily the wonder was wrought...than would have been possible in the streets of London. If the magic fan and word could only be imported for the use of our policemen, without losing their spell-like effect, there is no saying what amount might be saved in yearly police-rates.[4]

Nor was this an unusual occurrence. Henry Heusken, accompanying Townsend Harris to Edo a few years earlier, noted the "vast multitude," that had turned out to view their procession. "If

---

[3] The articles by Hayami, Rozman, and H. Smith in Marius Jansen and Gilbert Rozman, eds. (1986) deal with this era.

[4] Rutherford Alcock (1969).

people pressed too far forwards...an officer shaking his fan sufficed to cause hundreds of persons to step back." Contrasting Japan with Europe, Heusken's *Japan Journal* continued:

> If one of our great capitals found itself in the same situation as the city of Edo today, how many children would have been crushed under foot, and how many women would have died from lack of oxygen! How much profanity seasoned by a liberal use of spiritous beverages! What a tumult; how many hurrahs and shrill cries! And I have no doubt that rotten apples and even stones would have been thrown, aimed at the sacred features of the members of the Embassy.[5]

These direct observations, it should be emphasized, were made at a time when "feudal" authority was declining. How do such evidences of a comparatively firm social order balance off against the evidences of social conflict, and how do they relate to the processes leading to the Restoration?

More research has been done on late Tokugawa rural society and most of it is of high quality. In connection with it, some of the same kind of questions can be posed: what was the nature of local self-government and what was the balance between stability and instability? Few studies focus on the *bakumatsu* as such, but most works on Tokugawa rural society devote one or two chapters to it.

The backdrop for Western research in this area was the Japanese writings on social and economic history which had appeared during the 1920s and 1930s, and the Marxist historical writings which began during the same era and re-emerged with such force and vitality after World War II. Japanese historians put forth a variety of interpretations, but all agreed that the Meiji Restoration was a bourgeois revolution of sorts. They saw the driving force of the Restoration as emerging from the non-samurai sectors of the society. At first their emphasis was placed on big city merchants but later shifted to those involved in rural industries and commerce. They also agreed, following their model of a bourgeois revolution, that social conflict, and not social stability, was the key to understanding the processes leading to the Restoration. They discovered hundreds of peasant uprisings, protests, village disturbances, and the like in the thirty-year period between the Tempō reforms and the early 1870s. Their research laid to rest forever

---

[5] Henry Heusken (1964), 141.

the image—if it had ever existed—of the farmer as docile, passive, and submissive.

In Western writings, the pioneering work in this area was by Hugh Borton (1938). Borton formulated for a Western audience some of the research findings of Ono Takeo and Kokushō Iwao, two giants of the prewar school of social and economic history.

After World War II, the earliest work, and one that remains a landmark was by Thomas Smith (1959).[6] Smith was concerned to analyze the effect of the rising market economy on the traditional village, and the relationship between these changes and the emergence of a modern industrial labor force. He concluded:

> For upward of two hundred years the agricultural labor force had been unwittingly preparing for the transition to factory employment. Commercial farming and the experience of working for wages had taught peasants to respond with alacrity to monetary incentives....[7]

But Smith's study also documented the internal stability of the village. The balance between the newly rich and the old social elites, between the *hirakata* and *zakata*, shifted only glacially over the course of many decades.[8]

After Smith there was a hiatus during the sixties and seventies, followed by a rash of new research during the eighties and nineties. Most of the new works dealt with uprisings and protest and examined areas in eastern and northeastern Japan. A study by Neil Waters (1983) was exceptional for its focus on an area in which "nothing happened." He demonstrated that, in fact, a great deal was happening even without the drama of peasant uprisings. William Kelly, combining history and anthropology, wrote on four popular protest movements in the Shōnai domain in northeastern Japan (1985). The study was notable for its linkage of village-level events with *bakufu* and domain-level decision-making. The next year were published studies by Anne Walthall, with an Epilogue that covered "The Tenmei Period and Beyond"; Stephen Vlastos, with a focus on the Kanto region and Aizu; and Herbert Bix, the final part of which dealt with class conflict during the

---

[6] It was followed in 1977 by *Nakahara: Family, Farming, and Population in a Japanese Village*, and in 1988 by *Native Sources of Japanese Industrialization, 1750-1920*, a collection of Smith's many articles.

[7] Thomas Smith (1959), 212.

[8] Another early work, containing detailed information on the village in which Shibusawa Eiichi was born, was by William Chambliss (1965).

nineteenth century. In 1991, Walthall published a second work, translations of five histories of peasant uprisings written by peasants themselves, making primary materials on this topic available in English for the first time. In 1992, George Wilson's work on the *ee ja nai ka* movement came out. In 1995, James White, a historically-minded political scientist, published a work containing case studies which were not dissimilar to those in earlier works, but it broke new ground in its quantitative analysis of Japanese data on political protests.

Other works, peripheral to the Restoration but treating aspects of village economies, are by Conrad Totman (1989); Arne Kalland (1994); Kären Wigen (1995), a study of trade in the Ina Valley region near Mount Fuji; and David Howell (1995).

The above studies draw on both original sources and Japanese secondary works. Their findings, on the whole, are judicious. Disagreements between them usually are a matter of different regional patterns. A few of the conclusions and questions that emerge from these works are the following:

1) All studies agree that the rise of a market economy led to social stratification in the village. By the *bakumatsu* era, all villages in commercially advanced areas were composed of landlords, small farmers, and tenants. The land may have "belonged" to the lord, but it was "owned," as landlordism demonstrates, by commoners in the village. There is no consensus, however, regarding the baseline from which the change occurred. In some areas, early Tokugawa villages appear to have been communities of equals (*honbyakushō*) which gradually became more stratified. In others, in a pattern described by T. Smith, the ownership of land by hierarchically organized, extended families gave way to ownership by individual families. In still others, such as the Satsuma, Tosa, and Saga domains, the presence in the village of rural samurai shaped yet another pattern. In the English literature on the Tokugawa village we still lack a clear typology of regional patterns.

2) As landlords and landless peasants emerged, tensions arose within villages. Early Japanese research had focused on peasant uprisings (*ikki*), the most visible evidence of the rising tensions. In the early postwar era, the scholar Tōyama Shigeki in a now classic work, *Meiji ishin*, saw these tensions as the basic contradiction in Japanese society, the peasantry as the driving force behind the Meiji Restoration, and Japan as standing on the brink of peasant

wars of the sort that had raged in the Germanies several centuries earlier. Today such a view has few adherents. Scholars recognize, rather, a spectrum of village reactions to demands from above for increased taxation, that range from normal, quotidian, deferential resistance, to mild protests couched in language both polite and moralistic, to more strenuous protests which erupted only rarely in violent *ikki*.

3) The emphasis has shifted, accordingly, toward a recognition of the importance of village (or even regional) self-government by commoners, and of the competence of such bodies. Peasants—and by the 1850s "farmers" might be the better term—are no longer seen as *gumin*: illiterate, apathetic, docile, and passive. Instead, they are seen as locally active, with their own values and culture that defined clear notions of what was acceptable and what was not. They may not have had an abstract concept of "rights" as such, but they had clear expectations, which were based on past customs and practices. Even while accepting the existing sociopolitical order, they are seen as working consciously and consistently to forward their own interests. As M. William Steele puts it, they had "locally generated agendas," and they "attempted to right perceived wrongs and enhance the inherited tradition of local autonomy."[9] Moreover, they were often effective in advancing their interests. Vlastos writes that because of collective action by peasants, "tax extraction failed to keep pace with increases in agricultural output."[10] White, going a step further, argues: "One of the key reasons they [the samurai] were so poor is that lords found it easier to cut their stipends than to risk confrontation with the people over increased taxes."[11]

4) These writings raise questions about the position of village leaders. Most studies agree that early Tokugawa villages were politically united and socially homogeneous. As such, they often rose against samurai authority. But in the more socially stratified villages of the later Tokugawa era, poor peasants were more likely to attack village officials and other wealthy peasants.[12] Vlastos, for example, sees the wealthy *gōnō* of Fukushima as standing apart from others in the village, and becoming thereby the target for

---

[9] M. William Steele (unpublished paper), 22-23.
[10] Stephen Vlastos (1986), 160.
[11] James White (1995), 290.
[12] Vlastos (1986), 159; White, ibid., 307.

the resentments of poorer peasants. The existence of the rich in a society often terribly poor conflicted, he argues, with villagers' assumptions regarding a "moral economy." Waters has a similar view of the moral assumptions underlying village society but argues that, at least in Kawasaki, village leaders were a part of the social fabric. They joined in regional *kumiai*, which at times dunned the rich for the welfare of the poor. In short, he sees village leaders as participating in and contributing to the moral economy. A chapter in a recent Japanese book on the Restoration is closer to Waters. Kurushima Hiroshi (1995) looks at the Kinai region of western Japan where there were relatively few uprisings during the pre-Restoration era. In this region, he argues, the economic *kyōdōtai* of the early and middle eighteenth century was gradually replaced by a moral *kyōdōtai* in which village leaders were required to take on welfare responsibilities. He explains the paucity of uprisings in terms of their willingness to do so. Kurushima further claims that this "more advanced" Kinai pattern was the prototype for Japan's Meiji advance toward modernity.

If the gap between Waters and Vlastos reflects different regional patterns, we are faced with the question of distribution. White's quantitative analysis provides valuable answers, suggesting that contention was geographically skewed. He discovered that 3 percent of all counties accounted for 25 percent of all contentious events, and that close to 12 percent of counties recorded no contention whatsoever. Even more striking was his finding that "actual contention was rare, occurring in less than 5 percent of all the county-years of Tokugawa Japan."[13] And not only were uprisings rare, but most were local, of short duration, and concerned with particular grievances. There are instances, to be sure, in which feuds, generated by uprisings, continued over generations, but they are the exception. In most cases, when the protest ended, the local order was put back together again. After his fine-grained analysis of protest movements in Shōnai, Kelly concludes, "none of the four movements revealed or precipitated enduring solidarities of community, party, or class."[14]

5) Most accounts agree that peasant uprisings were not integral to the Restoration movement, that they were not used by one

---

[13] White, ibid., 278, 285.
[14] William Kelly (1985), 287.

side against the other, and had, in fact, little direct effect on it. Vlastos writes, "There is absolutely no evidence of...attempts to forge alliances with anti-Tokugawa samurai bands." White writes, "I have found no real link between contention [in the countryside] and Restoration."[15] Vlastos does point out, however, that peasant movements may have "hastened the collapse of Tokugawa feudalism, at least indirectly," since the majority of uprisings in the 1866-1869 years "occurred in eastern Japan in areas administered by the *bakufu* and fiefs of daimyo traditionally allied with the Tokugawa house."[16] This contention is plausible, and may some day be shown to be true. But so far all we have is a statistical correlation. Furthermore, if the uprisings weakened the *bakufu* during 1866 and 1867, why did they not weaken the newborn Meiji government during 1868 and 1869? Until 1871, the infant court government also was centered on the old *bakufu* lands in eastern Japan. The simple answer is that the *bakufu* tolerated uprisings and the Meiji government did not. If that is so, the emphasis shifts from the village to the nature of superordinate authority.

Finally, even if peasant uprisings made no direct contribution to the Restoration movement, the case can still be made that the condition of the countryside during the 1850s and 1860s was crucial to the movement in another sense. Taking several steps back and gazing at the whole of the society, we see it was composed of daimyo and shogunal domains. Each domain was self-governing. None collapsed during the *bakumatsu* years, none was taken over by a stronger neighbor, and virtually all continued to govern their areas until abolished in 1871. Within each domain were at least two layers of commoner self-government—subordinate to the domain but with large areas of autonomy. If only 5 percent of "county-years" saw contention, it follows that the other 95 percent did not. All in all, this suggests a fairly stable society.[17] This stabi-

---

[15] Vlastos (1986), 162; White (1995), 291.

[16] Vlastos, ibid., 165-66.

[17] My summation accords with the conclusions of the majority of works cited above. Wilson and Bix offer a higher appreciation of peasant uprisings, and might disagree. But let me reiterate that when I speak of stability, I am not speaking of a utopic state of harmony and tranquillity. Tensions over matters such as the allocation of taxes, communal labor, social rankings, village offices, water for irrigation, and the use of common lands, were universal. Yet as long as local leaders effectively managed the tensions and conflicts, villages remained stable. A second obvious point is that statistics are open to interpretation. If 5 percent

lity squares with the observations of Westerners. They noted and took for granted the peace and order of rural society. What amazed them was the effectiveness of public authority in the cities. The stability of the Japanese countryside contrasts markedly with conditions in mid-nineteenth-century China, where popular rebellions of incomparably greater scope almost overthrew the Ch'ing state. It also contrasts with village society in revolutionary France: in Japan taxes were collected throughout the Restoration era, whereas in France tax collection broke down during insurrections and the Great Fear.

If the Restoration movement can be seen as unfolding within a relatively stable society, then several of the movement's features can be more easily explained. One salient feature is that, for a nation of 30 million, so few were involved in Restoration politics. During the political tumult of 1862, Chōshū may have had fewer than one thousand troops in Kyoto. In 1863, the Chōshū forces were ousted from guard duty at the palace by two thousand Aizu troops and a smaller number from Satsuma. The numbers involved in the two most critical turning points of the period were also small. In the first, the 1866 second *bakufu* expedition against Chōshū, several tens of thousands of extremely reluctant troops were mobilized on the *bakufu* side, and they were defeated by fewer than ten thousand on the Chōshū side. The second turning point, which convinced the last shogun that further fighting was futile, was the battle of Toba-Fushimi where five or six thousand Satsuma and Chōshū troops fought against *bakufu* forces two or three times more numerous. Had even a few of the 270 domains sent troops in support of the *bakufu*, it might have won, and the history of the period would have been different. And had large scale peasant insurrections weighed in on either side, the outcome might also have been different. Satsuma could be Satsuma and Chōshū, Chōshū, just because most of the country tended more or less

---

of county-years saw contention, then, over the 15 years of the *bakumatsu* era, we could just as well conclude that 75 percent of Japan saw some contention. Correcting this figure for areas that were repeatedly contentious might bring the figure down, but further correcting it for the larger number of *ikki* in the late sixties might bring it back up again. The real question is how long did the effects of an uprising persist. Memories, no doubt, faded only slowly, but the functioning of a village usually returned to normal very quickly. Contention might well be measured in county-months, rather than county-years.

competently to its own affairs but was unwilling to become involved in national politics.

Even during the years after 1868, social stability remained a key variable. It afforded the new government a breathing space. In some areas the new government was effective from the start. Military threats and violence were dealt with summarily. When Aizu, Shōnai, and other northeastern domains, which had strongly upheld the *bakufu* during the sixties, refused to comply with the government's terms of surrender in 1868, armies were sent against them and they were quickly defeated. When foreigners were attacked, the new government severely punished the attackers. When peasants engaged in uprisings, they were speedily quashed, and, as White notes, the number of uprisings sharply declined after 1869.

But in other areas, the government's actions were far less decisive. The tasks facing the new government during the early years after the Restoration were enormous. The new leaders had to define what the new government would be, and what policies it would follow, while at the same time ridding themselves of the deadwood (mostly nobles, daimyo, and *shishi*) that had entered the government as a part of the Restoration settlement. Though the leaders were undeniably able, they managed to handle these tasks only because they could take for granted a nation composed of stable, self-governing building blocks, and not "a sheet of loose sand." They could afford, from time to time, to fumble, hesitate, and equivocate without penalty.

Faced with the difficult task of bringing the largely autonomous domains under government control, Kido once lamented that the new government was surrounded on all sides by "little *bakufu*." But had he looked at the advantages and not the drawbacks of the situation, he could just as well have said that the multitude of tasks that the new central government was as yet unprepared to take on were being handled quite adequately by local and domain governments. This leeway was critical. Had this stable regional and local order disintegrated after 1868, the new government might well have failed. Waters takes this argument a step further, suggesting that some "hasty" and "ill-conceived" government reforms during the early Meiji years were "modified" in Kawasaki by local leaders: "Their success at blunting the reforms redounded, willy-nilly, to the eventual benefit of the Meiji government because it allowed Meiji leaders to blunder without paying a full penalty."[18]

More research is needed to clarify the setting of the Restoration movement. Most recent research focuses on northeastern Japan. We need more case studies of local societies, including studies of *ikki*, in western Japan, Kyushu, and Shikoku. We need more studies of the normal modalities of local government—picking up where T. Smith left off. Stability and its sources need to be studied directly, and not just backed into in the course of studying contention. In studying local government, including commoner self-government of city wards, we need to examine more of its interaction with domain and *bakufu* governments. Kelly furnishes an example of this. On all of these counts we need to work toward a typology of local societies that will enable the historian to make sense of the obvious diversity of *bakumatsu* Japan.

The Restoration Movement

A second area of Restoration research focuses on the complex political processes which constituted the Restoration movement. Some of these processes continued past the Restoration itself into the first few years of the Meiji era. The actors in the drama were overwhelmingly samurai, though some from other classes also became involved.

Prewar treatments of this subject by McLaren, Murdoch, and others, were largely descriptive and dealt primarily with Japan's foreign relations. Then in 1940, E. H. Norman's pathbreaking work, *Japan's Emergence as a Modern State*, was published. Norman was the first Western historian to come to grips with the more interpretative schools of history that had developed in Japan during the twenties and thirties. As such, he is the starting point for postwar Western writings on the Restoration.

Norman based his interpretation, mainly, on the research of the moderate schools of social and economic history.[19] The names that appear in his footnotes were of economic historians such as Honjō Eijirō, Ono Takeo, Horie Yasuzō, and Takigawa Masujirō—

---

[18] Neil Waters (1983), 130.
[19] The Nihon Keizaishi Gakkai and the Shakai Keizaishi Gakkai were founded in 1930-1931.

scholars who had been influenced by British and German interpretations of the French Revolution as a bourgeois revolution. Norman followed their lead.[20] He emphasized *chōnin* gaining "admission to the warrior class," achieving "high official positions," and steering the "anti-*bakufu* forces through the troubled waters at the end of the Tokugawa period." He also stressed the early Meiji alliance between lower samurai and big merchants, such as the Mitsui, Sumitomo, Kōnoike, Ono, and Yasuda.[21] Today such views have been largely discarded, and Norman's writings are mainly of historiographical interest. But for the generation of scholars who came of age during the 1950s, it is worth recalling that Norman's book was a breath of fresh air, for he had an interpretation at a time when no one else did, and he presented it with style and vigor.

The next important work on the Restoration era was by William Beasley (1955). Where Norman had emphasized internal factors, Beasley re-emphasized the importance of foreign pressure on Japan. Certainly the unequal treaties and the warships that enforced them were the anvil against which the southwestern domains hammered the *bakufu*. Beasley's translations of key documents bearing on Japan's relations with the Western powers immensely clarified this dimension of history. Beasley's introduction to the documents provided a subtle analysis of the intellectual ambiguity of Japanese who would open their country and those who felt it should be kept closed. In 1972, Beasley followed with an overview of the Meiji period that was also particularly strong on Japan's international crisis. More recently, in 1995, he has published a volume on Japanese travellers in Europe and America in which he pursued Japan's encounter with the West on an individual level. Other books on the foreign relations of the Restoration era include works by Samuel Morison (1967), Grace Fox (1969), Meron Medzini (1971), and Masao Miyoshi (1979).

In 1961, two books appeared which offered new interpretations of the Restoration, one by me and one by Marius Jansen. Both spoke directly to the question of whether the Restoration could

---

[20] In *Japan's Emergence* he cited the Marxist historians Hattori Shisō and Tsuchiya Takao only in a footnote. In his 1943 *Soldier and Peasant* he used a few more Marxist writings, but still relied more on the earlier school. This is curious in that Norman himself was a Marxist during the late thirties.

[21] E. H. Norman (1940), 61,70.

be seen as a bourgeois, or incomplete bourgeois, revolution. Both books arrived at conclusions that differed fundamentally from Norman and the Marxist views dominant in Japan at the time. Their analysis of the Tosa and Chōshū domains made it clear that no formulaic overview would do for all of Japan. First, the books shifted away from a simplistic view of the Restoration as a "class alliance" toward a greater emphasis on domains. Most of the samurai in Japan were lower samurai, but most lower samurai did not participate in the Restoration—unless they happened to be from the handful of active domains. Why certain domains became active when most did not became a key historical question. Second, in the active domains, it was shown that the governmental bodies which made the important decisions included high-ranking as well as low-ranking members, and were devoid of either merchants or farmers. Third, it was demonstrated that the peasant soldiers in Chōshū's irregular militia had joined to escape their class, not to represent it. On count after count Norman's interpretation was disproved. Fourth, a closer look at domain-level politics showed the quicksilver role of the individual in history. Sakamoto cannot be separated from Tosa, but the role he played went beyond it.

The above books made clear the need for more domain studies. A few scholars responded: Harold Bolitho's (1974) publication opened a new dimension of Tokugawa history. The Epilogue, dealing with the *bakumatsu* era, analyzed the weakness of the *fudai* commitment to the *bakufu* cause. One wonders why no scholar has written a comparable book on the *shinpan* daimyo. During most of the *bakumatsu* era, the vital center of national politics was the movement for the union of court and *bakufu* (the *kōbu gattai* movement). Before the period of Ii's ascendency in the *bakufu*, the *shinpan* were its backbone, and even after Ii, their role continued to be critical. A book on the *shinpan* will make a major contribution. Other domain studies are by J. Victor Koschmann (1987) and Kate Nakai's translation of Yamakawa Kikue (1992). James McClain wrote an article (1988) and James Baxter, a book (1994), on Kaga during and after the Restoration era. Yet much remains to be done. We lack studies in English of many of the most important domains—Satsuma, Saga, Kumamoto, Fukuoka, Hiroshima, and Uwajima, and we know next to nothing of active pro-Tokugawa domains such as Aizu or Kuwana. Until such studies are in hand, large areas in our jigsaw puzzle of *bakumatsu* politics will remain tantalizingly blank.

From the late sixties, work on other important aspects of *bakumatsu* history also appeared. Herschel Webb wrote a volume on the Japanese Imperial institution (1968), the last third of which dealt with *bakumatsu* developments. His description of the Kyoto emperor as a captive in an area the size of the deck of an aircraft carrier must have caught many a reader's fancy.[22] Conrad Totman (1980) published an extremely detailed, major study of the two important *bakufu* reforms during the 1860s. His book makes it clear that the story of the Restoration hinged as much on the internal weaknesses of the *bakufu* as it did on the strengths of the southwestern domains.

Another genre in Restoration historiography, following in the footsteps of Jansen's study of Sakamoto, was biographical studies of individual actors. To list a few: in 1964, David Earl's informative account of the life and thought of Yoshida Shōin, and Masakazu Iwata's of Ōkubo Toshimichi; in 1970, Thomas Havens's volume; in 1971, that of Roger Hackett. Ivan Hall (1973) gave an original and detailed account of Mori Arinori's life that included materials from the United States and England that were previously unknown in Japan. Other works were by James L. Huffman (1980), Thomas Huber (1981), Andrew Fraser (his 1986 translation of Oka Yoshitake's work), and Charles Yates (1994).

Also important in the historiography of the Restoration are chapters in the many works with multiple authors. To list a few of the works in which such writings appear: the six volumes in the "Studies in the Modernization of Japan" series, which were edited, respectively, by Jansen (1965a), William Lockwood (1965), Ronald Dore (1967), Robert Ward (1968), Donald Shively (1971), and James Morley (1971); Bernard Silberman and H. D. Harootunian (1966); John Hall and Marius Jansen (1968); Craig and Shively (1970); Craig (1979); Robert Lifton, Shūichi Katō, and Michael Reich (1979); Tetsuo Najita and Victor Koschmann (1982); Jansen and Rozman (1986); and Jansen (1989). The last treats nineteenth-century Japan.

Lastly, there are the years after the Restoration. Should Restoration politics be seen as extending to the abolition of the do-

---

[22] Herschel Webb (1968), 129.

mains in 1871, or until the end of Satsuma's quasi-independence in 1878? Looking at government, the immediate post-Restoration years are particularly opaque. Even in Japan, detailed studies of this period, in the main, have appeared only recently. The transfer of power from the domains to the center was difficult and has not been adequately studied in the English literature. To give one example, we have no comparative study of the post-Restoration domain reforms in which conservative domain governments, hoping to curry favor with the new court government, gave power to pro-court activists who hastened the demise of the domains. And for the period to 1878, we need book-length studies of the 1871-73 "caretaker" government, the rise of the *seikanron*, conscription, post-Restoration samurai uprisings, the disestablishment of the samurai class, and land tax reform. Topics for research abound.

Among the English-language works on this period are the biographies mentioned earlier, the translation by Sidney Brown and Akiko Hirota of *The Diary of Kido Takayoshi* in three volumes (1983-86), and Silberman's two books on bureaucracy (1964, 1993). Books on the movement for the establishment of a national assembly usually include materials on the politics of the seventies. Among the important works are by Nobutaka Ike (1950); Robert Scalapino (1953); George Akita (1967); Roger Bowen (1980); and Arthur Stockwin's translation of Banno Junji (1992). Also important, though generally unavailable, are the many articles by Andrew Fraser.[23]

In economic history, there are excellent studies of the Tokugawa era such as those by Charles Sheldon (1958); William Hauser (1974); and Susan Hanley and Kozo Yamamura (1977). There are also superb works on the modern Japanese economy by G. C. Allen, William Lockwood, Henry Rosovsky, James Nakamura, Hugh Patrick, Kozo Yamamura, William Wray, and Andrew Gordon. But books on the Tokugawa economy wind down by the 1850s, while those on the modern economy usually pick up from the 1880s. In between is a trough. There is no book on the Restoration economy as such, no book, for example, that focuses on the opening

---

[23] Andrew Fraser, "Local Administration: the Example of Awa-Tokushima," can be found in Jansen and Rozman, eds. (1986). As far as I know, the rest of Fraser's very substantial research appears either in *Papers on Far Eastern History* or in the *Occasional Papers* put out by the Faculty of Asian Studies at Australian National University.

of Japan to foreign trade and its impact on society and politics.[24] For the first two decades of Meiji, the best book remains one that was published in 1955 by T. Smith. Abundant Japanese research is available in this area; the need for new studies in English is pressing.

The Cultural Revolution of Meiji

Beginning in the 1860s, and picking up steam in the decades that followed, Japan underwent a profound cultural change. Japan in the mid-nineteenth century may even be compared to Japan in the seventh and eighth centuries. In both periods, it reached out and took in a foreign culture, and the massive influx of new ideas, technologies, and institutions led to a national transformation. Without these changes, the Restoration movement would not have turned into a revolution. In fact, more than the particular configuration of domain forces that led to the emperor's restoration, it was these cultural changes that were central to the impact of the "Restoration."

But this cultural change is difficult to grasp. An initial problem is the nature of the "platform" on which Japanese thinkers stood as they reached out for new ideas during the 1860s. Was it primarily intellectual—the corpus of Tokugawa thought? If so, which elements counted, and which were discarded without further ado? The elaborate structures of thought of one age are rarely refuted; usually they are pushed to one side and ignored as new ideas come to the fore. Or was the platform constructed of those Tokugawa institutions that encouraged thinkers to inquire into new ideas and supported them while they did so—the medical profession, schools, and the stipends that made samurai a quasi-leisure class? Or was their relative openness to the West essentially a response to steamships, rifles, and cannon, a response that might have been elicited even had other sets of ideas and institutions been in place?

Whatever its ultimate evaluation, all of Tokugawa thought must be re-examined with the problem of the "platform" in mind.

---

[24] One monograph on a narrower topic that comes to mind is by Peter Frost (1970). The works by Wigen and Howell mentioned earlier also straddle this era. Two others are William Kelly (1982), and Johannes Hirschmeier (1964).

Tokugawa thought has been a particularly rich field in postwar research because of the many writings of Robert Bellah, Tetsuo Najita, George Elison, Herman Ooms, Kate Nakai, Peter Nosco, Samuel Yamashita, and others. To these must be added Mikiso Hane's translation of Maruyama Masao (1989), and the writings by Ronald Dore (1965) and Richard Rubinger (1982) on Tokugawa education. Also, it should be noted that the 1958 compilation by Ryusaku Tsunoda, W. Theodore de Bary, and Donald Keene is especially strong on Tokugawa thought and good on Meiji thought as well. Looking at the work done so far, the seminal thinkers of the late seventeenth century have been well studied, but far less has been done on the "syncretic" thinkers of the late eighteenth and early nineteenth centuries. Here, too, the backlog of Japanese research is immense.

The platform from which Japanese thinkers reached out for Western ideas, to the extent it was cultural, was primarily Confucian—if the term is understood to include Chinese histories as well as philosophical texts, and if the adaptations made to fit Confucian notions to the Japanese situation are forgiven. Looking at Japan, China, and Korea, there were interesting similarities in their approach to Western ideas. Yen Fu's reception of Western ideas was strikingly similar in many respects to that of Fukuzawa Yukichi, as was that of Yu Kil-Chan in Korea.[25] Yet the timetables were different. In Japan there occurred what might be called a compression of stages. Confucianism as a total system of thought withered and was largely discarded in Japan during the seventies, a change that did not occur in China until the May 4th movement about forty years later. Only a handful of ethical precepts survived.

Perhaps early Meiji thought may be seen as a double helix with emperorist and modern Western strands. The emperor-centered strand drew on elements from Confucianism, National Studies, and Shintō, but contained newer Western ideas as well. It informed the politics of the period. The baseline of Mito thought has been explored by Bob Wakabayashi (1986), and in the earlier-mentioned work by Koschmann (1987). The "honor the emperor and expel the barbarian" movement has been described in the several political histories mentioned earlier. Harry Harootunian (1970) treats

---

[25] See Benjamin Schwartz (1964), and Satō Seizaburō (1979).

Yoshida Shōin and other *bakumatsu* thinkers. Earl, Huber, and others, as noted earlier, have also written on Yoshida. After the Restoration, there was a short-lived movement to enhance the Imperial court by promoting Shintō and attacking Buddhism. This *shimbutsu bunri* and *haibutsu kishaku* movement has been studied in articles by Martin Collcutt (1986) and James Ketelaar (1990). Helen Hardacre (1986, 1989) has written on post-Restoration Shintō and on Shintō-tinged popular religions. Other scholarly writings, for example, Joseph Pittau's (1967) volume, treat the Charter Oath (1868), the Imperial Rescript to Soldiers and Sailors (1882), the Meiji Constitution (1889), and the Imperial Rescript on Education (1890). A recent article by John Breen (1996) focuses on the form of the Charter Oath as a Shintō ritual, rather than on its progressive content. Other works such as Jansen's translation of Irokawa Daikichi (1985) and works by Carol Gluck (1985) and Takashi Fujitani (1996), also offer broader interpretions of Japan's imperial institution and the ideology associated with it.

Despite the prominence of Japan's "emperor system," and the rituals and thought associated with it, scholars are not of one mind in their interpretations of it. Wakabayashi writes that later Mito thought "pointed to an emperor-centered government utilizing state religious teachings to infuse nationalism...in commoners."[26] That is to say, Mito thought already contained, in the egg as it were, the germ of the Meiji emperor-institution and modern Japanese nationalism. Certainly ideas such as *jōi*, *kaikoku*, *sonnō*, and *kokutai* are already quite developed in the Mito philosophy. Gluck and Fujitani present equally persuasive arguments that the modern emperor-institution was a late Meiji invention. Gluck writes, "Although the process began in the Restoration years, it required the entire Meiji period to weave the emperor's new clothes and display them effectively before the people."[27] And still another question that remains unaddressed is what the matrix of Shintō meant to the rise and spread of Mito thought and to the modern emperor cult.

The second strand of the double helix was Western modern thought. It had its origins in Dutch Studies (*rangaku*) (or what might better be called Confucian-*rangaku*), which developed into

---

[26] Bob Wakabayashi (1986), 15.
[27] Carol Gluck (1985), 73.

Western Studies (*yōgaku*) during the sixties, into the "civilization and enlightenment (*bunmei kaika*) movement" during the late sixties and seventies, and then on into the more complex thought of the late seventies and early eighties.

For this strand, the English literature has strengths and weaknesses. On Dutch Studies, there is the translation of Sugita Genpaku (1969), and works by Donald Keene (1969), Shigeru Nakayama (1969), Masayoshi Sugimoto and David Swain (1978), and Grant Goodman (1986). I have discussed Yamagata Bantō's reconciliation of Chu Hsi Confucianism and Western science (1965), and Hirakawa Sukehiro has discussed the relationship of the Confucian school of Ancient Studies to Dutch medicine (1989). But there is no book in English that systematically relates Dutch studies to the several schools of Confucianism, nor do we have an adequate picture of how the core study of Dutch language and medicine branched out into other sciences and then into geography, biography, and history.

For the *bakumatsu* period, Sir George Sansom (1949) published vignettes on Takashima Shūhan, Egawa Tarōzaemon, Sakuma Shōzan, and others concerned with Western technology and thought. Both Sakuma and Yokoi Shōnan have been treated in articles and chapters of various books. But little is available on the *bakumatsu* origins of the *bunmei kaika* movement—apart from Fukuzawa's *Autobiography*, gracefully but loosely translated by his grandson, Kiyooka Eiichi. This is a neglected topic. In 1853 the West was seen as barbarian and an open-the-country policy was adopted with the idea that the country, after self-strengthening, might later be closed. But by 1868, a new view of the West as civilized had appeared, and Japan had begun a wrenching reappraisal of its own place in the world. This shift occurred mainly between 1862 and 1868. The men who translated Western works during this period went on after 1868 to become the pamphleteers of the "civilization and enlightenment movement."

In Western writings, we encounter the civilization and enlightenment movement only in its fully developed form in the mid-1870s: translations of Fukuzawa (1969, 1973, and Kiyooka's translations of Fukuzawa's writings on education and on women). Carmen Blacker (1964) gives a lively picture of Fukuzawa's thought in mid-decade. I also have an article on Fukuzawa (1968). William Braistead's translation (1976) provides a sampler of the ideas of a broad range of key figures. Earl Kinmonth (1981) has chronicled the enthusiasm of contemporary Japanese for Samuel Smiles's *Self Help* and gives a sweeping interpretation of Meiji thought as well. The introduction of Western economic thought has been treated by Chūhei Sugiyama and Hiroshi Mizuta (1988). The relation between ideas and institutional change is dealt with by Eleanor Westney (1987). Several of the biographical studies mentioned earlier also fit in here. Mori Arinori and Nishi Amane were as much thinkers as doers. Most Meiji doers, in fact, had to be thinkers since they were doing something new.

The image of a double helix directs our attention to certain subjects, but may lead us to overlook others. In general, Japanese attention was absorbed by the ideas, sciences, and technologies of the contemporary West; anything not up-to-date was screened out. But we must remember that Christianity was a part of the contemporary West. Christian missionaries arrived early in Meiji Japan, and some Japanese thinkers felt Christianity was a source of Western cultural strength. Irwin Scheiner (1970) and Fred Notehelfer (1984) illuminate aspects of this topic. In this connection, William Clark's activities in Hokkaido also deserve a monograph.

When we look at Japanese thought during the seventies, we see a pastiche of ideas taken from various Western works. When we read the Meirokusha debates, we realize that opinion leaders held a variety of positions. Yet for most Japanese, the civilization and enlightenment movement of the seventies was perceived as having a kind of unity. This contrasts with the eighties, when *bunmei kaika* thought, like light refracted through a prism, broke up into different wavelengths: at one end of the spectrum was Nakae Chōmin's translation of Rousseau's *Social Contract*, at the other, a government-commissioned translation of Edmund Burke and Katō Hiroyuki's refutation of natural rights. In English, apart from the biographical studies already mentioned, the study of these decades has just begun.

Conclusion

How the above three areas of *bakumatsu* history fit together is, of course, the critical question. I see the villages, towns, and cities of Japan as the setting for the political movement that led to the Restoration. To say this is not to dismiss them, but rather to stress their importance, for it was only because they were involved with their own concerns, a different set of concerns than those of samurai, and only because of the competence of their self-government, that the political movement could unfold as it did. The political movement, by definition, is central to the story of the Restoration, but is still replete with problems of interpretation. Reading narratives of *bakumatsu* history, it sometimes seems as if the Tokugawa state was just waiting to crumble. Its willingness to compromise, and especially its loss of nerve after the death of Ii Naosuke in 1860, are notable. Yet for those involved in the anti-*bakufu* movement, the ancient regime seemed tremendously strong and enduring. When the Restoration had ended, Itō Hirobumi remarked, "looking back it seemed as if we could have done anything, but at the time it seemed a miracle that we survived each day."[28] Even on the day the Restoration was proclaimed, no one foresaw that nobles and daimyo would soon be swept away and radical reforms carried out. As for the cultural revolution, we note that, despite its rich antecedents, it came late. Katō Hiroyuki's *Tonarigusa* appeared in 1862 and the first volume of Fukuzawa's *Conditions in the West* in 1866. It began to have an impact during the closing years of the *bakumatsu* era, and blossomed during the seventies. The rapidity with which its ideas were accepted must still be explained.

BIBLIOGRAPHY

Akita, George. 1967. *Foundations of Constitutional Government in Modern Japan, 1868-1900*. Cambridge: Harvard University Press.
Alcock, Rutherford. 1969. *The Capital of the Tycoon*. New York: Greenwood.
Banno Junji. 1992. *The Establishment of the Japanese Constitutional System*. Translated by Arthur Stockwin. New York: Routledge.
Baxter, James. 1994. *The Meiji Unification through the Lens of Ishikawa Prefecture*. Cambridge: Council on East Asian Studies, Harvard University.
Beasley, William. 1955. *Select Documents on Japanese Foreign Policy, 1853-1868*. Oxford: Oxford University Press.
———. 1972. *The Meiji Restoration*. Stanford: Stanford University Press.

---

[28] This quotation is from a lecture for which I no longer have the original citation.

———. 1995. *Japan Encounters the Barbarian, Japanese Travellers in America and Europe.* New Haven: Yale University Press.
Bix, Herbert. 1986. *Peasant Protest in Japan, 1590-1884.* New Haven: Yale University Press.
Blacker, Carmen. 1964. *The Japanese Enlightenment: a Study of the Writings of Fukuzawa Yukichi.* Cambridge: Cambridge University Press.
Bolitho, Harold. 1974. *Treasures Among Men, the Fudai Daimyo in Tokugawa Japan.* New Haven: Yale University Press.
Borton, Hugh. 1968. "Peasant Uprisings in Japan of the Tokugawa Period." Reprint. New York: Paragon Book Reprint Corp. [*Transactions of the Asiatic Society of Japan*, 1938.]
Bowen, Roger. 1980. *Rebellion and Democracy in Meiji Japan.* Berkeley: University of California Press.
Braistead, William, trans. 1976. *"Meiroku zasshi," Journal of the Japanese Enlightenment.* Cambridge: Harvard University Press.
Breen, Joseph. Winter 1996. "The Imperial Oath of April 1868: Ritual, Politics, and Power in the Restoration." *Monumenta Nipponica* 51, no. 4.
Brown, Sidney, and Akiko Hirota, trans. 1983-86. *The Diary of Kido Takayoshi.* 3 vols. University of Tokyo Press.
Chambliss, William. 1965. *Chiaraijima: Land Tenure, Taxation, and Local Trade, 1818-1884.* Tucson: University of Arizona Press.
Collcutt, Martin. 1986. "Buddhism: the Threat of Eradication." In Jansen and Rozman, eds. (1986).
Craig, Albert. 1961. *Chōshū in the Meiji Restoration.* Cambridge: Harvard University Press.
———. 1965. "Science and Confucianism in Tokugawa Japan." In Jansen, ed. (1965).
———. 1968. "Fukuzawa Yukichi: The Philosophical Foundations of Meiji Nationalism." In *Political Development in Modern Japan*, edited by Robert Ward. Princeton: Princeton University Press.
Craig, Albert, ed. 1979. *Japan, a Comparative View.* Princeton: Princeton University Press.
Craig, Albert, and Donald Shively, eds. 1970. *Personality in Japanese History.* Berkeley: University of California Press. [Reprint. Ann Arbor: Center for Japanese Studies, University of Michigan, 1995.]
Dore, Ronald P. 1965. *Education in Tokugawa Japan.* Berkeley: University of California Press.
———. 1967. *Aspects of Social Change in Modern Japan.* Princeton: Princeton University Press.
Dower, John, with Timothy George. 1995. *Japanese History and Culture from Ancient to Modern Times: Seven Basic Bibliographies.* Princeton: Markus Wiener.
Earl, David. 1964. *Emperor and Nation in Japan.* Seattle: University of Washington Press.
Fox, Grace. 1969. *Britain and Japan, 1858-1883.* Oxford: Clarendon.
Frost, Peter. 1970. *The Bakumatsu Currency Crisis.* Cambridge: East Asian Research Center, Harvard University; distributed by Harvard University Press.
Fujitani, Takashi. 1996. *Splendid Monarchy, Power, and Pageantry in Modern Japan.* Berkeley: University of California Press.
Fukuzawa Yukichi. 1969. *An Encouragement of Learning.* Translated by David Dilworth and Umeyo Hirano. Sophia University.
———. 1973. *An Outline of a Theory of Civilization.* Translated by David Dilworth and G. Cameron Hurst. Sophia University.
Gluck, Carol. 1985. *Japan's Modern Myths.* Princeton: Princeton University Press.

Goodman, Grant. 1986. *Japan: the Dutch Experience*. London: Athlone; distributed in the U.S. and Canada by Humanities Press.
Hackett, Roger. 1971. *Yamagata Aritomo and the Rise of Modern Japan, 1838-1922*. Cambridge: Harvard University Press.
Hall, Ivan. 1973. *Mori Arinori*. Cambridge: Harvard University Press.
Hall, John W., and Marius Jansen, eds. 1968. *Studies in the Institutional History of Early Modern Japan*. Princeton: Princeton University Press.
Hanley, Susan, and Kozo Yamamura. 1977. *Economic and Demographic Change in Preindustrial Japan, 1600-1868*. Princeton: Princeton University Press.
Hardacre, Helen. 1986. *Kurozumikyō and the New Religions of Japan*. Princeton: Princeton University Press.
———. 1989. *Shintō and the State, 1868-1988*. Princeton: Princeton University Press.
Harootunian, H. D. 1970. *Toward Restoration, the Growth of Political Consciousness in Tokugawa Japan*. Berkeley: University of California Press.
Hauser, William. 1974. *Economic and Institutional Change in Tokugawa Japan*. Cambridge: Cambridge University Press.
Havens, Thomas. 1970. *Nishi Amane and Modern Japanese Thought*. Princeton, Princeton University Press.
Heusken, Henry. 1964. *Japan Journal, 1855-1861*. New Brunswick: Rutgers University Press.
Hirakawa, Sukehiro. 1989. "Japan's Turn to the West." In Jansen, ed. (1989).
Hirschmeier, Johannes. 1964. *The Origins of Entrepreneurship in Meiji Japan*. Cambridge: Harvard University Press.
Howell, David. 1995. *Capitalism from within: Economy, Society and the State in a Japanese Fishery*. Berkeley: University of California Press.
Huber, Thomas. 1981. *The Revolutionary Origins of Modern Japan*. Stanford: Stanford University Press.
Huffman, James L. 1980. *Politics of the Meiji Press: the Life of Fukuchi Gen'ichirō*. Honolulu: University of Hawai'i Press.
Ike, Nobutaka. 1969. *The Beginnings of Political Democracy in Japan*. New York: Greenwood Press. [Baltimore: Johns Hopkins Press, 1950.]
Irokawa Daikichi. 1985. *The Culture of the Meiji Period*. Translated by Marius Jansen. Princeton: Princeton University Press.
Iwata, Masakazu. 1964. *Ōkubo Toshimichi, the Bismarck of Japan*. Berkeley: University of California Press.
Jansen, Marius. 1961. *Sakamoto Ryōma and the Meiji Restoration*. Princeton: Princeton University Press.
Jansen, Marius, ed. 1965. *Changing Japanese Attitudes toward Modernization*. Princeton: Princeton University Press.
———. 1989. *The Nineteenth Century*. Vol. 5 of *The Cambridge History of Japan*. Cambridge: Cambridge University Press.
Jansen, Marius, and Gilbert Rozman, eds. 1986. *Japan in Transition from Tokugawa to Meiji*. Princeton: Princeton University Press.
Kalland, Arne. 1994. *Fishing Villages in Tokugawa Japan*. Richmond, Surrey: Curzon.
Keene, Donald. 1969. *The Japanese Discovery of Europe, 1720-1830*. Stanford: Stanford University Press.
Kelly, William. 1982. *Water Control in Tokugawa Japan: Irrigation Organization in a Japanese River Basin, 1600-1870*. Ithaca: China-Japan Program, Cornell University.
———. 1985. *Deference and Defiance in Nineteenth-Century Japan*. Princeton: Princeton University Press.
Ketelaar, James. 1990. *Of Heretics and Martyrs in Meiji Japan: Buddhism and its Persecutors*. Princeton: Princeton University Press.

Kinmonth, Earl. 1981. *The Self-Made Man in Meiji Japanese Thought from Samurai to Salaryman*. Berkeley: University of California Press.

Koschmann, J. Victor. 1987. *The Mito Ideology: Discourse, Reform, and Insurrection in Late Tokugawa Japan, 1790-1864*. Berkeley: University of California Press.

Kurushima Hiroshi. 1995. "Hyakushō to mura no henshitsu." In *Iwanami kōza Nihon tsūshi*. Vol. 15. Kinsei 5. Iwanami shoten.

Lifton, Robert, Shūichi Katō, and Michael Reich. 1979. *Six Lives, Six Deaths: Portraits from Modern Japan*. New Haven: Yale University Press.

Lockwood, William. 1965. *The State and Economic Enterprise in Japan*. Princeton: Princeton University Press.

Maruyama Masao. 1989. *Studies in the Intellectual History of Tokugawa Japan*. Translated by Mikiso Hane. Princeton: Princeton University Press.

McClain, James. 1988. "Failed Expectations: Kaga Domain on the Eve of the Meiji Restoration." *Journal of Japanese Studies* 14, no. 2.

McClain, James, John Merriman, and Kaoru Ugawa, eds. 1994. *Edo and Paris, Urban Life and the State in the Early Modern Period*. Ithaca: Cornell University Press.

Medzini, Meron. 1971. *French Policy in Japan during the Closing Years of the Tokugawa Regime*. Cambridge: East Asian Research Center, Harvard University; distributed by Harvard University Press.

Miyoshi, Masao. 1979. *As We Saw Them*. Berkeley: University of California Press.

Morison, Samuel. 1967. *"Old Bruin," Commodore Matthew Calbraith Perry*. Boston: Little, Brown.

Morley, James W. 1971. *Dilemmas of Growth in Prewar Japan*. Princeton: Princeton University Press.

Najita, Tetsuo, and J. Victor Koschmann. 1982. *Conflict in Modern Japanese History: The Neglected Tradition*. Princeton: Princeton University Press.

Nakayama, Shigeru. 1969. *A History of Japanese Astronomy*. Cambridge: Harvard University Press.

Norman, E. H. 1940. *Japan's Emergence as a Modern State*. New York: International Secretariat, Institute of Pacific Relations.

———. 1965 [1943]. *Soldier and Peasant in Japan: the Origins of Conscription*. Vancouver: Publication Centre, University of British Colombia.

Notehelfer, Fred. 1984. *American Samurai: Captain L. L. Janes and Japan*. Princeton: Princeton University Press.

Nouet, Noel. 1990 [1961]. *The Shogun's City: a History of Tokyo*. Translated by John and Michele Mills. Folkestone: Norbury.

Oka Yoshitake. 1986. *Five Political Leaders of Modern Japan*. Translated by Andrew Fraser. Tokyo: University of Tokyo Press.

Pittau, Joseph. 1967. *Political Thought in Early Meiji Japan, 1868-1889*. Cambridge: Harvard University Press.

Rozman, Gilbert. 1973. *Urban Networks in Ch'ing China and Tokugawa Japan*. Princeton: Princeton University Press.

Rubinger, Richard. 1982. *Private Academies of Tokugawa Japan*. Princeton: Princeton University Press.

Sansom, George. 1949. *The Western World and Japan*. New York: Alfred A. Knopf. [Reprint. Rutland, Vt.: Charles E. Tuttle, 1977.]

Satō, Seizaburō. 1979. "Response to the West: The Korean and Japanese Patterns." In Craig, ed. (1979).

Scalapino, Robert. 1970 [1935]. *Democracy and the Party Movement in Prewar Japan*. Berkeley: University of California Press.

Scheiner, Irwin. 1970. *Christian Converts and Social Protest in Meiji Japan*. Berkeley: University of California Press.
Schwartz, Benjamin. 1964. *In Search of Wealth and Power: Yen Fu and the West*. Cambridge: Belknap Press of Harvard University Press. [Pei-ching shih: Chih Kung chiso yu chu pan she, 1990.]
Seidensticker, Edward. 1983. *Low City, High City: Tokyo from Edo to the Earthquake*. New York: Alfred A. Knopf; distributed by Random House. [Reprint. Cambridge: Harvard University Press, 1991.]
Sheldon, Charles. 1958. *The Rise of the Merchant Class in Tokugawa Japan*. Locust Valley, N.Y.; published for the Association for Asian Studies by J. J. Augustin. [Reprint. New York: Russell and Russell, 1973.]
Shively, Donald. 1971. *Tradition and Modernization in Japanese Culture*. Princeton: Princeton University Press.
Silberman, Bernard. 1964. *Ministers of Modernization: Elite Mobility in the Meiji Restoration, 1868-73*. Tucson: University of Arizona Press.
———. 1993. *Cages of Reason*. Chicago: University of Chicago Press.
Silberman, Bernard, and H. D. Harootunian. 1966. *Modern Japanese Leadership*. Tucson: University of Arizona Press.
Smith, Thomas. 1955. *Political Change and Industrial Development in Japan: Government Enterprise, 1868-1880*. Stanford: Stanford University Press.
———. 1959. *Agrarian Origins of Modern Japan*. Stanford: Stanford University Press.
———. 1977. *Nakahara: Family, Farming, and Population in a Japanese Village*. Stanford: Stanford University Press.
———. 1988. *Native Sources of Japanese Industrialization, 1750-1920*. Berkeley: University of California Press.
Steele, M. William. 1990. "Edo in 1868: the View from Below." *Monumenta Nipponica* 45, no. 2.
———. Unpublished paper. "Everyday Politics in Restoration Period Japan."
Sugimoto, Masayoshi, and David Swain. 1978. *Science and Culture in Traditional Japan, A.D. 600-1854*. Cambridge: MIT Press. [Reprint. Rutland, Vt.: Charles E. Tuttle, 1989.]
Sugita Genpaku. 1969. *Dawn of Western Science in Japan, or Rangaku Kotohajime*. Translated by Ryozo Matsumoto. Hokuseido Press.
Sugiyama, Chūhei, and Hiroshi Mizuta, eds. 1989. *Enlightenment and Beyond, Political Economy Comes to Japan*. Tokyo: University of Tokyo Press.
Totman, Conrad. 1980. *The Collapse of the Tokugawa Bakufu, 1862-1868*. Honolulu: University of Hawai'i Press.
———. 1989. *The Green Archipelago: Forestry in Pre-Industrial Japan*. Berkeley: University of California Press.
Tsunoda, Ryusaku, W. Theodore de Bary, and Donald Keene, comps. 1965. *The Sources of the Japanese Tradition*. New York: Columbia University Press.
Vlastos, Stephen. 1986. *Peasant Uprisings in Tokugawa Japan*. Berkeley: University of California Press.
Wakabayashi, Bob. 1986. *Anti-Foreignism and Western Learning in Early-Modern Japan: The New Theses of 1825*. Cambridge: Council on East Asian Studies, Harvard University; distributed by Harvard University Press.
Walthall, Anne. 1986. *Social Protest and Popular Culture*. Tucson; published for the Association for Asian Studies by the University of Arizona Press.
———. 1991. *Peasant Uprisings in Japan*. Chicago: University of Chicago Press.
Ward, Robert E. 1968. *Political Development in Modern Japan*. Princeton: Princeton University Press.
Waters, Neil. 1983. *Japan's Local Pragmatists, the Transition from Bakumatsu to Meiji*

in the Kawasaki Region. Cambridge: Council on East Asian Studies, Harvard University; distributed by Harvard University Press.
Webb, Herschel. 1968. *The Japanese Imperial Institution in the Tokugawa Period*. New York: Columbia University Press.
Westney, D. Eleanor. 1987. *Imitation and Innovation: the Transfer of Western Organizational Patterns to Meiji Japan*. Cambridge: Harvard University Press.
White, James. 1995. *Ikki, Social Conflict and Political Protest in Early Modern Japan*. Ithaca: Cornell University Press.
Wigen, Kären. 1995. *The Making of a Japanese Periphery, 1750-1920*. Berkeley: University of California Press.
Wilson, George. 1992. *Patriots and Redeemers in Japan: Motives in the Meiji Restoration*. Chicago: University of Chicago Press.
Yamakawa Kikue. 1992. *Women of the Mito Domain*. Translated by Kate Nakai. University of Tokyo Press.
Yates, Charles. 1994. *Saigō Takamori: the Man Behind the Myth*. New York: Kegan Paul International.
Yazaki, Takeo. 1968. *Social Change and the City in Japan: From Earliest Times through the Industrial Revolution*. Tokyo: Japan Publications; distributed by Japan Publications Trading Co., San Francisco.

AMERICAN STUDIES OF JAPANESE FOREIGN RELATIONS

Akira Iriye

Recently I published a survey of modern Japanese foreign affairs (1997b), to which I appended a "Guide to Further Reading," an annotated list of some eighty English-language publications (books, not articles) that deal with various periods and aspects of the subject. With a few exceptions, I included only scholarly books that make use of Japanese-language material. (Since the overall concern of the essays in this volume is with American studies on Japan, popular writings, textbooks, policy documents, journalistic accounts, and the like, are of necessity excluded from consideration.)

Taking this bibliography as the point of departure, I would like to start by asking whether those on the list that are by American authors exemplify some unique characteristics, or whether scholars from all countries have cross-fertilized each other so that there is not much point in speaking of specifically American scholarly contributions in this field. It should be noted at the outset that by "American scholars" I mean not only those born and raised in the United States but also those from other countries who have been educated in American colleges and universities and who have made the United States their primary professional home. That would include American-trained Japanese scholars who publish in English.

First of all, it is evident that quantitatively American scholarship in the field of modern Japanese foreign affairs has been quite impressive. Of the eighty or so titles I included in the above "Guide," about eighty percent are by Americans, while the remaining twenty percent are by writers from other countries: Britain, Germany, the Netherlands, Canada, Australia, and Japan. (Scholars from many other countries, of course, have published on the subject, but I am focusing on important works written in English.) As far as English-language publications are concerned, it would seem that, outside of the United States, Britain stands out. No survey of the literature can ignore the enormous contributions made by Ian Nish (1972, 1985a, 1985b, 1993). His relentlessly multiarchival approach to the study of modern Japanese foreign policy would seem to represent the British tradition of diplomatic history. Likewise, William Beasley's interpretive volume on Japanese imperialism (1987) and Christopher Howe's monumental study of modern Japanese trade expansion (1995) reflect a keen interest in integrating the economic and political aspects of foreign policy, another trait that characterizes British (and perhaps European) scholarship.

Despite these distinguished works, however, it cannot be disputed that as far as English-language studies are concerned, American scholars have predominated in the field. This may be a reflection of the general development of Japanese studies since World War II; in various fields, ranging from Japanese literature to politics and economics, it would seem that the United States has produced more specialists and published more works in English than any other country. But there are also specific reasons why the study of Japanese foreign affairs has been particularly well developed in the United States.

First of all, there is the legacy of the war. Many of the wartime generation, i.e., those who entered the field during and immediately after the war, retained a strong interest in Japanese foreign affairs for obvious reasons; they wanted to understand the roots of modern Japanese imperialism and aggression. Historians such as Robert Butow, Marius Jansen, Hilary Conroy, and John White were keenly interested in the question and began publishing important monographs shortly after the war. Their studies of prewar Japanese relations with the United States (Butow, 1955), China (Jansen, 1954), Korea (Conroy, 1960), and Russia (White, 1964) were important contributions, and, taken together, they added enormously to examination of the complex story of modern Japanese responses to her Asian neighbors and the Western powers.

It was, however, James William Morley who, more than anyone else, acted decisively to ensure that the study of Japanese foreign affairs remained a major scholarly enterprise in the United States. Having published a pathbreaking monograph (1957) on the Siberian expedition of 1918, in 1963 he organized a conference at Buck Hills Falls, Pennsylvania, to conduct an in-depth discussion of where the field stood, and what subjects waited to be further explored. The participants included most of the senior and junior scholars from the United States interested in the history of

Japanese foreign affairs, who were joined by two from Japan (Hosoya Chihiro and Etō Shinkichi) and one from Britain (Nish). Morley succeeded in setting a research agenda for a generation, for it can be maintained that the participants at the conference would, each in his own way, make important scholarly contributions in the field during the remainder of the 1960s and into the 1970s.

By coincidence, in 1962 and 1963 Japan's specialists in diplomatic history published a monumental seven-volume *Taiheiyō sensō e no michi* (The Road to the Pacific War) which, in the sheer quantity of primary documents and the comprehensiveness of coverage, remains unparalleled to this day. This important landmark suggested that Japanese scholars, old and young, were making a serious attempt at understanding the recent past on the basis of thorough archival research. They chose not to put their findings in either a simple-minded nationalistic or a dogmatic anti-nationalist framework, instead seeking to trace in minute detail how decisions were made at each stage of the nation's march to the Pacific War. Because of the volumes' abundance of new documentary material and relative freedom from dogmatism, they were of potential value to students elsewhere, if they could be suitably translated. It was Morley's signal contribution to have undertaken the task. Starting immediately after the publication of the Japanese work, and going well into the 1990s, he supervised the translation of the seven volumes, a colossal task because each consisted of several chapters written by different authors. Thus the translated volumes were a testimony to Morley's initiative and leadership as well as his success in recruiting a large number of American scholars who shared his vision.[1] The translators included many American scholars who would publish important monographs of their own, even as they engaged in the translation project, thus ensuring that the field of Japanese foreign relations remained quite vigorous for decades to come.

Morley was also a force behind the epoch-making Hakone conference of Japanese and American historians in 1969 who gathered together to study the road to the war from a binational perspective. In cooperation with Dorothy Borg, Ernest R. May, and others who had established a national committee on American-

---

[1] The translated volumes are edited by James W. Morley (1976, 1980, 1983, 1984, 1994).

East Asian relations, Morley brought together Americanists from the United States and Japan specialists from Japan, who undertook to compare the two countries' decision-making systems, business organizations, the press, and the like prior to Pearl Harbor. The conference volume (Borg and Okamoto, eds., 1973) was a landmark in that for the first time a serious scholarly comparison of political, economic, and cultural institutions in Japan and the United States was undertaken. The stress on decision-making reflected the scholarly trend in both countries, in which various attempts were being made to develop theories in this area.

Morley and, by extension, his professional colleagues throughout the United States trained the next generation of Japanese studies scholars, many of whom specialized in Japanese foreign relations. Those who published important monographs in the field during the 1960s and the 1970s included James Crowley (1966), Shumpei Okamoto (1970), Peter Duus (1968), Mark Peattie (1975), Ben-Ami Shillony (1973), Roger Dingman (1976), Stephen Pelz (1974), Richard Minear (1971), John Dower (1979), and John Hunter Boyle (1972). These scholars served to enrich the field by offering diverse perspectives on prewar Japanese foreign affairs. Reflecting the general revisionist and radical trends in American scholarship from the mid-1960s into the 1970s, some works sought to portray Japan's decisions and decision-makers as no less "rational," or no more aggressive, than their counterparts elsewhere, while others were more interested in the peculiar political, social, and cultural settings in Japan that generated forces for war against both China and the United States. Since the 1980s, the ranks of specialists in Japanese foreign affairs have been joined by younger historians such as Michael Barnhart (1987), Joshua Fogel (1989), and Frederick Dickinson (volume forthcoming), as well as political scientists such as Michael Green (1995) and Daniel Okimoto (1989), working on more recent phenomena.[2]

Are there some characteristics shared by these generations of American students of Japanese foreign relations? It is hard to generalize, but at least it may be said that they have all made extensive use of Japanese sources, both primary and secondary,

---

[2] To this list one should add those who had entered the profession earlier but who published important monographs dealing with Japanese foreign affairs more recently. Examples would include: Stephen S. Large (1992), John J. Stephan (1984), Douglas R. Reynolds (1993), Herbert Bix (1992, 1995).

AMERICAN STUDIES OF JAPANESE FOREIGN RELATIONS   147

and that their works are products of often very close intellectual interchanges with their counterparts in Japan. Indeed, students of Japanese foreign relations, from the United States and from Japan, have developed a community of scholarly collaborators who see each other, exchange notes, and attend conferences together on numerous occasions. This, the growth of an intimate scholarly community across the Pacific, is one of the most remarkable developments since the war. It is ironic but significant that no topic has produced more binational scholarly cooperation than "the road to Pearl Harbor." Such instances as the above-noted 1969 Hakone conference, or the 1991 symposium, also held in the Hakone region on the fiftieth anniversary of Pearl Harbor, indicate that the gathering together of Japanese and American specialists on Japanese foreign relations has become common practice.

It is no accident, then, that some of the best recent examples of American scholarship in the field have taken the form of collaborative (often conference) volumes. Best exemplified by the work of Ramon Myers and Mark Peattie (1984), and of Peter Duus, Myers, and Peattie (1989, 1996), these volumes indicate the initiative taken by Americans to bring together specialists from the United States and Japan (and, increasingly, from other countries) for a collective re-examination of the past. Although scholars in other countries, notably Britain, have undertaken similar initiatives, collaborative enterprises have been a particularly notable feature of American studies on Japanese foreign relations.

An intriguing question suggests itself: has all this cross-fertilization among scholars of different countries produced shared outlooks and interpretations of the past? In particular, to what extent have Japanese and American scholarship on the subject become intertwined so as to be indistinguishable? In certain respects this seems to be what has happened. Japanese and American historians in most instances freely exchange information, and they both avail themselves of methodological innovations in political science, international relations theory, and the like. It is true that American works on the whole tend to be more "analytical," and Japanese more "descriptive." Some Japanese monographs are little more than documentary collections, with every unearthed document cited in order to indicate "what one clerk said to another." As a result, as David Titus has noted in his introduction to Tsunoda Jun's *The Final Confrontation* (Morley, 1994), there is a fascination with the minutiae of decision-making, with the locus of decisions going steadily down in the hierarchy until no single individual or group can be identified as having been responsible for a decision. Still, readers of recent Japanese monographs on the country's international relations will note that a good deal of analysis, often borrowed from conceptual schemes developed by Americans, is attempted. To that extent, Japanese and American specialists "speak the same language."

At the same time, however, there do appear to exist certain differences between Japanese and American scholarly products, some of which have recently become more marked. In part this is because the academic profession in the United States is far more internationalized than that in Japan. The influx of Asian scholars and students into the United States, in particular, has had a marked impact in sensitizing American scholars to the perspectives of different countries, in addition to those of Japan. Moreover, the development of American scholarly ties with China, including the opening of Chinese archives to researchers, has deepened an understanding of Chinese foreign affairs with which the study of Japanese foreign relations must be somehow connected. To talk of "the road to Pearl Harbor," for instance, primarily as a binational story, involving Japan and the United States, is no longer considered acceptable. China must be brought into the picture as a central player. Works like those by Parks Coble (1991) and You-li Sun (1993) reflect this recent trend in the American scholarly literature.

A related phenomenon, but something that goes even deeper in illustrating the contrast between Japanese and American studies of Japanese foreign relations, is that when it comes to the study of prewar Japanese imperialism, American scholars may be better situated, intellectually and psychologically, to undertake the task. Try as they might, many Japanese scholars of the subject, especially of the period 1931-1945, still find it difficult to be dispassionate or to avoid becoming conscious of the political and ideological implications of their work. True, there are notable examples, as seen in several monographs in Iwanami shoten's series (1992-1993). Some of the essays, especially by younger writers, are quite impressive, producing historical data with little awkwardness even when they document the country's unsavory and criminal behavior in China and elsewhere. Recent publications by Hatano Sumio (1996), Masuda Hiroshi (1995), and others suggest that it is perfectly possible for a Japanese historian to write about the imperialistic and militaristic past without having to feel apologetic, defensive, or politically correct (whatever "correctness" may mean in this context). Still, politicization of historical phenomena is a daily occurrence, as witness the controversies over the rape of Nanjing, compensation to "comfort women," or textbook accounts of these phenomena. Because scholars are often called upon to comment on public events, and because many of them, those in their sixties and seventies, were personally involved in the events of the 1930s and 1940s, it would be surprising if some self-consciousness did not seep into their studies of these decades.

American scholars, in contrast, do not have such political or psychological barriers. On such controversial episodes as the atomic bombings and the Vietnam War, American writers do manifest some of the same self-consciousness as Japanese. On the whole, however, it would appear that American studies of Japanese foreign relations have been free of such a tendency. Certainly, they have no reason to hesitate to study the history of Japanese colonialism and warfare otherwise than rigorously and non-ideologically. That may be why some of the best studies of Japanese imperialism and aggression have been written by American historians. Examples would include Peter Duus's (1995) detailed examination of the Japanese-Korean interactions on the peninsula prior to its formal annexation by Japan; Hilary Conroy's path-finding work (1960) contrasting the Meiji state's "realist" pragmatism with the "idealism" of its opponents; Marius Jansen's (1954) examination of Sun Yat-sen's dealings with many Japanese, including *shishi* (unemployed adventurers); James W. Morley's careful study (1957) of decision-making during the Siberian expedition; Stephen S. Large's volume (1992), the best account in existence of the role of the emperor at every juncture of the nation's road to war and aggression; Mark Peattie's superb analysis (1975) of the ideas of one of the architects of Japanese imperialism in the 1930s; John Dower's study (1979) of continuities between prewar and postwar Japan through a look at the career of Yoshida Shigeru; and Richard Minear's study (1971) of the Tokyo war crimes trials, a controversial topic which for that very reason could perhaps best be attempted by an American historian.

A notable recent development, to which I alluded earlier, has been the increasing number of historians originally from outside the United States to study, write, and work in American colleges and universities. Particularly remarkable have been young Chinese historians who have studied at American graduate schools and have published important monographs dealing with Japanese foreign affairs. Still a tiny number, we may confidently expect their ranks to swell in the years to come. They will enrich "American" studies of Japan by adding fresh material and perspectives they bring from China, and, needless to say, they will amplify the existing studies by introducing a wealth of material from Chinese archives.

I have noted some achievements and characteristics of American studies of Japanese foreign relations. These studies are quite well known among Japan specialists in the United States, Japan, and elsewhere. But the question arises whether these achievements, in themselves impressive, have made an impact on the study of international history in general. In other words, have historians of Japanese foreign relations, whether in the United States or elsewhere, contributed conceptual, methodological, or interpretive innovations comparable to those proposed by historians of European or North American international affairs? Have the latter incorporated the interpretations and findings of the Japan specialists into their own work so that there has developed an international history that is less parochial and more global, at least to the extent of bringing Western and Japanese (and, to an extent, East Asian) perspectives together?

Unfortunately, answers to these questions would appear to be mostly in the negative, or at best a very qualified positive. First of all, most works in the field of modern Japanese foreign policy tend to be couched in the framework of "realism," with a stress on such factors as national interest, geopolitics, and balance of power. The history of Japanese foreign affairs is fitted into a conception of world politics in which Japan is depicted as having sought to promote its own national interests, usually defined in terms of security and trade. The world is conceptualized as an arena for the interplay of geopolitical forces producing temporary alignments or, alternatively, conflicts among states. International relations are depicted essentially as relations among the great powers. In such a framework, Japan's story is one of a nation struggling to ensure its security and to emerge as a great power (throughout the Meiji period), then seeking to focus on the promotion of economic objectives (the 1920s), and finally challenging the other great powers in order to establish a hegemonic position in the region (the 1930s through 1945). After the defeat in World War II, Japan is seen to have redefined its national interests, with its security now tied to the global strategy of the United States and with a single-minded determination to transform itself into an economic superpower.

Such an interpretation easily fits itself into the "realist" framework which has characterized the bulk of writings on European and U.S. foreign affairs. That is to say, Japan specialists who work on the nation's foreign relations tend to accept the conceptual framework and the vocabulary of realism that have been developed by such influential writers as E. H. Carr (1940), Hans Morgenthau (1951), George Kennan (1951), and Henry Kissinger (1994). These latter, on their part, have incorporated work in Japanese diplomatic history when they discuss global affairs, although it has to be recognized that their writings are overwhelmingly Euro- and U.S.-centric. To cite one of the most recent examples, Kissinger's book, an excellent survey of modern international relations in the "realist" framework, contains simple factual mistakes (such as referring to the Japanese-USSR neutrality treaty of 1941 as a "non-aggression pact" signed in 1940). The distance between Eurocentric and Japan-focused works is still wide. But the point is that at this level, Japanese studies has done little else than offering facts and empirical data to historians of Western-oriented international relations, without suggesting novel conceptual approaches or interpretations.

A byproduct of the "realist" approach is the focus on decision-makers as they define and seek to promote national interests. Here geopolitical "realities" are perceived, and responded to, by a state's leaders, including, in democratic societies at any rate, politicians, intellectuals, and other opinion-molders. Sometimes it is not so much individuals as such but organizations (ministries, general staffs, and the like) that play critical roles, and intra-bureaucratic dynamics may yield policies beyond the control of specific individuals. Even so, the focus on the decision-making apparatus remains. Japan specialists have published numerous monographs centering on key individuals and organizations, and, indeed, as noted earlier, much published work on prewar Japanese foreign affairs falls into the category of decision-making studies. Their importance cannot be disputed; when they are incorporated into work by non-Japan specialists, the result is often an informative, well-balanced presentation. The best recent example is by Waldo Heinrichs (1988), a definitive study of Franklin D. Roosevelt's crucial decisions during 1941, a study whose value is enhanced by the author's detailed knowledge of Japanese decision-making which he has carefully assembled from secondary sources. The fact remains, however, that here again, the main contribution of Japan specialists has lain in providing information, not in offering conceptual innovations.

How about studies of imperialism? Modern international relations has to a great extent been synonymous with the history of empires, and certainly Japanese imperialism has been an integral part of the history. But here again, the Europeanists have been the innovators, and Japan specialists the adopters and adapters. One could write a historiographic essay on theories of imperialism—as, for instance, has Wolfgang Mommsen (1963, 1982)— without once mentioning theories developed by students of Japanese imperialism. From the Marxist and Leninist conceptualizations of imperialism to theories of social imperialism, of informal empire, of center-periphery interactions, and a host of other interpretations, imperialism has been one of the most exciting fields of scholarly inquiry in recent decades. Yet it would be fair to say that even the best examples of scholarly monographs on Japanese imperialism do not innovate conceptually but adopt one or another of theories and methodologies developed by Europeanists. Duus (1995), for instance, gives an excellent study of Japanese-Korean relations in the late nineteenth century that makes effective use of the concepts of "informal empire" and the "periphery." It would be fair to say, however, that Japan specialists have not significantly modified these concepts that have been developed in the context of the history of European imperialism. Maybe at the abstract conceptual level, Japanese and European imperialisms are interchangeable. Only the accumulation of more empirical studies will tell whether the Japanese experience compels a reformulation of the vocabulary in terms of which we discuss imperialism and colonialism.

This leads to a final observation. To ask whether Japanese imperialism was significantly different from European or American imperialism—was it more brutal? did it place greater stress on cultural control through language-teaching and other devices? did the "periphery" of the Japanese empire share common characteristics with the peripheries of other empires?—leads ultimately to the problems of cultural and civilizational patterns. It so happens that recently, students of European and U.S. international relations have been showing an unusual interest in the cultural aspects or underpinnings of international relations. Theirs have been attempts at going beyond "realism" with its stress on formal relations among sovereign states. Some fall in the category of what may be termed "climate of opinion" studies, that is, examinations of certain intellectual and cultural trends shared by leaders and publics within a country or, more interestingly, across countries. Superb monographs have been published, including those by David Kaiser (1990), Daniel Pick (1993), and James Joll (1992). Kaiser notes certain prevailing ideas about social relations, nationalism, and world politics shared by all European states since the seventeenth century; Pick describes contradictory impulses found in discussions of war and peace in the West since the nineteenth century; and Joll, in this and other writings, stresses the "mood" pervading Europe as defining a psychological context in which nations prepared for war. Others have examined the ideological underpinnings of a country's foreign policy. For instance, Michael Hunt (1987) suggests that certain ideologies have constituted the intellectual base-line on the basis of which Americans frame their approaches to external events; while Frank Ninkovich (1994) links U.S. foreign policy in the twentieth century to a growing concern over the dark forces of modern civilization. Still other scholars have described how individuals, civic societies, and non-governmental (or non-state) actors in various countries have developed contact across national boundaries.[3] These and many other studies in this genre have immensely enriched our understanding of international affairs. They compel us to consider these affairs not simply as interplays among states, each pursuing its own national interests, but products of cultural forces, many of which transcend national boundaries. Perhaps the extreme limit to which such study can be pushed may be seen in Samuel Huntington's work (1996),

---

[3] Studies of American missionaries abroad fall into this category. Among the most impressive is by Jane Hunter (1984). I explore the growth of contact among non-governmental organizations (1997a).

which sees contemporary international relations as being determined more by inter-civilizational than by inter-state accommodations and conflicts.

It may very well be that here, in the study of international relations as intercultural relations, Japan specialists have a great deal to contribute. Because by definition they are students of Japanese culture, they will be in a position to add substantially to the understanding of the cultural forces and issues involved in international affairs. For instance, John Dower, in a 1986 study of wartime American and Japanese perceptions of one another, shows that racism as a foundation of international affairs is a pervasive phenomenon, not a monopoly of one society or another. Similarly, through his numerous publications on Japanese-Chinese cultural relations, Joshua Fogel (1995, 1996) has demonstrated that Japan specialists can be at the forefront of those pushing for the study of intercultural affairs. If Japan specialists continue to produce similar monographs, they may be able to join specialists of European and American foreign affairs, so that together they may deepen our understanding of international relations as a cultural phenomenon. For instance, by accumulating monographs on Japan's cultural vocabulary as it has dealt with other societies, on Japanese perceptions of other cultures, or on individual Japanese interactions with individuals from other countries, students of Japanese foreign affairs will be able to respond constructively to the generalizations offered by Huntington. His book's main thesis, that civilizations are more likely to clash than to accommodate themselves with one another in the near future, calls for an informed response that can only be made after a careful examination of past trends and contemporary forces. Marius Jansen, Mark Peattie, and others have stressed the theme of pan-Asianism as a factor in prewar Japanese foreign relations, a theme that has been further explored by students of World War II, when Japan sought to eject the West from Asia. Such events suggest that a "clash of civilizations" was already taking place then, if not earlier, as far as Japan was concerned. At the same time, however, Matsumura Masayoshi's important recent book (1996) suggests that crosscultural relations have played a key role in modern Japanese foreign affairs. We need more empirical studies of this sort before jumping to conclusions about how the Japanese have perceived civilizations, whether being in harmony or in conflict, and how, to borrow from currently fashionable terminology, they have "imagined" or "reinvented" the world.

This brief essay has suggested some trends, achievements, and promise in American scholarship in the field of Japanese foreign affairs. One very promising trend has been the eagerness of the specialists to present their work in the framework of international history, not just Japanese history. This trend should be encouraged so that the entire field of Japanese studies will become an integral part of the study of the world. It is to be hoped that students of Japanese foreign relations will continue to internationalize themselves so as to make their scholarship a more vital part of the scholarship on international relations.

Bibliography

Alperovitz, Gar. 1995. *The Decision to Use the Atomic Bomb and the Architecture of an American Myth.* New York: Alfred A. Knopf.
Armacost, Michael H. 1996. *Friends or Rivals? The Insider's Account of U.S.-Japan Relations.* New York: Columbia University Press.
Bamba, Nobuya. 1972. *Japanese Diplomacy in a Dilemma: New Light on Japan's China Policy, 1924-1929.* Kyoto: Minerva.
Barnhart, Michael A. 1987. *Japan Prepares for Total War: The Search for Economic Security, 1919-1941.* Ithaca: Cornell University Press.
Beasley, William G. 1987. *Japanese Imperialism, 1894-1945.* Oxford: Clarendon.
Bix, Herbert. 1992. "The Showa Emperor's 'Monologue' and the Problem of War Responsibility." *Journal of Japanese Studies* 18, no. 2: 295-363.
——. 1995. "Japan's Delayed Surrender: A Reinterpretation." *Diplomatic History* 19, no. 2: 219-48.
Blaker, Michael. 1977. *Japanese International Negotiating Style.* New York: Studies of the East Asian Institute, Columbia University.
Borg, Dorothy, and Okamoto Shumpei, with the assistance of Dale K. A. Finlayson, eds. 1973. *Pearl Harbor as History: Japanese-American Relations, 1931-1941.* New York: Columbia University Press.
Boyle, John Hunter. 1972. *China and Japan at War, 1937-1945: the Politics of Collaboration.* Stanford: Stanford University Press.
Buruma, Ian. 1994. *The Wages of Guilt: Memories of War in Germany and Japan.* New York: Farrar, Straus, Giroux.
Butow, Robert. 1955. *Japan's Decision to Surrender.* Stanford: Stanford University Press.
——. 1974. *The John Doe Associates: Backdoor Diplomacy for Peace, 1941.* Stanford: Stanford University Press.
Carr, Edward Hallett. 1940. *The Twenty Years' Crisis, 1919-1939: An Introduction to the Study of International Relations.* London: Macmillan.
Coble, Parks M. 1991. *Facing Japan: Chinese Politics and Japanese Imperialism, 1931-1937.* Cambridge: Council on East Asian Studies, Harvard University Press.
Conroy, Hilary. 1960. *The Japanese Seizure of Korea, 1868-1910: A Study of Realism*

and Idealism in International Relations. Philadelphia: University of Pennsylvania Press.
Cook, Haruko Taya, and Theodore F. Cook. 1992. *Japan at War: An Oral History.* New York: New Press; distributed by W. W. Norton.
Crowley, James B. 1966. *Japan's Quest for Autonomy: National Security and Foreign Policy, 1930-1938.* Princeton: Princeton University Press.
Curtis, Gerald L., ed. 1994. *The United States, Japan, and Asia.* New York: W. W. Norton.
Destler, I. M. 1979. *The Textile Wrangle: Conflict in Japanese-American Relations, 1969-1971.* Ithaca: Cornell University Press.
Dickinson, Frederick. Forthcoming. *World War I and Japan.* Cambridge: Council on East Asian Studies, Harvard University. [Ph.D. diss., Yale University, 1993.]
Dingman, Roger. 1976. *Power in the Pacific: The Origins of Naval Arms Limitation, 1914-1922.* Chicago: University of Chicago Press.
Dower, John W. 1979. *Empire and Aftermath.* Cambridge: Harvard University Press.
———. 1986. *War Without Mercy: Race and Power in the Pacific War.* New York: Pantheon.
———. 1993. *Japan in War and Peace: Selected Essays.* New York: New Press; distributed by W. W. Norton.
Duus, Peter. 1968. *Party Rivalry and Political Change in Taishō Japan.* Cambridge: Harvard University Press.
———. 1995. *The Abacus and the Sword: the Japanese Penetration of Korea, 1859-1910.* Berkeley: University of California Press.
Duus, Peter, Ramon H. Myers, and Mark R. Peattie, eds. 1989. *The Japanese Informal Empire in China, 1895-1937.* Princeton: Princeton University Press.
———. 1996. *The Japanese Wartime Empire, 1931-1945.* Princeton: Princeton University Press.
Fletcher, William Miles. 1982. *The Search for a New Order: Intellectuals and Fascism in Prewar Japan.* Chapel Hill: University of North Carolina Press.
Fogel, Joshua A. 1984. *Politics and Sinology: The Case of Naitō Konan (1866-1934).* Cambridge: Council on East Asian Studies, Harvard University.
———. 1989. *Nakae Ushikichi in China: The Mourning of Spirit.* Cambridge: Council on East Asian Studies, Harvard University.
———. 1995. *The Cultural Dimension of Sino-Japanese Relations: Essay on the Nineteenth and Twentieth Centuries.* Armonk, N.Y.: M. E. Sharpe.
———. 1996. *The Literature of Travel in the Japanese Rediscovery of China, 1862-1945.* Stanford: Stanford University Press.
Fox, John P. 1982. *Germany and the Far Eastern Crisis, 1931-1938: A Study in Diplomacy and Ideology.* Oxford: Clarendon Press and New York: Oxford University Press.
Friend, Theodore. 1988. *The Blue-Eyed Enemy: Japan Against the West in Java and Luzon, 1942-1945.* Princeton: Princeton University Press.
Glaubitz, Joachim. 1995. *Between Tokyo and Moscow: The History of an Uneasy Relationship, 1972 to the 1990s.* Honolulu: University of Hawai'i Press.
Goodman, Grant K., ed. 1991. *Japanese Cultural Policies in Southeast Asia During World War 2.* Houndmills, U.K.: Macmillan.
Green, Michael J. 1995. *Arming Japan: Defense Production, Alliance Politics, and the Postwar Search for Autonomy.* New York: Columbia University Press.
Harootunian, H. D., and Bernard S. Silberman, eds. 1974. *Japan in Crisis: Essays on Taishō Democracy.* Princeton: Princeton University Press.
Hatano Sumio. 1996. *Taiheiyō sensō to Ajia gaikō* (The Pacific War and Japan's Asian Diplomacy). Tokyo daigaku shuppan kai.

Havens, Thomas R. H. 1978. *Valley of Darkness: the Japanese People and World War Two*. New York: W. W. Norton.
Heinrichs, Waldo H. 1988. *Threshold of War: Franklin D. Roosevelt and American Entry into World War II*. New York: Oxford University Press.
Howe, Christopher. 1995. *The Origins of Japanese Trade Supremacy: Development and Technology in Asia from 1540 to the Pacific War*. London: Hurst.
Hunt, Michael. 1987. *Ideology and U.S. Foreign Policy*. New Haven: Yale University Press.
Hunter, Jane. 1984. *The Gospel of Gentility: American Women Missionaries in Turn-of-the-Century China*. New Haven: Yale University Press.
Huntington, Samuel. 1996. *The Clash of Civilizations and the Remaking of World Order*. New York: Simon and Schuster.
Ienaga, Saburō. 1978. *The Pacific War, 1931-1945: A Critical Perspective on Japan's Role in World War II*. New York: Pantheon.
Inoue, Kyoko. 1991. *MacArthur's Japanese Constitution: A Linguistic and Cultural Study of its Making*. Chicago: University of Chicago Press.
Iriye, Akira. 1965. *After Imperialism: The Search for a New Order in the Far East, 1921-1931*. Harvard East Asian Series, 22. Cambridge: Harvard University Press.
———. 1972. *Pacific Estrangement: Japanese and American Expansion, 1897-1911*. Harvard Studies in American-East Asian Relations, 2. Cambridge: Harvard University Press.
———. 1981. *Power and Culture: The Japanese-American War, 1941-1945*. Cambridge: Harvard University Press.
———. 1987. *The Origins of the Second World War in Asia and the Pacific*. London: Longman.
———. 1992. *China and Japan in the Global Setting*. Edwin O. Reischauer Lecture Series, 1989. Cambridge: Harvard University Press.
———. 1997a. *Cultural Internationalism and World Order*. Baltimore: Johns Hopkins University Press.
———. 1997b. *Japan and the Wider World*. London: Longman.
Iriye, Akira, ed. 1980. *The Chinese and the Japanese: Essays in Political and Cultural Interactions*. Princeton: Princeton University Press.
Iriye, Akira, and Warren I. Cohen, eds. 1989. *The United States and Japan in the Postwar World*. Lexington: University Press of Kentucky.
———. 1990. *American, Chinese, and Japanese Perspectives on Wartime Asia, 1931-1949*. Wilmington, Del.: SR.
Iwanami shoten, ed. 1992-1993. *Iwanami kōza kindai Nihon to shokuminchi* (Modern Japan and Its Colonies). Iwanami shoten.
Jansen, Marius B. 1954. *The Japanese and Sun Yat-sen*. Cambridge: Harvard University Press.
———. 1995. *Japan and its World: Two Centuries of Change*. Reprint with a new preface by the author. Princeton: Princeton University Press.
Johnson, Chalmers A. 1982. *MITI and the Japanese Miracle: The Growth of Industrial Policy, 1925-1975*. Stanford: Stanford University Press.
Joll, James. 1992. *The Origins of the First World War*. London: Longman.
Kaiser, David. 1990. *Politics and War*. Cambridge: Harvard University Press.
Kennan, George Frost. 1951. *American Diplomacy, 1900-1950*. Chicago: University of Chicago Press.
Kennedy, Paul M. 1987. *The Rise and Fall of the Great Powers: Economic Change and Military Conflict from 1500 to 2000*. New York: Random House.
Kim, Key-Hiuk. 1980. *The Last Phase of the East Asian World Order: Korea, Japan, and the Chinese Empire, 1860-1882*. Berkeley: University of California Press.

Kissinger, Henry. 1994. *Diplomacy*. New York: Simon and Schuster.
Large, Stephen S. 1992. *Emperor Hirohito and Shōwa Japan: A Political Biography*. London: Routledge.
Lone, Stewart. 1994. *Japan's First Modern War: Army and Society in the Conflict with China, 1894-95*. New York: St. Martin's.
Lowe, Peter. 1977. *Great Britain and the Origins of the Pacific War: A Study of British Policy in East Asia, 1937-1941*. Oxford: Clarendon.
Marshall, Jonathan. 1995. *To Have and Have Not: Southeast Asian Raw Materials and the Origins of the Pacific War*. Berkeley: University of California Press.
Martin, Bernd. 1995. *Germany and Japan in the Modern World*. Providence: Berghahn.
Maruyama, Masao. 1963. *Thought and Behavior in Modern Japanese Politics*. New York: Oxford University Press.
Masuda Hiroshi. 1995. *Ishibashi Tanzan: riberaristo no shinzui* (Ishibashi Tanzan: the Spirit of a Liberal). Chūō kōronsha.
Matsumura Masayoshi. 1996. *Kokusai kōryūshi: kingendai no Nihon* (A History of International Cultural Relations: Modern and Contemporary Japan). Seiunsha.
Minear, Richard H. 1971. *Victors' Justice: The Tokyo War Crimes Trial*. Princeton: Princeton University Press.
Miyazaki Tōten. 1982. *My Thirty-three Years' Dream: The Autobiography of Miyazaki Tōten*. Translated with an introduction by Etō Shinkichi and Marius B. Jansen. Princeton: Princeton University Press.
Mommsen, Wolfgang J. 1982 [1963]. *Theories of Imperialism*. Translated by P. S. Falla. Chicago: University of Chicago Press.
Morgenthau, Hans. 1951. *In Defense of the National Interest*. New York: Alfred A. Knopf.
Morley, James W. 1957. *The Japanese Thrust into Siberia*. New York: Columbia University Press.
Morley, James W., ed. 1971. *Dilemmas of Growth in Prewar Japan*. Studies in the Modernization of Japan. Princeton: Princeton University Press.
Morley, James W., ed. and trans. 1976. *Deterrent Diplomacy: Japan, Germany, and the USSR, 1935-1940: Selected Translations from "Taiheiyō sensō e no michi, kaisen gaikō shi"*. New York: Columbia University Press.
——. 1980. *The Fateful Choice: Japan's Advance into Southeast Asia, 1939-1941: Selected Translations from "Taiheiyō sensō e no michi, kaisen gaikō shi"*. New York: Columbia University Press.
——. 1983. *The China Quagmire: Japan's Expansion on the Asian Continent, 1933-1941: Selected Translations from "Taiheiyō sensō e no michi, kaisen gaikō shi"*. New York: Columbia University Press.
——. 1984. *Japan Erupts: The London Naval Conference and the Manchurian Incident, 1928-1932: Selected Translations from "Taiheiyō sensō e no michi, kaisen gaikō shi"*. New York: Columbia University Press.
——. 1994. *The Final Confrontation: Japan's Negotiations with the United States, 1941: Selected Translations from "Taiheiyō sensō e no michi, kaisen gaikō shi"*. New York: Columbia University Press.
Morton, William Fitch. 1980. *Tanaka Giichi and Japan's China Policy*. New York: St. Martin's Press.
Mutsu Munemitsu. 1982. *Kenkenroku: A Diplomatic Record of the Sino-Japanese War, 1894-95 by Mutsu Munemitsu*. Edited and translated with historical notes by Gordon Mark Berger. Princeton: Princeton University Press.
Myers, Ramon H., and Mark R. Peattie, eds. 1984. *The Japanese Colonial Empire, 1895-1945*. Princeton: Princeton University Press.

Ninkovich, Frank. 1994. *Modernity and Power.* Chicago: University of Chicago Press.
Nish, Ian. 1972. *The Alliance in Decline: A Study in Anglo-Japanese Relations, 1908-23.* University of London, Historical Studies, 33. London: Athlone.
———. 1985a. *The Anglo-Japanese Alliance: The Diplomacy of Two Island Empires, 1894-1907.* 2nd ed. London: Athlone.
———. 1985b. *The Origins of the Russo-Japanese War.* London: Longman.
———. 1993. *Japan's Struggle with Internationalism: Japan, China, the League of Nations, 1931-33.* London: Kegan Paul International.
Nish, Ian, ed. 1982. *Anglo-Japanese Alienation, 1919-1952: Papers of the Anglo-Japanese Conference on the History of the Second World War.* Cambridge: Cambridge University Press.
Nye, Joseph S. 1990. *Bound to Lead: The Changing Nature of American Power.* New York: Basic.
Ogata, Sadako N. 1964. *Defiance in Manchuria: The Making of Japanese Foreign Policy, 1931-1932.* Berkeley: University of California Press.
Okamoto, Shumpei. 1970. *The Japanese Oligarchy and the Russo-Japanese War.* New York: Columbia University Press.
Okimoto, Daniel I. 1989. *Between MITI and the Market: Japanese Industrial Policy for High Technology.* Stanford: Stanford University Press.
Packard, George R. 1966. *Protest in Tokyo: The Security Treaty Crisis of 1960.* Princeton: Princeton University Press.
Peattie, Mark R. 1975. *Ishiwara Kanji and Japan's Confrontation with the West.* Princeton: Princeton University Press.
Pelz, Stephen E. 1974. *Race to Pearl Harbor: The Failure of the Second London Naval Conference and the Onset of World War II.* Cambridge: Harvard University Press.
Pick, Daniel. 1993. *War Machine.* New Haven: Yale University Press.
Reischauer, Edwin O. 1986. *My Life Between Japan and America.* New York: Harper and Row.
Reischauer, Haru Matsukata. 1986. *Samurai and Silk: A Japanese and American Heritage.* Cambridge: Belknap Press of Harvard University Press.
Renwick, Neil. 1995. *Japan's Alliance Politics and Defence Production.* Houndmills, U.K.: Macmillan in association with St. Anthony's College, Oxford University.
Reynolds, Douglas R. 1993. *China, 1898-1912: Xinzheng Revolution and Japan.* Cambridge: Harvard University Press.
Selden, Kyoko, and Mark Selden, eds. 1989. *The Atomic Bomb: Voices from Hiroshima and Nagasaki.* Armonk, N.Y.: M. E. Sharpe.
Sherwin, Martin J. 1975. *A World Destroyed: The Atomic Bomb and the Grand Alliance.* New York: Alfred A. Knopf; distributed by Random House.
———. 1987. *A World Destroyed: Hiroshima and the Origins of the Arms Race.* New York: Vintage.
Shillony, Ben-Ami. 1973. *Revolt in Japan: The Young Officers and the February 26, 1936 Incident.* Studies in Modernization of Japan. Princeton: Princeton University Press.
———. 1981. *Politics and Culture in Wartime Japan.* Oxford: Clarendon and New York: Oxford University Press.
Sigal, Leon. 1988. *Fighting to a Finish: the Politics of War Termination in the United States and Japan, 1945.* Ithaca: Cornell University Press.
Stephan, John J. 1984. *Hawaii under the Rising Sun: Japan's Plans for Conquest after Pearl Harbor.* Honolulu: University of Hawai'i Press.
Storry, Richard. 1957. *The Double Patriots: A Study of Japanese Nationalism.* Boston: Houghton Mifflin.

Sun, You-Li. 1993. *China and the Origins of the Pacific War, 1931-1941*. New York: St. Martin's.

Vogel, Ezra F. 1991. *The Four Little Dragons: The Spread of Industrialization in East Asia*. Edwin O. Reischauer Lectures, 1990. Cambridge: Harvard University Press.

Welfield, John. 1988. *An Empire in Eclipse: Japan in the Postwar American Alliance System: A Study in the Interaction of Domestic Politics and Foreign Policy*. London: Athlone.

White, John A. 1964. *The Diplomacy of the Russo-Japanese War*. Princeton: Princeton University Press.

Whiting, Allen Suess. 1989. *China Eyes Japan*. Berkeley: University of California Press.

JAPANESE ART STUDIES IN AMERICA SINCE 1945*

JOHN ROSENFIELD

How fast has the field grown? Langdon Warner, who long personified Japanese art studies in this country, died in 1955 at age seventy-four.[1] Warner was America's link to the pioneer days of Okakura Kakuzō (1862-1913), and his prestige was so high that the Japanese, searching for signs of compassion and favor after the furies of World War II, credited him (mistakenly) with saving Kyoto and Nara from aerial bombing.[2] Ten years after his death, however, there were still only three senior Japan specialists active in American colleges and museums—writing books and articles, training advanced students, or organizing scholarly exhibitions.[3] Today we number about thirty; new posts are opening steadily, and the demand exceeds the supply.

Indeed, the visual arts have proven to be one of the most effective of all branches of learning for introducing Japanese modes of expression and thought to general audiences in the West. The Japanese government has stimulated this interest by sending splendid art exhibitions overseas and by funding foreign scholars. It has encouraged public and private collecting abroad by adopting liberal policies toward the export of cultural properties. And in both Japan and the West publishers have issued a flood of lavishly illustrated books and exhibition catalogues.

---

* Author's note: This is a very personal effort to chart basic issues of ideology and historical method in studies of Japanese art in this country since the end of World War II. I make little attempt to survey scholars in the many subfields of Japanese art in a systematic fashion, and for reasons of space I am obliged to omit such important topics as archaeology, garden design, folk arts, and metalwork.

I wish to thank the following colleagues for their comments and advice: Sylvan Barnet, William Burto, Elizabeth ten Grotenhuis, Christine Guth, Howard Hibbett, Samuel Morse, Naomi Richard, Elizabeth Swinton, Cherie Wendelken, and Mimi Yiengpruksawan. Needless to say, however, all errors and all opinions cited here are my own.

[1] Theodore Bowie (1966).
[2] For Warner's wartime role, see Otis Cary (1987).
[3] Alexander Soper: see *In Memoriam Alexander Coburn Soper 1904-1993, 10 September 1993* (New York: Institute of Fine Arts, 1994). Robert T. Paine, Jr. (1900-1966): see *Ars Orientalis* 6 (1966), 243-47. Harold Stern (1922-1977): see *Archives of Asian Art* 31 (1977-78), 112-14.

Young scholars thus face the prospect of careers in a lively, expanding field. Paradoxically, however, our field is nowadays often described as troubled. Cited as a prime symptom of distress is the denial of tenure in American universities and museums to more than a dozen well-trained scholars over the past two decades; another dozen or so who received advanced training have dropped out of sight, and good positions are unfilled. The rate of attrition is painful in human terms. It is also a symptom of the intellectual challenges which beset not just the history of Japanese art but all branches of the humanities and social sciences.[4]

The suggestion of a crisis is even more puzzling in view of our field's many assets. At the most fundamental level—the root, the engine, the raison d'être of the entire art historical enterprise—is the vast corpus of Japanese art, an abundant array of profoundly moving aesthetic experiences. To be a historian of Japanese art, thus, is to gain privileged access not only to a splendid body of artistic material but also to Japan itself—its extraordinary traditional culture, its exciting urban life, and the fellowship of colleagues and friends there. With such assets and incentives why have a number of talented scholars failed to fulfill their promise? Why have they found it so difficult to publish? Why have the intellectual guidelines of our field become so clouded?

Many factors contribute to the problem, but I believe that two are especially germane. The first is the disjunction between the Japanese and Western scholarly worlds. Put simply, a substantial number of foreign art historians who successfully master the Japanese way of doing and seeing are ineffective when dealing with non-Japanese audiences. The second factor, and the more basic, is the confusion about the goals of scholarship caused by the waning of Modernism and the rise of Postmodernism in the practice and criticism of the arts.

I recognize that the terms Modern and Postmodern lead us into a semantic quagmire, since they do not denote commonly agreed meanings but are, rather, nicknames for tangled assortments of art forms and ideas.[5] I also recognize that my formulations—Jap-

---

[4] For similar problems in a cognate field, Islamic social studies, see Ernest Gellner (1992).

[5] In the social sciences the terms "modern" and "modernization" denote capitalist industrialism of the past century, the growth of large cities, and the ascendancy of the middle class; they also denote the development of mass politi-

anese versus Western modes of scholarship; Modern versus Postmodern outlooks—are simplistic. Japanese and Western scholars have influenced each other since the Meiji period; and many of the intellectual positions of Postmodern critics are restatements (in arcane language, to be sure) of older attitudes. Exceptions and contradictions abound, but I nonetheless want to use these rubrics to frame a discussion of intellectual challenges confronting our field.

Western and Japanese Modes of Scholarship

The first challenge is faced by all Western students of Japan and not by art historians alone. Except for those taking nationalist positions (*nihonjinron*), Japanology is not an autonomous field; its parts are usually absorbed into broader disciplines such as anthropology, social studies, literature, or art history.

Art History in Japan

It must be emphasized that Japan has long possessed a gigantic, perhaps overpowering, art-historical establishment. The Japanese have been writing treatises on art history and theory since the seventeenth century, a proclivity that continued into Meiji and thereafter. Adapting itself to European modes of scholarship, art history in Japan has been stimulated by a tireless publishing industry that produces a torrent of art history survey books, monographs, and learned journals. No other Asian nation has produced so many university posts for art historians, curatorships in public and private museums, research institutes, collectors, and dealers. No other Asian government appropriates so large a percentage of its budget to official organs like the Cultural Affairs Agency (Bunkachō), the Art Research Institute (Bijutsu kenkyūjo), and

---

cal movements, bureaucracies, and the empirical sciences, and the rise of individualism and secularism. In the visual arts "Modern" and "Modernism" denote rebellion against the canons of Beaux-arts Neo-classicism. In painting and sculpture they refer to extreme individualism, expressionism, and non-figural abstraction; in architecture and design the terms designate functionalism and the use of industrial materials. The connotations of these terms in the social sciences and visual arts are closely linked, for they reflect different aspects of the same phenomena. (The term "Postmodernism" is explored below.)

the national museums and theaters. No other branch of Asian art history requires foreign specialists to master such a vast and daunting array of published data.

In the decades since the end of World War II Japan has produced a phalanx of senior art historians whose published output is awesome in scale and authoritative in caliber: Akiyama Terukazu (Heian secular painting), Doi Tsugiyoshi (Momoyama painting), Fukuyama Toshio (architectural history), Kobayashi Takeshi (Buddhist arts), Mōri Hisashi (Buddhist sculpture), Narazaki Muneshige (*ukiyo-e*), Tanaka Ichimatsu (Muromachi ink painting), and Yamane Yūzō (Rinpa). This is but a sampling of those who have built the foundations of the art history subfields, and the list continues to grow.

At the core of their research is a science-like empiricism. Of course Japanese art historians write for the general public and discuss aesthetics and broad historical issues, but their efforts are primarily devoted to the concrete and particular: the discovery of a hitherto unrecognized work or a tombstone that clarifies an artist's family history; a comparative study of drapery patterns in Japanese and Korean Buddhist sculptures; the exploration of an iconographic motif; the analysis of a picture by infrared light to show how and when it was repainted. Hyper-specialization occurs everywhere, but it is encouraged to an extraordinary degree in Japan. Many scholars are known to concentrate on a single subject for their entire careers, virtually monopolizing it. Positivist, empirical research in art history accords closely with Japan's increasingly technocratic posture following World War II. Largely vanished are the polemical, nationalist (if not imperialist) sentiments found, for example, in the writings of Okakura Kakuzō.[6]

In the years between the two World Wars, most Western publications on Japanese art could best be characterized as art appreciation. Only a bare handful of Western scholars could read modern and premodern Japanese texts or converse easily with their Japanese colleagues. As in many other branches of Japanese studies, it was not until the 1960s that significant numbers of Western art historians achieved access to serious Japanese scholarship.

This development was accelerated by the appointment of ex-

---

[6] For overviews of Japanese art history after World War II, see Yashiro Yukio (1965, 1987).

pert Japanese-born art historians to faculties in the United States. Shimada Shūjirō (1907-1994), a specialist in Chinese painting, taught primarily at Princeton University and also at Harvard, imparting Japanese standards of meticulous scholarship.[7] His successor at Princeton, Shimizu Yoshiaki (1938-), is Japanese-born but educated in this country; as a scholar and teacher, he is wide-ranging in his studies in the history of painting.[8] Miyeko Murase, recently retired from Columbia University, has employed exacting positivist principles in her teaching and collection and exhibition catalogues.[9]

Professors in Japan began to open their seminar rooms to foreign graduate students in the late 1960s, assisting them generously and indoctrinating them in Japanese research topics and standards. Inevitably, perhaps, Western graduate art history students there began to measure themselves against their Japanese teachers and fellow students, and their art historical methods and goals were molded in that context. Returning to America to begin teaching in departments focused on Western art (and often with superficial grounding in Western art), a sizable number have found themselves ill-equipped to deal with the methodological controversies raging here.

To be sure, historians of Japanese art share many long-established interpretive topics with colleagues in the other national-regional subfields of art history (e.g., medieval European, Islamic, Renaissance, or Modern). These include the ritual uses of religious images; the forms by which the divine is depicted; the rise of secular imagery in religious contexts; modes of patronage; techniques of pictorial narration; technologies of the arts; modes of portraiture; doctrines of art-for-art's-sake; popular arts and urbanism; individualism and eccentricity—to list only a fraction. Sharing topics of universal interest should suffice to create a common bond between historians of Japanese art and their colleagues in Western art. Alas, the situation has been complicated by the rise of Postmodern critical theory.

---

[7] For his biography see *Archives of Asian Art* 58 (1995), 99-100; for his collected writings, see Shimada (1987, 1993).
[8] See Shimizu Yoshiaki (1980, 1981, 1988).
[9] Miyeko Murase (1975, 1986, 1994).

Modernist and Postmodernist Criticism

We should not ignore the fundamental role that Japanese art played in the rise of the Modern Art movements in Europe from the 1850s to their worldwide triumph after World War II. A passionate admiration of things Japanese was shared by five generations of leading Modernist artists, architects, and designers.[10] A list of the most prominent would include James Whistler, Vincent van Gogh, Paul Gauguin, Edgar Degas, Christopher Dresser, Frank Lloyd Wright, Bruno Taut, and Walter Gropius. Promethean figures, they not only incorporated Japanese styles into their own art forms, they lavishly praised Japan in their writings, thereby validating its art forms in Western minds with far more authority than did the efforts of academic historians and journalists.

In the rise of Modernism to its dominant position in the world, Japan (along with Islam and sub-Saharan Africa) provided formal systems much different from those taught in government-sponsored schools of art and architecture throughout the Western world.[11] Supported in Europe chiefly by monarchist regimes, the Beaux Arts academies promoted forms of art and architecture based, in simplest terms, on traditional Greco-Roman prototypes.

Seeking to create art forms suited to the new industrial age and the new (anti-monarchist) political regimes, the Modern movement comprised a host of subschools that rose and fell in rapid succession: chiefly Impressionism, Post-Impressionism, Cubism, Fauvism, Expressionism, Dada and Surrealism, Futurism, Constructivism and the International Style, and Abstract Expressionism. Though differing to greater or lesser degree from one another, the subschools were unified in their love of innovation and opposition to their common antagonist, the Beaux Arts academies. In tandem with their rejection of the Greco-Roman artistic heritage, Modernists promoted the vision of a more inclusive, more universal, civilization—a vision rooted in the rational doctrines of science and industrialism and made possible by the newly perfected steamships and railroads, electricity, and telegraphy.

By the 1960s Modernism, originally rebellious and avant-garde,

---

[10] See Gabriel Weisberg, et al. (1975), Yamada Chisaburō, ed. (1980), and Klaus Berger (1992).

[11] Nikolaus Pevsner (1940); Albert Boime (1971).

had become widely accepted throughout the West and an elitist orthodoxy in its own right, its triumph heralded by the geometric glass towers that punctuate the skylines of cities worldwide. The art historians of the era, as diverse as the artistic movements which they accompanied, created their own array of canonical writings. Some of the marquee names are Frederick Antal, Bernard Berenson, Henri Focillon, Max and Walter Friedlander, Roger Fry, Ernst Gombrich, Irwin Panofsky, Nikolaus Pevsner, Alois Riegl, Meyer Schapiro, and Heinrich Wölfflin.[12]

Postmodern Critical Theory

Worldwide turbulence in the 1960s (student protests, racial strife, tensions over Cuba and Vietnam) coincided with great upheavals in aesthetic values. The most enduring development, loosely called Postmodernism, stemmed largely from French criticism and American artistic practice.[13] Far from a unified system or settled body of ideas, its constituent parts have been as diverse as those of the Modernism from which it arose, and whatever unity it possesses came from its efforts to restructure its Modernist origins.

In studio arts the Postmodern subschools include Conceptual and Pop Art, Performance Art, the New Realism, and new forms of extreme expressionism. In architecture Postmodernism implies the use of historical references or vernacular building forms. Postmodern literary and art critics explore epistemological topics such as semiosis, deconstruction, poststructuralism, and psychoanalysis.[14] Some are more preoccupied by socio-ethical themes: sex, gender, class, race, nationalism, colonialism, and the environment. Pervading all of their writings is the subtext of power dynamics, an obsession with how the instruments of political power have affected the visual arts. This concern is often translated into a desire to control power within academe.

Present-day Postmodern criticism, a survivor of the collapse of fin-de-siècle socialism, claims (in the words of Michel Foucault)

---

[12] For a review of European art history up to the advent of Postmodern cultural theory, see Udo Kultermann (1993); for a critical anthology of basic essays, see W. E. Kleinbauer (1971).

[13] For overviews see Margaret Rose (1991), and Charles Jencks, ed. (1992).

[14] These critics have been accused of concentrating on philosophical issues at the expense of social problems. See Christopher Norris (1982), 131.

to be a "curative science."[15] Its advocates appeal to the idealism of the young. They oppose the spread of multinational corporations and the dehumanizing effects of industrial technology. They resist the hegemony of the professional middle class and its advocacy of the positive sciences ("bourgeois empiricism"). They strive to promote the well-being of marginalized groups, especially women, and they conspicuously embrace popular culture, which Modernists have rejected.

Graduate students in art history today tend to dismiss the paragons of traditional scholarship listed above in favor of writers like Georges Bataille, Roland Barthes, Jacques Derrida, Michel Foucault, Mikhail Bakhtin, Jean-François Lyotard, and Marcel Lacan. Though Postmodern critics employ baffling, obscurantist language (discussed below), their ideas have thoroughly permeated the intellectual atmosphere of present-day academe. The Postmodernist movements are at least three decades old, and a new generation of scholars and critics is emerging under the rubric of Cultural Studies (or Visual and Literary Studies), emphasizing such issues as sex and gender, postcolonialism, multiculturalism, and popular culture.[16]

A Personal Note

Now in my seventies, I was trained in the early 1950s in the so-called Warburg method, which links the history of artistic form to the history of ideas.[17] I have tried to apply that method to Japanese art, in which, for better or worse, I have been essentially self-taught.[18] I am neither an expert in Postmodern critical theory nor an apologist for it, but I do not join those who dismiss it as trendy nonsense (or worse).[19] I believe that it is the product of serious thought by serious people, and that it reflects larger developments

---

[15] Paul Rabinow, ed. (1984), 90.
[16] See Simon During, ed. (1993).
[17] Erwin Panovsky (1955); E. H. Gombrich (1970).
[18] See, for example, John Rosenfield (1968-69), 56-79; (1977), 205-25.
[19] "Postmodernism...is a tortuous, somewhat affected fad, practised by...academics living fairly sheltered lives; large parts of it are intelligible only and at most (and often with difficulty) to those who are fully masters of the nuances of three or four abstruse academic disciplines, and much of it is not intelligible to anyone at all. But it happens to be the currently fashionable form of relativism...." (Ernest Gellner, 1992, 72).

in the sociocultural environment of the West—changes in the technology of knowledge and communication, the collapse of long-established ideological systems, and the breakdown of political movements into single-issue factions. And I hope that my treatment of it is reasonably accurate.

In my view, Postmodern critical theory can be a tonic that clarifies and renovates obsolete ways of thinking—when correctly applied. When misapplied it can be harmful, even lethal, and the proper dosage is not easy to discern. Its impact on Japanese studies at large has already been noted.[20] And in the past decade, historians of Japanese art, either independently or under its influence, have been adopting many of its critical positions.[21]

The "Orientalist" Critique

One nagging question usually surfaces quickly in discussions of this kind: to what extent has the study of Japanese art in the West been distorted by Eurocentric or colonialist attitudes?—an accusation made by Edward Said (among others) against the Islamic, Near Eastern, and East Indian branches of Western Orientalism.[22] Said holds that, consciously or otherwise, Western Orientalists have adopted intellectual positions based on the political, economic, and technological prowess of the Euro-Atlantic powers. Those scholars, usually ill-informed about the East, posit the West as rational, humane, and advanced—in contrast to the Orient, which is the aberrant and undeveloped "Other." Said claims that this polarity, this binary division of the world into a superior "we" and inferior "they," helps Western powers to establish their cultural-political identity and to justify their unquenchable thirst for world domination.

As I will show presently, pioneer European and American art

---

[20] Miyoshi Masao and H. D. Harootunian, eds. (1989); Roland Barthes (1982).

[21] A study of provincial, non-elite art and folk religious traditions, for example, appears in Donald McCallum (1994). The interface between the dynamics of political power and the visual arts is explored in Mimi Yiengprukasawan's detailed study of Buddhist art and architecture at Hiraizumi, at present under production by the Harvard University Press. Timon Screech has explored the epistemological impact of science on Japanese popular imagery (1996, 1997). Pat Fister has applied feminist principles in her study of Japanese women artists (1988).

[22] Edward Said (1993); Ernest Gellner (1992), 43-52.

historians did indeed impose certain Western values on Japanese culture. And the legacy of their attitudes, vocabulary, and doctrines endures to the present day. Those pioneers did not, however, postulate the superiority of the West over the East; indeed, they were drawn to Japan because they credited its culture with important values missing in the West. And many were surprisingly well informed, having lived or traveled in Japan or worked with competent Japanese informants. From the beginning their approach blended European and Japanese values and attitudes. The development of our field has been far too tangled to serve as fodder for the "Orientalist" critique.

The most perceptive of the pioneer Western historians of Japanese art were (in my judgment) affiliates of Modernist movements. For example, Edmond de Goncourt (1822-1896) and his brother Jules (1830-1870), authors of biographies of Utamaro and Hokusai, were partisans of the French Impressionists; Louis Gonse (1846-1921) was an editor of the *Gazette des Beaux Arts* with encylopedic interests; Ernest Fenollosa's work on the *nō* theater was embraced by Ezra Pound (1885-1972); the British designer Christopher Dresser (1834-1904) praised the economy and simplicity of form in Japanese craft traditions, and quickly perceived that they expressed deep-seated religious and cultural values.

Religious Art: A Western Concept

The opening of Meiji Japan radically challenged that nation's traditional cultural outlook. Foreign concepts and terms—as basic as "art" and "craft"—required heroic efforts to master, as a new study by Satō Dōshin explains.[23] One of the most revolutionary changes was the classification of Buddhist and Shintō imagery as "art," which at first glance seems to have been a radical imposition of Western values. Not only had pre-Meiji Japanese never considered such material suitable for aesthetic contemplation and private collecting, a violently anti-Buddhist atmosphere prevailed at the beginning of the era. Prompted by Neo-Confucian doctrines and resurgent nationalism, an estimated five-sixths of Japanese Buddhist temples were closed, the clergy was reduced in number

---

[23] Satō Dōshin (1996).

by two thirds, and votive statues and paintings were treated as rubbish.[24]

By the 1890s, however, the Japanese Buddhist community had not only survived this extreme hostility, it attempted a thoroughgoing reform and adopted features of Western ecclesiastical organizations. At the same time Japanese and Western collectors alike began to extract devotional paintings and sculptures from their ritual contexts and to place them in private collections or in museums.[25] Ironically enough, this redefinition of votive objects as art was a by-product of Modernist secular values in which the spiritual authority of religion was eroded—as expressed in the enigmatic, unforgettable phrase "God is dead!" of Friedrich Nietzsche (1844-1900), one of the progenitors of Postmodern critical theory.[26] Votive paintings and sculptures came to be cherished for aesthetic qualities (beauty of proportion and craftsmanship, clarity of expression, or richness of ornament) and for their expressive powers as works of art—"the greatest stimulant to life," "the secret to the innermost being of the world," in the words of Nietzsche. Ignored were the holy mysteries and miraculous events that had given such images their original functions.

Furthermore, the countless hundreds of images preserved in temples and shrines provided Japanese art historians and cultural administrators with a ready-made corpus of "art" dating from the long periods of time whose secular imagery had largely vanished. Buddhist sculptures and paintings were registered as national treasures in far greater numbers than warranted by the role played by Buddhist values in the intellectual life of the modern nation. To this day, Buddhist material plays a strikingly prominent role in the overall history of Japanese art.

How does this fit into the current historiographic climate? Postmodern criticism, rooted in scientific epistemology, is a child of the radical skepticism and atheism of leftist European thought, which denounced organized religion for its superstition, mystification, and collusion with reactionary regimes. Following Nietzsche, it too proclaimed the death of God and of theology, and it has continued to undermine the intellectual credentials of tradition-

---

[24] Martin Collcutt (1986), 143-67; James Ketelaar (1990).
[25] Christine Guth (1993); Bernard Frank (1991).
[26] Bernd Magnus and Kathleen Higgins, eds. (1996): 35-36, 313-14.

al religions.[27] At the same time, however, the desiccated spiritual atmosphere of present-day culture has evoked an interest in (and longing for) sacerdotal values in all parts of the world. Astute thinkers within Postmodernism's orbit are returning to the study of religion as one of the many discursive ensembles of human thought.[28] They are focusing on the ritual uses of Buddhist art as elements in semiotic systems and as major factors in sociopolitical events.[29] In doing so they are calling into question many of the canons of establishment religious scholarship, like those of Suzuki Daisetz, for example.[30]

Historiographic Concepts

Until the advent of Postmodern critical theory most Western histories of Japanese art had been based on concepts introduced by the above-mentioned pioneer historians and artists. I shall list the more prominent of these concepts (called "epistemes" or "logocentrisms" in the new discourse), compare them with viewpoints of Postmodern critics, and offer (for what they are worth) my own observations. The reader will note that many of the issues listed here are closely intertwined; they also pertain not just to art history but to all branches of the humanities and social sciences.

Canons

From the Meiji period onward Western art historians and critics have sought Japanese equivalents of the prominent personalities around whom the history of European civilization was written. The first Japanese (and, indeed, the first Asian) artist to be so canonized was the master of Floating World imagery (*ukiyo-e*) Katsushika Hokusai, of whom some ten biographies in French, English, and German were published within a half-century after his death in 1859; he was likened variously to Gustave Doré, Honoré Daumier,

---

[27] Ernest Gellner (1992), 22-40.
[28] Philippa Berry and Andrew Wernick, eds. (1992).
[29] T. Griffith Foulk and Robert Sharf (1993-94); Helmut Brinker (1996); Samuel and Anne Morse (1996). For anthropological studies, see Catherine Bell (1997), and Victor Turner (1969, 1986).
[30] James Heisig and John Maraldo, eds. (1995); Bernard Faure (1993, 1991).

and William Blake.[31] Soon thereafter biographies of Ukiyo artists such as Katsukawa Shunshō and Utagawa Hiroshige, appeared in Western languages.

Though I will return to this subject below, I should mention here parenthetically that this was indeed an example of the imposition of Western opinion on an Eastern subject. Cultivated Japanese of the Meiji period considered Hokusai to be a vulgar, commercial artisan. Lionizing him as a genius was a Western misapprehension of Japanese culture, an affront to Japanese standards of good taste. This was, however, a curious by-product of the art market. *Ukiyo-e* prints and books, inexpensive and abundant, were the first major idiom of Asian art to arrive abroad in sufficient numbers to warrant serious study. Western artists and critics knew the names of the canonical masters of the past, but they had not seen original works of those masters in meaningful numbers. They were, however, perceptive enough to discern the great merits of Japanese pictorial design and draftsmanship even in the products of plebeian workshops. In doing so, they unwittingly endorsed a Postmodern principle of concern for popular culture and for the submerged, marginalized elements of society.

The outside world had received early instruction in traditional East Asian canons of great artists. The early surveys by Louis Gonse, William Anderson, Arthur Morrison, Oskar Münsterberg, and Ernest Fenollosa were all assisted by knowledgeable Japanese. The most influential book in English was that of Fenollosa, who had studied for nearly a decade with artists of the Kanō and Sumiyoshi schools and who expressed himself in tones of thunderous dogmatism.[32] At the top of his list of great East Asian painters he placed such Southern Song artists as Ma Yuan, Xia Gui, and Mu Qi, "in whom genius found its fullest means of expression"; "the state of things [in Hangchow] was much like that of Phidias under Pericles, or the Florentine artists under the Medici." At the top of his lists of Japanese masters were those who worked in Southern Song modes: Sesshū ("of such a fiery genius that he overmarks them all"), or Kanō painters such as Motonobu ("in whom was gathered the whole power of Kioto painting in the

---

[31] See bibliography in Richard Lane (1989), 315.
[32] Ernest Fenollosa (1912).

Hangchow style") and Tan'yū ("who went beyond Sesshū to the Chinese themselves").[33]

Openly elitist, Fenollosa focused on artists and objects associated with the imperial and shogunal courts and the great shrines and temples. His attitudes were entirely in accord with those of the Meiji government, which had inaugurated a system of registering and classifying works of art.[34] The system, which has undergone constant change, continues to exert powerful financial as well as intellectual influences. On the one hand, it fosters a highly efficient and reasonably honest mechanism governing the export of works of art; on the other, it has controlled the definition of what is important in art and what is not. It is a perfect example of the incorporation of aesthetic values into the functions of a state apparatus.

Postmodern critics challenge judgments of this kind and, indeed, the legitimacy of canons of all kinds. They consider canons to be mental traps, false hierarchies that repress and marginalize other values. Postmodern critics do not in principle endorse one canon over another; they seek instead to dissolve the kind of thinking that creates canons. This, of course, encourages the polysemia, the spirit of multiculturalism flourishing now in American academe.[35] It is also a useful prophylactic against the partisan monomania that afflicts highly fragmented subfields of Japanese scholarship. Some of Japan's hereditary cultural schools maintain rigid, absolute standards of judgment that allow for no dissent: in the Tea Ceremony, for example, flower arranging, or sword connoisseurship.

But any discussion of the value or utility of canons must recognize that traditional Chinese and Japanese cultural histories are filled with them—lists of artists and writers ranked in descending orders of quality ("inspired," "excellent," or "capable"); the Four Great Masters of Yuan; the Thirty-six Poetic Sages; the Three Master Calligraphers of the Kan'ei Period. These judgments are important historical artifacts in their own right, worthy subjects of analysis that sharpen our perception of the expressive values in the idioms that they represent. We should be skeptical of the claims

---

[33] Ibid., vol. 2, 32, 79, 88, 118.
[34] For a review of the registration system and its history, see Bunkazai hogo iinkai (1960).
[35] Ihab Hassan (1992).

that traditional canons are the loci of inherent truths, but we cannot ignore them as important vectors of traditional thought.

Biography

A by-product of the canons of masters is the focus on biography, the single most common research topic for art historians in both Japan and the West for more than a century. Indeed, one of the basic principles of traditional East Asian artistic and literary culture has been the concept of the autonomous creative individual, and most traditional East Asian art and literary criticism takes the form of biography, the individualization of the history of ideas.

Fundamental in Postmodern criticism, however, is the doctrine of the Death of the Author (or of the Artist) as articulated by Michel Foucault among others.[36] It denies the value of what it considers a basic postulate of Modernism, that the author/artist is the self-possessed creator of meaning. Postmodern criticism disparages the effort to establish the artist as the source of significance in works of art. Seeking to "escape from the tyranny of subjectivity," it sees the author/artist as merely one of many nodes in a network of significations. It focuses upon systems of expression, not their creators: "What are the modes of existence of this discourse? Where has it been used, how can it circulate, and who can appropriate it for himself?"[37]

The great majority of American doctoral dissertations on Japanese (and Chinese) art have been life-and-works monographs (*sakusha-sakuhin-ron*).[38] In general most of them have been strong on life and weak on art, or strong on art and weak on life. Complicating this issue is the fact that traditional East Asian biographic source materials are filled with unverified or legendary accounts. Finding detailed, accurate data for East Asian artists prior to 1800 is extremely difficult. To date, a bare handful of Japanese artists has received authoritative biographies that, by present-day standards, successfully balance artistic analysis and personal information.

---

[36] Michel Foucault, "What is an Author?" in Paul Rabinow, ed. (1984), 101-20.
[37] Ibid., 119.
[38] Those that have been published include Stephen Addiss (1987); similar in spirit is his catalogue of 1984; Calvin French (1974); Richard Wilson (1991).

The life-and-works monograph in art history has been falling out of favor owing to its inherent contradictions and difficulties—without being pushed by Postmodern critical theory.[39] Recent American dissertations in the visual arts of Japan have tended to be close studies of a monument, or a restricted group of objects, or a thematic topic. Biography itself has become a separate specialty, exemplified by the heroic efforts of the late Mori Senzō to unsnarl the biographies of Edo-period cultural figures.[40] Mori had the linguistic skills and temperament to sort through archaic land deeds, diaries, wills, and temple records. The art historian, freed from this kind of research, seeks to discover the mechanisms (training methods, discourse with friends and colleagues, demands of patrons) by which creative artists were drawn into the networks of significations of their day, and the manner by which they expressed those meanings.

Development of Style

Fenollosa's *Epochs of Chinese and Japanese Art* reflected a Hegelian (and Darwinian) view of history as an evolutionary process, progressive and teleologically determined. For Fenollosa, the role of the historian was to define and interpret the workings of this grand historical process—destined (in his mind) to create in the very near future a new world culture, a synthesis of the spiritual values of the East with the materialism and technological prowess of the West. Fenollosa's analysis of Buddhist sculpture was also influenced by Mediterranean archaeology. He had been trained in the history of Greek sculpture of the human figure, whose central tenet was the consistent, intelligible evolution from geometric and abstract shapes to realistic and highly expressive ones. Fenollosa sought to show that East Asian Buddhist statuary had evolved in roughly the same fashion.

The notion that stylistic evolution is an important clue to the inner workings and goals of human culture has largely been abandoned. Postmodern critics have discarded grand historical narra-

---

[39] The biographic approach has long ago been criticized by formalist art historians such as Heinrich Wölfflin or George Kubler.

[40] Mori Senzō (1970-95).

tives of this kind and replaced them with new agendas.[41] But as a device for ordering and dating works of art, the study of stylistic evolution is applicable to virtually every subfield of Japanese art, such as narrative painting, ink painting, ceramics, or *ukiyo-e*. Each of those idioms reveals evolutionary changes in the mastery of formal idioms or in the accumulation of technical sophistication. Stylistic evolution is no longer a worthy autonomous subject for research, and it is of little interest to non-specialists, but it remains an indispensable empirical tool for the art historian. It makes use of large numbers of photographs and thus benefits from new developments in computerized imaging.

Inherent in the study of stylistic development is the historian's device of periodization, whereby the evolutionary record is divided into stages, or periods, which are coordinated with developments in the sociopolitical background. Often used as an organizing principle in popular exhibitions and survey courses, period concepts tend to solidify into crippling distortions and over-simplifications. The Heian period, for example, has been called the age of aristocracy, feminized luxury, and aestheticism—at the expense of a more realistic interpretation of its history.[42] The Muromachi period has been subject to similar distortions: the age of the samurai, of Zen, of ink painting, and of manly vigor.

Iconology

Another major discipline in twentieth-century art history is iconology: assigning meanings to works of art on the basis of historical research. As practiced by its grand European masters such as Irwin Panofsky, iconology often identifies recurring themes that constitute the heart of cultural traditions. In Japanese art these include classical court literary subjects like the *Tale of Genji*, or Confucian ethical symbols such as the Seven Sages of the Bamboo Grove and the Four Sages of Mt. Shang.

This approach has been greatly affected by the new critical theories, which discredit the concept of a unified knowing subject (or viewer). Emphasizing the semiotic indeterminacy of works of art, they deride attempts to assign fixed meanings to symbols, claim-

---

[41] See Quentin Skinner (1985).
[42] See Mimi Yiengpruksawan (1994).

ing that the work of art cannot reflect a single, inherent unified significance. They maintain that the designation of grand themes in art is as meaningless as astronomers' maps of the constellations, which impose purely fictitious relationships upon unrelated stars. They place primary emphasis upon the present-day viewer/reader, who imparts significance to the work: "The work proposes; man disposes."[43]

This aspect of Postmodern criticism is largely redundant for much of Chinese and Japanese secular symbolism, especially those forms that treat nature and the human heart. East Asian natural symbols (orchids, bamboo, plums, cranes) were often made intentionally ambiguous, endowed with multiple meanings, and not susceptible to simple one-to-one designations. But given the vast number of Japanese paintings that bear inscriptions, the student of symbolic meanings has a rich palette of verbal and visual (word-image) data with which to explore this universe of fluid significance.

Contextualization

The large narratives of history have long been replaced by the more modest, empirical historicism practiced by mainstream Japanese art historians. This approach, seeking to discover the specific contexts from which given works of art arose, is based on the principle that the detailed record of how objects of great beauty were created is important in and of itself.

Here, however, one wing of Postmodern criticism has created a most dangerous challenge to standards of scholarship.[44] It declares that the past is essentially unknowable, that the positivist, scientific approach is fallacious, and that its presumed objectivity is a mirage. The critique dismisses the selection of subjects and topics of inquiry from the past as mere reflections of current priorities and judgments; it claims that the "objective history" of establishment scholarship creates a fictitious, sanitized past as a prototype for the flawed present. It derides traditional history for focusing upon "the most noble periods, the highest forms, and the purest individuals"; it claims that these judgments are "errors hardened

---

[43] Roland Barthes (1987), 69.
[44] See Ernest Gellner (1992), 2-26.

into an unalterable form in the long baking process of history." The new approach, by contrast, accepts all historical phenomena without distinction. It studies periods of decadence (or pettiness, or misfortune), and openly proclaims its contemporary affiliation: "No past is greater than your present."[45]

Though nothing in Postmodern doctrine prevents serious historical study, the formulation that the needs of the present supersede the achievements of the past has had the practical effect of presenting present-day issues disguised as history. Denying the possibility of objectivity and demeaning historical scholarship have resulted in a repetition of the Orientalist fallacy: presenting Eastern cultures according to Western criteria, and bringing to the task only superficial knowledge of the Eastern subject.

Shifting Paradigms of Scholarship

The fluidity of canons in the history of Japanese art is nowhere better illustrated than in the status of two of its major subfields: the Edo-period Floating World (Ukiyo) and Scholar-Amateur (Bunjin, or Nanga) movements. Other areas are undergoing changes as well, which I outline below. Some of these changes are the by-products of the Modernist ideals which flourished until the 1970s; others stem from Postmodern principles.

Ukiyo-e

As mentioned above, Japanese prints played a vital role in nineteenth-century japonisme, despite their low standing in Japanese traditional taste. Following this great surge of scholarship in the Meiji era, however, Western students and collectors turned toward other, more orthodox, topics, and their interest in *ukiyo-e* tended to fade. In the past two decades, however, responding to the changed intellectual climate, *ukiyo-e* has again come into prominence, along with the related *gesaku* literary idioms. Critical theorists have applauded this renewed interest as an assault on frozen concepts of Japanese elitist art and as an exploration of the liber-

---

[45] Michel Foucault, *Nietzsche, Genealogy, History*, quoted in Rabinow, ed. (1984), 77, 91.

ating taste of the masses (the carnival of popular culture, in the words of Mikhail Bakhtin).

Furthermore, the high sexual content in *ukiyo-e* and *gesaku* has appealed to the ethical wing of Postmodern criticism, which seeks to overcome the taboos on such subjects ("the image of the imperial prude...emblazoned on our restrained, mute, and hypocritical sexuality").[46] Noting that the Meiji regime, seeking to present a sanitized image of Japan to the West, discouraged study of the sexual content of *gesaku* and *ukiyo-e*, Indiana University organized an ambitious conference on the subject in 1995.[47] Accompanying this polemical interest in *ukiyo-e* has been a remarkably vigorous revival of the more traditional scholarly approaches (biographies, oeuvre catalogues).[48]

Arts of the Scholar-Amateur

Pioneer Western art historians either minimized the role of Nanga or ignored it entirely. In fact, Fenollosa's *Epochs* contains violent diatribes against the Scholar-Amateurs: "from any universal point of view their art is hardly more than an awkward joke."[49] This was a reflection of Japanese establishment taste, exemplified by the virtual exclusion of Nanga works from Meiji-era lists of national treasures.

The prejudice against literati painting prevailed in the West until the mid-1950s, when collectors and scholars, influenced by the growing acceptance of Expressionists (from El Greco and Salvador Rosa to Vincent van Gogh and Oskar Kokoschka), began to admire such Chinese Scholar-Amateurs as Zhuda (1625-after 1705) and Daoji (1641-1720) and Japanese such as Ike no Taiga (1723-1776) and Uragami Gyokudō (1745-1820). After the Japanese Cultural Affairs Agency (Bunkachō) was reorganized in 1950, it added over 150 Nanga paintings and calligraphies to its lists of registered works. And one of the most striking features of American scholarship in Japanese art since 1945 was the flower-

---

[46] Michel Foucault, *The History of Sexuality*, quoted in ibid., 292.
[47] Sumie Jones, ed. (1996).
[48] Timothy Clark (1992); Timothy Clark, et al. (1994); Asano Shūgō and Tyemoshi Kura-ku (Timothy Clark) (1995); Donald Jenkins (1993).
[49] Fenollosa (1912), vol. 2, 165.

ing of Nanga studies, led by James Cahill, Calvin French, and Stephen Addiss.[50]

Shift from Antiquarianism

Another major change is the admission of post-Meiji arts into academic art history and public exhibitions in this country. Despite the deep involvement of Fenollosa and Okakura in the living arts of their day, until recently establishment art historians in Japan and the West were doggedly antiquarian in their views. Space in the quasi-official Pelican history of Japanese art of 1955, for example, was allotted roughly as follows: eighty percent to Japanese art up to the Momoyama period, twenty percent to the Momoyama and Edo periods; the Meiji and post-Meiji eras were not discussed.[51] This proportion was roughly in accord with that of the objects then registered as Japanese national treasures.

Failure to confront the Modern era imbued the art-history field in America with an aura of romantic escapism at odds with the realities of the new Japan. (Surprisingly, this shortcoming did not afflict Western studies of Modern-era Japanese literature.) In the 1960s, however, art historians began to widen their perspectives; a number of major exhibitions with detailed catalogues explored various facets of twentieth-century Japanese art and culture.[52] Serious articles and doctoral dissertations have also begun to appear.[53] And the latest detailed survey book allots ample space to developments of the Meiji and post-Meiji eras.[54]

Architectural History

Avant-garde European and American architects have warmly praised Japanese buildings. Alexander Soper, one of the leading scholars of the post-World War II generation, was a masterful student of

---

[50] James Cahill (1972); Calvin French, et al. (1974); Stephen Addiss (1987). See also Melinda Takeuchi (1992).

[51] Robert Paine and Alexander Soper (1955).

[52] Museum of Modern Art (1966); Frederick Baekeland (1980); *Words in Motion: Modern Japanese Calligraphy* (1984); Mildred Friedman, ed. (1986); Takashina Shūji, et al. (1987); Frederick Baekeland and Robert Moes (1993); Alexandra Munroe, et al. (1994); Ellen Conant, et al. (1995).

[53] Mimi Yiengpruksawan (1993); Elizabeth Swinton (1986).

[54] Penelope Mason (1993).

Japanese architecture. But despite the self-evident majesty of building traditions there, architectural history has not yet become an integral part of humanistic studies in Japan.

In the West, where Renaissance aesthetic theory assigned it to the status of a Liberal Art, architecture has long been integrated into the teaching of art history departments, and scholars like Richard Krautheimer, Rudolf Wittkower, and James Ackerman have tied the evolution of architectural form to the larger themes of European cultural history. In Japan, however, architectural history has usually been taught in schools of engineering, and the extraordinary skills of specialists like Fukuyama Toshio, Ōta Hirotarō, and Naitō Akira have not ordinarily been integrated into the study of other artistic idioms.

This is a subfield that offers infinite possibilities for development, but due in large part to lack of intellectual and institutional support in Japan, the study of Japanese architecture has lagged far behind the other branches of the visual arts. Fortunately, well-trained younger Western specialists have recently begun to teach and publish in it.[55]

Crafts

Equally promising for future work is the vast area of Japanese handicrafts (*kōgei*). European collectors of the 1850s and 1860s, inspired by the theories of Gottfried Semper and the Arts and Industries movement in England, were wildly enthusiastic about Japanese export porcelains, cloisonné, and metalwork—the subject of some of the very first books on Japanese art.[56] By the turn of the century, however, Western attention had shifted to *ukiyo-e* and then to sculpture and painting. Japan, moreover, began to honor the Italian Renaissance distinction between the "fine" and "decorative" (or "minor") arts, even though this was foreign to traditional Japanese thought.

The crafts—ceramics, textiles, lacquer, and metalwork—have

---

[55] Historians of Japanese architecture have recently joined art history faculties at the University of Michigan (Jonathan Reynolds), Harvard (Cherie Wendelken), and the University of Melbourne in Australia (William Coaldrake; see his books of 1990, 1996).

[56] For a recent and detailed review of Meiji-period handicrafts, see Oliver Impey, et al. (1995).

historically played a central role in the evolution of Japanese taste and artistic technology. Fine craftsmen were often given the same status and honors as painters and sculptors, and artists in different media often exchanged design motifs and compositional patterns as they shared the same patrons. The crafts thus offer great opportunities for future scholarship—but with the same caveat that faces architectural historians: to integrate their study with the other branches of the visual arts and with the larger interpretative issues of the humanities. Enormous strides in this respect were made by Tsuji Nobuo in an ambitious exhibition (with detailed catalogue) that integrated arts and crafts in many media.[57] Richard Wilson, now at International Christian University in Tokyo, is successfully employing Japanese modes of empirical research in ceramics history.[58] And Louise Cort of the Freer-Sackler Galleries in Washington has made remarkable progress in her studies of the role of the crafts in Japan's folk culture.[59]

Interdisciplinary Studies

Postmodern critical theory attacks the tendency for scholarship to encapsulate itself in narrow specialties. A prime example of the weakness of a blinkered approach is the classic American study on Japanese court poetry, which omitted any mention of the fact that some of Japan's leading poets were gifted calligraphers and that calligraphy was an integral part of court literary culture.[60] On this point Postmodern criticism once again concurs with traditional East Asian values. The inherent unity of the "arts of the brush" (poetry, calligraphy, and painting) has long been a prime feature of Scholar-Amateur aesthetic doctrine. And the new criticism—as it extols indeterminacy, multivalence, and the interplay between discourses—discourages the narrow focus of extreme specialization.

Recent scholarship has increasingly crossed disciplinary lines. A Yale University Art Gallery exhibition demonstrated the impact of early court poetry on Edo-period decorative painting.[61] Stud-

---

[57] Tsuji Nobuo, et al. (1988).
[58] Richard Wilson (1991), and Richado Uiruson (Richard Wilson) and Ogasawara Seiko (1992).
[59] Louise Cort (1979, 1992, 1994).
[60] Robert Brower and Earl Miner (1981).
[61] Carolyn Wheelwright (1989).

ies in calligraphy have been obliged to integrate the analysis of artistic form with that of literary content.[62] Tsuji Nobuo has opened a linkage between art history and social studies by defining lineages of eccentric, individualistic artists of various cultural backgrounds.[63] And he has begun exploring the spiritual and ritual origins of Japanese decorative modes.[64] Tanaka Hisao has probed the history of patronage.[65] Others have explored the impact of the Japanese workshop system (*iemoto seido*) on the practice of the visual and theatrical arts.[66]

Younger Japanese scholars have joined in a recent fourteen-volume publication project to reappraise familiar masterpieces and employ new methodologies. The most controversial among these books has proposed a new identification and redating (in the fourteenth century) for one of the foundation works of traditional art history, the presumed portrait painting of Minamoto no Yoritomo.[67] Barbara Ruch, now at Columbia University, joined with Japanese colleagues in launching an ambitious interdisciplinary program to study so-called Nara Pictures (*nara-e*) and the texts which they illustrate. *Nara-e* is the misleading name given to usually naive narrative paintings of folk tales (*otogizōshi*) and religious subjects. Both the tales and the paintings had long been considered trivial by Japanese establishment scholars, but they embodied the forms by which traditional Japanese narrative painting survived during the Muromachi period, when Japanese high taste was focused on Chinese models.[68] Historian Henry Smith, also of Columbia University, has brought a social scientist's keen perspective to the interpretation of visual imagery.[69]

---

[62] John Rosenfield, Fumiko Cranston, and Edwin Cranston (1973); Shimizu Yoshiaki and John Rosenfield (1984).

[63] Tsuji Nobuo (1970, 1979, 1986, 1989).

[64] Tsuji Nobuo (1988, 1994).

[65] Tanaka Hisao (1990).

[66] Shimizu Yoshiaki (1980); John Rosenfield, ed. (1993).

[67] Yonekura Michio (1995).

[68] Nara e-hon kokusai kenkyū kai (Nara-e International Research Group), ed. (1981).

[69] Henry Smith (1986, 1988a, 1988b).

Art World Corruption

As a corollary of its rejection of canons of master artists and masterpieces, Postmodern criticism denigrates the very large sector of the art world populated by collectors, dealers, connoisseurs, and museum professionals.[70] This critique arises in part from the preoccupation of Postmodern critics with philosophy, a concern with pure ideation and theory that has been glibly summarized as "history bashing, museum bashing, and library bashing."[71] It is also fueled by a sense of outrage over unethical practices. Though Japan itself provides one of the world's most highly regulated and ethically correct environments for the art trade, young American students of Japanese art have been strongly influenced by this climate of hostile opinion.

Art dealers, collectors, and museum personnel are accused of wrenching works from their original contexts, treating them purely as aesthetic objects, and then debasing them as merchandise. They are said to engage in "merit scavenging"[72]—roaming like rag pickers over the refuse heaps of the past and appropriating to themselves the aesthetic and moral values inherent in the products of civilizations far more creative than their own. Museums, catering to the wealthy, are declared to be islands of elite culture, mausoleums of art isolated from the dynamic realities of society. Museums are further rebuked for glorifying masterpieces (and for advertising the vast sums of money paid for them), for flattering collectors to solicit gifts, and for promoting only those forms of art that fit into the museum environment. Exhibition catalogues, usually written against onerous deadlines, are disparaged as imperfect vehicles for scholarship; collection catalogues are decried as base tribute to vain collectors; and all catalogues are said to be ephemera—of no more enduring value than this week's television guide.

Condemnation of the dealer-collector-connoisseur-curator network raises still other allegations. Traffic in forgeries induces an air of suspicion and chicanery. Exploitation of tax laws undermines public support for museums. Third World monuments are plun-

---

[70] See, for example, Douglas Crimp (1983).
[71] Boris Groys (1997); see also James Cuno (1997).
[72] I owe this unforgettable expression to Sayeed Iqbal Jaffrey, a noted Pakistani painter and legal scholar, who used it in correspondence with the Harvard University Fine Arts Department during the mid-1960s.

dered; irreplaceable cultural relics are destroyed; the smuggling of works of art obscures their provenance and history. Not only does this increase the atmosphere of secrecy that pervades the art trade, it violates the candor, exactness, and propriety that should, in principle, motivate all scholarship.

The vast sums of money that flow through the art market are said to distort scholarship in much the same way that profits in the pharmaceutical industry disturb the field of biochemistry. Scholars shade their judgments in order to please powerful patrons. Dealers discover caches of obscure works, exaggerate their quality in publicity and exhibition campaigns, and commission scholars to substantiate the claims—with handsome profits flowing to all concerned.[73]

Postmodern critics have an especially low opinion of connoisseurship, the craft of verifying the authenticity, dating, original contexts, and relative quality of works of art. Long considered the root skill of the art historian, connoisseurship has been rapidly falling out of the curricula of graduate programs in art history because of its "materialism" and its crucial role in the art trade. Rarely heard today is the question that, some twenty years ago, was most often asked about an art historian: "Does that person have an 'eye'—a feeling for authenticity, quality, and expressive values?"

This critique, in my view, is both accurate and destructive. I have personally observed all of the ethical and intellectual transgressions cited above. But the art trade is also a legitimate medium of intellectual as well as financial exchange, and I know many honorable and learned dealers. I have worked with self-effacing collectors who acquire objects as an intellectual and aesthetic adventure and who encourage and support scholarship—and engage in it themselves. Their minds unencumbered by academic dogma, collectors often discover things that specialists overlook. I respect connoisseurs who elucidate the essential qualities of the works they authenticate. I admire museum curators who fulfill their mandates as scholars and public educators; they form insightful collections, organize pathfinding exhibitions, and publish catalogues which serve as important vehicles in the dissemination of knowl-

---

[73] Often described as a recent example of this phenomenon is the lavish catalogue of a private collection of Meiji-period handicrafts cited in note 56.

edge. The chicanery and greed that blemish collecting and the art trade are by no means purely modern phenomena; in Japan, as in China, they may be traced back to remote antiquity. Collecting, dealing, and the psychological and economic aspects of the art world are worthy subjects of scholarship in their own right.[74] The ethical transgressions of the art world are deplorable, and criticism is an essential engine of reform; but the absolutism and self-righteousness of Postmodern critics (the self-proclaimed exclusive franchise of virtue) have needlessly widened the chasm between academic scholarship and the art world, which historically have greatly nourished each other. To condemn the art world because of the misdeeds of some of its members is akin to condemning sex because of prostitution and pornography.

The Language of Scholarship

My final point here touches lightly on one of the largest and most sensitive issues of all, the language of scholarly discourse. Postmodern critics, seeking a revolution in intellectual standards, dismiss as fraudulent the claim that traditional scholarship is objective and universal; they state that establishment historians use vocabularies that are inherently biased in favor of positivist, rational, and middle-class professional values. (They assume, of course, that these are unworthy.)[75]

The "rhetorical sportiveness" (puns and neologisms) of Postmodern criticism is a weapon with which to attack establishment linguistic and intellectual orders. In fact, revolutionaries everywhere historically have sought to transform linguistic usage; the French Jacobins, for example, imposed new personal and calendrical names on the populace; the Maoist regime radically altered Chinese writing and transliteration systems. The arcane linguistic convolutions of Postmodern criticism, which can be traced back to Friedrich Nietzsche, have flourished in the distinctive atmosphere of Parisian cultural life, where language wars have long raged

---

[74] For studies in East Asian patronage, collecting, and dealing, see Yoko Woodson (1991) and Craig Clunas (1972). See Komatsu Shigemi (1972) for an account of the Kohitsu family of Japanese connoisseur-dealers.

[75] Barthes (1987), 9-12, 46-52.

among intellectual castes.[76] In the English-speaking world, however, "linguistic narcissism" of this kind is often accused of "obscurity, pretentiousness, faddiness, showmanship, and cultural name-dropping."[77] It is extremely painful to British and American writers who were trained to frame scholarship in plain terms and to strive for simplicity and clarity of expression.[78]

Traditional art history and criticism have indeed earned the reputation of outdated and fallible modes of discourse. Their core vocabularies have been debased by decades of careless use of terms such as "style," "value," "romantic," "plastic," "vitality." For English-language writers, however, the solution is not to substitute one set of jargon terms for another, but to employ language that responsibly reflects thought, and to insure that thought itself is clear and free of the constraints of orthodoxy. Some of the most gifted of the Postmodern critics have achieved that goal, but the most painful follies of the new criticism occur when its less gifted practitioners employ arcane vocabularies that totally occlude the works of art or literature they seek to explain.

Conclusion

The study of Japanese art in this country has never been stable, nor has it been conducted in an intellectual or social vacuum. Changes have been induced by the thinking of our Japanese colleagues, by developments in Chinese studies, by the insights and discoveries of collectors, by the economics of the art market, by the taste of the general public, by the directions of intellectual life in the nation's culture at large, and, of course, by the mighty tides of war and peace.

As historians of Japanese art, we must learn to cope with the turbulent intellectual climate of scholarship in the humanities if we are to survive the internecine wars of academe. In fact, I join with Mimi Yiengpruksawan in believing that we can render a distinct service by testing the relevance of present-day theoretical approaches by applying them to Asian models, and by develop-

---

[76] See Foreword by Philip Thody in ibid.
[77] Gellner (1992), 70.
[78] George Orwell (1988), 127-40.

ing our own interpretative strategies in the Japanese field.[79]

On the other hand, if we lose ourselves in theoretical concerns and ignore the positivist, empirical basis of Japanese studies, we run the risk of repeating one of the most flagrant crimes of Orientalism: applying Western standards and principles of analysis without a deep understanding of the Eastern subject. Moreover, if we lose ourselves in the dense thickets of theory, we run the danger of "substituting poetics for poetry," of ignoring the expressive properties of works of art—the vital experience, the felt excitement—that should serve as the prime focus of our efforts.[80] When we lose sight of that, we surrender the most powerful resource of our profession.

BIBLIOGRAPHY

Addiss, Stephen. 1984. *The World of Kameda Bōsai: the Calligraphy, Poetry, Painting, and Artistic Circle of the Japanese Literatus*. Exh. cat. New Orleans: New Orleans Museum of Art.

———. 1987. *Tall Mountains and Flowing Waters: The Arts of Uragami Gyokudō*. Honolulu: University of Hawai'i Press.

Asano Shūgo, and Tyemoshi Kura-ku (Timothy Clark). 1995. *Kitagawa Utamaro*. 2 vols. Exh. cat. Asahi shinbunsha.

Baekeland, Frederick. 1980. *Imperial Japan: the Art of the Meiji Era (1868-1912)*. Exh. cat. Ithaca: Johnson Museum of Art, Cornell University.

Baekeland, Frederick, and Robert Moes. 1993. *Modern Japanese Ceramics in American Collections*. Exh. cat. New York: Japan Society.

Barthes, Roland. 1975. *The Pleasure of the Text*. Translated by Richard Miller. New York: Farrar, Straus, and Giroux.

———. 1982. *Empire of Signs*. Translated by Richard Howard. New York: Farrar, Straus, and Giroux.

———. 1987. *Criticism and Truth*. Translated and edited by Katrine Keuneman. Minneapolis: University of Minnesota Press.

Bell, Catherine. 1992. *Ritual Theory, Ritual Practice*. Oxford: Oxford University Press.

———. 1997. *Ritual: Perspectives on the Practice of Religion*. New York: Oxford University Press.

Berger, Klaus. 1992. *Japonisme in Western Painting from Whistler to Matisse*. Cambridge: Cambridge University Press.

Berry, Philippa, and Andrew Wernick, eds. 1992. *Shadow of Spirit: Postmodernism and Religion*. London: Routledge.

Boime, Albert. 1971. *The Academy and French Painting in the Nineteenth Century*. London: Phaidon.

---

[79] As expressed in a letter from Mimi Yiengpruksawan to the author, dated April 1997.

[80] See Roland Barthes (1975).

Bowie, Theodore. 1966. *Langdon Warner Through His Letters*. Bloomington: Indiana University Press.
Brinker, Helmut, and Kanazawa Hiroshi. 1996. *Zen: Masters of Meditation in Images and Writings*. Exh. cat. *Artibus Asiae* supplementum 40. Zürich: Artibus Asiae.
Brower, Robert, and Earl Miner. 1981. *Japanese Court Poetry*. Stanford: Stanford University Press.
Bunkazai hogo iinkai (Commission for the Protection of Cultural Properties). 1960. *Bunkazai hogo no ayumi* (Progress in the Protection of Cultural Properties). Bunkazai hogo iinkai.
Cahill, James. 1972. *Scholar Painters of Japan: The Nanga School*. Exh. cat. New York: Asia Society.
Cary, Otis. 1987. *Mr. Stimson's "Pet City"—The Sparing of Kyoto, 1945: Atomic Bomb Targeting—Myths and Realities*. Kyoto: Amherst House, Dōshisha University.
Clark, Timothy. 1992. *Ukiyo-e Paintings in the British Museum*. London: British Museum.
Clark, Timothy, et al. 1994. *The Actor's Image: Print Makers of the Katsukawa School*. Chicago: Art Institute of Chicago.
Clunas, Craig. 1991. *Superfluous Things: Material Culture and Social Status in Early Modern China*. Urbana: University of Illinois Press.
Coaldrake, William. 1990. *The Way of the Carpenter: Tools and Japanese Architecture*. Tokyo: Weatherhill.
———. 1996. *Architecture and Authority in Japan*. London: Routledge.
Cohen, Warren. 1992. *East Asian Art and American Culture: A Study in International Relations*. New York: Columbia University Press.
Collcutt, Martin. 1986. "Buddhism: The Threat of Eradication." In *Japan in Transition: from Tokugawa to Meiji*, edited by Marius Jansen and Gilbert Rozman, 143-67. Princeton: Princeton University Press.
Conant, Ellen. 1995. *Nihonga. Transcending the Past: Japanese-Style Painting, 1868-1968*. Exh. cat. St. Louis: St. Louis Art Museum.
Cort, Louise. 1979. *Shigaraki, Potter's Valley*. Tokyo: Kodansha International.
———. 1992. *Seto and Mino Ceramics. Japanese Collections in the Freer Gallery of Art*. Washington: Freer Gallery of Art.
Cort, Louise, and Nakamura Kenji. 1994. *A Basketmaker in Rural Japan*. Exh. cat. Washington: Arthur M. Sackler Gallery.
Crimp, Douglas. 1983. "On the Museum's Ruins." In *The Anti-Aesthetic: Essays on Postmodern Culture*, edited with introduction by Hal Foster, 43-56. Seattle: Bay Press.
Cuno, James. March 1997. "Whose Money? Whose Powers? Whose Art History?" *Art Bulletin* 79, no. 1: 6-9.
Dresser, Christopher. 1882. *Japan: Its Architecture, Art, and Art Manufactures*. London: Longman, Greem.
During, Simon, ed. 1993. *The Cultural Studies Reader*. London: Routledge.
Faure, Bernard. 1991. *Rhetoric of Immediacy: A Cultural Critique of Chan/Zen Buddhism*. Princeton: Princeton University Press.
———. 1993. *Chan Insights and Oversights*. Princeton: Princeton University Press.
Fenollosa, Ernest. 1912. *Epochs of Chinese and Japanese Art, an Outline History of East Asian Design*. Rev. ed. 2 vols. New York: Frederick Stokes.
Fister, Pat. 1988. *Japanese Women Artists, 1600-1900*. Exh. cat. Lawrence: Spencer Museum of Art, University of Kansas.
Foster, Hal, ed. 1983. *The Anti-Aesthetic: Essays on Postmodern Culture*. Seattle: Bay Press.

Foulk, T. Griffith, and Robert Sharf. 1993-94. "On the Ritual Use of Ch'an Portraiture in Medieval China." *Cahiers d'extrême-orient* 7: 149-219.
Frank, Bernard. 1991. *Le panthéon bouddhique au Japon—Collections d'Émile Guimet*. Paris: Réunion des musées nationaux.
French, Calvin. 1974. *Shiba Kōkan: Artist, Innovator, and Pioneer in the Westernization of Japan*. Tokyo: Weatherhill.
French, Calvin, et al. 1974. *The Poet-Painters: Buson and his Followers*. Exh. cat. Ann Arbor: University of Michigan Museum of Art.
Friedman, Mildred, ed. 1986. *Tokyo: Form and Spirit*. Exh. cat. Minneapolis: Walker Art Center.
Gellner, Ernest. 1992. *Postmodernism, Reason and Religion*. London: Routledge.
Gombrich, Ernst. 1970. *Aby Warburg: An Intellectual Biography*. London: Warburg Institute.
Groys, Boris. April 6, 1997. "To Collect and be Collected." Public lecture, Harvard University.
Guth, Christine. 1993. *Art, Tea, and Industry: Masuda Takashi and the Mitsui Circle*. Princeton: Princeton University Press.
Hassan, Ihab. 1992. "Pluralism in Modern Perspective." In Jencks, ed. (1992), 196-207.
Heisig, James, and John Maraldo, eds. 1995. *Rude Awakenings: Zen, the Kyoto School, and the Question of Nationalism*. Honolulu: University of Hawai'i Press.
Impey, Oliver, Malcom Fairley, and Joe Earle. 1995. *Meiji no takara* (Treasures of Imperial Japan: Nasser D. Khalili Collection of Japanese Art). 8 vols. London: Kibo Foundation.
Jencks, Charles. 1992. "The Post-Modern Agenda." In Jencks, ed. (1992), 10-39.
Jencks, Charles, ed. 1992. *The Post-Modern Reader*. London: Academy Editions.
Jenkins, Donald. 1993. *The Floating World Revisited*. Exh. cat. Portland: Portland Art Museum.
Jones, Sumie, ed. 1996. *Imaging Reading Eros: Proceedings for the Conference, Sexuality and Edo Culture, 1750-1850*. Bloomington: East Asian Studies Center, Indiana University.
Ketelaar, James. 1990. *Of Heretics and Martyrs in Meiji Japan: Buddhism and its Persecution*. Princeton: Princeton University Press.
Kleinbauer, W. E. 1971. *Modern Perspectives in Western Art History*. New York: Holt, Rinehart, and Winston.
Komatsu Shigemi. 1972. *Kohitsu* (Account of the Kohitsu family of calligraphy connoisseur-dealers). Kodansha.
Koschmann, J. Victor. 1989. "Maruyama Masao and the Incomplete Project of Modernity." In Miyoshi and Harootunian, eds. (1989).
Kultermann, Udo. 1993. *The History of Art History*. New York: Abaris.
Lane, Richard. 1989. *Hokusai: His Life and Work*. New York: Dutton.
Magnus, Bernd, and Kathleen Higgins, eds. 1996. *The Cambridge Companion to Nietzsche*. Cambridge: Cambridge University Press.
Mason, Penelope. 1993. *History of Japanese Art*. New York: Abrams.
McCallum, Donald. 1994. *Zenkōji and Its Icon: A Study in Medieval Japanese Religious Art*. Princeton: Princeton University Press.
Miyoshi, Masao, and H. D. Harootunian, eds. 1989. *Postmodernism and Japan*. Post-Contemporary Interventions series. Durham: Duke University Press.
Mori Senzō. 1970-1995. *Mori Senzō choshaku-shū*. 30 vols. Chūō kōron shuppansha.
Morse, Samuel, and Anne Morse. 1996. *Object as Insight: Japanese Buddhist Art and Ritual*. Exh. cat. Katonah: Katonah Museum of Art.

Munroe, Alexandra, et al. 1994. *Scream Against the Sky: Japanese Art After 1945*. Exh. cat. New York: Harry Abrams.
Murase, Miyeko. 1975. *Japanese Art: Selections from the Mary and Jackson Burke Collection*. Exh. cat. New York: Metropolitan Museum of Art.
———. 1986. *Tales of Japan: Scrolls and Prints from the New York Public Library*. Exh. cat. New York: Oxford University Press.
———. 1994. *Jewel Rivers: Japanese Art from the Burke Collection*. Exh. cat. Richmond: Virginia Museum of Fine Arts.
Museum of Modern Art. 1966. *The New Japanese Painting and Sculpture*. Exh. cat. New York: Museum of Modern Art.
Nakano Genzō. 1982. *Nihon Bukkyō kaiga kenkyū* (Research on Buddhist Painting). Kyoto: Hōzōkan.
Nara e-hon kokusai kenkyū kai (*Nara-e* International Research Group), ed. 1981. *Zaigai Nara e-hon* (*Nara-e* in Foreign Collections). Kadokawa shoten.
Norris, Christopher. 1982. *Deconstruction: Theory and Practice*. Rev. ed. London: Routledge.
Norris, Christopher, and Andrew Benjamin. 1988. *What is Deconstruction?* London: Academy Editions.
Orwell, George. 1988. "Politics and the English Language." Reprint. In Vol. 4 of *In Front of Your Nose 1945-1950: The Collected Essays, Journalism, and Letters of George Orwell*, edited by Sonia Orwell and Ian Angus, 127-40. New York: Harcourt, Brace, Jovanovitch.
Paine, Robert, and Alexander Soper. 1955. *Art and Architecture of Japan*. 1st ed. Harmondsworth, U.K.: Penguin.
Panofsky, Erwin. 1955. *Meaning in the Visual Arts*. Chicago: University of Chicago Press.
Pevsner, Nikolaus. 1940. *Academies of Art, Past and Present*. Cambridge: Cambridge University Press.
Rabinow, Paul, ed. 1984. *Foucault Reader*. New York: Pantheon.
Rose, Margaret. 1991. *The Post-Modern and the Post-Industrial: A Critical Analysis*. Cambridge: Cambridge University Press.
———. 1993. *Parody: Ancient, Modern, and Post-Modern*. Literature, Culture, Theory series. Cambridge: Cambridge University Press.
Rosenfield, John. 1968-69. "The Sedgwick Statue of the Infant Shotoku Taishi." *Archives of Asian Art* 22: 56-79.
———. 1977. "The Unity of the Three Creeds." In *Japan in the Muromachi Age*, edited by John Hall and Toyoda Takeshi. Berkeley: University of California Press.
Rosenfield, John, ed. 1993. *Competition and Collaboration: Hereditary Schools in Japanese Culture*. Symposium papers. *Fenway Court*. Boston: Isabella Stewart Gardner Museum.
Rosenfield, John, Fumiko Cranston, and Edwin Cranston. 1973. *The Courtly Tradition in Japanese Art and Literature: Selections from the Hofer and Hyde Collections*. Exh. cat. Cambridge: Fogg Art Museum.
Said, Edward. 1978. *Orientalism*. 1st ed. New York: Pantheon.
———. 1993. *Culture and Imperialism*. 1st ed. New York: Alfred A. Knopf.
Satō Dōshin. 1996. *"Nihon Bijutsu" tanjō: kindai Nihon no "kotoba" to senryaku* (The Birth of "Japanese Art": Modern Japanese "Terminological" Strategies). Vol. 92 of *Kōdansha sensho mechie* (Kodansha Select Series "Métier"). Kodansha.
Screech, Timon. 1996. *The Western Scientific Gaze and Popular Imagery in Later Edo Japan: The Lens within the Heart*. Cambridge: Cambridge University Press.
———. 1997. *Edo no shintai o hiraku* (*Opening the Edo Body*). Translated by Takayama Hiroshi. Sakuhinsha.

Shimada Shūjirō. 1987. *Nihon kaigashi kenkyū* (Research on Japanese Painting). Chūōkōron bijutsu shuppan.
———. 1993. *Chūgoku kaigashi kenkyū* (Research on Chinese Painting). Chūōkōron bijutsu shuppan.
Shimizu, Yoshiaki. 1980. "Six Narrative Paintings by Yin T'o-lo: Their Narrative Content." *Archives of Asian Art* 33: 6-37.
———. 1981. "Workshop Management of the Early Kano Painters, ca. A.D. 1530-1600." *Archives of Asian Art* 34: 32-47.
Shimizu, Yoshiaki, ed. 1988. *Japan: The Shaping of Daimyo Culture 1185-1868.* Exh. cat. Washington: National Gallery of Art.
Shimizu, Yoshiaki, and John Rosenfield. 1984. *Masters of Japanese Calligraphy: 8th-19th Century.* Exh. cat. New York: Asian Society Galleries, Japan House Gallery.
Skinner, Quentin, ed. 1985. *The Return of Grand Theory in the Human Sciences.* Cambridge: Cambridge University Press.
Smith, Henry. 1986. *Hiroshige: One Hundred Famous Views of Edo.* New York: George Braziller.
———. 1988a. *Hokusai: One Hundred Views of Mt. Fuji.* New York: George Braziller.
———. 1988b. *Kiyochika: Artist of Meiji Japan.* Exh. cat. Santa Barbara: Santa Barbara Museum of Art.
Swinton, Elizabeth. 1986. "The Graphic Art of Onchi Kōshirō: Innovation and Tradition." Reprint. Outstanding Dissertation in the Fine Arts. New York: Garland. [Ph.D. diss., Harvard University, 1980.]
Takashina Shūji, et al. 1987. *Paris in Japan: The Japanese Encounter with European Painting.* Exh. cat. St. Louis: Washington University.
Takeuchi, Melinda. 1992. *Taiga's True Views: The Language of Landscape Painting in Eighteenth-Century Japan.* Stanford: Stanford University Press.
Tanaka Hisao. 1990. *Nihon bijutsu no enshutsusha: patoron no keifu* (Producers of Japanese Art: Lineages of Patrons). Kyoto: Shishindō.
Tsuji Nobuo. 1970. *Kisō no keifu* (Lineage of the Eccentric). Bijutsu shuppansha.
———. 1986. *Playfulness in Japanese Art.* Franklin Murphy Lectures. Vol. 7. Lawrence: Spencer Museum of Art, University of Kansas.
———. 1989. *Kisō no zufu* (Album of Eccentric Imagery). Heibonsha.
———. 1994. "Ornament (*kazari*), an Approach to Japanese Culture." *Archives of Asian Art* 47.
Tsuji, Nobuo, ed. 1979. *Enkū, Mokujiki, Hakuin, Sengai, Ryōkan: Edo no shūkyō bijutsu* (Edo-period Religious Arts: The Monks Enkū, Mokujiki, Hakuin, Sengai, and Ryōkan). Vol. 23 of *Nihon bijutsu zenshū* (Compendium of Japanese Art). Gakushū kenkyūsha.
Tsuji, Nobuo, et al. 1988. *Nihon no bi: "kazari no sekai" ten* (Japanese Beauty: "The Universe of Ornament" Exhibition). Exh. cat. NHK sābisu sentā.
Turner, Victor. 1969. *The Ritual Process: Structure and Anti-Structure.* Chicago: Aldine.
———. 1986. *The Anthropology of Performance.* New York: PAJ.
Uiruson, Richado (Wilson, Richard), and Ogasawara Seiko. 1992. *Ogata Kenzan: zensakuhin to sono keifu* (Ogata Kenzan: Complete Works and Lineage). Yūzankaku.
Weisberg, Gabriel, et al. 1975. *Japonisme: Japanese Influence on French Art 1885-1910.* Exh. cat. Cleveland: Cleveland Museum of Art.
Wheelwright, Carolyn. 1989. *Word in Flower: The Visualization of Classical Literature in Seventeenth-Century Japan.* Exh. cat. New Haven: Yale University Art Gallery.

Wilson, Richard. 1991. *The Art of Ogata Kenzan: Persona and Production in Japanese Ceramics*. Tokyo: Weatherhill.
——. See also under Uiruson Richado.
Woodson, Yoko. 1991. "Traveling *Bunjin* Painters and their Patrons: Economic Life Style and Art of Rai San'yō and Tanomura Chikuden." Ph.D. diss., University of California at Berkeley.
1984. *Words in Motion: Modern Japanese Calligraphy*. Exh. cat. Washington, D.C.: Library of Congress.
Yamada Chisaburō, ed. 1980. *Japonisme in Art: An International Symposium. Symposium Papers*. Tokyo: Committee for the Year 2001.
Yashiro Yukio. 1965. *Nihon bijutsu no tokushitsu* (Special Characteristics of Japanese Art). 2 vols. Iwanami shoten.
——. 1987. *Nihon bjutsu no saikentō* (Reappraisal of Japanese Art). Perikansha.
Yiengpruksawan, Mimi. 1993. "Japanese War Paint: Kawabata Ryūshi and the Emptying of the Modern." *Archives of Asian Art* 56: 76-90.
——. Winter 1994. "What's in a Name: Fujiwara Fixation in Japanese Cultural History." *Monumenta Nipponica* 49, no. 4: 423-53.
Yonekura Michio. 1995-. *Minamoto no Yoritomo zō: chinmoku no shōzōga* (The Image of Minamoto no Yoritomo: Portrait Painting of Reticence). Vol. 4 of *E wa kataru* (literally "Pictures Talk," formally "Cultural Memory in Arts"). 14 vols. Heibonsha.

THE POSTWAR DEVELOPMENT OF STUDIES OF JAPANESE RELIGIONS

Helen Hardacre

This essay documents the development of studies of Japanese religions undertaken in the United States since 1945. It addresses the relation of United States' religious studies of Japan to the development of Japanese studies as a whole and to the development of research on religion undertaken by Japanese scholars. Major subfields within the study of Japanese religions are examined and their development documented. This essay also examines the changing topics of United States Ph.D. dissertations on Japanese religions. It identifies the major topics of debate over the postwar decades, as well as areas which remain relatively underdeveloped. This essay is mainly limited to examination of book-length studies by scholars principally active in the United States (whatever their country of origin) and does not deal with periodical literature, nor, with a few exceptions, with essay collections, anthologies, translations, or reference works.

Before 1945, programs for the study of Japanese religions in United States universities were virtually non-existent, and only a few American scholars took a serious interest in the area. As courses of study began to be developed after 1945, like the study of non-Christian religions of any kind, most studies of the religions of Japan took place in divinity schools. In that setting it was routinely assumed that such studies would be relevant principally as an aid to studies of Christianity—as background information for prospective missionaries, or as comparative data broadening the training of specialists in theology and the like. As late as 1970 it was common for divinity schools to require advanced degrees in some area of the study of Christianity before a student could be permitted to undertake graduate study of Japanese religions. Many of those receiving Ph.D.'s in the study of Japanese religions before the 1970s were missionaries returned from Japan.

The study of religion as a secular academic discipline, providing programs of graduate and undergraduate study, free of theological baggage, came into existence in the United States in the 1970s, though some universities had had small programs before that time. Thereafter, it became possible to study Japanese religions independent of any relation to the study of Christianity, and without the presumption of a prior and pre-eminent personal commitment to Christianity, and without a theological "agenda" as the rationale for such study. As programs and departments of religious studies developed, an increasing number of courses on Japanese religions appeared. Student interest was sparked by the Vietnam War, which triggered a new awareness of various aspects of Asian societies and cultures. It was not uncommon at this time for faculty teaching courses on "World Religions," "Comparative Religions," or "Japanese Religions" to do so based entirely on study of secondary sources, and without any knowledge of the Japanese language.

During the 1970s Japanese language course offerings increased in major universities, though they remained absent at smaller and provincial institutions for another decade. Increasing availability of Japanese language training made it possible for graduate programs to require some standardized certification of competence in Japanese. It was some time later, however, before even the major universities ceased teaching Japanese on the model of Sanskrit or Latin (as a language that the student would read, but not speak) and incorporated training in speaking and hearing. This and other factors combined to channel students of Japanese religions toward thesis topics in premodern eras of history and away from religions of the modern and contemporary periods.

The professionalization of the study of Japanese religions was enhanced by the development of interdisciplinary area studies. The study of Japan emerged as a recognized area of expertise, along with the recognition that this area required a wide background in the study of history, literature, society, and culture. Eventually, specializations in such areas as Japanese history, Japanese literature, Japanese society, and Japanese religions were legitimated as representing one type of area studies. At the same time, however, it was widely assumed that professionalization in the discipline concerned was also required, along with a high level of language competence.

Area studies provided a powerful validation of ethnographic studies of modern and contemporary religious life, as well as an alternative to the "world religions" approach. Whereas world religions took a particular religion as the framework of analysis, area studies facilitated an approach in which a particular country or society, and religious life as practiced there, constituted the basic unit of analysis. Thus, whereas a world religions approach to Japan would inevitably give a dominant position to Buddhism, an area studies approach would tend to be more attentive to the variety of religious life, recognizing within the religious life of a single individual or community the influence of folk religious ideas, Shintō, new religions, and Christianity, as well as Buddhism. An area studies perspective tends to be more ethnographic and more interested in the actual practice of religion, being relatively less interested in global characterizations of Buddhism as a whole in idealized or theological terms. Based on an assumption of linguistic competence, an area studies approach to religion had the potential to encourage students to examine the roles of religion in actual social life. Ethnographic study was able to add a dimension to historical or textual study by focusing on questions of how particular ideas or practices were actually understood, appropriated, and changed by the particular individuals and communities concerned. This meant a change of focus from the macro- to the micro-level, and from the philosophical or historical to the anthropological or sociological.

Early Links with Japanese Scholarship

Until the mid-1970s, religious studies (*shūkyōgaku*) in Japan was much influenced by the perspective of History of Religions (*Religionswissenschaft*). Folklorist of religion Hori Ichirō and those who succeeded him as heads of the Department of Religious Studies at the University of Tokyo were well acquainted with Western scholarship on religion, which was incorporated into graduate training. One of Hori's books (1968) was translated through Joseph Kitagawa, head of the program on Japanese religions at the University of Chicago, and Kitagawa regularly sent his students to consult Hori and his successors. Folklore has been a continuing source of studies of religions, especially at the former Tokyo Kyōiku Daigaku and its successor Tsukuba University, and Kitagawa's ties to Yanagida Kunio, Wakamori Tarō, and Miyata Noboru helped stimulate an interest in Western scholarship among Japanese scholars of folklore.[1] Historical studies of religion also emerged from history departments, and these examined a variety of topics ignored by sectarian scholars of Buddhism, who tended to adopt the perspective of *shūgaku*, that is, studies of a particular Buddhist sect without more than passing reference to other religious traditions. Studies by Tsuji Zennosuke (1944-55) and Inoue Mitsusada (1985) are examples of historical scholarship on religion transcending sectarian frameworks and aiming to encompass the entire area of religion in a given era. The Department of Shintō and the Institute for the Study of Japanese Culture and Classics at Kokugakuin University have been important in sustaining links between Japanese and American scholars in studies of Shintō, a field which in Japan can include Shrine Shintō, Shintō-based new religions, some aspects of folk religion, and studies of religion and literature. Here again, Kitagawa's personal ties with key figures like Hirai Naofusa (1989), Ueda Kenji (1991), and Sonoda Minoru (1980) have been important.

Survey of Postwar United States Dissertations in Religion[2]

Dissertations provide a good index of the topics and approaches that have received particular significance at a given time. We can identify important shifts of emphasis in dissertations on Japanese religions. From 1895 to 1945, a total of thirty-three dissertations were written in the United States on Japanese religions. Studies of Japanese Christianity dominated the field, with a strong "applied" emphasis, investigating how the Christian churches in Japan could accommodate themselves to a totalitarian state, and attempting to identify approaches that would help Protestant missions attract converts. At the same time, however, studies of Shintō, folklore, religious philosophy, and Japanese Buddhism were also carried out. It is especially noteworthy with respect to studies of Japanese Buddhism that all dissertations in this field before 1945

---

[1] These prolific scholars produced a great number of studies which directly influenced the work of United States scholars of Japanese religions. Those listed here are merely some representative examples of their work. See Yanagida Kunio (1971); Wakamori Tarō (1980); and Miyata Noboru (1983, 1984, 1993).

[2] This section relies on unpublished research by Duncan Williams, Ph.D. candidate at Harvard in Japanese religions.

concerned the Jōdo and Jōdo Shinshū schools (the so-called Pure Land Schools). Studies of new religious movements, religious art and architecture, and religion and literature were also undertaken. The Divinity School of the University of Chicago emerged as the clear leader in the field, producing seventeen of the dissertations written before 1945, while Yale produced four, and Harvard and Columbia each produced two.

A group of five universities emerged from 1945 to 1995 as the leading sites for graduate study: Columbia produced 33 dissertations, followed by Harvard at 29, Berkeley with 27, Chicago at 26, and Claremont at 21. These outcomes were supported by strong university press lines in Japanese studies at Columbia and the University of California, Berkeley. Each university shows a slightly different mixture of resources, but strong programs in Japanese language formed a basic resource for graduate training at all of them. Columbia became a leading center of Japanese studies during these years, with major scholars in Japanese literature, history, and Buddhism. The university's Department of Religion emerged as a national leader and provided a significant aspect of necessary training. At Harvard, dissertations continued to be undertaken within the Divinity School, though the university's Committee on the Study of Religion in the Faculty of Arts and Sciences gradually came to provide a wider foundation in studies of religion, and to monopolize the right to grant the Ph.D., as opposed to theological degrees. Masatoshi Nagatomi, affiliated with the Divinity School, the Committee, and the Departments of East Asian Languages and Cultures, as well as the Department of Sanskrit, provided guidance for all areas of Buddhist studies. The University of California at Berkeley became a center of doctrinal and textual studies of Buddhism, with strong ancillary resources in Japanese literature and society. The University of Chicago's program on Japanese religions, situated within the History of Religions Program in the Divinity School, flourished through the guidance of Joseph Kitagawa and his ability (unmatched during the years of his tenure) to bring significant scholars of religion from Japan to Chicago for research and teaching. Claremont emerged as a center for studies in the area known as Buddhist-Christian dialogue, through the leadership of Masao Abe, a philosopher associated with the Kyoto School, who has written widely on Zen.

In addition to the five leading universities for the study of Japanese religions, another group of six universities trained ten or so Ph.D.'s each during the period 1945 to 1995: Yale, Princeton, Temple, Stanford, and the Universities of Michigan and Hawai'i. In Yale's case, this outcome represented a decline from its former position of leadership, while Princeton's strong East Asian Studies Department joined forces with the university's Department of Religion, a national leader. Princeton University Press, under the leadership of Miriam Brokaw, developed a strong line of publications on Japan, including a series of scholarly works in Japanese translated to English. Temple's eleven Ph.D.'s emerged from the university's mammoth religion program, with little guidance from specialists on Japan, with the result that none of them have found positions at leading institutions. Stanford's record is based on a combination of faculty resources in religion, and Japanese studies of history, literature, and society. The University of Michigan has strong resources in the areas of Japanese society, history, and literature to support specialists in Japanese religions. The University of Hawai'i has a similarly broad range of faculty resources, and in addition, its University Press has become a leading publisher of books on Japan. With the exceptions of Harvard and the University of Chicago, the majority of dissertations in Japanese religions since 1945 has been undertaken in Arts and Sciences departments, rather than in a divinity school.

The period 1945 to 1975 saw the production of 136 dissertations on Japanese religions, in a growing variety of fields. Studies of Japanese Christianity continued to dominate, accounting for about 20 percent of the dissertations produced in these years. Studies of Shintō, religious psychology, religion and literature, and religion and society accounted for about 10 percent each, while the remainder took up new religious movements and topics in Buddhism. In all, about 23 percent of the dissertations in these years concerned some aspect of Japanese Buddhism. An equal number of studies of the Pure Land Schools and Zen were undertaken (nine each), while studies of Buddhist philosophy continued, and investigations of the esoteric schools Tendai and Shingon appeared. A handful of studies were done in the areas of folk religion, Japanese Confucianism, and religion and arts.

The years 1976 to 1995 have seen further increases in the number and variety of dissertations on Japanese religions. Some 224 dissertations in the area were written during these years at United States universities. The year 1976 was the year during which the largest number, 24, were written in a single year, and each following year has produced an average of ten or so, with a slight tendency to decline after 1990. Significant changes also appeared in topics chosen for study. While studies of Shintō had previously accounted for about 10 percent of dissertations, this field dropped by two-thirds, to about 3 percent. The decline of Shintō itself probably played a role in producing this outcome, as well as the lack of strong, prolific faculty in the area, and the apparent declining salience of earlier investigations of Shintō's contributions to prewar Japanese militarism.[3] Added to this is the relative difficulty of research in this field, complicated by an arcane vocabulary and a lack of centralized archival resources. Studies of Japanese Christianity declined by about half, previously accounting for about 20 percent of all dissertations in the field, and dropping to about 10 percent in these years. While a small number of scholars of Japanese Christianity made this subject the core of a professional career, the majority of dissertation writers in this area did not contribute further to scholarship on Japanese religions. The decline in the number of Americans going to Japan as missionaries, coupled with the growing dominance of native Japanese clergy in Japanese Christian churches undoubtedly contributed to the decline of American dissertations on Japanese Christianity. Studies of Japanese Buddhism continued to account for 23 percent of all dissertations, and while studies of Zen continued to provide a significant focus, studies of the Pure Land Schools declined by over half, giving a new prominence to Zen studies. Studies of religion and literature also showed a significant decline. Studies of religious psychology continued to contribute about 10 percent of the total, but their long term influence on the field has been rather slight. The reason is that many of them addressed an "applied" topic, in which some technique derived from Japanese religions, usually Zen meditation, was suggested as an aid to psychological or counseling techniques developed in the West. The authors of these dissertations appear to have pursued careers in psychology, without contributing significantly to scholarship on Japanese religions after completing their dissertations. Fields achiev-

---

[3] Daniel Holtom's work (1922) had established this question as a significant area of Shintō studies.

ing significant gain during these years were studies of religion and the arts and studies of Japan's new religions. In the first case, several historians of the arts of Japan, such as John Rosenfield at Harvard, began to train graduate students, and in the second, the evident centrality of the new religions to contemporary Japanese religious life and society stimulated new interest. More studies of religions' roles in Japanese contemporary society have been produced since 1975, along with increasingly sophisticated studies of the historical roles of such religious institutions as Buddhist monasteries and Shintō shrines.

While overall one can point to a growing variety and sophistication in studies of Japanese religions, there are numerous areas which have not been addressed in proportion to their significance in Japanese religious history. Foremost among these is the Shugendō tradition, a cult of sacred mountains.[4] Also, the many varieties of folk religious life, including urban folklore and popular urban religious life (whether historical or modern), remain relatively unexplored. Similarly, the Pure Land and Nichiren schools of Buddhism remain insufficiently studied. Shintō deserves much more study in virtually every area, as does Japanese Confucianism. The proliferation of new religious movements and their deepening influence on modern society should become the subject of much new work, and, likewise, the nature of temple Buddhist life in modern and contemporary Japan.

The Development of Subfields of Religious Studies of Japan

There are several subspecialties within the study of Japanese religions, and each of these has followed a distinctive path of development. These can be identified with particular religious traditions (Buddhism, Shintō, Confucianism, Christianity, new religious movements, and folk religion) or with distinctive disciplinary perspectives (historical, anthropological/sociological, and studies of religion and the arts or literature). While some significant studies might be categorized under more than one of these head-

---

[4] Works by Byron Earhart (1969, 1974) have treated Shugendō, as have important journal articles by Allan Grapard.

ings, they provide a handy typology for the field overall. This section treats each in turn.

Histories

Scholars of Japanese religions active early in the postwar period were operating in an institutional context which frequently (if tacitly and implicitly) attributed to Christianity a definitive role in religious studies generally, erecting Christianity as a standard of judgment by which the religiosity of other traditions might be measured. Thus, for example, if participants in Japanese folk festivals were found to behave riotously or erotically, perhaps being drunk as well, the religiosity motivating the festival could be questioned as lacking the pious and somber attitude assumed, on the basis of (mostly) Protestant example, to be properly characteristic of religion. Or, given the primacy in Protestant piety of the idea of a personal relation to God, if it were discovered that worshippers at a Shintō shrine had little idea of which deities (*kami*) were actually enshrined there, the religiosity of shrine worship would be doubted, because it failed to exhibit the attitudes which worship on the Protestant model is assumed to have. One prewar study by Anesaki Masaharu (1930) attempted to demonstrate the integrity of Japanese religious history, though it proceeded on the assumption that "morality" as understood in Christianity set a universal standard. These Christo-centric attitudes cannot be said to have disappeared completely even at this writing, but they were much more influential upon the scholarly preoccupations of scholars writing in the 1950s, 1960s, and 1970s. For them, there was a clear necessity to demonstrate the integrity and coherence of Japanese religious life and Japanese religious history. Only by doing so could one create a basis on which to challenge the problematic assumptions derived from Christianity's pre-eminence within the divinity schools where religious studies of the day were largely carried out.

Kitagawa (1966) traced the chronological development of religion in relation to major trends in political and cultural history. His study thus follows the conventional periodization of major eras of Japan's political history and pays particular attention to relations between religions and the state in each age. Kitagawa also put particular importance upon the religious inspirations for important cultural works of art and literature. This work, which remains influential today, seeks also to identify transhistorical religious motifs which characterize Japan and identify its distinctiveness within the world's religious traditions. For example, he identified what he called "immanental theocracy" as the pattern which the motif of sacred kingship assumes in Japan, in the imperial institution. At the same time, the work is concerned to depict Japan as sharing religious motifs or patterns which are found more broadly in world history. Thus, he emphasized Japanese shamanism as a type of religious expression which is found in many other societies and stressed the contribution which comparative studies of shamanism could make to the study of Japanese religions, as well as asserting that the study of Japanese shamanism, in its many varieties, could offer important insights to studies of other shamanic traditions. Kitagawa's work remains virtually the only authoritative single-volume history of Japanese religions in English.

A work complementing Kitagawa's historical approach was Byron Earhart's survey (1969) and the companion volume of translations of primary sources (1974). The first of these treated Japanese religions thematically, identifying five themes characteristic of Japanese religious life through history. These included a close relation between religion and the state and a strong shamanic tradition. This work, which has become a standard textbook for elementary courses on Japanese religions, has achieved a wide influence.

In addition to the works by Kitagawa and Earhart just discussed, which treat the full span of religious history, many other works have treated specific eras. Jonathan Kidder's work on ancient Japan (1959, 1972) was largely based on the Japanese archaeological scholarship of the time. While it provided much useful information on material history, it did not recognize the important connections between ancient Japan and Korea, which subsequently came to light. Edwin O. Reischauer's studies (1955a, 1955b) on the monk Ennin (794-864) provided a vivid portrait of the flourishing world of Chinese Buddhism which served as such an inspiration for early Buddhist monks from Japan who traveled there in search of new texts and rites.

Robert Morrell (1987) initiated an important reconsideration of Japanese Buddhism during the Kamakura period. The received wisdom from earlier Japanese scholarship on the topic presented the Kamakura-era appearance of the new Buddhist schools of Zen, Jōdo, Jōdo Shinshū, and the Nichiren school as Japan's version of the Protestant Reformation and treated the leading figures associated with these schools as "founders." With all eyes upon these new developments, it was easy to overlook the continued existence of older Japanese Buddhist schools, or (worse) to assume that they had been swept away by these new brooms. Morrell's work particularly addressed the continuing vitality of the older Japanese Buddhist sects. The Reformation analogy furthermore produced the illusion that the appearance of Hōnen, Shinran, Nichiren, and Dōgen, the so-called "founders," led immediately to the generation of massive popular followings. In fact, the emergence of large-scale popular adherence to the new sects took several hundred years. These developments have been the subject of ongoing discussion at academic conferences and in the journals, as have pilgrimage and popular patronage of Buddhism, the subject of one monographic study by Janet Goodwin (1994).

United States studies of medieval Japanese Buddhism have been greatly influenced by the work of Kuroda Toshio. Kuroda struck a fatal blow at the "world religions" approach to the study of Japanese religions, by showing convincingly that throughout the medieval period Shintō and Buddhism were not understood or practiced as two separate religions, but as a unified system of rites and symbols better characterized as Esoteric Buddhism than as two religions. He called this unified system *kenmitsu taisei*. Kuroda's work also provoked a new approach to the study of Shintō, one which transcended the traditional concerns of Shintō scholars who were also members of the Shintō priesthood. Kuroda showed that the word *Shintō* in its modern sense as the name for a distinct religion was in fact an invention of the Meiji period, and that before that time it had had a variety of conflicting meanings and did not represent a continuous tradition for the great mass of the population outside its priesthood.[5]

American scholars pursuing Kuroda's insights are quite numerous and include Martin Collcutt, Allan Grapard, Neil McMullin, James Dobbins, and others. Their works have transformed the study of religion in this period, earlier conceptualized largely as the study of doctrines of the emergent Pure Land, Nichiren, and Zen sects,

---

[5] Kuroda's 1983 and 1990 works are representative of his approach.

to a new field of medieval religious life, which takes up medieval *jongleurs*, storytellers, popular preachers, popular pilgrimage, popular religious literature, arts, and more. McMullin's (1985) volume is notable for its stimulus to studies of the historical relations between religion and state in the period.

Robert Bellah (1957) wrote one of the most influential works on Japanese religious history in the postwar period. In it he proposed a direct relation between modernization and Japanese religious attitudes characterizing the Tokugawa period (1600-1868). Specifically, he described the attitudes toward work seen in the Jōdo Shinshū sect of Buddhism and the Shingaku movement, a popular movement based on Neo-Confucianism, as analogous to the Protestant work ethic. Japanese religions of the period produced values emphasizing thrift, diligence, and efficiency, accompanied by a desire to acquire education. Thus, popular, widespread religious sentiments in the era immediately preceding Japan's modernization can be said to have prepared the people for the experiences of industrialization, urbanization, compulsory education, and the other social dislocations that accompany modernization. Bellah's work stimulated studies seeking to apply Weberian theory to refine understanding of the relation between religion and modernization in Japan. Of these, the work of Winston Davis (1977, 1992) has been most influential.

An important contribution to historical studies of religion during the Meiji period comes from James Ketelaar (1990), who shows how Buddhist institutions were summarily dethroned from the position of state support they enjoyed during the preceding Tokugawa Period, and the diversity of reaction engendered by this experience. He shows convincingly how the nature of the religion's relation to the state was fundamentally changed, along with equally thoroughgoing changes in Buddhism's social position.

William Woodward's (1972) work is a study by an Occupation figure close to MacArthur and the officials in charge of creating specific legal frameworks for postwar religious institutions, removing the influence of State Shintō from the schools, and much more. He presents a significant collection of primary documents on the Occupation's roles.

Among younger American scholars, the work of Tamamuro Fumio (1977, 1987) is increasingly influential. Tamamuro bases his account of religious history on an unmatched ability to collect and analyze primary sources bearing on the history of religious institutions. He has worked on a wide variety of topics in Edo and early Meiji religious history, as well as on medieval subjects. His tenure in 1996 as Reischauer Institute Visiting Professor, as well as earlier stays at Princeton and in France, have attracted a large number of rising scholars to his methods. Recently, in part through his influence, a special seminar on religion during the Edo period has been established within the American Academy of Religion.

Buddhism

Studies of Japanese Buddhism form the largest subfield within the study of Japanese religions. Only a couple of postwar works have attempted to survey the whole field of Japanese Buddhism and its history, those by E. Dale Saunders (1964) and by Alicia Matsunaga and Daigan Matsunaga (1974-1976). The second of these has stood the test of time fairly well, but it is notable that the tendency to specialization among younger American scholars since the mid-1970s has tended to emphasize studies of more restricted topics and to militate against the undertaking of comprehensive histories of Buddhism. The largest cluster of specialized studies concerns Zen.

From 1955 a significant number of studies of Zen began to appear, led by the works of D. T. Suzuki, who published five widely-read works between 1955 and 1959. His influence on the American academy was very great, and his distinctive interpretation of Zen came to be popularly identified as encapsulating all of Japanese religiosity. In brief, Suzuki painted a highly idealized portrait of Zen as a religion of self-liberation through meditation and *kōan* practice, closely allied with the arts (ink painting, tea ceremony, flower arranging, and martial arts), and providing the historical faith of the samurai. While this image of Zen was highly attractive to American youth during the 1960s, it actually bore only fragmentary relation either to the practice of the Zen sects in Japan or to the larger history of the Zen tradition, except as idealized by some of its philosophers.

Studies of Zen Buddhism came to constitute a significant focus for studies of Japanese religions, and many young scholars pursued both a personal religious interest in Zen as well as academic studies of it. In addition, Japanese-trained American teachers of Zen as a religious practice, such as Alan Watts (1955) and others, began teaching in the United States, and their writings began to furnish numerous popular works on Zen which were adopted for classroom use.[6] As live-in facilities for Zen training and meditation (*zendō*) were established in the United States, they became centers for the promotion of knowledge about Japanese Buddhism generally. They could also provide a route by which a few might pursue further training in Japan, sometimes in a monastic setting and with the aim of becoming ordained. It is not too much to say that during the 1960s popular works on Zen achieved such an influence in American youth culture as to produce a widespread (though mistaken) impression that Zen meditation epitomized Japanese religion in general.

Several tendencies arose from these popular studies of Zen. First, a tendency to combine academic study with personal religious interest has produced trends analogous to divinity school training for those committed to Christianity as one's personal faith. That is, one can observe among scholars of Zen today close alliances with American Zen centers, and in their studies a commitment to the promotion of Zen. Second, the study of Zen has been powerfully shaped by its early popularizers such as Watts and D. T. Suzuki, for whom the center of Zen is meditation and *kōan* practice. Closely associated with Suzuki, Abe Masao has contributed studies of Zen examining its psychology and relation to Japanese culture. His works and those of Winston King and Thomas Kasulis can be likened in this emphasis and in perpetuating the impetus informing the works of Suzuki.[7]

By contrast with this approach, the historical reality of Zen's institutional history, the centrality in its actual practice of rites for ancestors, prayer rituals, and a strong connection to the imperial court have only recently come to receive attention by U.S. scholars. As we shall see below, a felt need to redress the Suzuki legacy has been a powerful stimulus to more recent studies of Zen.

Zen has continued to dominate United States studies of Japanese Buddhism, though a few volumes have appeared on other

---

[6] Paul Reps and Nyogen Senzaki (1957); Ruth Fuller Sasaki (1959); Gary Snyder and Gutetsu Kanetsuki (1961); and Philip Kapleau (1965).

[7] Abe Masao (1985, 1986, 1992, 1995, 1996); Winston King (1993); and Thomas Kasulis (1981).

sects, and although more diversity can be seen in the periodical literature. Biographical studies of significant Zen figures have provided one focus of study, and scholars making important contributions in this area include James Sanford (1981), biographer of Ikkyū Sōjun (1394-1481); Winston King (1986), writing on Suzuki Shōsan (1579-1655); Kenneth Kraft (1992) on the life of Daitō Kokushi (1282-1337); James Kodera (1980) and Steven Heine (1994) writing on Dōgen (1200-1253); and Abe Ryūichi and Peter Haskel (1996), biographers of Ryōkan (1758-1831).

The works of Carl Bielefeldt (1988) and Bernard Faure (1991, 1993) have provided an enlarged framework for Zen studies, by connecting Japanese developments to Chinese Ch'an and thus emphasizing the continuity between Japanese and Chinese religious history. This important innovation makes clear the importance of a larger historical context for Zen's development in Japan and brings to bear on it a larger body of relevant textual and historical knowledge. In addition, Faure's work is the first to rely upon postmodern theory to question the Suzuki legacy, and to call for a more historically grounded understanding of Zen.

Martin Collcutt's (1981) study of the institutional history of the Rinzai sect of Zen broke from the largely biographical or scriptural/textual mode of Zen studies by tracing the development of Zen institutions in Japan to their Chinese models. He further clarified the close connection of Zen institutions to the imperial court. Collcutt's work is complemented by a study of the institutional history of the Sōtō sect of Zen by William Bodiford (1993). In addition to sectarian histories of Zen, treatments of other significant areas of Japanese Buddhism include Byron Earhart's study of Shugendō (1970),[8] James Dobbins's study of Jōdo Shinshū (1989), and Minoru Kiyota's work on the Shingon sect (1978).

Significant biographical studies of Japanese Buddhist figures outside the Zen tradition include Alfred Bloom's (1968) study of Shinran (1173-1262); Yoshito Hakeda's (1972) work on Kūkai (774-835); Laurel Rodd's (1978) biography of Nichiren; Paul Groner's (1984) study of Saichō (766-822); Minor Rogers's (1991) treatment of Rennyo (1415-1499); and George Tanabe's (1992) book on Myōe (1173-1232).

---

[8] This study is not limited to "sectarian history," but also includes detailed study of pilgrimage in Shugendō, based on the history of religions approach.

Shintō

Studies of Shintō have undergone important changes during the postwar period. Prewar studies were greatly influenced by Japanese nationalism of the time, either promoting Shintō as legitimating nationalism and imperialism, as was the case with Katō Genchi's works, such as his (1926) study, or castigating it as "the spiritual engine of war." The understanding of Shintō as the religious force uniting the Japanese people in support of militarism was highly influential within the Allied Occupation of Japan, largely as filtered through Daniel Holtom's works, especially his (1943) publication. At the same time, a minor tradition of antiquarian scholarship, largely descriptive in nature and taking a highly positive attitude toward Shintō, was to be found in the works of Richard Ponsonby-Fane (1942).

Japanese prewar scholarship on Shintō had emphasized its unique character as providing the nation's "rites and creed" (*kokka no sōshi*), a rhetorical device implying that Shintō was not a religion, but was instead a suprareligious entity, unique to Japan, which all Japanese were obliged to honor, whatever their personal religious beliefs might be. In this guise, Shintō easily became linked with religious persecution in prewar Japan, especially of Japanese Christians, followers of heterodox new religious movements, and in Japan's overseas colonies. Early postwar scholarship on Shintō in Japan repented this recent history, and as Shintō scholars began to go overseas for study, especially to the University of Chicago, they and United States scholars began to produce studies promoting the idea that Shintō *is* a religion—potentially, at least, a world religion. To this end they emphasized universal ideas in Shintō and promoted ecumenical discussion with leaders of other religions. This impetus is clear in a 1968 volume published by the Institute for Japanese Culture and Classics, *Proceedings, The Second International Conference for Shinto Studies*. Meanwhile, the publication of many devotional or proselytizing works in English by the Shintō-affiliated new religions also helped to refine academic understanding of the diversity within Shintō, and to foster an understanding that only part of the Shintō world bore any direct connection to prewar militarism. The publication of bibliographies and other reference works in English, as well as the translation of significant primary texts also promoted studies of Shintō shorn of the prewar period's preoccupations,[9] as did English translations of significant works in Japanese, such as those by Muraoka Tsunetsugu (1964) or Ono Sokyō (1960), which was suitable for use as an introductory text for students.

During the late 1960s and early 1970s, a small number of studies on aspects of Shintō history appeared, including those by Wilhelmus Creemers (1968); Matsumoto Shigeru (1970), which originated as a Harvard dissertation; Robert Ellwood (1973); and Wilbur Fridell (1973). At this stage of research, each such work constituted virtually the only English-language study of its subject.

By the mid-1980s studies of Shintō came to include ethnographic treatments of Shintō new religions (cf. Hardacre, 1986a), while new studies on the topic of State Shintō were also written (Hardacre, 1989). David O'Brien and Yasuo Ohkoshi (1996) treat the legal case history of relations between Shintō and the state since 1945. Since 1990, studies of National Learning (*kokugaku*), one philosophical source of Shintō since the mid-Edo period, have been influential not only within religious studies of Japan, but also in the area of intellectual history. Significant examples of such work include books by Peter Nosco (1990) and Harry Harootunian (1988). An anthropological study of shrine life is available from John Nelson (1995).

In the early 1990s a group of three studies of the Kasuga shrine were published by Royall Tyler (1990), Allan Grapard (1992), and Susan Tyler (1992). These works represent the first "critical mass" of English-language studies of some Shintō topic, such that a perspective of views and divergent arguments emerge.

Confucianism

Confucianism in Japan has not historically been institutionalized in a way comparable to the tradition's existence in China; thus there is no formal priesthood, nor any explicitly articulated role in imperial ritual. With the exception of a few Confucian schools, there has been no ritual reverencing of Confucius, and the Japanese cult of ancestors is typically carried out in a Buddhist mode.

---

[9] Examples include Post Wheeler (1952); Katō (1953); works issued by the Association of Shintō Shrines (Jinja Honchō) (1958a, 1958b, 1958c); Donald Philippi (1959); Felicia Bock, (1970, 1972); Michiko Aoki (1971).

Thus, the conventional wisdom about Japanese Confucianism has held until recently that Confucianism in Japan is more accurately considered a philosophy than a religion.[10]

On the other hand, the influence of Confucian thought in the philosophy of political rule and in popular ethics is very strong. Confucian ideas can be recognized in so early a document as the so-called "Seventeen-Article Constitution" of Shōtoku Taishi (604). Confucian texts were used as copybooks in the commoner schools of the Tokugawa period, and they were the central curriculum of warrior education. Confucian thought was appropriated by both Buddhism and Shintō in diffuse ways, which is to say that both affirmed key Confucian concepts of hierarchy in society, the values of loyalty and obedience, and a premium on education and learning, but without any marked recognition of these as Confucian in origin.

Beginning in 1970, a religious dimension within Japanese Confucianism was recognized through the work of Theodore de Bary and his students and colleagues. De Bary published two highly influential collections (1970, 1979), which made clear that Neo-Confucianism as adopted in Japan embodied regimens of self-cultivation in service to the goal of becoming a sage, and that these were properly called "religious." His work further established the central importance of Korean Neo-Confucians in establishing this religiosity at the heart of the tradition as it was transmitted to Japan. De Bary's students, such as Mary Evelyn Tucker (1989), Peter Nosco (1984), and Samuel Yamashita (1994), have produced important works further clarifying the religious characteristics of Neo-Confucianism in Japan, and their insights have helped to clarify the nature of popular religious practice during the Tokugawa Period.

Among studies of Japanese Confucianism, Herman Ooms's work (1985) deserves special note. Until the publication of this work, it had been understood that Confucian thought provided the official, legitimating ideology of the Tokugawa shogunate, based largely on assertions to this effect by the Confucian scholar Hayashi Razan (1583-1657). Ooms showed convincingly how, while Razan and his school held rather minor official posts, far more influence was exerted upon the shogunate by such Buddhist leaders

---

[10] This perspective was represented, for example, by Warren Smith (1959).

as Tenkai (1536-1643). Ooms further demonstrated how the shogunate appropriated for its legitimation elements of Buddhism, Shintō, and Confucian thought, unconcerned about the distinctions among these traditions, tending instead to see them as mutually complementary and rightfully in service to the state.

Christianity

The survey of dissertations in the field of Japanese religions above showed that studies of Christianity have constituted a considerable, if declining, proportion of doctoral work in the area of religious studies of Japan. Over the postwar decades, the production of scholarly monographs on Japanese Christianity has dwindled to the point of near-extinction, and this phenomenon requires explanation. The growing independence of Japanese Christian churches, with a corresponding decline of foreign missions, is undoubtedly one important reason for the change. Fewer United States scholars of Japanese religions than previously begin as missionaries or come from missionary families, though one exception to this generalization is presented by those scholars who may have mission experience as members of the Church of the Latter Day Saints (the Mormons). But they do not tend to enter religious studies, being more prominent as scholars of literature. The more scholars of religion are trained in secular institutions, it seems, the less likely they are to specialize in Japanese Christianity. Another reason for the decline in studies in this area may relate to the small numerical presence of Christians in Japan. They have never exceeded one percent of the Japanese population, though it is widely recognized that the cultural significance of Christianity in Japan is far greater than this number suggests.

While the number of postwar scholarly studies of Christianity may be small, some of these works have made strong contributions to the development of the field of Japanese religions. Charles Boxer's study (1951) treats Christianity's first appearance in Japan and the remarkable development of Catholicism until its extirpation in the early seventeenth century. A couple of works devoted to the history of Catholic or Protestant churches have also been produced.[11] Several biographies of important Christian fig-

---

[11] Charles Iglehard (1959); Johannes Laures (1954).

ures have been written.[12] A notable contribution to the understanding of Meiji Christianity, by Irwin Scheiner (1970), was one of the first books on Japanese Christianity to be undertaken outside sectarian frameworks, aiming instead to understand the religion's relation to the social and cultural history of the period. Similarly, George Elison (1973) dramatically depicted the career of an early Christian apostate, showing the cultural forces impinging on the religion in its earliest history in Japan. More recently, social history works on Christianity have investigated the religion's relations with Buddhism during the Meiji period.[13] A new development is renewed interest in Japan's "hidden Christians," those who went underground after the religion's seventeenth-century proscription and perpetuated the faith in hiding for over two and a half centuries.[14]

New Religions

Significant research within religious studies of Japan during the postwar period has addressed the phenomenon of Japan's new religions. The term *new religions* is an awkward one, designating popular religious movements and organizations founded outside the ecclesiastical or ordination structures of Buddhism and Shintō, from the early nineteenth century to the present. Thus, these movements tend to be centered on laity, and some express a frank anti-clericalism against temple Buddhism. Doctrinally, they may originate in Buddhist, Shintō, folk, or (more rarely) Christian beliefs. Most have adopted the conventional morality of Japanese society, whatever their theological beliefs, and thus on the whole they tend to uphold the family and the work ethic, to value education and hard work in all areas. They may originate in revelations from some deity to a founder, many of whom are women. While overwhelmingly socially conservative in their understandings of the proper roles of women and men, they nevertheless have offered distinctive possibilities to women to transcend the bounds of the domestic sphere. Perhaps for this reason, their membership typically is skewed to a predominance of women. With-

---

[12] John F. Howes (1960); George Bickle (1976); Robert Schildgen (1988); F. Calvin Parker (1990).
[13] See, for example, Notto Thelle (1987).
[14] Ann Mary Harrington (1993); Christal Whelan (1996).

out a doubt, the new religions constitute the most vital area of postwar Japanese religious life, and this vitality has attracted the attention and interest of numerous scholars.

Studies of the new religions have profited greatly from association with the "People's History School" (*minshūshi*) of Japanese scholarship, as well as from Japanese sociologists of religion. The "People's History" movement, particularly associated with Irokawa Daikichi, Yasumaru Yoshio, and Kano Masanao, has been highly influential upon studies of Japanese early modern and modern history, but it has also had a profound impact upon studies of religion from 1600 to the present.[15] Whereas cultural prejudice against contemporary religious movements was sometimes heard in scholars' remarks to the effect that such movements were not "genuinely" religious, the "People's History School" took a very positive view of the historical predecessors of such religions. Their sympathetic portrayals of Tenrikyō, Konkōkyō, and Ōmotokyō strengthened the rationale for studies of contemporary "descendants" of these religions which treated them also as genuinely religious in nature and deserving serious scholarly study. More recently, however, studies have emerged which question "People's History" portrayals of religions, especially those flourishing at the end of the Edo period, criticizing them for idealizing such religions as democratic and egalitarian, positioning them as prefiguring the People's Rights Movement of the Meiji period. The question has also been raised whether religious movements spanning such a long time period as the early nineteenth century to the present can be characterized as a unitary group, except in superficial terms.

Sociology of religions in Japan has also focused on new religious movements. Largely concerned with religions of the modern and early modern periods, it developed in the 1970s, through the efforts of the first generation of scholars born after World War II. It is one of the largest and most vital areas of scholarship on religion in Japan today. Its professional society, the Association for the Study of Religion and Society (Shūkyō to Shakai Gakkai) has nearly 400 members internationally. For these scholars, the antiquarian analytic categories of History of Religions and the ten-

---

[15] See, for example, Irokawa Daikichi (1985); Kano Masanao (1977); Yasumaru Yoshio (1974).

dency to idealize the ancient period proved to be impediments in the study of modern and contemporary religious life, far less useful than an approach based on social science. Two of the most prominent scholars in this area are Inoue Nobutaka (1990) and Shimazono Susumu (1992).[16] While sociology of religion in the United States is highly quantified and has been historically preoccupied with documenting such things as changing statistics of church attendance, this field in Japan includes historical scholarship and manifests an interest in religious world view and types of religious experience. It attempts to document the entire spectrum of contemporary religious life.

Two early, influential works on new religions by United States scholars were those of Harry Thomsen (1963) and Neil McFarland (1967). The first of these, an encyclopedic volume, was principally descriptive in nature, presenting information on a wide variety of new religions, while the second portrayed new religions, which had arisen in great number immediately after World War II, as reactions to social crisis. The new religions were publishing many devotional-proselytizing works in English in the early postwar years, and these also helped increase scholarly awareness, but perhaps no development was more dramatic in its impact than the appearance of the mammoth Sōka Gakkai, and the political party it formed in 1964, the Clean Government Party (Kōmeitō). Following this event, a number of influential studies of this religion were written, and it continues to be a major focus of inquiry into the new religions.[17]

A number of monographs focused on specific new religions have appeared. A stimulating and provocative ethnographic study of Mahikari by Winston Davis (1980) depicts this religion as perpetuating a magical world view in the midst of Japanese society's increasing priority upon science and technology. Minoru Kiyota (1982) and Byron Earhart (1989) have both written on Gedatsukai, a new religion derived from Shingon Buddhism, which also incorporates aspects of Shintō and Shugendō. Earhart's study is especially comprehensive in its ethnographic coverage, and it represents the result of extremely fruitful collaboration between

---

[16] Both these scholars are extremely prolific; the works here merely exemplify their approaches.

[17] See James Dator (1969); James White (1970); Daniel Métraux (1988, 1994).

Earhart and Miyake Hitoshi and his students at Keio University (1978). Hardacre's (1984) study of Reiyūkai Kyōdan, a Buddhist new religion derived from the Nichiren tradition, took issue with McFarland's thesis about the new religions originating as a reaction to crisis and emphasized instead the coherence of Reiyūkai's beliefs and practices on their own terms. As against portrayals of the new religions as mere hodgepodges of miscellaneous beliefs and practices, Hardacre's study of the Shintō new religion Kurozumikyō (1986a) proposed that the new religions as a whole share a common world view, whatever their doctrinal origins.

Religion and Society

Studies of religions' roles in Japanese society have been a sustained interest in the United States, and it is frequently the case that sociological and anthropological studies touch upon aspects of religion. In this section works specifically focused on religion and society are described. Several significant essay collections have tried to present comprehensive sociological treatments of Japanese religions.[18] Anthropologist Edward Norbeck's (1970) work was particularly influential. One focus for anthropological scholarship has been the religious practices of "minority" communities of the Ainu, Okinawans, and other small groups.[19]

Robert J. Smith's (1974) study of Japanese ancestor worship combined the insights of comparative anthropological scholarship with rich ethnographic research in a variety of settings in Japan, as well as a sophisticated understanding of the Buddhist and other religious ideas bearing on the cult of ancestors in Japan. It remains the most comprehensive work in English on this fundamental aspect of Japanese religious life.

More specialized studies have also appeared. Anthropologists Emiko Ohnuki-Tierney (1987) and Walter Edwards (1989) have discussed the monkey as a cultural symbol and Japanese weddings, respectively. David Goodman has produced a study of Japanese anti-Semitism (1995). William LaFleur (1992) and Helen Hardacre (1997) have both written on the phenomenon of *mizuko kuyō*,

---

[18] Morioka Kiyomi and William Newell (1968); Gotō Akira and Nakane Chie (1972); Morioka Kiyomi (1975); George De Vos and Takao Sofue (1984).
[19] Neil Munro (1962); William Lebra (1966); David Plath, with Yoshie Sugihara (1969); Helen Hardacre (1986b).

a ritual widely popularized and intensely commercialized after the mid-1970s to pacify the souls of aborted fetuses.

Works on folk religion may be considered as a distinct, if small, category within studies of religion and society, inasmuch as the study of Japanese folklore in the United States has been closely associated with the disciplines of anthropology and sociology. Few American universities maintain departments of folklore, but Indiana University is one exception. Richard Dorson of that institution produced a much-used collection (1962), but his untimely death meant that no continuing teaching program for Japanese folklore went forward. Other noteworthy studies of Japanese folklore, influential in the United States though not in all cases written by American scholars, include Blacker's study of shamanism (1975); Bownas's study of Japanese rainmaking (1963); Casal's on festivals (1967); and Statler's on pilgrimage (1983).

Studies of Religion in Relation to Art and Literature

It has long been recognized that there is a close relation between religion and the arts in Japan, and that an aesthetic dimension is a regular part of most Japanese religious life, of whatever kind. Studies of religion in relation to the arts have thus provided a distinctive aspect of Japanese religious studies. Buddhist iconography is the subject of a book by Saunders (1960), while Fontein examined the arts of Zen (1970). Shintō arts have been the subject of two books by Christine Guth (1976, 1985). John Rosenfield examined Buddhist painting while Grotenhuis studied the Taima Mandala (1979), and Willa Tanabe (1988) examined paintings relating to the Lotus Sutra. Donald McCallum (1994) studied the Amida image at the Nagano temple Zenkōji, extending his research to the larger world of medieval arts.

Significant studies have also been produced in the area of religion and literature. Many of these have included translations. Religious poetry has been one focus of such studies, as seen in the works of Ury (1977), LaFleur (1978), Kamens (1990), Heine (1989), and Ebersole (1989). Two notable studies of medieval Buddhist writing have been produced by Edward Kamens (1988) and Margaret Childs (1991). David Goodman (1988) examines religious aspects of contemporary theater, and LaFleur (1983) explicitly attempts to clarify medieval understandings of karma through an examination of literature.

Conclusion

It can be seen from the foregoing examination that United States studies of Japanese religions have ranged over a very considerable area and have developed distinct subfields which each show growing vitality. Three hundred sixty United States dissertations on Japanese religions have been written between 1945 and 1995. Within Japanese studies as a whole, studies of religion comprise the fifth or sixth largest field.[20] Like other areas of Japanese studies, studies of religion have profited greatly from the rising standards of linguistic competence now expected of the field. Religious studies has also benefited enormously by the secularization of studies of religion, and their removal in most instances from divinity schools. Since religious studies itself is interdisciplinary in nature, its findings have enriched numerous cognate disciplines. In many different areas of religious studies, United States scholars have entered into highly productive association with Japanese scholars, and these links have also enriched graduate training. Religious studies can be expected to continue to contribute strongly to the growth and development of Japanese studies in the United States.

Bibliography

Abe Masao. 1985. *Zen and Western Thought*. Honolulu: University of Hawai'i Press.
———. 1986. *A Zen Life: D. T. Suzuki Remembered*. New York: Weatherhill.
———. 1992. *A Study of Dōgen: His Philosophy and Religion*. Albany: State University of New York Press.
———. 1995. *Buddhism and Interfaith Dialogue*. Honolulu: University of Hawai'i Press.
———. 1996. *Zen and Comparative Studies*. Honolulu: University of Hawai'i Press.
Abe, Ryūichi, and Peter Haskel. 1996. *Great Fool: Zen Master Ryōkan—Poems, Letters, and Other Writings*. Honolulu: University of Hawai'i Press.
Anesaki Masaharu. 1930. *History of Japanese Religion: With Special Reference to the Social and Moral Life of a Nation*. London: Kegan Paul, Trench, Trubner.
Aoki, Michiko, trans. 1971. *Izumo Fudoki*. Sophia University Press.
Ashkenazi, Michael. 1993. *Matsuri: Festivals of a Japanese Town*. Honolulu: University of Hawai'i Press.
Association of Shintō Shrines. 1958a. *Basic Terms of Shintō*. Tokyo: Jinja Honchō,

---

[20] The Japan Foundation (1996). Religion's ranking among the other areas of Japanese studies varies slightly according to the standard of measurement employed, but it clearly has increased in the last ten years. Ahead of it are history, literature, art history, and political science.

Kokugakuin University and Institute for Japanese Culture and Classics.
———. 1958b. *An Outline of Shintō Teaching*. Tokyo: Jinja Honchō, Kokugakuin University and Institute for Japanese Culture and Classics.
———. 1958c. *Shintō Shrines and Festivals*. Tokyo: Jinja Honchō, Kokugakuin University and Institute for Japanese Culture and Classics.
Bellah, Robert. 1957. *Tokugawa Religion: The Values of Pre-Industrial Japan*. Glencoe, Ill.: Free Press.
Bickle, George. 1976. *The New Jerusalem: Aspects of Utopianism in the Thought of Kagawa Toyohiko*. Tucson: University of Arizona Press.
Bielefeldt, Carl. 1988. *Dōgen's Manuals of Zen Meditation*. Berkeley: Center for Japanese Studies, University of California, Berkeley, University of California Press.
Blacker, Carmen. 1975. *The Catalpa Bow, A Study of Shamanistic Practices in Japan*. London: Allen and Unwin.
Bloom, Alfred. 1968. *The Life of Shinran: A Journey to Self Acceptance*. Leiden: E. J. Brill.
Bock, Felicia, trans. 1970. *"Engi-shiki": Procedures of the Engi Era, Books I-V*. Tokyo: Monumenta Nipponica Monographs, Sophia University Press.
———. 1972. *"Engi-shiki": Procedures of the Engi Era, Books VI-X*. Tokyo: Monumenta Nipponica Monographs, Sophia University Press.
Bodiford, William. 1993. *Sōtō Zen in Medieval Japan*. Honolulu: University of Hawai'i Press.
Bownas, Geoffrey. 1963. *Japanese Rainmaking and Other Folk Practices*. London: Allen and Unwin.
Boxer, Charles. 1951. *The Christian Century in Japan, 1549-1650*. Berkeley: University of California Press.
Casal, Ugo. 1967. *The Five Sacred Festivals of Ancient Japan: Their Symbolism and Historical Development*. Tokyo: Monumenta Nipponica Monographs no. 26, Sophia University Press and Charles E. Tuttle.
Childs, Margaret. 1991. *Rethinking Sorrow: Revelatory Tales of Late Medieval Japan*. Ann Arbor: Center for Japanese Studies, University of Michigan.
Collcutt, Martin. 1981. *Five Mountains: The Rinzai Zen Monastic Institution in Medieval Japan*. Cambridge: Harvard East Asian Monograph no. 85, Harvard University Press.
Creemers, Wilhelmus. 1968. *Shrine Shinto after World War II*. Leiden: E. J. Brill.
Dator, James. 1969. *Sōka Gakkai: Builders of the Third Civilization, American and Japanese Members*. Seattle: University of Washington Press.
Davis, Winston. 1977. *Toward Modernity: A Developmental Typology of Popular Religious Affiliations in Japan*. Ithaca: East Asia Papers Series no. 12, Cornell University Press.
———. 1980. *Dojo: Magic and Exorcism in Modern Japan*. Stanford: Stanford University Press.
———. 1992. *Japanese Religion and Society: Paradigms of Structure and Change*. Albany: State University of New York Press.
de Bary, Wm. Theodore, ed. 1970. *The Unfolding of Neo-Confucianism*. New York: Columbia University Press.
de Bary, Wm. Theodore, and Irene Bloom, eds. 1979. *Principle and Practicality: Essays in Neo-Confucianism and Practical Learning*. New York: Columbia University Press.
De Vos, George, and Takao Sofue, eds. 1984. *Religion and the Family in East Asia*. Osaka: National Museum of Ethnology.

Dobbins, James. 1989. *Jōdo Shinshū: Shin Buddhism in Medieval Japan.* Bloomington: Indiana University Press.
Dorson, Richard. 1962. *Folk Legends of Japan.* Rutland, Vt.: Charles E. Tuttle.
Earhart, H. Byron. 1969. *Japanese Religion: Unity and Diversity.* Belmont, Calif.: Dickenson.
——. 1970. *A Religious Study of the Mount Haguro Sect of Shugendō: An Example of Japanese Mountain Religion.* Tokyo: Monumenta Nipponica Monographs, Sophia University Press.
——. 1974. *Religion in the Japanese Experience: Sources and Interpretations.* Encino, Calif.: Wadsworth.
——. 1989. *Gedatsu-kai and Religion in Contemporary Japan: Returning to the Center.* Bloomington: Indiana University Press.
Ebersole, Gary. 1989. *Ritual Poetry and the Politics of Death in Early Japan.* Princeton: Princeton University Press.
Edwards, Walter. 1989. *Modern Japan Through Its Weddings: Gender, Person, and Society in Ritual Portrayal.* Stanford: Stanford University Press.
Elison, George. 1973. *Deus Destroyed: The Image of Christianity in Early Modern Japan.* Cambridge: Harvard East Asia Series, Harvard University Press.
Ellwood, Robert. 1973. *The Feast of Kingship: Accession Ceremonies in Ancient Japan.* Tokyo: Monumenta Nipponica Monographs no. 50, Sophia University Press.
Faure, Bernard. 1991. *The Rhetoric of Immediacy: A Cultural Critique of Chan/Zen Buddhism.* Princeton: Princeton University Press.
——. 1993. *Chan Insights and Oversights.* Princeton: Princeton University Press.
Fontein, Jan, with Money Hickman. 1970. *Zen Painting and Calligraphy.* Boston: Boston Museum of Fine Arts.
Fridell, Wilbur. 1973. *Japanese Shrine Mergers 1906-12: State Shinto Moves to the Grassroots.* Tokyo: Sophia University Press.
Goodman, David. 1988. *Japanese Drama and Culture in the 1960s: The Return of the Gods.* Armonk, N.Y.: M. E. Sharpe.
Goodman, David, with Masanori Miyazawa. 1995. *Jews in the Japanese Mind: The History and Uses of a Cultural Stereotype.* New York: Free Press.
Goodwin, Janet. 1994. *Alms and Vagabonds: Buddhist Temples and Popular Patronage in Medieval Japan.* Honolulu: University of Hawaiʻi Press.
Gotō Akira, and Nakane Chie, eds. 1972. *The Symposium on Family and Religion in East Asian Countries.* Tokyo: Center for East Asian Cultural Studies.
Grapard, Allan. 1992. *The Protocol of the Gods: A Study of the Kasuga Cult in Japanese History.* Berkeley: University of California Press.
Groner, Paul. 1984. *Saichō: The Establishment of the Japanese Tendai School.* Berkeley: Berkeley Buddhist Studies Series 7, Asian Humanities Press.
Guth, Christine. 1985. *Shinzō: Hachiman Imagery and its Development.* Cambridge: Harvard University Press.
Guth, Christine, with Haruki Kageyama. 1976. *Shinto Arts: Nature, Gods, and Man in Japan.* New York: Japan Society.
Hakeda Yoshito, trans. 1972. *Kūkai: Major Works Translated with an Account of his Life and a Study of his Thought.* New York: Columbia University Press.
Hardacre, Helen. 1984. *Lay Buddhism in Contemporary Japan: Reiyūkai Kyōdan.* Princeton: Princeton University Press.
——. 1986a. *Kurozumikyō and the New Religions of Japan.* Princeton: Princeton University Press.
——. 1986b. *The Religion of Japan's Korean Minority, The Preservation of Ethnic Identity.* Berkeley: University of California Korean Studies Monograph Series, University of California Press.

———. 1989. *Shintō and the State: 1868-1988*. Princeton: Princeton University Press.
———. 1997. *Marketing the Menacing Fetus in Japan*. Berkeley: University of California Press.
Harootunian, Harry. 1988. *Things Seen and Unseen: Discourse and Ideology in Tokugawa Nativism*. Chicago: University of Chicago Press.
Harrington, Ann Mary. 1993. *Japan's Hidden Christians*. Chicago: Loyola University Press.
Heine, Steven. 1989. *A Blade of Grass: Japanese Poetry and Aesthetics in Dōgen Zen*. New York: Peter Lang.
———. 1994. *Dōgen and the Kōan Tradition: A Tale of Two Shōbōgenzō Texts*. Albany: State University of New York Press.
Hirai Naofusa. 1989. *Izumo kunitsukuri hitsugi jinji no kenkyū* (A Study of the Izumo Fire-Striking Ritual). Taimeidō.
Holtom, Daniel. 1922. *The Political Philosophy of Modern Shinto, a Study of the State Religion of Japan*. Chicago: University of Chicago Press.
———. 1943. *Modern Japan and Shinto Nationalism: A Study of Present-Day Trends in Japanese Religions*. Chicago: University of Chicago Press.
Hori, Ichiro. 1968. *Folk Religion in Japan: Continuity and Change*. Edited and translated by Joseph Kitagawa and Alan Miller. Chicago: University of Chicago Press.
Howes, John F. 1960. *Japan's Modern Prophet: Uchimura Kanzō*. Kyoto: Dōshisha and Amherst, Mass.: Amherst College Presses.
Iglehard, Charles. 1959. *A Century of Protestant Christianity in Japan*. Rutland, Vt.: Charles E. Tuttle.
Inoue Mitsusada. 1985. *Kodai bukkyō no tenkai* (The Development of Ancient Buddhism). Iwanami shoten.
Inoue Nobutaka, ed. 1990. *Shinshūkyō jiten* (An Encyclopedia of New Religions). Kōbundō.
Institute for Japanese Culture and Classics. 1968. *Proceedings, The Second International Conference for Shinto Studies*. Tokyo: Kokugakuin University.
Irokawa Daikichi. 1985. *The Culture of the Meiji Period*. Princeton: Princeton University Press.
Japan Foundation. 1996. *Japanese Studies in the United States: The 1990s*. Ann Arbor: Japan Foundation and Association for Asian Studies.
Kamens, Edward. 1988. *The Three Jewels: A Study and Translation of Minmoto Tamenori's "Sanbōe"*. Ann Arbor: Center for Japanese Studies, University of Michigan.
———. 1990. *The Buddhist Poetry of the Great Kamo Priestess: Saisaiin Senshi and the "Hosshin Wakashū"*. Ann Arbor: Center for Japanese Studies, University of Michigan.
Kano Masanao. 1977. *Kindai Nihon no minshū undō to shisō* (Thought in the Popular Movements of Modern Japan). Yūhikaku.
Kapleau, Philip, ed. and comp. 1965. *The Three Pillars of Zen: Teaching, Practice, and Enlightenment*. New York: Weatherhill.
Kasulis, Thomas. 1981. *Zen Action/ Zen Person*. Honolulu: University of Hawai'i Press.
Katō Genchi. 1926. *A Study of Shinto: The Religion of the Japanese People*. Tokyo: Meiji Japan Society.
———. 1953. *A Bibliography of Shinto in Western Languages from the Oldest Times till 1952*. Tokyo: Meiji jingu shamusho.
Ketelaar, James. 1990. *Of Heretics and Martyrs in Meiji Japan: Buddhism and Its Persecution*. Princeton: Princeton University Press.

Kidder, Jonathan E. 1959. *Japan Before Buddhism*. New York: Praeger.
——. 1972. *Early Buddhist Japan*. New York: Praeger.
King, Winston. 1986. *Death Was His Kōan: The Samurai Zen of Suzuki Shōsan*. Berkeley: Asian Humanities Press.
——. 1993. *Zen and the Way of the Sword*. New York: Oxford University Press.
Kitagawa, Joseph M. 1966. *Religion in Japanese History*. New York: Columbia University Press.
Kiyota, Minoru. 1978. *Shingon Buddhism: Theory and Practice*. Los Angeles: Buddhist Books International.
——. 1982. *Gedatsukai: Its Theory and Practice (A Study of a Shinto-Buddhist Syncretic School in Contemporary Japan)*. Los Angeles: Buddhist Books International.
Kodera, James. 1980. *Dōgen's Formative Years in China: An Historical and Annotated Translation of the "Hōkyōki"*. London: Routledge and Kegan Paul.
Kraft, Kenneth. 1992. *Eloquent Zen: Daitō and Early Japanese Zen*. Honolulu: University of Hawai'i Press.
Kuroda Toshio. 1983. *Ōbō to buppō: chūseishi no kōzō* (Imperial Law and Buddhist Law: The Structure of the History of the Middle Ages). Kyoto: Hōzōkan.
——. 1990. *Nihon chūsei no shakai to shūkyō* (Japanese Society in the Middle Ages and Religion). Iwanami shoten.
LaFleur, William. 1983. *The Karma of Words: Buddhism and the Literary Arts in Medieval Japan*. Berkeley: University of California Press.
——. 1992. *Liquid Life: Abortion and Buddhism in Japan*. Princeton: Princeton University Press.
LaFleur, William, trans. 1978. *Mirror for the Moon: A Selection of Poems by Saigyō (1118-1190)*. New York: New Directions.
Laures, Johannes. 1954. *The Catholic Church in Japan: A Short History*. Rutland, Vt.: Charles E. Tuttle.
Lebra, William. 1966. *Okinawan Religion: Belief, Ritual, and Social Structure*. Honolulu: University of Hawai'i Press.
Matsumoto Shigeru. 1970. *Motoori Norinaga, 1730-1801*. Cambridge: Harvard University Press.
Matsunaga, Alicia, and Daigan Matsunaga. 1974, 1976. *Foundations of Japanese Buddhism*. 2 vols. Vol. 1: *The Aristocratic Age*. Los Angeles: Buddhist Books International; Vol. 2: *The Mass Movement: Kamakura and Muromachi Periods*. Los Angeles: Buddhist Books International.
McCallum, Donald. 1994. *Zenkōji and Its Icon: A Study in Medieval Japanese Religious Art*. Princeton: Princeton University Press.
McFarland, H. Neil. 1967. *The Rush Hour of the Gods: A Study of New Religious Movements in Japan*. New York: Macmillan.
McMullin, Neil. 1985. *Buddhism and the State in Sixteenth-Century Japan*. Princeton: Princeton University Press.
Métraux, Daniel. 1988. *The History and Theology of Soka Gakkai: A Japanese New Religion*. Lewiston, N.Y.: Studies in Asian Thought and Religion no. 9, Edwin Mellen Press.
——. 1994. *The Soka Gakkai Revolution*. Lanham, Md.: University Press of America.
Miyake Hitoshi. 1978. *Shugendō: yamabushi no rekishi to shisō* (Shugendō: The History and Thought of the Yamabushi). Kyōikusha shuppan sabisu.
Miyata, Noboru. 1983. *Kami to hotoke: minzoku shūkyō no shosō* (Kami and Buddhas: Aspects of Folk Religion). Shōgakkan.
——. 1984. *Miroku shinkō* (The Cult of Maitreya). Yūzankaku shuppan.
——. 1993. *Edo no hayarigami* (Popular Deities in the Edo Period). Chikuma shobō.

Morioka, Kiyomi. 1975. *Religion in Changing Japanese Society*. Tokyo: University of Tokyo Press.
Morioka, Kiyomi, and William Newell, eds. 1968. *The Sociology of Japanese Religion*. Leiden: E. J. Brill.
Morrell, Robert. 1987. *Early Kamakura Buddhism: A Minority Report*. Berkeley: Asian Humanities Press.
Munro, Neil. 1962. *Ainu Creed and Cult*. London: Routledge and Kegan Paul.
Muraoka Tsunetsugu. 1964. *Studies in Shinto Thought*. Translated by Delmer M. Brown and James T. Araki. Japanese Ministry of Education.
Nelson, John. 1995. *A Year in the Life of a Shinto Shrine*. Seattle: University of Washington Press.
Norbeck, Edward. 1970. *Religion and Society in Modern Japan: Continuity and Change*. Houston: Tourmaline Press/Rice University Press.
Nosco, Peter. 1990. *Remembering Paradise: Nativism and Nostalgia in Eighteenth-Century Japan*. Cambridge: Council on East Asian Studies, Harvard University.
Nosco, Peter, ed. 1984. *Confucianism and Tokugawa Culture*. Princeton: Princeton University Press.
O'Brien, David, and Yasuo Ohkoshi. 1996. *To Dream of Dreams: Religious Freedom and Constitutional Politics in Postwar Japan*. Honolulu: University of Hawai'i Press.
Ohnuki-Tierney, Emiko. 1987. *The Monkey as Mirror: Symbolic Transformations in Japanese History and Ritual*. Princeton: Princeton University Press.
Ono Sokyō. 1960. *Shinto, The Kami Way*. Tokyo: International Institute for the Study of Religions, Bulletin no. 8.
Ooms, Herman. 1985. *Tokugawa Ideology: Early Constructs 1570-1680*. Princeton: Princeton University Press.
Parker, F. Calvin. 1990. *Jonathan Goble of Japan: Marine, Missionary, Maverick*. Berkeley: University Press of America.
Philippi, Donald L., trans. 1959. *"Kojiki": Translated with an Introduction and Notes*. Tokyo: The Institute for Japanese Culture and Classics, Kokugakuin University.
Plath, David, with Yoshie Sugihara. 1969. *Sensei and His People: The Building of a Japanese Commune*. Berkeley: University of California Press.
Ponsonby-Fane, Richard. 1942. *Studies in Shinto and Shinto Shrines*. Kyoto: The Ponsonby Memorial Society.
Reischauer, Edwin O.1955a. *Ennin's Diary: The Record of a Pilgrimage to China in Search of the Law*. New York: Ronald.
——. 1955b. *Ennin's Travels in T'ang China*. New York: Ronald.
Reps, Paul, and Nyogen Senzaki, eds. 1957. *Zen Flesh, Zen Bones: A Collection of Zen and Pre-Zen Writings*. Rutland, Vt.: Charles E. Tuttle.
Rodd, Laurel. 1978. *Nichiren: A Biography*. Tucson: Center for Asian Studies, Arizona State University.
Rogers, Minor Lee, with Ann T. Rogers. 1991. *Rennyo: The Second Founder of Shin Buddhism*. Berkeley: Asian Humanities Press.
Rosenfield, John, with Elizabeth ten Grotenhuis. 1979. *Journey of the Three Jewels: Japanese Buddhist Painting from Western Collections*. New York: Asia Society/Weatherhill.
Sanford, James. 1981. *Zen-Man Ikkyū*. Chico, Calif.: Harvard Studies in World Religion no.2, Scholars Press.
Sasaki, Ruth Fuller. 1959. *Zen: A Method for Religious Awakening*. Kyoto: The First Zen Institute of America in Japan.

Saunders, E. Dale. 1960. *Mudra: A Study of Symbolic Gestures in Japanese Buddhist Sculpture.* New York: Bollingen Foundation/Pantheon.
——. 1964. *Buddhism in Japan, With An Outline of Its Origins in India.* Philadelphia: University of Pennsylvania Press.
Sawada, Janine Anderson. 1993. *Confucian Values and Popular Zen: Sekimon Shingaku in Eighteenth-Century Japan.* Honolulu: University of Hawai'i Press.
Scheiner, Irwin. 1970. *Christian Converts and Social Protest in Japan.* Berkeley: University of California Press.
Schildgen, Robert. 1988. *Toyohiko Kagawa: Apostle of Love and Social Justice.* Berkeley: Centenary.
Shimazono Susumu. 1992. *Gendai kyūsai shūkyōron* (A Theory of Contemporary Religions of Salvation). Seikyūsha.
Smith, Robert J. 1974. *Ancestor Worship in Contemporary Japan.* Stanford: Stanford University Press.
Smith, Warren. 1959. *Confucianism in Modern Japan: A Study of Conservatism in Japanese Intellectual History.* Tokyo: Hokuseido.
Snyder, Gary, and Gutetsu Kanetsuki. 1961. *The Wooden Fish: Basic Sutras and Gathas of Rinzai Zen.* Kyoto: First Zen Institute of America in Japan.
Sonoda Minoru. 1980. *Matsuri no genshōgaku* (A Phenomenological Study of Festivals). Kōbundō.
Statler, Oliver. 1983. *Japanese Pilgrimage.* New York: William Morrow.
Suzuki, Daisetz Teitarō. 1955. *Studies in Zen.* London: Rider.
——. 1956. *Zen Buddhism: Selected Writings.* Garden City: Doubleday.
——. 1957. *Mysticism: Christian and Buddhist.* London: Allen and Unwin.
——. 1958. *Zen and Japanese Buddhism.* Tokyo: Japan Travel Bureau.
——. 1959. *Zen and Japanese Culture.* New York: Pantheon.
Tamamuro Fumio. 1977. *Shinbutsu bunri* (The Separation of Buddhism and Shintō). Kyōikusha.
——. 1987. *Nihon Bukkyōshi. Kinsei* (The History of Japanese Buddhism: The Edo Period). Yoshikawa kōbunkan.
Tanabe, George. 1992. *Myōe the Dreamkeeper: Fantasy and Knowledge in Early Kamakura Buddhism.* Cambridge: Harvard University Press.
Tanabe, Willa. 1988. *Paintings of the Lotus Sutra.* New York: Weatherhill.
Thelle, Notto. 1987. *Buddhism and Christianity in Japan: From Conflict to Dialogue, 1854-1899.* Honolulu: University of Hawai'i Press.
Thomsen, Harry. 1963. *The New Religions of Japan.* Rutland, Vt.: Charles E. Tuttle.
Tsuji Zennosuke. 1944-55. *Nihon Bukkyōshi* (The History of Japanese Buddhism). 10 vols. Iwanami shoten.
Tucker, Mary Evelyn. 1989. *Moral and Spiritual Cultivation in Japanese Neo-Confucianism: The Life and Thought of Kaibara Ekken (1630-1714).* Albany: State University of New York Press.
Tyler, Royall. 1990. *The Miracles of the Kasuga Deity.* New York: Columbia University Press.
Tyler, Susan. 1992. *The Cult of Kasuga Seen Through Its Art.* Ann Arbor: Center for Japanese Studies, University of Michigan.
Ueda Kenji. 1991. *Shintō shingaku ronkō* (Essays on Shintō Theology). Taimeidō.
Ury, Marian. 1977. *Poems of the Five Mountains: An Introduction to the Literature of the Zen Monasteries.* Tokyo: Mushinsha.
Wakamori Tarō. 1980. *Kodai no shūkyō to shakai* (Religion and Society in the Ancient Period). Kōbundō.
Watts, Alan. 1955. *The Way of Liberation in Zen Buddhism.* San Francisco: American Academy of Asian Studies.

Wheeler, Post. 1952. *The Sacred Scriptures of the Japanese*. New York: Henry Schuman.
Whelan, Christal. 1996. *The Beginning of Heaven and Earth: The Sacred Book of Japan's Hidden Christians*. Honolulu: University of Hawai'i Press.
White, James. 1970. *The Sōkagakkai and Mass Society*. Stanford: Stanford Studies in Comparative Politics 4, Stanford University Press.
Woodward, William. 1972. *The Allied Occupation of Japan 1945-1952 and Japanese Religions*. Leiden: E. J. Brill.
Yamashita, Samuel. 1994. *Master Sorai's Responsals*. Honolulu: University of Hawai'i Press.
Yanagida Kunio. 1971. *Teihon Yanagida Kunio shū* (The Collected Works of Yanagida Kunio). 36 vols. Chikuma shobō.
Yasumaru Yoshio. 1974. *Nihon no kindaika to minshū shisō* (Popular Thought and the Modernization of Japan). Aoki shoten.

"THE WAY OF THE WORLD": JAPANESE LITERARY STUDIES IN THE POSTWAR UNITED STATES*

NORMA FIELD

Preliminary Map with Precautions

Hamlet was thirty, textually speaking, and not a young man by Renaissance standards; yet he lives on as quintessential youth in the minds of modern readers in Europe and elsewhere. It is by exploiting this discrepancy that Franco Moretti launches his study of the *Bildungsroman* (1987) from which I have borrowed the first part of my title. In his argument, youth, as that period in life most open to mobility and contradiction, plays a key role in the culture of modernity; indeed, beginning with the classic novels of development appearing from the turn of the eighteenth century, youth—assumed to be fleeting but tantalizingly open-ended—comes to symbolize not merely a stage but a mode of life capable of interiorizing contradiction and, moreover, of flourishing in just such instability.

I invoke Moretti's title and study as a guiding spirit for this essay. The linkage proposed between a society in the throes of historical transformation, the culture developing in such a society (in part produced by and producing those throes), and a particular literary genre—in other words, between the socio-economic-political process of modernization, the culture of modernity, and the *Bildungsroman*—is certainly suggestive for the study of Japanese literature. More generally, the paradox surrounding Hamlet's age

---

* Warm thanks to Bill Sibley, Haraoka Fumiko, Mitamura Masako, Mitani Kuniaki, and Melissa Wender for discussion, information, and stories. Multiple respondents to the electronic JLit-L list confirmed that there is no easy way to track with specificity the translation of Euro-American theoretical works into Japanese; but in so confirming, they variously demonstrated the value of the list. Amanda Seaman and Alisa Freedman were heroic with research assistance.

I am grateful to Helen Hardacre for giving me the opportunity to undertake this study. It has provided me the occasion to reflect with some humility upon the labors of predecessors and peers, whether I have agreed with their inclinations or not. Finally, I would like to pay tribute to my own teacher, Earl Miner, for his sustained intellectual commitment to the study of Japanese literature.

is useful as a mental icon of literature's relatedness to the ways of the world. Both these registers inform the project at hand, the study of the study of Japanese literature.

Moretti's example, among many others, suggests an understanding of literature in which it finds its place among the forces defining the world just as it, too, is defined by it. The world—the past and present of literary works, that is, of their authors and readers, of the conditions of production and reproduction—mediates any understanding of a literary text. Such mediation is necessarily complex. The biography of an author, for example, is an undismissable element of the historical matrix of a work; yet its relationship to the reception of a work varies according to time and place and, in any case, cannot be the equivalent of the work or the arbiter of its meaning. One reason for this is the linguistic density of the literary artifact, salient among the elements mediating between a work and our reading. Writers are also readers, and readers are formed and reformed from work to work and according to the circumstances of their reading. Mediation operates mutually and multidimensionally. Now, recourse to the language of "mediation" rather than of "causality" may seem merely prudent if not outright cowardly, but a text and its contexts of production and reproduction can never be reduced to each other, and among available terms, "mediation" best captures the shifting relations between the two. This said, however, the devil still lurks in the details of elaboration.

The task at hand, then, is to pursue the implications of this stance for the study of Japanese literature in the United States. First, though, let me pause over the geopolitical choice in my title. There are other plausible candidates, such as "Anglo-American" Japanese literary studies, that may be more desirable because more inclusive, though it remains a question whether it is sufficiently more representative so as to signal, say, Australian scholarship. But it is incumbent upon us to recognize the salience of the U.S.-Japan relationship as well as the consequences of American dominance in the postwar world, such that even the work in English of non-U.S. nationals virtually requires publication in the U.S. to command notice. I say this in part by way of apology for one kind of omission among others inevitable in an overview but also to underscore the character of the historical matrix within which the study of Japanese literature has evolved. Incidentally, if, as a matter of intellectual hygiene, we were to acknowledge the degree to which "the" West in the opposition West/non-West has really meant only the U.S., it might go some way to overcoming that increasingly inadequate dichotomy itself.

What, then, might a history of Japanese literary studies in the postwar U.S. look like? First and foremost, it would be tenaciously *relational*. What kinds of literature and what kinds of criticism were produced in Japan during, say, the first two postwar decades, and what was selected for introduction into the U.S.? Equally important, what was not transmitted? How do such selections and omissions relate to the legacy of the war in Japan, the role of the Occupation, American domestic politics, and the dominance of New Criticism in the American academy? What impact, if any, did U.S. reception have on Japanese literary production? What are the dynamics of methodological shifts in criticism, the two- and three-way character of the traffic? Why, for example, beginning in the 1970s, did French-based structuralist and poststructuralist theories become influential in Japan, much more so than Frankfurt School critical theory or first-generation British cultural studies?[1] When and how did such influence register in the work of American scholars studying Japanese literature? How might the emergence of these theories and their complex routes of transmission—some running directly between France and Japan or the U.S. and Japan, others between French philosophers and American scholars of English and comparative literature, thence to American scholars of Japan, and finally to Japan, there to join the circuit of direct transmission from France—relate to the Civil Rights Movement and the Vietnam War in the U.S., the 1960 and 1970 student/citizen movements in Japan, or Algerian independence and the student/labor uprising of 1968 in France? As with literary production, theoretical production is not to be explained immediately by its historical context, but it is not as detached from it as the aura of theoretical authority would suggest. As theories move from the urgency of their origins—as they inevitably do if they survive long enough—they are likely to foreground differ-

---

[1] A representative summation of this history may be seen in the citations and bibliography in Fuhara Yoshiaki, ed. (1985). My thanks to Linda Chance and John Treat for this title.

ent kinds of works. Do such works in Japan then commend themselves to American scholarly attention?

The writing, reading, and viewing of fiction, poetry, and drama, as well as their translation, criticism, and theorizing are overlapping but never equally sustained or valued activities. This is a consequence of their being embedded in their historical moments and therefore social spaces. "Literature" itself is an object produced in history. The premodern breadth suggested both by the etymological presence of "letters" in "literature" and "*bun*" in "*bungaku*" was both narrowed and intensified as literature, and *bungaku* came, in the course of the multiple social transformations of modernity, to connote aesthetic objects more-or-less (but never completely) separate from other spheres, whose study came increasingly to be consigned to specialist professionals, and less and less the producers themselves. The vanishing stability and diminished prominence of literature/*bungaku* as object of study is one feature of the current age of social transformation. On both sides of the Pacific, technological change and the vast expanse of mass culture have favored the image, and especially, the moving image, over the printed word. Literature is no longer a principle vehicle for discovering oneself, learning about others, or being entertained. The dominance of textualist, and even pan-textualist (world-as-text) theories has combined uncannily with socio-politico-economic forces to erode literature as a coherent, not to say prestigious, entity. Institutions of higher education in Japan have steadily dismantled their programs of general education, a principal venue for the dissemination of literature; pressures for accelerated professionalization have been proceeding apace in American higher education as well. Added to that are new challenges to area studies, the common institutional base for the study of Japanese literature, in the post-Cold War order and the frenzy for downsizing in the academy. Will the residues of multiculturalism help the study of Japanese literature survive along with other literatures in departments of comparative literature or the currently popular though institutionally unfixed programs in cultural studies? Will it be obliged to shed its heavy burden of language-learning in the process? And for those of us who continue to read, study, and teach literature in the face of its seeming obsolescence, what is at stake in our continued engagement, if such we are able to choose? What is at stake in the academic pursuit of literature?

What is at stake in the academic pursuit of Japanese literature in the United States?

What I have done thus far is to sketch an agenda for writing a literary history and secondarily, for making the literary history of the future—in other words, I have tried to address historical and existential registers. The latter is necessarily speculative, and I can only symptomatically respond to the former. In doing so, I have resorted to a hybrid mode of organization. I begin with a category based on historical periodization, 1945-1960. Though far fewer works were published in English during that period than subsequently, they were formative for the contours of Japanese literary studies. Thereafter, though I initially sought to follow the same chronological principle, I found that I would be having to argue my way unpersuasively around the next cut-off date, somewhere in the 1980s. Periodization is a complex matter, and in any case, it began to seem more useful to recognize different temporalities operating within the study of Japanese literature. Accordingly, all subsequent sections address work produced from the 1960s on. Although it is notoriously difficult to separate poetry and prose in premodern literature, both the volume of publication and the different trajectories of scholarship prompted me to treat their study in two separate sections. The discussion of premodern prose all too glancingly addresses medieval (*chūsei*) and early modern (*kinsei*, or Tokugawa in American historiography) literature, with a focus on theater in the former and prose fiction in the latter. The final section reviews the post-1960 study of literature written from the Meiji period on.

Before proceeding, let me say a word about the Bibliography, major credit for which goes to Melissa Wender,[2] who, in consultation with me, compiled a core list of monographs that attempts to be broadly inclusive (though hardly comprehensive) about the resources available in English today for the study of Japanese literature. To the extent that translations are included, they are usually those with enough supporting material to count as translation-cum-study, i.e., most often studies of premodern literature. Since they are so few in number, even sparingly introduced translations of modern poetry are included. (Anything like a complete list of

---

[2] A graduate student at the University of Chicago working on a dissertation on Zainichi (Resident Korean) literature.

literary translations into English would constitute a volume in itself. Guides are listed in the first section of the Bibliography, however.) The Bibliography is a combination of this list of selected works and of the sources cited in the Notes. The Notes give special attention to extended reviews, and especially, clusters of reviews. In an area of study where the volume of secondary work is still relatively small, reviews can make significant contributions to scholarship, and multiple reviews of a given work are as much as we are apt to have of a debate. The Notes also attempt, however unevenly, to call attention to scholarship in Japanese.

Getting Started: 1945-1960

Any effort to survey the development of Japanese studies in the U.S. must be mindful of the role of World War II and of the U.S. Occupation of Japan. The evidently effective language schools set up by the Army and the Navy in several centers around the country produced a group who, upon their return from war and further study, were to constitute the first cohort of scholars.[3] The friendliness of the Occupation, the receptiveness of Japanese to American tutelage, the rapidity with which the erstwhile enemy became not only a friend but a valued ally are the stuff of mythologized history in both countries.[4] The scholarly rehabilitation of Japan got under way quickly with publications by Edwin Reischauer (1946, 1950) and George B. Sansom (also in 1950). This was the context in which the first postwar translations and discussions of Japanese literature appeared: Reischauer and Yamagiwa's (1951) selection of early (Heian and Kamakura) prose narratives; Donald Shively's translation (1953); and two modern titles from a commercial publisher, Alfred A. Knopf, in 1955 by Tanizaki Jun'ichirō and Osaragi Jirō. That same year, Grove Press in New York brought out Donald Keene's *Anthology* (1955b), followed by his collection of *Modern Japanese Literature* in 1956. Within the decade, there would be a second title by Tanizaki (1957); two titles by Kawabata Yasu-

---

[3] Marius B. Jansen (1988), 19-21.
[4] Mightily contested, of course, by such figures as Etō Jun. See, for example, his *Amerika to Watakushi* (1965). For a brief but probing analysis of the peaceful Occupation, see John Dower (1986), 301-11.

nari (1956, 1959); four titles by Mishima Yukio (1957a, 1957b, 1958, 1959); two titles by Dazai Osamu (1956, 1958); and one title each by Yoshikawa Eiji (1956), Ōoka Shōhei (1956), and Natsume Sōseki (1957).

By the end of the 1950s, a pattern becomes discernible: the mutual constitution of a canon of *modern* Japanese literature and a *general* readership of English speakers. Many of these titles found British publishers and were also reissued by Charles E. Tuttle in Tokyo, where they not only met and created the appetites of foreign residents but tantalized Japanese readers with an intriguing image of their own literature as an international literature. (A powerful foretaste of this phenomenon was had by those Japanese writers traveling to prewar Europe and encountering Arthur Waley's translation of *The Tale of Genji*.) The remarkable convergence of commercial interest and translation talent of this initial period was crucial to defining the place of Japanese literature in the U.S. cultural and academic milieu well into the 1980s. With the exception of *The Tale of Genji* (especially in its one-volume Doubleday-Anchor edition of 1955), which found its way into many a college literature course long before the age of multiculturalism and the haiku of Bashō, premodern literature was primarily the province of the scholar for output from university presses.[5] What distinguished this formative period was that the scholar who toiled away at producing the supporting apparatus for the premodern translation—notably, Donald Keene, Edward Seidensticker, or Ivan Morris—was so often he who produced the graceful translation for the cosmopolitan readers of titles from Knopf, Grove, or New Directions. Doubtless, it was not only the still modest proportions of the academic study of Japan but the identity of scholar and translator that adjusted the relative weight of apparatus to work somewhat differently from what it has been since. No doubt, too, this was a sort of golden age precisely because the confluence of talent and commercial support enabled a degree of symbiosis between the world of the academy and that of a larger public—a rare thing in any case in the U.S.[6]

---

[5] The one-volume edition contained the first nine chapters of the *Genji*. Waley is ever the exception. His *The Nō Plays of Japan* (1957) included a substantial Introduction but minimal footnotes. See also Helen McCullough (1959) and Howard S. Hibbett (1959), which with its accessible introduction and generous sampling of Edo fiction, lent itself to reissue in 1975.

[6] The scope and success of the marketing may be gauged from Kawabata's

It is worth pausing over the nature of the canon produced in the first fifteen postwar years. It was overwhelmingly a canon that conferred aesthetic allure upon the erstwhile enemy, and to the extent that the war appeared, it was in the depoliticized response of common humanity. Even the works that seem aberrant at first glance are consonant with the ethos of the period: Osaragi's *Homecoming* and Yoshikawa's *The Heike Story* belong to the domain of popular literature, but the former depicts sympathetically the alienation awaiting the soldier returning from war, and the latter displaces recent images of Japanese militarism with the romance of the medieval warrior.[7] Ōoka's *Fires on the Plain* is a frontal confrontation with the horrors of war, but its hallucinatory, metaphysical quality is an invitation to universalizing. It is actually *Kokoro* that is the exceptional translation from this period; despite its author's status, it failed to grip the English-speaking reader's imagination in the same way as did the works of Tanizaki, Kawabata, and Mishima. The canon created during the golden age was a canon centered on the works of this triumvirate, making them synecdochic of Japanese culture; or more succinctly, the golden age created the triumvirate as such, and thereby consolidated a certain version of Japanese culture.[8] (Dazai does not literally belong to the triumvirate but the two early Keene translations are thoroughly compatible both in the politically untroubling view of the war of the one and the existential torment of the other; an expanded view of Dazai does not become available until the 1980s.)[9]

Now, it is of course hardly novel to suggest that Japanese literature as represented by the triumvirate was a comfortably enticing thing. What is important today is to understand with some specificity how that exotic effect was produced, which in part entails identifying the kinds of writing omitted in the course of canon-formation. It may be useful to review contemporary assessments as represented by Donald Keene's influential introduction to Jap-

---

Snow Country's garnering thirteen listings in *Book Review Digest 1957* (482), well before he won the Nobel Prize (and no doubt important to his doing so).

[7] See Edward Fowler's persuasive argument for the similarity of *Homecoming*'s appeal to that of *Some Prefer Nettles* in his provocative and informative article (1992): 6-7.

[8] Ibid., 8-9, for the triumvirate phenomenon (I borrow the expression from Fowler) and especially for its impact on Japanese writers.

[9] Through, for instance, James O'Brien (1983), Phyllis I. Lyons (1985), and James Westerhove (1985).

anese literature (1955a). Here is a description of the "terrible years of 1946 and 1947":

> Certain left-wing writers who had been imprisoned or exiled returned to write memoirs, and their books, together with translations of foreign works, especially American, took up a large part of the booksellers' lists. But of genuine literary production there was very little. Pornographic novels, detective stories, and other types of escapist literature began to appear, reflecting the low standard of the tastes of the reading public.[10]

Thirty years later, Keene observes of that same period in his chapter on "Postwar Literature" (1984) that "The year or two following the end of the war was a period of extraordinary literary activity."[11] What accounts for this change of assessment? Given the conditions of life during the immediate postwar years, it may in fact have been difficult to gauge from a distance just how "extraordinary" the literary activity was, and Keene, after his wartime experience with the navy, was unable to return to Japan until 1953.[12] But surely, more than any particulars of individual experience—for of course this view is not Keene's alone—the intellectual dimensions of that politico-historical moment, combined with more confident notions of what constituted authentic literature than are available at present, account for the long dismissal of that period of ferment. To glance at a summary chronology such as to be found in the back of literary dictionaries (*bungaku jiten*) is to recognize the riches produced by people emerging from and confronting catastrophe even as they struggled for day-to-day survival. The roster of the first postwar decade is astonishing for its quality and variety: of course, there were writers already established before the war, such as Nagai Kafū, Shiga Naoya, or Ishikawa Jun; there were the "decadents" (Buraiha) associated with Dazai, notably Sakaguchi Ango and Oda Sakunosuke; and then Miyamoto Yuriko, Umezaki Haruo, Hanada Kiyoteru, Noma Hiroshi, Shiina Rinzō, Kaneko Mitsuharu, Fukunaga Takehiko, Hara Tamiki, Ōta Yōko, Takeda Taijun, Tamura Taijirō, Enchi Fumiko, Kojima Nobuo,

---

[10] Donald Keene (1955a), 105-6.

[11] Donald Keene (1984), 17. Keene also has two informative essays on wartime literary production in the chapter "The Japanese and the Landscapes of War," the first on "The Sino-Japanese War of 1894-95 and Japanese Culture" (first published in 1971) and the second on "Japanese Writers and the Greater East Asia War" (first published in 1964): in Keene (1971), 259-321.

[12] Donald Keene (1978), 65-84.

Hayashi Fumiko, Nakamura Shin'ichirō....Some of them have subsequently been introduced, others have not. As noted above, the English-language canon as it was established in the postwar decade-and-a-half is characterized by the minimal presence of literature dealing with the war and its aftermath, not to mention the atomic bombs. Relatedly, there is almost no sign of attention to contemporary Japanese debates about literature.[13] The social experience of devastation is at least as likely to provoke intense scrutiny of the conditions of existence as "escapist" pornography and detective fiction. Postwar critics and writers argued fervently about the relationship of politics and literature, the place of national identity in literature, about subjectivity, about writers' war responsibility, about political apostasy (*tenkō*).[14] No doubt such concerns would have been labeled ideological by scholars of Japan and therefore deemed unliterary in a United States under the gentlemanly spell of New Criticism combined with the onset of McCarthyism. The writings of the triumvirate, unclouded by the passionate polemics of their context, projected an unthreatening because aestheticized exoticism not only compatible with but agreeably enhancing what might have been a merely humdrum, safely liberal, and modern subject—indeed, one more and more like "us" thanks to the maturation proceeding under American tutelage—presented in the new history books and the Cold War mass media learning to see Japan as the pillar of freedom in the Far East.

The confluence of the worldviews of the Japan historian and of the literature scholar is suggested in the lavish praise by Edwin O. Reischauer for an article by Donald Keene ending with the following claim:

> A large proportion of the Japanese economists and historians are under the influence of Marxism. This is not true of the writers of literature, and in this lies a source of the strength of the Japanese urge to spiritual independence.[15]

---

[13] Joseph K. Yamagiwa's 1953 article is an early exception. It provides a matter-of-fact guide to contemporary critical debates as well as a sociology of literature through reader surveys.

[14] Usui Yoshimi (1975) excerpts from the major postwar debates. Keene, disappointingly, does not address the postwar debates in his "Modern Criticism" section (1984). The interdisciplinarity, so to speak, of postwar debates is attested by Maruyama Masao's 1949 essay in Ivan Morris (1963). See J. Victor Koschmann (1996).

[15] Donald Keene (1957), 152.

Reischauer's review calls this essay

> a most penetrating and often amusing analysis of the Japanese public's omnivorous reading habits, the way authors make a handsome living, the leading writers of the present day, the sad state of popular and scholarly literary criticism, and the deleterious influence of politics on both original writing and criticism.[16]

Let me clarify several points. First, I am not claiming intentionality on the part of translators or publishers, or even, necessarily, the historians, to collude in the seemingly depoliticizing politics of the Cold War rehabilitation of Japan. Intentions, in any case, are difficult to demonstrate, and it is generally more productive to deal with effects. Second, in calling attention to certain politico-cultural effects, I am denying neither the value of the symbiosis of general public, commercial press, and scholar-translator referred to earlier, nor the interest of Tanizaki, Kawabata, and Mishima as writers. (Still less do I deny the value of Americans developing a sense of friendship for the reviled enemy!) They are, regardless of individual taste, remarkable writers for whom we are collectively fortunate to have had such talented translators. Moreover, insofar as they are available (publishers please take note), we can always contextualize them and read their works differently from the ways in which they were introduced.

But let me offer other specific examples for thinking about the historicity of interpretation along with the unexamined ground of such interpretation, namely, an understanding of literature as ahistorical, whose identity, therefore, is not subject to argument: you know literature when you see it, in Japan or anywhere else. Hayashi Fumiko's desolate 1951 novel, *The Drifting Cloud*, for example, was praised by Keene (1955a) as an evocation of postwar Japan but criticized for being "*too close to the facts* which inspired it to permit any real *literary* quality" (107; emphasis added. My examples inevitably come from Keene because he has been the most consistently prolific scholar-promoter of Japanese literature throughout the postwar decades). What the requisite distance from "the facts" might be and whether the nature of "the facts" in question has any bearing on the literary success of a work are never discussed. Keene's *Modern Japanese Literature*, a catholic collection

---

[16] Edwin O. Reischauer (1958): 202.

still effective in jump-starting the English-speaking reader's acquaintance with modern Japanese literature, includes a passage from "Earth and Soldiers" (1938), extracted from the diaries of Hino Ashihei, who was a reporter officially assigned to cover troop activities during the Sino-Japanese War beginning in 1937. Neither the *Introduction* (at 104) nor the preface to the selection in *Modern Japanese Literature,* presumably by Keene, mentions that Hino was purged for his contributions to the war effort between 1947 and 1950. The latter asserts that "Hino has been denounced for his lack of a more critical attitude toward these wars of aggression, but it is undeniable that he accomplished brilliantly the task of making *reportage* into a work of *artistry*" (357; emphasis added). Thirty years later, however, Keene's account of Hino in the "War Literature" chapter (1984) concludes with the view that his "reputation is unlikely to improve with time. He will probably be remembered as the archetypal war writer, the chief spokesman for the *heitai* during the fifteen long years of war" (926). Lastly, as for Kobayashi Takiji, the best-known writer of the proletarian literature movement: although the *Introduction* concludes its account of his *Crab-Canning Boat*[17] with a description of the ship coming into "contact with a party of charming Soviet subjects," including a Japanese-speaking Chinese who "communicates the glad tidings of Marxism" (103), it nonetheless helpfully situates its "crude" qualities in relation to an American contemporary, Clifford Odets's play *Waiting for Lefty* (1935). The preface to the anthology selection, "The Cannery Boat," while referring to its "gross imperfections," manages to refer to its author's death by prison torture (333). What is most striking, however, is that of the thirty-six selections in the anthology, this one alone lacks a named translator. It is chilling to encounter the phrase "Translated Anonymously" (332)—without further comment—in a collection published in 1955, and to realize from the bibliography that it must be the same anonymous (how different from the "*yomibito shirazu*" of the imperial anthologies of poetry!) translator of a New York edition of 1933. The assessment of Kobayashi remains consistent over the decades: he is still denied "*literary* excellence" in *Dawn to the West* (616; emphasis added).

This rapid sketch shows how, just in the work of one promi-

---

[17] Translation in Kobayashi Takiji (1973).

nent scholar, the relationship between politics and literature shifts, affected in part by which politics are understood to be most objectionable in a given age. What is consistent is a reliance on distancing from life as a source of literary value. The persistent tendency in American criticism of Japanese literature to subtract points qua literature from works whose contents seem to resemble too closely their contexts of production has something of an equivalent in the contentious debate amongst Japanese writers and critics on the subject of the *shishōsetsu*, or the I-novel, so called. In any case, the unargued discounting of autobiographical and of more broadly realist works as literature has contributed to the narrowing of Japanese works for introduction into English together with the dismissal of much Japanese criticism and scholarship for being, precisely, biographical. In the process, the autobiographical, the political, and the realist in fiction, and the biographical in criticism, have been usefully conflated, resulting in the almost exclusive validation of literature and literary study that are unworldly without, however, the production of an account of literary autonomy.[18]

Before taking leave of this formative period, I would like to pause over the possibilities represented by postwar Japanese literary scholarship, specifically of the Tokugawa period. We know that in the world of the historians, this was a period that attracted heated debate. Schematically put, the often Marxist Japanese historians as well as E. H. Norman[19] concentrated on its feudal and repressive dimensions, while the modernization-theorist American historians emphasized its rational promise for Japanese modernity. Robert Bellah's influential Weberian analysis appeared in 1957,[20] one year before the formation of the Conference on Modern Japan, which led to the famous Hakone modernization conference of 1960 and subsequent string of publications. The question here is, what was the role of the presentation, through translation and

---

[18] The choice of "unworldly" is contrastively inspired by Edward Said's discussions throughout his 1983 essays.

[19] See John W. Dower's contextualizing introduction (1975).

[20] Tokugawa historiography has been considerably complicated since, on both sides of the Pacific. It will be interesting to watch the impact of Amino Yoshihiko's materialist self-revision of his earlier more orthodox Marxist work. Amino is a medievalist whose research has been enormously influential on other periods. Two volumes of translation are scheduled from the Center for Japanese Studies at the University of Michigan Press in 1998.

discussion, of Tokugawa cultural production in this debate? Earlier, I referred to Bashō's haiku as an exception, along with *Genji*, to the tendency for premodern literature to be confined to the scholarly world of weighty annotation and university presses. But in addition to haiku, Kabuki together with the puppet theater also had nonspecialist appeal,[21] and of course, *ukiyo-e* had a venerable presence in modern Europe. The fiction never enjoys the same status, but the *Anthology of Japanese Literature* does offer a sampling, including three pieces by Ihara Saikaku, who would find a number of translators in the coming decades.[22] Might the appeal of the peculiarly accessible-yet-profound spirituality of haiku, the fascinating stylization of Kabuki and the puppet theater, and even the alien exuberance of Saikaku, have been roughly equivalent to the lure of the writings of the Mishima-Tanizaki-Kawabata triumvirate?

Japanese scholarship suggested other possibilities, ones not altogether unknown to American scholars. Richard Lane's articles (1955, 1957) make refreshing reading even today in their respect for Japanese scholarship and uncondescending attitude toward the fiction itself on the one hand and attention to "material factors" such as the development of printing technology and the "rise of capitalism" on the other.[23] The former begins by quoting the Tokugawa literature and linguistics scholar Ebara Taizō proclaiming in 1948 that "'the *real* study of Saikaku is only now beginning.'"[24] Lane glosses the assertion with reference to the availability of texts and government censorship, which are unquestionably pertinent considerations. But Ebara's statement comes to life only when we concretely sense what was at stake in Saikaku scholarship for those engaged in the study of Japanese literature during the prewar and wartime years. Modern literature scholar Ino Kenji, who was a student during the period when state oppression led to massive leftist apostasy, recalls why he chose Saikaku for his graduation thesis as he anticipated military conscription two years hence:

> ...people were talking a lot in those days about Japaneseness, or the archaic, or about *yūgen* or *sabi* or *shiori* as representative of medieval [values], and they valorized even those literary traditions as [expressive

---

[21] Faubion Bowers (1976 [1952]).
[22] Theodore de Bary, for example, has an early book-length translation (1956).
[23] Richard Lane (1957), 644.
[24] Richard Lane (1955), 182. Emphasis in original.

of] the genius of the Japanese nation, but in Saikaku you could see elements that parodied such medieval traditions. Or [you could see] the heroic grace of an amoral stance that transcended the common sense of *giri ninjō*. So at the least I can say that those aspects tied in with my sense of alienation from the academicism of national literature [studies] in those days, the philology that had lapsed into miscellany or political opportunism....[25]

Ino's remembrances are offered in the context of reflections on the contributions of the "historico-sociological school" (Rekishi shakaigakuha) to postwar literary studies. One of the leaders of that school, Masuda Katsumi (1977 [1961]), reflects critically and therefore all the more compellingly on its efforts to transcend the mechanical reflectionism or reductivism of prewar approaches or its contestation of philological positivism (often held to be nonideological both before and after the war). The very collaboration between historians and literary scholars encouraged by the movement prompted such scholars as Saigō Nobutsuna to seek principles proper to literary history.[26] The bottom line of the historico-sociological school, at least as articulated by a prewar scholar, Ishiyama Tetsurō, and quoted approvingly by Masuda, was that:

> "In 'Japanese Literary Arts Studies' [Nihon Bungeigaku], a mistaken notion of the 'purity' of the object of study led to what must be specified as the serious defect of cutting off and abstracting 'literariness' from historical and social human life....No literary art whatsoever can exist apart from concrete human life...."[27]

The horizon of aspiration of the historico-sociological school has been effaced in Japanese scholarship today, in part by the challenges of the 1970 Zenkyōtō generation. It was never known in the United States. This is wasteful.

---

[25] Ino Kenji (1987), 238.

[26] At least partly in response to historian of ancient Japan Ishimoda Shō's review of Saigō's (1963 [1948]) volume, as reported in Ino (1987), 252. Saigō (1964) published a memorable study of early Japanese poetry and prose fiction.

[27] Quoted in Masuda (1977 [1961]), 77. Nihon Bungeigaku is the name by which Okazaki Yoshie's ethnocentric prewar approach to the study of the Japanese literary arts is known. For another antireductivist specimen of historico-sociological school writing, see Hirosue Tamotsu (1987). For a refreshing antidote to an etherealized Bashō, see Hirosue (1988). Nishiwaki Junzaburō's provocative denunciation (1995 [1946]) of haiku on the grounds that it could not achieve autonomy and therefore could not be considered an art, published shortly after the war, exemplifies the sort of formalist aestheticism prompted by heightened consciousness of "the West" in defeat.

Onward from the Sixties (I): The Study of Classical Poetry

As everyone knows, it is an act of violence to separate poetry and prose in premodern Japanese literary texts. Nevertheless, I do so in an effort to understand how the study of premodern literature has developed. I begin with an essay that was published in 1958 because it and its author, Konishi Jin'ichi, are so important to that monumental work published three years later, *Japanese Court Poetry*.[28] The translation of "Association and Progression" is, alas, still remarkable for the effort it represents on the part of American scholars in making Japanese scholarship available in English. (We ought to pause over the phrase "translated *and adapted* by" under Konishi's name on the title page of the article [emphasis mine].) The article's argument remains important in contesting the still common view of the irreducibly if appealingly brief character of Japanese fixed-form poetry; it furthermore demonstrates principles whereby that brevity is regularly overcome. *Japanese Court Poetry* itself remains remarkable: no subsequent work to date approaches its sustained examination—spanning 527 pages, with a section of the bibliography devoted to Japanese scholarship—of a central, perhaps the central genre of Japanese literature over time. Considerable space is necessarily allotted to the presentation of the poetry itself in translation, but our attention is consistently directed to how the poems themselves might be understood. From the vantage point of the present, the book suggests a leap of faith on the part of the authors that their field was ready for such a prolonged encounter with the workings of *uta* (*waka*). Understandably, points of comparison (e.g., Dryden, Milton) that may seem idiosyncratic today appear throughout to legitimize this effort. The approach might be generalized as New Critical (and Konishi is exceptional among *kokubungakusha* for his familiarity with New Criticism) though with generous gesturings toward institutional context and genre history. It served to valorize *waka* by demonstrating that it could withstand such sustained formal analysis. To judge from contemporary reviews[29] and subsequent scholarship, however, this demonstration was not soon absorbed and devel-

---

[28] The article, "translated and adapted" by Robert H. Brower and Earl Miner, is "Association and Progression" (Konishi, 1958). Brower and Miner are the authors of *Japanese Court Poetry* (1961).
[29] For example, D. E. Mills (1961-62) and Donald Keene (1961).

oped, whether by contestation or agreement; questions of translation attracted more energy.

Despite the continued efforts of the authors of *Japanese Court Poetry*, including both the distillation and extension of content (down to 159 pages of text, with coverage stretched to the year 1500) of the 1968 book by Miner, we must wait until 1980 or so for the beginning of lively and substantive discussion of premodern Japanese poetry. The trigger was to be another ambitious study by Miner (1979). In this study of linked verse, interest in *waka*'s connectedness first introduced in "Association and Progression" is developed into evaluative/interpretive codes synthesized from the rules governing sequence composition. The merit of such an elaboration of rules lies in providing readers a participatory introduction to the genre. Reviewers responded to the challenge of the book by giving it bracing criticism extending far beyond the common recitation of errors in translation.[30] Linked verse was to prove a fruitful topic of investigation, as shown by such publications as those by Steven D. Carter in 1987, and Esperanza Ramirez-Christensen in 1994. The former gives a detailed sense of what rule-bound composition and reading might be, with suggestive but sober comparisons to structuralist and especially Barthesian writerly reading practices. In the latter the possibilities of the literary biography are vivified in the presentation of Shinkei's life as interwoven sociopolitical world and aesthetico-religious practice. The Shinkei "Reader" in the text demonstrates a tenacious commitment to the urgency of artful translation along with critical engagement. H. Mack Horton (1993) is persuasive on the role of the oral, social performance producing the written texts through which we apprehend the poetry today, a practice that informed even solitary, individual composition. The argument here most definitely does not reduce the written to its prior oral text; rather, each acquires a palpable reality.

Linked verse, in short, seems to be a genre that is singularly good-to-think-with, entailing as it did the social enactment of formal splitting and combining; the rich production of meaning through mastery of convention; and the expression of challenges

---

[30] For example, Wílllíam R. LaFleur (1982) and especially, Esperanza Ramirez-Christensen (1981). Ueda Makoto's review (1979) reminds us of the significance of this publication.

to convention as *renga* ceded to *haikai*. And if we follow the further movement from still link-conscious *haikai* to the isolated *hokku*, yielding the familiar haiku surrounded by profoundly blank space, we shall also have traced an aspect of what used to be called the "transition from feudalism," crudely speaking.[31] Here is a practice that should stimulate students with a substantive sense of aesthetic "difference" from the presumptions of modernity, in Japan as elsewhere.

Though I have dwelt on how linked verse has been productive for the study of so-called traditional Japanese poetry generally, I do not mean to suggest that the study of *waka* stood still in the meanwhile. A flurry of translations and studies sparked lively reviews during the 1980s, with some of the coals still warm in the current decade. First, pre-imperial anthology poetry, an important part of which is in the long *chōka* form, appeared on the table: Ian Levy's initial volume of translation of the *Man'yōshū* appeared in 1981; Paula Doe's study of Ōtomo no Yakamochi with multiple translations appeared in 1982; Ian Levy's study of Hitomaro appeared in 1984; and somewhat later, in 1992, came Gary Ebersole's study of "ritual poetry." The Levy translation certainly provided an alternative vision of the selections translated in *Japanese Court Poetry* or the widely circulated 1965 Columbia University Press's reissue of a selection published by the Japan Classics Translation Committee of the Nippon Gakujutsu Shinkōkai in, of all years, 1940.[32] Levy's translations, unencumbered by notes, are clearly meant to appeal to the reader's eye as poetry in English; his Hitomaro book, besides directing a passionate attention to the early poems that they have not received since, argues for a historical person, Hitomaro, who took the *chōka* form on a leap from the world of myth to the world of lyric—for the most part, remarkably enough, in the vehicle of praise for the imperial family. Gary Ebersole used texts from the *Kojiki* and the *Nihon Shoki* as well as the *Man'yōshū* to contest the notion of "primitive" mythic beliefs and practices of the eighth-century court with an argument for

---

[31] This and much more explored in a lengthy essay in two parts by Mark Morris (1984/1985).

[32] The translation and publication history of the *Man'yōshū* are detailed in Edwin Cranston (1983); also see Eric Rutledge (1983), which concludes with an interesting comparison of Levy's translation into English to Orikuchi Shinobu's into modern Japanese.

the conscious political manipulation of ritual.[33] In an article published in 1981, Roy Andrew Miller had introduced the work of two Japanese scholars that complicated by anticipation both Levy's and Ebersole's arguments with claims for the reworkings of indigenous oral narratives along Chinese models and the particular impact of foreign conceptualizations of time. This cluster of writings, along with reviews of Levy's *Hitomaro* book,[34] suggested the possibility of a sustained argument about the relationship between lyric, myth, and ritual; among anthropological, historical, and literary discourses; and about the stakes for scholarship (and even for the poetry-loving common reader imagined by Levy) in the U.S. and Japan. Such a discussion did not materialize, however, perhaps because the issues raised, and most especially, the training required to join the debate, unfortunately seemed too specialized.

For somewhat later poetry, the back-to-back appearance of two translations of the *Kokinshū*, the tenth-century imperial anthology, the first in Japanese, evidently provided the occasion for explicit debate. The Laurel Rodd-Mary Henkenius translation (1984) experimented with spacing to convey the effects of *waka* prosody. Such discussion as this elicited, however, was eclipsed by the controversy over Helen McCullough's two 1985 volumes, one a translation of *Kokinshū* plus *Tosa nikki* and *Shinsen waka*, the other of commentary.[35] It is almost as if the very heft of the two volumes (with half the translations in the one reproduced in the other) provoked the urge to balk in the ranks of our patient, decorous profession: no, we won't have those *waka*s rolling off the conveyor belt any more; we won't learn how to judge them according to Heian taste (and why should we believe that this is what they— who were they, anyway—believed?); and no, we don't care about how it was all imitation Chinese; and we might as well stop pretending that this works as poetry in English....

Well, I exaggerate. No doubt it was an overdetermined moment. Hiroaki Sato and Burton Watson's labors had resulted in another

---

[33] This may be the place to refer to Donald Philippi's memorable translation with detailed commentary of the *Kojiki* (1967).

[34] See Esperanza Ramirez-Christensen (1987), Paula Doe (1987), and especially, Mark Morris (1986b).

[35] Among the reviews were those by Roy Andrew Miller (1987), Richard H. Okada (1988), and Thomas H. Rohlich (1988).

tome (1981), which included a major sampling of *waka* with mostly unsatisfactory if intriguing results. Edward Said's vastly influential *Orientalism* appeared in 1979, prompting a symposium in the *Journal of Asian Studies* in 1980. And a number of students of Japanese literature had become familiar enough with poststructuralist ideas which, combined with both the specific analyses and the political charge of Said's book, caused them to pause before unexamined appeals to individual persons authoring expressive poems. Such resistance has itself thrown up further issues for sorting out. How, for instance, is the insistence on Japanese difference to be distinguished from generic Japanese exceptionalism, not to mention the prewar variety? Beyond objecting to a simplistic notion of influence, how should we understand the place of "China"—and of course, "Korea"—in early "Japanese" letters? (How, that is, can we avoid reading back into the Nara and Heian past identities attached to modern nation-states?)[36] A number of these issues are incisively presented in the most challenging analysis of *waka* to appear in English to date, namely, "Waka and Form, Waka and History."[37] Although the nature of the comma in the title remains opaque—how is the argument about form itself (*waka* as unilinear and not a stack of English lines) being related to history?—the implied quest is at any rate begun.

Before leaving this section, I want to make an observation that applies not only to the copiously annotated translation (or study-cum-translation) of classical poetry but of prose as well: with a few exceptions, most scholars' engagement with Japanese scholarship is confined to their choice of base text. It is surely a pity that there is not more constant curiosity about ongoing debates, however distracting they may be in the progress of one's translation.[38] For example, a major collection of essays by Suzuki Hideo pertinent to so many of the issues that are either under discussion or should be under discussion—the role of Chinese poetry and poetics, shifts

---

[36] Addressed by Thomas LaMarre (1994). Developed in a manuscript forthcoming from Duke University Press.

[37] Mark Morris (1986c). Response by Earl Miner (1990). See also Edwin A. Cranston (1988). For another sampling of Morris on *waka*, see his review of Steven D. Carter (1993).

[38] It's always worth a quick check to see if the journal *Kokubungaku* from Gakutōsha has produced a *hikkei* (handbook) on the topic in question, premodern or modern.

in rhetorical figures between collections, individual vs. group, poetry composed by women and by men in the persona of women, poetry and prose fiction—goes uncited. The book was published in 1990, but a number of the essays date back to the early 1970s. One of them, "Waka no hyōgen ni okeru shimbutsu taiō kōzō," is potentially as useful as "Association and Progression" has been.

Onward from the Sixties (II): The Study of Premodern Prose

In contrast to the case of poetry, there is a steady march of translations (often with appended "study") of prose forms with poetry such as diaries and tales, from the *Gikeiki* in 1966 (McCullough) to a one-volume selection from *Genji* and *Heike* in 1994 (McCullough). In between, there appeared, among others, translations of the *Makura no sōshi* (Morris, 1967); two translations of the *Ōkagami* (Yamagiwa, 1967; McCullough, 1980); the *Tsurezuregusa* (Keene, 1967); two translations of the *Izumi Shikibu nikki* (Cranston and Miner, both 1969); two translations of the *Ise monogatari* (McCullough, 1968; Harris, 1972); two translations of the *Tosa nikki* (Miner, 1969; McCullough, 1985b); the *Uji shūi monogatari* (Mills, 1970); the *Sarashina nikki* (Morris, 1971); the *Ochikubo monogatari* (Whitehouse and Yanagisawa, 1971); the *Nihon ryōiki* (Nakamura, 1973); two translations of the *Towazugatari* (Brazell, 1973; Whitehouse and Yanagisawa, 1974); two translations of the *Heike monogatari* (Kitagawa and Tsuchida, 1975; McCullough, 1988); the *Genji monogatari* (Seidensticker, 1976); the *Sanuki no Suke nikki* (Brewster, 1977); the *Yowa no nezame monogatari* (Hochstedler, 1979); the *Konjaku monogatari* (Ury, 1979); the *Eiga monogatari* (McCullough and McCullough, 1980); the *Yamato monogatari* (Tahara, 1980); the *Murasaki Shikibu nikki* (Bowring, 1982); the *Hamamatsu Chūnagon monogatari* (Rohlich, 1983); the *Torikaebaya monogatari* (Willig, 1983); the *Mumyōzōshi* (Marra, 1984); the *Tsutsumi Chūnagon monogatari* (Backus, 1985); the *Soga monogatari* (Cogan, 1987); the *Sanbō ekotoba* (Kamens, 1988); the *Heichū monogatari* (Videen, 1989); the *Genmu monogatari, Sannin hōshi, Shichinin bikuni* (Childs, 1991); and the *Matsura no Miya monogatari* (Lammers, 1992).[39] Culled

---

[39] See Bibliography (Section III, "Premodern Literature—Studies/Translations of Prose and General Studies") for information on this and preceding translations/studies.

from several of the above and reconstructively translated are the stories in the beguiling *Japanese Tales*, a volume in the Pantheon Fairy Tale and Folklore Library.[40] *The Yanagita Kunio Guide to the Japanese Folktale*, by contrast, beckons in the direction of folklore studies.[41]

The above looks like a list in prose. Could it have been anything else? Of course, having presented the information in this way, I can be charged with having invidiously created a problem, but I believe there is more to this than presentation. The air of miscellany—quiet, painstaking, sometimes inspired, but miscellany nonetheless—hangs over this branch of scholarship, interrupted only by the Seidensticker *Genji* and its reviews, subsequent monographs on *Genji* by Haruo Shirane (1987), by me (1987), by Richard Bowring (1988), and by Richard Okada (1991), and their reviews, the sum total of which does begin to look like a veritable discourse.[42] *Genji*'s being the perennial exception, however, is arguably nonsalutary for both the study of premodern literature generally and for *Genji* itself. (Indeed, Okada's book takes *Taketori* and *Ise* as well as associated poetry within its compass and is much the stronger for it.) To be sure, there have been memorable articles and reviews associated with works other than *Genji* by Janet A. Walker back in 1977; Mark Morris in 1980 and 1986a; and Richard J. Bowring in 1992. These shine, however, without cumulative impact. Collaborating with the annotated translation with commentary is the this-is-wrong (usually), this-is-right (more rarely) school of reviewing, punctilious enough to enumerate typos. Of course, this is necessary, it is how the profession polices itself and maintains credibility. There is also the plain fact that those who toil in the fields of premodern Japanese literature are usually deprived of the pleasure of discussing their crops in de-

---

[40] Royall Tyler (1987).
[41] Fanny Hagin Mayer (1986). Also see Keigo Seki (1963).
[42] Principal reviews of the Seidensticker *Genji* are by Helen C. McCullough (1977), Earl Miner (1977), Marian Ury (1977), Edwin Cranston (1978), and Masao Miyoshi (1979). Belonging with this group is Marian Ury (1976). There now exists a third partial translation in English in the selections included in Helen McCullough, trans. (1994), reviewed by Thomas H. Rohlich (1995). Reviews of Field and Shirane: Mark Morris (1990), Richard H. Okada (1990), Janet Goff (1991b), and Marian Ury (1991). Reviews of Okada: Haruo Shirane (1994), and Esperanza Ramirez-Christensen (1995).

tail, and sometimes, though rarely, a sense of joyful learning does come through to the reader of the painstaking review.[43]

To return to the list and its salient feature, namely, its representing a staggering amount of congealed industry. Who are the intended consumers? Presumably, beneath the most dutiful thicket of sources beats a passion to bring a richly remote world to a new reader. (And a number of the translations far exceed the dutiful.) And yet, is it not the case that the majority of readers will be the author's peers, or peers in the making, those graduate students in the early stages of their study of classical Japanese or those interested primarily in other periods or genres and wanting a quick take? What does it mean, then, this production of densely annotated translations? Surely anyone interested in that degree of detail would turn to the Japanese editions and reference tools? Or is there a sort of pride in the supporting apparatus that aims to produce the "most complete version" of Japanese text x "in any language," an ambition that may be relatively indifferent to the desires of the reader who can only access the text through English translation? Can we imagine the translations qua translation contributing to the study of their "original" texts in Japan, that is, in a way other and more than serving as an entry in yet another survey of "overseas study" of Japanese literature? The question of readership applies to *Genji* scholarship as well, insofar as studying the *Genji* and writing about it in English in the U.S. are a categorically different activity from doing the same in Japan in Japanese. We ought not avoid considering the implications of studying and presenting texts that most of our colleagues will never be able to read, let alone care to. Now, it just may be that these are philistine concerns, and the slow, patient labor invested in the production of these texts is its own justification. (And would that more occupations were as blameless.)

As I write this essay, the Pulitzer-prize winning novelist of the Vietnam War Larry Heinemann is traveling the country with a group of Vietnamese writers. They are sponsored by a Boston-based foundation dedicated to the study of the social consequences of war. The group's translator is a man who, during the war, was sent by his country ("North" Vietnam) to study Russian literature in the

---

[43] E.g., Cranston's "The Seidensticker *Genji*," which juxtaposes three versions of a series of passages.

Soviet Union, where he learned English as well. He has been translating Shakespeare's sonnets, Byron, and Robert Burns. This is his first experience of an English-speaking land, an experience he had never counted on having in his lifetime. Translations, in other words, can be obscure in more ways than one.

I imagine that perfecting *Don Juan* in Vietnamese is somehow critical to this man's life. Literary activity is animated by urgency, and so it would not be wrong for us to envy him. But it would be absurd, for which of us would choose the devastation underlying that urgency; and in any case, urgency of this kind can hardly be manufactured and chosen as if it were a consumer good. So we are back to the challenge of lighting a spark from time to time within the altogether different exigencies (not inarduous) of academic routine. What directions might be explored—absolutely new ones being unavailable, to be sure, but ones that might be more regularly or boldly pursued? One is the systematic experimentation with the language of translation itself, experimentation whose yearning is radical whether its end product be novel or conservative. Another is rigorous trial of a theoretical paradigm such that both text and theory, and concomitant notions of West and non-West, are transformed—a necessary ideal at all times.[44] If we take theoretical paradigms beyond the textualism dominant in recent years, a broader vista opens up. Concern with gender and sexuality generates work such as that by Gregory M. Pflugfelder (1992) and recalls to our attention Rosette Willig's fine translation of *Torikaebaya*. (Let me register a historicizing plea, though, before this topic adds the force of its current prestige to the use of Japanese literature as raw material for the in-praise-of-destabilization industry: just as the site of difference is not ipso facto one of emancipation for its inhabitants, destabilization is in the first instance a conceptual issue for those of us who deploy it and not necessarily a carnivalesque or any other actuality for those who lived or are living it.) In Carole Cavanaugh's "Text and Textile" (1997), the yoking of reading practices informed by textualist theory to socio-historical knowledge demonstrates that texts exist *in* worlds at least as much as they *are* worlds. Cavanaugh presents a stunning vision of Heian texts that breathes social life into Ro-

---

[44] A *Genji* example again, but a superbly thoroughgoing one, is Amanda Mayer Stynchecum's work (1980, 1988).

man Jakobson's old metaphor-metonymy dichotomy, making it newly productive for literary analysis.[45]

It becomes necessary to acknowledge—as earlier I did not—the importance of works in translation as well as research aids in English to interdisciplinary scholarship. I am thinking of the *Princeton Companion to Classical Japanese Literature*, of course, but also of the histories produced over the past two decades by Donald Keene, Shūichi Katō, and Jin'ichi Konishi, which assuredly serve as pleasure reading as well.[46]

The variety of Heian-Kamakura-Muromachi and hard-to-date premodern texts now available in English could also gain new coherence were we willing to look in more sustained fashion at their relationship to one another as well as to their worlds: how are religious concerns, the politics and economics of eros, or gender and status definitions manifested in the different combinations of prose and verse? What does the interplay of prose narrative and verse look like in this context? Formalist concerns about narration? It is probably not surprising that these questions have been most often broached in the case of the *Genji*, but it may be surprising to see how succinctly this has been accomplished in the slim volume on teaching edited by Edward Kamens (1993). In these "approaches," research—including the contributors' own—quickens as it is sifted and reshaped for the purposes of pedagogy. Anthologies, those indispensable teaching tools, would also benefit from attention to these concerns. Might it not be worthwhile to experiment with constructing them more as arguments than as smorgasbords?[47] Being mindful of the classroom in our research and translation might give the latter both more force and coherence. The classroom is, after all, the world most readily available to us, the place where we live out our routine relation-

---

[45] Joshua S. Mostow (1992) gives signs of more work to look forward to. Indispensable to this scholarship is the kind of knowledge first offered in English by William H. McCullough (1967). There is further work now available in English such as that by Wakita Haruko (1984).

[46] See Bibliography (Section I, "Bibliographies/Guides/Survey Histories in English").

[47] Not that smorgasbords are without argument. The newest anthology is by Helen McCullough (1990). Sonja Arntzen in her review (1991) says that this cannot replace Keene's anthology of 1955 because of the latter's comprehensiveness but goes on to wonder only too sensibly if it isn't the from-beginning-to-end survey course of literature in translation that doesn't need rethinking. Also reviewed by Aileen Gatten (1991).

ship to literature. Kamens gives a lively reminder of the place of the classroom in locating our objects of study in relation to other texts, in the larger historical world, and in kindling the creative passion buried in the disciplinary mundane.

Now, I would like to take the theme of worldliness and literary study back to Japan for a look at a transformational period in the study of Heian prose that emerged from the Zenkyōtō movement of the late 1960s. In retrospect, the protest mobilized around the 1970 Security Treaty (Ampo) renewal was the last high point in the long, resistive closing of the postwar era itself, beginning with the 1960 anti-Security Treaty movement, continuing throughout the sixties and the early seventies in various forms of citizen and student activism, and indisputably complete with general political indifference by the early 1980s.[48] Prior to the eruption of eastern Europe in 1989, the student movements of the late sixties seemed to be the last contestation of the postwar settlement in many parts of the world. The late sixties and early seventies activism in Japan had its impact on national literature (*kokubungaku*) studies, too; here I sketch the formation and subsequent trajectory of a group called the Monogatari Kenkyūkai ("Monoken"), dedicated to the study of prose narrative, especially the central texts of the Heian Period. Monoken is an apt subject for case study in this context for several reasons: it was formed self-consciously at a particular historical moment; it has maintained a degree of reflexivity throughout its existence and most especially on the occasion of its twenty-fifth anniversary, just observed; from its inception it has engaged Euro-American theory, hardly the norm for a *kokubungaku* group; and lastly, it has gone from being a rebel to constituting the establishment. Monoken is now quite influential in the academy and has also had impact on American scholars of the post-Seidensticker *Genji* generation, myself included, to the present day.

A remarkable article written by one Monoken founder, poet and prominenent scholar Fujii Sadakazu, in 1969, several months after the "fall" of Yasuda Auditorium of the University of Tokyo to the riot police, gives a glimpse into the encounter between na-

---

[48] I acknowledge this is an idiosyncratic way of periodizing the postwar. Of course, the project of periodization is shaped by the periodizers' priorities. For the record, the Japanese government's priorities were such as to result in an economics white paper in 1956 declaring the end of the postwar ("*mohaya sengo de wa nai*").

tional literature studies and the student movement.[49] Titled "Barikēdo no naka no *Genji monogatari*" (*Genji monogatari* Behind the Barricades), it briefly describes the history of national literature studies as one of consistent linkage to state power (the term *kokubungaku* itself being connected to the founding of a department at the Imperial University in 1889), a linkage that was not broken even in the ascendancy of liberal-to-leftist scholarship in the wake of the postwar purges. In the subsequent routinization of national literature studies, the issues of responsibility for the war and the postwar settlement were made taboo, and an academic industry expanded, dominated by positivism and careerism, promoting the depoliticization of students (124). In the eyes of graduate student Fujii, the linkage to power fatally ruled out the possibility of scholarship as science (128). But it is not a clinical scientificity that Fujii advocates. In the closing passages, he affirms:

> [To reject *Genji* studies at the University of Tokyo] is at the same time to struggle to take back the work in order to free our imagination and sensibility....When the student of national literature achieves self-negation, a new human being will be born from within. Should we not be pushing ourselves to that place where we as fully human selves shall confront the work?
>
> . . . .
>
> Through the long period of struggle, the *Genji monogatari* has come to seem in my eyes closer to the primeval energy of the world of poetry than of prose. I cannot help thinking that the hellish home of poetry in the present age is not in the site of Japanese lyric as *waka* but in the passionate chaos that is the world of *monogatari* (134).

It cannot be accidental that Abe Yoshiomi cites this passage in the opening essay of the twenty-fifth anniversary issue of the Monoken *Kaihō* (Bulletin) (1996). Other founding documents[50] develop the themes of encounter between scholar and work as subjects, rather than reified researcher and objectified work, the importance of methodological self-consciousness in such an en-

---

[49] The issue of *Tenbō* in which Fujii's article appears has other valuable articles juxtaposing the thoughts of the sixties generation and of postwar progressive intellectuals. Subsequent references in text.

[50] For example, "*Genji monogatari* kenkyū no kanōsei" (The Potential of *Genji* Studies), a 1971 discussion with Fujii Sadakazu, Hasegawa Masaharu, Katō Shigefumi, and Mitani Kuniaki as participants (Fujii, et al., 1982); and Mitani Kuniaki (1977).

deavor, and a notion of the unconscious that draws both on Freud and the neonativism (*shinkokugaku*) of Orikuchi Shinobu and Yanagita Kunio, especially with respect to their focus on the unwritten. Historicism (including that of the Historico-sociological School) is held at arm's length for its positivist associations although in fact many Monoken scholars have been consistently attentive to the role of history.

There are numerous accounts, a few written, but mostly oral, of the reading material of the first generation "behind the barricades," in the independent study groups organized while the universities were closed. On the one hand, Lévi-Strauss, Barthes, Foucault, Derrida, the Russian Formalists, Engels on the origins of the state; on the other, Yanagita, Orikuchi, Yoshimoto Takaaki (Ryūmei). Monoken's annual themes (pursued in presentations at monthly meetings), set on the basis of group debate commonly took the form of "*monogatari* and x," with "x" consisting of such topics as *waka*, legends (*setsuwa*), time and space, narratology, intertextuality, metaphor, or sexual difference, with, however, the telling absence of ideology though it had been proposed more than once.[51] The concerted work on narration (*katari*) in the late 1970s was to be transmitted to modern Japanese literary studies in the 1980s.[52]

The political urgency of a particular historical moment that inspired the first generation is—necessarily—long gone. Some tendencies, such as a focus on narratology, survived long after the early years of the group. This is surely because of the group focus on the genre of premodern prose narrative, a choice in turn presumably explained by contrast with the privileged status of *waka* as seen in the compilation of imperial anthologies. Still, narratology and Zenkyōtō are not an obvious pair. It might be clarified by comparison with Frederic Jameson's description of a reverse phenomenon in France, namely, the "transformation of structuralist approaches into active ideologies in which ethical, political, and historical consequences are drawn from the hitherto more epistemological 'structuralist' positions."[53] Could it be that in Japan the "ethical, political, and historical" desires roused in the

---

[51] Abe Yoshiomi (1966), 4-5.
[52] See, for example, Komori Yōichi (1988a or 1988b).
[53] Frederic Jameson (1988), 187.

late sixties found in structuralist and poststructuralist methodologies a decisive instrument for breaking with the past? An underrecognized effect of formalist approaches is a decontextualization that frees the object of analysis for a new contextualization.

It is not yet clear what such contextualization(s?) might be.[54] The initial political urgency has been replaced by the drive for ever greater theoretical sophistication. Monoken members have not only been absorbed into the mainstream but have taken on leadership roles.[55] The first generation's search for a methodology useful in revealing the deep structure of premodern Japanese narratives seems to have produced a textualist orthodoxy that is no doubt more rigid in summary description than in practice. At the same time, it may be that the fixation on narratology concealed an unrecognized or embryonic and certainly ironic acquiescence on the part of the Zenkyōtō generation founders to the technologism of the age. Abe pregnantly observes in his anniversary article that Monoken more than once considered "ideology" for an annual theme but never adopted it. We are all familiar with the opportunistic use of theories—including those that are unmistakably worldly in their genesis, such as feminism—that presumes their availability to any end (the other side of the horror of essentialism) or exploits the commodity value of their novelty. Monoken seems to have resisted this tendency to a degree, and it would be worth understanding why this has been so and seeing the extent to which commitment to a particular body of texts has contributed to this. (This may be a challenge to a too easy dismissal of canons as well as a query about the differences between the researcher qua *kenkyūsha* versus the critic qua *hihyōka*. See, for example, the hesitation over joining the rush to cultural studies.)[56]

No question that the present is an expansive moment, with multiple new publications offering more points of contact than

---

[54] Mitamura Masako suggests that in contrast to the dominant Monoken work on Heian texts, medieval (*chūsei*) scholars have been more and more critically engaged with history (personal communication). See, for example, Hyōdō Hiromi (1985, 1995); Akasaka Norio, Hyōdō Hiromi, Yamamoto Hiroko, eds. (1994). Another young scholar, Tanaka Takako, works with women, Buddhism, folk religion, and literature. See, for instance, her *"Akujo" ron* (1992).

[55] See their prominence in, for example, Akiyama Ken, ed. (1993).

[56] Muroki Hideyuki, et al. (1996), 65-70.

ever with scholars working in English as ties are forged with art history, modern literature, and popular culture.[57] The new prominence of women as writers and editors is especially welcome.[58] Can this pace of fin-de-siècle production continue? The question returns us to the United States, for, as I have suggested above, the conditions of work and the corresponding stakes (including the pedagogical) are markedly different depending upon whether one is studying the canonical literature of one's own country or that of another.

Now, I must shift another set of gears and pay meager penance for having separated poetry and prose and for having paid insufficient attention to periodization, conventional or otherwise. The literary study of "medieval" Japan (*chūsei*)—spanning some portion of the eleventh through the fifteenth centuries depending on the activity in question—especially demands an interdisciplinary approach when it comes to its best-known genre, the *nō* theater. The *nō*, which may seem more tidily enclosed than many enterprises, is in fact most successfully studied as interactive poetry, music, and dance.

This has been far more actively acknowledged than in the days of Waley's volume (1921) or even the 1970 Keene anthology, both of which unquestionably played a part in attracting the attention to *nō* that has made the fine studies of today available. The translations included in Kenneth Yasuda's collection were completed long before the 1989 publication, showing him to have been one of the pioneers in insisting on the three-dimensional structure. Thomas Blenman Hare (1986) gives a detailed stylistic analysis combined with translation and a "documentary biography." Monica Bethe and Karen Brazell's series (1982) is accompanied by video cassettes. Janet Goff's intertextual study of *nō* and the *Genji* (1991a) is especially rewarding for its discussion of the craft of text com-

---

[57] A recent instance is the publication in Japan of papers gathered from the first Midwest Association for Japanese Literary Studies meeting in 1995: Sekine Eiji, ed. (1996).

[58] Chino Kaori, a pioneer in incorporating gender issues in Heian art history, appears in two promising new publications: the (annual) journal *Genji kenkyū* (*Genji* Studies), edited by Mitamura Masako, Kawazoe Fusae, and Matsui Kenji; and in Kojima Naoko (1996). Feminist modern literature scholar Yonaha Keiko and Hashimoto Osamu, author of the wildly popular *Yōhen Genji* (1991-92), a rewriting of *Genji* with an androgynous Genji as narrator, also appear in the inaugural issue of *Genji kenkyū*.

position. Mae J. Smethurst (1989) actually did what many talk about, namely, compare *nō* with Greek tragedy. The translations by Royall Tyler (1992a) are breathtaking, works to enjoy as well as to study, for so much of the effect of the *nō* text has been transmitted into English without becoming padded paraphrase or disappearing into supporting apparatus.[59]

Nine of Zeami's treatises, previously known only in snatches—such as the especially heady ones in *Sources of Japanese Tradition*[60]—became available in J. Thomas Rimer and Yamazaki Masakazu's translation in 1984, allowing readers to experience that intense combination that modernity has sorted out as philosophy, religion, and craft. This text had a wide-ranging predecessor in Ueda Makoto's compilation and translation (1967).[61] The very use of the word *theory* in this premodern context, where practitioners (not only in Japan) were also the theorists of their craft, has a defamiliarizing, salutary effect for us who exult or are trapped in abstract specialization. Going this route enriches the reading of such works as those by William R. LaFleur (1983) or David Pollack (1986). Susan Matisoff's work on Semimaru (1978) and Carolyn Anne Morley's on Kyōgen (1993) invoke a different register of medieval social and therefore cultural variety.[62] Barbara Ruch's work is an important contribution to a broader conception of medieval society and culture.[63]

With Michele Marra's two volumes (1991, 1993), we get explicit ideological analyses of medieval Japanese cultural production as part of a projected new literary history. Steven T. Brown (1996), referring to New Historicism's most fruitful home in Renaissance studies and particularly in the drama, demonstrates the application of New Historicist procedures to Hideyoshi's patronage of

---

[59] Tyler's reviews are also reliably pleasurable to read (for example, 1991, 1992b).

[60] Selections from "Seami" in "The Vocabulary of Japanese Aesthetics II," in Tsunoda, et al. (1958), 277-97.

[61] Also see Shūichi Katō (1981 [1971]).

[62] Walter Giesen's review of the former (1979) provides a prescient sketch for an expanded view of medieval studies.

[63] See Ruch's collection of essays in Japanese (1991), reviewed by the distinguished historian Wakita Haruko (1994). Some of the essays have appeared in English, beginning as early as 1977 and as recently as 1992. The latter is a promising example of interdisciplinary effort.

and participation in *nō* performances.[64] The mutual challenge of these works and those listed earlier that focus on aesthetic specificities lies in seeing how much each can take on of the material of the other in making its arguments.

To state the obvious, the terrain of Tokugawa period literary studies is different from that of medieval literary studies; it is, after all, the period many Japanese scholars refer to as *kinsei*, the proximate era. Is it now possible to translate this as "early modern" without endorsing the happy teleology of the postwar modernization theorists, and if so, what would it mean? I cannot answer this question, but there have been signs of new kinds of interest in the period. Paul Schalow observes in his review of the late Andrew Lawrence Markus's (1993) work that in contrast to translations and studies of haiku (*haikai*) and Kabuki and puppet theater, as well as translations of the fictions of Saikaku, studies of *gesaku*, or late Tokugawa narratives, have appeared at the rate of "on average—once a decade."[65] Other than a chapter in Donald Keene's (1976) survey, there had previously been work by Leon Zolbrod (1967) and Robert Leutner (1985). The problem with Tokugawa fiction generally for English-language scholars seems to be the same one felt by Meiji Japanese writers including Tsubouchi Shōyō: its crudeness and its frivolity. Even Saikaku, the acknowledged master, is subjected to unfavorable comparison with Murasaki Shikibu, "let alone Balzac."[66]

If the Cold War U.S. was not a promising place for the enthusiastic study of such fiction, history has brought us a more favorable moment. Credit must be given to the now well established critique of Orientalism in promoting non-Eurocentric evaluations of narrative form (augmented by an assortment of postmodernist desiderata); but perhaps even more pertinently, to feminism's insistence on gender, and increasingly, sexuality, as part of the academic agenda and especially, the new prominence of gay-lesbian scholarship; and finally, to the current humanistic interest in "visuality." There is now a fine history on Tokugawa "homosexuality" by Gary Leupp (1995). The book is mostly focused on men,

---

[64] MAJL's *Proceedings* offers a sampling of some of the most refreshing work being done in Japanese literary studies today.
[65] Paul Schalow (1994). Quotation from 524.
[66] Donald Keene (1976), 211.

but since it is careful to situate homosexuality in relationship to gender, it addresses women's social and sexual roles as well. Important new translations are by Paul Schalow (1990) and Stephen D. Miller (1996), the latter including selections of medieval and contemporary as well as Tokugawa literature.[67] Suggesting the great range of scholarship to be anticipated in the near future is Sumie Jones's (1996) proceedings for the conference on "Sexuality and Edo Culture, 1750-1850," held at Indiana University in Bloomington in August of 1995. This remarkable collection encompasses several generations and disciplines, Tokugawa and non-Tokugawa scholars from Japan as well as the U.S. (and one from Korea), and includes a generous number of illustrations, their variety augmented by the (apparent) recent lifting of the ban on the depiction of pubic hair—an unusual instance of state action, or rather, nonaction, having an unintended impact on scholarship.[68] The essays are alert to the importance of historical specificity, demonstrate a variety of methodologies, and receive succinct, probing commentary from their discussants. One of the obvious gains of a timely engagement with mainsteam discourse (if gay-lesbian studies may provisionally be called that) in a political and methodologically reflexive way is the initiation of dialogue with scholars outside the field. Thus, art historian Norman Bryson, having disagreed with Gary Leupp's use of demography, then concedes that insisting on how discourse "produce[s] social effects out of itself" makes it "difficult to establish why it is that certain forms of discourse come into being, and their relation to other social processes."[69] Schalow's (1990) translation of Saikaku, by the way, is thoughtfully reviewed by David M. Halperin (1991), author of the influential *One Hundred Years of Homosexuality And Other Essays on Greek Love* (1990).

Of course, it isn't possible to know where this great rush of interest in Tokugawa sexuality will lead. But we can hope that through its encounters with social, cultural, and intellectual his-

---

[67] This collection consists entirely of fiction and poetry except for one selection, the translation of the "Correspondence on Gay Lifestyles" between the distinguished naturalist Minamata Kumagusu (1867-1941) and the much younger essayist and bibliographer of Japanese male homosexuality, Iwata Jun'ichi (1900-1945), by William F. Sibley (134-71).
[68] Henry Smith, in Sumie Jones, ed. (1996), 33.
[69] Norman Bryson, in ibid., 120. Cf. Leupp's article in ibid., 105-9.

tory, with anthropology, with art history, with linguistics, it might contribute to a transformed analysis of literary production and in turn, of the social and economic dynamics themselves.[70] If the remarkable visualization of the erotic is investigated in dialogue with these various disciplines, it might just be possible to understand this historically determinate, exorbitant passion for the body without being trapped into the reification of The Body that occurred in recent memory in anthropology and other disciplines. Could we also hope that the quietly aestheticized parts of Edo literature that have long been familiar in English—say, the Bashō of *Oku no Hosomichi*[71] – will begin to look different? Perhaps there will even be a chance to take up the missed engagement with postwar Japanese Edo scholarship, in a more productive way than might have been possible earlier.[72]

Onward from the Sixties (III): Modern Literature and Questions of Modernity in Japan and Elsewhere

Four decades after the beginnings of the postwar study of Japanese literature in English, there is a sprawling corpus of translations, studies, and reviews. Of course, the change is not simply quantitative. On the one hand, there has been a palpable diminution of the condescending, bemused tone that so regularly crept into the writing of the earlier generation of "friends/experts" of Japan (*shinnichiha, chinichiha*). On the other, with the days of impressionistic New Criticism long gone, the American literary scholarship on Japan has acquired, often via English and comparative literary and anthropological studies, an array of tools and

---

[70] Texts to be brought into this discussion include Naoki Sakai (1991) and H. D. Harootunian (1995). Then there is the essay by the late Andrew L. Markus (1985), which, not being about sexual display, might be all the more useful in thinking about Tokugawa sexuality.

[71] Ueda Makoto translates the title as "The Narrow Road to the Far North" (1991).

[72] For example, the work of Hirosue Tamotsu, which almost never shows up in bibliographies. C. Andrew Gerstle exceptionally refers to him, noting that Hirosue's work on Chikamatsu may be the only one to have gone through several editions, but dismisses him for his "Aristotelian," i.e., Western views (1986), 84-88. In this context, I note that one of the titles of the prolific Hirosue, which I have not been able to read, is *Bashō to Saikaku* (1963). Certainly see his *Kanōsei to shite no Bashō* (1988) along with Mark Morris's "Buson and Shiki" (1984/1985).

topics, shaped in good measure by French poststructuralism, some Frankfurt School-style cultural Marxism, Bakhtinian narratology, a touch of British but more American-style cultural studies, several feminisms, and lately, colonial and postcolonial studies.

What are the consequences? They are naturally many and contradictory, but it may be helpful to refer to two framing works, both by Masao Miyoshi, the first published in 1974, the second in 1991.[73] When *Accomplices of Silence* came out, it instantly energized the field.[74] It gave the reader—this reader, at any rate—the exhilarating sense that here were writers whose works could be discussed like any others. Never mind that the analyses were pointing up those notorious lacks in Japanese character. They still make fine reading, and it is a good thing that this lively and learned book has been made available again from the Center for Japanese Studies at the University of Michigan. *Accomplices* argues that "the Japanese attitude toward personality is...negative," that characters are "types, and not living individuals" (xi), comprising, moreover, the "myth of a collectivized self" (xii), that the various "problems" of language and style culminate in the "typical Japanese dislike of the verbal" (xv). The more recent *Off Center*, which strictly refers to Japanese prose fictions as *shōsetsu*, says that "events occur without being conscripted into the unreal time of cosmogony," and that the *shōsetsu* "is the expression not of order and suppression, as the novel is, but of space, decentralization, and dispersal" (22). The *shōsetsu* "disperses and decentralizes art so that the reader as well as the author may become aware of the space outside the work" (23). Between the two works, there is a certain consistency in the description of the object; what has changed is the evaluation, from a troubled ambivalence to enthusiastic embrace. Where there had been silence and death, there is now a joyous, oral, Third World plenitude. What happened between 1974 and 1991? One thing that happened was poststructuralism, especially deconstruction, with its thematics of decentering, playful mobility of the signifier, and above all, the centrality of language, at once the site of self-reference and perpetual deferral. (The endorsement of orality is a bit of a glitch, though

---

[73] Subsequent references in text.
[74] See reviews by William Currie (1974), Edwin McClellan (1975), and Jay Rubin (1975).

the commodified "oralization" of transcribed and reconstructed interviews and discussions dubbed "conversationalism" is attacked in the last chapter, 225). *Off Center* manifests a convergence of these poststructuralist themes with the postmodernist critique of the Enlightenment with its allegedly singular identities and totalizing worldview, a critique much strengthened by the critique of Orientalism.

Such motifs and sympathies have been enormously influential. Okada's (1991) work referred to earlier, and volumes by James A. Fujii (1993) and Edward Fowler (1988) share many of the premises of *Off Center*, especially of its title essay, "Against the Native Grain" (9-36).[75] What are the stakes in the discourse represented by these works? The shared practice of using the term *shōsetsu* foregrounds the thematics of "difference." In trying to understand this particular valorization of "difference," I have often wondered why Bakhtin's capacious notion of the novel as opposed to epic (1982) hasn't been explored in these contexts. Might the concept of the "non-West," and therefore the underlying West/non-West binarism, be as much a limitation as an asset in these deliberations? What would happen if we were to adopt the view of Egyptian economist Samir Amin that "the modern world culture is not Western but capitalist"?[76] I put this tentatively because I am sobered by the warning of political scientist Ellen Meiksins Wood that to "conflat[e] 'modernity' with capitalism encourages us to throw out the baby with the bath water, or, more precisely, to keep the bath water and throw out the baby."[77] Nevertheless, there are several good reasons for questioning our reliance on the ahistorical pair West/non-West: it homogenizes each, it effaces other important categories such as North/South, and it obscures Japan's own early modern trajectory. This certainly is not to imply that we can forget the history of imperialism or the present of neocolonialist practices, in which Japan and other East and Southeast Asian countries are participants. Inasmuch as the features of a recently identified "native taxonomy" curiously overlap with those

---

[75] Fujii reviews by Irmela Hijiya-Kirschnereit (1994), Hosea Hirata (1993), Paul Anderer (1994) (combined with a review of David Pollack's 1992 work). Fowler reviews by Irmela Hijiya-Kirschnereit (1989), Mary Layoun (1989), Janet A. Walker (1989) (combined with a review of Kazuo Ozaki [1988]).

[76] Samir Amin (1994), 222.

[77] Ellen Meiksins Wood (1996): 27-28.

of poststructuralism, however, we need to probe the implications; for the motifs of decentered mobility, self-reference (the self being without content), open-ended dispersal—whether these are deployed within a deconstructive discourse, *écriture féminine,* Japanese narrativity, or a generic postmodernism, resemble nothing so much as the characteristics of capital itself. One synonym of open-endedness is uncertainty; to thrive on it is to be flexible, to be a creature consonant with the regime of capital. (Hence the youth of Hamlet underscored by Moretti.) Can there be anything *necessarily* emancipatory, let alone indigenous (non-Western), about that? Might this be one source of the contradictory assessments of Japan that appear throughout *Off Center?*[78]

Freeing analysis from the obligation to uncover the native and to find it decentered, mobile, playful, and good (i.e., counterhegemonic) frees us to make comparisons *across* modernities and to look at cultural forms as responses to problems that are at once *internal* to societies as well as externally *imposed* upon them. It remains to be said that in fact Fowler and Fujii go on to make just such observations. Fujii's chapter on Sōseki's *Kokoro* and the absence of Empire connect with the multidisciplinary work now being done in Japan on Japanese colonialism.[79] The apparent linguistic determinism of Fowler's argument surely requires complication at the very least ("Language and the Illusion of Presence"), but the book's overall argument about the centrality of *shishōsetsu* to *shōsetsu* is an enabling one. Certainly, the topics of *shishōsetsu,* Naturalism, and the self have never been far from the center of concern throughout the history of modern Japanese literature. Irmela Hijiya-Kirschnereit's (1996) reconstruction from her 1981 publication in German is also committed to a study of literature in its (native) context, "reconstructing the discourse, and reflecting the relevant research within its contextual limitations...."[80] By contrast, Suzuki Tomi posits the *shishōsetsu* as a phenomenon constructed retroactively by discourse.[81]

---

[78] What Dennis Washburn refers to as the "Boo/Hurrah paradigm" (1994); also see Charles Inouye (1992), Robert J. Smith (1992), and Ted Goossen (1993).

[79] Such as literary critic Kawamura Minato's (1994, 1995) work.

[80] Irmela Hijiya-Kirschnereit (1996), 325.

[81] Some other texts to be considered here would be Paul Anderer's translation of Kobayashi Hideo (1995); Janet A. Walker (1979); William F. Sibley (1968), as well as his review article of Arima Tatsuo (1971); and Marleigh Grayer Ryan (1965).

For discussions of discursive formation, one of the most influential volumes of all is by Karatani Kōjin (1994).[82] In arguing for the "discovery" of landscape or childhood or illness, and most especially, of interiority, Karatani posits them as key features of modernity. Is there a paradoxical ahistoricism at work here? Was not a kind of "interiority" being produced in the long monologues of the *Genji* or in aristocratic diaries or in the various arrangements of *waka* or in the introspection that accompanied Heian Buddhism's focus on salvation? The combinations of modern and premodern texts in J. Thomas Rimer's (1978) work become a pedagogical preparation for addressing such questions. A more recent contribution is from Dennis Washburn (1995).

In any case, the Karatani translations have been extremely productive, and we should encourage more such translation projects. We do need, of course, to be thoughtful in promoting the circulation of theory. A symptomatic text here is a discussion hosted by Karatani and Asada Akira as part of their series on modern Japanese criticism on the pages of *Hihyō kūkan* (Critical Space), a popular theory journal they coedit.[83] Their discussion with Hasumi Shigehiko and Miura Masashi on criticism produced during the period 1965-89 produces an interesting account of the incorporation of French theory into Japan, said by Asada to have been an entirely different affair from the mediated, superficial importation of Foucault, Derrida, et al., into the U.S. According to this account, Karatani is described as the equivalent of the French antihumanist poststructuralists emerging after 1968 (129). What is striking about this discussion, which is explicitly concerned with the transnational circulation of postmodernism, is how, occasional references to the oil crisis or the Tokyo Olympics notwithstanding, there is no reflection on how the theory relates to its contexts, which leaves the assertion about superficial American importation just that, an unsupported assertion. No doubt this happens in part because this is felt to be an in-group discussion, in which such

---

Mary Layoun (1990) suggests a way to think about the genre of the novel and modernity, about capitalism and imperialism, through comparison of Greek, Palestinian, and Japanese examples.

[82] Reviews by Charles Shirō Inouye (1993) and Stephen Snyder (1994).

[83] "Shōwa hihyō no shomondai" (Various Issues in Shōwa Criticism), in Karatani Kōjin, ed. (1991). See Asada Akira's timeline, especially prepared for this discussion, 122-23.

specification would be superfluous, not to say uncool. The sense of a self-sufficient world of (a species of) theory is confirmed by Karatani in a 1995 interview in which he suggests that criticism as the activity of introducing new works and evaluating them is over, and that it has been superseded by theory, which is more widely read than novels in both Japan and the U.S.[84] There is already in place a theory circuit that requires little or no contact not only with the world either as history or as sociopolitical present but even with the literary works that are, however nominally, its own occasions. A contextualized, comparative history of theory importation into the U.S. and Japan would not only be an interesting intellectual project but might serve as a modest antidote to this hermeticism.[85]

But surely the more direct antidote is focused study and translation, which themselves are of course not atheoretical. And there have been many fine contributions that have immeasurably deepened and widened our sense of Japanese literature. The late Robert Lyons Danly (1981) made available a selection from the writings of the only canonical modern woman writer, Higuchi Ichiyō. Ōe Kenzaburō's receipt of the Nobel Prize has been the greatest boost to translation in recent years, not only of his works, one hopes, but of a range of Japanese literature. (We must also let publishers know how important it is for titles to be kept in print; even the other Nobel laureate Kawabata's major works float in and out of print.) Alan Wolfe (1990) gives us a chance to further our thinking about a writer who has been quite generously translated, Dazai Osamu. Miriam Silverberg's 1990 work remains sui generis and therefore invites others to join that exploration of art and politics.[86] A contrasting approach to poetry and modernism,

---

[84] Karatani Kōjin (1995): 15. Karatani's apocalyptic leap at the end of the interview to global ecological disaster is unexplained.

[85] There is no handy *jiten* for this purpose. See John Treat's entries for Japan in Ralph Cohen, ed. (1988), 121-29. It is always sobering to recall that Saussure was translated by Kobayashi Hideo in 1928 and critiqued by the grammarian Tokieda Motoki (1941). The *Course in General Linguistics* becomes available in English only thirty years later.

There aren't many models for the sort of history I am suggesting, which are in principle just as susceptible to charges of "reductivism" as the contextualization of literary works themselves. Kristin Ross (1995) situates language-centered structuralism as a technicism of 1950s and 1960s France (190-91).

[86] Of a very different nature, but not to be forgotten, is G. T. Shea's work on left wing writers (1964).

as impassioned in its way, is explored by Hosea Hirata (1993). Then there is John Whittier Treat's informative and polemical work on "atomic bomb literature" (1995a).[87] Ernestine Schlant and J. Thomas Rimer's recent work comparing Germany and Japan (1991) makes one wonder why such a project hadn't been undertaken earlier and hope that more such efforts will be made. A feminist interest in the aftermath of war and in the context-sensitivity of theory motivates Sharalyn Orbaugh's forthcoming study. Feminists have been extremely active, both here and in Japan. Paul Schalow and Janet Walker's new anthology (1996) was preceded by such pioneering translations as those by Yukiko Tanaka and Elizabeth Hanson (1982); Noriko Mizuta Lippit and Kyoko Iriye Selden (1991); and Yukiko Tanaka (1987).[88] Livia Monnet (1996) criticizes the ongoing canonization of Nakagami Kenji.[89] I have tried (1994) to introduce the topic of literature produced by Zainichi (Resident Korean) women writers.[90]

Quite recent fiction has been introduced in such collections as those by Alfred Birnbaum (1991) or Helen Mitsios (1990). Susan J. Napier (1996) situates very recent writings in a history going back to the late nineteenth century.[91] The works of Murakami Haruki or Yoshimoto Banana are reviewed in the trade press, but they are also discussed by scholars in collections devoted not to literature but to cultural studies. See, for example, essays by Stephen

---

[87] For collections of translations of atomic-bomb literature, see Richard H. Minear, trans. and ed. (1990); Kenzaburō Ōe, ed. (1985); and Kyoko and Mark Selden, eds. (1989).

[88] There is an enormous volume of feminist scholarship in Japan now. Two samples: Ueno Chizuko, Ogura Chikako, and Tomioka Taeko (1992) turn the tables on the conventional male discussion of "female literature" (*joryū bungaku*); Yamamoto Chie (1992) gives a succinct history of postwar women's writings that shows new facets even of familiar figures.

[89] Livia Monnet (1996). For an opposing view, see Nina Cornyetz (1995).

[90] See also Norma Field (1996). Perhaps "minority literature" will become a category in U.S. Japanese literary studies. There is Steve Rabson's fine translation of two Okinawan novellas (1989); Rabson and Michael Molasky are preparing a collection of fiction by Okinawan writers in translation.

It is interesting to note that even though Edward Said's *Orientalism* (1978) was translated into Japanese in 1986, it had little impact until the recent prominence of Zainichi intellectuals in conjunction with the sudden popularity of cultural studies. See Kang Sang-jung (1996). *Orientalism*'s importance to Japanese and East Asian Studies is explicitly marked by a symposium in the *Journal of Asian Studies* (Kapp, 1980).

[91] Also see her earlier study (1995).

Snyder (1996) or Aoki Tamotsu (1996). John Treat has published two extended discussions of Yoshimoto Banana, one in a collection on Japanese women and consumption, the other in a collection on popular culture that he edited, with an introduction titled, significantly enough, "Japanese Studies into Cultural Studies."[92]

The Future Today

In that introductory essay, Treat refers to a "crisis" in literary studies that is not confined to Japanese literary studies but nonetheless has specific bearing on the "nexus of Japanese studies with cultural studies":

> The crisis in literary studies precipitated by the shift in our literacy away from the printed word and towards other varieties of signifiers, and to a lesser extent the crises brought on by contending methods in history, sociology and anthropology, parallel the disruption of multidisciplinary area studies in the wake of both a post-Cold War world and one where the naturalness of even a place name ('Japan') is questioned by the ascendancy of theories of discourse and difference (8-10).

Treat closes the Introduction with the hope for

> more work by those of us trained in a traditional discipline [modern Japanese literature in his case] but who are now interested in the potential of a multidisciplinary, transnational cultural studies that might better capture our experience of how the world, including Japan, has changed (13).

The modern Chinese literature and film scholar Rey Chow has written an essay (1993) in which she approaches the same issue from a somewhat different angle.[93] (Chow uses the homogenizing category of "Asian" literatures self-consciously and critically.) The section is titled "The Question of Literature in 'Cultural Studies'":

> If the rationale for cultural studies programs across the U.S. begins with the apprehension of the insufficiencies of models of learning

---

[92] The first essay is "Yoshimoto Banana's *Kitchen*" (1995b). The second is "Yoshimoto Banana Writes Home," in John W. Treat (1996). Subsequent references to the Introduction of this volume in text. For a feminist discussion of Yoshimoto, see Shinsawa Hiroko (1991).

[93] Subsequent references in text.

> "culture" that are based on the nation-state... the question remains as to what is to be done after the traditional boundaries of knowledge-production have been overthrown.

. . . .

> Because modern Asia is not "literary" any more, the close and patient attention that classicists devote to literary texts simply evaporates. Instead, works of modern literature become mere research documents for the historian or political scientists (131).

Chow is neither affirming "traditional" methods applied to "classical" texts (a form of Orientalism within the American academy), nor asserting that there is something wrong per se with the use of literature as social document. What is problematic, she argues, is the character of our age, in which knowledge is all too readily processed and reproduced as information. Literature's common marginalization within cultural studies is disturbing because

> not only does literature's potential in subverting the increasing trend toward *informationalization* remain unrealized, but literature itself becomes an instrument in that process of informationalization and a subordinate part to the world historical record.
>
> The informationalization of literature produces the illusion that there is no real need to pay attention to literature and to the work it performs upon its readers (132; emphasis in the original).

If there is a general crisis in literary studies, it has specific implications for the study of a marginal literature. If Japanese literature (among others) has had one kind of constrained yet varied existence within area studies, its release into cultural studies may be so transformational as to signify its evaporation as object of study.

Are we ready to say, so be it? Both Treat's and Chow's analyses, albeit with different accents, direct us to think again about the features of literature, about the stakes of literary study in the academy, and specifically, the stakes for the study of Japanese literature. Is there some distinctive way in which literature works upon its readers? Are there in addition special ways in which a marginal literature affects its readers because of the historical circumstances in which it does its work? Are these important enough for us to fight to preserve and pursue? On what grounds?

In order to answer such questions, we will have to return to the question of language: language as in language teaching and translation, but also as in the language of film, in order to sharpen our understanding of verbal art by comparison with visual art. It only makes good intellectual and pedagogical sense for us to become film literate. We will need to do this thinking with our eyes resolutely open to institutional context, to budget cuts, to demands for ever- accelerated professionalization, to the claims of "globalization" that may paradoxically produce a new parochialism as English's lingua franca status is reinforced. We will need to explore regional ties with different aims from earlier geopolitical or current economic appetites for domination, on the one hand, and consider how we relate to the vitality of Asian America, on the other.

We have been sensitized by the critique of Orientalism, but we need to remember the power of the new and the different that cannot be reduced to a hierarchical exoticism. Literature is also a distinctive place for discovering oneself as stranger, and we must never become too knowing to recognize and transmit that possibility.

Bibliography

The Bibliography is divided into the following sections. Since many entries fall into more than one category, a degree of arbitrariness in the interest of economy has been unavoidable. Premodern translations appear under their translators; modern, their authors.

I. Bibliographies/Guides/Survey Histories in English
II. Premodern Literature – Studies/Translations of Poetry
III. Premodern Literature – Studies/Translations of Prose and General Studies
IV. Premodern Literature—*Genji*
V. Modern Literature – General Works and Collections
VI. Modern Literature – Studies/Translations of Single Authors
VII. Women and Modern Literature
VIII. Poetry – Modern
IX. Theater – Traditional
X. Theater – Modern
XI. Film
XII. Popular/Mass Culture
XIII. Translated Works by Japanese Critics
XIV. Other Cited Works
XV. Resources on the World Wide Web

I. Bibliographies/Guides/Survey Histories in English

Buehrer, Beverley Bare. 1990. *Japanese Films: A Filmography and Commentary, 1921-1989*. Jefferson, N.C.: McFarland.

Dower, John W., with Timothy S. George. 1995. *Japanese History and Culture from Ancient to Modern Times: Seven Basic Bibliographies.* 2nd rev. ed. Princeton: Markus Weiner.
Erickson, Joan, and Midori Y. McKeon, comps. 1997. "Selected Bibliography of Japanese Women's Writing." In *The Woman's Hand: Gender and Theory in Japanese Women's Writing,* edited by Paul Gordon Schalow and Janet Walker. Stanford: Stanford University Press.
Fujino, Yukio, ed. 1979. *Modern Japanese Literature in Translation: A Bibliography.* New York: Kodansha America.
Fukuda, Naomi, ed. 1986. *Japanese History: A Guide to Survey Histories, Part II, Literature.* Ann Arbor: Center for Japanese Studies, University of Michigan.
Galbraith, Stuart. 1996. *The Japanese Filmography: A Complete Reference to 209 Filmmakers and the Over 1250 Films Released in the United States, 1900 through 1994.* Jefferson, N.C.: McFarland.
Gessel, Van C. 1997. *Japanese Fiction Writers, 1868-1945.* Detroit: Gale Research.
Huber, Kristina Ruth. 1992. *Women in Japanese Society: An Annotated Bibliography of Selected English Language Materials.* Chapters on Women Writers and Women's Spoken Language by Kathryn Sparling. Westport, Conn.: Greenwood.
Japan P.E.N. Club, ed. 1990. *Japanese Literature in Foreign Languages, 1945-1990.* Tokyo: Japan Book Publishers Association.
Kato Shuichi. 1979a. *A History of Japanese Literature: The First Thousand Years.* Translated by David Chibbett. Kodansha.
———. 1979b. *A History of Japanese Literature: The Years of Isolation.* Translated by Don Sanderson. Kodansha.
———. 1981. *A History of Japanese Literature: The Modern Years.* Kodansha.
Keene, Donald. c1976. *World within Walls: Japanese Literature of the Pre-modern Era, 1600-1867.* New York: Holt, Rinehart, and Winston.
———. 1984. *Dawn to the West: Japanese Literature of the Modern Era.* 2 vols. New York: Holt, Rinehart, and Winston.
———. 1995. *Seeds in the Heart: Japanese Literature from Earliest Times to the Late Sixteenth Century.* New York: Henry Holt.
Kokusai Bunka Kaikan. 1979. *Modern Japanese Literature in Translation: A Bibliography.* New York: Kodansha International and Harper and Row.
Konishi Jin'ichi. 1984. *The Ancient and Archaic Ages.* Vol. 1 of *A History of Japanese Literature.* Edited by Earl Miner. Translated by Aileen Gatten and Nicholas Teele. Princeton: Princeton University Press.
———. 1986. *The Early Middle Ages.* Vol. 2 of *A History of Japanese Literature.* Edited by Earl Miner. Translated by Aileen Gatten. Princeton: Princeton University Press.
———. 1991. *The High Middle Ages.* Vol. 3 of *A History of Japanese Literature.* Translated by Aileen Gatten and Mark Harbison. Princeton: Princeton University Press.
Lewell, John. 1993. *Modern Japanese Novelists: A Biographical Dictionary.* New York: Kodansha International.
Makino, Yasuko, and Mihoko Miki. 1996. *Japan and the Japanese: A Bibliographic Guide to Reference Sources.* Westport, Conn.: Greenwood.
Makino, Yasuko, and Masaei Saito, eds. 1994. *A Student Guide to Japanese Sources in the Humanities.* Ann Arbor: Center for Japanese Studies, University of Michigan.
Mamola, Claire Zebroski. 1992 [1989]. *Japanese Women Writers in English Translation: An Annotated Bibliography.* 2 vols. New York: Garland.

Marks, Alfred H., and Barry D. Bort. 1975. *Guide to Japanese Prose.* Boston: G. K. Hall.
Miller, Barbara Stoler. 1994. *Masterworks of Asian Literature in Comparative Perspective: A Guide for Teaching.* Armonk, N.Y.: M. E. Sharpe.
Miner, Earl, Hiroko Odagiri, and Robert E. Morrell. 1985. *The Princeton Companion of Classical Japanese Literature.* Princeton: Princeton University Press.
Mulhern, Chieko I., ed. 1994. *Japanese Women Writers: A Bio-critical Sourcebook.* Westport, Conn.: Greenwood.
Putzar, Edward. 1973. *Japanese Literature: A Historical Outline.* Adapted and translated from Hisamatsu Sen'ichi, ed., *Nihon bungakushi.* Tucson: University of Arizona Press.
Rimer, J. Thomas. 1988. *A Reader's Guide to Japanese Literature: From the Eighth Century to the Present.* Tokyo: Kodansha International.
Schilling, Mark. 1997. *The Encyclopedia of Japanese Pop Culture.* New York: Weatherhill.

II. Premodern Literature—Studies/Translations of Poetry

Brazell, Karen, and Lewis Cook. 1975. "The Art of Renga." *Journal of Japanese Studies* 2: 29-61.
Brower, Robert H., trans. 1992. *Conversations with Shōtetsu (Shōtetsu monogatari).* Ann Arbor: Center for Japanese Studies, University of Michigan.
Brower, Robert H., and Earl Miner. 1961. *Japanese Court Poetry.* Stanford: Stanford University Press.
Carter, Steven D. 1983. *Three Poets at Yuyama.* Berkeley: Institute of East Asian Studies, University of California.
———. 1987. *The Road to Komatsubara: A Classical Reading of the "Renga Hyakuin".* Cambridge: Council on East Asian Studies, Harvard University.
———. 1993. *Literary Patronage in Late Medieval Japan.* Ann Arbor: Center for Japanese Studies, University of Michigan.
Carter, Steven D., trans. 1991. *Traditional Japanese Poetry: An Anthology.* Stanford: Stanford University Press.
———. 1994. *Waiting for the Wind: Thirty-six Poets of Japan's Late Medieval Age.* New York: Columbia University Press.
Cranston, Edwin A. 1983. "The Ramifying Vein: An Impression of Leaves." *Journal of Japanese Studies* 9, no. 1: 97-138.
———. 1988. "A Web in the Air." *Monumenta Nipponica* 43, no. 3: 305-52.
Cranston, Edwin A., trans. 1993. *The Gem-Glistening Cup.* Vol. 1 of *A Waka Anthology.* Stanford: Stanford University Press.
Crihfield, Liza. 1979. *Ko-uta: "Little Songs" of the Geisha World.* Rutland, Vt.: Charles E. Tuttle.
Doe, Paula. 1982. *A Warbler's Song in the Dusk: The Life and Work of Ōtomo Yakamochi (718-784).* Berkeley: University of California Press.
———. 1987. Review of Levy (1984). *Journal of Japanese Studies* 13, no. 1: 162-65.
Ebersole, Gary L. 1992. *Ritual Poetry and the Politics of Death in Early Japan.* Princeton: Princeton University Press.
Halperin, David M. 1991. Review of Schalow (1990). *Journal of Japanese Studies* 17, no. 2: 398-403.
Hirosue Tamotsu. 1963. *Bashō to Saikaku.* Miraisha.
———. 1988. *Kanōsei to shite no Bashō* (Bashō as Potentiality). Agora Sōsho.
Horton, H. Mack. 1993. "Renga Unbound: Performative Aspects of Japanese Linked Verse." *Harvard Journal of Asiatic Studies* 53, no. 2: 443-512.

Huey, Robert N. 1989. *Kyōgoku Tamekane: Poetry and Politics in Late Kamakura Japan*. Stanford: Stanford University Press.

Isaku, Patia R. 1981. *Mountain Storm, Pine Breeze: Folk Song in Japan*. Tucson: University of Arizona Press.

Kamens, Edward. 1990. *The Buddhist Poetry of the Great Kamo Priestess Daisaiin Senshi and "Hosshin Wakashū"*. Ann Arbor: Center for Japanese Studies, University of Michigan.

Keene, Donald. 1961. Review of Bowers and Miner (1961). *Harvard Journal of Asiatic Studies* 24: 274-81.

Konishi Jin'ichi. 1958. Translated and adapted by Robert H. Brower and Earl Miner. In "Association and Progression: Principles of Integration in Anthologies and Sequences of Japanese Court Poetry, A.D. 900-1350." *Harvard Journal of Asiatic Studies* 21: 67-127.

———. 1971. *Sōgi*. Chikuma shobō.

Kwon, Yung-Hee K. 1994. *Songs to Make the Dust Dance: The "Ryōjin Hishō" of Twelfth-century Japan*. Berkeley: University of California Press.

LaFleur, Willliam R. Summer 1982. Review of Miner (1979). *Journal of Japanese Studies* 8, no. 2: 384-88.

———. 1983. *The Karma of Words: Buddhism and the Literary Arts in Medieval Japan*. Berkeley: University of California Press.

LaMarre, Thomas. 1994. "Writing Doubled Over, Broken: Provisional Names, Acrostic Poems, and the Perpetual Contest of Doubles in Heian Japan." *positions: east asia cultures critique* 2, no. 2: 250-73.

Lee, Peter H. 1979. *Celebration of Continuity: Themes in Classic East Asian Poetry*. Cambridge: Harvard University Press.

Levy, Ian Hideo. 1981. *The Ten Thousand Leaves: A Translation of the "Man'yōshū," Japan's Premier Anthology of Classical Poetry*. Vol. 1. Princeton: Princeton University Press.

———. 1984. *Hitomaro and the Birth of Japanese Lyricism*. Princeton: Princeton University Press.

McCullough, Helen Craig. 1985a. *Brocade by Night: "Kokin Wakashū" and the Court Style in Japanese Classical Poetry*. Stanford: Stanford University Press.

McCullough, Helen Craig, trans. 1985b. *"Kokin Wakashū": The First Imperial Anthology of Japanese Poetry, with "Tosa Nikki" and "Shinsen Waka"*. Stanford: Stanford University Press.

Miller, Roy Andrew. 1981. "Time, Space, and Texts." Review of Shirakawa Shizuka's *Shiki Man'yōron* (Early *Man'yōshū* Studies) (1979), and Nagafuji Yasushi's *Kodai Nihon bungaku to jikan ishiki* (Ancient Japanese Literature and Time Consciousness) (1979). *Journal of Japanese Studies* 7, no. 1: 202-14.

———. 1987. "No Time for Literature." Review of Helen McCollough (1985a, 1985b). *Journal of the American Oriental Society* 107, no. 4: 745-60.

Mills, D. E. 1961-62. Review of Brower and Miner (1961). *Journal of Asian Studies* 21: 557-58.

Miner, Earl. 1968. *An Introduction to Japanese Court Poetry*. With translations by the author and Robert H. Brower. Stanford: Stanford University Press.

———. 1979. *Japanese Linked Poetry: An Account with Translations and Haikai Sequences*. Princeton: Princeton University Press.

———. 1990. "*Waka*: Features of its Constitution and Development." *Harvard Journal of Asiatiac Studies* 50, no. 2: 669-706.

Miner, Earl, and Hiroko Odagiri, trans. 1981. *The Monkey's Straw Raincoat and Other Poetry of the Bashō School*. Princeton: Princeton University Press.

Mori, Masaki. 1997. *Epic Grandeur: Toward a Comparative Poetics of the Epic*. Albany: State University of New York Press.
Morris, Mark. 1984/1985. "Buson and Shiki." *Harvard Journal of Asiatic Studies* 44, no. 1: 381-425; and 45, no. 1: 255-321.
———. 1986b. Review of Levy (1984). *Harvard Journal of Asiatic Studies* 46, no. 2: 638-53.
———. 1986c. "Waka and Form, Waka and History." *Harvard Journal of Asiatic Studies* 46, no. 2: 551-610.
———. 1993. Review of Carter (1991). *Monumenta Nipponica* 48, no. 1: 116-19.
Mostow, Joshua S. 1996. *Pictures of the Heart: the "Hyakunin Isshu" in Word and Image*. Honolulu: University of Hawai'i Press.
Okada, Richard H. 1988. "Translation and Difference – A Review Article." Review of Helen McCullough (1985a, 1985b). *Journal of Asian Studies* 47, no. 1: 29-40.
Ooka Makoto. 1991. *The Colors of Poetry: Essays in Classic Japanese Verse*. Translated by Takako U. Lento and Thomas V. Lento. Rochester, Mich.: Katydid.
Pekarik, Andrew J. 1983. *The Thirty-six Immortal Women Poets*. New York: George Braziller.
Ramirez-Christensen, Esperanza. December 1981. "The Essential Parameters of Linked Poetry." *Harvard Journal of Asiatic Studies* 41, no. 2: 555-95.
———. 1987. Review of Levy (1984). *Journal of Asian Studies* 46, no. 3: 664-67.
———. 1994. *Heart's Flower: The Life and Poetry of Shinkei*. Stanford: Stanford University Press.
Raud, Rein. 1994. *The Role of Poetry in Classical Japanese Literature: A Code and Discursivity Analysis*. Tallinn: Eesti Humanitaarinstituut.
Rodd, Laurel, and Mary Henkenius, trans. 1984. *"Kokinshū": A Collection of Poems Ancient and Modern*. Princeton: Princeton University Press.
Rohlich, Thomas H. 1988. Review of Helen McCullough (1985a, 1985b). *Journal of Japanese Studies* 14, no. 1: 125-31.
Rutledge, Eric. 1983. "The *Man'yōshū* in English." *Harvard Journal of Asiatic Studies* 43, no. 1: 263-90.
Saigō Nobutsuna. 1964. *Shi no hassei: bungaku ni okeru genshi, kodai no imi* (The Emergence of Poetry: The Significance of the Primitive and the Ancient Eras in Literature). Rev. ed. Miraisha.
Sato, Hiroaki. 1983. *One Hundred Frogs: From Renga to Haiku to English*. New York: Weatherhill.
Sato, Hiroaki, and Burton Watson, trans. 1981. *From the Country of Eight Islands: An Anthology of Japanese Poetry*. Seattle: University of Washington Press.
Smits, Ivo. 1995. *The Pursuit of Loneliness: Chinese and Japanese Nature Poetry in Medieval Japan, ca. 1050-1150*. Stuttgart: F. Steiner.
Suzuki Hideo. 1990. "Waka no hyōgen ni okeru shimbutsu taiō kōzō" (The Structure of Psychological-Material Equivalence in the Language of Waka). In his *Kodai wakashiron* (Studies in the History of Early Waka). Tokyo Daigaku Shuppankai.
Ueda, Makoto. 1965. *Zeami, Bashō, Yeats, Pound: A Study in Japanese and English Poetics*. The Hague: Mouton.
———. 1970. *Matsuo Bashō*. New York: Twayne.
———. 1979. Review of Earl Miner (1979). *Journal of Asian Studies* 39, no. 1: 353-55.
———. 1991. *Bashō and His Interpreters: Selected Hokku with Commentary*. Stanford: Stanford University Press.

Verity, Kenneth. 1996. *Awareness beyond Mind: Verses in Haiku and Senryū Style.* Shaftesbury, Dorset: Element.
Walker, Janet A. 1977. "Poetic Ideal and Fictional Reality in the *Izumi shikibu nikki.*" *Harvard Journal of Asiatic Studies* 37, no. 1: 135-82.
Yasuda, Kenneth. 1957. *Japanese Haiku: Its Essential Nature, History and Possibilities in English with Selected Examples.* Rutland, Vt.: Charles E. Tuttle.

III. Premodern Literature—Studies/Translations of Prose and General Studies

Abe Yoshiomi. August, 1966. "Monoken 25 nen" (Twenty-five Years of Monoken). *Monogatari Kenkyūkai kaihō: Monogatari Kenkyūkai sōsetsu 25 shūnen kinen* (Bulletin of the Monogatari Kenkyūkai: 25th Anniversary of the Founding of the Monogatari Kenkyūkai), no. 27: 4-5.
Akasaka Norio, Hyōdō Hiromi, Yamamoto Hiroko, eds. 1994. *Monogatari sabetsu tennōsei* (Tales, Discrimination, and the Emperor System). Satsukisha.
Akiyama Ken, ed. 1993. *"Genji monogatari" jiten* (A *Tale of Genji* Dictionary). *Bessatsu Kokubungaku*, no. 36 (Special Issue, *Kokubungaku*). Gakutōsha.
Arntzen, Sonja. 1991. Review of Helen McCullough (1990). *Journal of Asian Studies* 50, no. 3: 694-95.
Backus, Robert L., trans. 1985. *The "Riverside Counselor's Stories": Vernacular Fiction of Late Heian Japan (Tsutsumi Chūnagon monogatari).* Stanford: Stanford University Press.
Bowring, Richard J. 1992. "The *Ise monogatari*: A Short Cultural History." *Harvard Journal of Asiatic Studies* 52, no. 2: 401-80.
Bowring, Richard J., trans. 1982. *Murasaki Shikibu, Her Diary and Poetic Memoirs: A Translation and Study.* Princeton: Princeton University Press.
Brazell, Karen, trans. 1973. *Confessions of Lady Nijō.* Garden City, N.Y.: Anchor.
Brewster, Jennifer, trans. 1977. *The Emperor Horikawa Diary (Sanuki no Suke nikki).* Honolulu: University of Hawai'i Press.
Bryson, Norman. 1996. "Response to: 'Configurations of Gender.'" In Jones, ed. (1996).
Chance, Linda H. 1997. *Formless in Form: Kenkō, Tsurezuregusa and the Rhetoric of Japanese Fragmentary Prose.* Stanford: Stanford University Press.
Childs, Margaret Helen, trans. 1991. *Rethinking Sorrow: Revelatory Tales of Late Medieval Japan (Genmu monogatari, Sannin hōshi, Shichinin bikuni).* Ann Arbor: Center for Japanese Studies, University of Michigan.
Cogan, Thomas J., trans. 1987. *The Tale of the Soga Brothers.* University of Tokyo Press.
Cranston, Edwin A., trans. 1969. *The Izumi Shikibu Diary: A Romance of the Heian Court.* Cambridge: Harvard University Press.
de Bary, Theodore, trans. 1956. *Five Women Who Loved Love* (Ihara Saikaku's *Kōshoku gonin onna*). Rutland, Vt.: Charles E. Tuttle.
Gatten, Aileen. 1991. Review of Helen C. McCullough (1990). *Monumenta Nipponica* 46, no. 3: 369-72.
Giesen, Walter. 1979. Review of Matisoff (1978). *Journal of Japanese Studies* 5, no. 2.
Hare, Thomas, ed. 1996. *The Distant Isle: Studies and Translations of Japanese Literature in Honor of Robert H. Brower.* Ann Arbor: Center for Japanese Studies, University of Michigan.
Harris, Jay, trans. 1972. *The Tales of Ise.* Tokyo: Charles E. Tuttle.
Hibbett, Howard. 1959. *The Floating World in Japanese Fiction.* New York: Grove Press.

Hirosue Tamotsu. 1987. "Jiritsuteki janrushikan ni tsuite" (On the Theory of Autonomous Genre History). In *Nihon bungaku kōza 1: Hōhō to shiten* (Readings in Japanese Literature, 1: Method and Point-of-View), edited by Nihon Bungaku Kyōkai, 166-79. Taishūkan.
Hochstedler, Carol, trans. 1979. *The Tale of Nezame: Part Three of "Yowa no nezame monogatari"*. Ithaca: China-Japan Program, Cornell University.
Hyōdō Hiromi. 1985. *Katarimono josetsu: "Heike" gatari no hassei to hyōgen* (Introduction to Oral Narratives: The Origins and Expressions of "Heike" Recitation). Yūseidō.
———. 1995. *"Taiheiki" "yomi" no kanōsei* (*Taiheiki*: The Possibilities for "Reading"). Kodansha.
Ino Kenji. 1987. "Nihon bungaku kenkyū ni okeru 'rekishi' to 'shutai': toku ni 'rekishi-shakaigakuha' no nagare ni sotte" ("History" and "the Subject" in Japanese Literary Studies, Especially Along the Lines of the "Historico-sociological School"). In *Nihon bungaku kōza 1: hōhō to shiten* (Readings in Japanese Literature, 1: Method and Point-of-View), edited by Nihon Bungaku Kyōkai. Taishūkan.
Jones, Sumie, et al. 1985. *Principles of Classical Japanese Literature*. Edited by Earl Miner. Princeton: Princeton University Press.
Jones, Sumie, ed. 1996. *Imaging Reading Eros: Proceedings for the Conference, Sexuality and Edo Culture, 1750-1850*. Held at Indiana University in August of 1995. Bloomington: East Asian Studies Center, Indiana University.
Kamens, Edward, trans. 1988. *The Three Jewels: A Study and Translation of Minamoto Tamenori's "Sanbōe"*. Ann Arbor: Center for Japanese Studies, University of Michigan.
Kato Shuichi. 1981 (1971). *Form Style Tradition: Reflections on Japanese Art and Society*. New York: Kodansha International.
Kawai, Hayao. 1996. *The Japanese Psyche: Major Motifs in the Fairy Tales of Japan*. 2nd ed. Woodstock, N.Y.: Spring Publications.
Keene, Donald. 1955a. *Japanese Literature: An Introduction for Western Readers*. New York: Grove Press.
Keene, Donald, ed. 1955b. *Anthology of Japanese Literature: From the Earliest Era to the Mid-Nineteenth Century*. New York: Grove Press.
Keene, Donald, trans. 1967. *Essays in Idleness: The "Tsurezuregusa" of Kenkō*. New York: Columbia University Press.
Kelsey, W. Michael. 1982. *Konjaku monogatari-shū*. Boston: Twayne.
Kitagawa, Hiroshi, and Bruce T. Tsuchida, trans. 1975. *The Tale of the Heike*. Tokyo: University of Tokyo Press.
Kobayashi Hiroko. 1979. *The Human Comedy of Heian Japan: A Study of the Secular Stories in the Twelfth-century Collection of Tales, "Konjaku monogatarishū"*. Tokyo: Centre for East Asian Cultural Studies.
Kojima Naoko, ed. 1996. *Ōchō monogatari no sei to shintai: Itsudatsu suru monogatari* (Sex and the Body in Monarchic [Age] Monogatari: Monogatari as Deviance). Shinwasha.
Lammers, Wayne P., trans. 1992. *The Tale of Matsura: Fujiwara Teika's Experiment in Fiction*. Ann Arbor: Center for Japanese Studies, University of Michigan.
Lane, Richard. 1955. "Postwar Japanese Studies of the Novelist Saikaku." *Harvard Journal of Asiatic Studies* 18: 181-99.
———. 1957. "The Beginnings of the Modern Japanese Novel: *Kana-Zōshi*, 1600-1682." *Harvard Journal of Asiatic Studies* 20: 644-701.
Leutner, Robert. 1985. *Shikitei Samba and the Comic Tradition in Edo Fiction*. Cambridge: Council on East Asian Studies, Harvard University.

Markus, Andrew Lawrence. 1985. "The Carnival of Edo: *Misemono* Spectacles from Contemporary Accounts." *Harvard Journal of Asiatic Studies* 45, no. 2: 499-541.
——. 1992. *The Willow in Autumn: Ryūtei Tanehiko, 1783-1842*. Cambridge: Council on East Asian Studies, Harvard University.
Marra, Michele. 1991. *The Aesthetics of Discontent: Politics and Reclusion in Medieval Japanese Literature*. Honolulu: University of Hawai'i Press.
——. 1993. *Representations of Power: The Literary Politics of Medieval Japan*. Honolulu: University of Hawai'i Press.
Marra, Michele, trans. 1984. "Mumyōzōshi." *Monumenta Nipponica* 39, no. 3: 409-34.
Masuda Katsumi. 1977 [1961]. "Rekishi-shakaigakuteki kenkyū" (Historico-sociological Studies). In *Nihon bungaku kenkyū hōhō koten hen* (Methodologies for the Study of Japanese Literature, Classical Volume), in *Nihon bungaku kenkyū shiryō sōsho* (Japanese Literature Research Materials Series), edited by Nihon Bungaku Kenkyū Shiryō Kankōkai, 77-83. Yūseidō.
Matisoff, Susan. 1978. *The Legend of Semimaru, Blind Musician of Japan*. New York: Columbia University Press.
Mayer, Fanny Hagin, ed. and trans. 1986. *The Yanagita Kunio Guide to the Japanese Folktale*. Nagoya: Asian Folklore Studies, Nanzan University.
McCullough, Helen Craig, ed. 1990. *Classical Japanese Prose: An Anthology*. Stanford: Stanford University Press.
McCullough, Helen, trans. 1959. *The "Taiheiki": A Chronicle of Medieval Japan*. New York: Columbia University Press.
——. 1966. *Yoshitsune: A Fifteenth-century Japanese Chronicle (Gikeiki)*. Tokyo: Tokyo University and Stanford: Stanford University Press.
——. 1968. *Tales of Ise*. Tokyo: University of Tokyo Press and Stanford: Stanford University Press.
——. 1980. *Ōkagami, The Great Mirror: Fujiwara Michinaga (966-1027) and His Times*. Princeton: Princeton University Press.
——. 1986. "A Tosa Journal." In *"Kokin Wakashū": The First Imperial Anthology of Japanese Poetry, with "Tosa Nikki" and "Shinsen Waka"*. Stanford: Stanford University Press.
——. 1988. *The Tale of the Heike*. Stanford: Stanford University Press.
McCullough, William H., and Helen Craig McCullough, trans. 1980. *A Tale of Flowering Fortunes: Annals of Japanese Aristocratic Life in the Heian Period (Eiga monogatari)*. 2 vols. Stanford: Stanford University Press.
Miller, Marilyn Jeanne. 1985. *The Poetics of Nikki Bungaku: A Comparison of the Traditions, Conventions, and Structure of Heian Japan's Literary Diaries with Western Autobiographical Writings*. New York: Garland.
Mills, D. E., trans. 1970. *A Collection of Tales from Uji*. Cambridge: Cambridge University Press.
Miner, Earl. 1990. *Comparative Poetics: An Intercultural Essay on Theories of Literature*. Princeton: Princeton University Press.
——. 1996. *Naming Properties: Nominal Reference in Travel Writings by Bashō and Sora, Johnson and Boswell*. Ann Arbor: University of Michigan Press.
Miner, Earl, ed. 1985. *Principles of Classical Japanese Literature*. Princeton: Princeton University Press.
Miner, Earl, trans. 1969. *Japanese Poetic Diaries (Tosa nikki, Izumi Shikibu nikki, Oku no hosomichi, Botan kuroku)*. Berkeley: University of California Press.
Mitani Kuniaki. 1977. "Kaisetsu: sakuhin to no 'taiwa' o motomete" (Afterword: in Search of "Dialogue" with the Work). In *Nihon bungaku kenkyū shiryō sōsho:*

Nihon bungaku kenkyū hōhō koten hen (Japanese Literature Research Materials Series: Methodologies for the Study of Japanese Literature, Classical Volume), edited by Nihon Bungaku Kenkyū Shiryō Kankōkai, 303-12. Yūseidō.

Morris, Ivan, trans. 1967. The "Pillow-Book" of Sei Shōnagon (Makura no sōshi). 2 vols. New York: Columbia University Press.

———. 1971. As I Crossed a Bridge of Dreams: Recollections of a Woman in Eleventh-Century Japan (Sarashina nikki). New York: Dial Press.

Morris, Mark. 1980. "Sei Shōnagon's Poetic Catalogues." Harvard Journal of Asiatic Studies 40, no. 1: 5-54.

———. 1986a. Review of Backus (1985). Monumenta Nipponica 41, no. 3: 349-51.

Mostow, Joshua S. 1992. "The Amorous Statesman and the Poetess: The Politics of Autobiography and the Kagerō Nikki." Japan Forum 4, no. 2: 305-15.

Nakamura, Yoko Motomochi, trans. 1973. Miraculous Stories from the Japanese Buddhist Tradition: The "Nihon Ryōiki" of the Monk Kyōkai. Cambridge: Harvard University Press.

Pflugfelder, Gregory M. 1992. "Strange Fates: Sex, Gender, and Sexuality in Torikaebaya monogatari." Monumenta Nipponica 47, no. 3: 347-68.

Philippi, Donald, trans., with commentary. 1967. Kojiki. Tokyo University Press.

Plutschow, Herbert E. 1990. Chaos and Cosmos: Ritual in Early and Medieval Japanese Literature. Leiden: E. J. Brill.

Pollack, David. 1986. The Fracture of Meaning: Japan's Synthesis of China from the Eighth through the Eighteenth Centuries. Princeton: Princeton University Press.

Reischauer, Edwin O., and Joseph K. Yamagiwa, eds. and trans. 1951. Translations from Early Japanese Literature. Cambridge: Harvard University Press.

Rohlich, Thomas A. 1983. A Tale of Eleventh-Century Japan: "Hamamatsu Chūnagon monogatari". Princeton: Princeton University Press.

Rosenfield, John, ed. 1973. The Courtly Tradition in Japanese Art and Literature; Selected from the Hofer and Hyde Collections. New York: Japan Society Gallery.

Ruch, Barbara. 1977. "Medieval Jongleurs in the Making of a National Literature." In Japan in the Muromachi Age, edited by John W. Hall and Toyoda Takeshi, 279-309. Berkeley: University of California Press.

———. 1991. Mō hitotsu no chūsei zō: bikuni, otogizōshi, raise (For Another Image of the Medieval Period: Nuns, Tales, the Afterlife). Kyoto: Shibunkaku.

———. 1992. "Coping with Death: Paradigms of Heaven, Hell, and the Six Realms in Early Japanese Literature and Painting." In James H. Sanford, et al., eds. (1992), 93-130.

Saigō Nobusuna. 1963 [1948]. Nihon kodai bungaku no kenkyū (Studies in Ancient Japanese Literature). Rev. ed. Iwanami Shoten.

Sakai, Naoki. 1991. Voices of the Past: The Status of Language in Eighteenth-Century Japanese Discourse. Ithaca: Cornell University Press.

Sanford, James H., William R. LaFleur, and Masatoshi Nagatomi, eds. 1992. Flowing Traces: Buddhism in the Literary and Visual Arts of Japan. Princeton: Princeton University Press.

Schalow, Paul. 1994. Review of Markus (1993). Journal of Japanese Studies 20, no. 2: 524-28.

Schalow, Paul, trans. 1990. The Great Mirror of Male Love (Saikaku's "Nanshoku ōkagami"). Stanford: Stanford University Press.

Seki Keigo, ed. 1963. Folktales of Japan. Translated by Robert J. Adams. Chicago: University of Chicago Press.

Sekine Eiji, ed. 1996. Uta no hibiki, monogatari no yokubō (Echo of Poems, Desire for Narratives). Shinwasha.

Tahara, Mildred M., trans. 1980. *"Tales of Yamato": A Tenth-Century Poem-Tale.* Honolulu: University of Hawai'i Press.
Tanaka Takako. 1992. "*Akujo*" ron (On the "Bad" Woman). Kinokuniya shoten.
Tsunoda, Ryusaku, Wm. Theodore de Bary, and Donald Keene, comps. 1958. *Sources of Japanese Tradition.* Vol. 1. New York: Columbia University Press.
Tyler, Royall, trans. 1987. *Japanese Folk Tales.* New York: Pantheon.
———. 1990. *The Miracles of the Kasuga Deity.* New York: Columbia University Press.
Ueda Makoto, trans. and comp. 1967. *Literary and Art Theories in Japan.* Cleveland: The Press of Western Reserve University.
Ury, Marian, trans. 1979. *Tales of Times Now Past: Sixty-two Stories from a Medieval Japanese Collection (Konjaku monogatari).* Berkeley: University of California Press.
Varley, Paul. 1994. *Warriors of Japan, As Portrayed in the War Tales.* Honolulu: University of Hawai'i Press.
Videen, Susan Downing, trans. 1989. *Tales of Heichū.* Cambridge: Council on East Asian Studies, Harvard University.
Wakita, Haruko. 1994. Review of Ruch (1991). *Journal of Japanese Studies* 20, no. 2: 498-505.
Wheelwright, Carolyn. 1989. *Word in Flower: The Visualization of Classical Literature in Seventeenth-century Japan.* New Haven: Yale University Art Gallery.
Whitehouse, Wilfrid, and Eizo Yanagisawa, trans. 1971. *The "Tale of the Lady Ochikubo": A Tenth Century Japanese Novel.* Garden City, N.Y.: Anchor.
———. 1974. *Lady Nijo's Own Story: The Candid Diary of a Thirteenth-Century Japanese Imperial Concubine (Towazugatari).* Rutland, Vt.: Charles E. Tuttle.
Willig, Rosette F., trans. 1983. *"The Changelings": A Classical Court Tale (Torikaebaya).* Stanford: Stanford University Press.
Yamagiwa, Joseph K., trans. 1967. *"The Okagami," a Japanese Historical Tale.* London: George Allen.
Yoshida, Kogorō. 1984. *Tanrokubon, Rare Books of Seventeenth Century Japan.* Translated and adapted by Mark A. Harbison. Tokyo: Kodansha International and New York: Harper and Row.
Young, Blake Morgan. 1982. *Ueda Akinari.* Vancouver: University of British Columbia Press.
Zolbrod, Leon. 1967. *Takizawa Bakin.* New York: Twayne.

IV. Premodern Literature—Genji

Bargen, Doris G. 1997. *A Woman's Weapon: Spirit Possession in the "Tale of Genji".* Honolulu: University of Hawai'i Press.
Bowring, Richard. 1988. *Murasaki Shikibu: The "Tale of Genji".* Oxford: Oxford University Press.
Cavanaugh, Carole. 1997. "Text and Textile: Unweaving the Female Subject in Heian Writing." *positions: east asia cultures critique* 4, no. 3.
Cranston, Edwin A. 1978. "The Seidensticker *Genji.*" *Journal of Japanese Studies* 4, no. 1: 1-25.
Field, Norma. 1987. *The Splendor of Longing in the "Tale of Genji".* Princeton: Princeton University Press.
Fujii Sadakazu. July 1969. "Barikēdo no naka no *Genji monogatari*" (*Genji monogatari* Behind the Barricades). *Tenbō (Prospects),* no. 127: 123-34.
Fujii Sadakazu, et al. 1982. "*Genji monogatari* kenkyū no kanōsei" (The Potential of *Genji* Studies). 1971. Reprint. In *Nihon bungaku kenkyū shiryō sōsho: Genji*

monogatari IV (Japanese literature research materials series: *Tale of Genji*, Vol. IV), 100-14. Yūseidō.
Goff, Janet Emily. 1991a. *Noh Drama and the "Tale of Genji": The Art of Allusion in Fifteen Classical Plays*. Princeton: Princeton University Press.
———. 1991b. "The Pleasure of Reading the *Genji*." *Journal of Japanese Studies* 17, no. 2: 345-58.
Hashimoto Osamu. 1991-92. *Yōhen Genji (Kiln-warped Genji)*. 14 vols. Chūō Kōronsha.
Kamens, Edward, ed. 1993. *Approaches to Teaching Murasaki Shikibu's "The Tale of Genji"*. New York: Modern Language Association of America.
Loui, Shirley M. 1991. *Murasaki's "Genji" and Proust's "Recherche": A Comparative Study*. Lewiston, N.Y.: Edwin Mellen.
McCullough, Helen Craig. 1977. "The Seidensticker *Genji*." *Monumenta Nipponica* 32, no. 1: 93-110.
McCullough, Helen Craig, trans. and ed. 1994. *Genji and Heike: Selections from "The Tale of Genji" and "The Tale of the Heike"*. Stanford: Stanford University Press.
McMullen, I. J. 1991. *Genji Gaiden: The Origins of Kumazawa Banzan's Commentary on the "Tale of Genji"*. Ithaca: Ithaca Press and Oxford: Oxford Oriental Institute.
Miner, Earl. 28 January 1977. "The Rise of the Radiant Prince." *Times Literary Supplement*, p. 98.
Mitamura Masako, Kawazoe Fusae, and Matsui Kenji, eds. *Genji kenkyū (Genji Studies)*.
Miyoshi, Masao. February 1979. "Translation as Interpretation." *Journal of Asian Studies* 38, no. 2: 299-302.
Morris, Mark. 1990. "Desire and the Prince: New Work on *Genji monogatari*: A Review Article." *Journal of Asian Studies* 49, no. 2: 291-304.
Murasaki Shikibu: The Greatest Lady Writer in Japanese Literature. 1970. Tokyo: (Monbushō) Japan National Commission for Unesco.
Murase, Miyeko. 1984. *Iconography of the "Tale of Genji": Genji monogatari ekotoba*. New York: Weatherhill.
Muroki Hideyuki, et al. 1996. "Zadankai: *Genji monogatari* kenkyū no tenbō" (Panel Discussion: Prospects for *Genji* Studies). In *Shin monogatari kenkyū 4: "Genji monogatari" o "yomu"* (New Monogatari Studies 4: "Reading" the *Tale of Genji*), edited by Monogatari Kenkyūkai, 65-70. Wakakusa shobō.
Okada, H. Richard. 1990. "Domesticating *The Tale of Genji*." *Journal of the American Oriental Society* 110: 60-70.
———. 1991. *Figures of Resistance: Language, Poetry, and Narrating in the "Tale of Genji" and Other Mid-Heian Texts*. Durham: Duke University Press.
Pekarik, Andrew J. 1991. *Ukifune: Love in the "Tale of Genji"*. New York: Columbia University Press.
Puette, William J. 1992. *The "Tale of Genji" by Murasaki Shikibu: A Reader's Guide*. Tokyo: Charles E. Tuttle.
Ramirez-Christensen, Esperanza. 1995. "Resisting Figures of Resistance." *Harvard Journal of Asiatic Studies* 55, no. 2: 179-218.
Rohlich, Thomas H. 1995. Review of Helen McCullough, trans. and ed. (1994). *Monumenta Nipponica* 50, no. 3: 387-89.
Seidensticker, Edward. 1978. *Genji Days*. New York: Kodansha International.
Seidensticker, Edward, trans. 1976. *The Tale of Genji*. New York: Alfred A. Knopf.

Shirane, Haruo. 1987. *The Bridge of Dreams: A Poetics of the "Tale of Genji"*. Stanford: Stanford University Press.
———. 1994. Review of Okada (1991). *Journal of Japanese Studies* 20, no. 1: 221-28.
Stynchecum, Amanda Mayer. 1980. "Who Tells the Tale? 'Ukifune': A Study in Narrative Voice." *Monumenta Nipponica* 35, no. 4: 375-403.
———. 1988. *Narrative Voice in "The Tale of Genji"*. Illinois Papers in Asian Studies. Vol. 5. Urbana: University of Illinois Press.
Tyler, Royall. 1992b. Review of Goff (1986) and Marra (1992). *Journal of Japanese Studies* 18, no. 2: 611-18.
Ury, Marian. 1976. "The Imaginary Kingdom and the Translator's Art; Notes on Re-reading Waley's *Genji*." *Journal of Japanese Studies* 2, no. 2: 267-94.
———. 1977. "The Complete *Genji*." *Harvard Journal of Asiatic Studies* 37, no. 1: 183-201.
———. 1991. "Tales of *Genji*." *Harvard Journal of Asiatic Studies* 51, no. 1: 263-308.
Waley, Arthur, trans. 1955. *The Tale of Genji*. New York: Doubleday-Anchor.

V. Modern Literature—General Works and Collections

Anderer, Paul. 1984. *Other Worlds: Arishima Takeo and the Bounds of Modern Japanese Fiction*. New York: Columbia University Press.
———. 1994. "Brave New History." *Journal of Japanese Studies* 20, no. 2: 459-76.
Anderer, Paul, trans. and ed. 1995. *Literature of the Lost Home: Kobayashi Hideo – Literary Criticism 1924-1939*. Stanford: Stanford University Press.
Aoki, Tamotsu. 1996. "Murakami Haruki and Japan Today." In Treat, ed. (1996), 265-74.
Arima Tatsuo. 1969. *The Failure of Freedom: A Portrait of Modern Japanese Intellectuals*. Cambridge: Harvard University Press.
Birnbaum, Alfred, ed. 1991. *Monkey Brain Sushi: New Tastes in Japanese Fiction*. New York: Kodansha.
Borton, Hugh, ed. 1957. *Japan Between East and West*. New York: Harper and Brothers, for the Council on Foreign Relations.
Colligan-Taylor, Karen. 1990. *The Emergence of Environmental Literature in Japan*. New York: Garland.
Currie, William. 1974. Review of Miyoshi (1974). *Monumenta Nipponica* 29, no. 4: 483-84.
Doak, Kevin Michael. 1994. *Dreams of Difference: The Japan Romantic School and the Crisis of Modernity*. Berkeley: University of California Press.
Field, Norma. 1994. "Beyond Envy, Boredom, and Suffering: Toward an Emancipatory Politics for Resident Koreans and Other Japanese." *positions: east asia cultures critique* 1, no. 3: 640-70.
———. 1996. "Texts of Childhood in Inter-Nationalizing Japan." In *Text and Nation: Cross-disciplinary Essays on Cultural and National Identities*, edited by Laura García-Moreno and Peter C. Pfeiffer, 143-71. Columbia, S.C.: Camden House.
Fogel, Joshua A. 1996. *The Literature of Travel in the Japanese Rediscovery of China, 1862-1945*. Stanford: Stanford University Press.
Fowler, Edward. 1988. *The Rhetoric of Confession: Shishōsetsu in Early Twentieth-Century Japanese Fiction*. Berkeley: University of California Press.
———. 1992. "Rendering Words, Traversing Cultures: On the Art and Politics of Translating Modern Japanese Fiction." *Journal of Japanese Studies* 18, no. 1.
Fuhara Yoshiaki, ed. 1985. *Bungaku no juyō: gendai hihyō no senryaku* (Literary Reception: The Strategies of Contemporary Criticism). Kenkyusha.

Fujii, James A. 1993. *Complicit Fictions: The Subject in the Modern Japanese Prose Narrative*. Berkeley: University of Calfornia Press.
Gessel, Van C. 1989. *The Sting of Life: Four Contempoary Japanese Novelists*. New York: Columbia University Press.
———. 1993. *Three Modern Novelists: Soseki, Tanizaki, Kawabata*. Tokyo: Kodansha International.
Goossen, Ted. 1993. Review of Miyoshi (1974). *Journal of Asian Studies* 52, no. 2: 461-62.
Hijiya-Kirschnereit, Irmela. 1996. *Rituals of Self-revelation: Shishosetsu as Literary Genre and Socio-Cultural Phenomenon*. Cambridge: Council on East Asian Studies, Harvard University.
Homma, Kenshiro. 1983. *The Literature of Naturalism: An East-West Comparative Study*. Kyoto: Yamaguchi Publishing House.
Inouye, Charles. 1992. Review of Miyoshi (1974). *Monumenta Nipponica* 47, no. 3: 400-404.
Kang Sang-jung. 1996. *Orientarizumu no kanata e* (Beyond Orientalism). Iwanami shoten.
Karatani Kōjin. July 1995. "Intabyū: Ikani taishō suruka; Karatani shi ni kiku" (Interview: how should we deal with it; asking Mr. Karatani Kojin). *Kokubungaku kaishaku to kenkyū no kyōzai* (National Literature: Resources for Interpretation and Research) 40, no. 8: 15.
Karatani Kōjin, ed. 1991. *Kindai Nihon no hihyō, Shōwa hen, ge* (Criticism in Modern Japan, Shōwa Volume, 2). Fukutake shoten.
Kawamura Minato. 1994. *Umi o watatta nihongo: shokuminchi no "kokugo" no jikan* (The Japanese that Crossed the Seas: "National Language" Class in the Colonies). Seidosha.
———. 1995. *Sengo bungaku o tou: sono taiken to rinen* (Interrogating Postwar Literature: Experience and Principle). Iwanami shoten.
Keene, Donald. 1956. *Modern Japanese Literature*. New York: Grove Press.
———. 1957. "Literary and Intellectual Currents in Postwar Japan and Their International Implications." In *Japan Between East and West*, edited by Hugh Borton. New York: Harper and Brothers, for the Council on Foreign Relations.
———. 1971. *Landscapes and Portraits: Appreciations of Japanese Culture*. Tokyo: Kodansha International.
———. 1978. *Meeting with Japan*. Tokyo: Gakuseisha.
Kimball, Arthur G. 1972. *Crisis in Identity and Contemporary Japanese Novels*. Tokyo: Charles E. Tuttle.
Kizer, Carolyn. 1995. *Picking and Choosing: Essays on Prose*. Cheney: Eastern Washington University Press.
Komori Yōichi. 1988a. *Buntai to shite no katari* (Narration as Style). Shin'yōsha.
———. 1988b. *Kōzō to shite no katari* (Narration as Structure). Chikuma shobō.
Kornicki, Peter F. 1982. *The Reform of Fiction in Meiji Japan*. Concord: Paul and Company Publishers Consortium.
Koschmann, J. Victor. 1996. *Revolution and Subjectivity in Postwar Japan*. Chicago: University of Chicago Press.
Layoun, Mary. 1989. Review of Fowler (1988). *The Journal of Asian Studies* 48, no. 1: 158-60.
———. 1990. *Travels of a Genre: The Modern Novel and Ideology*. Princeton: Princeton University Press.
Lippitt, Noriko Mizuta. *Reality and Fiction in Modern Japanese Literature*. Armonk, N.Y.: M. E. Sharpe, 1980.

Maruyama, Masao. "From Carnal Literature to Carnal Politics." 1949. In *Thought and Behavior in Modern Japanese Politics*, edited by Ivan Morris. Oxford: Oxford University Press, 1963.

Matthew, Robert. 1989. *Japanese Science Fiction: A View of a Changing Society*. London: Routledge and Oxford: Nissan Institute of Japanese Studies, University of Oxford.

McClellan, Edwin. 1969. *Two Japanese Novelists: Soseki and Toson*. Chicago: University of Chicago Press.

———. 1975. Review of Miyoshi (1974). *Journal of Asian Studies* 34, no. 4: 1017-20.

Miller, Stephen D., ed. 1996. *Partings at Dawn: An Anthology of Japanese Gay Literature*. San Francisco: Gay Sunshine Press.

Minear, Richard H., trans. and ed. 1990. *Hiroshima: Three Witnesses*. Princeton: Princeton University Press.

Mitsios, Helen, ed. 1990. *New Japanese Voices: The Best Contemporary Fiction from Japan*. New York: Atlantic Monthly Press.

Miyoshi, Masao. 1974. *Accomplices of Silence: The Modern Japanese Novel*. Berkeley: University of California Press.

———. 1991. *Off Center: Power and Culture Relations Between Japan and the United States*. Cambridge: Harvard University Press.

Morrison, John W. 1955. *Modern Japanese Fiction*. Salt Lake City: University of Utah Press.

Napier, Susan Jolliffe. 1991. *Escape from the Wasteland: Romanticism and Realism in the Fiction of Mishima Yukio and Ōe Kenzaburō*. Cambridge: Council on East Asian Studies, Harvard University.

———. 1996. *The Fantastic in Modern Japanese Literature: The Subversion of Modernity*. London: Routledge.

Orbaugh, Sharalyn. Forthcoming. *The Japanese Fiction of the Allied Occupation, 1945-1952*. Stanford: Stanford University Press.

Ōshiro Tatsuhiro, and Higashi Mineo. 1989. *Okinawa: Two Postwar Novellas*. Translated by Steven Rabson. Berkeley: Institute for East Asian Studies, University of California.

Petersen, Gwenn Boardman. 1979. *The Moon in the Water: Understanding Tanizaki, Kawabata, and Mishima*. Honolulu: University of Hawai'i Press.

Pollack, David. 1992. *Reading Against Culture: Ideology and Narrative in the Japanese Novel*. Ithaca: Cornell University Press.

Powell, Irena. 1983. *Writers and Society in Modern Japan*. Tokyo: Kodansha International.

Reischauer, Edwin O. 1958. Review of Borton, et al. (1957). *Harvard Journal of Asiatic Studies* 21.

Rimer, J. Thomas. 1978. *Modern Japanese Fiction and Its Traditions: An Introduction*. Princeton: Princeton University Press.

———. 1988. *Pilgrimages: Aspects of Japanese Literature and Culture*. Honolulu: University of Hawai'i Press.

Rubin, Jay. 1975. Review of Miyoshi (1974). *Journal of Japanese Studies* 1, no. 2: 466-85.

———. 1984. *Injurious to Public Morals: Writers and the Meiji State*. Seattle: University of Washington Press.

Schlant, Ernestine, and J. Thomas Rimer, eds. 1991. *Legacies and Ambiguities: Postwar Fiction and Culture in West Germany and Japan*. Washington, D.C.: Woodrow Wilson Center Press and Baltimore: Johns Hopkins University Press.

Selden, Kyoko, and Mark Selden, eds. 1989. *The Atomic Bomb: Voices from Hiroshima and Nagasaki*. Armonk, N.Y.: M. E. Sharpe.

Shea, George Tyson. 1964. *Leftwing Literature in Japan: A Brief History of the Proletarian Literary Movement.* Tokyo: Hosei University Press.
Sibley, William F. 1968. "Naturalism in Japanese Literature." *Harvard Journal of Asiatic Studies* 28: 157-69.
———. 1971. Review of Arima (1969). *Harvard Journal of Asiatic Studies* 31.
Smith, Henry. 1996. "Overcoming the Modern History of Edo 'Shunga.'" In Jones, ed. (1996).
Smith, Robert J. 1992. Review of Miyoshi (1991). *Journal of Japanese Studies* 18, no. 2: 565-68.
Snyder, Stephen. 1994. Review of Karatani (1994). *Journal of Asian Studies* 53, no. 1: 208-9.
———. 1996. "Two Murakamis and Marcel Proust: Memory as Form in Contemporary Japanese Fiction." In *In Pursuit of Contemporary East Asian Culture,* edited by Tang Xiaobing and Stephen Snyder, 69-83. Boulder: Westview.
Suzuki, Tomi. 1996. *Narrating the Self: Fictions of Japanese Modernity.* Stanford: Stanford University Press.
Takahashi, Tsutomu. 1994. *Parallelisms in the Literary Vision of Sin: Double-Readings of Natsume Sōseki and Nathaniel Hawthorne, Akutagawa Ryūnosuke and Ambrose Bierce, and Hagiwara Sakutarō and Stephen Crane.* New York: Peter Lang.
Thunman, Noriko. 1983. *Nakahara Chūya and French Symbolism.* Stockholm: Institute of Oriental Languages, University of Stockholm.
Treat, John Whittier. 1995. *Writing Ground Zero: Japanese Literature and the Atomic Bomb.* Chicago: University of Chicago Press.
Treat, John Whittier, ed. 1996. *Contemporary Japan and Popular Culture.* Honolulu: University of Hawai'i Press.
Tsuruta, Kinya, ed. 1989. *The Walls Within: Images of Westerners in Japan and Images of the Japanese Abroad: Selected Proceedings, the University of British Columbia May 8-10, 1988.* Vancouver: Institute of Asian Research, University of British Columbia.
———. 1993. *The Proceedings of Nature and Selfhood in Japanese Literature: A Conference Held at the University of British Columbia, August 25-26, 1992.* Vancouver: Department of Asian Studies, University of British Columbia.
Tsuruta, Kinya, and Thomas E. Swann, eds. 1976. *Approaches to the Modern Japanese Novel.* Tokyo: Sophia University.
Twine, Nannette. 1991. *Language and the Modern State: The Reform of Modern Written Japanese.* London: Routledge.
Ueda, Makoto. 1967. *Literary and Art Theories in Japan.* Cleveland: Press of Western Reserve University.
———. 1976. *Modern Japanese Writers and the Nature of Literature.* Stanford: Stanford University Press.
———. 1986. *Explorations: Essays in Comparative Literature.* Lanham, Md.: University Press of America.
Usui Yoshimi. 1975. *Kindai bungaku ronsō* (Debates about Modern Literature). Vol. 2. Chikuma shobō.
Walker, Janet A. 1979. *The Japanese Novel of the Meiji Period and the Ideal of Individualism.* Princeton: Princeton University Press.
———. 1989. Review of Fowler (1988). *Journal of Japanese Studies* 15, no. 2: 447-54.
Washburn, Dennis. 1994. Review of Miyoshi (1991). *Harvard Journal of Asiatic Studies* 54, no. 1: 280-312.
———. 1995. *The Dilemma of the Modern in Japanese Fiction.* New Haven: Yale University Press.

Yamagiwa, Joseph K. November 1953. "Fiction in Post-war Japan." *The Far Eastern Quarterly* 13, no. 1: 3-22.
Yamanouchi, Hisaaki. 1980. *The Search for Authenticity in Modern Japanese Literature*. Cambridge: Cambridge University Press.

VI. *Modern Literature—Studies/Translations of Single Authors*

Bowring, Richard J. 1979. *Mori Ōgai and the Modernization of Japanese Culture*. Cambridge: Cambridge University Press.
Chambers, Anthony H. 1994. *The Secret Window: Ideal Worlds in Tanizaki's Fiction*. Cambridge: Council on East Asian Studies, Harvard University.
Copeland, Rebecca L. 1992. *The Sound of the Wind: The Life and Works of Uno Chiyo*. Honolulu: University of Hawai'i Press.
Cornyetz, Nina. 1995. "Nakagami Kenji's Mystic Writing Pad; or, Tracing Origins, Tales of the Snake, and the Land as Matrix." *positions: east asia cultures critique* 3, no. 1: 224-54.
Dazai Osamu. 1956. *The Setting Sun (Shayō)*. Translated by Donald Keene. New York: New Directions.
——. 1958. *No Longer Human (Ningen shikkaku)*. Translated by Donald Keene. New York: New Directions.
——. 1983. *Dazai Osamu: Selected Stories and Sketches*. Translated by James O'Brien. Ithaca: Cornell University East Asia Program.
——. 1985. *The Return to Tsugaru: Travels of a Purple Tramp (Tsugaru)*. Translated by James Westerhoven. Kodansha International.
Doi, Takeo. 1976. *The Psychological World of Natsume Soseki*. Cambridge: Harvard University Press.
Hijiya-Kirschnereit, Irmela. 1989. "The Darkness at the Foot of the Lighthouse: Recent Research on *Shishōsetsu*." *Monumenta Nipponica* 44, no. 3: 337-45.
——. 1994. Review of James Fujii (1993). *Monumenta Nipponica* 49, no. 1: 102-5.
——. 1996. *Rituals of Self-Revelation: Shishōsetsu as Literary Genre and Socio-Cultural Phenomenon*. Cambridge: Council on East Asian Studies, Harvard University Press.
Hirata, Hosea. 1993. Review of James Fujii (1993). *Journal of Asian Studies* 52, no. 4: 1012-13.
Ito, Ken Kenneth. 1991. *Visions of Desire: Tanizaki's Fictional Worlds*. Stanford: Stanford University Press.
Kawabata Yasunari. 1956. *Snow Country (Yukiguni)*. Translated by Edward G. Seidensticker. New York: Alfred A. Knopf.
——. 1959. *Thousand Cranes (Semba zuru)*. Translated by Edward G. Seidensticker. New York: Alfred A. Knopf.
Keene, Dennis. 1980. *Yokomitsu Riichi, Modernist*. New York: Columbia University Press.
Kobayashi Hideo. 1995. "Discourse on Fiction of the Self." Translated by Paul Anderer. In *Literature of the Lost Home: Kobayashi Hideo – Literary Criticism 1924-1939*, edited by Paul Anderer, 67-93. Stanford: Stanford University Press.
Kobayashi Takiji. 1973. *The Factory Ship (Kani kōsen)*. Translated by Frank Motofuji along with *The Absentee Landlord*. Tokyo University Press.
Liman, A. V. 1992. *A Critical Study of the Literary Style of Ibuse Masuji: As Sensitive as Waters*. Lewiston, N.Y.: Edwin Mellen Press.
Lyons, Phyllis I. 1985. *The Saga of Dazai Osamu: A Critical Study with Translations*. Stanford: Stanford University Press.

Mishima Yukio. 1957b. *The Sound of Waves (Shiosai)*. Translated by Meredith Weatherby. New York: Alfred A. Knopf.
——. 1958. *Confessions of a Mask (Kamen no kokuhaku)*. Translated by Meredith Weatherby. New York: New Directions.
——. 1959. *Temple of the Golden Pavilion (Kinkakuji)*. Translated by Ivan Morris. New York: Alfred A. Knopf.
Nathan, John. 1974. *Mishima: A Biography*. Boston: Little, Brown.
Natsume Sōseki. 1957. *Kokoro*. Translated by Edwin McClellan. Chicago: Henry Regnery.
Ōoka Shōhei. 1956. *Fires on the Plain (Nobi)*. Translated by Ivan Morris. New York: Alfred A. Knopf.
Osaragi Jirō. 1955. *Homecoming (Kikyō)*. Translated by Brewster Horwitz. New York: Alfred A. Knopf.
Ozaki Kazuo. 1988. *Rosy Glasses and Other Stories*. Translated by Robert Epp. Ashford, Kent: Norbury.
Rimer, J. Thomas. 1975. *Mori Ōgai*. Boston: Twayne Publishers.
Ryan, Marleigh Grayer. 1975. *The Development of Realism in the Fiction of Tsubouchi Shōyō*. Seattle: University of Washington Press.
Ryan, Marleigh Grayer, trans., with commentary. 1967. *Japan's First Modern Novel: "Ukigumo" of Futabatei Shimei*. New York: Columbia University Press.
Scott-Stokes, Henry. 1995. *The Life and Death of Yukio Mishima*. New York: Noonday Press.
Seidensticker, Edward. 1990 [1965]. *Kafu the Scribbler: The Life and Writings of Nagai Kafu, 1879-1959*. Ann Arbor: Center for Japanese Studies, University of Michigan.
Sibley, William F. 1971. *The Shiga Hero*. Chicago: University of Chicago Press.
Starrs, Roy. 1994. *Deadly Dialectics: Sex, Violence, and Nihilism in the World of Yukio Mishima*. Honolulu: University of Hawai'i Press.
Tanizaki Jun'ichirō. 1955. *Some Prefer Nettles (Tade kuu mushi)*. Translated by Edward G. Seidensticker. New York: Alfred A. Knopf.
——. 1957. *The Makioka Sisters (Sasame yuki)*. Translated by Edward G. Seidensticker. New York: Alfred A. Knopf.
Tansman, Alan M. 1993. *The Writings of Koda Aya, a Japanese Literary Daughter*. New Haven: Yale University Press.
Torrance, Richard. 1994. *The Fiction of Tokuda Shusei and the Emergence of Japan's New Middle Class*. Seattle: University of Washington Press.
Treat, John Whittier. 1988. *Pools of Water, Pillars of Fire: The Literature of Ibuse Masuji*. Seattle: University of Washington Press.
Wilson, Michiko N. 1986. *The Marginal World of Oe Kenzaburo: A Study of Themes and Techniques*. Armonk, N.Y.: M. E. Sharpe.
Wolfe, Alan Stephen. 1990. *Suicidal Narrative in Modern Japan: The Case of Dazai Osamu*. Princeton: Princeton University Press.
Yasko, Guy. 1995. *Mishima Yukio vs. Tōdai Zenkyōtō: The Cultural Displacement of Politics*. Durham: Asian/Pacific Studies Institute, Duke University.
Yoshikawa Eiji. 1956. *The Heike Story (Shin Heike monogatari)*. Translated by Fuki Wooyenaka Uramatsu. New York: Alfred A. Knopf.
Yourcenar, Marguerite. 1986. *Mishima: A Vision of the Void*. Translated by Alberto Manguel in collaboration with the author. Henley on Thames: A. Ellis.

VII. Women and Modern Literature

Birnbaum, Phyllis, trans. 1982. *Rabbits, Crabs, Etc.: Stories by Japanese Women.* Honolulu: University of Hawai'i Press.

Danly, Robert Lyons. 1981. *In the Shade of Spring Leaves: The Life and Writings of Higuchi Ichiyō, a Woman of Letters in Meiji Japan.* New Haven: Yale University Press.

Kitada Sachie. 1994. "Contemporary Feminist Literary Criticism." Translated by Miya E. M. Lippit. *U.S.-Japan Women's Journal,* English Supplement, no. 7: 72-97.

Knapp, Bettina Liebowitz. 1992. *Images of Japanese Women: A Westerner's View.* Troy, N.Y.: Whitston.

Lippit, Noriko Mizuta, and Kyoko Iriye Selden, trans. and eds. c1991. *Japanese Women Writers: Twentieth Century Short Fiction.* Armonk, N.Y.: M. E. Sharpe. Originally published as *Stories by Contemporary Japanese Women Writers.* Armonk, N.Y.: M. E. Sharpe, 1982.

Monnet, Livia. 1996. "Ghostly Women, Displaced Femininities and Male Family Romances: Violence, Gender and Sexuality in Two Texts by Nakagami Kenji." *Japan Forum* 8, nos. 1 and 2: 13-34 and 221-39.

Mulhern, Chieko I. 1991. *Heroic with Grace: Legendary Women of Japan.* Armonk, N.Y.: M. E. Sharpe.

Schalow, Paul Gordon, and Janet A. Walker, eds. 1997. *The Woman's Hand: Gender and Theory in Japanese Women's Writing.* Stanford: Stanford University Press.

Schierbeck, Sachiko Shibata. 1994. *Japanese Women Novelists in the 20th Century: 104 Biographies, 1900-1993.* Copenhagen: Museum Tusculanum Press, University of Copenhagen. New York: Distribution in USA, Paul.

Shimer, Dorothy Blair, ed. 1982. *Rice Bowl Women: Writings by and about the Women of China and Japan.* New York: New American Library.

Shinsawa Hiroko. 1991. "Banana kara Chibi Maruko e: Ren'airon būmu no riyū" (From Banana to Chibi Maruko: Why the Boom in Theories of Love). In *New Feminism Review* 2: *Onna, hyōgen: feminizumu hihyō no tenkai* (Women, Language: The Development of Feminist Criticism), edited by Mizuta Noriko: 266-71.

Sievers, Sharon L. 1983. *Flowers in Salt: The Beginnings of Feminist Consciousness in Modern Japan.* Stanford: Stanford University Press.

Tanaka, Yukiko, ed. c1987. *To Live and to Write: Selections by Japanese Women Writers, 1913-1938.* Seattle: Seal.

Tanaka, Yukiko, ed. and trans. c1991. *Unmapped Territories: New Womens's Fiction from Japan.* Seattle: Women in Translation.

Tanaka, Yukiko, and Elizabeth Hanson, eds. 1982. *This Kind of Woman: Ten Stories by Japanese Women Writers, 1960-1976.* Stanford: Stanford University Press.

Treat, John Whittier. 1995b. "Yoshimoto Banana's *Kitchen,* or the Cultural Logic of Japanese Consumerism." In *Women, Media and Consumption in Japan,* edited by Lise Skov and Brian Moeran, 274-309. Honolulu: University of Hawai'i Press.

Ueno Chizuko, Ogura Chikako, and Tomioka Taeko. 1992. *Danryū bungakuron* (A Theory of Male Literature). Chikuma shobō.

Vernon, Victoria V. 1988. *Daughters of the Moon: Wish, Will, and Social Constraint in Fiction by Modern Japanese Women.* Berkeley: Institute of East Asian Studies, University of California.

Yamamoto Chie. 1992. *Oikaze no onnatachi: josei bungaku to sengo* (Tailwind for Women: Women's Literature and the Postwar Era). Ōtsuki shoten.

VIII. Poetry—Modern

Asawa, Margaret Benton. 1993. *Kitahara Hakushū: His Life and Poetry*. Ithaca: East Asia Program, Cornell University.
Fitzsimmons, Thomas, and Yoshimasu Gozo, eds. 1993. *The New Poetry of Japan: The 70s and 80s*. Santa Fe: Katydid Books; distributed by University of Hawai'i Press.
Hijiya, Yukihito. 1979. *Ishikawa Takuboku*. Boston: Twayne.
Hirata, Hosea. 1993. *The Poetry and Poetics of Nishiwaki Junzaburō: Modernism in Translation*. Princeton: Princeton University Press.
Kaneko Mitsuharu. 1988. *"Shijin": Autobiography of the Poet Kaneko Mitsuharu, 1895-1975*. Honolulu: University of Hawai'i Press.
Kijima, Hajime, ed. 1975. *The Poetry of Postwar Japan*. Iowa City: University of Iowa Press.
Kirkup, James, trans. 1978. *Modern Japanese Poetry*. Edited and introduced by A. R. Davis. St. Lucia, Queensland: University of Queensland Press.
Ko, Won. 1977. *Buddhist Elements in Dada: A Comparison of Tristan Tzara, Takahashi Shinkichi, and their Fellow Poets*. New York: New York University Press.
Morton, Leith, ed. and trans. 1993. *An Anthology of Contemporary Japanese Poetry*. New York: Garland.
Nishiwaki Junzaburō. November 1946. "Daini geijutsuron: gendai haiku ni tsuite" (A Theory of Secondary Art: On Contemporary Haiku). *Sekai* (The World). 1995. Reprint. *Sekai: shuyō rombunsen 1946-1995* (*Sekai*: Selection of Principal Articles 1946-1995), 24-47. Iwanami shoten.
Ōoka Makoto. 1994. *A Poet's Anthology: The Range of Japanese Poetry*. Translated by Janine Beichman. Preface by Donald Keene. Santa Fe: Katydid Books; distributed by University of Hawai'i Press.
Rexroth, Kenneth, and Ikuko Atsumi, eds. and trans. 1977. *The Burning Heart: Women Poets of Japan*. New York: Seabury Press.
Rimer, J. Thomas. 1984. *Guide to Japanesle Poetry*. New York: Macmillan.
Silverberg, Miriam Rom. 1990. *Changing Song: The Marxist Manifestos of Nakano Shigeharu*. Princeton: Princeton University Press.
Stryk, Lucien, ed. and trans. 1993. *Cage of Fireflies: Modern Japanese Haiku*. Athens, Oh.: Swallow.
Ueda, Makoto. 1983. *Modern Japanese Poets and the Nature of Literature*. Stanford: Stanford University Press.
Ueda, Makoto, ed. and trans. 1996. *Modern Japanese Tanka: An Anthology*. New York: Columbia University Press.

IX. Theater—Traditional

Bethe, Monica, and Karen Brazell. 1982. *Dance in the Nō Theatre*. 3 Vols. Ithaca: China-Japan Program, Cornell University.
Bowers, Faubion. 1976 [1952]. *Japanese Theatre*. Westport, Conn.: Greenwood.
Brown, Steven T. Summer 1996. "Theatricalities of Power: New Historicist Readings of Japanese Noh Drama." *Revisionism in Japanese Literary Studies* (*Proceedings of the Midwest Association for Japanese Literary Studies*) 2: 156-87.
Ernst, Earle. 1974. *The Kabuki Theatre*. Honolulu: University of Hawai'i Press.
Gerstle, C. Andrew. 1990. *Circles of Fantasy: Convention in the Plays of Chikamatsu*. Cambridge: Harvard University Press.
Hare, Thomas Blenman. 1986. *Zeami's Style: The Noh Plays of Zeami Motokiyo*. Stanford: Stanford University Press.

Inoura, Yoshinobu. 1981. *The Traditional Theater of Japan.* New York: Weatherhill.
Keene, Donald, ed. 1970. *Twenty Plays of the Nō Theatre.* New York: Columbia University Press.
Keene, Donald, trans. 1990. *The Major Plays of Chikamatsu.* New York: Columbia University Press.
Kominz, Laurence R. 1995. *Avatars of Vengeance: Japanese Drama and the Soga Literary Tradition.* Ann Arbor: Center for Japanese Studies, University of Michigan.
Lombard, Frank A. 1994. *An Outline History of the Japanese Drama.* Honolulu: University of Hawai'i Press.
Morley, Carol Anne. 1993. *Transformations, Miracles, and Mischief: The Mountain Priest Plays of Kyōgen.* Ithaca: Cornell East Asia Series.
Murray, Christopher. 1990. *Yeats and the Noh: A Comparative Study.* Savage, Md.: Barnes and Noble.
Ortolani, Benito. 1995. *The Japanese Theatre: From Shamanistic Ritual to Contemporary Pluralism.* Princeton: Princeton University Press.
Poorter, Erika de. 1986. *Zeami's Talks on Sarugaku: An Annotated Translation of the Sarugaku Dangi.* Amsterdam: J. C. Gieben.
Pronko, Leonard C. 1984. *Guide to Japanese Drama.* 2nd ed. Boston: G. K. Hall.
Rimer, J. Thomas, and Yamazaki Masakazu, trans. 1984. *On the Art of the Nō Drama: The Major Treatises of Zeami.* Princeton: Princeton University Press.
Scott, A. C. (Adolphe Clarence). 1966. *The Kabuki Theatre of Japan.* New York: Collier.
Shively, Donald, trans. 1953. *The Love Suicide at Amijima: A Study of a Japanese Domestic Tragedy by Chikamatsu Monzaemon.* Cambridge: Harvard University Press.
Smethurst, Mae J. 1989. *The Artistry of Aeschylus and Zeami: A Comparative Study of Greek Tragedy and Nō.* Princeton: Princeton University Press.
Thornbury, Barbara E. 1982. *Sukeroku's Double Identity: The Dramatic Structure of Edo Kabuki.* Ann Arbor: Center for Japanese Studies, University of Michigan.
Toita, Yasuji. 1970. *Kabuki: The Popular Theater.* Translated by Don Kenny. New York: Walker/Weatherhill.
Tyler, Royall. 1991. Review of Smethurst (1989) and Yasuda (1989). *Journal of Japanese Studies* 17, no. 1: 220-28.
Tyler, Royall, trans. 1992a. *Japanese Nō Dramas.* Harmondsworth, U.K.: Penguin.
Waley, Arthur, trans. 1957. *The Nō Plays of Japan.* Reprint. New York: Grove Press. [London: Allen and Unwin, 1921.]
Yasuda, Kenneth, trans. 1989. *Masterworks of the Nō Theatre.* Bloomington: University of Indiana Press.

X. Theater—Modern

Concerned Theater Japan. Spring 1970-Spring 1973. 1-2. Tokyo: Concerned Theatre Japan Co.
Goodman, David G. 1988. *Japanese Drama and Culture in the 1960s: The Return of the Gods.* Armonk, N.Y.: M. E. Sharpe.
Mishima Yukio. 1957a. *Five Modern Noh Plays* (*Kindai nōgakushū*). Translated by Donald Keene. New York: Alfred A. Knopf.
Morioka, Heinz. 1990. *Rakugo: The Popular Narrative Art of Japan.* Cambridge: Harvard University Press.
Rimer, J. Thomas. 1974. *Toward a Modern Japanese Theatre: Kishida Kunio.* Princeton: Princeton University Press.

Senda, Akihiko. 1996. *The Voyage of Contemporary Japanese Theater.* Honolulu: University of Hawai'i Press.
Shields, Nancy K. 1996. *Fake Fish: The Theater of Kōbō Abe.* New York: Weatherhill.
Toyotaka Komiya, ed. 1969. *Japanese Music and Drama in the Meiji Era.* Translated and adapted by Donald Keene. Reprint. Tokyo bunko.

XI. Film

Anderson, Joseph L., and Donald Richie. 1982. *The Japanese Film: Art and Industry.* Expanded ed. Princeton: Princeton University Press.
Barrett, Gregory. 1989. *Archetypes in Japanese Film: The Sociopolitical and Religious Significance of the Principal Heroes and Heroines.* Selinsgrove, Pa.: Susquehanna University Press and London: Associated University Presses.
Bock, Audie. 1985. *Japanese Film Directors.* New York: Kodansha International.
Breakwell, Ian. 1995. *An Actor's Revenge (Yukinojo Henge).* London: British Film Institute.
Broderick, Mick, ed. 1996. *Hibakusha Cinema: Hiroshima, Nagasaki, and the Nuclear Image in Japanese Film.* London: Kegan Paul International.
Burch, Noël. 1979. *To the Distant Observer: Form and Meaning in the Japanese Cinema.* Revised and edited by Annette Michelson. Berkeley: University of California Press.
Davis, Darrell W. 1996. *Picturing Japaneseness: Monumental Style, National Identity, Japanese Film.* New York: Columbia University Press.
Desser, David. 1988. *Eros Plus Massacre: An Introduction to the Japanese New Wave Cinema.* Bloomington: Indiana University Press.
Dissanayake, Wimal, ed. 1988. *Cinema and Cultural Identity: Reflections on Films from Japan, India, and China.* Lanham, Md.: University Press of America.
———. 1993. *Melodrama and Asian Cinema.* Cambridge: Cambridge University Press.
Erhlich, Linda C., and David Desser, eds. 1994. *Cinematic Landscapes: Observations on the Visual Arts and Cinema of China and Japan.* Austin: University of Texas Press.
Galbraith, Stuart. 1994. *Japanese Science Fiction, Fantasy and Horror Films: A Critical Analysis of 103 Features Released in the United States, 1950-1992.* Jefferson, N.C.: McFarland.
Goodwin, James, ed. 1994. *Perspectives on Akira Kurosawa.* New York: Maxwell Macmillan International.
Hirano, Kyoko. 1992. *Mr. Smith Goes to Tokyo: The Japanese Cinema under the American Occupation, 1945-1952.* Washington, D.C.: Smithsonian Institution.
Kirihara, Donald. 1992. *Patterns of Time: Mizoguchi and the 1930s.* Madison: University of Wisconsin Press.
McDonald, Keiko I. 1983. *Cinema East: A Critical Study of Major Japanese Films.* Rutherford, N.J.: Farleigh Dickinson University Press.
———. 1994. *Japanese Classical Theater in Films.* Rutherford, N.J.: Farleigh Dickinson University Press and Cranbury, N.J.: Associated University Presses.
Mellen, Joan. 1975. *Voices from the Japanese Cinema.* New York: Liveright.
———. 1976. *The Waves at Genji's Door: Japan through Its Cinema.* New York: Pantheon.
Nolletti, Arthur, Jr., and David Desser, eds. 1992. *Reframing Japanese Cinema: Authorship, Genre, History.* Bloomington, Indiana University Press.
Oshima, Nagisa. 1992. *Cinema, Censorship, and the State: The Writings of Nagisa Oshima, 1956-1978.* Edited and with an introduction by Annette Michelson. Translated by Dawn Lawson. Cambridge: MIT Press.

Rayns, Tony, ed. 1984. *EIGA: 25 Years of Japanese Cinema*. Edinburgh: Edinburgh International Film Festival.
Reader, Keith. 1981. *Cultures on Celluloid*. London: Quartet Books.
Richie, Donald. 1971. *Japanese Cinema; Film Style and National Character*. Garden City, N.Y.: Doubleday.
——. 1982. *The Japanese Movie*. Rev. ed. Tokyo: Kodansha International.
——. 1990. *Japanese Cinema: An Introduction*. Hong Kong and New York: Oxford University Press.
——. 1996. *The Films of Akira Kurosawa*. 3rd ed., expanded and updated. Berkeley: University of California Press.
Satō, Tadao. 1982. *Currents in Japanese Cinema: Essays*. Translated by Gregory Barrett. New York: Kodansha International/USA.

XII. Popular/Mass Culture

Allison, Anne. 1996. *Permitted and Prohibited Desires: Mothers, Comics and Censorship in Japan*. Boulder: Westview.
Buruma, Ian. 1984. *Japanese Mirror: Heroes and Villains of Japanese Culture*. London: J. Cape.
——. 1985. *Behind the Mask: On Sexual Demons, Sacred Mothers, Transvestites, Gangsters, and Other Japanese Cultural Heroes*. New York: New American Library.
Fields, George. 1983. *From Bonsai to Levi's: When West Meets East, An Insider's Surprising Account of How the Japanese Live*. New York: Macmillan.
Goto Kazuhiko, et al. 1991. *A History of Japanese Television Drama: Modern Japan and the Japanese*. Tokyo: The Japan Association of Broadcasting Art.
Jagusch, Sybille A., ed. 1990. *Window on Japan: Japanese Children's Books and Television Today: Papers from a Symposium at the Library of Congress, November 18-19, 1987*. Washington, D.C.: Library of Congress: Supt. of Docs. U.S. G.P.O.
Kasza, Gregory James. 1988. *The State and the Mass Media in Japan, 1918-1945*. Berkeley: University of California Press.
Kobayashi, Akiyoshi. 1992. *TV News Flow in Asia Pacific Regions*. Tokyo: NHK Broadcasting Culture Research Institute.
Lent, John A., ed. 1995. *Asian Popular Culture*. Boulder: Westview.
McCormack, Gavan, and Yoshio Sugimoto, eds. 1988. *The Japanese Trajectory: Modernization and Beyond*. Cambridge: Cambridge University Press.
McFarland, H. Neill (Horace Neill). 1987. *Daruma: The Founder of Zen in Japanese Art and Popular Culture*. Tokyo: Kodansha International.
Moeran, Brian. 1989. *Language and Popular Culture in Japan*. Manchester: Manchester University Press.
——. c1996. *A Japanese Advertising Agency: An Anthropology of Media and Markets*. Honolulu: University of Hawai'i Press.
Pharr, Susan J., and Ellis S. Krauss, eds. 1996. *Media and Politics in Japan*. Honolulu: University of Hawai'i Press.
Powers, Richard Gid, and Hidetoshi Kato, eds., and Bruce Stronach, assoc. ed. 1989. *Handbook of Japanese Popular Culture*. New York: Greenwood.
Rimer, J. Thomas, ed. 1990. *Culture and Identity: Japanese Intellectuals during the Interwar Years*. Princeton: Princeton University Press.
Schodt, Frederik L. 1996. *Dreamland Japan: Writings on Modern Japan*. Berkeley: Stone Bridge.
Seidensticker, Edward. 1983. *Low City, High City: Tokyo from Edo to the Earthquake*. New York: Alfred A. Knopf.

———. 1991. *Tokyo Rising: The City since the Great Earthquake.* Cambridge: Harvard University Press.
Shisō no Kagaku Kenkyūkai. 1959. *Japanese Popular Culture: Studies in Mass Communication and Cultural Change.* Rutland, Vt.: Charles E. Tuttle.
Skov, Lise, and Brian Moeran, eds. 1995. *Women, Media and Consumption in Japan.* Honolulu: University of Hawai'i Press.
Tobin, Joseph J., ed. 1992. *Re-made in Japan: Everyday Life and Consumer Taste in a Changing Society.* New Haven: Yale University Press.
Treat, John Whittier, ed. 1996. *Contemporary Japan and Popular Culture.* Honolulu: University of Hawai'i Press.
Tsurumi, Shunsuke. 1987. *A Cultural History of Postwar Japan: 1945-1980.* London: KPI.
Yang, Jeff, et al., eds. 1997. *Eastern Standard Time: A Guide to Asian Influence on American Culture from Astro Boy to Zen Buddhism.* Boston: Houghton Mifflin.

XIII. Translated Works by Japanese Critics

Eto, Jun. 1980. *One Aspect of the Allied Occupation of Japan: The Censorship Operation and Post-war Japanese Literature.* Washington, D.C.: The Wilson Center, Smithsonian Institution.
Inoue, Charles. 1993. Review of Karatani (1994). *Monumenta Nipponica* 48, no. 4: 489-91.
Karatani Kōjin. 1994. *Origins of Modern Japanese Literature.* Translation edited by Brett de Bary. Duke University Press.
Kawabata Yasunari. 1969. *Japan the Beautiful and Myself.* Translated by Edward G. Seidensticker. Kodansha International.
Kobayashi Hideo. 1995. *Literature of the Lost Home: Kobayashi Hideo – Literary Criticism, 1924-1939.* Edited and translated by Paul Anderer. Stanford: Stanford University Press.
Nakagawa Yoichi. 1975. *Nakagawa's "Ten no Yūgao": With a Commentary on the Relevance of Yoichi Nakagawa's Novel in Japanese Literature.* Translation and commentary by Jeremy Ingalls. Boston: Twayne.
Nakamura Mitsuo. 1968. *Modern Japanese Fiction 1868-1926.* Rev. ed. Kokusai bunka shinkōkai.
———. 1969. *Contemporary Japanese Fiction, 1926-1968.* Kokusai bunka shinkōkai.
Ōe, Kenzaburō. 1995. *Japan, the Ambiguous, and Myself: The Nobel Prize Speech and Other Lectures.* Translated by Yamanouchi Hisaaki, et al. Kodansha International.
Tsuda, Sōkichi. 1988. *An Inquiry into the Japanese Mind as Mirrored in Literature: The Flowering Period of Common People Literature.* Translated by Fukumatsu Matsuda. Westport, Conn.: Greenwood.

XIV. Other Cited Works

Amin, Samir. 1994. *Re-reading the Postwar Period: An Intellectual Itinerary.* Translated by Michael Wolfers. New York: Monthly Review Press.
Bakhtin, M. M. 1982. "Epic and Novel." In *The Dialogic Imagination: Four Essays by M. M. Bakhtin,* edited by Michael Holquist, translated by Caryl Emerson and Michael Holquist, 3-40. Austin: University of Texas Press.
Bellah, Robert. 1957. *Tokugawa Religion: The Cultural Roots of Modern Japan.* New York: The Free Press.
Chow, Rey. 1993. "The Politics and Pedagogy of Asian Literature." In *Writing*

Diaspora: Tactics of Intervention in Contemporary Cultural Studies, edited by Rey Chow, 120-34. Bloomington: Indiana University Press.

Cohen, Ralph, ed. 1988. *New Literary History: International Bibliography of Literary Theory and Interpretation, 1984-85.* Baltimore: Johns Hopkins University Press.

Dower, John W. 1986. *War without Mercy: Race and Power in the Pacific War.* New York: Pantheon.

Dower, John W., ed. 1975. *Origins of the Modern Japanese State: Selected Writings of E. H. Norman.* New York: Pantheon.

Etō Jun. 1965. *Amerika to Watakushi* (America and I). Kodansha.

Halperin, David M. 1990. *One Hundred Years of Homosexuality and Other Essays on Greek Love.* New York: Routledge.

Harootunian, H. D. 1995. "Late Tokugawa Culture and Thought." In *The Emergence of Meiji Japan,* edited by Marius B. Jansen, 53-143. Cambridge: Cambridge University Press.

Jameson, Frederic. 1988. "Periodizing the 60s." In *The Ideologies of Theory: Essays 1971-1986; Vol. 2: The Syntax of History.* Minneapolis: University of Minnesota Press. This essay from 1984.

Jansen, Marius B. 1988. "Stages of Growth." In *Japanese Studies in the United States; Part I: History and Present Condition,* in *Japanese Studies Series XVII,* edited by the Japan Foundation, 19-21. Ann Arbor: Association for Asian Studies.

Kapps, Robert A., et al. 1980. "Review Symposium: Edward Said's *Orientalism.*" *Journal of Asian Studies* 34, no. 3: 481-517.

Leupp, Gary. 1995. *Male Colors: The Construction of Homosexuality in Tokugawa Japan.* Berkeley: University of California Press.

———. 1996. "Male Homosexuality in Edo During the Late Tokugawa Period, 1750-1850: Decline of a Tradition?" In Jones, ed. (1996), 105-9.

McCullough, William H. 1967. "Japanese Marriage Institutions in the Heian Period." *Harvard Journal of Asiatic Studies* 27: 103-67.

Moretti, Franco. 1987. *The Way of the World: The Bildungsroman in European Culture.* London: Verson.

Reischauer, Edwin O. 1946. *Japan – Past and Present.* New York: Alfred A. Knopf.

———. 1950. *The United States and Japan.* Cambridge: Harvard University Press.

Ross, Kristin. 1995. *Fast Cars, Clean Bodies: Decolonization and the Reordering of French Culture.* Cambridge: MIT Press.

Said, Edward. 1983. *The World, the Text, and the Critic.* Cambridge: Harvard University Press.

Sansom, George B. 1950. *The Western World and Japan.* New York: Alfred A. Knopf.

Tokieda Motoki. 1941. *Kokugogaku genron* (The Principles of the National Language). Iwanami shoten.

Wakita Haruko. 1984. "Marriage and Property in Premodern Japan from the Perspective of Women's History." Translated by Suzanne Gay. *Journal of Japanese Studies* 10, no. 1: 73-99.

Wood, Ellen Meiksins. July-August 1996. "Modernity, Postmodernity, or Capitalism?" *Monthly Review*: 27-28.

XV. Resources on the World Wide Web

HORAGAI (online magazine presented by critic Kato Koiti, featuring Isikawa Jun, Abe Kōbō, and new Japanese writers including recent Akutagawa Prize winners. As is naturally the case with many Japanese websites—of which this list is only a minuscule sampling—much more information is available if

you can access in Japanese: http://www.win.or.jp/Ihoragai/english.html
Kokubungaku Kenkyū Shiryōkan (National Institute of Japanese Literature) website: http://www.nijl.ac.jp/
(Literature/Language/Culture) website established by a Mr/s Matsuoka with numerous links to other sites, including the NIJL one above: http://lang.natoya-u.ac.jp/~matsuoka/Japan.html
Nichibunken (The International Research Center for Japanese Studies, run by the Ministry of Education, Science, and Culture): http://www.nichibun.ac.jp/Welcome.html
Film bibliographies at the University of Iowa: http://www.lib.uiowa.edu/eac/japanfil.html and kinema club: http://pears.lib.ohio-state.edu/Markus/Welcome.html
JLIT-L (a Japanese literature electronic mail list; information requested and received; subscribe by sending a message to <listserv@vm.cc.purdue.edu> with a message stating "sub JLIT-L xyxy" with your name in place of "xyxy"): <JLIT-L@vm.cc.purdue.edu >

WHEN AND WHERE JAPAN ENTERS: AMERICAN ANTHROPOLOGY SINCE 1945*

Jennifer Robertson

Introduction

"Assignment: Japan" was the title of the first chapter of Ruth Benedict's now classic book, *The Chrysanthemum and the Sword*, commissioned by the Office of War Information and published in 1946.[1] This essay in turn is the result of my own "Assignment: Japan Anthropology" in which Benedict figures prominently as an omnipresent ancestral spirit. It is the latest of several attempts over the past twenty-five years to review postwar trajectories of Japan Anthropology in the United States.[2] Taking a clue from the Victorian explorer-writer Isabella Bird, who titled her travelogue *Unbeaten Tracks in Japan* (1880), I was challenged to compose a different sort of review.[3] Thus, rather than compose my essay as a summary of the specific (Anglophone) texts that embody "new" directions in Japan Anthropology, I have instead explored the "historical memory" active within that field, focusing my discussion and bibliography on sociocultural and historical dimensions of anthropology. It is in the process of surveying the repeating patterns of the representations of Japan that I refer the reader to specific texts,

---

* I wish to thank Helen Hardacre for inviting me to compose this essay on Japan Anthropology. I benefited from the discussion following my presentation of a rough draft of this essay on 21 March 1996 at the Edwin O. Reischauer Institute of Japanese Studies, Harvard University. In addition to thanking my Harvard colleagues for their feedback, I wish to thank Robert J. Smith for reading that draft and Celeste Brusati for her many critical readings of this essay. Of course, the argument developed in this essay is my own. Finally, my thanks to Ms. Gesine Bottomley and the library staff of the Wissenschaftskolleg (Institute for Advanced Study), Berlin, for their kind assistance.

[1] Translated into Japanese soon after its publication, the eighth edition in that language was released in 1952. It was also reprinted in English in 1989 (Boston: Houghton Mifflin) with a forward by Ezra Vogel, author of the controversial book *Japan as Number One* (1979).

[2] John Bennett (1970), Japan Foundation (1988), William W. Kelly (1991), Edward Norbeck and Susan Parman (1970), David Plath and Robert Smith (1992), Takao Sofue (1960, 1970, 1992), Patricia Steinhoff (1995), and Mariko Tamanoi (1990).

[3] Isabella Bird (1973 [1880]).

emphasizing those produced since 1990, for they are not covered in state-of-the-field reports to date. My essay also differs from existing reviews in that I incorporate information about doctoral dissertations and conference papers (presented at the annual meetings of the American Anthropological Association), two types of texts which, theoretically, both reflect and respond more directly to trends in the discipline of anthropology. Because the general subject of my review is "American" Anthropology, I include at the outset a brief consideration of the dominant perception of that field today. This also provides a framework for locating when and where Japan enters the field as a site for the ongoing development of anthropological theory.

The title of my essay is borrowed from Paula Giddings's book, *When and Where I Enter: The Impact of Black Women on Race and Sex in America* (1984). Giddings undertook to assess and demonstrate the impact black women have made on both ideas and actual relations of race, sex, and gender, rather than the reverse. Similarly, I have interpreted my primary assignment as a matter of assessing the impact—or lack thereof – of Japan on the development of anthropological theory. Like the "American" automobile, "American" Anthropology today is a transnational phenomenon, no longer easily distinguished as cultural to British Anthropology's social. The influence of European social scientists and culture critics is especially obvious—currently, the work of Michel Foucault stands out in this regard just as the structuralist theory of Lévi-Strauss informed the shape of American (sociocultural) Anthropology in the 1970s. Nevertheless, as I discuss, the work of an American woman, Ruth Benedict, has reverberated in the manner of a basso continuo through American anthropological studies of Japan ever since the publication of *The Chrysanthemum and the Sword* in 1946. I use "American" in reference to an institutional nexus rather than as an isolable thing in itself; I use it to identify dissertations produced not by American citizens but for American universities, and conference papers delivered at the annual meetings of the American Anthropological Association.[4]

---

[4] In the same spirit and in the interest of informing the community of readers about important Anglophone works recently published in the field of Japan Anthropology in general, I have included references to scholarship on Japan by a range of international scholars. Among the edited volumes (not cited in Kelly, 1991) which serve as useful guides and references to a broad range of anthro-

Anthropology as Entropy

Transnational or not, anthropology in the United States today was recently described, in a 1994 review, as a "discipline in a stage of disintegration and fragmentation into myriad subdisciplines, subspecialities, and interest groups."[5] Many colleagues may see their own departments in that description, and indeed, volatile departmental politics and disciplinary transformations are often conflated in internecine endgame scenarios. These are, after all, lean and hungry times. The question remains, however, as to whether the *discipline* of anthropology itself is disintegrating into a myriad of subspecialities, or whether *departments* of anthropology are fragmenting into a myriad of discordant and incompatible interest groups which are perceived as subspecialties. Thus, discipline and department must be distinguished for analytical purposes.

The compromised interpersonal dynamics which characterize many anthropology departments can be attributed in part to the rather crude market forces accompanying the corporatizing university which deform collegial behavior and erode professional courtesy. This unfortunate trend has emerged irrespective of sex, gender, sexuality, ethnicity, and so forth, which, over the past two decades, singly and collectively have complicated the social texture of departments—for the better, in my view. But the characterization of the discipline itself as in a stage of disintegration would appear to be informed by a notion of history as entropy—as an inevitable dissipation from an earlier, more integral state. Sherry Ortner for example, begins her famous article "Theory in Anthropology since the Sixties," published a decade ago, with the sober pronouncement (after Eric Wolf) that "the field of anthropology is coming apart":

> The field appears to be a thing of shreds and patches, of individuals and small coteries pursuing disjunctive investigations and talking mainly to themselves....Although anthropology was never actually unified in the sense of adopting a single shared paradigm, there was at least a period when there were a few large categories of theoretical

---

pological interest in Japan are those by Harumi Befu and Josef Kreiner, eds. (1992); Adriana Boscaro, Franco Gatti, and Massimo Raveri, eds. (1990); Roger Goodman and Kirsten Refsing, eds. (1992); and Amy Heinrich, ed. (1997).

[5] Paula Rubel and Abraham Rosman (1994): 335; see also Sherry Ortner (1984): 126-27.

affiliation, a set of identifiable camps or schools, and a few simple epithets one could hurl at one's opponents. Now there appears to be an apathy of spirit....[6]

Ortner acknowledges that anthropology was never a unitary discipline and yet seems to share Wolf's nostalgia for a "shared discourse, a shared set of terms to which all practitioners address themselves, a shared language we all, however idiosyncratically, speak."[7]

The notion of history as entropy and the operation of a willful nostalgia are mutually constitutive; nostalgia is not just a sentiment provoked by the perception of fragmentation and loss, it also a rhetorical practice, used by the right and the left alike, through which to recuperate wholeness, spontaneity, energy, and community. As both a mnemonic and a rhetorical practice, nostalgia retrieves from the past an authentic, original, and stable referent around which to reconstitute an unstable present. Of course, the particular configuration of this particular past is itself a product of mnemonic and textual strategies[8]—a composite of selective memories and practices separated out from their messy milieux.

Ortner conjures up a vision of a more integral past which she then recuperates as an antidotal prescription for the future health of the discipline. She points to the emergence since the eighties of a general, unified "practice theory" which, in her view, provides a desirable theoretical agenda for the nineties and beyond.[9] For Ortner, practice theory amalgamates as well as surpasses the limitations of prior—but actually coeval – theoretical schools or approaches of symbolic anthropology, cultural ecology, structural Marxism, and political economy. She acknowledges feminist anthropology only in a footnote, ostensibly due to a lack of space, as one of the primary contexts in which practice theory has been developing.[10] Whether consciously or unconsciously, more than spatial logistics may have influenced the exclusion of feminist anthropology from Ortner's review. Because feminist theory challenges the ideological underpinnings of anthropological concepts

---

[6] Eric Wolf (1980), E9, cited in Ortner, ibid., 126.
[7] Ortner, ibid., 126.
[8] Janice Doane and Devon Hodges (1987), 8.
[9] Sharon Stephens (1989), 75.
[10] Ortner (1984), 145 n. 15.

and theories to date, it therefore is not and cannot be part of the integral past which is invoked in the nostalgic rhetoric bemoaning the dissipation of anthropology and urging its recuperation through a unified theory.

As others have noted, also missing from Ortner's masterly review is the importance of grounding theoretical prescriptions in particular places, such as Japan, insofar as practices are locally enacted.[11] Arjun Appadurai, for example, observed that although the idea of culture as a "*local* dimension of human behavior is a tenacious and widespread assumption," there is a dearth of "systematic [analyses] of locality, as a conceptual issue, and of place, as the empirical counterpart to it."[12] How certain places—Bali as opposed to Japan, for instance—are endowed with conceptual and theoretical significance is another matter which I address further on.

Something Crystal[13]

There is at least one other way of interpreting the historical trajectory of the discipline of anthropology that both avoids ensnarement in the entropy-nostalgia loop and accommodates coeval theoretical approaches and their application and refinement in diverse places. Instead of describing American anthropology today as a "discipline in a stage of disintegration and fragmentation," one might describe anthropology in constructive terms as a resilient and plastic discipline of expanding objective referents and multiplying discursive potentialities.

The image of expansion and multiplication I have in mind is that of crystallization: namely, the ongoing formation of a multifaceted body of knowledge(s). "Multifaceted" suggests a body of knowledge that is historical and collective without being unitary, while "fragmented" alludes to the rupture of a form unified in the past. (This is an important distinction.) Moreover, crystals form in saturated solutions, a rather neat way of imagining the differ-

---

[11] Cf. Stephens (1989).
[12] Arjun Appadurai (1986): 356.
[13] The subheading is a pun on the *Nantonaku Kurisutaru* (Something Crystal), an award-winning novel cum guidebook by Tanaka Yasuo about vapid Tokyo yuppies and their patterns of conspicuous consumption.

ent, coeval configurations of knowledge emerging constantly in a rich brew—a space-time manifold—of histories, places, sites, theories, methods, practices, and interpretations. These ingredients can also be conceptualized as the strings—which are, ideally, braided – around which a crystal grows.

While drafting this essay, I happened to read a review by the film critic Stuart Klawans of the movie "12 Monkeys," a big-budget Hollywood remake of the 1962 film, "La Jetée"—"a black and white fantasy about memory, loss and the intersection of public and private catastrophe."[14] In a description that captures my use of crystallization with reference to the totality of anthropology, Klawans writes that the script for "12 Monkeys" "uses 'La Jetée' as a string in a crystal; facet builds on facet, but you keep circling around the buried core of the source, which itself becomes like an obsessive memory."[15] I shall borrow the motifs of "time-travel" and "obsessive memory" as devices helpful in locating when, where, and how Japan entered the mainstream of postwar American anthropology.

For anthropologists such as myself who work in and on Japan, the image of a crystal calls to mind the wartime expression coined by military ideologues to beautify self-sacrifice and mass deaths in combat: *gyokusai*. *Gyokusai* literally means "jewel smashed."[16] It was precisely such baroque expressions and drastic acts that occasioned the Office of War Information to commission Ruth Benedict to write *The Chrysanthemum and the Sword*, in which she attempted to

> understand Japanese habits of thought and emotion and the patterns into which these habits fell....The Japanese were the most alien enemy the United States had ever fought in an all-out struggle. In no other war with a major foe had it been necessary to take into account such exceedingly different habits of acting and thinking....We had to understand their behavior in order to cope with it.[17]

---

[14] Stuart Klawans (1996): 34.
[15] Ibid.
[16] As John Dower explains (1986), "The expression derived from a line in the sixth-century Chinese history Chronicles of the Northern Ch'i, where it was stated that on matters of principle, the man of moral superiority would break his precious jade rather than compromise to save the roof tiles of his home" (231). "The conventional interpretation of *gyokusai* appears to have been that it was better to die gloriously, like a shattered gem, than to live meaninglessly, like a mundane roof tile" (352 n. 61).
[17] Benedict (1974 [1946]), 4 and 1.

Earlier, in 1943, anthropologist John Embree published *The Japanese* as part of the Smithsonian's War Background Studies series. This was followed by *The Japanese Nation* in 1945. Benedict cites the latter along with Embree's more well-known ethnography, *Suye Mura* (1939), but Embree himself is conspicuously absent from her acknowledgments. Embree too directed his wartime studies toward better understanding and determining Japanese attitudes and behavior, but whereas Benedict sought to explain "the Japanese" in terms of a timeless cultural profile fabricated from fragments of data, Embree (1945) focused on providing a socio-historical and ethnographic "context for the interpretation of the behavior of Japanese and some basis for an understanding of future developments in Japan."

In a nutshell, Benedict's intellectual project was one of selective incorporation and containment, and Embree's one of linear unfolding. She collapsed past and present, and fused shreds and patches of data in formulating a unique and timeless janusian core (aka the "chrysanthemum" and the "sword") that was "the Japanese" cultural personality. He, on the other hand, acknowledged the effects of historical transformations and political ideologies in shaping particular configurations of individual and collective behavior without denying altogether the continuity of certain cultural patterns. Writing against national character studies, Embree historicized his portrayal of Japan and questioned

> the validity of using culture patterns which determine individual behavior within a social group as an "explanation" for national and international socio-economic-political developments....[A] summary (even when accurate) of a nation's citizens' behavior traits...does not provide a magic explanation for a nation's aggressive warfare whether it be Japanese, British, American, or Russian.[18]

I do not wish to simply cast Benedict as the "bad guy" and Embree as the "good guy"—the methods of both are equally problematic, although Benedict's work has occupied more mnemonic space in American anthropology. Rather, I have invoked Ancestors Benedict and Embree for two basic reasons. First, their work, but especially Benedict's, might usefully be regarded as constituting the historical—perhaps even obsessive—memory shaping the practice of Japan Anthropology in the United States since the end of World

---

[18] John Embree (1950): 443.

War II. Second, it is through their efforts that Japan first entered the mainstream of American anthropology as a contested discourse on, simultaneously, Japanese culture, ethnographic representation, and anthropological theory, especially with respect to the pros and cons of National Character Studies and of the Culture and Personality school. One might even argue that the 1940s was the only period (thus far) in which Japan was the place of and for mainstream anthropological debates and controversy. Whatever the case, Japanese imperialist designs in Asia and the Pacific, and the attack on Pearl Harbor; the Axis Alliance; the internment of Japanese Americans; and the atomic bombing of Hiroshima and Nagasaki followed by the largely American occupation of Japan, were all events which helped to overdetermine the salience of Japan as a particularly rich and controversial site of and for anthropological inquiry in the 1940s.

What about today? Although the two nation-states are no longer fighting each other in a "hot" war, it remains the case that Japan is of vital interest to the United States on every conceivable level, from the geopolitical to the gustatory. Americans had unprecedented exposure to Japan during the war and subsequent Occupation, and today Japan is a ubiquitous presence as a dominant economic power. I am not alone in wondering why Japan, unlike, say, Bali or Morocco or Oaxaca, Mexico, is not thus one of the cultural areas of choice, or "prestige zones,"[19] represented in the development of anthropological theory and in the areal spread of anthropology departments. To reframe the question in terms of my metaphor of crystallization: what has happened to the Japan string?

The existence of prestige zones has partly to do with the distance from current affairs of anthropological theorizing, and partly to do with the colonial history of Euro-American anthropology and the canonical emphasis since the nineteenth century on the cultures of peoples of color with a history of domination by "the West." (For largely the same reason Europe and North America are still underrepresented in anthropology.) But Japan confounds the simple binarism informing the construction of Anthropology's Other: it was never a colony of "the West," and in the first half of this century, Japan occupied the ambivalent position of an anti-

---

[19] Lila Abu-Lughod (1989): 279.

colonial colonizer, although its ambiguity in this regard was overshadowed in the United States first by its status as absolute enemy and later by its unconditional surrender in 1945. Moreover, the discipline of anthropology in Japan was itself facilitated if not motivated by Japanese colonialism in Asian and Pacific Rim countries. The rhetorical question thus arises: Is Japan, like Europe and the United States, somehow perceived as too much like "us" to be a worthwhile subject of anthropological inquiry?

In mulling over the implications of this state of affairs, it occurred to me that perhaps some—or many—people believe that there is nothing left to learn about Japan, or nothing really new and interesting—apart from gee-whiz factoids about rampant consumerism, such as the price in square centimeters of Ginza real estate, or the number of $500 musk melons sold during one of the two annual gift-giving periods. Perhaps they believe that Ruth Benedict said it all: namely, that despite their hi-tech veneer, the Japanese are a people unified in their confidence in hierarchy, whose public acts are regulated by shame, and who put a premium on cleanliness, education, and self-discipline. Ironically, Benedict never went to Japan nor did she know the language. Yet, she proceeded to construct "cultural regularities" from fragmentary data, including novels, movies, interviews with interned Japanese Americans, and the small—described by Benedict as "vast"—corpus of existing scholarly literature on Japan.[20] I do not wish to diminish Benedict's formidable anthropological skills and scholarly legacy, but by the same token, neither do I want to diminish the consequences of her work. In a sense, Benedict made getting to know Japan look too easy, and the Japan she profiled seemed all too knowable: once inscrutable, the Japanese were suddenly crystal clear.

Embree did not attempt to encapsulate Japanese cultural history within a formula, although he acknowledged the persistence of certain cultural practices and attitudes, and his books are certainly very formulaic in terms of their organization.[21] Although

---

[20] Benedict (1974 [1946]), 6.

[21] It is instructive in this connection to compare the matter-of-fact Table of Contents in Embree's *The Japanese Nation*: Historical Background, Modern Economic Bases, Government Structure, Social Class System, Family and Household, Religion, etc., with Benedict's more evocative and psychological headings in *The Chrysanthemum and the Sword*: Taking One's Proper Station, Repaying One-

both Benedict and Embree constitute the braided memory of Japan Anthropology, Benedict's bold bricolage has been far more influential in shaping people's image of Japan than has been either Embree's rather dry, methodical ethnography or his sharp critiques of national character studies.[22]

I believe that the easy and monolithic knowability of Japan construed from *The Chrysanthemum and the Sword* is fundamentally related to the double agenda of that book. A didactic book, *The Chrysanthemum and the Sword* was as much an attempt to explain a hitherto inscrutable Japan to a hostile American audience as it was an effort to evince and highlight American national character against the foil of Japan. Benedict's humane objective with her double agenda was to encourage Americans, dizzy from propaganda proclaiming the Japanese a "most alien enemy," to see the Japanese as human too. To this end she positioned each people as the mirror image of the other. Benedict declared that "[t]he arc of life in Japan is plotted in opposite fashion to that in the United States": whereas Americans increase their freedom of choice during the course of their lives, "the Japanese rely on maximizing the restraints upon [them]."[23] In Benedict's mirror, the Japanese reliance on hierarchy is reflected back as the American faith in freedom (43). Whereas "sensitivity about trifles" is virtuous behavior in Japan, it is recognized as "neurotic" and "adolescent" in the United States (108). If the Japanese "play up suicide," Americans "play up crime" (167). And whereas in Japan performance deteriorates under competition, in the United States competition stimulates performance, yielding socially desirable results (153). These are but a few of the oppositional representations of "the Japanese" and "the Americans" developed by Benedict, who concluded that in Japanese life, "the contradictions, as they seem to us, are as deeply based in their view of life as our uniformities are in ours (197)."

Like her colleague Clyde Kluckhohn (1949), Benedict used anthropology as a mirror held before us to allow and encourage

---

In-Thousandth, Clearing One's Name, The Dilemma of Virtue, Self-Discipline, The Child Learns, etc.

[22] The 1982 publication by Robert J. Smith and Ella Lury Wiswell (the widow of John Embree) based on Wiswell's field notes of 1935-1936, adds flesh to Embree's somewhat skeletal account of everyday life in Suye-mura.

[23] Benedict (1974 [1946]), 253-54 and 254. Subsequent references in text.

a better understanding of ourselves through the study of others.[24] But a mirror is not an inert device and can be deployed as an agent in the resolution of difference and opposition. In the bamboo mirror held before Americans, Japanese national character was rendered intelligible as American national character the other way around. The potential for solipsism should be obvious; the apparent wholeness of the mirrored image can deflect recognition of the need to learn more about Japan on terms relevant to the dynamic and intertwined histories of localities and subjective cultural formations and practices within that country. As Embree noted in his 1947 review of *The Chysanthemum and the Sword*, the only way to begin to really know the Japanese people

> is to accumulate comparative data on the basis of a series of field studies in different areas of the culture....So far these are lacking for Japan.[25]

Today, ethnographies based on fieldwork in Japan are certainly more plentiful than in 1947, but I will argue that anthropologists since then have, in one way or another, continued to work both through and against a conventionalized conception of Japan as enantiomorphic with the United States—and by extension, with "the West." The ever-growing anthropological literature on "the Japanese self," for example, works both to locate "indigenous" constructions of selfhood and to distinguish the Japanese from the American (or Western) self. Similarly, and not surprisingly, "mirror" and "mask" are popular words in titles of books on Japan, and the objective of revealing, unmasking, or unwrapping the "real" Japan has motivated many a Japan scholar.[26] Ian Buruma, the saucy Dutch journalist with a penchant for sensationaliz-

---

[24] Cf. Helen Mears (1948).

[25] Embree (1947): 246.

[26] In this connection, Kelly (1991) has remarked that "Selfhood is a field of argument among multiple, competing, and shifting cultural representations, and the best of these recent studies underscore this. Where they have stressed the ideological construction and institutional nexus of self-expression, they succeed in problematizing the relation between cultural construct and social praxis. Where they remain cast in broad and ahistorical terms, they are dangerously essentialist and suspiciously Orientalist" (403). Among the most recent studies of Japanese selfhood are by Jane Bachnik and Charles Quinn, Jr., eds. (1994), Wimal Dissanayake, ed. (1996), Emiko Ohnuki-Tierney (1993), Alan Roland (1988), and Nancy Rosenberger, ed. (1992). See also the relevant sources up to 1991 cited in Kelly. Joy Hendry (1993) writes of Japan as the epitome of "wrapping," which she describes as a "veritable cultural template" and a "cultural design."

ing the prurient and political extremes of Japanese society, has capitalized on the salience of both tropes: his 1984 book *Japanese Mirror* was republished a year later under the title *Behind the Mask*.

One last factor to consider with respect to Benedict's central role in facilitating the knowability of "the Japanese" concerns the influence of *The Chrysanthemum and the Sword* in Japan, where it was published in translation in 1948. In their 1953 review of the critical reception of the book among Japanese scholars, John Bennett and Michio Nagai point out that,

> [i]t should be understood that the translation of *The Chrysanthemum and the Sword* has appeared in Japan during a period of intense national self-examination—a period during which Japanese intellectuals and writers have been studying the sources and meaning of Japanese history and character, in one of their perennial attempts to determine the most desirable course of Japan's development.[27]

In recent years, the Japanese social critic and philosopher Aoki Tamotsu has suggested that *The Chrysanthemum and the Sword* "helped invent a new tradition for postwar Japan."[28] Benedict's homogenizing and timeless portrait of "the Japanese" added momentum to the growing interest in "ethnic nationalism" in Japan, evident in the hundreds of ethnocentric *nihonjinron*—treatises on Japaneseness—published since the postwar period.[29] As I have argued elsewhere (1997, 1998a), the obsession today in Japan with cultural distinction mirrors a similar obsession with internationalization; in fact, the two obsessions can be understood as enantiomorphic: that is, the same impulse the other way around.

My point in this digression on the reception in Japan of *The Chrysanthemum and the Sword* is to suggest that despite criticisms of Benedict's failure to discriminate among historical developments and "differing institutional contexts of data,"[30] Japanese culture critics were especially interested in her attempt to portray the whole or total structure (*zentai kōzō*) of Japanese culture—a goal which, Bennett and Nagai note, had been "common enough in certain branches of Japanese humanistic studies."[31] In short, Benedict's

---

[27] John Bennett and Michio Nagai (1953): 404.
[28] Aoki Tamotsu (1991 [1990]): 30-52. See also Kevin Doak (1996): 77-103.
[29] For a thorough analysis of *nihonjinron*, see Harumi Befu (1993): 107-35. A recent dissertation on the fetishization of "women's language" in *nihonjinron* is by Janet Kay Fair (1996).
[30] Bennett and Nagai (1953): 408.
[31] Ibid., 406.

totalizing ensemble of fragments reinforced and was reinforced by similar efforts on the part of her Japanese counterparts, for whom the widest and thickest line of difference lies between a unique Japan and the rest of the world (basically, "the West") as if both entities were internally coherent.[32] Thus, ongoing Japanese attempts to locate cultural uniqueness mirror the attempts of non-Japanese anthropologists, among others, to unmask, unwrap, and to otherwise reveal the authentic core or essence of Japanese society.

Paper Trails

Up to now, I have described the work of Embree and especially Benedict as a persistent memory shaping the postwar anthropology of Japan.[33] I now want to look more closely at the shape of Japan Anthropology in the United States. I shall focus briefly on two types of ethnographic production underrepresented in earlier reviews of the field: namely, doctoral dissertations and conference papers delivered at the annual meetings of the American Anthropological Association.[34] As I noted in the Introduction, these genres theoretically both reflect and respond to trends in the discipline.

If, as Ortner has claimed, anthropology is "coming apart," then Japan Anthropology must have missed the entropy train. As we shall see, postwar doctoral dissertations on Japan demonstrate a surprising amount of continuity and contiguity of topic, along with, as I have argued above, continuity in the general assumptions and characterizations of Japanese culture and peoples irrespective of an author's theoretical framework or orientation. There are of course some exceptions—exceptions which, I shall venture to generalize, are contingent upon several (necessarily) interrelated factors.

---

[32] Cf. Aoki (1991), 31-32.

[33] Robert J. Smith (1989) has given this memory a genealogical twist by his reference to American anthropologists of Japan as Benedict's "children and grandchildren" (360-74).

[34] I elected not to peruse the abstracts of the Association for Asian Studies (AAS) annual meetings. Many Japan anthropologists present their work at that international venue in addition to the AAA. The programs and abstracts of the AAS are also a useful index of the current interests of Japan anthropologists.

First, perhaps the most important of these factors are reading and speaking fluency in Japanese and a contingent effort to utilize information from a diverse number of individuals and groups (who are not presumed a priori to represent "the Japanese" voice), as well as from a range of Japanese texts. The relative dearth and narrow scope of the Japanese-language materials utilized in a significant proportion of Japan Anthropology dissertations (and published works) is dismaying, especially given the high premium placed in Japan, past and present, on writing and the generation of documents on every conceivable subject. Without sufficient efforts to broaden the range and scope of Japanese-language materials utilized, patterns of Japanese culture canonized in the Anglophone literature can be accorded, almost by default, the status of truisms which are then reproduced by successive generations of Japan anthropologists. It is not that these patterns and truisms are wrong or misleading per se, but that they should be subjected now and then to what is known colloquially as a "reality check." If there is one gatekeeping concept that is unequivocally appropriate for Japan scholars to employ it ought to be "bibliophilia": the long cultural history of literacy and enormity and diversity of textual production in Japan are reasons compelling enough to demand (greater) attention to bibliography. In the context of bibliography, one type of "reality check" would involve exploring the multifarious ways in which a topical issue, say, organ transplantation, has been debated among sundry constituencies, as opposed to presenting unproblematically "the Japanese" position.[35]

Other factors (also unconnected to one's ethnicity or nationality) which are instrumental in generating research that works to complicate the received picture of Japan include extended periods of residence in Japan and regular long and short return visits; a familiarity with history, the product and process, and concomitant attention to the historical vicissitudes of social and cultural formations; and, ideally, a familiarity with a wide range of idea-generating literatures outside the purview of Japanese studies.

What are the dominant topical rubrics that characterize postwar dissertations in Japan Anthropology? The vagaries of family life and work; rural lifeways; modes of urbanization; schools, day-

---

[35] In this connection, see the pioneering work of Helen Hardacre (1994), Margaret Lock and Christine Honde (1990), and Emiko Ohnuki-Tierney (1994).

care centers, and strategies of socialization in education; types of language and linguistic patterns; and religious affiliations and practices are the overarching rubrics for research sites and topoi that have predominated since 1947, the year of the first postwar dissertation in Japan Anthropology.[36] Japanese management practices and business culture emerged as popular topics in the mid-1960s – the so-called miracle sixties, when the Japanese GNP registered double digit growth. Similarly, a number of dissertations written in the 1980s shared an interest in exploring the by then highly visible and tangible preoccupation, of certain Japanese groups and institutions, with the politics of tradition and nostalgia in urban (and urbanizing) areas.[37] Another salient development within the corpus of postwar Japan Anthropology has been the increased—if still inadequate – analytical attention paid to the sex-gender system, although as I discuss further on, much rigorous research remains to be done on the complex, norm-bending operations of this system. The various theoretical approaches employed in the interrogation and analysis of these longstanding and emerging topics alike have often, but not always, followed general trends in the discipline as a whole, depending on the autonomy or acumen of the student and/or the authoritarian disposition of her or his chair and professors.

As an aside, with respect to chairs and professors, of the seventy-three faculty members listed in the *1995 AAA Guide to Departments* who indicated some expertise in Japan, twenty-seven (37 percent) are female, fifteen (55 percent) of whom have tenure, and forty-six (63 percent) male, thirty-eight (83 percent) of whom are tenured. The most senior anthropologist earned his doctorate in 1946, the most junior earned hers in 1993. Of the female faculty, eighteen (67 percent of the total number) earned their doctorates in the 1980s and 1990s.[38] The statistics show that post-

---

[36] The first postwar dissertation was by Robert Spencer (1947).

[37] Among those who wrote dissertations on this topic which were sooner or later reconfigured as books are Theodore Bestor (1989), Marilyn Ivy (1995), and Jennifer Robertson (1994 [1991]).

Dissertations on this topic continue to be written, as exemplified by Mikako Iwatake (1993), Sug-In Kweon (1994), John Nelson (1993), Scott Schnell (1993), and Karen Smyers (1993).

[38] Several new Japan Anthropology positions have been filled since the 1995 guide was published, and some of the new faculty hired earned their doctorates as late as 1996.

war Japan Anthropology was a virtual male bastion up to the mid-1980s, when an almost equal number of female and male faculty earned their doctorates—which is not to suggest that the playing field is now level. One would need to factor in such data as the number of years between earning the doctorate and being hired, the characteristics of the employing institution (two-year or four-year college, university, etc.), years to tenure, and so forth in order better to interpret these numbers and percentages, an undertaking not central to the objective of this essay.

According to my figures compiled from the CD ROM listing of dissertation abstracts, between 1947 and 1995 a total of 239 persons (120 women and 119 men) submitted dissertations to American universities which were catalogued under the subject heading "Anthropology and Japan, Japanese."[39] I noticed a striking demographic pattern in the group of dissertation writers from 1989 onward: there was a precipitous growth in the number of Japanese students from Japan graduating with doctorates in Japan Anthropology from American universities. Forty-one, or 35.3 percent, of the 116 graduates from 1989 to 1995 were Japanese, twenty-nine (about 71 percent) of whom were female. This pattern peaked in 1993, when twelve Japanese, nine of whom were female, earned doctorates in anthropology. In comparison, only twelve anthropology doctorates—18 percent of the total—were earned by Japanese students at American universities between 1945 and 1988.[40]

Suffice it to say that these numbers reflect a combination of several recent, intersecting developments: the increasing strength of the yen relative to the dollar; the growing presence of independent (and mostly female) twenty-somethings in Japan; and the

---

[39] Dissertations by women began to outnumber those by men from roughly 1990, although 1992 was an exception: that year, only three of the eleven doctorates were earned by women.

A caveat: the dissertation abstracts entry "Anthropology and Japan, Japanese" does not correspond exactly to dissertations produced for actual anthropology departments. Also classified under that rubric are dissertations from other departments having anthropological content.

Although I tried to limit my statistics to anthropology dissertations proper, they doubtless include some theses from other departments. Robert J. Smith (1989) notes that 119 dissertations in Japan Anthropology were completed between 1950 and 1988, but does not indicate the source of this figure.

[40] Admittedly, these figures, and especially the pre-eighties figures, are tentative as my criteria for establishing Japanese identity and probable Japanese citizenship were based on a combination of names and personal knowledge.

intensifying hunger of American institutions for the "real" money of students who pay their own tuition—and the majority of students from Japan fit that description. Among the most popular topics pursued by the Japanese contingent of dissertation writers were self-consciously selected "roots quest"-related projects, including explorations of self cum cultural identity and gendered family roles, and the investigation of programs to resocialize children and adolescents who have lived abroad for many years. One might even entertain the possibility that the presence of a critical mass of Japanese graduate students in the U.S. may consolidate further the dominant tendency for anthropologists of Japan on both sides of the Pacific Ocean to mirror each other's attempts to reveal the "real" Japan.[41]

In so saying, I am not suggesting that postwar, and especially recent scholarship on Japan paints a cultural portrait that is invariant and homogeneous. Far from it; that portrait has been complicated by the proliferation in the number of both dominant and marginal sites, situations, and actors (including the ethnographer), in part due to theoretical attention in anthropology to such matters of late. Consequently, the archetypal peasant of Embree's *Suye Mura* is now many ethnographic subjects, including weekday white-collar worker and weekend farmer; local tourist attraction and custodian of the landscape of nostalgia; migrant worker; dispensible day laborer in the automotive and nuclear energy industries; political activist; and victim of industrial pollution, to name some of the more conspicuous ones.[42]

Nevertheless, some scholars have argued that Benedict's unitary portrait of "the Japanese" remains the backdrop in front of which these new actors have debuted and back into which they are reabsorbed. This was a charge that motivated the publication in 1988 of a volume titled *The Other Japan*, identified as a book "about the other side of the story"; a book about "the unresolved conflicts beneath the smooth surface of managed capitalism in

---

[41] Cf. Bennett and Nagai (1953).

[42] See, for example, the sources cited in Kelly (1991). Among those relevant sources published from 1991 to the present, and/or not cited by Kelly, are David Apter (1984); *Bulletin of Concern Asian Scholars*, ed. (1988 [1987]); Ivy (1995); Kamata Satoshi (1982); Yukiko Kawahara (1990); Shizuko Oshima (1989); Jennifer Robertson (1994 [1991], 1997, 1998a). Among the relevant dissertations completed between 1990 and 1996 are: Junko Goto (1993); Richard Hara (1994); Sug-In Kweon (1994); Ellen Schattschneider (1996a); and Martin Weiss (1996).

Japan today."[43] The title of and rationale for this book alerts us to the catch-22 confounding the matter of representation in Japan Anthropology: it seems that cultural portraits contrary to the tenaciously normative template constructed by Benedict and subsequently reproduced can only always be "alternative" or "other" as opposed to unacknowledged facets of the complex, composite, and integrated whole of "Japanese culture." This crisis of representation, as it were, has as much to do with the dominant mythos *in* Japan of a homogenous society as it does with the perception *of* Japan as knowable in opposition to "the West," and more specifically, the United States. In this connection, Arjun Appadurai has argued that the "anthropology of complex civilizations...exists in a peculiar form...[in which] a few simple theoretical handles become metonyms and surrogates for the civilization or society as a whole; hierarchy in India, honor-and-shame in the circum-Mediterranean, filial piety in China...."[44] As I see it, paradox and contradiction are two generic gatekeeping concepts that have both opened up and limited anthropological theorizing about Japan since *The Chrysanthemum and the Sword*.

The Bamboo Mirror

As a prelude to redressing the crisis of representation in Japan Anthropology, let me offer a more specific examination of the modal Japanese cultural personality first portrayed by Benedict. It was a Janus-faced thing. Her bamboo mirror revealed a version of Japan that was the United States the other way around. Whereas the Americans operated on the basis of consistent and indivisible moral principles (part and parcel of the allegedly irreducible so-called Western "I"), the Japanese were contradictory and

---

[43] *Bulletin of Concerned Asian Scholars*, ed. (1988 [1987]), 3. The journal, *Bulletin of Concerned Asian Scholars* (*BCAS*) is an excellent source for articles "that challenge the accepted formulas for understanding Asia, the world, and ourselves," as noted on the inside cover of every issue. *AMPO* and *positions: east asia cultures critique* are similarly oriented if differently conceptualized journals. Generally speaking, the former, along with *BCAS*, tends to deal more directly, empirically, and analytically with practices and policies of social, economic, and political consequence, while the latter tends to offer articles of a more "current" literary critical and critical theoretical bent.

[44] Appadurai (1986): 357.

opportunistic (and possessors of a so-called relational, shifting "I").

> The Japanese are, to the highest degree, both aggressive and unaggressive, both militaristic and aesthetic, both insolent and polite, rigid and adaptable, submissive and resentful of being pushed around, loyal and treacherous, brave and timid, conservative and hospitable to new ways.[45]

This litany of oppositions would seem to be reinforced by certain dyadic subject positions and concepts, namely *uchi/soto* (inside/outside), *tatemae/honne* (public face/private feelings), *ura/omote* (back/front, inner/outer), frequently invoked today by "ordinary" Japanese and anthropologists of Japan alike to explain the dynamics of interpersonal and social relations. These specific dyads are not noted by Benedict. Nevertheless, in a passage that also illustrates my argument about the discursive construction of Japan as a mirror-image of "the West," one scholar suggests that Benedict's

> interpretation of the importance of personal ties within Japanese culture initiated Western recognition of Japanese *uchi/soto* "in-group/out-group" relationships, and this recognition has been expanded and refined by anthropologists (Nakane 1970; Lebra 1976), psychologists (DeVos 1985; Roland 1988), political scientists (Pye 1985), and others, drawing together much of Japanese behavior that is otherwise inexplicable (at least from a Western perspective).[46]

The perception today of an ur-concept of in-group/out-group in *The Chrysanthemum and the Sword* seems to be a byproduct of the sociological adaptation of Benedict's developmental psychological model in which Japanese character appears as a "deeply implanted dualism."[47] As key, dyadic sociological concepts, *uchi/*

---

[45] Benedict (1974 [1946]), 2. Benedict saw her task as one to find or fashion a cultural Rosetta stone that would enable her and all Americans to decode and understand the paradoxical Japanese. See especially her first chapter, "Assignment: Japan," 1-19.

[46] Patricia Wetzel (1994), 74.

[47] Benedict (1974 [1946]), 291. See especially her chapter "The Child Learns" (253-98), in which the pattern of children's socialization and maturation also reads as a metaphor of and for Japanese national and cultural character.

Children's socialization and schooling remains one of the most prevalent topics in the general anthropological literature on Japan, and not a few ethnographers were able to observe and participate in the schools attended by their own children. Among the books not cited in William W. Kelly's "Directions in the Anthropology of Contemporary Japan" and/or which were published after 1991 are by Eyal Ben-Ari (1996), Gail Benjamin (1997), Catherine Lewis (1995), Lois Peak (1991), *soto, tatemae/honne,* and *ura/omote* are probably of postwar vintage. The scholarship on these dyads does not locate the historical juncture(s) where they emerged as critically and discursively salient patterns of Japanese social behavior. Rather, their explanatory validity notwithstanding, they tend to be treated as timeless axioms. It appears that Benedict's own, now canonized—even reified—set of oppositions derived from notions of the dualistic structure of "the Japanese" cultural personality already circulating among an Anglophone public as early as the 1890s. Witness how closely her litany of contradictory subject positions resembles that detailed by Eliza Scidmore in her travelogue cum commentary published in 1891:

> The Japanese are the enigma of this century; the most inscrutable, the most paradoxical of races. They and their outward surroundings are so picturesque, theatrical, and artistic that at moments they appear a nation of *poseurs*—all their world a stage, and all their men and women merely players; a trifling, superficial, fantastic people, bent on nothing but pleasing effects....To generalize, to epitomize is impossible; for they are so opposite and contradictory, so unlike all other Asiatic peoples, that analogy fails. They are at once the most sensitive, artistic, and mercurial of human beings, and the most impassible, conventional, and stolid; at once the most logical, profound, and conscientious, and the most irrational, superficial, and indifferent; at once the most stately, solemn, and taciturn, and the most playful, whimsical, and loquacious. While history declares them aggressive, cruel, and revengeful, experience proves them yielding, merciful, and gentle. The same centuries in which was devised the elaborate refinement of cha no yu saw tortures, persecutions, and battle-field butcheries unparalleled. The same men who spent half their lives in lofty meditation, in indicting poems, and fostering art, devoted the other half to gross pleasures, to hacking their enemies in pieces, and watching a hara kiri with delight. Dreaming, procrastinating, and referring all things to that mythical *mionichi* (tomorrow), they can yet amaze one with a wizard-like rapidity of action and accomplishment.[48]

Although and because the dyads noted earlier have acquired,

Thomas Rohlen and Gerald LeTendre, eds. (1996), James Shields, Jr. (1989), and David Shwalb and Barbara Shwalb, eds. (1996). See also Byung-Ho Chung (1992).

Among the most recent publications on Japanese education more generally are those by Kaori Okano (1993), Edward Beauchamp and James Vardaman, eds. (1994), and Thomas Rohlen and Gerald LeTendre, eds. (1996).

[48] Eliza Scidmore (1891), 369.

almost by default, the status of gatekeeping concepts (or truisms), it is all the more important that they be historicized and that their usages be investigated separately and collectively, over time and across space. Only by doing so can we complicate our understanding and calibrate our investigations of the vicissitudes of Japanese cultural history and contingent social practices. Another widely repeated, formulaic explanation for what Benedict identified as the deep dualism of "the Japanese" character is that the Japanese are both traditional and modern: in the words of a new book titled *Unmasking Japan Today*, Japan is characterized by "a dual structure where traditional values and modern practices co-exist."[49]

The same or similar sets of contradictions are also reproduced, if unevenly valenced, in a hefty percentage of the general literature on postwar Japan which has been categorized dichotomously under the rubrics Japan-bashing and Japan-apology. These generic categories themselves are often hypostatized in work that fits into neither camp.[50] For example, Robert J. Smith (1983) effectively mediates between harsh and Pollyanaish judgments of Japanese cultural formations and practices in positioning himself as a sensible ethnographer.

So, in addition to working through and against Benedict's now conventionalized conception of Japan as a mirror-image of the United States, Japan anthropologists also find themselves negotiating sets of oscillating contradictions.[51] For some, taking stock of, elaborating on, and even attempting to resolve these apparent contradictions and dyadic gatekeeping concepts have been overarching objectives. I have already cited the new book *Unmasking Japan Today* as one such example; another is the more nuanced and scholarly volume by Bachnik and Quinn (1994).[52] Lewis Austin's edited volume (1976) is also exemplary of the conception of Japan in terms of oppositions, as is Edward Norbeck's volume (1965) published ten years earlier. Norbeck, in fact, began his book with contrasting vignettes: "Japan is a land of jet airplanes..." and it is a "land where oxen plough rice paddies...and the average citizen...

---

[49] *1996 Catalogue* (1996), 36.

[50] William W. Kelly (1988), Ross Mouer and Yoshio Sugimoto (1986), and Kosaku Yoshino (1992). For a different perspective on the politics of "Japan bashing," see Norma Field (1993 [1991]).

[51] For example, William W. Kelly (1992).

[52] Recent dissertations on selfhood are by Karen Kelsky (1996c), Gordon Mathews (1993), and Eiko Tada (1991).

has never ridden in an airplane."[53] These apparently contradictory images allowed him to "express the familiar saying that Japan is a land of contrasts"; contrasts which "have grown rather than diminished as the years have passed."[54]

For Japanese and non-Japanese alike, "tradition" has represented and continues to represent a metaphysical place from which postwar progress—referred to as modernization, Americanization, and now internationalization—can be measured, in both senses of the term: estimated and regulated. Inspired in part by the "invention of tradition" scholarship of the 1980s, together with the tangible politics of nostalgia in Japan, several anthropologists have shown how "tradition" has been reified, by different agents with different agendas, as a place of nostalgic return and recuperation: the greater the perceived distance from a more unified past, the greater in turn the nostalgic impulse.[55] Likewise, "internationalization" has been scrutinized recently and its apparent contradictions and symbiotic relationship to "tradition" analyzed critically.[56]

Mainstreaming Japan

The postwar literature on Japan may be rife with negotiations of paradox and analyses of dyadic concepts, but anthropological theory today is virtually devoid of references to Japan. Twenty-five years ago John Bennett remarked that social research on Japan "has not yet made significant contributions to social and cultural theory,"[57] and it seems that Japan is still not regarded as an efficacious site for the development of anthropological theory—although it has served as a proving ground where numerous theories have been deployed in efforts to "unwrap" and "unmask" Japanese everyday practices.

As I see it, we Japan anthropologists need to attend more con-

---

[53] Edward Norbeck (1984 [1965]), 1.
[54] Ibid., 2.
[55] See the sources cited in note 37.
[56] See Amy Borovoy (1995), Seung-Mi Han (1995), Laura Hein and Ellen Hammond (1995), Karen Kelsky (1996b), Mark Lincicome (1993), David McConnell (1991), John Nelson (1993, 1996), Hiroshi Mannari and Harumi Befu, eds. (1983), Jennifer Robertson (1997, 1998a), and Stephen Vlastos, ed. (1998).
[57] John Bennett (1970), 11.

sciously and conscientiously to at least two simultaneous agendas in our work. First, we need to pay attention to and address and redress, as opposed to simply conform to, current issues and developments in anthropology, the discipline, and to thicken, layer, texture, and complicate our representations of Japan and Japanese peoples. Second, we need to emphasize "the vision thing"; that is, we need to exercise at least as much initiative and creative chutzpah as the Geertzs, Bourdieus, and Ortners in demonstrating the relevance of Japan to the processes of anthropological theorizing and modifying theory.

A third important agenda is a sustained analysis of the history of intersections of Japanese and Euro-American strategies of cultural critique. So, for example, instead of (or, at the very least, in addition to) superimposing a Freudian or Lacanian interpretive framework onto Japanese sexual and gendered practices past and present, one might fruitfully look at the history of sexology in Japan, or at the history of Freudian theory in Japan, and its adaptations and transformations there as well as in Europe and the United States. Locating and historicizing theory in this way would help to temper and moderate a tendency I have observed in certain recent monographs on Japan to use theory, sometimes in lieu of sufficient Japanese archival and empirical material, as a totalizing explanation, rather than as a reasonable conjecture resonant with specific historical circumstances in Japan, or as a guide for further investigations. Obviously, the mere invocation of a theory of practice is not a viable substitute for exploring and recording actual, everyday practices and collective activities in particular places and times.[58]

The annual meetings of the American Anthropological Association (AAA) have long been a forum where "Japan" can enter the mainstream of anthropological discourse. Generally, the papers presented at the AAA meetings tend to be formative and consequently embody a more diverse range of topical and theoretical material than do doctoral dissertations to date. At the 1994 meeting, for example, there were thirty-nine papers on or dealing with Japan but not a single "Japan" panel, although there were four "East Asia" panels. However, the following year, there were four specifically "Japan" panels and a total of fifty-three papers

---

[58] Cf. Ortner (1984), 158-59.

on Japan were delivered, a figure amounting to 15 percent of all AAA presentations that year. Of the four, only one panel aimed explicitly to position Japan as an illuminating site for the exploration of practices and processes with a view toward contributing to the development of anthropological theories, in this case on the subject of ritual.[59] (In so saying, I do not mean to suggest that the other "Japan" panels and papers fell short of this overall aim; rather, my point pertains to the *specifically articulated aim* of the panels.)

In 1994, the vast majority of AAA presentations on Japan were part of intercultural and international panels which dealt with such topics and thematic clusters as nationalism, gender, and tropes of kinship; the psychological interpretation of the body and sexuality; sexuality and fieldwork; lesbian and gay rights and communities; globalization; female religious practioners; family businesses; and cross-cultural differences in request and refusal.[60] The papers themselves ranged over many topics: colonialism, class consciousness, censorship and obscenity, transnationalism, motherhood, environmental destruction, suicide, schools and social discipline, women and the festishization of "the West," prostitution, and multiculturalism. The 1995 panels focused on, in addition to ritual practices, incest and sexual child abuse; the politics of land reclamation; Japanese linguistic diversity; political parties and hegemony; toxic waste and the politics of pollution; the politics of representation; changes in political ("fathers'") authority; life course; women's work; working class culture in Japan; and types of apprenticeship in Japan. Among the subjects explored in the individual papers were such "Japan" staples as women's speech, *uchi/soto* and domesticity, religious ritual, recreation, the figure of the emperor, gardens, minorities, death and mortuary rituals, Okinawa, and rituals of human reproduction, and several relatively newer anthropological concerns, such as the politics of museums and the operations of fandom. In addition, the subject of Japanese colonialism and empire-building has begun to receive some much needed if still very limited critical attention, as reflected in

---

[59] This was the panel titled, "Ritual Practice in the Formation, Negotiation, and Reconstitution of Community: Models from Japan."

[60] The East Asia panels dealt specifically with transnationalism and the global in the local, family businesses, and female religious practices.

several of the AAA papers delivered over the past three years. This nascent trend seems to be informed both by the blossoming interest in this subject in post-Shōwa Japan itself, and by a renewed interest among anthropologists in general in colonial legacies and neocolonial practices, although this new literature focuses mostly on Euro-American forms of colonialism.

The general pattern of a greater number of panels that are cross-cultural and not Japan-specific in focus has prevailed since at least 1968 (the earliest AAA data I was able to collect),[61] although the number of Japan papers delivered has increased steadily. One mainstreaming strategy would be the organization at the AAA meetings of "Japan" panels organized around issues and events that resonate with those in the so-called real world past and present, and which address focal trends in the discipline of anthropology. To have a Japan paper included in a panel on, say, fatherhood is important, but it is equally important to have a panel rethinking the category of "father" using a variety of cases and historical practices from Japan. To put this point more polemically: it is important but not enough to insert "the Japanese" perspective into an otherwise Eurocentric panel in order to achieve a speck of multicultural diversity—even though cross-cultural panels do help, ultimately, to diversify the sites of anthropological theorizing.

Mending the Smashed Jewel

Anthropologist Carol Vance has qualified, in reference to her research on gender and sexuality, that "[t]heory can only be developed through reference to an ever-expanding body of information, [which in turn is] made possible through more intensive use of historical [– and I would add, empirical –] material...."[62] How can Japan, in the double sense of a concrete, objective referent and a discursive formation, become a more obvious and cogent site for and source of anthropological theorizing? It seems to me that a crucial first step would involve two actions: first, making

---

[61] According to my research assistant, senior colleagues had disposed of early copies of the program and abstracts, and, following its recent move, the AAA could no longer locate its own collection of these materials.

[62] Carol Vance (1985), 18.

its monolithic knowability problematic, and second, decentering the more Eurocentric premises of anthropological theory.[63]

Gender is a very good place to start. The unstable relationship among sex, gender, and sexuality is a highly visible and salient subject in current anthropological and interdisciplinary theorizing that could be significantly transformed if Japanese practices past and present were brought into play. Another good place to start is the twinned subject of imperialism and colonialism. Once in play, "Japan" would be transformed and rendered less easily knowable, at least not by way of any overdetermined gatekeeping concepts (with the one exception of bibliophilia!). I would like to conclude this essay with a consideration of some topical issues and theoretical and methodological directions in which we might profitably move.

Many visitors to and scholars working in Japan are quite aware of the existence of a colorful and lively variety of gender identities and sexual practices, including some exploitative and abusive ones. Evidence of their existence pervades the mass media and streets of Tokyo and other cities alike. Although some writers have capitalized on the sensational and prurient dimensions of Japanese social institutions,[64] rigorous and grounded studies on these subjects are, unfortunately, few and far between. More often than not, the varied experiences of the female and male members of Japanese society continue to be underacknowledged and/or collapsed with dominant, naturalized gender ideals (for example, "the Japanese" housewife and "the Japanese" businessman).[65] But even as some anthropologists begin to challenge this stereotype, collectively they have tended to resist exploring gender identities and sexual practices that muddy the a priori image of uncompromised

---

[63] Cf. Michael Herzfeld (1987), 7.

[64] Some of these writers and their works include William Bohnaker (1990), Nicholas Bornoff (1991), Ian Buruma (1984, 1985), Boye De Mente (1966), and Karl Taro Greenfeld (1994).

[65] Recently, I received a letter from a prospective graduate student who has lived in Japan for several years, from which I shall quote, not to "prove" my point, but to underscore the problem: "...I noticed that my experiences and acquaintances did not reflect those described in most mainstream publications on the Japanese, and the salaryman/wise wife, loving mother models did not apply to anyone I knew. That is why at the time, I was so fascinated with Taro's [sic] [Karl Taro Greenfeld] *Speed Tribes*, although I realize that much of it is fabricated sensationalism." Letter from Vincent Fike, 26 November 1996.

heterosexuality whether inside or outside the institution of monogamous marriage (itself only a century old in Japan). With relatively few exceptions, the literature on so-called unconventional—but are they really?—gender identities and sexual practices is monopolized by callow and fleetingly sensationalistic "documentaries" and exposés of the "pink" underbelly of Japan, Inc.[66] The absence of a critical mass of unself-censored, rigorous, historically grounded scholarship on the relationship among sex, gender, and sexuality in Japan has left a huge space in the anthropological literature that has been colonized by journalists with an eye on the bestseller list. We need to know more about the salient discourses on gender and sexuality that emerged at different historical junctures in Japanese cultural history if we are to redress and reconfigure some of the more obfuscatory stereotypes of Japanese women and men—stereotypes of domestic and foreign creation alike.[67]

One of the more obvious solutions is to pay more attention to all the different venues in which gender identities and sexual practices figure centrally. Especially now that mass and popular cultural formations are being taken seriously in the academy, there is not even a limp argument to be made about the inappropriateness of all-female revue theaters, comic books, television, bars, pulp fiction, nightclubs, animation, advertisements, and the like as subjects of serious anthropological study.[68] After all, these are

---

[66] "Pink" (*pinku*) is a Japanese euphemism for "prurient." See note 64 for examples of such texts.

[67] Among the new and recent scholarship (not all by graduates or members of anthropology departments) that helps to correct this unfortunate tendency are works by Sharman Babior (1993), Makoto Furukawa (1994), Helen Hardacre (1990), Karen Kelsky (1994, 1996a), Yasue Kuwahara (1994), Gary Leupp (1995), Elizabeth Miller (1994), Donald Roden (1990), Miriam Silverberg (1991), and Tsuneo Watanabe and Jun'ichi Iwata (1989 [1987]). At the risk of appearing immodest, I should also like to cite some of my own work in this connection (1989, 1992, 1995, and 1998b.)

[68] Among the recent dissertations and publications (not cited by Kelly and not already cited by me elsewhere in this essay) that engage with the topic of popular culture are Anne Allison (1996), Jennifer Beer (1993), Millie Creighton (1993), Darrel Davis (1996), Kinko Ito (1994), Brian Moeran (1996), Chieko Irie Mulhern (1989), Susan Napier (1993), Paul Noguchi (1994), Peter Oblas (1995), Andrew Painter (1991, 1993), Richard Powers and Hidetoshi Kato (1989), John Russell (1991), Miyoko Sasaki and Heinz Morioka (1981), Lise Skov and Brian Moeran, eds. (1995), Miriam Silverberg (1992), Ron Tanner (1994), Joseph Tobin, ed. (1992), John W. Treat, ed. (1996), and Christine Yano (1995).

Japanese creations used and abused by Japanese people and deserve our critical attention.

Just as the archetypal peasant of *Suye Mura* is now many actors, so too the monolithic category "Japanese Woman" has been dismantled by scholars representing a wide range of disciplines. Recent Anglophone literature informs us of the historical presence of female emperors;[69] unruly women, feminist activists, and "flappers" in nineteenth- and early twentieth-century Japan;[70] gender-bending female religious leaders who advanced unconventional interpretations of ritual practices;[71] cross-dressing female revue actors and their fans who have provoked continual debate since the 1910s on the relationship among sex, gender, and sexuality;[72] and the tens of thousands of "comfort women" whose brutal treatment was a sine qua non of militarization and imperialist aggression,[73] to name a few female "types" whose existence and legacies complicate the timeless, normative portrait of "the Japanese Woman." The scholarship on these "types" has been augmented by research devoted to giving voice to the various underacknowledged people who inhabit "the other Japan," among whom are included members of the working class, ethnic minorities, the aged and disabled, delinquents and criminals, "internationalized" youth, and the invisible nobility.[74] Nevertheless, it remains the case that even

---

[69] Joan Piggot (1997, forthcoming), and Patricia Tsurumi (1982).

[70] Mikiso Hane, ed. and trans. (1988), Sharon Sievers (1983), Miriam Silverberg (1991), Mariko Asano Tamanoi (1991), Anne Walthall (1994).

[71] Hardacre (1990) and Emily Groszos Ooms (1993). See also Jody Okun (1987) and Ellen Schattschneider (1996b).

[72] Refer to my work on the politics of gender and sexuality in Japan (e.g., 1998b). See also Kimi Coaldrake (1996).

[73] Ustinia Dolgopol and Snehal Paranjape (1994), George Hicks (1995), and Kazuko Watanabe (1994b).

[74] Recent publications and dissertations on these diverse categories of people include Kazuhiro Abe (1989), Diana Bethel (1993), Mary Brinton (1993), Louisa Cameron (1996), George De Vos (1992), Frank Dikötter, ed. (1997), Edward Fowler (1996), Anne Freed (1992), Roger Goodman (1990), David Howell (1996), Janet Hunter (1993), Yoko Kawashima (1987), Kenji Kosaka, ed. (1994), Robin Le Blanc (1994), Takie Sugiyama Lebra (1993), Margaret Lock (1993), John Maher and Gaynor Macdonald, eds. (1995), Pyong Gap Min (1992), Barbara Molony (1995), Shunta Mori (1995), Stephen Murphy-Shigematsu (1993/1994), Peter Oblas (1995), Christopher Reichl (1995), James Roberson (1993), Glenda Roberts (1994), Ikuya Sato (1991), Richard Siddle (1996), Katarina Sjöberg (1993), Herman Smith (1995), Carolyn Stevens (1995), Patricia Tsurumi (1994), Christena Turner (1995), Mamoru Tsukada (1991). See also Takie Sugiyama Lebra, ed. (1992).

as our knowledge of unorthodox, marriage resisting, status-quo upsetting females increases appreciatively, books and articles continue to be published on the normative subject of "the Japanese Woman."[75] In contrast, comparatively few scholarly articles and fewer books (in English) exist on the *explicit*—as opposed to implied or de facto—subject, normative or otherwise, of Japanese men.[76]

Japanese women have long been mystified as the essence of Japanese culture, and one could argue that collectively, they and their white-collar husbands (*sarariiman*) – for, according to the regnant stereotype, "the Japanese Woman" today is a married, professional housewife with 1.5 children—have been too knowable, like the nation and culture they embody and represent. But, what if...? What if we separated Japanese females from the cult of femininity and stressed instead that femininity as such is both male-inscribed and, as Japanese (male) critics have insisted, is best performed by males, notably Kabuki *onnagata*, or woman's-role specialists. What if we knew that a certain professional housewife was a former *otokoyaku*, or man's-role player, in the Takarazuka Revue, who once was infamous for her many offstage love affairs with female fans; or what if we knew that her husband was a lifetime member of a "New Half" or transvestite[77] club for males who express a need to cross-dress and explore their so-called feminine temperament? Or what if we knew that their daughter was a member of one of the more notorious all-female motorcycle gangs who are cozy with tatooed gangsters? And what if we knew that the entire family had in common a passion for New Half comic books and the music of the androgynous Gao, the Japanese version of K. D. Lang whose ambiguous sexuality is advertised (in English) as a virtue?

---

[75] For example, Sumiko Iwao (1992). Recent works, in addition to those already cited which help to complicate to varying degrees this stereotype and/or explore its emergence and reproduction, include *AMPO, Japan Asia Quarterly Review*, ed. (1996), Kumiko Fujimura-Fanselow and Atsuko Kameda, eds. (1995), Anne Imamura, ed. (1996), Brian McVeigh (1996), and Kazuko Watanabe (1994a). See also Kristina Huber (1992).

[76] Several recent exceptions are by Anne Allison (1994), Janet Kay Fair (1996), Karen Kelsky (1996c), Gary Leupp (1995), Donald Roden (1990), and James Thomas (1993).

[77] "New Half" refers to the representation, usually in comic books and animated cartoons, of fantastical, intersexed bodies, most typically portrayed in the form of a figure with breasts and a penis. In reference to humans, New Half is a euphemism for "androgyne" or "transvestite."

Incorporating these hitherto repressed "what if" variables into anthropological theorizing about sex, gender, and sexuality and the ethnographic representation of Japan would (and should) texture and complicate both processes. The addition of more empirical, historical, practical evidence would help to modify and refine anthropological theories premised on (a) a rather slim body of actual, mostly European, practices, and (b) a large body of literary and film characters, rather than actual people. Likewise, the ethnographic representation of Japan would be enhanced by the addition of vivid, living colors to the black and white, and pastel, portraits of Japanese women and men. In other words, anthropologists of Japan must be as supple in their interpretive abilities as Japanese are ambiguous and inventive in their everyday practices and desires.

And what of colonialism? Over the past two decades the relationship between anthropology and colonialism has crystallized into a significant facet of the discipline's history. Earlier, I noted the advent in recent years of dissertations and AAA conference papers on aspects of Japanese colonialism. As an anti-colonial colonizer, Japan poses a challenge to literature on colonialism presented in the guise of a "Western self-critique" wherein critical reappraisals of anthropology and the colonial encounter nevertheless retain an asymmetrical relationship between "the West" and "the Third World." Although neither "the West" nor "the Third World" exists as an internally coherent entity, there is a tendency to treat both as singular formations defined in terms of their experience of colonialism and imperialism, where "the West" is the supreme change agent and "the Third World" the irreversibly changed reactant. Moreover, this formula ignores the histories of multiple non-Euro-American colonizers and imperialist regimes. Applied anthropology publications concerned with "cultural survival" have long focused on certain neo-colonial practices, often under the rubric of human and environmental rights. Much, however, remains to be done in anthropological publications of a more literary and historical bent, although I sense a growing interest among Japanese and foreign scholars alike in scrutinizing from different disciplinary vantage points Japanese imperialism and Japan's role in colonizing Asia past and present.[78]

---

[78] Among the recent dissertations that deal, differentially, with the cultural

Few would disagree with the observation that whether First or Third, the world was *never not* transcultural. Cultural encounters and their effects are the sine qua non of human life – whether that life takes the form of a New Guinea hill tribe or an urbanized population in Japan. Of course, one must never forget that there have been imbalances of varying proportions associated with "the crossing of cultural borders: conquest, colonialism, imperialism, tourism, or scholarly interest all involve choice and require power, even if only buying power."[79] Neither can one forget, as Latin American anthropologists have reminded us, that transcultural encounters, while not strictly dialectical and however uneven or unequal in power or degree, are "shifting processes" and do not constitute unidirectional teleologies.[80] All parties to and involved in the encounter are affected and modified by it albeit with different consequences.

Japan, the product and synthesis of manifold inter-regional and international encounters over 2000 years, is one of many non-Euro-American societies and states which confounds the binarist (il)logic of the Western self-critique. To the substantial and growing historical literature on Japanese colonialism is needed the addition of anthropological analyses of the affective and cultural strategies employed by the Japanese imperial state and its agencies. Such analyses would both augment and animate the picture of imperial Japan evident in scholarship focusing on the more bureacratic, military, economic, and political aspects of Japanese colonialism. Equally important, inserting Japan into the anthropological discourse on colonialism would both problematize the easy foil of "the Third World" and offset the Eurocentric production of meaning of the colonial encounter. Such a move would also focus

---

aspects of Japanese imperialism and colonialism are Leo Tsu-Shin Ching (1994b), Shiaw-Chian Fong (1993), Kazuko Furuno (1990), Keiko Matsuki (1995), Eiko Tai (1993), and Lisa Yoneyama (1993).

Additional published references on the "culture" of Japanese imperialism and colonialism include those by Yoji Akashi (1993), Ernest Allen, Jr. (1994), Leo Ching (1994a), Haruko Cook and Theodore Cook (1992), John Dower (1993), Grant Goodman, ed. (1991), Chih-Ming Ka (1995), Roger Purdy (1992), Vincente Rafael (1990), Jennifer Robertson (1995), Sasaki Chikara (1992), Shigeru Sato (1994), Rob Steven (1990), and Michael Weiner (1994, 1995). See also Peter Duus (1995), Peter Duus, Ramon Myers, and Mark Peattie, eds. (1996), and Mark Peattie (1988).

[79] Diane Taylor (1991): 63.
[80] Refer to Taylor, ibid.

much needed attention within Japan on the relationship between colonialism and anthropological practices. Only in the past several years have several Japanese anthropologists of Japan themselves pondered the anthropological legacy of colonialism and vice versa. And finally, the same move would make more visible the relationship between militarization and the invention of certain social institutions in Japan, such as neighborhood organizations and the educational curriculum, which tend to be viewed from a presentist perspective insofar as the wartime period is (mostly) glossed over in otherwise informative postwar ethnographies on these subjects.

To conclude, I would like to return to the metaphors of time travel and the crystal that I invoked at the outset. The image of a "smashed jewel" informed Benedict's normative (and normalized) portrait of Japan as the mirror-image of America. It seems to me that our own "Assignment: Japan" is to recover and mend the smashed jewel as a multi-faceted crystal. By historicizing the salient trends and themes in the anthropology of Japan, I have sought to emphasize the need for us to remember our complex disciplinary genealogy and associated memories. This is hardly a nostalgic exercise, but rather a way of re-membering the components of that genealogy in order both to realize new relationships, and to recognize old relationships anew.

Bibliography

Abe, Kazuhiro. 1989. "Japanese Capitalism and the Korean Minority in Japan: Class, Race, and Racism." Ph.D. diss., University of California at Los Angeles.

Abu-Lughod, Lila. 1989. "Zones of Theory in the Anthropology of the Arab World." *Annual Review of Anthropology* 18: 267-306.

Akashi, Yoji. 1993. "The Greater East Asia War and Bunkajin, 1941-1945." *War and Society* 11, no. 1: 129-77.

Allen, Ernest, Jr. Winter 1994. "When Japan was 'Champion of the Darker Races': Satokata Takahashi and the Flowering of Black Messianic Nationalism." *The Black Scholar* 24: 23-46.

Allison, Anne. 1994. *Nightwork: Sexuality, Pleasure, and Corporate Masculinity in a Tokyo Hostess Club.* Chicago: University of Chicago Press.

——. 1996. *Permitted and Prohibited Desires: Mothers, Comics, and Censorship in Japan.* Boulder: Westview.

AMPO, Japan Asia Quarterly Review, ed. 1996. *Voices from the Japanese Women's Movement.* Armonk, N.Y.: M. E. Sharpe.

Aoki Tamotsu. 1991 [1990]. *"Nihon bunkaron" no hen'yō* (The Transformation of Treatises on Japanese Culture). Chūō kōronsha.

Appadurai, Arjun. 1986. "Theory in Anthropology: Center and Periphery." *Comparative Studies in Social History* 28: 356-61.

Apter, David. 1984. *Against the State: Politics and Social Protest in Japan.* Cambridge: Harvard University Press.

Austin, Lewis, ed. 1976. *Japan: Paradox of Progress.* New Haven: Yale University Press.

Babior, Sharman. 1993. "Women of a Tokyo Shelter: Domestic Violence and Sexual Exploitation in Japan." Ph.D. diss., University of California at Los Angeles.

Bachnik, Jane, and Charles Quinn, Jr., eds. 1994. *Situated Meaning: Inside and Outside in Japanese Self, Society, and Language.* Princeton: Princeton University Press.

Beauchamp, Edward, and James Vardaman, eds. 1994. *Japanese Education Since 1945: A Documentary Study.* Armonk, N.Y.: M. E. Sharpe.

Beer, Jennifer. 1993. "Packaged Experiences: Japanese Tours to Southeast Asia." Ph.D. diss., University of California at Berkeley.

Befu, Harumi. 1993. "Nationalism and *Nihonjinron.*" In *Cultural Nationalism in East Asia: Representation and Identity,* edited by Harumi Befu, 107-35. Berkeley: Institute of East Asian Studies, University of California.

Befu, Harumi, and Joseph Kreiner, eds. 1992. *Otherness of Japan: Historical and Cultural Influences on Japanese Studies in Ten Countries.* Munich: Iudicium Verlag.

Ben-Ari, Eyal. 1996. *Japanese Childcare: An Interpretive Study of Culture and Organization.* New York: Kegan Paul International.

Benedict, Ruth. 1974 [1946]. *The Chrysanthemum and the Sword: Patterns of Japanese Culture.* Reprint. New York: Meridian.

Benjamin, Gail. 1997. *Japanese Lessons: A Year in a Japanese School through the Eyes of an American Anthropologist and her Children.* New York: New York University Press.

Bennett, John. 1970. "Some Observations on Western Anthropological Research on Japan." In Norbeck and Parman, eds. (1970), 11-27.

Bennett, John, and Michio Nagai. 1953. "The Japanese Critique of the Methodology of Benedict's *The Chrysanthemum and the Sword.*" *American Anthropologist* 55: 404-11.

Bestor, Theodore. 1989. *Neighborhood Tokyo.* Stanford: Stanford University Press.

Bethel, Diana. 1993. "From Abandonment to Community: Life in a Japanese Institution for the Elderly." Ph.D. diss., University of Hawai'i at Manoa.

Bird, Isabella. 1973 [1880]. *Unbeaten Tracks in Japan.* Reprint. Rutland, Vt.: Charles E. Tuttle.

Bohnaker, William. 1990. *The Hollow Doll.* New York: Ballantine.

Bornoff, Nicholas. 1991. *Pink Samurai: Love, Marriage, and Sex in Contemporary Japan.* London: Grafton.

Borovoy, Amy. 1995. "Good Wives and Mothers: The Production of Japanese Domesticity in a Global Economy." Ph.D. diss., Stanford University.

Boscaro, Adriana, Franco Gatti, and Massimo Raveri, eds. 1990. *Social Sciences, Ideology and Thought.* Vol. 2 of *Rethinking Japan.* Sandgate: Japan Library.

Brinton, Mary. 1993. *Women and the Economic Miracle: Gender and Work in Postwar Japan.* Berkeley: University of California Press.

Bulletin of Concerned Asian Scholars, ed. 1988 [1987]. *The Other Japan.* Armonk, N.Y.: M. E. Sharpe.

Buruma, Ian. 1984. *Japanese Mirror: Heroes and Villains of Japanese Culture.* London: J. Cape.

———. 1985. *Behind the Mask: On Sexual Demons, Sacred Mothers, Transvestites, Gangsters and Other Japanese Cultural Heroes.* New York: Meridian.

Cameron, Louisa. 1996. "Women and Gender in the Japanese Workplace and Society." Ph.D. diss., Columbia University.
Ching, Leo Tsu-Shin. Spring 1994a. "Imaginings in the Empires of the Sun: Japanese Mass Culture in Asia." *Boundary 2* 21: 198-219.
———. 1994b. "Tracing Contradictions: Interrogating Japanese Colonialism and Its Discourse." Ph.D. diss., University of California at San Diego.
Chung, Byung-Ho. 1992. "Childcare Politics: Life and Power in Japanese Day Care Centers." Ph.D. diss., University of Illinois at Urbana-Champaign.
Coaldrake, Kimi. 1996. *Women's Gidayu and the Japanese Theatre Tradition*. New York: Routledge.
Coleman, Samuel. 1991 [1983]. *Family Planning in Japanese Society: Traditional Birth Control in a Modern Urban Culture*. Princeton: Princeton University Press.
Cook, Haruko, and Theodore Cook. 1992. *Japan at War: An Oral History*. New York: W. W. Norton.
Creighton, Millie. Winter 1993. "'Sweet Love' and Women's Place: Valentine's Day, Japan Style." *Journal of Popular Culture* 27: 1-19.
Davis, Darrel. 1996. *Picturing Japaneseness: Monumental Style, National Identity, Japanese Film*. New York: Columbia University Press.
De Mente, Boye. 1966. *Bachelor's Japan*. Rutland, Vt.: Charles E. Tuttle.
De Vos, George. 1992. *Social Cohesion and Alienation: Minorities in the United States and Japan*. Boulder: Westview.
Dikötter, Frank, ed. 1997. *The Construction of Racial Identities in China and Japan*. Honolulu: University of Hawai'i Press.
Dissanayake, Wimal, ed. 1996. *Narratives of Agency: Self-Making in China, India, and Japan*. Minneapolis: University of Minnesota Press.
Doak, Kevin. Winter 1996. "Ethnic Nationalism and Romanticism in Early Twentieth-Century Japan." *Journal of Japanese Studies* 22: 77-103.
Doane, Janice, and Devon Hodges. 1987. *Nostalgia and Sexual Difference: The Resistance to Contemporary Feminism*. New York: Methuen.
Dolgopol, Ustinia, and Snehal Paranjape. 1994. *Comfort Women: An Unfinished Ordeal. Report of a Mission*. Geneva: International Commission of Jurists.
Dower, John. 1986. *War Without Mercy: Race and Power in the Pacific War*. New York: Pantheon.
———. 1993. *Japan in War and Peace*. New York: New Press.
Duus, Peter. 1995. *The Abacus and the Sword: The Japanese Penetration of Korea, 1895-1910*. Berkeley: University of California Press.
Duus, Peter, Ramon Myers, and Mark Peattie, eds. 1996. *The Japanese Wartime Empire, 1931-1945*. Princeton: Princeton University Press.
Embree, John. 1939. *Suye Mura, A Japanese Village*. Chicago: University of Chicago Press.
———. 1945. *The Japanese Nation: A Social Survey*. New York: Farrar and Rinehart.
———. 1947. Review of Benedict (1946). *American Sociological Review* 12, no. 1: 245-46.
———. 1950. "A Note on Ethnocentrism in Anthropology." *American Anthropologist* 52, no. 3: 430-32.
Fair, Janet Kay. 1996. "Japanese Women's Language and the Ideology of Japanese Uniqueness." Ph.D. diss., University of Chicago.
Field, Norma. 1993 [1991]. *In the Realm of a Dying Emperor: Japan at Century's End*. New York: Random House, Vintage.
Fike, Vincent. 26 November 1996. Letter to the author.
Fong, Shiaw-Chian. 1993. "Achieving Weak Hegemony: Taiwanese Cultural

Experience under Japanese Rule, 1895-1945." Ph.D. diss., University of Chicago.
Fowler, Edward. 1996. *Sanya Blues: Laboring Life in Contemporary Tokyo.* Ithaca: Cornell University Press.
Freed, Anne. 1992. *The Changing Worlds of Older Women in Japan.* Manchester, Conn: Knowledge, Ideas and Trends, Inc.
Fujimura-Fanselow, Kumiko, and Atsuko Kameda, eds. 1995. *Japanese Women: New Feminist Perspectives on the Past, Present, and Future.* New York: Feminist Press at the City University of New York.
Furukawa, Makoto. 1994. "The Changing Nature of Sexuality: The Three Codes Framing Homosexuality in Modern Japan." Translated by Alice Lockyer. *U.S.-Japan Women's Journal* (English Supplement), no. 7: 98-127.
Furuno, Kazuko. 1990. "The Emperor and the Japanese: Power and Faith in Japanese Culture." Ph.D. diss., New School for Social Research.
Giddings, Paula. 1985 [1984]. *When and Where I Enter: The Impact of Black Women on Race and Sex in America.* Reprint. New York: Bantam Classics.
Goodman, Grant, ed. 1991. *Japanese Cultural Policies in Southeast Asia during World War 2.* New York: St. Martin's.
Goodman, Roger. 1990. *Japan's "International Youth": The Emergence of a New Class of Schoolchildren.* New York: Oxford University Press.
Goodman, Roger, and Kirsten Refsing, eds. 1992. *Ideology and Practice in Modern Japan.* New York: Routledge.
Goto, Junko. 1993. "Rural Revitalization (*Chiiki-Okoshi*) in Japan: A Case Study of Asuke Township." Ph.D. diss., University of California at Los Angeles.
Greenfeld, Karl Taro. 1994. *Speed Tribes: Days and Nights with Japan's Next Generation.* New York: Harper Collins.
Han, Seung-Mi. 1995. "From Regional Craft to National Art: Politics and Identity in a Japanese Regional Industry." Ph.D. diss., Harvard University.
Hane, Mikiso, ed. and trans. 1988. *Reflections on the Way to the Gallows: Rebel Women in Prewar Japan.* Berkeley: University of California Press.
Hara, Richard. 1994. "Dividing Harvests: Household and Property in Contemporary Rural Japan." Ph.D. diss., City University of New York.
Hardacre, Helen. 1990. "Gender and the Millenium in Ōmotokyō, A Japanese New Religion." In *Japanese Civilization in the Modern World VI: Religion,* edited by Tadao Umesao, Helen Hardacre, and Hirochika Nakamaki, 47-62. Osaka: Senri Ethnological Studies 29, National Museum of Ethnology.
———. 1994. "Response of Buddhism and Shintō to the Issue of Brain Death and Organ Transplant." *Cambridge Quarterly of Healthcare Ethics* 3: 585-601.
Hein, Laura, and Ellen Hammond. 1995. "Homing in on Asia: Identity in Contemporary Japan." *Bulletin of Concerned Asian Scholars* 27, no. 3: 3-17.
Heinrich, Amy, ed. 1997. *Currents in Japanese Culture: Translations and Transformations.* New York: Columbia University Press.
Hendry, Joy. 1993. *Wrapping Culture: Politeness, Presentation, and Power in Japan and Other Societies.* Oxford: Clarendon.
Herzfeld, Michael. 1987. *Anthropology Through the Looking-Glass: Critical Ethnography in the Margins of Europe.* Cambridge: Cambridge University Press.
Hicks, George. 1995. *The Comfort Women: Japan's Brutal Regime of Enforced Prostitution in the Second World War.* New York: W. W. Norton.
Howell, David. January 1996. "Ethnicity and Culture in Contemporary Japan." *Journal of Contemporary History* 31: 171-90.
Huber, Kristina. 1992. *Women in Japanese Society: An Annotated Bibliography of Selected English Language Materials.* Westport, Conn.: Greenwood.

Hunter, Janet. 1993. *Japanese Women Working.* New York: Routledge.
Imamura, Anne, ed. 1996. *Re-Imaging Japanese Women.* Berkeley: University of California Press.
Ito, Kinko. 1994. "Images of Women in Weekly Male Comic Magazines in Japan." *Journal of Popular Culture* 27: 81-95.
Ivy, Marilyn. 1995. *Discourses of the Vanishing: Modernity, Phantasm, Japan.* Chicago: University of Chicago Press.
Iwao, Sumiko. 1992. *The Japanese Woman: Traditional Image and Changing Reality.* New York: Free Press.
Iwatake, Mikako. 1993. "The Tokyo Renaissance: Constructing a Postmodern Identity in Contemporary Japan." Ph.D. diss., University of Pennsylvania.
Japan Foundation. 1988. *Japanese Studies in the United States.* Japanese Studies Series XVII. Tokyo: Japan Foundation.
Ka, Chih-Ming. 1995. *Japanese Colonialism in Taiwan: Land Tenure, Development, and Dependency, 1895-1945.* Boulder: Westview.
Kamata Satoshi. 1982. *Japan in the Passing Lane: An Insider's Account of Life in a Japanese Auto Factory.* Translated by Tatsuru Akimoto. New York: Pantheon.
Kawahara, Yukiko. 1990. "Women Left Behind: Wives of Seasonal Migrant Workers in Japan." *Asian Profile* 18, no. 2: 127-35.
Kawashima, Yoko. 1987. "The Place and Role of Female Workers in the Japanese Labor Market." *Women's Studies International Forum* 10, no. 6: 599-611.
Kelly, William W. 1988. "Japanology Bashing." *American Ethnologist* 15, no. 2: 172-76.
———. 1991. "Directions in the Anthropology of Contemporary Japan." *Annual Review of Anthropology* 20: 395-431.
———. 1992. "Finding a Place in Metropolitan Japan: Transpositions of Everyday Life." In *Postwar Japan as History*, edited by Andrew Gordon. Berkeley: University of California Press.
Kelsky, Karen. Spring 1994. "Intimate Ideologies: Transnational Theory and Japan's 'Yellow Cabs.'" *Public Culture* 6, no. 3: 465-78.
———. 1996a. "Flirting with the Foreign: Interracial Sex in Japan's 'International' Age." In *Global/Local: Cultural Production in the Transnational Imaginary*, edited by Rob Wilson and Wimal Dissanayake. Durham: Duke University Press.
———. 1996b. "The Gender Politics of Women's Internationalism in Japan." *International Journal of Politics, Culture and Society* 10, no. 1: 29-50.
———. 1996c. "Self as Other, Other Selves: Gender, Identity, and Narratives of Internationalism in Japan." Ph.D. diss., University of Hawai'i.
Klawans, Stuart. 22 January 1996. "12 Monkeys." *The Nation* 262: 34.
Kluckhohn, Clyde. 1949. *Mirror for Man: the Relation of Anthropology to Modern Life.* New York: Whittlesey House.
Kosaka, Kenji, ed. 1994. *Social Stratification in Contemporary Japan.* London: Routledge and Kegan Paul International.
Kuwahara, Yasue. Spring 1994. "Make Me Sick: Perceptions of Traditional Sex Roles in Japanese Society in Novels by Yamada Amy." *Journal of Popular Culture* 27: 107-16.
Kweon, Sug-In. 1994. "Politics of Furusato in Aizu, Japan: Local Identities and Metropolitan Discourses." Ph.D. diss., Stanford University.
Le Blanc, Robin. 1994. "Homeless as Citizens: The Political World of the Japanese Housewife." Ph.D. diss., University of Oklahoma.
Lebra, Takie Sugiyama. 1993. *Above the Clouds: Status Culture of the Modern Japanese Nobility.* Berkeley: University of California Press.

Lebra, Takie Sugiyama, ed. 1992. *Japanese Social Organization*. Honolulu: University of Hawai'i Press.

Leupp, Gary. 1995. *Male Colors: The Construction of Homosexuality in Tokugawa Japan*. Berkeley: University of California Press.

Lewis, Catherine. 1995. *Educating Hearts and Minds: Reflections on Japanese Preschool and Elementary Education*. Cambridge: Cambridge University Press.

Lincicome, Mark. May 1993. "Nationalism, Internationalization, and the Dilemma of Educational Reform in Japan." *Comparative Education Review* 37, no. 2: 123-51.

Lock, Margaret. 1993. *Encounters with Aging: Mythologies of Menopause in Japan and North America*. Berkeley: University of California Press.

Lock, Margaret, and Christine Honde. 1990. "Reaching Consensus about Death: Heart Transplants and Cultural Identity in Japan." In *Social Science Perspectives on Medical Ethics*, edited by G. Weisz, 99-119. Dordrecht: Kluwer.

Maher, John, and Gaynor Macdonald, eds. 1995. *Diversity in Japanese Culture and Language*. London: Kegan Paul International.

Mannari, Hiroshi, and Harumi Befu, eds. 1983. *The Challenge of Japan's Internationalization: Organization and Culture*. Tokyo: Kwansei Gakuin University and Kodansha International.

Mathews, Gordon. 1993. "Ikigai: The Pursuit of a Life Worth Living in Japan and the United States." Ph.D. diss., Cornell University.

———. 1996. *What Makes Life Worth Living: How Japanese and Americans Make Sense of Their Worlds*. Berkeley: University of California Press.

Matsuki, Keiko. 1995. "Creating Showa Memories in Contemporary Japan: Discourse, Society, History and Subjectivity." Ph.D. diss., University of Arizona.

McConnell, David. 1991. "Educational Policy for Global Integration: The Social and Political Construction of Internationalization in Japan." Ph.D. diss., Stanford University.

McVeigh, Brian. 1996. *Life in a Japanese Women's College: Learning to be Ladylike*. New York: Routledge.

Mears, Helen. 1948. *Mirror for Americans, Japan*. Boston: Houghton, Mifflin.

Miller, Elizabeth. 1994. "A Borderless Age: AIDS, Gender, and Power in Contemporary Japan." Ph.D. diss., Harvard University.

Min, Pyong Gap. Spring 1992. "A Comparison of the Korean Minorities in China and Japan." *International Migration Review* 26: 4-21.

Moen, Darrell. 1996. "The Emergent Culture of the Japanese Organic Farming Movement and Its Implications for Political Economy." Ph.D. diss., University of Wisconsin at Madison.

Moeran, Brian. 1996. *A Japanese Advertising Agency: An Anthropology of Media and Markets*. Honolulu: University of Hawai'i Press.

Molony, Barbara. 1995. "Japan's 1986 Equal Employment Opportunity Law and the Changing Discourse on Gender." *Signs* 20, no. 2: 268-302.

Mori, Shunta. 1995. "The Social Problems of Students Returning to Japan from Sojourns Overseas: A Social Constructionist Study." Ph.D. diss., University of California at Santa Cruz.

Mouer, Ross, and Yoshio Sugimoto. 1986. *Images of Japanese Society*. New York: Routledge and Kegan Paul.

Mulhern, Chieko Irie. 1989. "Japanese Harlequin Romances as Transcultural Woman's Fiction." *Journal of Asian Studies* 48, no. 1: 50-71.

Murphy-Shigematsu, Stephen. Winter 1993/1994. "Multiethnic in Japan and the Monoethnic Myth." *MELUS* 18: 63-80.

Napier, Susan. Summer 1993. "Panic Sites: The Japanese Imagination of Disaster from Godzilla to Akira." *Journal of Japanese Studies* 19: 327-51.
Nelson, John. 1993. "Enduring Identities: The Guise of Shinto in Contemporary Japan." Ph.D. diss., University of California at Berkeley.
———. 1996. *A Year in the Life of a Shinto Shrine.* Seattle: University of Washington Press. *1996 Catalogue.* 1996. Westport, Conn: Greenwood.
Noguchi, Paul. Fall 1994. "Savor Slowly: Ekiben—The Fast Food of High-Speed Japan." *Ethnology* 33: 317-30.
Norbeck, Edward. 1984 [1965]. *Changing Japan.* Reprint, 2nd ed. New York: Waveland.
Norbeck, Edward, and Susan Parman, eds. 1970. *The Study of Japan in the Behavioral Sciences. Rice University Studies* 56, no. 4.
Oblas, Peter. 1995. *Perspectives on Race and Culture in Japanese Society: The Mass Media and Ethnicity.* Lewiston, N.Y.: E. Mellen.
Ohnuki-Tierney, Emiko. 1993. *Rice as Self: Japanese Identitites through Time.* Princeton: Princeton University Press.
———. June 1994. "Brain Death and Organ Transplantation: Cultural Bases of Medical Technology." *Current Anthropology* 35, no. 3: 233-54.
Okano, Kaori. 1993. *School to Work Transition in Japan: An Ethnographic Study.* Clevedon: Multilingual Matters.
Okun, Jody. 1987. "Kyoso: Opportunity and Role Constraint for Shamanic Women in Modern Japan." *Journal of Asian Culture* 11: 69-82.
Ooms, Emily Groszos. 1993. *Women and Millenarian Protest in Meiji Japan: The Case of Deguchi Nao and Omotokyo.* Ithaca: East Asia Program, Cornell University.
Ortner, Sherry. 1984. "Theory in Anthropology Since the Sixties." *Comparative Studies in Social History* 26, no. 1: 126-66.
Oshima, Shizuko. 1989. *Japan through the Eyes of Women Migrant Workers.* Tokyo: Japan Woman's Christian Temperance Union.
Painter, Andrew. 1991. "The Creation of Japanese Television and Culture." Ph.D. diss., University of Michigan at Ann Arbor.
———. Summer 1993. "Japanese Daytime Television, Popular Culture, and Ideology." *Journal of Japanese Studies* 19: 295-325.
Peak, Lois. 1991. *Learning to Go to School in Japan: The Transition from Home to Preschool Life.* Berkeley: University of California Press.
Peattie, Mark. 1988. *Nan'yō: The Rise and Fall of the Japanese in Micronesia, 1885-1945.* Pacific Islands Monograph Series, no. 4. Honolulu: University of Hawai'i Press.
Piggot, Joan. 1997. *The Emergence of Japanese Kingship.* Stanford: Stanford University Press.
———. Forthcoming. "Chieftain Pairs and Co-Rulers: Female Sovereignty in Early Japan." In *Gender in Japanese History*, edited by Hitomi Tonomura. Ann Arbor: Center for Japanese Studies, University of Michigan.
Plath, David, and Robert Smith. 1992. "How 'American' are Studies of Modern Japan Done in the United States?" In Befu and Kreiner, eds. (1992), 201-29.
Powers, Richard, and Hidetoshi Kato. 1989. *Handbook of Japanese Popular Culture.* New York: Greenwood.
Purdy, Roger. 1992. "Nationalism and News: 'Information Imperialism' and Japan, 1910-1936." *Journal of American-East Asian Relations* 1, no. 3: 295-325.
Rafael, Vincente. 1990. "Collaboration and Rumor: The Philippines Under Japanese Occupation." *Culture and History* 8: 87-106.

Raz, Jacob. 1992. *Aspects of Otherness in Japanese Culture.* Tokyo: Institute for the Study of Languages and Cultures of Asia and Africa.
Reichl, Christopher. 1995. "Stages in the Historical Process of Ethnicity: Japanese in Brazil." *Ethnohistory* 42, no. 1: 31-62.
Roberson, James. 1993. "Work Hard, Play Hard: Japanese Working Class Lives." Ph.D. diss., University of Hawai'i at Manoa.
Roberts, Glenda. 1994. *Staying on the Line: Blue-Collar Women in Contemporary Japan.* Honolulu: University of Hawai'i Press.
Robertson, Jennifer. 1989. "Gender-Bending in Paradise: Doing 'Female' and 'Male' in Japan." *Genders* 5: 188-207.
——. 1992. "The Politics of Androgyny in Japan: Sexuality and Subversion in the Theater and Beyond." *American Ethnologist* 19, no. 3: 419-42.
——. 1994 [1991]. *Native and Newcomer: Making and Remaking a Japanese City.* Berkeley: University of California Press.
——. 1995. "Mon Japon: The Revue Theater as a Technology of Japanese Imperialism." *American Ethnologist* 22, no. 4: 970-96.
——. 1997. "Empire of Nostalgia: Rethinking 'Internationalization' in Japan Today." *Theory, Culture and Society* 14, no. 4: 97-122.
——. 1998a. "It Takes a Village: Internationalization and Nostalgia in Postwar Japan." In Steven Vlastos, ed. (1998), 209-39.
——. 1998b. *Takarazuka: Sexual Politics and Popular Culture in Modern Japan.* Berkeley: University of California Press.
Roden, Donald. 1990. "Taishō Culture and the Problem of Gender Ambivalence." In *Culture and Identity: Japanese Intellectuals During the Interwar Years*, edited by J. Thomas Rimer, 37-55. Princeton: Princeton University Press.
Rohlen, Thomas, and Gerald LeTendre, eds. 1996. *Teaching and Learning in Japan.* Cambridge: Cambridge University Press.
Roland, Alan. 1988. *In Search of Self in India and Japan: Toward a Cross-Cultural Psychology.* Princeton: Princeton University Press.
Rosenberger, Nancy, ed. 1992. *Japanese Sense of Self.* Cambridge: Cambridge University Press.
Rubel, Paula, and Abraham Rosman. 1994. "The Past and Future of Anthropology." *Journal of Anthropological Research* 50: 335-43.
Russell, John. 1991. "Race and Reflexivity: The Black Other in Contemporary Japanese Mass Culture." *Cultural Anthropology* 6: 3-25.
Sasaki, Chikara. 1992. "Science and the Japanese Empire 1868-1945: An Overview." In *Science and Empires: Historical Studies about Scientific Development and European Expansion*, edited by Patrick Petitjean, Catherine Jami, and Anne Marie Moulin, 243-46. Dordrecht: Kluwer.
Sasaki, Miyoko, and Heinz Morioka. 1981. "Rakugo: Popular Narrative Art of the Grotesque." *Harvard Journal of Asiatic Studies* 41, no. 2: 417-59.
Sato, Ikuya. 1991. *Kamikaze Bikers: Parody and Anomy in Affluent Japan.* Chicago: University of Chicago Press.
Sato, Shigeru. 1994. *War, Nationalism and Peasants: Java Under Japanese Occupation, 1942-1945.* Armonk, N.Y.: M. E. Sharpe.
Schattschneider, Ellen. 1996a. "Circuits of Discipline: Production, Reproduction, and the Work of the Gods in Tsugaru." Ph.D. diss., University of Chicago.
——. 1996b. "The Labor of Mountains." *positions: east asia cultures critique* 4, no. 1: 1-30.
Scidmore, Eliza. 1891. *Jinrikisha Days in Japan.* New York: Harper and Brothers.
Schnell, Scott. 1993. "The Rousing Drum: Ritual, Change, and Adaptation in a

Rural Mountain Community of Central Japan." Ph.D. diss., Ohio State University.

Shields, James Jr. 1989. *Japanese Schooling: Patterns of Socialization, Equality, and Political Control.* University Park: Pennsylvania State University Press.

Shwalb, David, and Barbara Shwalb, eds. 1996. *Japanese Childrearing: Two Generations of Scholarship.* New York: Guilford.

Siddle, Richard. 1996. *Race Resistance, and the Ainu of Japan.* New York: Routledge.

Sievers, Sharon. 1983. *Flowers in Salt: The Beginnings of Feminist Consciousness in Modern Japan.* Stanford: Stanford University Press.

Silverberg, Miriam. 1991. "The Modern Girl as Militant." In *Recreating Japanese Women, 1600-1945,* edited by Gail Bernstein, 239-66. Berkeley: University of California Press.

——. 1992. "Constructing the Japanese Ethnography of Modernity." *Journal of Asian Studies* 51, no. 1: 30-54.

Sjöberg, Katarina. 1993. *The Return of the Ainu: Cultural Mobilization and the Practice of Ethnicity in Japan.* Philadelphia: Harwood.

Skov, Lise, and Brian Moeran, eds. 1995. *Women, Media, and Consumption in Japan.* Honolulu: University of Hawai'i Press.

Smith, Herman. 1995. *The Myth of Japanese Homogeneity: Socio-Ecological Diversity in Education and Socialization.* Commack, N.Y.: Nova Science.

Smith, Robert J. 1983. *Japanese Society: Tradition, Self, and the Social Order.* Cambridge: Cambridge University Press.

——. 1989. "Beikoku ni okeru Nihon kenkyū—minzokugaku" (Japan Studies in the United States—Ethnology). *Minzokugaku kenkyū* 54, no. 3: 360-74.

Smith, Robert J., and Ella Lury Wiswell. 1982. *The Women of Suye Mura.* Chicago: University of Chicago Press.

Smyers, Karen. 1993. "The Fox and the Jewel: A Study of Shared and Private Meanings in Japanese Inari Worship." Ph.D. diss., Princeton University.

Sofue Takao. 1960. "Japanese Studies by American Anthropologists: Review and Evaluation," translated by Douglas Haring. *American Anthropologist* 62: 306-18.

——. 1970. "The Japanese Viewpoint." In Norbeck and Parman, eds. (1970): 305-9.

——. 1992. "An Historical Review of Japanese Studies by American Anthropologists: The Japanese Viewpoint." In Befu and Kreiner, eds. (1992), 231-40.

Spencer, Robert. 1947. "Japanese Buddhism in the United States, 1940-1945: A Study in Acculturation." Ph.D. diss., University of California at Berkeley.

Steinhoff, Patricia. 1995. "Trends in Japanese Studies in North America: A Tale of Two Directories." *Japan Foundation Newsletter* 23: 1-7, 10.

Stephens, Sharon. 1989. "Anthropology Since the 60s, Theory for the 90s?" Working Papers. Ann Arbor: Program in Comparative Studies of Social Transformation, University of Michigan.

Steven, Rob. 1990. *Japan's New Imperialism.* Houndmills, U.K.: Macmillan.

Stevens, Carolyn. 1995. "A *Purehabu* With a View: Volunteer Activities and Social Marginality in Urban Japan." Ph.D. diss., Columbia University.

Tada, Eiko. 1991. "Maintaining a Balance: Between '*Hito*' (Person) and '*Kojin*' (Individual) in a Japanese Farming Community." Ph.D. diss., University of California at San Diego.

Tai, Eiko. 1993. "Taiwanese in Japan: A Legacy of Japanese Rule in Taiwan." Ph.D. diss., University of California at Berkeley.

Tamanoi, Mariko. 1990. "Women's Voices: Their Critique of the Anthropology of Japan." *Annual Review of Anthropology* 19: 17-37.

——. 1991. "Songs as Weapons: The Culture and History of *Komori* (Nursemaids) in Modern Japan." *Journal of Asian Studies* 50, no. 4: 793-817.
Tanaka Yasuo. 1981. *Nantonaku kurisutaru* (Something Crystal). Kawade shobō.
Tanner, Ron. Winter 1994. "Toy Robots in America, 1955-1975: How Japan Really Won the War." *Journal of Popular Culture* 28: 125-54.
Taylor, Diane. 1991. "Transculturating Transculturation." In *Interculturalism and Performance*, edited by Bonnie Marranca and Gautam Dasgupta. New York: PAJ.
Thomas, James. 1993. *Making Japan Work: The Origins, Education and Training of the Japanese Salaryman*. Sandgate: Japan Library.
Tobin, Joseph, ed. 1992. *Re-Made in Japan: Everyday Life and Consumer Taste in a Changing Society*. New Haven: Yale University Press.
Treat, John W., ed. 1996. *Contemporary Japan and Popular Culture*. Honolulu: University of Hawai'i Press.
Tsukada, Mamoru. 1991. *Yobiko Life: A Study of the Legitimation Process of Social Stratification in Japan*. Berkeley: Institute of East Asian Studies, University of California.
Tsurumi, Patricia. 1982. "The Male Present Versus the Female Past: Historians and Japan's Ancient Female Emperors." *Bulletin of Concerned Asian Scholars* 14, no. 4: 71-75.
——. 1994. "Yet to Be Heard: The Voices of Meiji Factory Women." *Bulletin of Concerned Asian Scholars* 26, no. 4: 18-27.
Turner, Christena. 1995. *Japanese Workers in Protest: An Ethnography of Consciousness and Experience*. Berkeley: University of California Press.
Vance, Carol. 1985. "Pleasure and Danger: Toward a Politics of Sexuality." In *Pleasure and Danger: Exploring Female Sexuality*, edited by Carol Vance. Boston: Routledge and Kegan Paul.
Vlastos, Stephen, ed. 1998. *Mirror of Modernity: Invented Traditions in Modern Japan*. Berkeley: University of California Press.
Vogel, Ezra. 1979. *Japan as Number One: Lessons for America*. Cambridge: Harvard University Press.
Walthall, Anne. 1994. "Devoted Wives/Unruly Women: Invisible Presence in the History of Japanese Social Protest." *Signs* 20, no. 1: 106-36.
Watanabe, Kazuko. 1994a. "Japanese Women's Studies." *Women's Studies Quarterly* 22, nos. 3-4: 73-88.
——. 1994b. "Militarism, Colonialism, and the Trafficking of Women: 'Comfort Women' Forced into Sexual Labor for Japanese Soldiers." *Bulletin of Concerned Asian Scholars* 26, no. 4: 3-17.
Watanabe Tsuneo, and Jun'ichi Iwata. 1989 [1987]. *The Love of the Samurai: A Thousand Years of Japanese Homosexuality*. Translated by D. R. Roberts. London: GMP.
Weiner, Michael. 1994. *Race and Migration in Imperial Japan*. New York: Routledge.
——. July 1995. "Discourses of Race, Nation and Empire in Pre-1945 Japan." *Ethnic and Racial Studies* 18: 433-56.
Weiner, Michael, ed. 1997. *Japan's Minorities: The Illusion of Homogeneity*. London: Routledge.
Weiss, Martin. 1996. "Japanese Immigrants in Brazil: A Quantitative Study of Exchange and Cooperation in Two Postwar Agricultural Colonies." Ph.D. diss., Columbia University.
Wetzel, Patricia. 1994. "A Movable Self: The Linguistic Indexing of *uchi* and *soto*." In Bachnick and Quinn, eds. (1994).
Wolf, Eric. 30 November 1980. "They Divide and Subdivide and Call It

Anthropology." *New York Times*, p. E9. Cited in Ortner (1984).

Yano, Christine. 1995. "Shaping the Tears of a Nation: An Ethnography of Emotion in Japanese Popular Song." Ph.D. diss., University of Hawai'i at Manoa.

Yoneyama, Lisa. 1993. "Hiroshima Narratives and the Politics of Memory." Ph.D. diss., Stanford University.

Yoshino, Kosaku. 1992. *Cultural Nationalism in Contemporary Japan: A Sociological Enquiry*. New York: Routledge.

THE TURBULENT PATH TO SOCIAL SCIENCE: JAPANESE POLITICAL ANALYSIS IN THE 1990S*

Kent E. Calder

The study of Japanese politics today is a microcosm of Japanese politics itself. Like the turbulent world that it attempts to analyze, that intellectual enterprise finds itself in a state of disarray and transition. From a traditional pluralism of perspectives, it has been steadily consolidating into two warring camps, with uneasy premonitions of major methodological change. As the longstanding isolation of Japanese political analysis from its parent discipline of political science steadily erodes, the field tries realistically to analyze Japanese political phenomena, even as it also strives to increase methodological and theoretical rigor.

Compared to the situation fifteen years ago, Japanese political analysis today is more sophisticated in at least five major respects. First, it is much more self-conscious about methodology. Varieties of method are rapidly proliferating, and testable hypotheses are becoming increasingly common and central to scholarly work. Second, the field is growing systematically comparative, with both those affirming and those denying Japanese uniqueness testing their claims, at least implicitly, against a backdrop of multiple national and historical cases.

Japanese political analysis is also growing more contentious, as it becomes more closely related to actual policy debates, and as analysts divide with increasing fervor on such real-world policy questions. The emergence and critique of "revisionism" over the past decade is only one evidence of this drift toward contention. Such controversy, to be sure, has had the positive effect of forcing protagonists to clarify the logic and empirical bases of their positions. Yet it has also had unsettling consequences as well. Chief among these have been an intensification of ad hominem arguments and personal vendettas within the field, together with a disquieting decline in the quality of primary Japanese-language

---

* The author expresses special thanks to the Harvard University Japan Forum and to Bill Grimes for comments on the manuscript, and to Edna Lloyd and Margot Chamberlain for assistance with publication.

data relating to sensitive political-economic topics, and a rise of propagandism.

A fourth hallmark of Japanese political analysis today is the rising importance in the field of non-traditional modes of dialogue, information dissemination, and debate—many influenced strongly by the emergence and steady expansion of the Internet. Several vigorous, highly interactive Internet discussion groups like the SSJ Forum, the U.S.-Japan Policy Forum, and the Dead Fukuzawa Society have arisen, together with rapidly proliferating home page offerings by both U.S. and Japanese educational institutions, government agencies, think tanks, and corporations. Such new forums for electronic communication provide much more rapid dissemination of both factual information and commentary about Japanese political events than has been previously possible. They are also supplemented, for those without Japanese-language ability, by intelligent new condensed summaries of the Japanese press, such as *The Japan Digest*, compiled in Washington, D.C., and *The Quick Read*, produced by USIS Tokyo. Many are disseminated rapidly by facsimile or E-mail.

A final trend, becoming rapidly more pronounced in the field of Japanese political analysis, is a growing integration between foreign and Japanese analyses of how Japan's political system and its political economy actually function. Several established Western scholars of Japanese politics, such as Terry MacDougall at the Kyoto Stanford Center and Steven Reed at Chūō University, have taken up long-term appointments in Japan. A few Japanese scholars have done the reverse, and the number of visiting appointments in Japanese politics outside Japan is rising. The United Nations University, through the efforts of its former Senior Vice Rector Inoguchi Takashi among others, is becoming more vigorous in cross-national analysis and exchange. International conferences relating to Japanese politics are proliferating. And the Internet, as suggested above, is clearly accelerating the momentum and intimacy of cross-national interaction.

This paper chronicles the foregoing, broadly positive trends in detail. It also, however, points out shadows in the ongoing evolution of Japanese political analysis. Research continues to have difficulty developing cumulative qualities, although there are some important partial exceptions to this tendency, such as the subfield of political economy. Despite the proliferation of basic information available to researchers, there are unsettling indications that its quality is declining, amidst the rising politicization of Japanese political analysis. And the rush toward developing comparative as well as methodological skills and experience has arguably meant a decline in the intuitive feel that many younger non-Japanese specialists in Japanese politics have for the historical and cultural dimensions of the phenomena they study. For better or worse, the study of Japanese politics is rapidly, if unevenly, becoming a social science rather than a branch of the humanities, particularly in the United States.

Methodological Innovation

Japanese studies generally has emerged from a culturalist perspective,[1] just as political science has emerged from law. The study of Japanese politics per se was given particular impetus for nearly four decades after World War II by two streams: political philosophy and political economy. The humanistic, philosophical stream, with strong sensitivity also to psychology, was well represented in the classic work of Maruyama Masao (e.g., 1963). Although often brilliantly insightful, it did not systematically test empirical propositions and was not in the usual social science conception centrally concerned with methodology. The political-economic stream, pioneered in the West by the Canadian E. H. Norman and in Japan by a series of Marxist intellectuals,[2] typically employed historical-institutional analysis that elaborated the relationship of economics and politics across various sectors in taxonomic form,[3] without developing clearly testable hypotheses.

Japanese political analysis has typically been a "concept taker" rather than a "concept maker" in relation to its discipline.[4] Yet the field has nevertheless, from time to time, fleshed out the meaning and implication of concepts with much broader application. Most of those broader concepts have centered in the area of political-economic development. In that field Japan's early in-

---

[1] One prototypical case, ironically not by a professional Japan specialist, is, of course, by Ruth Fulton Benedict (1946).
[2] See John W. Dower (1975).
[3] See, for example, Daniel I. Okimoto (1989); Richard J. Samuels (1987).
[4] See Richard J. Samuels (1992).

dustrial successes employing a state-led development model prompted both Japan specialists and others simultaneously to specify the Japanese model itself and probe its broader relevance. During the 1960s Japan specialists were prominent articulators of "modernization theory."[5] Similarly, Chalmers Johnson (1982) developed the notion of the "developmental state," which has also been applied elsewhere in East Asia, as well as Europe.[6]

To a greater degree than in political science as a whole, research on Japanese politics since World War II has been in either a humanistic vein, like the work of Maruyama, or historical-institutional in character, like the modernization studies and the work of Chalmers Johnson described above. Electoral studies, of course, have frequently been more quantitative.[7] Yet this latter orientation has been relatively unusual in the Japanese politics field as a whole.

One major recent methodological trend in Japanese political analysis has been an increasingly determined quest, both within and outside the historical-institutional persuasion, for testable, falsifiable hypotheses. To be sure, there are conspicuous exceptions to this tendency even among prominent literature; it is virtually impossible to test, for example, whether a nation's industrial-policy behavior is or is not "developmental" in character. Semantic arguments thus rage about both the meaning and the application of the concept. Major advances in testability have been made in Japanese politics, particularly where clear, quantifiable dependent variables are available.

Much of this new wave of hypothesis-testing is occurring in the analysis of budgetary politics, where clearly political dependent variables are available for consideration. Over fifteen years ago John Campbell (1977), for example, presented the notion of "balance" as an operative principle in Japanese budgeting. In recent years a number of scholars on both sides of the Pacific have refined this concept and explored its implications, using clearly testable hypotheses.[8]

---

[5] See Robert Ward and Dankwart Rustow (1964); Marius B. Jansen (1965); William Lockwood (1965); Ronald P. Dore (1967); Robert E. Ward (1968); and Donald H. Shively (1971).

[6] See, for example, John Zysman (1983); Jung-en Woo (1991).

[7] See Scott C. Flanagan, et al. (1991).

[8] See, for example, the work of Noguchi Yukio and Gregory Noble, as well as Kent E. Calder (1988).

The most important—and controversial—recent methodological innovation in Japanese political analysis is clearly the introduction of rational choice theory into the field. Mark Ramseyer and Frances Rosenbluth (1993, 1995) argued (1) that the rules of the game among political players decisively shape the character of political competition, and (2) that those rules can be rationally comprehended. Many of the rules that they deduce, such as the suggestion that both bureaucracy and judiciary are agents of the legislative majority, are furiously contested on empirical grounds.[9] Yet the approach has, as in the discipline of political science more generally, begun to acquire an increasing critical mass of adherents.

A recent variant of rational choice theory that factors in more sensitivity to institutional context than conventional presentations is the "microanalytic" approach of Kohno Masaru (1997). Kohno's work, attempting to explain the evolution of post-World War II Japanese party politics from multi-party to dominant single party and back again, focuses on the incentive structure and bargaining power of individual political actors, rather than broader groups, and embeds the analysis in historical context. The approach does not easily account for phenomena in a falsifiable manner, and cannot account for exogenous influences outside the political system. In one critical transformation of party politics that Kohno examines, namely the 1955 conservative merger, such external developments, especially rising corporate debt-equity ratios and deteriorating cash flows after the Korean War, were in fact important in triggering political change.[10] Yet the "microanalytic" approach does seem to aid in establishing forward-looking and internally consistent interpretations, giving it significant prospective heuristic value.

A third recent methodological innovation of potential importance is the introduction of "institutionalized norms" as an object of study. Employing this approach, the distinguished comparativist Peter Katzenstein (1996), not himself a Japan specialist, undertakes to explain the distinctive and sharply contrasting scope of police activities (very broad) and military responsibilities (unusually narrow) in Japan. The concept of norms, which Kat-

---

[9] See especially Chalmers Johnson and E. B. Keehn (1994).
[10] See Calder (1988), chap. 1.

zenstein views as being "made and unmade by history,"[11] is more dynamic and protean than that of most anthropologists. Yet Katzenstein does reintroduce a recognition of culture as a central explanatory variable that has not been common in Japanese political studies for a generation.

Toward Systematic Comparison

One powerful advantage of the rational choice approach, of course, is that it facilitates comparative analysis, *provided* that the analyst is sensitive to the nuances of differing political, social, psychological, and economic contexts. The trend toward systematic comparison, however, had been proceeding long before the emergence of rational choice as a popular political science methodology in the early 1990s. Indeed, the origins of systematic comparison can be traced to the modernization studies of the 1960s, although its progress since then has been checkered.

Japan has long been a two-fold anomaly in comparative terms: as the first—and for many years the only—non-Western industrialized democracy, and as a nation with a highly distinctive language and culture. The process of transnational comparison involving Japan is consequently inherently compelling, probing the limits of classical social science concepts like democracy and market-based economic management. Yet distinctive cultural and institutional variables make comparison inherently difficult.

Recent Pacific regional political-economic trends, especially the broadening since the late 1980s of pluralist democracy to South Korea, Taiwan, Thailand, and once again to the Philippines, coupled with the collapse of one-party dominance in Japan itself, have made cross-Asian comparisons more plausible, however. In similar fashion Japan's own increasing affluence and growing interaction with Western nations is also rendering comparisons with G-7 countries, especially between Japan, on the one hand, and larger European continental democracies like Germany, France, and Italy, on the other, more increasingly meaningful. These dual real-world trends make cross-national comparisons involving Japanese politics ever more plausible and attractive.

---

[11] Peter J. Katzenstein (1996), 2-3.

Following the early modernization-based comparative studies like that of Ward and Rustow, it was another two decades before cross-national comparison was given further momentum by Chalmers Johnson's "developmental state" paradigm. The process of qualifying, refining, and rebutting that model of state involvement in economic policy-making has been a further stimulus to comparative analysis.[12]

The original concept was laid out in Johnson's (1982) institutional history of Japan's well-known industrial-policy ministry that accorded it a determining role in the nation's economic development. In the book Johnson distinguished between a "regulatory state" that adopts a quietistic, legalistic approach to the economy, and a "developmental state" that seeks to transform economic structure through activist bureaucratic intervention. He identified the Anglo-Saxon democracies with the former paradigm and Japan with the latter, clearly implying from growth-rate differentials prevailing from the 1950s through the 1970s that the "developmental" system of *dirigiste* state intervention produced superior economic results.

Johnson's developmental state paradigm assumes the state to be a decisive, unified rational actor with powerful—indeed, almost unlimited—capabilities to transform the national economy. It also assumes political parties to be inert or ineffective actors, largely inconsequential in economic policy-making except as agents of all-powerful bureaucrats. And it further assumes that the private sector—in contrast to the decisive, proactive bureaucrats—plays a secondary and deferential role in the economic development process.

Through the presentation of his MITI institutional history within the more general framework of the "developmental state" and "regulatory state" categories, Johnson opened the way for a productive discussion of Japanese political-economic institutions, particularly the industrial-policy bureaucracy, in comparative perspective. His work first stimulated searches for "developmental" institutions and political-economic systems elsewhere,[13] particularly in France and Northeast Asia. These often involved a high

---

[12] Okimoto (1989); Samuels (1989); and Calder (1993).

[13] See, for example, John Zysman (1983); Fred Deyo (1987); and Alice Amsden (1989).

degree of positive approval of the pattern. Within six years, however, his work was stirring much more complex and critical reactions, questioning and qualifying the cross-national utility of his "developmental state" concept, as well as its applicability to even the Japanese case.[14]

Johnson's assessment of the Japanese political economy was challenged on four major grounds: (1) his assumption of MITI pre-eminence within the state in economic-policy formation; (2) his assumption of bureaucratic pre-eminence in the transformation of the economy; (3) his assumption of bureaucratic omniscience and efficacy; and (4) his assumption that the world of political parties was irrelevant to economic success. It is important to consider each of these critiques in detail, as they influenced the ensuing flow of Japanese political analysis. In total they cast considerable doubt on the relevance of the "developmental state" paradigm to the realities of the Japanese political economy, especially as it entered the turbulent "information age" of the late 1990s. Yet the debate that Johnson began greatly deepened scholarly analysis of Japanese industrial policy. It also led to a settled acceptance by most observers in the field that understanding the distinctive historical-institutional circumstances in which Japan entered the modern global economy is a crucial precondition for appreciating how Japan behaves even today, and that such understanding can have broader theoretical relevance.[15]

The first objection to Johnson's work was, as noted, its assumption of MITI pre-eminence within the Japanese state. In reality, critics pointed out, MITI lacked operating responsibility for many important sectors of the economy: banks, security companies, shipbuilding, pharmaceuticals, railways, airlines, and telecommunications, to name a few. Many other ministries—several of which were powerful in their own right, and adamantly opposed to MITI control—had important roles in policy-making.[16] And their modus operandi was by no means universally "developmental."

Johnson's assumption that the bureaucracy—pre-eminently,

---

[14] On the applicability to France, for example, see, for example, Jack Hayward (1986).

[15] See David Williams (1996), especially 259-73.

[16] The Ministry of Finance and the Bank of Japan, for example, were both important in industrial finance, and neither deferred much to MITI even in its heyday during the 1950s and 1960s. See Calder (1993), 72-102.

MITI—engineered Japan's post-World War II "economic miracle" was also sharply questioned.[17] Critics pointed out that Johnson did not even look at alternative possibilities in coming to his conclusion of bureaucratic pre-eminence. Samuels pointed to the important role of industry associations and "reciprocal consent"— rather than bureaucratic fiat—in the industrial-policy process. Okimoto and Calder pointed more generally to rich and often highly proactive private-sector institutions such as industrial groups, industrial banks, and trading companies. These bodies played decisive roles in economic growth, especially in successful consumer goods industries like consumer electronics and automobiles, the "Johnson revisionists" maintained.

In reassessing the role of bureaucracy, the "Johnson revisionists" often expressed a skepticism of bureaucratic efficiency that contrasted sharply with Johnson's a priori assumption of its omniscience and efficacy. In particular, the new wave pointed to the clientelism and captive regulation that often followed an ambitious arrogation of power by MITI and other ministries. The bureaucratic pathologies of standard operating procedures and obliviousness to market forces were also emphasized,[18] drawing on works in organization theory transcending Japan.[19] The "Johnson revisionists" thus deepened the integration of Japanese political-economic studies into the broader discipline of political science that Johnson had begun, albeit with a contradictory analytic intent.

The "Johnson revisionists" challenged a fourth assumption of *MITI and the Japanese Miracle*: that the Japanese political world had little impact on economic policy formation, and was essentially a puppet of the bureaucracy. They pointed both to the decisive role of politicians in brokering policy innovations in times of political crisis[20] and to their hand in frustrating bureaucratic efforts at industrial management on a wide variety of occasions.[21] The explicit critiques of Johnson on the role of political parties in economic policy-making were part of a broader stream of literature

---

[17] See, in particular, Okimoto (1989); Samuels (1987); and Calder, ibid.

[18] On the operation of all these forces in the process of government credit allocation, for example, see Calder, ibid.

[19] See, for example, Anthony Downs (1966); Graham T. Allison (1971).

[20] Calder (1988), especially 156-230.

[21] Calder (1993), especially 45-71.

stressing the proactive role of political parties in Japan more generally.[22] This argument was employed not only to elucidate the changing character of Japanese domestic politics, but also to suggest prescriptions for the policies of foreign economic partners dealing with Japan.[23]

Following the "Johnson revisionists" came a wave of systematic analysis re-emphasizing certain enduring roles of the state in the political economy. The most provocative and most systematically comparativist of these was by Steven Vogel (1996). Although bureaucracies may not be able readily to control whole economies in an era of globalization and interdependence, they are remarkably tenacious and effective in asserting their institutional influence. This is true, Vogel maintains, even in such market-driven sectors as finance and telecommunications, drawing on evidence from the Japanese and British cases.

Aside from the debate over industrial policy, a second intellectual force propelling a more comparative approach to Japanese politics has been the continuing controversy over the character of Japanese democracy. As suggested above, Japan's distinctive standing as one of the first non-Western nations with nominally democratic institutions, preceding even India, naturally makes Japanese democracy of broader theoretical interest. Simultaneously, the distinctive way in which those institutions function (simultaneously supporting both one-party dominance and rapid economic growth) naturally makes their democratic character controversial.

Edwin O. Reischauer and E. H. Norman, early pioneers in the cross-disciplinary Japanese studies field, were also, together with Reischauer's elder brother, Robert Reischauer, among the earliest students of Japanese democracy.[24] Edwin Reischauer, drawing on evidence of pluralism in Meiji Japan, including the *jiyū minken undō* and Diet assertion of budget-review prerogatives, stressed the proto-democratic character of pre-World War II Japanese institutions, a line of argument echoed and deepened by Robert Scalapino (1962). Norman, by contrast, emphasized feudal-authorita-

---

[22] See, for example, Gerald L. Curtis (1988); Bradley Richardson (1997).
[23] See, for example, Kent Calder (1989); Leonard J. Schoppa (1997).
[24] See Robert Karl Reischauer (1939); Edwin O. Reischauer (1946); John Dower (1975).

rian elements of the prewar system and transwar continuities,[25] a line subsequently pursued also by John Dower (1979).

Only in the 1970s did the analysis of Japanese democracy begin to grow explicitly comparative. While there was no intellectual catalyst as clear or controversial as Johnson's *MITI and the Japanese Miracle* in the industrial-policy arena, a key role was played by the debate over progressive local government. Terry MacDougall, in particular, pioneered cross-national comparison with Western democracies, in his (1975) analysis of how Japanese progressive local governments served as a pluralizing agent and a catalyst for policy change, in the ostensibly conservative one-party dominant system of the high-growth period. Mike Mochizuki (1982) and Dick Samuels (1983), students of MacDougall, extended this comparative analysis of pluralizing features of Japanese one-party democracy in the legislative and local economic policy arenas.

In the debate over Japanese democracy, as in other aspects of explicit cross-national analysis, Japanese politics has been more of a "concept taker" than a "concept maker."[26] Yet Japan specialists have flagged some promising areas for emphasis that hopefully will lead to development of new relevant concepts for comparative politics. T. J. Pempel (1990), for example, has used the Japanese case to probe the meaning of one-party dominant democracy in comparative perspective, attempting to draw systematic comparisons with Sweden, India, and Israel. Terry MacDougall (1982) and Ian Neary (1996), among others, have deepened concepts of interactive low-profile leadership with notions of "king making" and "brokerage" based on Japanese experience. Susan Pharr (1990) has likewise made provocative contributions to the comparative understanding of democracy through her concepts of "marginalization" and status politics, based on examining the role of women, outcaste groups, and the young in Japanese political experience.

---

[25] Dower, ibid.
[26] On this distinction, see Samuels (1992), 17–56.

A More Contentious Field

Japanese political studies, like Japanese politics itself, has long had a bias toward superficial consensus and toward the marginalization of fundamental debate.[27] To be sure, this consensus tendency has been periodically breached by iconoclastic intellectuals like E. H. Norman, and was ruptured at times by the Vietnam War. Yet the prevailing interpretation until the late 1980s typically neglected the darker side of Japanese politics, and presented an optimistic view of Japan's capacity and propensity to change in ways congruent with American interests. That view was not frequently questioned among students of Japanese politics until the late 1980s.

The first sharp and influential critique to this optimistic view of Japan's ability to change, and to pursue a course congenial to the Western industrial world, was the work of the *Handelsblad* Tokyo correspondent Karel van Wolferen (1989). Building on van Wolferen's view of Japan as "a system, not a state," incapable of decisive action, fellow journalist and social commentator James Fallows (1990) ventured the policy conclusion that Japan should be "contained." Clyde Prestowitz (1988) and Chalmers Johnson (1995) joined the so-called "revisionist" bandwagon, also calling for tougher U.S. policies toward Japan, although their analysis was based on a view of the Japanese state as coherent and strategic that contrasted sharply with—indeed, contradicted—the fragmented, autistic model presented by van Wolferen.

The new "revisionist" views naturally stirred controversy, both because they contrasted so sharply to more optimistic prevailing views of the Japanese political economy's flexibility and democratic qualities, and because they presented a challenge to prevailing public policies. The debate over new policy approaches to Japan and over an appropriate paradigm of the Japanese political economy to use as a point of departure was given increased urgency and bitterness by the growing trade deficits with Japan, which expanded steadily throughout the early 1990s.

Japanese surpluses have now crested, at least momentarily. The United States is once again the largest automobile and semiconductor manufacturer in the world, and China's trade surplus with

---

[27] On the marginalization concept, see Susan J. Pharr (1990).

the U.S. now periodically exceeds that which the U.S. confronts with Japan. The Japanese and the American private sector, if not Japan's government, have shown considerably more capacity to adjust than many revisionists thought possible. Some analysts think the "revisionist" debate is now passé.

Yet other analysts see the policy problem as being reform, in broader transnational terms. Political economist Kozo Yamamura, for example, has recently argued that Japanese industrial groups, in collusion with government, now dominate all of Asia through their transnational networks. The trade surplus of Japan's Asian industrial base with the United States, he argues, in admittedly speculative fashion, is at least $15 billion greater than that which the United States confronts with territorial Japan.[28] The debate thus continues, with anti-revisionists depreciating the danger of Japanese transnational networks to Western interests, and emphasizing the possibility of liberalizing changes in the Japanese domestic political economy itself.

Non-Traditional Forms of Dialogue

Historically, scholars of Japanese politics have gathered at professional meetings, subject-specific conferences, and informal gatherings. Across the vast expanse of the Pacific and the continental U.S. itself, divorced from European and other scholarly centers, personal contact has been at best intermittent. This isolation is being radically and fatefully reconfigured by the coming of the Internet.

Where these changes will lead is difficult to foresee. At a minimum, insights, together with groundless speculations, are being diffused much more quickly than before, along with the need for rebuttal. The traditional gulf between Japanese and Western scholarly understanding of Japanese politics may also be eroding, thanks to efforts like that of the Tokyo University Institute of Social Science, which has pioneered the field of interactive new-media dialogue in Japan with its innovative SSF Forum.

---

[28] Walter Hatch and Kozo Yamamura (1996).

Conclusion

The study of Japanese politics is clearly in a historic state of flux. Traditionally rather loosely integrated with its parent discipline of political science, the field is becoming more tightly linked to scholarship on politics outside Japan, both by the professional concerns of younger scholars in the field, and by the increasing convergence of Japanese political patterns with those elsewhere, particularly in Asia. Students of Japanese politics are growing more comparative and more methodologically sophisticated, even as they are also growing more contentious.

They are also drawing impressions and information from a much broader range of sources than before and forming them more quickly with the coming of a new electronic era. Yet the quality of the massive new information flows still remains in question. Japanese politics itself has always been a field of endeavor where crucial insights often flow in subtle, subterranean fashion. Indeed, one of the best known proverbs in the field is "Issun saki wa yami" (one inch forward is darkness), referring to the opaqueness of surface political phenomena. Rising controversy in the field of Japanese politics, as it becomes more tightly linked with policy processes in the United States, Japan, and elsewhere, may be leading to a troubling decline in the quality of scholarly data, coupled with propagandization. New methods and new technology should help to improve the quality of insight. Yet they must not stand in the way of gaining—and respecting—the intuitive insights that traditionalists hold dear.

Bibliography

Allison, Graham T. 1971. *Essence of Decision: Explaining the Cuban Missile Crisis.* Boston: Little, Brown.
Amsden, Alice. 1989. *Asia's Next Giant: South Korea and Late Industrialization.* New York: Oxford University Press.
Anchordoguy, Marie. 1989. *Computers, Inc.: Japan's Challenge to IBM.* Cambridge: Council on East Asian Studies, Harvard University.
Baerwald, Hans H. 1986. *Party Politics in Japan.* Boston: Allen and Unwin.
Benedict, Ruth Fulton. 1946. *The Chrysanthemum and the Sword.* Boston: Houghton Mifflin.
Calder, Kent E. 1988. *Crisis and Compensation: Public Policy and Political Stability in Japan.* Princeton: Princeton University Press.
———. 1989. *International Pressure and Domestic Policy Response: Japanese Informatics*

Policy in the 1980s. Princeton: Center for International Studies, Princeton University.
——. 1993. *Strategic Capitalism: Private Business and Public Purpose in Japanese Industrial Finance.* Princeton: Princeton University Press.
Campbell, John Creighton. 1977. *Contemporary Japanese Budget Politics.* Berkeley: University of California Press.
——. 1992. *How Policies Change: The Japanese Government and the Aging Society.* Princeton: Princeton University Press.
Curtis, Gerald L. 1971. *Election Campaigning Japanese Style.* New York: Columbia University Press.
——. 1988. *The Japanese Way of Politics.* New York: Columbia University Press.
Deyo, Fred, ed. 1987. *The Political Economy of the New Asian Industrialism.* Ithaca: Cornell University Press.
Dore, Ronald P., ed. 1967. *Social Change in Modern Japan.* Princeton: Princeton University Press.
Dower, John W., ed. 1975. *Origins of the Modern Japanese State: Selected Writings of E. H. Norman.* New York: Pantheon.
——. 1979. *Empire and Aftermath: Yoshida Shigeru and the Japanese Experience, 1878-1954.* Cambridge: Council on East Asian Studies, Harvard University.
Downs, Anthony. 1966. *Inside Bureaucracy.* Boston: Little, Brown.
Fallows, James. May, 1990. "Containing Japan." *The Atlantic.*
Flanagan, Scott C., Shinsaku Kōhei, Ichirō Miyake, Bradley Richardson, and Joji Watanuki. 1991. *The Japanese Voter.* New Haven: Yale University Press.
Fukui, Haruhiro. 1970. *Party in Power: The Liberal Democrats and Japanese Policymaking.* Berkeley: University of California Press.
Hatch, Walter, and Kozo Yamamura. 1996. *Asia in Japan's Embrace: Building a Regional Production Alliance.* Cambridge: Cambridge University Press.
Hayao, Kenji. 1993. *The Japanese Prime Minister and Public Policy.* Pittsburgh: University of Pittsburgh Press.
Hayward, Jack. 1986. *The State and the Market Economy: Industrial Patriotism and Economic Intervention in France.* New York: New York University Press.
Ike, Nobutaka. 1957. *Japanese Politics: Patron-Client Democracy.* New York: Alfred A. Knopf.
——. 1978. *A Theory of Japanese Democracy.* Boulder: Westview.
Inoguchi Takashi. 1993. *Gendai Nihon gaikō* (Contemporary Japanese Diplomacy). Chikuma shobō.
Ishida Takeshi. 1956. *Kindai Nihon seiji kōzo no kenkyū* (A Study on Modern Japanese Political Structure). Mirai sha.
——. 1961. *Sengo Nihon no seiji taisei* (Postwar Japan's Political System). Mirai sha.
Jansen, Marius B., ed. 1965. *Changing Japanese Attitudes toward Modernization.* Princeton: Princeton University Press.
Johnson, Chalmers. 1982. *MITI and the Japanese Miracle.* Stanford: Stanford University Press.
——. 1995. *Japan: Who Governs?* New York: W. W. Norton.
Johnson, Chalmers, and E. B. Keehn. Summer, 1994. "A Disaster in the Making: Rational Choice and Asian Studies." *The National Interest.*
Kataoka, Tetsuya. 1991. *The Price of a Constitution: The Origin of Japan's Postwar Politics.* New York: Crane Russak.
Katzenstein, Peter J. 1996. *Cultural Norms and National Security: Politics and Military in Postwar Japan.* Ithaca: Cornell University Press.

Kawai, Kazuo. 1960. *Japan's American Interlude.* Chicago: University of Chicago Press.
Kohno, Masaru. 1997. *Japan's Postwar Party Politics.* Princeton: Princeton University Press.
Komiya Ryutarō, Masahiro Okuno, and Kotaro Suzumura, eds. 1988. *Industrial Policy of Japan.* Translated under the supervision of Kazuo Sato. Academic Press Japan.
Kyōgoku Jun'ichi. 1987. *Nihon no seiji* (*The Political Dynamics of Japan*). English edition. Tokyo University Press. [Tokyo daigaku shuppan kai, 1983.]
Lockwood, William, ed. 1965. *The State and Economic Enterprise in Japan: Essays in the Political Economy of Growth.* Princeton: Princeton University Press.
MacDougall, Terry E. 1975. "Political Opposition and Local Government in Japan: The Significance of Emerging Progressive Local Leadership." Ph.D. diss., Yale University.
MacDougall, Terry E., ed. 1982. *Political Leadership in Contemporary Japan.* Ann Arbor: Papers in Japanese Studies, University of Michigan.
Maruyama, Masao. 1963. *Thought and Behavior in Japanese Politics.* Oxford: Oxford University Press.
Mason, Mark. 1992. *American Multinationals and Japan: The Political Economy of Japanese Capital Controls, 1899-1980.* Cambridge: Council on East Asian Studies, Harvard University.
Masumi Junnosuke. 1985. *Gendai seiji* (Contemporary Politics). Tokyo daigaku shuppan kai.
McNelly, Theodore. 1959. *Contemporary Government of Japan.* Boston: Houghton Mifflin.
Mendel, Douglas H., Jr. 1961. *The Japanese People and Foreign Policy.* Berkeley: University of California Press.
Mochizuki, Mike. 1982. "Managing and Influencing the Japanese Legislative Process: The Role of Parties and the National Diet." Ph.D. diss., Harvard University.
Morris, I. I. 1960. *Nationalism and the Right Wing in Japan.* Oxford: Oxford University Press.
Neary, Ian, ed. 1996. *Leaders and Leadership in Japan.* Richmond, Surrey: Curzon.
Okimoto, Daniel I. 1989. *Between MITI and the Market.* Stanford: Stanford University Press.
Otake Hideo. 1979. *Gendai Nihon no seiji kenryoku, keizai kenryoku* (Political Power and Economic Power in Contemporary Japan). San'ichi shobō.
———. 1986. *Adenaua to Yoshida Shigeru* (Adenauer and Shigeru Yoshida). Chūō kōronsha.
Packard, George R., III. 1960. *Protest in Tokyo: The Security Treaty Crisis of 1960.* Princeton: Princeton University Press.
Pempel, T. J. 1982. *Policy and Politics in Japan.* Philadelphia: Temple University Press.
Pempel, T. J., ed. 1976. *Policymaking in Contemporary Japan.* Ithaca: Cornell University Press.
———. 1990. *Uncommon Democracies: The One-Party Dominant Regimes.* Ithaca: Cornell University Press.
Pharr, Susan J. 1981. *Political Women in Japan.* Berkeley: University of California Press.
———. 1990. *Losing Face: Status Politics in Japan.* Berkeley: University of California Press.
Prestowitz, Clyde. 1988. *Trading Places.* New York: Basic.

Quigley, Harold S., and John E. Turner. 1956. *The New Japan: Government and Politics.* Minneapolis: University of Minnesota Press.
Ramseyer, J. Mark, and Frances McCall Rosenbluth. 1993. *Japan's Political Marketplace.* Cambridge: Harvard University Press.
———. 1995. *The Politics of Oligarchy.* Cambridge: Cambridge University Press.
Reed, Steven R. 1986. *Japanese Prefectures and Policymaking.* Pittsburgh: University of Pittsburgh Press.
Reischauer, Edwin O. 1946. *Japan Past and Present.* New York: Alfred A. Knopf.
———. 1950. *The United States and Japan.* Cambridge: Harvard University Press.
———. 1970. *Japan: The Story of a Nation.* New York: Alfred A. Knopf.
Reischauer, Robert Karl. 1939. *Japan: Government-Politics.* New York: Thomas Nelson.
Richardson, Bradley. 1997. *Japanese Democracy: Power, Coordination, and Performance.* New Haven: Yale University Press.
Rosenbluth, Frances. 1989. *Financial Politics in Contemporary Japan.* Ithaca: Cornell University Press.
Samuels, Richard J. 1983. *The Politics of Regional Policy in Japan.* Princeton: Princeton University Press.
———. 1987. *The Business of the Japanese State: Energy Markets in Comparative and Historical Perspective.* Ithaca: Cornell University Press.
———. 1992. "Japanese Political Studies and the Myth of the Independent Intellectual." In *The Political Culture of Foreign Area and International Studies: Essays in Honor of Lucian Pye,* edited by Richard J. Samuels and Myron Weiner. Washington, D.C.: Brassey.
Scalapino, Robert. 1962. *Democracy and the Party Movement in Prewar Japan.* Berkeley: University of California Press.
Scalapino, Robert, and Junnosuke Masumi. 1964. *Parties and Politics in Contemporary Japan.* Berkeley: University of California Press.
Schoppa, Leonard J. 1997. *Bargaining with Japan: What American Pressure Can and Cannot Do.* New York: Columbia University Press.
Shively, Donald H., ed. 1971. *Tradition and Modernization in Japanese Culture.* Princeton: Princeton University Press.
Steiner, Kurt. 1965. *Local Government in Japan.* Stanford: Stanford University Press.
Stockwin, J. A. A. 1975. *Japan: Divided Politics in a Growth Economy.* London: Weidenfeld and Nicholson.
Thayer, Nathaniel B. 1969. *How the Conservatives Rule Japan.* Princeton: Princeton University Press.
van Wolferen, Karel. 1989. *The Enigma of Japanese Power.* New York: Alfred A. Knopf.
Vogel, Steven K. 1996. *Freer Markets, More Rules.* Ithaca: Cornell University Press.
Ward, Robert E. 1967. *Japan's Political System.* Englewood Cliffs: Prentice Hall.
Ward, Robert E., ed. 1968. *Political Development in Modern Japan.* Princeton: Princeton University Press.
Ward, Robert E., and Dankwart Rustow, eds. 1964. *Political Modernization in Japan and Turkey.* Princeton: Princeton University Press.
Watanuki, Joji. 1977. *Politics in Postwar Japanese Society.* Tokyo: University of Tokyo Press.
Williams, David. 1996. *Japan and the Enemies of Open Political Science.* London: Routledge.
Woo, Jung-en. 1991. *Race to the Swift: State and Finance in Korean Industrialization.* New York: Columbia University Press.
Woodall, Brian. 1996. *Japan under Construction: Corruption, Politics, and Public Works.* Berkeley: University of California Press.
Yanaga, Chitoshi. 1956. *Japanese People and Politics.* New York: John Wiley.

———. 1968. *Big Business in Japanese Politics.* New Haven: Yale University Press.
Zhao, Quansheng. 1993. *The Politics behind Politics: Informal Mechanisms and the Making of China Policy.* Westport, Conn.: Praeger.
Zysman, John. 1983. *Governments, Markets, and Growth: Financial Systems and the Politics of Industrial Change.* Ithaca: Cornell University Press.

THE DEVELOPMENT OF JAPANESE LEGAL STUDIES IN AMERICAN LAW SCHOOLS*

Frank K. Upham

Introduction

Students of Japanese law suffer from a disadvantage that is unusual in the law school environment: most observers think that their object of study either does not exist or is a trivial add-on to a society that functions quite well without any reference to law. This view is by no means limited to foreigners bewitched by visions of Kabuki and the *Tale of Genji*. It is apparently shared by American political scientists. How else explain the lack of a single entry for "law" or similar terms in the index of a volume entitled *Conflict in Japan*? It is also widely shared by the Japanese. Shortly after becoming a law professor, I was asked by a Ministry of Finance bureaucrat, apparently bewildered by the idea of an American specialist in Japanese law, why I would want to study anything so irrelevant. And she was a graduate of a faculty of law.

Despite this peculiar handicap, the field of Japanese law is now established in American law schools. Although in 1970 there was only one American law professor specializing in Japan and only one or two law schools offering a course, as of 1996 one count put the number of law schools with courses on Japanese law taught by full-time professors with Japanese language ability at over a dozen.[1] If the criteria for inclusion were broadened to include

---

* I want to thank David Lee and Valerie Leipheimer for their excellent research assistance. I presented somewhat different versions of this essay at the conference on "New Approaches to Comparative and Foreign Law" held at the University of Utah, October 11 and 12, 1996, and at the Reischauer Institute of Japanese Studies at Harvard University on November 14, 1996. In addition to the useful comments I received at these times, I have benefited from the comments of William Alford, Mary Anne Case, Jorge Escoril, Mary Ann Glendon, Donald Horowitz, Duncan Kennedy, Richard Rabinowitz, Michael Reich, and Arthur Rosett. I asked for substantial help from my colleagues in Japanese law and am very grateful for detailed comments, corrections, and suggestions received from Eric Feldman, Daniel Foote, John Haley, Dan Henderson, Curtis Milhaupt, and Mark Ramseyer. I have tried to incorporate their views into the essay, but the opinions and mistakes remain mine.

[1] John O. Haley (1996), n. 5. Most of the statistics on the state of Japanese legal studies in the United States that I use in this essay come from that article.

schools using adjuncts and professors with research interests but not linguistic competence, the number would probably reach two dozen. Nor is interest in Japanese law limited to the full-time professoriat. A title search of a single legal data base for the first half of the 1990s turned up more articles on Japan than on either France or Germany.

The field remains tiny, however, with no more than a dozen scholars able to use Japanese sources in research and a smaller group of active specialists that until recently was heavily dependent on a cohort of scholars born between 1942 and 1954. Since the study of Japanese law has not traditionally been considered within the core of comparative law, the place of Japan in law school curricula remains unclear, and sustained intellectual contact between scholars of Japanese law and mainstream comparativists has been disappointingly rare. Thus, while it is unlikely that the situation will return to that of 1970, the field is far from mature.

In the first section of this essay, I describe the development of the field, the number and nature of Japanese law courses, the emergence of a critical mass of well-trained scholars, and the place of Japanese law as area studies within American law schools. In the second section, I attempt to portray and explain the relationship between Japanese law and mainstream comparative law, which has been self-defined as the study of European civil law. In this section, I also address briefly the intellectual influence of Japanese scholars, particularly Kawashima Takeyoshi, on the nature and direction of Japanese law scholarship in the United States.

The Growth of Japanese Legal Studies in American Law Schools

The Japanese American Program for Cooperation in Legal Studies

As may be common in the study of Asian cultures in American universities, postwar Japanese legal studies in the United States began with a project justified not so much in terms of learning about Japan but rather as teaching the Japanese how better to import Western ideas and institutions. Thus, Prof. David F. Cavers, then Chairman of the Committee on International Legal Studies and later Associate Dean of Harvard Law School, began the Japanese American Program for Cooperation in Legal Studies in 1954 with funding from the Ford Foundation and supplemented by the Fulbright Commission with encouragement from the Department of State. The core of the program was a series of educational exchanges to bring Japanese judges, procurators, and scholars to the Harvard, Michigan, and Stanford law schools to study American law, and to send American law professors to Japan to teach. Cavers stated the purpose of the program as follows:

> [T]he concern from which the idea of a cooperative program grew [was] our belated realization of the predicament which the bold experiment of the United States in transplanting American laws and legal institutions into the Japanese system had created for the legal profession and the legal scholars of Japan. American law faculties had not been participants in that experiment, nor were they, of course, committed to strive for its success. However, the risk that such an experiment would fail because the transplanted laws had not been properly understood and hence could not be properly employed and evaluated was one to which American law schools, as institutions responsible for the exposition and transmission of the American legal tradition, could not remain insensitive. As I noted in reporting to the...Ford Foundation: "The American laws are not entitled to preservation in the Japanese system simply because of their source or the good intentions with which they were put forward. However, they should be weighed by people who understand them and who can evaluate their usefulness in Japanese society in light of the functions they have played in the United States."[2]

The ostensible focus of the Program, therefore, was on American law, but there were three features that Cavers hoped would contribute to the development of American studies of Japanese law. The first was the dispatch of four American law professors to Japan to lecture. Although not an intended consequence of the program, one of them, Prof. B. J. George of the University of Michigan and later of New York University Law School, began the study of Japanese language and eventually became one of the pioneers of Japanese legal studies in the United States. A more intentional consequence was the training of three young Ameri-

---

[2] David F. Cavers (1963), xvii-xviii. Richard Rabinowitz reports that Cavers intended that the program would build American expertise in Japanese law as well as train Japanese in American law. For purposes of the funding institutions, however, the latter was emphasized in public documents. (Rabinowitz letter dated October 3, 1997, on file with the author.) Cavers hoped that at least one of the young Americans involved in the program would become a permanent full-time teacher of Japanese law. As it turned out, none did.

can law school graduates in Japanese language and law, one of whom, Rex Coleman, went on to be the first American scholar of Japanese tax law and an occasional teacher of Japanese law. It was a third aspect of the program, the convening of a conference on Japanese law at Harvard Law School in 1961, however, that marked the beginning of coordinated attention to Japanese law in American law schools.

The conference reassembled the Japanese who had studied in the United States in the 1950s and paired them with American collaborators to produce chapters in a symposium volume entitled *Law in Japan: The Legal Order in a Changing Society*, edited by Prof. Arthur von Mehren with the assistance of Coleman. The editorial collaborators included not only young American lawyers with Japanese language and experience like Thomas Blakemore, Coleman, and Richard Rabinowitz, but also well known American professors with no prior particular interest in Japan. These included not only Cavers, George, and von Mehren, but also Robert Braucher (Harvard), Walter Gellhorn (Columbia), Nathaniel Nathanson (Northwestern), and Max Rheinstein (Chicago). Also attending the conference from other disciplines were established scholars such as Richard Beardsley (anthropology, Michigan), Robert Bellah (sociology, Harvard), Albert Craig (history, Harvard), John Hall (history, Yale), William Lockwood (Woodrow Wilson School, Princeton), James Morley (political science, Columbia), Benjamin Schwartz (history, Harvard), and Kurt Steiner (political science, Stanford).

The editor divided the resulting volume into three sections: The Legal System and the Law's Processes; The Individual, the State, and the Law; and The Law and the Economy. The twelve chapters focused on the areas of Japanese law most affected by Occupation reforms, such as constitutional law, criminal procedure, labor law, family law, the judicial review of administrative action, antitrust, and corporate governance. The contributors included some of the giants of the legal profession in postwar Japan: Kawashima Takeyoshi, the founder of Japanese legal sociology, perhaps the most influential scholar on the nature of Japanese legal culture and the only Japanese author to make do without an editorial collaborator; Hattori Takaaki, later to serve as Chief Justice of the Japanese Supreme Court; Itō Masami, then a constitutional law professor and later a Supreme Court justice; Hirano

Ryūichi, a criminal law professor, later to serve as President of Tokyo University; and Katō Ichirō, a civil law professor and another future President of Tokyo University.

Law in Japan became the first general book on Japanese law. Several of its chapters laid the groundwork for later scholarship but foremost among them was Kawashima's, which introduced the concept of weak legal consciousness and which has had a profound effect on the course of American scholarship on Japanese law. The holding of the conference at Harvard, the close involvement of several of its faculty, the involvement of Michigan and Stanford law schools in the Japanese American Program for Cooperation in Legal Studies, and the participation of professors from other law schools gave the study of Japanese law visibility in the American law school world that it has not lost. Shortly thereafter, Rex Coleman taught the first Japanese law course at Harvard, and in 1964 the Japanese American Society for Legal Studies (JASLS) was founded, again at Harvard. JASLS sponsored the publication of the journal *Law in Japan: An Annual*, and Coleman became its first editor.

The Japanese Law Program at the University of Washington

Despite this early momentum, Harvard did not emerge as the leading center for Japanese legal studies in the United States. Nor did Michigan or Stanford or any of the other elite law schools involved in the early exchanges or represented at the 1961 conference. That position has been occupied since the late 1960s by the Asian Law Program founded by Dan Fenno Henderson at the University of Washington School of Law in 1962. As it was with the activities centered at Harvard, financial support from the Ford Foundation was instrumental in the creation of Washington's program.

Henderson has had a remarkable career. He joined the Japanese and Korean bars during the brief time in the 1950s when they were open to foreigners and then practiced for several years in Tokyo and the West Coast. With this experience, a political science Ph.D. from Berkeley, and a law degree from Harvard, Henderson had qualifications that were unique at the time and are unlikely to be repeated in the future.[3] He joined the Wash-

---

[3] There was one other person in the 1950s with a background equivalent to

ington faculty in 1962 and did not leave it until 1993. During those three decades he and his colleagues John O. Haley, who joined the faculty in 1974 and replaced Henderson as Director of the Asian Law Program, and Daniel H. Foote, who joined the faculty in 1988, have created the only comprehensive program on Japanese law outside Japan.

Henderson started the first regularly offered course on Japanese law in the mid-sixties and developed course materials that were eventually distributed in successive editions in 1978 and 1988 as *Law and the Legal Process in Japan.* Henderson was a prolific scholar and unchallenged as America's pre-eminent academic expert on Japanese law well into the seventies, but it was the law school's and university's determination to build on his presence that established Washington as the center of Japanese law studies outside of Japan. The most impressive evidence of this institutional commitment has been the constant presence of at least two and at times three Japanese law specialists (Foote, Haley, and Henderson) on the regular faculty, but also important has been the creation of a master's in law program in Japanese and the comprehensive curriculum on which it is based. The key to creating both was Henderson's practice of inviting Japanese specialists (often with American counterparts) to teach particular subjects like transnational litigation, sales and contracts, business associations, intellectual property, administrative law, antitrust, and tax. Although they have not been generally distributed, the materials are a unique resource to scholars and teachers as well as to Washington's students. The experience of teaching at Washington has also served as the foundation for several Japanese professors to go on to teach elsewhere in the United States and to publish as monographs what were originally Washington teaching materials.

Henderson's. Richard Rabinowitz was also a member of the Japanese bar, had excellent Japanese language and practice experience, and a Ph.D. from Harvard in Social Science. An article drawn from his dissertation on the development of the Japanese legal profession was published in the *Harvard Law Review* 70 (1956) as "The Historical Development of the Japanese Bar." Rabinowitz was a graduate of Yale Law School and, as Program Secretary of the Japanese American Program for Cooperation in Legal Studies, he had played a large role in the exchange programs administered from Harvard. Unfortunately for the field, Rabinowitz did not enter full-time academics, instead practicing law in Tokyo until semi-retirement in the 1990s. As of 1996 Rabinowitz continues to be engaged in practice, but is now devoting much of his energy to writing a legal history and analysis of Japan's foreign investment control regulations and policies of the postwar period.

Washington's undergraduate (J.D. degree) and graduate (LL.M.) programs in Japanese law remained unsurpassed in the mid-1990s, and it is not hyperbole to consider them as an important and unique part of the structure of Japanese studies around the world. Washington has educated dozens of Americans, Canadians, Europeans, Australians, and others more thoroughly in Japanese law than any other institution could have done. It has created a comprehensive library collection on Japanese law, and the Washington program, through Henderson, then Haley, and finally Foote, maintained the publication of *Law in Japan: An Annual* through twenty-five issues from the late 1960s to 1995, when it became the editorial responsibility of the Japanese side of JASLS. Washington's record is all the more remarkable given the status and resources of the law school and university. The School of Law is small with a full-time faculty of less than thirty-five and an undergraduate enrollment of 510 students. (These figures compare, for example, to over sixty faculty and twelve hundred J.D. students at New York University School of Law.) It is also public, and the Washington state legislature has not always been generous with its institutions of higher learning in general and the law school in particular.

The record is not of course one of total success. It is notable that not a single one of the tenured Japanese law specialists at United States law schools is a J.D. graduate of Washington, and only Haley is an LL.M. graduate.[4] This may have more to do with the practice of American law schools of limiting hiring largely to J.D. graduates of a narrow range of schools than with the quality of Washington's program, as is perhaps demonstrated by the presence of Washington graduates on law faculties in Australia, Canada, and Japan.

Another possible shortcoming was the treatment of *Law in Japan:*

---

[4] University of Washington Asian Law Program graduates in law teaching include Mark Levin, who joined the University of Hawai'i School of Law in 1997; Vicki Beyer, who has been the Director of the Temple University Law School Program in Japan; Stephan Salzberg and Pittman Potter (Chinese law) at the University of British Columbia Faculty of Law in Canada; and Veronica Taylor at University of Melbourne in Australia. This count does not include Lawrence Beer, a Ph.D. graduate of the University of Washington who spent a great deal of time at the Asian Law Program and should perhaps be considered its product. Beer writes extensively on Japanese law but is a political scientist, not a law professor.

An Annual. On the one hand, Washington deserves the credit for overseeing the editing and publication of the journal through 25 issues. On the other hand, only for one issue was a Japanese law specialist from another United States law school closely involved in the journal. Rex Coleman was followed by Henderson, then Haley, who was usually the editor until Foote took over in 1989. (Others have included Australian law professor Malcolm Smith three times and Amelia Porges of the Office of the United States Trade Representative.) Nor were other American professors closely or consistently brought into editorial decisions. There are many reasons for this pattern, the most obvious being that for much of this period, there were very few other Japanese law professors. Another certainly was the difficulty of coordinating with colleagues at other schools, and a third may have been the reluctance of the Japanese members of the Japanese American Society for Legal Studies, *Law in Japan: An Annual*'s sponsor, to entrust publication to a person or institution with a less established track record within Japanese academic circles. Nonetheless, had a wider group been brought into the enterprise, perhaps there would have been a broader commitment to its continuation when its survival became problematic in the late 1980s and its publication was taken over by the Japanese branch of JASLS.

As the account of the history of Japanese law in other American law schools demonstrates, however, these criticisms of the University of Washington program are minor flaws in what remains a record of educational and scholarly accomplishment unsurpassed not only in the area of Japanese law but perhaps in the area of comparative law in general.

Japanese Legal Studies Outside of Washington

Besides Washington, only Columbia and Harvard have maintained a significant commitment to Japanese legal studies from the seventies through the nineties. Both have offered introductory courses in Japanese law since the late sixties, and Columbia has had a program since Michael Young joined the faculty in 1980. The program gained greater depth when Lance Liebman came from Harvard Law School to become dean in 1992. Although not a Japan expert, Liebman had worked closely with Tokyo University professors, particularly with labor law specialist Sugeno Kazuo on issues of employment security and social welfare. Under his deanship, Columbia established a faculty exchange program whereby Columbia and Tokyo University faculty teach at each other's campus for a few weeks at a time every other semester. Similar exchange programs exist at Washington and Michigan, the former with Kobe University, the latter with Tokyo again.

Harvard's program began in 1971, when the Mitsubishi Corporation endowed a chair in Japanese law. As of 1997, the chair had not been filled with a permanent appointment, but it has provided a focal point for a series of visiting professors, around whom Harvard's Chinese law professors, first Jerome A. Cohen and then William Alford, created an uneven but often interesting program on Japanese law. The visitors have included American law professors, including (in chronological order) Dan Henderson, Frank Upham, Mark Ramseyer, John Haley, and Dan Foote; American practitioners like Charles Stevens and Richard Rabinowitz; and a long and distinguished list of Japanese professors and practitioners.[5] Continuity has inevitably suffered and the teaching has been uneven and occasionally disastrous, but the record of accomplishments is nonetheless impressive. Although undoubtedly due more to Harvard's traditional position as America's top producer of legal academics than to its Japanese law program, Harvard has produced the lion's share of American Japanese law teachers: Tamie Bryant (UCLA), Foote (Washington), Rob Leflar (University of Arkansas, Fayetteville), Percy Luney (Duke and North Carolina Central), Ramseyer (Chicago), Upham (New York University), and Young (Columbia).[6]

---

[5] After consultation with East Asian Legal Studies at Harvard, I believe that the following is the full list of Japanese professors who have taught as the Mitsubishi Visiting Professor: Fujikura Kōichirō, Hanami Tadashi, Iwahara Shinsaku, Kanda Hideki, Kitagawa Zentarō, Matsushita Mitsuo, Miyazawa Setsuo, Owada Hisashi, Sugeno Kazuo, Tanaka Hideo, Tanase Takao, Taniguchi Yasuhei, and Uga Katsuya. Japanese lawyers have included Nagashima Yasuhara and Yanagida Yukio.

[6] Dan Henderson also graduated from Harvard, but well before Harvard had any program in Japanese law. Haley (1996), n. 5, attempted a list of law schools and faculty with, as he put it, at least the potential to teach Japanese law courses. His list is as follows with my addition of the legal degrees of the professors (unless noted degrees are undergraduate, i.e., either LL.B. or J.D.): Albany (Alex Seita, Stanford), Arizona State (Dennis S. Karjala, U.C. Berkeley), University of Arkansas, Fayetteville (Robert B. Leflar, Harvard), U.C. Hastings (Dan F. Henderson, Harvard, and Leo Kanowitz, U.C. Berkeley), UCLA (Tamie L. Bryant, Harvard), Colorado (Hiroshi Motomura, U.C. Berkeley), University of Hawai'i (Mark Levin,

Harvard has also been the site for the development of a series of teaching materials, of which three have been commercially published: those by Professor Tanaka Hideo of Tokyo University (1976); Professor Fujikura Kōichirō of Dōshisha and later Tokyo and Waseda Universities, Professor Morishima Akio of Nagoya University, and American practitioner Julian Gresser (1981); and Tokyo practitioner Yanagida Yukio and his co-editors Foote, Edward S. Johnson, Jr., Ramseyer, and Hugh T. Scogin (1994).

After Harvard and Columbia, interest in Japanese law at American law schools has been primarily driven by availability of personnel. Although many schools beyond the dozen or so with full-time professors teaching about Japan have indicated substantial interest in hiring full-time faculty to teach Japanese law, the supply has lagged well behind demand. As a consequence, many schools that would like to offer courses have either not done so on a regular basis, used adjunct professors from practice, or brought a series of visitors from Japan. Among such schools are Duke, which for several years used Percy Luney of North Carolina Central and Fujikura Kōichirō of Tokyo University as visiting professors to teach Japanese law; and Michigan, which used a series of Japanese visitors in conjunction with Whitmore Gray, a comparativist who combined a strong interest in Japan with similar interests in China and Russia.

The latest law school to invest seriously in Japanese law, New York University, has done so as part of a new model of integrating foreign law into the law school curriculum. Instead of either bringing a series of different individuals as visiting professors as Harvard has done or having an ongoing connection with one person who could teach for only a short period each year as did Duke with Fujikura, NYU hires foreign faculty for extended terms to

---

Yale, LL.M., Washington), Marquette (Kenneth L. Port, Wisconsin), New York Law School (B. J. George, Michigan), New York University (Eric Feldman, U.C. Berkeley, Ph.D., U.C. Berkeley, Harry First, Pennsylvania, and Frank K. Upham, Harvard), North Carolina Central (Percy R. Luney, Jr., Harvard), Washington University (Curtis J. Milhaupt, Columbia), and the University of Washington (Daniel H. Foote, Harvard, and John O. Haley, Yale and LL.M. Washington). To this list, one might add Dan Rosen (Southern Methodist, LL.M. and J.S.D., Yale) who taught at Loyola of New Orleans until 1996 when he moved permanently to the Faculty of Law at Dōshisha University. Mark West (Columbia) is likely to join an American law faculty in 1998, giving Columbia two of the four most recent entries into the field while Harvard has none.

visit for one half to a full semester each year. The goal is to integrate the foreign faculty into the intellectual life of the school and to allow them time to accommodate their courses and teaching to the demands of American law students. Significantly, three of the first faculty chosen under this program in 1994-95 were Japanese: Japan's Permanent Representative to the United Nations, Ambassador Owada Hisashi of the Ministry of Foreign Affairs, Fujikura, and Prof. Taniguchi Yasuhei of Kyoto University. NYU then hired the author in 1994 and Eric Feldman in 1996, a Ph.D./ J.D. from University of California, Berkeley, who specializes in Japanese law and society. With the arrival of Feldman, NYU became the only school outside of Washington with more than one Japan specialist.

But it has not been only area specialists that have studied Japan in American law schools. As Japan's economic power has grown, law professors without language competence or formal area studies training have begun to write about Japan. This effort includes the work of Harry First, a domestic antitrust expert at NYU, on the Japanese Fair Trade Commission and the Antimonopoly Law; that of Dan Rosen, a communications and constitutional law scholar originally of Loyola of New Orleans now permanently at Dōshisha in Kyoto, on privacy and constitutional law issues; and that of Geoffrey Miller, a banking and financial law expert at NYU, on the legal status of the Bank of Japan and the loan crisis of the nineties. Non-Japan specialists' contribution has been most highly developed in the area of corporate governance, beginning in earnest when Mark Roe of Columbia Law School needed comparative support for his argument that the American system of financial regulation and its resulting impact on industrial organization was a product of historical accident and domestic politics. The result was a 1993 *Yale Law Journal* article co-authored with his Columbia colleague Ron Gilson that argued that the *keiretsu* system supported and helped explain the prevalence of long-term relational contracting in Japan as compared to the United States. Roe then broadened the argument (1993) with an article comparing corporate structure in Germany, Japan, and the United States in a symposium volume devoted to "economic competitiveness and the law," which article in turn provoked a critical response from Mark Ramseyer (1993) entitled with typical wit, "Columbian Cartel Launches Bid for Japanese Firms." There followed numerous articles by nonspecialists examining such features of Japanese corporate organization as the main bank system, life-time employment, and corporate cross shareholding.[7]

The best of the scholars involved in these exchanges have been able to overcome their lack of language ability by judicious use of Japanese graduate students studying in the United States and consultation with colleagues on Japanese law faculties. When strengthened by an ongoing dialogue with American specialists such as Curtis Milhaupt of Washington University School of Law and Ramseyer, the result has been an expansion of work on Japanese law that goes well beyond what would be possible by the small corps of specialists. As is common in the work of first time observers of Japan, however, their work sometimes portrays items of general knowledge to Japan specialists as pathbreaking discoveries by the authors, as when Gilson and Roe breathlessly referred to their observation that the *keiretsu* system was not principally designed by the Japanese as a means of corporate governance as a "critical insight" seemingly unknown to the Western world before their article.

Japanese Legal Studies as Area Studies

One of the striking aspects of the place of Japanese legal scholars in American academics is their intellectual integration with general Japanese studies. Probably for reasons having to do with their training and personal backgrounds, they have consistently been involved with other disciplines and departments at a depth and level of frequency unusual for law professors. Thus, Mark Ramseyer's co-authored books (with political scientist Frances Rosenbluth) are as well known for their arguments on Japanese politics and economic history as they are for their attention to legal issues, and the author's book on law and social change is probably used more frequently in undergraduate courses on Japan than in law schools. Similarly, legal specialists have served consistently in interdisciplinary positions relating to Japanese studies: Haley on the Social Science Research Council and the Fulbright Commission; Ramseyer as Chair of the University of Chicago's Committee on Japanese Studies and on the SSRC; and the author on the SSRC

---

[7] See, e.g., Marleen O'Connor (1993): 1529; Miller and Macey (1995).

and the American Advisory Committee to the Japan Foundation. Despite the lingering effects of the "law is irrelevant in Japan" tradition, legal specialists are included in symposia volumes on modern Japan, whether political science, economics, or history, more frequently than other foreign law specialists are likely to be on, e.g., modern Europe.[8] They have also served on interdisciplinary bodies outside of Japanese studies, either within their own universities, as exemplified by Haley's tenure as Director of the University of Washington's Henry M. Jackson School of International Studies or Michael Young's service as Director of Columbia's Program on Religion, Human Rights and Religious Freedom, or beyond, as exemplified by Ramseyer's service on the Board of Directors of the American Law & Economics Association and as co-editor of the *Journal of Legal Studies*.

Despite their close relationship with Japanese studies, professors of Japanese law have not suffered from the tension between "area studies" and "theory building" that has plagued their colleagues in the social sciences.[9] In the first place, legal education retains a professional as well as an academic function, and at even the most elite schools there are faculty who argue for an emphasis on teaching and practical training. They are supported by the students, most of whom are uninterested in academic careers, and the alumni, who are generally much more involved in school activities than are alumni of, for example, the UCLA political science department. Since students and alumni agree on Japan's practical importance and since many Japanese law teachers have also taught basic domestic law courses, the pressure to engage in theory-building has never been much of a factor in individual academic choices.

A second reason for the relative comfort of even the most descriptive of area specialists is the fragmented nature of theory in contemporary legal academics. There is no unitary cutting edge. Theory arguably includes innovative pedagogy, as demonstrated by the best of clinical education, as well as substantive and meth-

---

[8] See, e.g., John O. Haley (1990), Mark Ramseyer (1994a), and Frank K. Upham (1993a and b).

[9] James A. Bill (1985): 810-12, summarizes this tension as "Many of the theoreticians have lost the capacity to bring into focus the important fine-grained detail while some area specialists only seem to have the capacity to focus narrowly and myopically upon that detail."

odological approaches that range from the various "law and..." fields of economics, literature, and society through rational and public choice theory, critical legal studies, feminism, and critical race theory to traditional jurisprudence. In this fractured universe, where the scholarship is more likely to be done by jacks than masters of the disciplinary trades, area studies can exist without apology. As we will see in the next section, however, it remains unclear exactly where Japanese law fits, especially in regard to other forms of comparative law.

The Place of Japanese Legal Studies in Comparative Law

The Separation of Japanese Legal Studies from Mainstream Comparative Law

One would assume that a logical place for Japanese legal studies within American law schools would be alongside, for example, German, Chinese, or Islamic law as one part of the broader subject of comparative law. To make this assumption, however, would be to make the error that Oliver Wendell Holmes warned us against in the search for the origin of legal doctrine—that the essence of law is not logic, but experience.[10] So too, the essence of legal curricula is history, not logic. And the history of comparative law in American law schools does not include Japan.

The separation of the study of Japanese law (and perhaps of all non-Western law) from what has been considered comparative law since World War II can most simply be illustrated by data from the *American Journal of Comparative Law*, the publication of the American Association of Comparative Law. The *AJCL* is only one of approximately ninety journals dealing with either comparative law or international law (totally distinct subjects blithely lumped together in American legal culture primarily because they both deal with foreigners), but as one of the very few dedicated only to comparative law and as the only one edited by the recognized leaders in the field, it is arguably representative of what I refer to as mainstream comparative law.

---

[10] Oliver Wendell Holmes (1995), 109, 115: "The life of the law has not been logic: it has been experience....In order to know what it is, we must know what it has been; and what it tends to become."

In the forty-six years from 1950 to the middle of 1996, the *AJCL* published approximately 1450 book reviews. Sixty percent of reviewed books were written in English and all but one of the rest in other European languages, including 35 percent in German or French. The one book was in Chinese. Of course, the language of a book is not a certain guide to its subject. A book in French could be written by a Vietnamese scholar about Vietnamese law, and an English book could be a translation of a foreign original. But such is not likely to have often been the case. Of over 1100 articles in the *AJCL* during this period, twenty-six or 2.32 percent concerned Japan. (Alas, for those of us in Japanese studies always looking over our shoulders at China, there were twenty-seven about China!) In the same time period there were ninety-one and seventy-four articles about Germany and France respectively, and Europe as a whole occupied 41.12 percent versus 8.67 percent for Asia, including South Asia. (Latin America had 7.06 percent, Africa 1.79 percent, and the Middle East 3.31 percent.)

These statistics may be unsurprising when we remember the relative prominence of Japan and Europe in the American consciousness of the 1950s and 1960s, but they become more interesting when we discover that there were more articles written about Japan in the fifties than in any decade since. Perhaps reflecting the same approach that animated the Japanese American Program for Cooperation in Legal Studies, there were nine articles about Japan in the fifties. In the subsequent three decades, an extraordinary period in the economic and political development of Japan and the time when the Occupation reforms became naturalized Japanese law, there were only eleven articles about Japan, fewer than about Sweden (fifteen) and one sixth as many as about Germany (sixty-four). In the 1980s, when many in Japan and the United States were convinced that Japan represented the next world hegemon, there were as many or more articles about Germany, France, Belgium, the United Kingdom, Italy, Spain, Switzerland, USSR, China, Yugoslavia, Mexico, Vietnam, and Iran as there were about Japan (two). Ironically as Japan lost its invincible aura in the 1990s, the pattern changed, and Japan became, after Germany, the second most written about country (six articles as of 1996 versus thirteen).

There are three possible reasons for the neglect of Japan by mainstream comparative law. One is that the American legal world in general is not interested in Japan, at least in comparison to Germany or France, so that it would be natural that comparative law is not either. This is not the case. A survey of one legal publications data base from approximately 1980 to mid-1996 revealed 617 articles about Japan compared to 591 about Germany and 448 about France. Indeed, from these data, we can conclude that the general legal reader is more interested in Japan than in any single European country. To discover why this general interest is not reflected in the pages of the *AJCL*, therefore, we have to look inside the structure of American legal academics.

When we do so, we encounter two possible explanations: that the scholars of mainstream comparative law who dominate the American Association of Comparative Law and the *American Journal of Comparative Law* are professionally uninterested in Japan (and the rest of the non-European world), or that scholars of Japanese law are uninterested in what constitutes mainstream comparative law. In my opinion, both explanations are partially correct and are largely unavoidable given the training and background of the two groups.

From the Perspective of Mainstream Comparative Law: The Importance of "Culture"—Japan's and Comparative Law's

The field of general comparative law was dominated for most of the postwar era by a small group of distinguished European jurists who immigrated to the United States, many as refugees from Nazism, in the 1930s and 1940s.[11] As accomplished scholars from the most prestigious universities of the continent, especially Germany, they quickly established themselves at top law schools and began to build American comparative law scholarship in their images. They wrote about Europe, used European methodologies and concepts in their scholarship, and, perhaps most important, viewed the nature of law and legal systems through the lens of nineteenth-century German Legal Science, one of the richest traditions in legal thought.

Legal Science began with Friedrich Carl von Savigny's success-

---

[11] John H. Langbein (1995) at 547, lists the most prominent of these as Rheinstein at Chicago, Schlesinger at Cornell, Ehrenzweig and Reisenfeld at Berkeley, Kessler and Damaska at Yale, and Rabel and Stein at Michigan. See also Ugo Mattei (1994).

ful opposition to early nineteenth-century attempts to unify and codify German law in response to the French Civil Code of 1804. Savigny rejected the French argument that law could be derived solely by reasoning from abstract principles of natural law. On the contrary, Savigny argued that law was like language, a part of the genius and culture of a people and therefore knowable only through the methods of historical research. He maintained that a satisfactory legal system had to be based on the principles of law that had historically been in force in Germany. It followed that a prerequisite to codification was a thorough historical study of the legal order to identify and properly state these principles and to arrange them in a coherent system.[12]

Despite Savigny's initial appeal to history and culture, it was the drive to classify and categorize that came to dominate Legal Science. Germany's legal history, particularly its grounding in Roman law, became data for the "scientific" enterprise of identifying the underlying principles of law. The natural phenomena of law—the statutes, regulations, customary rules, etc.—became the equivalent of the experimental and observational data of chemistry or physics, and the goal of the legal scientist was to use definitions and classifications of data to create a systemic explanation of the law.

Although perhaps not necessary to the enterprise, the emphasis on systematic coherence and conceptual validity—critics have described Legal Science as "conceptual jurisprudence"—led to a high level of abstraction and a tendency to "make the facts recede," especially when they interfered with the ultimate objective of "a general theory of law from which all but the essential elements have been removed." Accompanying the emphasis on logical coherence was an attempt at purity. Legal Scientists focused their attention on pure legal phenomena to the exclusion of the nonlegal data, insights, and theories of other social sciences, ironically including history. Nor was the legal scientist interested in the ends of law, such as justice, which was the realm of the philosophers. The result of this narrowing disciplinary process was in

---

[12] I have drawn heavily on the work of Mary Ann Glendon and John Merryman in developing this section. Readers interested in more than this extremely superficial account are urged to consult, inter alia, Mary Ann Glendon, et al. (1982, 1985); John Henry Merryman and David S. Clark (1978); and John Henry Merryman, David S. Clark, and John O. Haley (1994).

the words of John Merryman, a leading American comparativist, "a highly artificial body of doctrine that is deliberatively insulated from what is going on outside in the rest of culture."[13]

Of course there is more to the story of German Legal Science than the outline given above, and the giants of postwar American comparative law were highly critical of the excessive formalism of much of their intellectual heritage.[14] It remains true, however, that even a more detailed and nuanced account of the intellectual tradition of Continental legal scholarship would retain two seemingly contradictory characteristics that become of central importance when we try to relate this heritage to the development of Japanese legal studies in the 1950s through the 1990s. First, the school is predicated on the assumption that law is deeply embedded in and dependent on culture. Second, the school developed a highly conceptual and abstract methodology where legal scholarship was defined to exclude the social, political, economic, and practical dimensions of law that became central to American legal research and teaching with the emergence of the Legal Realists in the 1920s and 1930s.

At least to the extent that these two characteristics influenced American comparative law, there was little chance that it would bring Japan into its core concerns.[15] If law is as culturally specific as language, there was little reason to compare legal systems from two very different cultural traditions. The tendency within comparative law was indeed to divide the legal universe conceptually into "families" of legal cultures and to limit most comparisons to legal systems within the same cultural environment in order to

---

[13] Merryman and Clark (1978), 228-29.

[14] Rudolf von Jhering actually wrote a biting satire of Legal Science in which he placed its leaders in a "Heaven of Conceptions [where] [t]he conceptions can not endure contact with the real world. Where they live and rule[,] the real world, and everything connected with it, must remain distant. In the Heaven of Conceptions..., there is no life in your sense, it is a realm of abstract thoughts and conceptions which have formed themselves out of themselves by means of the logical generatio aequivoca and which, therefore, shy from any contact with the real world. A person who desires to enter here must even give up all memory of the real world, otherwise he is not worthy or capable of looking upon the pure conceptions in which the highest pleasure of our heaven consists." Excerpted in Arthur Taylor von Mehren and James Russell Gordley (1977), 71.

[15] Just how unlikely that would be can be sensed from John Langbein's statement in 1995 of his "amazement" that half of the twenty-five top American law schools offered courses on Japanese law. Langbein (1995), 546.

find what worked there so that it could be used to improve one's own legal system and to advance the goal of the conceptual unification of the civil law family of national legal systems.

While comparisons might be extended to the common law world of England and North America, places with a culture as distinct as Japan's posed severe problems. A fundamentally Western cultural environment could no longer be taken for granted and comparative law as normally practiced—to discern technical variations or innovations within a fundamentally unitary legal culture—became impossible. One option would have been to adopt a functionalist approach, to investigate, for example, the treatment of traffic accidents in several different legal systems without reference to legal culture. Since the heritage of Legal Science was to eschew empirical (and thus nonlegal) research, however, such work was not only well outside the core inquiry but also demanded methodological training that comparativists rarely receive. A second option would have been to redefine the legal families from categories dependent on history and intellectual tradition to families defined on criteria like levels of economic, technical, or political development. To do so, however, would have meant turning away from the central questions of the Continental civil law tradition and from Savigny's original insight that law cannot be taken out of its cultural context.

The chances that countries like Japan would become significant objects of comparative scrutiny, therefore, were slim, but Japan was not ignored completely. The part of the Continental tradition that valued the classification of the world legal systems into families based on culture had to deal with Japan, although of course China loomed much larger in the comparativists' imaginations. How they dealt with Japan, however, was not necessarily satisfactory to Japan scholars. Consistent with the assumption that law arises from and should be studied within its national culture and history, the tendency was to emphasize the way that Japanese culture shaped its law, rather than investigating the role that law played in politics, economics, or society.

The result sometimes verged on silliness, at least from the perspective of American scholars of Japanese law. Even when the scholars are serious, the conclusions interesting, and the insights provocative, most Japan scholars don't like it, partly because of their own background, partly because of the method. Although perhaps inevitably taken out of context, an example may help illustrate what it is about the comparative law methodology that irritates American scholars of Japanese law. In 1976, Roberto Mangabeira Unger used "the comparative method" to gain perspective on the evolution of postliberal society, by which he meant the West, and to create a taxonomy of modernity and of modern legal systems.[16] In doing so he had to address the troubling diversity of modern societies that challenged the idea of modernity itself. To get a comparative grasp on this diversity, he had to expand his conception of modernity to include two nonliberal types of society. Inevitably, given its Orientalist appeal, one was the People's Republic of China, which represented for Unger "revolutionary socialist society"; the other was Japan from Meiji to the present, which Unger classified as "traditionalistic." Each faced social dilemmas analogous to those of the postliberal West but exhibited its own distinctive form of consciousness, mode of organization, and law.

For Unger, "the dualism of traditionalistic society" creates "two very different kinds of legal life" that exist simultaneously within society. "[First], there is the central legal order, formulated by the indigenous elite or imposed by the colonial authorities in imitation of foreign models" (227-28). For Japan this is the German-inspired codes of the turn of the century and the constitutional and other reforms of the Occupation. "[Second], alongside the central legal order, there is an informal system of customary law that embodies the dominant consciousness of traditionalistic society and buttresses its rank order" (228). For Unger this becomes the informal dispute resolution, the low litigation rates, and Kawashima's weak legal consciousness, which combine to constitute the customary legal system. But "[e]ven more important than the interpenetration of custom and legal order in the history of traditionalistic societies is the growth of a sprawling body of bureaucratic law that mainly regulates the economy. This law is often designed to circumvent the central legal system, which is perceived as remote and rigid or as committed to procedures, interests, and ideals opposed by the dominant elite" (228).

No one familiar with Japanese law would dispute the plausibil-

---

[16] Roberto Mangabeira Unger (1976). He deals with Japan at pp. 224-31. Subsequent references in text.

ity of these characterizations, although many would dispute their accuracy, bemoan their generality, and question their distinctiveness from American law. If one is to categorize and characterize "modern" law in a single volume and "traditionalistic society" in seven pages, however, corners must be cut, and nuanced interpretation may be impossible. What is most objectionable, therefore, is not Unger's generality or accuracy; it is his sources. For his conclusions on Japanese law, he cites sociologists (Vogel, Ishida, and Nakane), historians (T. Smith and Beasley), anthropologists (Dore), and a business school professor (Yoshino) as well as of course Kawashima's *Law in Japan* chapter and the second volume of Dan Henderson's study of conciliation. Except for the last two, there is little or no attention to law in these sources, and the Kawashima and Henderson sources focus directly only on the informal and "nonlegal" aspects of Japanese law, precisely those aspects that reinforce what Unger got from the nonlegal sources.

Although it probably would not have mattered, Unger would have had some excuse for not consulting legal sources in his attempt to explain Japanese law: in 1976, there was not much available on concrete legal phenomena in Japan. By 1991 when Stephen C. Hicks[17] critiqued Unger's treatment of Japanese law, however, there was a great deal of translated primary sources such as statutes, cases, and scholarship and a large secondary literature interpreting them, and yet Hicks makes almost no use of these empirical data.

Hicks's argument is that the notion of the self in Japan is very different from Unger's assumptions and that his misapprehension of the Japanese self led Unger to misunderstand Japanese law. Hicks is best understood in his own words:

> For us in the West, benevolence, respect, altruism, or disinterestedness are not culturally prominent....In Japan, however, [these values] are self-consciously acknowledged to be the cement of all social relations. Thus *giri* (duty) and *on* (responsibility) should be fulfilled with *ninjo* (warmth) (822-23).
> In Japan the private sphere of autonomy is not only less fulfilling but detracts from the sense of group unity. Dignity comes from belonging. Again, what guides this is an emotionally felt harmony, not a principle of authority whether in one's conscience or in a creed....One significant effect of this is that law works differently. It

---

[17] Stephen C. Hicks (1991): 789.

is not an important social force except in a formal sense. A dispute is not an isolated case separate from its social setting (823).

Hence law does not preexist the occurrence of a dispute and predict the parameters of its resolution. Social order is maintained without law as a system of rules....The emphasis in Japanese society is on relationships, not transactions. Law is considered determinate and impersonal, two characteristics which contradict the very personal and conciliatory nature of Japanese ways of resolving disputes (823-24).

The key [to resolving conflict] seems to be the disassociation of fault from the person for the sake of the relationship....Rather than restore the status quo of mutual respect by compensation or the legitimation of rights and wrongs, the Japanese seek to reestablish the original harmony underlying the relationship before the breach. One's vulnerability to the other is in effect confessed in the affirmation of the preexisting relatedness (825-26).

In reaching these conclusions about Japanese law and the Japanese, Hicks relied exclusively on titles like "The Implications of Apology: Law and Culture in Japan and the United States"; "Ajase and Oedipus: Ideas of the Self in Japanese and Western Legal Consciousness"; "Some Cultural Assumptions about the Japanese"; "The Law of the Subtle Mind: The Traditional Japanese Conception of Law"; "The Status of the Individual in the Notion of Law, Right and Social Order in Japan"; "Consciousness of the Individual and the Universal among the Japanese"; *The Anatomy of Dependence*; and "The Status and Role of the Individual in Japanese Society."[18] While one would be foolish to dismiss the role of apology or dependence (*amae*) in Japanese law, one might wonder whether a glance at a translated case or two might not have deepened Hicks's insight into how these cultural values work themselves out in the legal system. Or perhaps a close look at empirical data on the reality of, e.g., family court mediation in Japan might have given Hicks a somewhat more grounded view of the roles of self and hierarchy and rights and harmony.

While I admit to doubts as to the usefulness of observations about law at their level of abstraction, my point is not that Hicks and Unger are wrong. My point is that they are both representative of a comparative law method that is anathema to most American scholars of Japanese law.[19] It is revealing that Hicks's primary

---

[18] Hicks cited and then dismissed Haley's work on the non-cultural explanations for Japanese attitudes toward law (824 n. 114).

[19] The methodology of Hicks and Unger is not representative of all comparative

criticism of Unger is that Unger failed to "look at the Japanese social order through its own self-image." In stating the comparative law project thusly, Hicks is very much in the spirit of current discussion of a "crisis" in comparative law, a discussion that leads one to conclude that Savigny's influence remains strong among late twentieth-century comparativists.

To an outsider like myself this dissatisfaction with contemporary comparative law scholarship in the United States seems remarkably widespread. William Ewald has spoken of a "malaise" in comparative law and of the field's devotion to the Muse Trivia, "the same Goddess who inspires stamp collectors, accountants and the hoarders of baseball statistics."[20] Others have described the state of the field as a matter of "concern" (Joachim Zekoll)[21] and "dispersed" and "scattered" (Arthur von Mehren),[22] or complained that its scholarship is "superficial" (Alan Watson)[23] or that it deals only with "irrelevant problems" (Jaro Mayda),[24] or despaired about a comparative law curriculum that enjoys only "marginal relevance" (Zekoll) or is a "curricular Potemkin Village" (Langbein). John Langbein captured the sense of this literature well when he stated, "If the study of comparative law were to be banned from American law schools tomorrow morning, hardly anyone would notice."[25]

Although some blame the malaise on parochial and monolingual American students or the obsession with case analysis in law school pedagogy, most commenters eventually conclude that the prevailing method of studying foreign legal systems does not lead to a satisfactorily inside understanding of that system, what Hicks

---

law work now being done in the United States. Three examples of comparative scholarship that eschews the cultural abstractions that irritate Japanese law scholars are Mary Ann Glendon (1987); Donald Horowitz (1994): 233; and Joseph Weiler (1986): 1103. There are many other possible examples. Indeed, as the "crisis" in American comparative law discussed infra suggests, many comparativists may share Japanese law scholars' methodological unease. The fact remains, however, that when comparativists turn their attention to Japan, the temptation to focus on abstract cultural differences to the exclusion of close analysis of concrete social and legal phenomena seems often irresistible.

[20] William Ewald (1995): 1891, 1892.
[21] Joachim Zekoll (1996): 2722.
[22] Arthur Taylor von Mehren (1971): 624.
[23] Alan Watson, *Legal Transplants: An Approach to Comparative Law*, 2nd. ed. (Athens: University of Georgia Press, 1993), 10-16, quoted in Ewald (1995): 1963.
[24] Quoted in Ewald, ibid.
[25] Langbein (1995), 549.

meant when he stressed the importance of looking at Japan's social order from within the Japanese' own self-image and perhaps what Savigny meant when he stressed that law was as embedded in culture as language. According to this view, comparativists must overcome their American biases and attempt to understand alien legal practice as a native would. Before they can begin to gather concrete legal data, therefore, they must be able to understand on a subjective level the natives' range of experience and way of thinking and feeling about the world. Otherwise, comparative law is no more than the assembly of facts with no hope of a true understanding of what the system means to the foreigners living and practicing within it.

From the Perspective of Japanese Law Scholars: The Importance of "Culture"—Japan's and Ours

The American law professors who specialized in Japanese law were a very different group from mainstream comparativists. First, they were native Americans, with no Japanese expatriate prominent among them. Second, they came to law after having studied or lived in Japan. Some were born and raised in Japan as the children of American missionaries or businessmen; others encountered Japan via such means as Princeton-in-Asia or the Mormon Church; others went first as graduate students in Japanese studies. Their training was therefore usually first as Japan specialists who added law to their area studies training, rather than as legal specialists who came to Japan after formal training in law.

As American-trained scholars approaching Japan, they immediately faced the "is law relevant?" question. Here the Kawashima chapter in *Law in Japan* is again important. Despite repeated and persuasive attacks by a number of Japanese and American scholars led on the American side by John Haley, it probably remains the most influential text on Japanese law for those without specialist training in Japan. Both Unger and Hicks, for example, cited Kawashima, and many of the other works cited by them are derivative of Kawashima. Even if their previous area studies training had not predisposed them to do so, therefore, scholars of Japanese law would have been forced to look at law within a social context simply to prove its worth as an object of a scholarly career.

If instead they had simply started talking about the transplant from Germany to Japan of a particular theory of obligation in the Civil Code, everyone would have assumed their total irrelevance. Other American scholars of Japan would have been totally bewildered: not only have these people chosen a subject of dubious importance, but they also are talking about it with an incomprehensible vocabulary and at a level of abstraction that makes it meaningless to others interested in Japan. Nor is it likely that legal comparativists would have paid much attention. First, they would have doubted, perhaps unfairly, that the Japanese echoes of European debates on civil code theories had much to teach scholars thoroughly familiar with the originals. Second, the importance that the European tradition ascribes to national culture would have made comparativists wary of the relevance of Japanese interpretations of Western theories.

On the latter point, it is useful to recount one of the rare encounters between mainstream comparativists and Japan scholars. It occurred at the 1985 meeting of the American Association of Comparative Law. The Association had chosen to meet at the University of Washington so that Asian law could be a focus of attention. John Haley, who perhaps more than anyone else has tried to bridge this intellectual divide, and Arthur Rosett, who has championed the teaching of Asian law at UCLA, addressed the group on "Teaching Japanese Law as Comparative Law." They argued that it was possible to teach the basic civil law course through a single country, Japan. The response of one of the leading comparativists in the audience, one of those whom Rosett remembered as "the hecklers from the East," was incredulity: that it was unthinkable to try to teach the civil law tradition through Japan because "Japan has a distinct culture." Since it is unlikely that the speaker believed that Germany and France do not have distinct cultures, the conclusion must be that the civil law system is not a system outside of the particular cultural context in which one studies it. In other words, if one wants to compare law, it must be Europe. Otherwise, one has to compare law and culture. Hence we have articles about Japanese law that do not get beyond *giri* and *ninjō*.

So the unavoidable first task for Japanese legal scholars was to prove law's relevance to a full understanding of postwar Japan. Fortunately, this was not difficult. First Dan Henderson's 1965 study of judicially-based conciliation in Tokugawa and contemporary Japan demonstrated the institutional, as opposed to solely cultural, foundations of alternative dispute resolution in Japan. Then in the 1970s, the use of litigation by citizens' and residents' movements forced even those observers trained to see only harmony and consensus, first, to face the role of conflict in Japanese society and, second, to acknowledge the role of formal law in articulating and channeling that conflict. The Big Four Pollution Cases were the most celebrated of these litigation campaigns, but litigation played a substantial role in virtually every environmental dispute and was present throughout the social upheaval of the period, including the campaign for women's rights in employment. Although not denying the relevance of culture in some ultimate sense, these events demonstrated the importance of studying law as an independent factor in society, rather than as the passive reflection of culture.

Perhaps most corrosive of the culturalist view of Japanese law, however, was John Haley's "The Myth of the Reluctant Litigant," published in 1978. In it Haley directly challenged the by then conventional wisdom attributed to Kawashima but repeated by Unger, Hicks, and innumerable other Westerners and Japanese that Japan's legal system was an amalgam of modern rules—Germany's from the turn of the twentieth century and America's from the Occupation—and premodern attitudes, Kawashima's weak legal consciousness. Haley cited data on the cost and delays of litigation in Japan, gaps in the doctrines needed for the effective enforcement of judgments, institutional weaknesses in the judicial system, and secular trends in national litigation rates that led many to believe that Japan's low rate of litigation, which as Haley pointed out was not all that low once the comparison went beyond the U.S., had as much to do with deliberate government policy as it did with culture. Once Mark Ramseyer began in the 1980s to apply, with devastating effect, the principles of economic analysis and rational choice theory to Japanese legal phenomena, therefore, the idea that law is either socially or politically insignificant or culturally determined in a strong sense was pretty well dead within the coterie of Japanese law scholars.

Given this background, it is unlikely that Japanese law scholars will turn away from their sociolegal approach any time soon and begin to explore the way in which European civil law theories or scholarly traditions have worked themselves out in Japan. First, they would have to become thoroughly competent in French or German. Second, they would have to delve deeply into what they have been trained both as American lawyers and area studies specialists to see as the epiphenomena of scholarly theory. Third, there is the fear that civil law theories are of very limited relevance in Japan, something learned in undergraduate law faculties and forgotten on graduation. To shift from relating law to Japanese politics, economics, or society to focusing on the intricacies of doctrine would mean forsaking the audience that Japanese legal scholars have painstakingly created among other American legal academics and Japan specialists, U.S.-Japan relations gurus, and governmental agencies on both sides of the Pacific for the uncertain embrace of mainstream comparative law, a field that, at least from a reading of its own literature, appears in crisis.

To engage the intellectual challenges of the Europeanists, therefore, would not only be psychologically difficult, it would be personally and professionally expensive and risky. While most in the field would agree that an in-depth knowledge of, for example, the evolution of German administrative law doctrine would be very useful in explaining Japanese courts' approach to government action, none of the current generation of Japan scholars is likely to become as broadly comparative as would be necessary to understand the jurisprudential, as opposed to social or political, bases of Japanese administrative law.

At this point a brief digression, courtesy of John Haley, into German scholarship on Japanese law can provide an interesting perspective on the nature of the gulf between mainstream comparativists and Japanese law scholars.[26] Germans write more about Japanese law than any foreigners except Americans. They understand the technical doctrine wonderfully well and can explain its origins and meanings in a depth that escapes the Americans. The nature of the administrative law doctrines of standing or justiciability in Japan, for example, becomes much clearer with a knowledge of their German equivalents. The importance of this perspective is not limited to the clarification of doctrine; indeed, it can at times point out the limited importance of doctrine per se. In the case of the administrative law "threshold" doctrines men-

---

[26] See Haley (1982a).

tioned above, a review of the liberalization of the doctrines by German courts would show that it was not simple fidelity to German doctrine that has kept Japanese judges from expanding access to administrative litigation.

To discover what has motivated the Japanese judiciary, therefore, one needs to go beyond doctrinal analysis to social or political reasons for judicial conservatism in this area, and in this effort, the German scholars of Japanese law have little to add. In fact, according to Haley, they tend to be uncritically accepting of American area studies literature. Because legal education in Germany is undergraduate, German scholars come to Japan after studying law and generally have very little area studies training. Furthermore, German Japanese studies programs are largely philological—focusing on history, literature, and culture at the expense of contemporary economics, politics, or sociology. The result is a body of scholarship on Japanese law that is in ways the mirror image of and therefore complements the American literature.

The gap between mainstream comparative law and American scholarship on Japanese law may have its intellectual origins in a broader phenomenon than the differences in background and training described above. Mainstream comparativists, with their ambition to bring the whole world into a system of families of laws, are acting out, albeit on a smaller stage, the same drama as Samuel P. Huntington, a professor of international relations, performed when he published his 1993 declaration that the future of world politics could best be understood and predicted as a "clash of civilizations."[27] For Huntington, "the fundamental course of conflict in [the] new world will not be primarily ideological or primarily economic. The great divisions among humankind and the dominating source of conflict will be cultural....The clash of civilizations will dominate global politics. The fault lines between civilizations will be the battle lines of the future."

The penchant for categorization and the reliance on culture for assigning nations, civilizations, and legal systems to different categories appear to run deep in Americans who focus their con-

---

[27] Samuel P. Huntington (1993): 22. For those readers who are curious—and who would not be?—but too lazy to look up the article: Huntington lists "seven or eight major civilizations...Western, Confucian, Japanese, Islamic, Hindu, Slavic-Orthodox, Latin American and possibly African."

cept of foreigners on Europe. They seem to have a view of Asia (and Japan) that is so culturally sensitive that it is, ironically, extraordinarily ethnocentric. Apparently they believe that cultural differences between the United States and Japan—*giri* and *ninjō* rather than individualism—overwhelm the fundamental similarities of political organization and ideology, of social and economic structure, and of levels of education and income, not to mention similarities in law.

This approach, however, is anathema to scholars of Japanese law. They see cultural explanations of the world not only as depriving them of their hard won claim to relevance (as well as profoundly misleading), but also as invariably using Europe as the starting point and implicit norm. Thus, René David's famous classification of world law left Japan to the "other" category, and Unger characterized Japan as representative of "traditionalistic" societies. The idea that contemporary Japan is more bound by tradition than the United States, Italy, Spain, Ireland, or any number of other countries is bizarre to most students of Japan, and yet Unger's classification continues to be influential.[28] As long as this continues to be the case and the Japanese specialists remain focused almost entirely on their own concerns, the two cultures of comparative law and Japanese law are likely to persist in their separate courses.

Bibliography

(This bibliography is highly selective. Except for bibliographies, I have limited the choices to materials of interest to a non-legal audience, but I have not included works by legal scholars that are already generally known to Japan specialists.)

I. Bibliographies

Coleman, Rex, and John O. Haley. 1975. *An Index to Japanese Law, Law in Japan: An Annual* [Special Issue] Occasionally supplemented in *Law in Japan: An Annual.*

Feldman, Eric. 1988. "Annotated Bibliography: Japanese Law and Society." *Law in Japan: an Annual.*

---

[28] See Ugo Mattei (1997). Mattei divides the world's legal systems into professional law, political law, and traditional law. All of Europe and North America belong to the first. China and Japan belong to the third.

Oda, Hiroshi, and Sian Stickings. 1996. *Japanese Law in English*. London: University College, London.
Scheer, Matthias K. 1992. *Japanese Law in Western Languages*. Hamburg: German-Japanese Lawyers Association.

II. Translated Case Reports

Beer, Lawrence W., and Hiroshi Itoh. 1978. *The Constitutional Case Law of Japan: Selected Supreme Court Decisions 1961-1970*. Seattle: University of Washington Press.
———. 1996. *The Constitutional Case Law of Japan: Selected Supreme Court Decisions 1970-1990*. Seattle: University of Washington Press.
Maki, John M. 1964. *Court and Constitution of Japan: Selected Supreme Court Decisions 1948-1960*. Seattle: University of Washington Press.
Milhaupt, Curtis. 1996. "A Relational Theory of Japanese Corporate Governance: Contract, Culture, and the Rule of Law." *Harvard International Law Journal* 37: 3.
———. Spring 1997. "The Market for Innovation in the United States and Japan: Venture Capital and the Comparative Corporate Governance Debate." *Northwestern University Law Review* 91, no. 3: 865-98.

III. Books

Gresser, Julian, Fujikura Koichiro, and Morishima Akio. 1981. *Environmental Law in Japan*. Cambridge: MIT Press.
Haley, John O. 1991. *Authority Without Power: Law and the Japanese Paradox*. New York: Oxford University Press.
Henderson, Dan Fenno. 1965. *Conciliation and Japanese Law*. 2 vols. Tokyo: University of Tokyo Press.
Ramseyer, Mark. 1996. *Odd Markets in Japanese History*. New York: Cambridge University Press.
Tanaka, Hideo, with the assistance of Malcolm Smith. 1976. *The Japanese Legal System*. Tokyo: Tokyo University Press.
Upham, Frank K. 1987. *Law and Social Change in Postwar Japan*. Cambridge: Harvard University Press.
von Mehren, Arthur Taylor, ed. 1963. *Law in Japan: The Legal Order in a Changing Society*. Cambridge: Harvard University Press.
Yanagida Yukio, et al. 1994. *Law and Investment in Japan: Cases and Materials*. Cambridge: East Asian Legal Studies Program, Harvard University.

IV. Articles, Essays, and Chapters in Books

Bryant, Tamie. 1992. "'Responsible' Husbands, 'Recalcitrant' Wives, 'Retributive' Judges: Judicial Management of Contested Divorce in Japan." *Journal of Japanese Studies* 18: 407.
Cavers, David F. 1963. "The Japanese American Program for Cooperation in Legal Studies." In *Law in Japan: The Legal Order in a Changing Society*, edited by Arthur Taylor von Mehren, xv-xxxviii. Cambridge: Harvard University Press.
Feldman, Eric. 1988. "Defining Death: Organ Transplants, Tradition, and High Technology in Japan." *Social Science and Medicine* 27.
Foote, Daniel. 1992. "The Benevolent Paternalism of Japanese Criminal Justice." *California Law Review* 80: 317.

———. 1995. "Resolution of Traffic Accident Disputes and Judicial Activism in Japan." *Law in Japan* 25: 19.
Haley, John O. 1978. "The Myth of the Reluctant Litigation." *Journal of Japanese Studies* 4: 359.
———. Summer 1980. "Sheathing the Sword of Justice in Japan: An Essay on Law Without Sanctions." *Journal of Japanese Studies* 8: 265-81.
———. Spring 1982a. "Comment, The Revival of German Scholarship on Japanese Law." *The American Journal of Comparative Law* 30: 335-42.
———. 1982b. "The Politics of Informal Justice: The Japanese Experience, 1922-1942." In *The Politics of Informal Justice*, edited by R. Adel. Vol. 2, 125-47. New York: Academic Press.
———. 1989. "Mission to Manage: The U.S. Forest Service as a 'Japanese' Bureaucracy." In *The U.S. Japanese Economic Relationship: Can It Be Improved?*, edited by Kichiro Hayashi, 196-225. New York: New York University Press.
———. 1990. "Weak Law, Strong Competition, and Trade Barriers: Competitiveness as a Disincentive to Foreign Entry into Japanese Markets." In *Japan's Economic Structure: Should It Change?*, edited by Kozo Yamamura, 203-36. Seattle: Society for Japanese Studies.
———. Spring 1996. "Educating Lawyers for the Global Economy." *The Michigan Journal of International Law* 17: 733-46.
Leflar, Robert B. 1996. "Informed Consent and Patients' Rights in Japan." *Houston Law Review* 33: 1.
Miller, Geoffrey, with Jonathan R. Macey. 1995. "Corporate Governance and Commercial Banking: A Comparative Examination of Germany, Japan, and the United States." *Stanford Law Review* 48: 73.
Miyazawa, Setsuo. 1993. "Long-term Strategies in Japanese Environmental Litigation." *Law and Social Inquiry* 18: 605.
Ramseyer, Mark J. 1988. "Reluctant Litigant Revisited: Rationality and Disputes in Japan." *Journal of Japanese Studies* 14: 111.
———. 1989. "Water Law in Imperial Japan: Public Goods, Private Claims, and Legal Convergence." *Journal of Legal Studies* 18: 51.
———. 1993. "Columbian Cartel Launches Bid for Japanese Firms." *Yale Law Journal* 102: 2005.
———. 1994a. "Explicit Reasons for Implicit Contracts: The Legal Logic to the Japanese Main Bank System." In *The Japanese Main Bank System: Its Relevance for Developing and Transforming Economies*, edited by Masahiko Aoki and Hugh T. Patrick. Oxford: Oxford University Press.
———. 1994b. "The Puzzling (In)dependence of Courts: A Comparative Approach." *Journal of Legal Studies* 23: 721.
Roe, Mark. 1993. "Some Differences in Corporate Structure in Germany, Japan, and the United States." *Yale Law Journal* 102: 1927-2002.
Roe, Mark, and Ron Gilson. 1993. "Understanding the Japanese Keiretsu: Overlaps between Corporate Governance and Industrial Organization." *Yale Law Journal* 102: 871-906.
Rosen, Dan. 1990. "Private Lives and Public Eyes: Privacy in the United States and Japan." *Florida Journal of International Law* 6: 141.
Salzberg, Stephen M. 1991. "Japan's New Mental Health Law: More Light Shed on Dark Places?" *International Journal of Law and Psychiatry* 14: 137.
Upham, Frank K. Summer 1976. "Litigation and Moral Consciousness: An Interpretive Analysis of Four Japanese Pollution Suits." *Law and Society Review*.
———. 1991. "The Man Who Would Import: A Cautionary Tale About Bucking the System in Japan." *Japanese Studies* 17: 323.

———. 1993a. "Privatizing Regulation: The Implementation of the Large-Scale Retail Stores Law." In *Political Dynamics in Contemporary Japan*, edited by Gary D. Allison and Yasunori Sone, 264. Ithaca: Cornell University Press.
———. 1993b. "Unplaced Persons and Movements for Place." In *Postwar Japan as History*, edited by Andrew Gordon, 325-46. Berkeley: University of California Press.
Wagatsuma, Hiroshi, and Arthur Rosett. 1986. "The Implications of Apology: Law and Culture in Japan and the United States." *Law and Social Review* 20: 461.
West, Mark. 1997. "Legal Rules and Social Norms in Japan's Secret world of Sumo." *The Journal of Legal Studies* 26: 165.
Young, Michael. 1984. "Judicial Review of Administrative Guidance: Governmentally Encouraged Consensual Dispute Resolution in Japan." *Columbia Law Review* 84: 923.

V. Other Cited Works

Bill, James A. Fall 1985. "Area Studies and Theory-Building in Comparative Politics: A Stocktaking." *Political Science*: 810-12.
Ewald, William. 1995. "Comparative Jurisprudence (I): What Was It Like to Try a Rat?" *University of Pennsylvania Law Review* 143: 1889.
Glendon, Mary Ann. 1987. *Abortion and Divorce in Western Law*. Cambridge: Harvard University Press.
Glendon, Mary Ann, Michael Wallace Gordon, and Christopher Osakwe. 1982. *Comparative Legal Traditions in a Nutshell*. St. Paul: West Publishing.
———. 1985. *Comparative Legal Traditions*. St. Paul: West Publishing.
Hicks, Stephen C. 1991. "On the Citizen and the Legal Person: Toward the Common Ground of Jurisprudence, Social Theory, and Comparative Law as the Premise of a Future Community, and the Role of the Self Therein." *University of Cincinnati Law Review* 59: 789.
Holmes, Oliver Wendell. 1995. *The Common Law*. In *The Collected Works of Justice Holmes*, edited by Sheldon M. Novick. Chicago: University of Chicago Press.
Horowitz, Donald. 1994. "The Qur'an and the Common Law: Islamic Law Reform and the Theory of Legal Change." *American Journal of Comparative Law* 42: 233.
Huntington, Samuel P. Summer 1993. "The Clash of Civilizations?" *Foreign Affairs*.
Langbein, John H. 1995. "The Influence of Comparative Procedure in the United States." *The American Journal of Comparative Law* 43: 545-54.
Mattei, Ugo. Winter 1994. "Why the Wind Changed: Intellectual Leadership in Western Law." *The American Journal of Comparative Law* 42, no. 1: 195-218.
———. Winter 1997. "Three Patterns of Law: Taxonomy and Change in the World's Legal Systems." *The American Journal of Comparative Law* 45, no. 1: 5-44.
Merryman, John Henry, and David S. Clark. 1978. *Comparative Law: Western European and Latin American Legal Systems*. Indianapolis: Bobbs-Merrill Company.
Merryman, John Henry, David S. Clark, and John O. Haley. 1994. *The Civil Law Tradition: Europe, Latin America, and East Asia*. Charlottesville: Michie.
O'Connor, Marleen. 1993. "A Socio-Economic Approach to the Japanese Corporate Governance Structure." *Washington and Lee Law Review* 50: 1529.
Unger, Roberto Mangabeira. 1976. *Law in Modern Society*. New York: Free Press.
von Mehren, Arthur Taylor. 1971. "An Academic Tradition for Comparative Law?" *The American Journal of Comparative Law* 19: 624.

von Mehren, Arthur Taylor, and James Russell Gordley. 1977. *The Civil Law System*. 2nd ed. Boston: Little, Brown.
Weiler, Joseph. 1986. "Eurocracy and Distrust: Some Questions Concerning the Role of the European Court of Justice in the Protection of Fundamental Human Rights Within the Legal Order of the European Communities." *Washington Law Review* 61: 1103.
Zekoll, Joachim. 1996. "Kant and Comparative Law—Some Reflections on a Reform Effort." *Tulane Law Review* 70: 2719.

TAKING JAPANESE STUDIES SERIOUSLY

Andrew Gordon

In the spring of 1996 the Joint Committee on Japanese Studies (JCJS) of the American Council of Learned Societies and the Social Science Research Council was "decommissioned." For nearly 30 years this committee had been a central actor in the effort to promote Japanese studies in North America, part of the two Councils' larger postwar effort to support the enterprise called "area studies." It is no surprise that the decision to dissolve the JCJS along with 11 other joint area committees occasioned impassioned protest, although the sensational journalistic coverage of shouting and tears in the hallways of these venerable institutions was unusual.[1] Defenders of the area studies project convened emergency meetings, while supporters of the new turn at the SSRC and ACLS assured all who cared to listen of their ongoing commitment to what they now called "local knowledge."[2]

One of the most striking features of this latest round of what the *Chronicle of Higher Education* called a "clash over [the] value of area studies" is what Yogi Berra would have called déjà vu all over again.[3] Some buzz words were new—globalization instead of modernization, for example—and the context was the post-Cold War era and not the Cold War itself. But the issue was framed in familiar ways.

In this essay, keeping the focus on Japanese studies but aware that the issues are more general, I try to clarify the common ground on which both defenders and detractors of area studies stand, suggest a different way to assess the value of the enterprise, and examine some works that indeed make a case for taking Japanese studies seriously.

As a first step, consider how the historian John W. Hall justified the founding of the Japan Committee thirty years ago.

---

[1] Jacob Heilbrunn (1996).
[2] For example, a meeting of the National Council of Area Studies Associations (NCASA) in Washington, D.C., September 18, 1996. A report is published in the *Asian Studies Newsletter* (1991): 12.
[3] Christopher Shea (1997).

> Having passed beyond the state of strategic concern—of knowing the enemy—or even of area studies—knowing the foreigner—the leaders of Japanese studies in the United States have begun to look upon their work as much more an integral part of disciplinary studies in general. As Japan is accepted as part of the "modern world", as Japanese scholars mix freely with ours, Japan-based data and findings become increasingly relevant to even the most theoretical work in the social sciences. This deep but subtle change in the role and importance of Japanese studies in the realm of social science research has not been sufficiently explained to those outside of the field...*A CJS [Committee on Japanese Studies] would contribute greatly to this process of reuniting area studies with the main stream of methodological and theoretical advance in the social sciences and of enriching that stream with an element of cultural sophistication and understanding that it now so frequently and so conspicuously lacks.*[4]

Compare this to a memo sent by the staff of SSRC to "Friends of the Council interested in Japan" in 1996, describing the new, post-JCJS order.

> We are excited to announce the receipt of a major grant from the Ford Foundation in support of the core activities of our joint international programs. The grant is intended to further the Councils' efforts to redesign and strengthen their jointly sponsored program of international, interdisciplinary research and training in the social sciences and humanities. The new program architecture is designed to build on the previous system by bringing local knowledge to bear on global and comparative issues and by renewing our commitment to link the world of scholarship with debates and practical efforts that take place outside the academy. *Intellectually, our aim is to integrate discipline-based scholarship with the often unique perspectives provided by local—or area-based—knowledge.* Practically, the task is to provide insights and theories to those struggling to cope with global forces that threaten to generate new inequalities, inequities and injustices. Organizationally, the objective is to create a truly international community of scholars focused on issues of common concern around the globe.

If we consider the heart of these two statements as they address the intellectual case for area studies, we see that Hall's call for enriching the social sciences with "cultural sophistication" has dropped out of the later pronouncement, and "area knowledge" has been re-labeled "local knowledge," a slip that increases a nega-

---

[4] Letter from John Whitney Hall to Joseph Slater of the Ford Foundation, October 3, 1967. I am indebted to Dr. Rudolf Janssen for bringing this document to my attention. Italics added in this and the next quote.

tive connotation of narrowness. But the fundamental positioning of area-based research is the same. In 1967 the call was made to "reunite area studies" with "methodological and theoretical advance in the social sciences." In 1996 the order was reversed but the order of the day was the same: to "integrate discipline-based scholarship"—another way of referring to theory framed by a coherent method—with the "often unique perspectives provided by local—or area-based—knowledge."

Only the means to this end are said to be changing. The single acronym of the JCJS will be replaced by an alphabet soup of Collaborative Research Networks (CRN), Regional Advisory Panels (RAP) and a Human Capital Committee (HCC), together with a rump Japan Advisory Board (JAB). For scholars of Japan, the new order promises a seat at several tables, including perhaps multiple CRNs, and an East Asia RAP. Clearly, as the SSRC and the ACLS transformed their area programs in general, including the Japan program, these two organizations continued to believe that "local knowledge" mattered. At the same time, by eliminating the JCJS and all the other standing area committees they repudiated the idea that a consistent and explicit effort to organize and focus intellectual energies on the study of an entity called Japan, or any other specific place, is the best way to integrate local knowledge into broader systems of knowledge.

Beyond False Dichotomies

At the heart of this complicated affirmation and challenge to area and Japanese studies, and indeed also at the heart of John Hall's initial call for a Japan Committee, are two deeply entrenched, related dichotomies. One sets area studies against theory and science, and another sets area against disciplines, in both cases to the explicit disadvantage of area. The political scientist Robert Bates echoed these perspectives in 1996 with a blunt and provocative statement that has served as a lightning rod for contentious debate despite his stated goal of reconciliation. He wrote that "within the academy, the consensus has formed that area studies has failed to generate scientific knowledge." In most political science departments, he continued, area specialists "constitute a center of resistance to new trends in the discipline. They tend to lag behind others in terms of their knowledge of statistics [and] their commitment to theory."[5]

John Hall in 1967 had accepted this dichotomy between "Japan-based data" and the "most theoretical work in the social sciences" but he was optimistic about the potential for a Committee on Japanese Studies to bridge the dichotomy by "reuniting" area studies and social sciences. Critiques such as Bates's and the fact that the SSRC in 1996 restated Hall's view of the problem, and its solution, show either a failure of work in Japanese and area studies to fulfill this potential or a failure to communicate its achievements.

I believe the failure is more one of communication (or reception) than of execution. But it is very important not simply to rebut this charge on its own terms, answering that the consensus is wrong and that Japanese studies or area studies *has* generated theory and scientific knowledge, or to assert that we could "reunite" the two given proper organization and funding. First one must take on the premise of all the critics, that something called "scientific knowledge," or theory, or social sciences, or the disciplines, stands outside and above area knowledge.

A dichotomized understanding of area studies and social science always leads to models of intellectual activity in which practitioners classed as area studies people are the fetchers and carriers of the academy. A separate category of scholars, the "theorists," this thinking has it, need them to prepare the ground so they can do the really important intellectual work of abstracting. Thus, Bates in fact *defends* area studies as "a necessary complement to the social sciences. Social scientists will be weaker, the weaker our colleagues in area studies." The value of area studies scholars –"ethnographers, historians, students of culture"—in this view is as a source of "data" which will then be analyzed by properly trained theorists.[6] Disciplines here are the sites or providers of theoretical method and rigor, area students the diligent fact finders. Meta-

---

[5] Robert Bates (1996): 1. Also quoted in Christopher Shea (1997), p. A13. Bates slightly distances himself from this consensus, calling for a "mutual infusion" of area studies and theoretical work. He has earlier argued that area studies has contributed to social science, as co-editor, with V. Y. Mudimbe and Jean O'Barr (1993). This book is dedicated to showing how study of Africa is central to the work of many academic disciplines.

[6] Bates, ibid., 1-2.

phorically speaking, area studies is considered an artisanal craft akin to brickmaking, and theorizing is a grander pursuit akin to architecture. With defenders like this, one scarcely needs detractors.

This metaphor posits a division of labor that is misleading as well as invidious. Granted, the acts of theorizing and gathering and sifting evidence can be spoken of separately as a heuristic device. But in the best scholarly work in humanities as well as social science disciplines from literary studies, anthropology, and history to political science (and even economics once upon a time), these pursuits are inseparable. A different way to model this intellectual enterprise might think of theory and discipline as lens and camera, the scholar as a photographer, filmer (or painter), and the area (or human experience in a specific time and space) as the object or subject being imagined. The investigator's goal, in this rendering, is to create a study, or a picture, of human experience. We all must use lenses or tools. A pure theoretician is akin to a lens maker. Some area specialists simply take their theoretical lenses off the shelf, without much thought to the choice. They may not give much thought to the fact that their particular lens has an impact on the picture that results. Others get involved in both analyzing, selecting, and improving the lenses as well as taking the pictures. And of course many lens makers take pictures, too. Usually the best photographers pay attention to their lenses, and the top lens makers know something about taking fine pictures.

Put this way, the researcher is engaged in an integrated process of creative activity. Such an understanding of academic inquiry assigns a higher value to the study of experience through the use of tools of analysis than the brickmaking and architecture rendition allows for. Analytically speaking, a dichotomy between generating abstractions and understanding experience remains, but it has been refigured in a way that is closer to the integrated practice of the best scholars.

Characterizing area studies in this way is just a first step toward taking them seriously. The next step could be to argue that the pictures themselves are the ultimate objects of value, the lenses incidental tools. One should take Japanese studies seriously because it has produced pictures worth having, even by those outside the field. This may be the line of argument many people who see themselves as humanists of a certain old school would be inclined to take. They would emphasize that the finest works on Japanese subjects are worth reading in and of themselves, for what they say about their topics and about human experience that speaks to readers broadly. Indeed, I think such works are numerous. But to justify the area studies project in these terms goes to an opposite extreme from the proud claims of pure theorists. It enters a silly contest about which is more important, taking pictures or designing lenses.

A more promising second step would be to focus attention on the indivisibility of picture taking and lens making and stress that most scholars do both, if with different degrees of emphasis. Neither activity is possible or meaningful without the other. Japanese studies has most value when it does two things at once: makes good pictures and improves lens design. Put in negative terms, if the study of a place—say Japan—never does more than use throw-away cameras, never contributes to better lens design, there may be grounds for criticism even in terms of this refigured metaphor. Can Japanese studies, that is, be dismissed as a selfish or narrow enterprise that takes from but does not give back to the guilds of lenscrafters? A brief survey of some important works in fields close to my own research interests, together with an unsystematic and not comprehensive look at some others that have happened to catch my attention, should make it clear that it cannot.

Japanese Studies as Lens Redesign

One of the pioneers and most accomplished historians of Japan over the postwar era has been Thomas C. Smith. He is best known for his series of books and articles on the agrarian origins of modern Japan.[7] In this work Smith offered brilliant evidence of the extent and contours of economic development in Tokugawa Japan, and he argued that the Tokugawa economy provided an important legacy to Meiji and twentieth-century Japan.

In addition, in the 1980s Smith returned to an old fascination with the history of labor in Japan and wrote two important essays.

---

[7] In addition to his 1955 and 1959 publications, many of his most important works are collected in the book *Native Sources of Japanese Industrialization, 1750-1920* (1988).

In one (1988 [1986]) he offers a fine example of the historian as picture taker and lens designer both. He begins with E. P. Thompson's famous work on the time consciousness of workers in England in the transition from an agrarian to an industrial capitalist society, "Time, Work-Discipline, and Industrial Capitalism." Thompson himself drew on the analyses of scholars looking at non-Western societies, including Edward Evans-Pritchard and Pierre Bourdieu, to make a distinction between the task orientation of pre-industrial, agricultural labor, and the time-orientation of factory labor. These writers might then be considered "area specialists" of an earlier generation, although Bourdieu especially has since emerged as a much-quoted cultural theorist. His place as a supplier of empirical evidence to Thompson, thence Smith, is a nice example of the difficulty of separating out camps of "theorists" and "area specialists."

Thompson argues that with the rise of industrial capitalism in England came a sharp break with the past, as working people were forced to internalize a new sense of time discipline. Thompson's work drew on and enriched local knowledge of England, and was itself a form of area studies, although not so named. At the same time, he offered a generalized model or theory of the social transformations that accompany capitalism in any society.

Smith turned to Japan and asked if Thompson's model applied to the experience of agrarian society in the Tokugawa era and the subsequent industrial transformation. He examined a rich body of evidence such as manuals written by and for farmers, and he concluded these farmers were not possessed of a casual time sense or a "task orientation" akin to Thompson's presentation of the English, Evans-Pritchard's of the Nuer, or Bourdieu's of the Algerian peasant. He argued that to the contrary, Tokugawa peasants strictly monitored the use of time. They had a keen awareness of its economic and social value. At the end of his exploration of the Tokugawa and Meiji era evidence, Smith comes back to the larger notion of "pre-industrial" time discipline itself, and he questions it with subtlety and force. He writes:

> Tokugawa peasants seem so far removed from the attitudes attributed to pre-industrial English working people by Thompson that I cannot help wondering if he has not exaggerated the strength and prevalence of task-orientation in eighteenth-century England.... Thompson quotes the complaint of a writer in an agricultural maga-

zine in 1800 that "When a labourer becomes possessed of more land than he and his family can cultivate in the evenings...the farmer can no longer depend on him for constant work." This sounds like a wish for independence on the worker's part rather than necessarily a casual attitude towards time....Perhaps the conflict over time between employers and workers in eighteenth-century England was not over the value of time, but over who owned it and on what terms....

Then, turning to the United States, Smith continues:

The Boston carpenters, masons and stonecutters in 1835 proclaimed that the "God of the Universe has given us time, health and strength. We utterly deny the right of any man to dictate to us how much of it we shall sell." Many English working people in the late 18th century would have understood and sympathized with this statement. No Japanese in 1835 could possibly have understood the statement or taken a favorable view of it if they did....The source of the divergence would seem to have less to do with time-sense (as Thompson uses the term) than with different conceptions of the individual in society.

Here, in a brilliant analysis that deserves wide reading, Thomas Smith ends up not only saying something important about time and money in Japan, but in England and the United States. He presents a strong case that the connections between time and money have been differently understood in different times and places. This is a historian's work, and historians rarely proceed by constructing formal models in the manner of game theorists. But only an obtuse reader could fail to read Smith's work as profoundly theoretical. He challenges a *discontinuous* theory of change in which a pre-industrial time sense gives way to an industrial one. He offers instead a theory of *continuity* in the transition to capitalism or industrial society. He posits and shows that in these three societies, at least, differing culturally constructed time senses crossed the divide of the industrial revolution partly intact. This essay stands as a fine example of a work of Japanese studies that both offers a picture of Japan and contributes to the redesign of the lenses used to make sense of modern history more generally.

A more recent and quite different sort of historical study offers another example of an important dual contribution. Takashi Fujitani's book (1996) both helps us make sense of Meiji Japan and suggests ways to rethink aspects of a Foucauldian approach to modern history. Fujitani analyzes the way the elites of the time deployed the Meiji emperor to achieve their end of building a powerful nation-state. He uses Foucault's concepts (the lens metaphor would be particularly apt in this case) of the "society of surveillance" and the "disciplinary society" to make sense of the political uses of the emperor in Meiji times. But he also shows us that an unamended Foucauldian model fails to capture an essential feature of the Japanese story. For Foucault, the modern "disciplinary society" with its dispersed, omnipresent systems of power emerged in the West upon the ruins of monarchic power. Foucault understands monarchic power as a polar opposite to modern forms of disciplinary power. But in Japan, a society that was arguably in every respect the model of a "disciplinary society" was created by bolstering, indeed newly inventing, monarchic power in a process that included the very sophisticated manipulation of the imperial gaze.[8] This book forces those who heed its message to modify an important aspect of a Foucauldian approach that posits two theoretically and experientially distinct forms of power. Again, a work of Japanese studies contributes on a variety of levels.

Also in the realm of cultural studies, this time psychological, consider a work that brings a seemingly esoteric bit of Japanica into the gaze of "gaze theorists" and psychoanalytic theory. Anne Allison writes about Japanese comics (*manga*), and in the process she takes on Western, Freudian-derived theories of how pictures of women, whether in pornography or art, are presented through a power-laden "male gaze." She looks at the way the gaze of the presumed male reader and characters focuses on women's naked bodies in *manga*, and finds that it doesn't fit the Freudian paradigms of "power-gazing." In particular, she sees a continuity from the gazing of children to that of adults, one that contradicts Freudian assumptions about a "development of subjectivity away from mothers assumed to start at puberty."[9]

While Freud-bashing is old hat, the gaze theorists here addressed are recent, and they have been much noticed. Allison, like Thomas Smith, has demonstrated a culturally bounded character to theories, psychological ones in this case. One thus has a valuable picture of Japanese society as well as ideas for redesigning the analytic lens.

---

[8] Takashi Fujitani (1996), 141-45.
[9] Anne Allison (1993), 34.

Japanese Studies and "New" Models

One could perhaps say, at the risk of belaboring the metaphor, that the examples so far are all too "Japanese." That is, they fall into the realm of improvement engineering of lenses. They take an existing model first produced in study of elsewhere (usually the West), and they modify or improve it in study of Japan. Improvement engineering is not an unworthy activity, as anyone who has traded up from a Ford to a Toyota can tell you, but neither is it a high status achievement.

One might ask: are there no examples where one must take Japanese studies seriously because a work has devised a new model from the ground up? That is probably an unreasonable question. Is there any important idea that has not been prefigured someplace by someone? Arguably, any "new" theoretical approach owes a debt to earlier thinking. A more realistic approach may be to look not for pure originality but for major innovations that take on a life of their own, that come to be seen as fresh and productive of interesting thinking by a larger community of scholars. In addition to the works introduced above, I believe one can point to a number of analytic approaches that were generated in important ways first or at an early stage from studies of Japan by Japanese scholars as well as others.

Professor Doi Takeo, for example, first articulated his concept of psychological dependence, or *amae*, as a tool to better understand the behavior and psychodynamics of Japanese people (1971). In the wrong hands, the notion of *amae* as a particular trait of Japanese culture can produce simplistic essentializing of the peculiarities of "the Japanese." But most powerful tools are dangerous ones as well, and Doi's analysis, which originated as he thought about Japanese society, has also been of good use as a lens to examine other cases.[10] This was recognized from the start by many readers. As Doi's English translator noted:

> But to explain the Japanese is only half of the author's aim. Just as *amae* in the Japanese [people] is of course tempered by various other characteristics superficially associated with the West, such as personal freedom, objectivity, and so on, so *amae* is an essential part of the

---

[10] For example, Doi in a 1981 addition to his original book notes Joseph de Rivera (1977), 127.

humanity of Western man also. Just as the value attached to *amae* has accounted for both the virtues and the failings of Japanese society, so its suppression, or diversion into different channels, explains much of what is most admirable and detestable in the Western tradition.[11]

Doi himself made this point clear in a chapter written for a later edition of his book: "while my whole argument depends on the assertion that *amae* is a peculiarly Japanese emotion, I also assert that it has universal relevance." Thus, he continues, "even in Western societies where there is no convenient word corresponding to *amae* and feelings of *amae* would seem not to exist, a surprising amount of a similar kind of feeling can be observed if one looks at the phenomenon with Japanese eyes."[12]

Closer to my own area of interest, the modern history of economy, society, and polity in Japan, one can identify at least two important, related cases of conceptual innovation emerging from studies focused on Japan. First, there is a long tradition of scholarship that articulates some concept of the timing of development, especially "late development." These authors theorize on global time. They argue that the same processes unfolding at different times in global history are not, in fact, the same processes. The dynamics of industrialization in a latecomer, or of a later capitalist revolution, reflect their relative timing.

One pioneer, perhaps the first, who made the point that "a precipitate move out of medievalism into the modern system of industry and science" gave both Germany and especially Japan a great although transient "opportunity" to challenge the advanced powers was Thorstein Veblen (1943). Another important scholar who focused more systematically on the dynamics of late development, although looking solely at Europe, was Alexander Gerschenkron. His provocative analysis (1966) had obvious implications for Japan, which he recognized. But perhaps the first extended work to develop this argument in depth for Japan was Ronald Dore's now classic study (1973), in which Dore identifies and articulates "a general late capitalist development syndrome." He defines a late developing nation or society as a place that, to choose selectively from his list of defining features:

---

[11] John Bester (1981 [1973]), 10.
[12] Doi Takeo (1981 edition), 169.

1) is "less likely to be dominated by a laissez-faire philosophy" and more likely to see a "predominant" state role;

2) experiences no slow buildup of rural proto-industry that can evolve gradually from peasant to capitalist agriculture before industrialization;

3) develops mass education concurrent with or prior to building large manufacturing industries;

4) faces a larger technological leap from traditional skills to those of imported new technologies than an early developer;

5) faces a larger organizational leap, as well, so that industry is likely from the outset to be marked by "rationalized bureaucratic forms";

6) is likely from the outset to incorporate labor management practices and rules that are already in place in "advanced" cases;

7) is dominated by more secure large firms and plan-oriented management;

8) has a sharper dualism of large versus small firms, with workers in the former sector relatively privileged.[13]

This book has had major impact. While historians might challenge some of the particulars of Dore's catalogue of the distinguishing marks of late developers in general or Japan in particular, the essence of this work stands up to scrutiny twenty-five years after publication. Dore also adds an important final twist to the logic of his late developer theory in what is arguably the most provocative aspect of the book. He suggests that Britain, once the proud first industrial "developer," now finds itself in the late twentieth century to be a latecomer forced to scramble to catch up to and "converge" toward the organization-oriented practices found in Japan.[14]

Twenty-five years later, the notion that Japan as late developer is now a world leader to whom former hegemons look for models is so widely accepted as to be a cliché. And the state of clichéhood is perhaps the greatest sign that a theory or model designed for a particular topic has taken on a wide-ranging life of its own. Dore has recently provoked new controversy by arguing that now it is the German system of industrial relations that is pressed to converge toward a version of the Japanese model.[15] Here, then,

---

[13] Ronald Dore (1973), 408-15.
[14] Ibid., 338-71, chapter titled "Britain Catching Up?"
[15] Ronald Dore (1966).

is a fine example of the importance of taking Japanese studies seriously, both for the picture it offers of Japan and as a source of ideas for wider application.[16]

Clearly and intimately related to the theory of late development is the model of the "developmental state." This concept, first articulated with rigor and depth by Chalmers Johnson (1982), has proven of value not only to picture-takers of Japan, but to lens-makers and photographers all around the world. For Johnson, the developmental state is a political formation growing out of "the situational nationalism of the late industrializers."[17] He writes that "in states that were late to industrialize, the state itself led the industrialization drive, that is, it took on *developmental* functions."[18] The state was not simply active in regulating society, setting forth rules and a framework for economic behavior. The state also set substantive social and economic goals—what industries should exist? which should be phased out?—and it intervened directly to help private actors achieve these. Focusing particularly on the institutional history of the Ministry of Commerce and Industry and the trials of depression, war, and recovery that led it to become the Ministry of International Trade and Industry (MITI), Johnson traces the course from the 1920s through the 1970s of one critical project of Japan's developmental state, industrial policy.

Not all of his colleagues are convinced that the Japanese state achieved its goals to the extent Johnson suggests. Many object that the state's tools were neither so well honed nor so effective as he claims. But the most vociferous critics, especially economists, are in fact missing the point when they criticize the developmental state for being inefficient compared to the market. This may or may not be true, in some or in many cases. But Johnson makes an important distinction between "efficiency" and "effectiveness" early in the book, and for him the crucial point is that the state in Japan has been effective, that is to say, consequential, in its meso- and micro-level interventions.[19] To challenge the efficiency of the state does not deny its "effectiveness" in achieving essentially political goals. Indeed the chorus of calls in the mid-1990s, in Japan and outside it, for the deregulation of the Japanese economy (*kisei*

---

[16] I should note that the title of this chapter is a take-off on that of another book by Dore (1987).
[17] Chalmers Johnson (1982), 24.
[18] Ibid., 19. Emphasis in the original.
[19] Ibid., 21.

kanwa) in the interests of economic "efficiency" fundamentally affirms that the existing bureaucratic state is effective. If it were not, there would be no need to deregulate.

Others who have described the political economy in recent years have argued persuasively that Japan is home to a more negotiated set of relationships between state and society than Chalmers Johnson admits.[20] But most of these critics end with some modified formulation of a political economy where the state is surely present and vigorous in ways that place Japan toward one end of a spectrum of "capitalisms." The important point is not whether every claim on behalf of the developmental state is sustained. The notion of multiple capitalisms, with an idealized "developmental state" as one (and any model must be idealized to be usable outside its original context) has been productive and provocative to other researchers. It has helped them take better pictures, which is one important standard for theoretical "significance."

None of these achievements, it is important to note, would have been possible without in-depth study of Japanese society and history, knowledge of the language and attention to its nuance, careful examination of institutions past and present, as well as attention to larger issues of the various ways of knowing and framing that we call method and theory. The scholars who produced these works were both brickmakers and architects, both lensmakers and careful picture takers, one and the same.

Embedding the "Rational" Individual

This case for area studies asserts that Japanese studies requires both creative picture taking and innovative tool design. At base, I believe this case rests on what will be for some a subversive or counter-intuitive idea, especially for swimmers in the recently surging stream of the academic river known as rational choice theory. It is worth pausing to develop this point.

Rational choice begins with the assumption that all individuals are consistent seekers of maximum utility, whose preferences are internally consistent and predictable in a given context. The premise for this sort of social science is unapologetically reductive and

---

[20] For example, Richard Samuels (1987) and Daniel Okimoto (1989).

proudly universalistic.[21] Contra rational choice, I would argue that knowledge in the social sciences and humanities is in some fundamental ways in fact *not* about universal political or social behavior. It is about the particular. It is less a search for regularities across the globe than an effort to understand socially embedded contingencies of place and of time. Taking rational choice seriously in the long run is unlikely to leave us much wiser in our understanding of the diversity of human experience. A more enduring and measured theorizing would assume that something about experience in and around a certain place at a certain moment has a particularity not found elsewhere. This particularity will require special tools of analysis or will lead to the design of such, for example the concept of late development or the developmental state (neither of these, after all, could have emerged from study of American or British evidence alone). These tools should then, despite their particular origins, prove of use in comparative, international, or other investigations.

To argue that knowledge is particular certainly does not mean that Japan or any place should be understood as particular to the extreme of being uniquely unique. Such claims are the property of narrow-minded advocates of so-called "theories of the Japanese" (*nihonjinron*). Work in the field of Japanese studies must take these theories of the Japanese seriously by examining and relativizing them, trying to understand where they come from and why they are so powerful in contemporary or past culture, without falling victim to their seductive claims.[22] But in our enthusiasm to repudiate the crude culturalism of the Japanese (or any other) essentialists, our work must not reject a nuanced understanding of contextualized human behavior.

To be sure, some rational choice analysts of Japan are deeply familiar with Japanese language, laws, institutions, even customs. But the fundamental premises of their undertaking deny that the study of a particular place has intrinsic meaning. Theoretically correct work in the rational choice tradition sees no particular substance to the human subject. He or she (and gender differences, too, would evaporate as insubstantial reflections of the "rules

---

[21] A valuable discussion of rational choice and the study of Japanese politics and history is by Joseph P. Gownder and Robert Pekkanen (1996).

[22] Tessa Morris-Suzuki's (1995) article is an excellent example of such an effort.

of the game") is a utility-seeking atom. Rational choice theorists recognize that this individual is constrained by political, economic, or even cultural arrangements, but they begin by assuming that a calculating, thinking individual exists prior to and separate from any social or cultural context. As Robert Bates makes clear in a fascinating brief memoir of his experience studying the African coffee trade, the point of departure for his learning "real world lessons about politics and scholarship" is a Hobbesian view of humanity as originating in a "natural condition" in which individuals exist as scattered beings, without society, condemned to lives that are "solitary, poor, nasty, brutish and short."[23] As the Japanese political thinker, Katō Hiroyuki, argued in the 1870s, students of the human condition who take concepts such as Hobbes's or Rousseau's state of nature or Locke's social contract as descriptions of the "real world" are replacing analysis of reality with a mythic fiction about the origins and functioning of society.[24]

The problem with taking Hobbes seriously, as it were, is that one throws out the socially embedded baby with the culturalist bathwater. One fails to explore the complicated mutual implication of rules and institutions with human subjectivity and cultural systems. A rational choice advocate might counter that "economic institutions and rules of the game" are simply "the rational choice jargon for culture."[25] I would reply that a culture is more than a structure of rules and incentives, although it includes these. It also includes a set of received ideas and understandings about how the world works and ought to work and the symbolic representation of these ideas. Such understandings have evolved in any one time and place out of such a long and complicated process, and taken on such a degree of meaning to those who participate in a given community, that they cannot simply be reduced to a reflection of the rules of the game in force at that time. These understandings inhere in the consciousness and behavior of individuals. They constitute the rules and direct their practice in place and time as much as they reflect them.

Think, for example, of the way in which young girls and boys in Japan are educated and then, as adults, enter the world of work.

---

[23] Robert Bates (1997): 34.
[24] Bob T. Wakabayashi (1984): 485 and passim.
[25] Cited from May 4, 1994 E-mail posting by Thomas Roehl.

One way to understand this process is to argue that the "rules of the game" of education and employment make it a rational choice for many women to opt out of struggles for mainstream "male" careers. Instead they choose to become part-time workers who focus primary energy on the raising of the next generation of children in a way that will reinforce future gender-divided choices about careers and life course. Certainly, this analysis makes a lot of sense. But ending the argument here fails to recognize that curriculum and tracking at school and at work constitute a system of "rules" that is tightly bound up with a received but contested structure of ideas about proper gender roles. The ideas account for or generate the system of rules, as much as the reverse. Neither can be seen as residual or prior, and the system is full of tensions. Actors and rules, Hobbes's individual in "nature" and the collective "society," can only be separated as acts of analytic convenience. Change does not come first to one or the other, so much as it comes simultaneously to both in their mutual implication in the social lives of people.

Conclusion

Taking Japanese studies seriously, one discovers an impressive stock of achievements. Only some of them have been introduced here. If the problem is not one of execution, why the consensus that area studies does not produce scientific knowledge? The answer is not simply a failure to communicate. Part of the answer lies in the treachery of the question, the way it dichotomizes scientific knowledge and area study to the disadvantage of area. One response must be to argue vigorously against the terms of the question, asserting that the processes of theorizing and studying areas are integrated ones, and then to beat the drums loudly on behalf of work that succeeds in both dimensions, and proceed to produce more in that tradition. Of course, it would be naive to think that louder drum beating itself will carry the day. The dichotomized thinking that gives pride of place to a certain concept of social science over mere "description" of areas is deeply rooted in the political and cultural structure of the academic world and is unlikely to change.

But the stubborn persistence and reproduction of different

cultural and institutional formations around the world offers some reason to carry on. Of course, we are ceaselessly told by the pundits of our day that we live in an era of extraordinary "globalization." This talk needs to be taken seriously insofar as institutions like GATT and NAFTA allow ever-easier flows of goods, capital, and even people, creating a so-called borderless world. One implication is that local areas do not much matter. As the universal rules of the market economy proliferate, local anomalies will disappear. Taking seriously the study of Japan or any other place should make it clear that particular local formations are no more likely to wither away under capitalism than the state is likely to disappear under socialism. The trick is to negotiate the channel between marginalizing the local as the accidental detail of the particular, and romanticizing it as a transcendent cultural essence or a heroic site of resistance.

Bibliography

Allison, Anne. 1993. "A Male Gaze in Japanese Children's Cartoons Or, Are Naked Female Bodies Always Sexual?" *Working Papers in Asian Pacific Studies*. Durham: Duke University Asian Pacific Studies Institute.
Association for Asian Studies. November/December 1991. *Asian Studies Newsletter*. Ann Arbor: Association for Asian Studies.
Bates, Robert. Winter 1996. "Letter from the President: Area Studies and the Discipline." *APSA-CP: Newsletter of the American Political Science Association Organized Section in Comparative Politics* 7, no. 1.
——. March-April 1997. "With One Ear Cocked: Studying the Coffee Trade, A Social Scientist Learns Real-World Lessons about Politics and Scholarship." *Harvard Magazine* 99, no. 4: 34.
Bates, Robert, V. Y. Mudimbe, and Jean O'Barr, eds. 1993. *Africa and the Disciplines: The Contributions of Research in Africa to the Social Sciences and Humanities*. Chicago: University of Chicago Press.
Bester, John. 1981 [1973]. "Foreword." *The Anatomy of Dependence*. Tokyo: Kodansha International.
de Rivera, Joseph. 1977. *A Structural Theory of the Emotions*. New York: International University Press.
Doi Takeo. 1971. *Amae no kōzō*. Kōbundō. Translated with foreword by John Bester as *The Anatomy of Dependence*. 1981 [1973]. Tokyo: Kodansha International.
Dore, Ronald. 1966. "Unions Between Class and Enterprise." *Industrielle Beziehungen* 3 Jg., Heft 1: 154-97.
——. 1973. *British Factory-Japanese Factory*. Berkeley: University of California Press.
——. 1987. *Taking Japan Seriously: A Confucian Perspective on Leading Economic Issues*. Stanford: Stanford University Press.
Fujitani, Takashi. 1996. *Splendid Monarchy: Power and Pageantry in Modern Japan*. Berkeley: University of California Press.

Gerschenkron, Alexander. 1966. *Economic Backwardness in Historical Perspective.* Cambridge: Harvard University Press.

Gownder, Joseph P., and Robert Pekkanen. Summer 1996. "The End of Political Science? Rational Choice Analyses in Studies of Japanese Politics." *Journal of Japanese Studies* 22, no. 2: 363-84.

Hall, John Whitney. October 3, 1967. Letter to Joseph Slater. Folder: Conference on Modern Japan, Box 3. Ann Arbor: Collection of the Center for Japanese Studies, Bentley Historical Library, University of Michigan.

Heilbrunn, Jacob. May/June 1996. "The News from Everywhere: Does Global Knowledge Thinking Threaten Local Knowledge? The Social Science Research Council Debates the Future of Area Studies." *Lingua Franca.*

Johnson, Chalmers. 1982. *MITI and the Japanese Miracle: The Growth of Industrial Policy, 1925-1975.* Stanford: Stanford University Press.

Morris-Suzuki, Tessa. August 1995. "The Invention and Reinvention of 'Japanese Culture.'" *Journal of Asian Studies* 54, no. 3: 759-80.

Okimoto, Daniel. 1989. *Between MITI and the Market: Japanese Industrial Policy for High Technology.* Stanford: Stanford University Press.

Roehl, Thomas. May 4, 1994. E-mail posting from International Business, University of Illinois, to the JAPAN list at Princeton (Japan@pucc.princeton.edu).

Rosovsky, Henry. 1961. *Capital Formation in Japan, 1868-1940.* New York: Free Press of Glencoe.

Samuels, Richard. 1987. *The Business of the Japanese State.* Ithaca: Cornell University Press.

Shea, Christopher. 10 January 1997. "Political Scientists Clash Over Value of Area Studies." *Chronicle of Higher Education*, pp. A13-A14.

Smith, Thomas C. 1955. *Political Change and Industrial Development in Japan: Government Enterprise, 1868-1880.* Stanford: Stanford University Press.

———. 1959. *The Agrarian Origins of Modern Japan.* Stanford: Stanford University Press.

———. May 1986. "Peasant Time and Factory Time." *Past and Present*, no. 111. [Reprint. His *The Native Sources of Japanese Industrialization, 1750-1920*, 199-235. Berkeley: University of California Press, 1988.]

Thompson, E. P. December 1967. "Time, Work-Discipline, and Industrial Capitalism." *Past and Present*, no. 38.

Veblen, Thorstein. 1943. "The Opportunity of Japan." *Essays in Our Changing Order.* New York: Viking Press.

Wakabayashi, Bob T. December 1984. "Katō Hiroyuki and Confucian Natural Rights." *Harvard Journal of Asiatic Studies* 44, no. 2: 485 and passim.

INDEX

Abe, Kazuhiro, 321n
Abe, Masao, 199, 208, 208n
Abe, Ryūichi, 209
Abe, Yoshiomi, 253-54, 254n
Abu-Lughod, Lila, 301n
Addiss, Stephen, 175n, 181, 181n
Aizu, 117, 120, 125, 129
Akasaka, Norio, 255n
Akita, George, 131
Akiyama, Ken, 255n
Akiyama, Terukazu, 164
Alcock, Rutherford, 115, 118, 118n
Alford, William, 354n, 362
Allen, Ernest, 324n
Allen, G. C., 131
Allinson, Gary, 32n
Allison, Anne, xxvii, 320n, 322n, 395, 395n
Allison, Graham, 344n
American Council of Learned Societies (ACLS), viin, 387, 389
    see also Joint Committee on Japanese Studies
Amin, Samir, 262, 262n
Amino, Yoshihiko, 239n
Amsden, Alice, 342n
Amstutz, Galen, xxviii, 58, 62
Anchordoguy, Marie, 13n
Anderer, Paul, 262n, 263n
Anderson, Benedict, 14n
Anderson, William, 173
Anesaki, Masaharu, 203
anthropology, anthropological, xiv, xvii, xviii, xxiii-xxiv, 9n, 163, 218, 260, 357
    individualism and, 10, 13
    invented traditions and, xxii, xxiv, 14, 15n
    methods and, 120, 202, 245, 260, 267, 391
    religion and, 172n, 217
    Robertson on, xxiii-xxiv, 294-335
Aoki, Michiko, 211n
Aoki, Tamotsu, 267, 305, 305n, 306n
Appadurai, Arjun, 298, 298n, 311, 311n
Apter, David, 310n
archaeology, archeological sites, xviii, 37-44, 59, 161n, 176, 204
architecture, architectural history, 41, 164, 169, 181-82, 182n, 183, 199
    modernism and, 163n, 166, 167
area studies, viii, 196-97, 230, 268
    Cold War and, xiii, 267
    legal studies and, xxvi, 355, 365-67, 377, 380, 381
    methodology and, ix, xvii, 387-93, 390n, 403
    Orientalism and, xi, xii
    rational choice theory and, xiv-xv, xxvii, 400-403
Arima, Tatsuo, 263n
Arnesen, Peter, 57, 58n, 61
Arntzen, Sonja, 251n
art studies, 161-94
Asada, Akira, 264, 264n
Asano, Shūgō, 180n
Asao, Naohiro, 60n, 110n
Ash, James, 47
Association for Asian Studies, viin, 64, 306n
Aston, William, 45
Asuka period, 42-44, 46
Atwell, William, 62, 64
Austin, Lewis, 314

Babior, Sharman, 320n
Bachnik, Jane, 304n, 314
Backus, Robert, 247
Baekeland, Frederick, 181n
bakufu, 56-58, 59
    bakumatsu period and, 117, 120, 123-29, 137
    Tokugawa period and, 89, 95, 97, 102
bakumatsu period, 32, 124, 125n, 129-30, 134, 135, 136-37
    cities and, 118, 127
    emperor system and, 15, 137
    rural society and, 119, 121
Banno, Junji, 131
Barnes, Gina, 37, 42, 46
Barnhart, Michael, 146
Barshay, Andrew, 30n
Barthes, Roland, 108, 168, 169n, 178n, 187n, 189n, 243, 254
Bashō, 233, 240, 241n, 260, 260n
Bates, Robert, 389-90, 390n, 402, 402n
Baxter, James, 129

Beardsley, Richard, 357
Beasley, William G., 4n, 44, 128, 144, 374
Beauchamp, Edward, 313
Beer, Jennifer, 320n
Beer, Lawrence, 360n
Befu, Harumi, 10n, 14n, 296n, 305n, 315n
Bell, Catherine, 172n
Bellah, Robert, 92-95, 93n, 103, 133, 206, 239, 357
Ben-Ari, Eyal, 312n
Bender, Ross, 48
Benedict, Ruth
  classic book, 294-95, 306n, 338n
  essentialist images of Japan and, viii, xxiii, 11, 299-306, 302n, 303n, 310-13, 312n, 314, 325
  shame culture and, 5, 9, 13
  see also Orientalism
Benjamin, Gail, 312
Bennett, John, 294n, 305, 305n, 315, 315n
Berger, Klaus, 166n
Bernstein, Gail, 26n, 100n
Berry, Mary Elizabeth, 21-22, 21n, 23n, 61, 63
Berry, Philippa, 172n
Bester, John, 397n
Bestor, Theodore, 15n, 308n
Bethe, Monica, 256
Bethel, Diana, 321n
Beyer, Vicki, 360n
Bickle, George, 214n
Bielefeldt, Carl, 58, 209
Bill, James, 366n
biographic, biographies, 175-76, 176n, 180, 228, 239
  Meiji figures and, 198
  nō and, 256
  religion and, xxii, 209, 213-14
  Restoration figures and, xx, 130, 131
  samurai and, 148
Bird, Isabella, 294, 294n
Birnbaum, Alfred, 266
Birt, Michael, 57, 61
Bito, Masahide, 104
Bix, Herbert, 23n, 96, 98, 120, 124n, 146n
Blacker, Carmen, 135, 218
Blakemore, Thomas, 357
Bloom, Alfred, 209
Bock, Felicia, 53, 211n

Bodart-Bailey, Beatrice, 85n
Bodiford, William, 58, 209
Bohnaker, William, 319n
Boime, Albert, 166n
Bolitho, Harold, xvi, xvii, xix, xxviii, 96, 104, 104n, 129
Borg, Dorothy, 145-46
Borgen, Robert, 53, 55
Bornoff, Nicholas, 319n
Borovoy, Amy, 315n
Borton, Hugh, xix, 85, 120
Boscaro, Adriana, 296n
Bourdieu, Pierre, 108, 316, 393
Bowen, Roger, 26n, 131
Bowers, Faubion, 240n
Bowie, Theodore, 161
Bownas, Jeffrey, 218
Bowring, Richard, 3n, 52, 247, 248
Boxer, C. R., 60, 63, 213
Boyle, John Hunter, 146
Braistead, William, 135
Braithwaite, John, 13
Braucher, Robert, 357
Brazell, Karen, 247, 256
Breen, John, 134
Brewster, Jennifer, 247
Brinker, Helmut, 172n
Brinton, Crane, 115
Brinton, Mary, 321n
Brower, Robert, 52, 183n, 242n
Brown, Delmer M., 48, 51, 61, 62
Brown, L. Keith, 9n
Brown, Philip, 62, 96, 97
Brown, Sidney, 131
Brown, Steven, 257
Brownlee, John, 44
Bryant, Tamie, 362, 362n
Bryson, Norman, 259, 259n
Buckley, Sandra, 32n
Buddhism, Buddhist, 22
  area studies and, 197
  art and, xxi, 164, 169n, 170-72, 176
  early history and, 43-44, 46, 47, 50, 52, 55
  Hardacre on, xxi-xxii, 198-209, 211-14, 216-18
  literature and, 255n, 264
  medieval history and, 61-62
  Restoration and, 134
  Tokugawa history and, 99
Buruma, Ian, 304, 319n
Butow, Robert, 144

Cahill, James, 181, 181n
Calder, Kent, xvi, xvii, xxiv, 27n, 339n, 340n, 342n, 343n, 344, 344n, 345n
Cambridge History of Japan, 1, 2, 5n, 18, 19, 20n, 21, 24, 55
Cameron, Louisa, 321n
canon, canons
 anthropology and, 301, 307, 313
 art and, 163n, 167, 172-75, 179, 185
 literature and, 233-36, 256, 265
capitalism, capitalist, 23-24, 30, 32
 comparative study and, 393-94, 397-400, 404
 Japan and, 2-4, 6-8, 10, 12, 16-17, 20, 25, 310
 literature and, 240, 264n
 modernization and, 162n, 262-63
Carr, E. H., 4, 151
Carter, Stephen D., 63, 243, 246n
Cary, Otis, 161n
Casal, Ugo, 218
Cavanaugh, Carole, 250
Cavers, David, 355-56, 356n, 357
Chambliss, William, 120n
Childs, Margaret, 218, 247
Ching, Leo Tsu-Shin, 324n
Chino, Kaori, 256n
Chiyonobu, Y., 50
Chōshū, 117, 125, 129
Chow, Rey, 267-68
Christianity, 22
 Japanese religious studies and, xxi-xxii, 195-97, 198-201, 202-3, 208, 210, 213-14
 missionary encounter with Japan, 63, 136
 Orientalism and, 2, 16
Chronicle of Higher Education, 387
Chung, Byung-Ho, 313n
Clark, David, 370n, 371n
Clark, Timothy, 180n
Clement, Ernest, 86, 87, 88n
Clunas, Craig, 187n
Coaldrake, Kimi, 321n
Coaldrake, William, 50, 182n
Coble, Parks, 148
Cogan, Thomas, 247
Cohen, Jerome, 362
Cohen, Ralph, 265
Cold War, xiii
 area studies and, xiii-xiv, xvii, 230, 387
 historical study and, 32

literature and, 258, 267
modernization theory and, 5, 6, 11, 24, 94, 236-37
Cole, Robert, 12, 14n
Coleman, Rex, 357, 358, 361
Collcutt, Martin, xvi, xvii, xviii, 55, 58, 59, 134, 171n, 205, 209
colonialism, colonialist
 cultural studies and, xiv, 261, 317-19, 323-25
 Japan and, 149, 152, 262, 263, 301-2, 324n, 373
 postmodernism and, xxi, 167-68
 West and, 30, 169
Columbia University, 165, 184, 199, 244, 357, 361-62, 363n, 364, 366
comparative law, xxvi, 355, 361, 367-82
Conant, Ellen, 181
Confucian, Confucianism
 art and, 177
 diffusion in Japan, 43-44, 48, 50
 institutions and, 12n, 13, 15, 381n
 Meiji period and, 133, 134-35, 170
 studies of, xxi-xxii, 200, 202, 211-13
 Tokugawa period and, 87, 99, 102, 206
Conroy, Hilary, 23n, 144, 149
convergence, convergence theory, xv, xvii, 2, 5-8, 12, 23, 32
Cook, Haruko, 324n
Cook, Theodore, 324n
Cooper, Michael, 63
Cornell, Laurel, 100
Cornyetz, Nina, 266n
Cort, Louise, 63, 183, 183n
crafts, handicrafts, 13, 182-83, 182n, 186
Craig, Albert, xvi, xvii, xix-xx, 27, 128, 130, 135, 357
Craig, Teruko, 98
Cranston, Edwin, 50-51, 184n, 244n, 246n, 247, 248n
Cranston, Fumiko, 184n
Crawcour, Sydney, 14n
Crawford, Gary, 42
Creemers, Wilhelmus, 211
Creighton, Millie, 320n
Crimp, Douglas, 185n
critical theory, 16, 18, 229
 art and, 165, 167-72, 176, 183
 see also poststructuralism, postmodernism, deconstruction
Crowley, James, 146

Crump, J. I., 48
Cumings, Bruce, 32n
Cuno, James, 185n
Currie, William, 261n
Curtis, Gerald, 345n
Cusumano, Michael, 13, 13n

Dale, Peter, 14n
Danly, Robert, 265
Dator, James, 216n
Davis, Darrel, 320n
Davis, David, 62
Davis, Winston, 206, 216
Dazai, Osamu, 233-35, 265
de Bary, William Theodore, 133, 212, 240n
deconstruction, x, 16, 20, 167, 261
  see also poststructuralism, postmodernism, critical theory
De Mente, Boye, 319n
de Rivera, Joseph, 396n
developmental state thesis, xxvii, 8, 339, 342-43, 399-401
De Visser, M. W., 55
De Vos, George, 18n, 321n
Deyo, Fred, 342n
Dickinson, Frederick, 146
Dickson, Walter, 86, 90, 91n
Dikötter, Frank, 321n
Dingman, Roger, 146
Dissanayake, Wimal, 304n
dissertations (Ph.D.)
  on anthropology, 295, 306-10, 309n, 316, 320n, 323
  on art, 175-76, 181
  on religion, 195, 198-202, 213, 219
divergence, divergence theory, xvii, 2, 5, 8, 10-13, 20, 32
Doak, Kevin, 305n
Doane, Janice, 297n
Dobbins, James, 58, 62, 205, 209
Doe, Paula, 244, 245n
Doi, Takeo, xxvii, 396-97, 396n, 397n
Doi, Tsugiyoshi, 164
Dolgopol, Ustinia, 321n
Dore, Ronald, xvii, 14-15n, 130, 339n, 374
  Confucianism and, 12n, 15
  divergence/convergence and, 12, 397-99, 398n, 399n
  education and, 93, 93n, 99, 108, 133
Dorson, Richard, 218

Dower, John, xvi, xvii, 4n, 115n, 146n, 232n, 239n, 324n, 338n, 345n
  gyokusai and, 299n
  postwar history and, xvii-xviii, 31, 149, 346, 346n
  racism and, 19, 31n, 154
  E. H. Norman and, 6n, 23n
Downs, Anthony, 344n
Dresser, Christopher, 166, 170
During, Simon, 168
Dutch Studies, 134-35
Duus, Peter, 1, 20n, 146, 147, 149, 152, 324n

Earhart, Byron, 202n, 204, 209, 209n, 216-17
Earl, David, 130, 134
Ebara, Taizō, 240
Ebersole, Gary, 218, 244-45
economics (discipline), xii, xiv, 144, 391
  law and, 366, 367, 372, 380, 381
Edwards, Walter, 45, 217
Egami, Namio, xviii, 45
Elison, George, 61, 63-64, 95, 133, 214
Elisonas, Jurgis (George Elison), 61
Ellwood, Robert, 211
Embree, John, 300, 300n, 302-4, 302n, 303n, 304n, 306, 310
emperor, emperor system, 23, 317
  early history and, 51-53, 57, 321
  invented tradition and, 14-15
  modern period and, 115, 133-34, 149, 394-95
  Tokugawa period and, 87, 130, 134
ethnographic, ethnography
  anthropology and, 300, 301, 303, 304, 306, 310, 314, 323, 325
  area studies and, 196, 390
  education and, 312n
  religion and, 211, 216, 217
Etō, Jun, 232n
Etō, Shinkichi, 145
Eurocentric, Eurocentrism, xv, xxii, 17-18, 95, 151, 169, 258, 318-19, 324
Evans-Pritchard, E., 393
Ewald, William, 376, 376n

Fair, Janet Kay, 305n, 322n
Fallows, James, 347
Farris, Wayne, 49-50, 54-55
fascism, fascist, 19, 23, 28, 29
Faure, Bernard, 58, 172n, 209

Fawcett, Clare, 37n
Feldman, Eric, 354, 363n, 364
feminism, feminist, xii, 169n
  anthropology and, 297, 321
  law and, 367
  literature and, 255, 256n, 258, 261, 266, 266n, 267n
Fenollosa, Ernest, 170, 173-74, 173n, 176, 180, 180n, 181
feudal, feudalism, ix, 11, 95, 239, 244, 345
  Tokugawa period and, xvii, 1, 3-6, 93-94, 119, 124
Field, Norma, xvi, xvii, xxii-xxiii, 52, 248, 248n, 266, 266n, 314n
First, Harry, 363n, 364
Fisher, Galen, 85
Fister, Pat, 169n
Flanagan, Scott, 339n
Fletcher, William Miles, III, 30n
Fogel, Joshua, 30n, 146, 154
folklore, 197-98, 202, 218, 248
Fong, Shiaw-Chian, 324n
Fontein, Jan, 218
Foote, Daniel, 354, 359-63, 363n
foreign relations, foreign affairs, xiv, 4, 127, 128, 364
  Iriye on, xx, 143-60
Foucault, Michel, xxvii, 108, 167, 175, 175n, 179n, 180n, 254, 264, 295, 394-95
Foulk, T. Griffith, 172n
Fowler, Edward, 234n, 262, 262n, 263, 321n
Fox, Grace, 128
Frank, Bernard, 171n
Frankfurt School, 229, 261
Fraser, Andrew, 130, 131, 131n
Freed, Anne, 321n
French, Calvin, 175n, 181, 181n
Friday, Karl, 54
Fridell, Wilbur, 211
Friedman, Mildred, 181n
Frost, Peter, 132n
Fruin, W. Mark, 14n
Fuhara, Yoshiaki, 229n
Fujii, James, 262, 262n, 263
Fujii, Sadakazu, 252-53, 253n
Fujiki, Hisashi, 61
Fujikura, Kōichirō, 362n, 363
Fujimura-Fanselow, Kumiko, 322n
Fujitani, Takashi, xxvii, 23n, 134, 394-95, 395n

Fukui, Haruhiro, 27n
Fukuyama, Toshio, 164, 182
Fukuzawa, Yukichi, 133, 135, 137
Furukawa, Makoto, 320n
Furuno, Kazuko, 324n

Garon, Sheldon, 26n, 29, 32n
Gatten, Aileen, 251n
Gatti, Franco, 296n
Gellhorn, Walter, 357
Gellner, Ernest, 162n, 168n, 172n, 178n, 188n
gender, gender roles
  anthropology and, xxiv, 295, 296, 308-10, 317, 319-23, 321n
  cultural studies and, 167-68, 316
  homosexuality and, 258-59
  literature and, 250, 251, 256n
  rational choice theory and, 401, 403
  religion and, xxii
  see also sexuality
Genji (monogatari, *Tale of Genji*), 53, 177, 354
  literary studies and, xxiii, 233, 233n, 240, 247-49, 248n, 249n, 250n, 253n, 256, 256n, 264
George, B. J., 356-57, 363n
George, Timothy, 1, 115n
Gerschenkron, Alexander, 397
Gerstle, C. Andrew, 101n, 260n
Giddings, Paula, 295
Giesen, Walter, 257n
Gilson, Ron, 364, 365
Glendon, Mary Ann, 354, 370n, 376n
globalization, xiii, xv, 269, 317, 345, 387, 404
Gluck, Carol, 15, 29, 32n, 134, 134n
Goble, Andrew, 57
Goff, Janet, 248n, 256
Gombrich, E. H., 167, 168n
Goncourt, Edmond de, 170
Goncourt, Jules de, 170
Gonse, Louis, 170, 173
Goodman, David, 217, 218
Goodman, Grant, 135, 324n
Goodman, Roger, 296n, 321n
Goodwin, Janet, 58, 205
Goossen, Ted, 263n
Gordley, James, 371n
Gordon, Andrew, xvi, xvii, xxvi-xxvii, 22, 28, 23n, 26n, 32, 131
Goto, Junko, 310n

Gotō, Akira, 217n
Gownder, Joseph, 401n
Grapard, Alan, 50, 58, 202, 205, 211
Gray, Whitmore, 363
Green, Michael, 146
Greenfield, Karl Taro, 319n
Gresser, Julian, 363
Groner, Paul, 55, 209
Grossberg, Kenneth, 57
Grotenhuis, Elizabeth ten, 161n, 218
Groys, Boris, 185n
Guth, Christine, 161n, 171n, 218

Hackett, Roger, 130
Hakeda, Yoshihito, 55, 209
Hakone conference, xx, 145, 147, 239
Haley, John, 12n
    divergence theory and, 8-9, 12
    Japanese legal studies and, 354n, 359-61, 362, 362n, 363n, 365-66, 366n, 370n, 375n, 377, 378, 379-81, 380n
Hall, Ivan, 130
Hall, John Whitney, 5, 357
    area studies and, 387-88, 388n, 389
    bakumatsu studies and, 118, 130
    Cambridge History and, 1, 5n, 22-23
    early history and, 45-46, 48-49, 49n, 54, 56, 57, 58n, 61, 61n
    Tokugawa studies and, 86n, 92-94, 93n, 97
Halperin, David, 259
Hammond, Ellen, 315n
Han, Seung-Mi, 315n
Hanayama, Shinsho, 45
Hane, Mikiso, 26n, 26, 28, 133, 321n
Hanihara, Kazuro, 42
Hanley, Susan, 98, 131
Hanson, Elizabeth, 266
Hara, Richard, 310n
Hardacre, Helen, xvi-xvii, xxi-xxii, 15n, 50, 55, 134, 211, 217, 217n, 307n, 320n, 321n
Hare, Thomas, 256
Harootunian, Harry, 133, 169n, 211, 260n
    modernization theory and, 10n, 17-18, 22, 25n, 130, 169n
    Tokugawa studies and, 99, 103-6, 106n, 108
Harrington, Ann Mary, 214n
Harrington, Lorraine, 58n
Harris, Jay, 247

Harvard University, xvi, xvin, 11, 27, 165, 294
    art studies and, 182n, 185n, 202
    Japanese legal studies and, xxv, 354n, 355-58, 359n, 361-63, 362n
    religious studies and, 199-200, 211
Hasegawa, Masaharu, 253n
Hashimoto, Osamu, 256n
Haskel, Peter, 209
Hassan, Ihab, 174n
Hasumi, Shigehiko, 264
Hatada, Takashi, 47
Hatano, Sumio, 149-50
Hatch, Walter, 348n
Hattori, Takaaki, 357
Hauser, William, 22, 23n, 96, 97, 131
Havens, Thomas, 130
Hayami, Akira, 118, 118n
Hayashi, Fumiko, 236, 237
Hayashiya, T., 59
Hayward, Jack, 343n
Hazard, Benjamin, 59
Heian period
    art studies and, 164, 177
    historical studies and, 37, 49-55
    literary studies and, 232, 245, 246, 250-52, 255n, 256n, 264
Heilbrunn, Jacob, 387
Hein, Laura, 23n, 32n, 315n
Heine, Steven, 102n, 209, 218
Heinrich, Amy, 296n
Heinrichs, Waldo, 152
Heisig, James, 172n
Hellman, Donald, 12n
Henderson, Dan Fenno, 354, 358-61, 362, 362n, 374, 378
Hendry, Joy, 304n
Henkenius, Mary, 245
Herzfeld, Michael, 319n
Heusken, Henry, 90, 118, 119n
Hibbett, Howard, 92, 94, 161n, 233n
Hicks, George, 321n
Hicks, Stephen, 374-77, 374n, 375n, 379
Hideyoshi, 61
Higgins, Kathleen, 171n
Higuchi, Ichiyō, 265
Hijiya-Kirschnereit, Irmela, 262n, 263, 263n
Hino, Ashihei, 238
Hirai, Atsuko, 30n
Hirai, Naofusa, 198
Hirakawa, Sukehiro, 135

Hirano, Kunio, 47
Hirano, Ryūichi, 357-58
Hirata, Hosea, 262n, 266
Hirosue, Tamotsu, 241n, 260n
Hirota, Akiko, 131
Hirschmeier, Johannes, 132n
Hobbes, Thomas, 95, 402-3
Hobsbawm, Eric, 13, 15n
Hochstedler, Carol, 247
Hodges, Devon, 297n
Hokusai, Katsushika, 170, 172
Holtom, Daniel, 201n, 210
Honde, Christine, 307n
Honjō, Eijirō, 127
Hori, Ichirō, 197
Hori, Kyotsu, 57
Horie, Yasuzō, 127
Horioka, Charles, 32n
Horowitz, Donald, 354, 376n
horserider invasion thesis, xviii, 45, 46-47
Horton, H. Mack, 243
Hosoya, Chihiro, 145
Hoston, Germaine, 30n
Howe, Christopher, 144
Howell, David, 96, 99, 121, 132n, 321n
Howes, John, 214n
Huber, Kristina, 322n
Huber, Thomas, 130, 134
Hudson, Mark, 42
Huffman, James, 130
Hunt, Michael, 153
Hunter, Jane, 153n, 321n
Huntington, Samuel, 153, 154, 381, 381n
Hurst, Cameron, 53, 57
Hutterer, Karl, 42
Hyōdō, Hiromi, 255n

iconology, 177-78
Iglehard, Charles, 213n
Ihara, Saikaku, 240-41, 258, 259, 260n
Ike, Nobutaka, 131
Ikegami, Eiko, 98
Ikegami, Yoshihiko, 14n
ikki, 22, 58, 62, 121, 125n, 127
Imamura, Anne, 322n
imperialism, imperialist, 262, 264n, 319
  Japan and, ix, xx, 26, 30n, 144, 148-49, 152, 301, 321, 323-24, 324n
  religion and, 210
  Western culture and, 11, 19, 20, 30
Impey, Oliver, 182n

individualism, 9, 10, 10n, 13, 19, 163n, 165, 382
Ino, Kenji, 240-41, 241n
Inoguchi, Takashi, 337
Inoue, Mitsusada, 48, 198
Inoue, Nobutaka, 216
Inouye, Charles, 264n
I-novel, 10, 239
  see also shishōsetsu
international relations, *see* foreign relations
Internet, xxiv, 42, 337, 348
  see also Tokyo University Institute of Social Science
Internet discussion groups, xxiv, 337
invention of tradition, 13-14, 15, 15n, 16, 315
Iriye, Akira, xvi, xvii, xx, 116, 143, 153n
Irokawa, Daikichi, 134, 215, 215n
Ishimoda, Shō, 241n
Ishiyama, Tetsurō, 241
Ito, Kinko, 320n
Itō, Masami, 357
Ivy, Marilyn, 32n, 308n, 310n
Iwanami shoten, 148
Iwao, Seiichi, 62, 64
Iwao, Sumiko, 322n
Iwata, Jun'ichi, 259n, 320n
Iwata, Masakazu, 130
Iwatake, Mikako, 308n

Jameson, Frederic, 108, 254, 254n
Jannetta, Ann, 96
Jansen, Marius, 9n, 61, 232n, 339n
  bakumatsu studies and, 118n, 128-30, 131n, 134
  Cambridge History and, 1, 22-23
  foreign relations studies and, 144, 149, 154
Japan Digest, The, 337
Japan Foundation, viin, 219n, 294n, 366
Jencks, Charles, 167n
Jenkins, Donald, 180n
Johnson, Chalmers, 8n, 12, 15, 32n, 340n, 399n
  developmental state and, xxvii, 8, 8-9n, 27n, 31-32, 339, 342-47, 399-400
Johnson, Edward S., Jr., 363
Joint Committee on Japanese Studies (JCJS), viin, 387-89
  see also American Council of Learned Societies

Joll, James, 153
Jōmon period, xviii, 2, 37, 38-42
Jones, Sumie, 100, 180n, 259, 259n
Journal of Japanese Studies, 9, 21, 24-25

Ka, Chih-Ming, 324n
Kaempfer, Engelbert, 85
Kahn, Herman, 12n
Kaiser, David, 153
Kaitokudō, 106, 107
Kaizuka, Shigeki, 50
Kalland, Arne, 99, 121
Kamakura period, 55-59, 204-5, 232, 251
Kamata, Satoshi, 310n
Kameda, Atsuko, 322n
Kamens, Edward, 52, 218, 247, 251-52
Kami Takamori site, xviii, 37, 39, 42
Kamstra, J. H., 46
Kanda, James, 61
Kanetsuki, Gutetsu, 208n
Kang, Sang-jung, 266n
Kano, Masanao, 215, 215n
Kanowitz, Leo, 362n
Kapleau, Philip, 208n
Karatani, Kōjin, 264-65, 264n, 265n
Karjala, Dennis, 362n
Karsh, Bernard, 14n
Kassel, Marleen, 99, 103
Kasulis, Thomas, 208, 208n
Kato, Hidetoshi, 320n
Katō, Genchi, 210, 211n
Katō, Ichirō, 358
Katō, Shigefumi, 253n
Katō, Shūichi, 130, 251, 257n
Katsumata, Shizuo, 61
Katzenstein, Peter, 340-41, 341n
Kawabata, Yasunari, xxiii, 232-33, 233-34n, 234, 237, 240, 265
Kawahara, Yukiko, 310n
Kawai, Hayao, 14n
Kawamura, Minato, 263n
Kawashima, Takeyoshi, 355, 357-58, 373, 374, 377, 379
Kawashima, Yoko, 321n
Kawazoe, Fusae, 256n
Keehn, E. B., 340n
Keene, Donald, 52
 literary studies and, 232-38, 235n, 236n, 242n, 247, 251, 251n, 256, 258, 258n
 Tokugawa studies and, 92-94, 93n, 133, 135

Kelly, William, 15n, 25n, 32n, 96, 98, 120, 123, 123n, 127, 132n, 294n, 295n, 304n, 310n, 312n, 314n, 320n
Kelsky, Karen, 314n, 320n, 322n
Kennan, George, 151
Kern, Adam, xxviii
Ketelaar, James, 134, 171n, 206
Kidder, J. E., Jr. (Jonathan Edward), 37, 44-46, 50, 204
Kiley, Cornelius, 46, 53, 57
Kiley, Neil, 54
King, Winston, 208n, 209
Kinmonth, Earl, 136
Kinzley, W. Dean, 15n
Kirkwood, Kenneth, 89
Kissinger, Henry, 151
Kitagawa, Hiroshi, 247
Kitagawa, Joseph, 197-99, 203-4
Kitajima, Ken, 106n
Kiyota, Minoru, 209, 216
Klawans, Stuart, 299, 299n
Kleinbauer, W. E., 167n
Kluckhohn, Clyde, 303
Knox, William, 85
Kobata, Atsushi, 62
Kobayashi, Hideo, 263n
Kobayashi, Takeshi, 164
Kobayashi, Takiji, 238, 238n
Kobori, Kazumasa, 107n
Kodera, James, 209
kofun, 43, 44
 see also Tumulus
Kohno, Masaru, 340
Kojima, Naoko, 256n
Kokushō, Iwao, 120
Komatsu, Shigemi, 187n
Komori, Yōichi, 259n
Konishi, Jin'ichi, xxiii, 242, 242n, 251
Kornicki, Peter, 3n
Kosaka, Kenji, 321n
Koschmann, J. Victor, 25, 25n, 32n, 129, 130, 133, 236
Kōzaha, 5
 see also Marxism
Kraft, Kenneth, 209
Kreiner, Josef, 296n
Kultermann, Udo, 167n
Kumakura, Isao, 57n
Kurata, Bunsaku, 45, 46
Kuroda, Toshio, 205, 205n
Kuroita, Katsumi, 45
Kuwahara, Yasue, 320n

INDEX 415

Kweon, Sug-In, 308n, 310n
Kyoto School, 19, 199

labor, labor studies, labor history, 14n,
 25, 26n, 32, 310, 398
 legal studies and, 357, 361
 politics and, 28-29, 229
 pre-20th century study of, 50, 54, 98,
  120, 124n, 392-94
Lach, Donald, 64
LaFleur, William, 217, 218, 243n, 257
LaMarre, Thomas, 246n
Lammers, Wayne, 247
Lane, Richard, 173n, 240, 240n
Langbein, John, 369n, 371n, 376, 376n
language training, ix, xi, xii, 96, 196-97,
 199, 230, 268
 area studies and, xiii-xiv, 400, 401
 legal studies and, 354, 356, 359n, 365
 military experience and, viii, 232
Large, Stephen, 146n, 149
Laures, Johannes, 213n
law, legal studies, xiv, xvii, 185, 338
 historical study of, 61, 89, 97, 98
 Japanese difference and, 9, 9n, 10,
  401
 religion and, 206, 211
 Upham on, xxv-xxvii, 354-86
Layoun, Mary, 262n, 264n
Le Blanc, Robin, 321n
Lebra, Takie, 312, 321n
Lebra, William, 217n
Ledyard, Gari, 45
Leflar, Robert, 362, 362n
LeTendre, Gerald, 313n
Leupp, Gary, 96, 98, 100, 258-59, 259n,
 320n, 322n
Leutner, Robert, 258
Levin, Mark, 360n, 362-63n
Levine, Solomon, 14n
Levy, Ian, 244-45, 244n
Lewis, Catherine, 312n
Lewis, Michael, 26n
Lidin, Olof, 103
Lieberman, Joseph, 13n
Liebman, Lance, 361
Lifton, Robert, 130
Lincicome, Mark, 315n
Lippit, Noriko, 266
literature, literary studies, viii, xii, xv,
 xvii, 9n, 10, 311n, 391
 anthropology and, 323

 art studies and, 163, 167, 168, 175,
  177, 179, 181, 184, 188
 early history and, 50-53, 62
 Field on, xxii-xxiii, 227-93
 legal studies and, 367, 381
 religious studies and, 196, 199-201,
  202, 204, 206, 213, 218, 219n
 Tokugawa period and, 101
Lock, Margaret, 307, 321
Lockwood, William, 130, 131, 339n, 357
Luney, Percy, 362, 363, 363n
Lyons, Phyllis, 234n

Macdonald, Gaynor, 321n
MacDougall, Terry, 337, 346
Macey, Jonathan, 365n
Madoka Kanai, 1
Magnus, Bernd, 171n
Maher, John, 321n
Mannari, Hiroshi, 315n
Mannheim, Karl, 14n
Maraldo, John, 172n
Markus, Andrew Lawrence, 258n, 260n
Marra, Michele, 247, 257
Maruyama, Masao, xxiv, 29, 133, 236,
 338, 339
Marxist, Marxism, Marx, 16, 18, 20n, 27,
 108, 128n, 129, 152, 239n, 261, 297,
 338
 literary studies and, 236, 238-39
 modernization theory and, 6, 8, 21,
  22, 119
Maske, Andrew, 64
Mason, Penelope, 181n
Mass, Jeffrey, 53, 57, 58, 58n
Massarella, Derek, 63
Massey, Elizabeth, viin
Massey, Joseph, viin
Masuda, Hiroshi, 149
Masuda, Katsumi, 241, 241n
Mathews, Gordon, 314n
Matisoff, Susan, 257
Matsui, Kenji, 256n
Matsuki, Keiko, 324n
Matsumoto, Sannosuke, 104
Matsumoto, Shigeru, 211
Matsumura, Masayoshi, 154
Matsunaga, Alicia, 207
Matsunaga, Daigan, 207
Matsuo, Takayoshi, 28
Mattei, Ugo, 369n, 382n
May, Ernest R., 145

Mayer, Fanny Hagin, 248n
McCallum, Donald, 58, 169n, 218
McClain, James, 1, 5n, 96, 97, 118, 129
McClellan, Edwin, 9n, 261n
McConnell, David, 315n
McCullough, Helen, 52, 233n, 245, 247, 248n, 251n
McCullough, William, 52, 247, 251n
McEwan, J. R., 92, 103
McFarland, Neil, 216, 216n
McMullin, Neil, 62, 205-6
McVeigh, Brian, 322n
Mears, Helen, 304n
medieval (*chūsei*) period, 21
    Collcutt on, xviii-xix, 37, 41, 55-59, 58n, 61, 62
    literary studies and, 231, 234, 239n, 240-41, 256-59, 257n
    religious studies and, 205-7, 218
Medzini, Meron, 128
Meiji Ishin Shigakkai, 116
Meiji period, 24, 149, 150, 345, 373, 392, 393
    art studies and, 163, 170, 173-74, 179-80, 182n, 186n
    invented tradition and, 14-15, 29, 394-95
    literary studies and, 231, 258
    modernization and, 5, 16, 89
    religious studies and, 205-6, 214, 215
    Tokugawa period and, 103
Meiji Restoration, ix, xiv, xvii, xix, 32
    Craig on, xix-xx, 115-42
    modernization and, ix, 5, 18-19, 22-23, 94
Mercer, Rosemary, 103
Merriman, John, 118
Merryman, John, 370n, 371, 371n
Métraux, Daniel, 216n
Milhaupt, Curtis, 354, 363n, 365
militarism, 5, 6, 28, 29, 30, 201, 210, 234
Miller, Elizabeth, 320n
Miller, Geoffrey, 364, 365n
Miller, Richard J., 45, 48
Miller, Roy Andrew, 245, 245n
Miller, Stephen, 259
Mills, C. Wright, 16
Mills, D. E., 242n, 247
Min, Pyong Gap, 321n
Minamata, Kumagusu, 259n
Minear, Richard, 103, 146, 149, 266n
Miner, Earl, xxiii, 52, 183n, 227, 242n, 243, 246n, 247, 248n

Minichiello, Sharon, 30n
Mishima, Yukio, xxiii, 233, 234, 237, 240
Mitamura, Masako, 227, 255n, 256n
Mitani, Kuniaki, 227, 253n
Mitchell, Richard, 26n
MITI (Ministry of International Trade and Industry), 8, 12, 31, 342-45, 343n, 346, 399
Mito, 133-34
Mitsios, Helen, 266
Mitsubishi Visiting Professors (Harvard University), 362, 362n
Miura, Masashi, 264
Miyake, Hitoshi, 217
Miyata, Noboru, 197, 198n
Miyoshi, Masao, 10n, 17, 17n, 101n, 128, 169n, 248n, 261
Mizuta, Hiroshi, 136
Mochizuki, Mike, 32, 346
modern, modernism, modernity
    Dower on modernization theory, xvii-xviii, 5-23, 6n, 23n, 25, 27, 30-31
    "early modern" periodization, 5, 5n, 22, 41, 61, 231
    legal studies and modernization (modernity) theory, 373-74
    literary studies and modernization (modernity) theory, 227, 230, 239, 244, 257, 258, 260, 262-68, 264n
    Meiji period and, 123, 130
    Modern Art, modernism in art, 20, 21, 162, 163n, 165-68, 170-71, 175, 179, 181
    modern literary canon, 232-37
    "modern" periodization, 232-33
    modernization (modernity) theory, ix-x, xii, xiii, xxv, 162n, 206, 315, 387
    political science and, 339-42
    Tokugawa studies and modernization (modernity) theory, xix, 93, 95, 100
Moeran, Brian, 320n
Moes, Robert, 181n
Molasky, Michael, 266n
Molony, Barbara, 321n
Mommsen, Wolfgang, 152
Monnet, Livia, 266, 266n
Monoken (Monogatari kenkyūkai), xxiii, 252-55, 255n
Moore, Joe B., 26n

moral economy, 123
Moretti, Franco, 227, 263
Morgenthau, Hans, 151
Mori, Senzō, 176, 176n
Mori, Shunta, 321n
Mōri, Hisashi, 164
Morioka, Heinz, 320n
Morioka, Kiyomi, 217n
Morishima, Akio, 363
Morison, Samuel, 128
Morley, Carolyn, 257
Morley, James W., xx, 130, 145-46, 145n, 147, 149, 357
Morrell, Robert, 204
Morris, Dana, 49
Morris, Dixon, 59
Morris, Ivan, 233, 236, 247
Morris, Mark, 244n, 245n, 246n, 248, 248n, 260n
Morris-Suzuki, Tessa, 401n
Morrison, Arthur, 173
Morse, Anne, 172n
Morse, S. E., 38
Morse, Samuel, 161n, 172n
Mostow, Joshua, 251n
Motomura, Hiroshi, 362n
Mouer, Ross, 14n, 314n
Mudimbe, V. Y., 390n
Mulhern, Chieko, 320n
Munro, Neil, 217n
Munroe, Alexandra, 181n
Münsterberg, Oskar, 173
Murakami, Haruki, 266
Murakami, Yasusuke, 14n
Muraoka, Tsunetsugu, 211
Murase, Miyeko, 165, 165n
Murdoch, James, 86, 127
Muroki, Hideyuki, 255n
Muromachi period, 55-59, 164, 177, 184, 251
Murphy-Shigematsu, Stephen, 321n
Murray, David, 86
Myers, Ramon, 147, 324n

Nagahara, Keiji, 58, 61
Nagai, Michio, 305, 305n, 310n
Nagatomi, Masatoshi, 199
Naitō, Akira, 182
Najita, Tetsuo
  bakumatsu studies and, 130, 133
  modernization theory and, 18-20, 19n, 25

Tokugawa studies and, 96, 99, 102n, 103-4, 105n, 107
Nakagami, Kenji, 266
Nakai, Kate, 96, 99, 103, 129, 133
Nakamura, James, 131
Nakamura, Kyoko, 55
Nakane, Chie, 217n, 312n, 374
Nakayama, Shigeru, 135
Nanga painting, 179
Naoki, Kōjirō, 48
Napier, Susan, 266, 320n
Nara period, 37, 42, 47-51, 55, 184, 246
Narazaki, Muneshige, 164
Nathanson, Nathaniel, 357
nationalism, nationalist, 14n, 145, 153, 167, 170, 317, 317n, 399
  Japanese cultural essence and, 11, 15, 17-19, 29, 163, 164, 305
  Shintō and, 210
  Tokugawa thought and, 134
  see also nihonjinron
Natsume, Sōseki, 233, 263
Neary, Ian, 346
Nelson, John, 211, 308n, 315n
neoclassical economics, 8, 27
new religions, xxii, 197, 198, 202, 210, 211, 214-17
New Criticism, 229, 236, 242, 260
Newell, William, 217n
nihonjinron, xxiii, 11, 14, 14n, 15, 18, 26, 163, 305, 305n, 401
Ninkovich, Frank, 153
Nish, Ian, 143, 145
Nishiwaki, Junzaburō, 241n
Noble, Gregory, 339n
Noguchi, Paul, 320n
Noguchi, Yukio, 339n
Norbeck, Edward, 217, 294n, 314-15, 315n
Norman, E. Herbert, 338, 345-47
  interpretation of Restoration and, 127-28, 128n
  Marxism and, 21, 128n, 239
  modernization theory and, 5-6, 6n, 15, 23, 23n
  Tokugawa studies and, 92, 94, 94n, 108
Norris, Christopher, 167n
Nosco, Peter, 99, 103, 133, 211, 212
Notehelfer, Fred, 25n, 136
Nouet, Noel, 118

O'Barr, Jean, 390n
Oblas, Peter, 320n, 321n
O'Brien, David, 211
O'Brien, James, 234n
Occupation period, 5, 23, 232n
    generational influence on scholarship about, viii, xii, 94, 206, 210, 229, 232, 301
    law and, 357, 368, 373, 379
O'Connor, Marleen, 365n
Ōe, Kenzaburō, 265, 266n
Ogasawara, Seiko, 183n
Ogura, Chikako, 266n
Ohkoshi, Yasuo, 211
Ohnuki-Tierney, Emiko, 217, 304n, 307n
Oka, Yoshitake, 130
Okada, Richard, 52, 245n, 248, 248n, 262
Okakura, Kakuzō, 161, 164, 181
Okamoto, Shumpei, 146
Okano, Kaori, 313n
Okazaki, Yoshie, 241n
Okimoto, Daniel, 146, 338n, 344, 344n, 400n
Okochi, Kazuo, 14n
Okun, Jody, 321n
Ono, Sokyō, 211
Ono, Takeo, 120, 127
Ōoka, Shōhei, 233, 234
Ooms, Emily, 321n
Ooms, Herman, 62
    Tokugawa studies and, 96, 98, 99, 104, 104n, 133, 212-13
Orbaugh, Sharalyn, 266
Orientalism, Orientalist, xi, xii, xxi, 2, 3, 3n, 13, 15, 16, 26, 169-70, 179, 189, 246, 258, 262, 266n, 268, 269, 304n, 373
    see also Benedict; Said
Orikuchi, Shinobu, 244n, 254
Ortner, Sherry, 296-98, 296n, 297n, 306, 316, 316n
Orwell, George, 188n
Osaragi, Jirō, 232, 234
Oshima, Shizuko, 310n
Ōta, Hirotarō, 182
Other, Otherness, xix, 18, 19, 31, 85, 169, 301
    Tokugawa studies and, 91-92, 94-95, 100-101, 106-9
Owada, Hisashi, 362n, 364
Oyama, Kyōhei, 58n
Ozaki, Kazuo, 262n

Paine, Robert, 161n, 181n
Painter, Andrew, 320n
Paleolithic period, 37, 38
Panovsky, Erwin, 168n
Paranjape, Snehal, 321n
Parker, F. Calvin, 214n
Parker, Geoffrey, 61, 63
Parman, Susan, 294n
party politics, parties, 6, 9, 10, 340-46
Patrick, Hugh, 131
Peak, Lois, 312n
Pearl Harbor, 146-48, 301
Pearson, Richard, 37, 37n, 42
peasants, 49, 87, 98-99, 128n, 129
    anthropology and, 310, 321
    economic development and, 393-94, 398
    protest and, 22, 25, 25n, 85, 96, 119-121
Peattie, Mark, 146-47, 149, 154, 324n
Pekkanen, Robert, 401n
Pelz, Stephen, 146
Pempel, T. J., 27, 27n, 346
People's History School, 22, 25-26, 215
Pevsner, Nikolaus, 166n, 167
Pflugfelder, Gregory, 250
Pharr, Susan, 346, 347n
Philippi, Donald, 211n, 245n
Pick, Daniel, 153
Piggot, Joan, 46, 50, 51, 58, 321n
Pittau, Joseph, 134
Plath, David, 14n, 217n, 294n
Pollack, David, 17n, 257, 262n
Ponsonby-Fane, Richard, 210
Porges, Amelia, 361
Port, Kenneth, 363n
postmodern, postmodernism, x-xiv, xvi, xviii, xix, xxi, xxiii, 10, 13, 27, 32n, 162, 167n, 209
    art studies and, 163, 163n, 165-66, 167-68, 168n, 171-80
    divergence/convergence theory and, 10, 13, 16-18, 20, 23n
    literary studies and, 258, 262, 263, 264
    Tokugawa studies and, 106-7, 110
    see also poststructuralism, deconstruction, critical theory
poststructuralism, x, 16, 18, 20, 167, 229
    literary studies and, 246, 255, 261-63, 264
    see also postmodernism, deconstruction, critical theory

Potter, Pittman, 360n
Pound, Ezra, 170
Powers, Richard, 320n
Prestowitz, Clyde, 347
professionalization, xiii, 196, 230, 269
professors, professorial chairs in schools, xviii, 20, 165, 308
  law and, xxvi, 354, 356-58, 360-66, 362n, 362-63n, 374, 377, 381
  psychology (discipline), xiv, 200, 201, 338
Pulleyblank, E.g., 44
Purdy, Roger, 324n
Pure Land (Buddhism), xxii, 55, 61, 199, 200-202, 205
Pye, Michael, 103
Pyle, Kenneth, 25n

Quick Read, The, 337
Quinn, Charles, 304n, 314

Rabinovitch, Judith, 53
Rabinow, Paul, 15n, 175n, 179n
Rabinowitz, Richard, 354, 357, 358-59n, 362
Rabson, Steve, 266n
racism, racist, viii, 31, 109, 154
Rafael, Vincente, 324n
Ramirez-Christensen, Esperanza, 243, 243n, 245n, 248n
Ramseyer, Mark, 340, 354, 362, 364, 365-66, 366n, 379
Ranger, Terence, 13, 15n
rational choice theory, xi, xiii-xv, xvi, xxv, xxvii, 340-41, 379, 400-403, 401n
Raveri, Massimo, 296n
Reed, Steven, 337
Refsing, Kirsten, 296n
Reich, Michael, 130, 354
Reichl, Christopher, 321n
Reischauer, Edwin O., 4n, 6, 6n, 55, 204, 232, 236-37, 237n, 345, 345n
Reischauer, Robert Karl, 43, 45, 345, 345n
religions, religious studies, xiv, xv, 29, 134, 302n
  art studies and, 170-72
  early history and, 38, 55, 58, 60
  Hardacre on, xxi-xxii, 195-226
  literary studies and, 255n, 257
  Tokugawa history and, 92, 95
Reps, Paul, 208n

Reynolds, Douglas, 146n
Reynolds, Jonathan, 152n
Rheinstein, Max, 357, 369n
Richardson, Bradley, 345n
Richmond, Carol, 62
Rimer, J. Thomas, 30n, 257, 264, 266
ritsuryō system, 47-50, 53-54
Roberson, James, 321n
Roberts, Glenda, 321n
Roberts, Luke, 96
Robertson, Jennifer, xvi, xvii, xxiii-xxiv, 15n, 95, 308n, 310n, 315n, 320n, 321n, 324n
Robinson, G. W., 51
Rodd, Laurel, 209, 245
Roden, Donald, 320n, 322n
Roe, Mark, 364, 365
Rogers, Minor, 209
Rohlen, Thomas, 13, 313n
Rohlich, Thomas, 245n, 247, 248
Roland, Alan, 304n, 312
Rōnōha, 5
  see also Marxism
Rose, Margaret, 167n
Rosen, Dan, 363n, 364
Rosenberger, Nancy, 304n
Rosenbluth, Frances, 340, 365
Rosenfield, John, xvi, xvii, xx-xxi, 50, 168n, 184n, 202, 218
Rosett, Arthur, 354, 378
Rosman, Abraham, 296n
Rosovsky, Henry, 131
Ross, Kristin, 265n
Rousseau, Jean Jacques, 136, 402
Rozman, Gilbert, 118, 118n, 130, 131n
Rubel, Paula, 296n
Rubin, Jay, 261n
Rubinger, Richard, 96, 99, 133
Ruch, Barbara, 59, 184, 257, 257n
Russell, John, 320n
Rustow, Dankwart, 339n, 342n
Rutledge, Eric, 244n
Ryan, Marleigh Grayer, 263n

Sadler, A. L., 86, 90
Said, Edward, xi, 2, 3n, 16, 169, 169n, 239n, 246, 266n
  see also Orientalism
Saigō, Nobutsuna, 241, 241n
Saikaku, *see* Ihara Saikaku
Sakai, Naoki, 104, 260n
Sakai, Yukichi, 104

Sakamoto, Tarō, 44, 51
Salzberg, Stephan, 360n
Samuels, Richard, 4, 4n, 10n, 27, 27n, 338n, 342n, 344, 344n, 346, 346n, 400n
samurai, 60, 62, 177
  as image of Japan, 3-4, 207
  emergence of, 52, 54, 55
  Meiji period and, 117, 119, 121-24, 127-29, 130-31, 137
  Tokugawa and, 87, 98, 99, 101, 132
Sanford, James, 209
Sannai Maruyama site, xviii, 39-40
Sansom, George, 45, 48, 60, 63, 86, 135, 232
Sasaki, Chikara, 324n
Sasaki, Miyoko, 320n
Sasaki, Ruth, 208n
Sato, Hiroaki, 245
Sato, Ikuya, 321n
Sato, Shigeru, 324n
Satō, Dōshin, 170, 170n
Satō, Elizabeth, 50, 54
Satō, Seizaburō, 133n
Satsuma, 121, 125, 129
Saunders, E. Dale, 207, 218
Savigny, F. Carl von, 369-70, 372, 376, 377
Sawada, Janine, 95, 96, 99
Scalapino, Robert, 131, 345
Schalow, Paul, 258, 258n, 259, 266
Schattschneider, Ellen, 310n, 321n
Scheiner, Irwin, 20n, 24, 98, 98n, 103, 135, 214
Schildgen, Robert, 214n
Schlant, Ernestine, 266
Schnell, Scott, 308n
Schoppa, Leonard, 345n
Schwartz, Benjamin, 133n, 357
Scidmore, Eliza, 313, 313n
Scogin, Hugh, 363
Screech, Timon, 102n, 169n
Seidensticker, Edward, 12n, 52, 118, 233, 247, 248, 248n, 249n, 252
Seigle, Cecelia, 100
Seita, Alex, 362n
Seki, Keigo, 248n
Sekine, Eiji, 256n
Selden, Kyoko, 266, 266n
Selden, Mark, 266n
Senzaki, Nyogen, 208n
sexuality, 96, 180n, 187
  art and, 179-80
  theory and anthropology and, 167, 295, 296, 308, 316-17, 318-23, 321n
  literary studies and, 250, 254, 258-60, 259n, 260n
  Tokugawa and, 90, 100, 101, 258-60, 260n
  see also gender
shamanism, 204, 218
Sharf, Robert, 172n
Shea, Christopher, 387n
Shea, G. T., 265n
Sheldon, Charles, 92, 94, 107n, 131
Shields, James, 313n
Shillony, Ben-Ami, 146
Shimada, Shūjirō, 165, 165n
Shimazono, Susumu, 216, 216n
Shimizu, Yoshiaki, 56, 165, 165n, 184n
Shingaku, 93, 95, 99, 206
Shinkei, 243
Shinobu, Seizaburō, 28
shinpan, 129
Shintō
  art and, 170
  early history, 44, 50, 52
  Meiji period and, 133-34
  religious studies and, xxi-xxii, 22, 197-98, 200-203, 201n, 205, 206, 210-14, 216-17, 218
  Tokugawa period and, 99, 133-34
Shirane, Haruo, 52, 248, 248n
shishōsetsu, 10, 239, 263
Shively, Donald, 92, 94, 130, 232, 339n
Shōji, Kawazoe, 59
Shōnai, 120, 123, 126
Shotoku, 45
Shōwa period, 15, 30n, 31, 32, 264n, 318
Shwalb, Barbara, 313n
Shwalb, David, 313n
Sibley, William, 227, 259n, 263n
Siddle, Richard, 321n
Sievers, Sharon, 26n, 321n
Silberman, Bernard, 130
Silverberg, Miriam, 265, 320n
Sippel, Patricia, 98
Sjöberg, Katarina, 321n
Skinner, Quentin, 105, 177n
Skov, Lise, 320n
Smethurst, Richard, 26n
Smethurst, Mae, 257
Smith, Bardwell, 60n
Smith, Henry, 22, 23n, 118, 118n, 184, 184n, 259n

INDEX

Smith, Herman, 321n
Smith, Malcolm, 361
Smith, N. Skene, 85, 115
Smith, Robert J., 118, 217, 263n, 294, 294n, 303n, 306n, 309n, 314
Smith, Thomas C., xix, xxvii, 92-94, 93n, 98, 120, 120n, 121, 127, 132, 374, 392-95, 392n
Smith, Warren, 212n
Smyers, Karen, 308n
Snyder, Gary, 208n
Snyder, Stephen, 264n, 266-67
Social Science Research Council (SSRC), vii, 7, 10, 365, 387-90
sociology (discipline), xiv, 9n, 13, 236n, 267, 357, 381
    religious studies and, 202, 215-16, 217-18
Sofue, Takao, 217n, 294n
Solomon, Michael, 58, 62
Sonoda, Minoru, 198
Soper, Alexander, 161n, 181, 181n
Sōseki, *see* Natsume
Spae, Joseph, 92
Spencer, Robert, 308n
Statler, Oliver, 218
Steele, William, 117n, 118, 122, 122n
Steenstrup, Carl, 9, 9n, 57
Steiner, Kurt, 357
Steinhoff, Patricia, 294n
Stephan, John, 146n
Stephens, Sharon, 297n, 298n
Stern, Harold, 161n
Steslicke, William, 7, 7n
Steven, Rob, 324n
Stevens, Carolyn, 321n
Stevens, Charles, 362
Stockwin, Arthur, 131
Stone, Alan, 25n
strong state theory, 24, 27n, 32
Strong, Kenneth, 25n
stylistic evolution, 176-77
Suematsu, Yasukazu, 46
Sugihara, Yoshie, 217n
Sugimoto, Masayoshi, 135
Sugimoto, Yoshio, 14n, 314n
Sugita, Genpaku, 135
Sugiyama, Chūhei, 136
Sugiyama, Hiroshi, 58
Sun, You-li, 148
Suzuki, D. T., xxii, 172, 207-9
Suzuki, Hideo, 246

Suzuki, Tomi, 363
Swain, David, 135
Swinton, Elizabeth, 161, 181n

Tada, Eiko, 314n
Tahara, Mildred, 247
Tai, Eiko, 324n
Taiheiyō sensō e no michi, 145
Taira, Koji, 32n
Taishō period, 6, 15, 23
Takagi, Yasaka, viin
Takamiya, Hiroto, 42
Takashina, Shūji, 181n
Takeuchi, Melinda, 181n
Takigawa, Masujirō, 127
Tamamuro, Fumio, 206-7
Tamanoi, Mariko Asano, 294n, 321n
Tanabe, George, 209
Tanabe, Willa, 218
Tanaka, Hideo, 362n, 363
Tanaka, Hisao, 184, 184n
Tanaka, Ichimatsu, 164
Tanaka, Stefan, 31n
Tanaka, Takako, 255n
Tanaka, Takeo, 59
Tanaka, Yukiko, 266
Taniguchi, Yasuhei, 362n, 364
Tanizaki, Jun'ichirō, xxiii, 19, 20, 232, 234, 237, 240
Tanner, Ron, 320n
Tanuma, 92
Taylor, Diane, 324n
Taylor, Veronica, 360n
Thelle, Notto, 214n
Thody, Philip, 188n
Thomas, James, 322n
Thompson, E. P., xxvii, 393-94
Thomsen, Harry, 216
Titus, David, 147
Tobin, Joseph, 320n
Toby, Ronald, 51, 52n, 53, 64, 96
Tokieda, Motoki, 265n
Tokugawa, Ieyasu, 86
Tokugawa period, xix, xx, xxvii, 16, 24-25, 379
    as feudal exemplar, 1-3, 5
    Bolitho on, xvii, xix, 85-114
    historical studies of, 60-63, 239n
    literature and, 231, 239-40, 258-60, 260n
    Meiji transition and, 116-18, 119, 121-24, 128-30, 131-33, 137

religion and, 206, 212
  Smith on economics of, 392-94
Tokyo, University of, 253, 358, 361-62, 363
Tokyo University Institute of Social Science, 348
Tomioka, Taeko, 266n
Tonomura, Hitomi, 58-59
Tosa, 61, 121, 129
Totman, Conrad, 56, 95, 99, 100, 121, 130
Tōyama, Shigeki, 121
Toyoda, Takeshi, 58
Transactions of the Asiatic Society of Japan, 85, 115
Treat, John, 17n, 21, 21n, 229n, 265n, 266-67, 267n, 268, 320n
Tsang, *see* Richmond
Tsubouchi, Shōyō, 258
Tsuchida, Bruce, 247
Tsuji, Nobuo, 183, 183n, 184, 184n
Tsuji, Tatsuya, 110n
Tsuji, Zennosuke, 198
Tsukada, Mamoru, 321n
Tsukahira, Toshio George, 92
Tsunoda, Jun, 147
Tsunoda, Ryusaku, 133, 257n
Tsurumi, E. Patricia, 26n, 48, 321n
Tucker, Mary Evelyn, 103, 212
Tumulus (*kofun*) period, 42-43
Turner, Christena, 321n
Turner, Victor, 172n
Twitchett, Denis, 1
Tyler, Royall, 58, 211, 248n, 257, 257n
Tyler, Susan, 58, 211

Ueda, Kenji, 198
Ueda, Makoto, 243n, 257, 260n
Ueno, Chizuko, 266n
Ugawa, Kaoru, 118
Uiruson, Richado, *see* Richard Wilson
ukiyo-e, 164, 172, 173, 177, 179-80, 182, 240
Unger, Roberto, 373-74, 373n, 375-76, 375n, 377, 379, 382
Uno, Kathleen, 32n
Upham, Frank, xvi, xvii, xxv-xxvi, 9, 9n, 32n, 362, 363n, 364, 365
Ury, Marian, 218, 247, 248n
Utamaro, 170

Vance, Carol, 318, 318n

Vaporis, Constantine, 96, 97
Vardaman, James, 313n
Varley, H. Paul, 57, 57n, 59
Veblen, Thorstein, 397
Videen, Susan, 247
Vietnam War, Vietnam, 149, 249-50, 368
  generational influence on scholarship, xii, 24, 96, 167, 196, 229, 347
Vlastos, Stephen, 15n, 22, 25n, 96, 98, 120, 122, 122n, 123, 315n
Vogel, Ezra, xvii, 11, 12n, 294n, 374
Vogel, Steven, 345
von Mehren, Arthur, 357, 371n, 376, 376n

waka, 242-46, 246n, 253-54, 264
Wakabayashi, Bob, 96, 99, 103, 133, 134, 134n, 402n
Wakamori, Tarō, 197, 198n
Wakita, Haruko, 59, 251n, 257n
Wakita, Osamu, 61
Waley, Arthur, 233, 233n, 256
Walker, Janet, 248, 262n, 263n, 266
Walthall, Anne, 25n, 96, 98, 100, 120, 321n
Wang, Yi-tung, 59
Wang, Zheng-ping, 51, 55
Ward, Robert, 130, 339n, 342n
Warner, Langdon, 161, 161n
Washburn, Dennis, 263n, 264
Washington, University of, xxv, 358-61, 360n, 363n, 366, 378
Waswo, Ann, 26n
Watanabe, Kazuko, 321n, 322n
Watanabe, Tsuneo, 320n
Waters, Neil, 120, 123, 126, 127n
Watsky, Andrew, 63
Watson, Alan, 376, 376n
Watson, Burton, 245
Watts, Alan, 208
Webb, Herschel, 130, 130n
Weiler, Joseph, 376n
Weiner, Michael, 324n
Weinstein, Stanley, 46, 58, 62
Weisberg, Gabriel, 166
Weiss, Martin, 310n
Wendelken, Cherie, 161n, 182n
Wender, Melissa, 227, 231, 231n
Wernick, Andrew, 172n
West, Mark, 363n
Westerhove, James, 234n
Westney, Eleanor, 136

Wetzel, Patricia, 312n
Wheeler, Post, 211n
Wheelwright, Carolyn, 63, 183n
Whelan, Christal, 214n
White, James, 32n, 98, 121, 122, 122n, 123, 126, 216n
White, John, 144
Whitehouse, Wilfred, 247
Wigen, Kären, 98, 99, 121, 132n
Wigmore, John Henry, 85
Williams, David, 343n
Williams, Duncan, 198n
Willig, Rosette, 247, 250
Wilson, George, 121, 124n
Wilson, Richard, 175n, 183, 183n
Wintersteen, Prescott B., Jr., 57
Wiswell, Ella, 303n
Wolf, Eric, 296-97, 297n
Wolfe, Alan, 265
Wolferen, Karel van, 347
women, 25, 29, 100
  anthropology and, 305n, 309, 309n, 317, 320-23
  art and, 169n, 395
  comfort women, 149
  discrimination and, xiii, 168, 295
  Fukuzawa on, 135
  history of, 22, 23, 26n, 29, 258-59
  literature and, 247, 255n, 256, 265-66, 266n, 267
  religion and, 214
  politics and, 26, 346, 379, 403
Woo, Jung-en, 339n
Wood, Ellen Meiksins, 262, 262n
Woodson, Yoko, 187n
Woodward, William, 206
World War I, 29, 164
World War II, 4n, 19, 31, 115, 119, 120, 161, 164-65, 164n, 166, 181, 367
  Japanese studies attitudes and, vii-ix, xii, xx, xxii-xxiii, xxv, 4, 161n, 232, 300-301, 338, 339
  religious studies and, 216, 217
  study of foreign relations and, 144, 151, 154
  study of political science and, 338, 339, 340, 344, 345

  Tokugawa studies and, xix, 92
Wray, Harry, 23
Wray, William, 27, 27n, 131

Yamada, Chisaburō, 166n
Yamagiwa, Joseph, 232, 236n, 247
Yamamoto, Chie, 266n
Yamamoto, Hirofumi, 110n
Yamamoto, Hiroko, 255n
Yamamura, Kozo, 21, 54, 56, 57, 58, 58n, 62, 98, 131, 348, 348n
Yamane, Yūzō, 164
Yamashita, Samuel, 85n, 103, 104n, 105, 133, 212
Yamato, 43-47, 49
Yamazaki, Masakazu, 257
Yanagida, Kunio, 19, 20, 197, 198n
Yanagida, Yukio, 362n, 363
Yanagisawa, Eizo, 247
Yano, Christine, 320n
Yashiro Yukio, 164n
Yasuda, Kenneth, 256
Yasumaru, Yoshio, 215, 215n
Yates, Charles, 130
Yayoi period, 2, 37-39, 40-42
Yazaki, Takeo, 118
Yiengpruksawan, Mimi, 161, 177n, 181n, 188, 189n
Yoji, Akashi, 324n
Yonaha, Keiko, 256n
Yonekura, Michio, 184n
Yoneyama, Lisa, 324n
Yoshikawa, Eiji, 233, 234
Yoshimoto, Banana, 266-67, 267n
Yoshimoto, Takaaki, 254
Yoshino, Kosaku, 314n
Yoshino, Michael, 374
Yoshinogari site, xviii, 38, 40-42
Young, Michael, 361, 362, 366
Yuba, Janet, 63

Zekoll, Joachim, 376, 376n
Zen, viii, xxii, 58, 177, 199-201, 205, 207-9, 218
Zenkyōtō, 241, 252, 254
Zolbrod, Leon, 258
Zysman, John, 339n, 342n

LIST OF CONTRIBUTORS

HAROLD BOLITHO is Professor of Japanese History at Harvard University.

KENT E. CALDER is Director, Program on U.S.-Japan Relations, Woodrow Wilson School, Princeton University (on leave) and Special Advisor to the U.S. Ambassador to Japan.

MARTIN COLLCUTT is Professor of East Asian Studies and History at Princeton University.

ALBERT M. CRAIG is Harvard-Yenching Professor of History at Harvard University.

JOHN W. DOWER is Elting Morison Professor of History at the Massachusetts Institute of Technology.

NORMA M. FIELD is Professor of East Asian Languages and Civilizations at the University of Chicago.

ANDREW GORDON is Professor of History at Harvard University.

HELEN HARDACRE is Reischauer Institute Professor of Japanese Religions and Society at Harvard University.

AKIRA IRIYE is Charles Warren Professor of American History at Harvard University.

JENNIFER ROBERTSON is Professor of Anthropology at the University of Michigan.

JOHN M. ROSENFIELD is Abby Aldreich Rockefeller Professor of Oriental Art, Emeritus, at Harvard University.

FRANK K. UPHAM is Professor of Law at New York University School of Law.

BRILL'S JAPANESE STUDIES LIBRARY

ISSN 0925-6512

1. H.E. PLUTSCHOW, *Chaos and Cosmos*. Ritual in Early and Medieval Japanese Literature. 1990. ISBN 90 04 08628 5
2. Th.F. LEIMS, *Die Entstehung des Kabuki*. Transkulturation Europa-Japan im 16. und 17. Jahrhundert. 1990. ISBN 90 04 08988 8
3. Chr. SEELEY, *A History of Writing in Japan*. 1991. ISBN 90 04 09081 9
4. A. VOVIN, *A Reconstruction of Proto-Ainu*. 1993. ISBN 90 04 09905 0
5. Y. YODA, *The Foundations of Japan's Modernization*. A Comparison with China's Path Towards Modernization. Transl. by K.W. Radtke. 1996. ISBN 90 04 09999 9
6. H. HARDACRE and A.L. KERN (eds.), *New Directions in the Study of Meiji Japan*. 1997. ISBN 90 04 10735 5
7. J.A. TUCKER, *Ito Jinsai's Gomō Jigi and the Philosophical Definition of Early Modern Japan*. 1998. ISBN 90 04 10992 7
8. H. Hardacre (Ed.) *The Postwar Developments of Japanese Studies in the United States*. 1998. ISBN 90 04 10981 1

HARVARD-YENCHING LIBRARY

This book must be returned to the Library on or before the last date stamped below. A fine will be charged for late return. Non-receipt of overdue notices does not exempt the borrower from fines.